Major Problems
in American Women's History

MAJOR PROBLEMS IN AMERICAN HISTORY SERIES

GENERAL EDITOR

THOMAS G. PATERSON

Major Problems
in American Women's History

DOCUMENTS AND ESSAYS

THIRD EDITION

EDITED BY

MARY BETH NORTON

CORNELL UNIVERSITY

RUTH M. ALEXANDER

COLORADO STATE UNIVERSITY

HOUGHTON MIFFLIN COMPANY
Boston   New York

For Grael and Lia
and
for Genny Nicole and Natalie

Editor in Chief: Jean L. Woy
Senior Development Editor: Frances Gay
Senior Project Editor: Christina M. Horn
Associate Project Editor: Lindsay Frost
Associate Production/Design Coordinator: Christine Gervais
Production/Design Assistant: Bethany Schlegel
Senior Manufacturing Coordinator: Marie Barnes
Senior Marketing Manager: Sandra McGuire

Cover image: *Three Women,* by Margaret Peterson (1902–1997). Gift of friends of the artist, courtesy of the Oakland Museum of California. Photo by M. Lee Fatherree.

Printed in the U.S.A.

Library of Congress Catalog Card Number: 2001133319

ISBN: 0-618-12219-2

3456789-QWF-07 06 05 04 03

Contents

C H A P T E R   6
Women and Slavery
Page 132

C H A P T E R   7
White Women in the Civil War Crisis
Page 160

C H A P T E R   8
Women in the Trans-Mississippi Frontier West
Page 187

C H A P T E R   9
Work and Work Cultures in the Era of the "New Woman," 1880–1920s
Page 213

C H A P T E R   1 0
The "New Woman" in Public Life and Politics, 1900–1930
Page 246

CHAPTER 13
Women and the Disputed Meanings of Gender, Race, and Sexuality During World War II
Page 358

CHAPTER 14
Women and the Feminine Ideal in Postwar America
Page 394

CHAPTER 15
*Women Confront Oppression and Demand Change,
the 1960s and 1970s*
Page 427

CHAPTER 16
*Women, Social Change, and Reaction from
the 1980s to the New Millennium*
Page 476

Preface

Today, a slim majority of all college students in the United States are female. A large majority of all adult women work for wages, at least part time, even if they are married with young children. Most married couples practice some form of birth control, and residents of the United States, on average, have only enough children to replace themselves (recent population growth stems almost entirely from immigration). Fifty years ago, none of those statements was true; indeed, most would have seemed outlandish. What has changed the lives of American women and families so dramatically? Only by studying the relatively new field of women's history can we learn the answers.

The first books on women's history published in the United States appeared in the mid-nineteenth century; yet as a subject of serious scholarly inquiry, the field is less than four decades old. For generations the only authors who concerned themselves with women's past were women with no formal training in the discipline of history. Until the mid-1960s, graduate education in history was dominated by men who showed little interest in studying the history of the other sex.

But that pattern changed dramatically when two interrelated developments had an enormous impact on the practice of history in the country. First, the modern feminist movement erupted in the general turmoil of that most turbulent decade, the sixties, and women pressed for equality with men in all areas of life. Second, appreciable numbers of women began to enter the historical profession, partly as a result of the new employment opportunities that had become available to them. The demonstrations, riots, and iconoclastic atmosphere of the 1960s and 1970s helped to create a revolution in the way history was studied, bringing to the fore questions about ordinary people, their families, and their work lives in what has come to be called "the new social history."

The earliest works of social history, like those written on more traditional topics, concerned themselves almost exclusively with men. But by the mid-1970s an increasing number of books and articles on women's experiences, most of them written by young female historians, began to appear in print. A new field was being born: courses on the subject proliferated in undergraduate and graduate curricula, journals such as *Gender & History* and *The Journal of Women's History* were founded to publish articles on the new subject, and women's studies programs were organized, most with a strong historical component. Graduate and undergraduate women could now study the history of their own sex in a formal educational setting, and men could learn the history of women just as women had long studied the history of men.

Today the field of American women's history is lively, characterized by disparate approaches to the subject and full of fervent debates. Women's historians have gone beyond their roots in the new social history to study women through different

xiii

methodologies and in a variety of contexts. Most recently, cultural history and an attention to language and categorization (commonly called "the linguistic turn") have achieved greater prominence in the field, as have studies that attempt to integrate women's history with the better known history of men in such contexts as politics and law. Moreover, some scholars have now begun to study the history of gender, examining both women and men and how their lives, roles, and experiences differ because of their sexual identities. Most, still, however, focus primarily on women, as do the essays in this volume.

The essays and documents in *Major Problems in American Women's History,* like those that appear in other books in this series, introduce students to a wide range of current scholarly approaches to key issues in the field. The book focuses on interpretive dialogues—that is, subjects on which historians disagree, either in their conclusions or in their emphases. In either case, the historians are engaging in perhaps their most important professional function: learning from and challenging each other's viewpoints in order to arrive at a better, more complete, and more accurate understanding of the past.

For this third edition, we have continued the emphasis on multicultural diversity in women's experiences, an emphasis that brings into sharp focus the differences and similarities in women's experiences along lines of race and class. In addition, we have made major changes in the contents of the volume to reflect current scholarly trends. Just one chapter (on the American Revolution) remains the same as in the second edition. Overall, two-thirds of the essays and two-thirds of the documents are new. In five chapters, the contents are entirely new; in most others, new documents and essays both highlight changes in historians' approaches to their subjects. We have added essays by such well-known scholars as Nancy Cott, Julie Roy Jeffrey, Paula Baker, Judy Yung, Leisa Meyer, Ruth Rosen, James F. Brooks, and Gloria L. Main. Emphases new to this third edition are women and war (for example, Chapter 7, on women in the Civil War crisis, and Chapter 13, on World War II), and on issues of health, sexuality, marriage, and reproduction (a new Chapter 11, as well as individual essays in other chapters, including Chapters 2, 7, 12, 13, 14, 15, and 16).

Like other volumes in this series, each chapter opens with a brief introduction that gives the background and context for the topic of the chapter. There follows a selection of pertinent documents giving voice to participants in the issue explored by the chapter. Two or three essays then examine the subject from different viewpoints or approaches. Headnotes, setting the readings in historical and interpretive perspective, introduce each chapter's documents and essays sections. All writings are aimed at allowing students to reach their own conclusions. Each chapter ends with suggestions for further reading for students who would like to do additional research. Sources for all documents and essays are also provided.

Instructors and students who want to continue their study of women's history are encouraged to join organizations and subscribe to journals specializing in this subject area. The most important organizations promoting women's history in the United States are regional: the Western Association of Women Historians (http://www.wawh.org/), the Southern Association for Women Historians (http://www2.h-net.msu.edu/~sawh/), the Berkshire Conference of Women Historians (http://berksconference.org/) and Women and Gender Historians of the Midwest (http://www4.wittenberg.edu/academics/hist/whom/whom.html). The most important American journal is

The Journal of Women's History, published by Indiana University Press (http://iupjournals.org/jwh/).

We are grateful to the following scholars who reviewed the second edition and offered helpful suggestions for this revision: Cara Anzilotti, Loyola Marymount University; Carolyn Lawes, Old Dominion University; Heather Munro Prescott, Central Connecticut State University; Pamela Tyler, North Carolina State University; and Nancy C. Unger, Santa Clara University.

For help in locating and copying documents and essays for this edition, the authors thank Mary Miles, Krissa Swain, Lorraine Vokolek Scott, Sierra Standish, and Carolyn Hartl. Ruth Alexander acknowledges financial assistance from a Professional Development grant at Colorado State University; Mary Beth Norton received aid from the Return Jonathan Meigs III Fund at Cornell University. Finally, we are grateful for the editorial assistance offered by Frances Gay at Houghton Mifflin.

M.B.N.
R.M.A.

Major Problems
in American Women's History

CHAPTER
1

Current Issues in American

Women's History

As the field of women's history has matured in the United States over the past three decades, scholars' emphases have changed significantly. Initially concerned with rescuing from undeserved obscurity those women who had played a leadership role in the American past, historians later moved on to investigating women's lives in the "private sphere," broadening the definition of "politics" to encompass many aspects of women's "public" activities, examining the experiences of ordinary working women (both free and enslaved), and, more recently, considering the implications of the development of the conceptual category "woman" in and of itself. Throughout, historians have kept women—a previously ignored component of the population— at the center of their inquiry, even when they have added a consideration of men and masculinity to their studies, thus creating the new field of gender history.

Historians today confront a series of important issues when they set out to write "women's" history. Initially they have to define which women they are studying, because past scholarship has clearly demonstrated that women's lives differed dramatically, most obviously because of their race, ethnicity, or class background, but also for other reasons (such as their level of education or their sexual orientation). Then historians have to develop useful analytical questions in order to go beyond the mere retrieval of information, however intrinsically interesting that information might seem to be. And finally they have to place the women they are studying in the appropriate historical contexts, for abstracting women's experiences from particular times and places can lead to ahistorical misunderstandings. While accomplishing all these tasks, contemporary historians must also remain mindful of key historiographical and theoretical concerns that they address both implicitly and explicitly in their works.

◆ E S S A Y S

The three essays reprinted here provide an introduction to contemporary thinking about women's history in the United States. The German historian Manuela Thurner briefly surveys the changing theories and paradigms in the field of American women's history since its inception in the 1970s, offering readers a useful summary of trends and disputes. Another German, Gisela Bock, critically examines the dichotomous approaches that, in her view, have too often dominated debates among women's historians on key interpretive issues. Evelyn Brooks Higginbotham of Harvard University, developing in detail a theme touched on here by Thurner, points out that most works in American "women's" history focus solely on whites, while most works in American "black" history focus solely on men. What, she asks, does that mean for African American women?

Issues and Paradigms in American Women's History

MANUELA THURNER

Emerging out of the women's liberation movement of the 1960s and 1970s, women's history has always been linked to an avowedly political agenda. This agenda, in short, was to denounce sexism and discrimination against women, to expose the origins, foundations, and workings of patriarchy, and subsequently to formulate and implement strategies for its eventual demolition. Due to the fact that the second-wave women's rights movement shared historical space and cultural momentum with, among others, the antiwar, civil rights, and gay liberation movements, attention was also paid to other forms of inequality and discrimination, variously seen to be independent of or related to the patriarchal oppression of women. History was considered to be an especially relevant and important helpmate in this enterprise, both because of its potential to create and sustain a community through a sense of a shared past, and through its promise to provide a more precise map of the varieties, limitations of, as well as possible alternatives to patriarchal structures and power. Although or maybe because they were not yet bound by institutionalized structures, women's historians in the 1960s and early 1970s were a varied group, buoyed by a sense that by (re)writing history they were in fact making history. . . .

. . . [F]aced with a daunting array of tasks and challenges, both empirical and theoretical, early women's history comprised an immense and eclectic variety of approaches and concerns. Yet according to many contemporary and later accounts of the development and state of women's history up to the mid-1970s, the field's concentration was seen to be in three major areas: first, in the research into historical ideals of femininity, culled from all kinds and genres of writing; second, in biographies of extraordinary women, the so-called "great women" or "women worthies"; and, finally, in studies and analyses of feminist and collective women's movements, especially the women's suffrage movement. Extremely self-conscious and self-critical both vis-à-vis their scholarly colleagues as well as their broader feminist constituency, women's historians soon recognized and criticized the fact that, by and large, these approaches were imitating the parameters and categories of traditional "patriarchal history." Analyses of prescriptive writings, in addition to providing little insights into women's "real" lives, often served to underwrite further the canonical status of the texts under scrutiny, most of them authored by men. While histories of great women copied the elitist and exclusivist "great men of history paradigm,"

[handwritten marginalia: womens history to 1970's]

Manuela Thurner, "Subject to Change: Issues and Paradigms of U.S. Feminist History," *Journal of Women's History 9,* no. 2 (summer 1997): 122–146. Reprinted by permission of Indiana University Press.

analyses of "organized womanhood," facilitated by the richness of sources, were seen to imply that analyses of female activities were worthy of historical attention only if set in the public arena of electoral politics. In addition, many studies of single or collective womanhood were seen to follow a teleological narrative pattern, bolstered by the "whiggish" belief in a steadily progressive democratization and modernization of U.S. society. Inquiries into the status of women, which could perhaps be called the fourth major topic of early women's history, also served to call into question traditional historical periodization. Realizing that it was not enough simply to add women to the historical record on terms not their own, women's historians increasingly became interested in devising new methodologies and conceptual models more specific to their questions and concerns.

Since it accomplished just that, Carroll Smith-Rosenberg's 1975 essay, "The Female World of Love and Ritual," quickly became a model for women's historians. Analyzing nonelite white women's correspondence of 35 families between circa 1760 and 1880, Smith–Rosenberg drew a picture of a specifically middle-class female (sub)culture with its own rituals, values, and ways of communicating, thus lending credence to Barbara Welter's 1966 postulation of the existence of "separate spheres" for Victorian men and women. In contrast to Welter's interpretation, which was based on male-authored prescriptive writings, Smith-Rosenberg's reading of the female sphere did not make it out to be a highly restrictive and crippling realm; rather, she imagined it as a social space that offered women many opportunities for autonomy, agency, and a variety of activities. In subsequent years, this idea of a woman's sphere and a women's culture grounded in this sphere arguably became the major subject of U.S. women's history. Not the least of its attractions was the fact that it opened up a vast space for research, discovery, and interpretation, a space, moreover, in which women wielded power and enjoyed their lives. Wherever women lived and worked together, whether at home, work, or church, under ordinary or extraordinary circumstances, a specific women's culture was seen to form and function.

While the idea of separate spheres was, on the one hand, clearly a subject of empirical investigation and analysis, its power to produce new perspectives and knowledge made it as much an analytical tool as a topic of women's history. The paradigm's appeal was such that it was adapted and adopted by feminist historians specializing in a variety of areas. Since it portrayed a world where women's intense homosocial bonding may have included more explicitly homosexual activities, historians of lesbian women, eager to find foremothers and historical antecedents for their experiences and struggles, greeted Smith-Rosenberg's article as a groundbreaking piece. Labor historians' analyses of women's work throughout the centuries— from the midwives of colonial times to the factory girls of the early nineteenth century and the saleswomen of the turn of the century—furnished further evidence of a female culture outside the private sphere of the home. Historians of feminism came to see woman's sphere, which encompassed religious, social, and charitable work, as the birthplace of both feminist activists and ideology. Throughout the nineteenth century, Paula Baker saw an increasing "domestication of American politics," which found its logical and timely consequence in the granting of women's suffrage in 1920. The postulation of a "separate, public female sphere" thus opened a path for a variety of analyses into the relationship between the private and the public; the subsequent redefinitions of the political arguably are among the most far-reaching reformulations and revisions of U.S. history. Generating insights and debates that not only expanded the boundaries of women's history but changed the face of much received historical wisdom, the separate spheres paradigm thus achieved theoretical as well as topical prominence. . . .

[But] historians from racial and ethnic minorities charged that the concept of women's separate sphere was basically restricted to white, middle-class Protestant women and thus held little promise to explain African-American or immigrant women's experiences. Historians of lesbian women soon saw the need for a more accurate definition of the female networks and relationships constituting this homo-social sphere, and historians of periods other than the nineteenth century asked for an increasing historicization of the paradigm, questioning its usefulness to explain women's lives beyond a specific moment in history and location in culture. Others disliked the too positive portrayal and romanticization of a female world and warned against forgetting that this female sphere existed in a men's world that largely determined its contours. Over and against an increasing "culturalization" of women's history, they demanded that an analysis of patriarchy had to be the central concern of women's history, that the emphasis had to be on analyses of the inequalities and hierarchical interdependency of those two separate, but hardly equal spheres. . . .

Deconstructing Discourses

In the mid 1980s, the linguistic turn in the social sciences and the reception of post-structuralist theories of French provenance coincided with growing uneasiness with a variety of herstory approaches, leading to a new model for historical scholarship—gender history. According to Joan Scott, who has in the meantime come to be designated the primary spokesperson for this paradigm, women's history, by adhering too closely to the methodology of social history, was either too integrationist or, by imagining a history of their own, too separatist fundamentally and lastingly to transform the discipline of history. Thus, in 1986, Scott introduced "gender" as a new and "useful category of historical analysis" and thus initiated a new phase in U.S. women's history, even, as Barbara Melosh put it, "a departure from women's history."

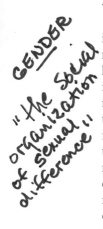

When the term "gender" began to be more frequently used in the 1980s, it was initially taken to be a substitute for "women." As a neutral, euphemistic term, it did not immediately conjure up visions of radical feminism and thus helped women's history to win a broader acceptance within academic structures. . . . Gender, according to Scott, is the "knowledge about sexual difference," with knowledge . . . defined not only as ideas and insight, but denoting all the institutions, structures, daily practices, and rituals by which and through which a society organizes and understands itself. Thus, gender is "the social organization of sexual difference," the knowledge that assigns meaning to bodily difference." . . Gender and race, since seemingly rooted in immutable, "natural," biological facts, are metaphors of difference par excellence; as discursive constructs, however, meaning and power produced through reference to gender can be "deconstructed," demystified, and thus made open to change. Deconstructing gender, which is according to Scott, "a primary way of signifying relationships of power," thus constitutes a highly political enterprise.

Since meaning is produced through and in language, this approach to gender takes leave of a belief in "material" experiences of "real men and women," and

instead takes discourse, rhetoric, and representation to be the subject that really
matters. . . . In Scott's view, herstorians fail to address or, even worse, frustrate this
agenda by simply accepting the category "women" as well as other historical terminology instead of questioning the very production and workings of these categories.
As long as historians take their task to be writing the history of "women" and their
"experiences," she sees them as contributing to the further consolidation of an epis-
temology which always constructs women as the Other and thus as deviant of and
secondary to a male norm. The only strategy to break free of the vicious circle of
tautological arguments of women's discrimination based on specifically female
experiences, Scott argues, is to change the very subject of historical inquiry. Only
"when historians take as their project *not* the reproduction and transmission of
knowledge, but the analysis of the production of knowledge itself," can feminist
history redeem its promise to change the way history is written and perceived by a
larger public. . . .

 . . . [W]hile women's historians generally agree on the significance as well as
usefulness of gender as a category for historical analysis, Joan Scott's theoretical
tour de force has started a lively debate among historians. Discomfort with what
some take to be an elitist, near-unintelligible vocabulary of poststructuralist theorizing constitutes the least important critique. More frequently, critics contend that
poststructuralist gender theory often claims to be the one and only theory by criticizing all other approaches as naive, inappropriate, or ineffective. . . . Other critics of
Scott's poststructuralist approach worry that the abstract debates about discourse,
language, and gender as a metaphor of difference are of little help when it comes to
the description of and the attack on real, material inequalities within and without
academic circles. Joan Hoff, who for many years has probably been the harshest
critic of poststructuralist theory, perceives gender history to be a symbol and symp-
tom of a dangerous indifference and apolitical relativism, even a "deliberate depoliti-
cization of power through representations of the female self as totally diffuse and
decentered." She deplores poststructuralism's abstract theorizing, its emphasis on
intertextuality rather than on human interrelationships, and castigates it for being
ethnocentric, sexist, and thus profoundly antifeminist. In her worst-case scenario,
the price paid for a deconstructivist approach is not only the very subject women's
historians and women's activists have been concerned with —women—but even
history itself. . . .

 . . . Is all history only text, discourse, and representation, or can historians get
at the materiality of the past, a "reality behind language," in order to record the
experiences and activities of men and women? Is individual or collective action
based in concrete, material experiences or is it, according to Scott, purely a "discursive effect"? Does the emphasis on language and discourse deflect attention
from issues of power, oppression, and discrimination or is discourse the central,
maybe even the only, area through which struggles for power are articulated and
consequently the arena in which those struggles need to be fought? Is it sufficient
to define gender as a metaphor of sexual difference if it needs to be understood as a
system or structure of oppression?

 Stimulated by these sometimes quite acerbic debates about the uses and abuses
of gender history, some have tried to make concrete proposals for the integration of
poststructuralist approaches into their analyses of male and female identities and

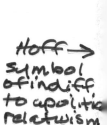

subjectivities. Lesbian and gay history has been a field that, for many years, has debated and successfully practiced a combination of essentialist and deconstructivist approaches, always aware of the interplay between the construction of social categories and the formation of subjective identities. In addition, gender as a category of analysis holds special promise for those interested in the construction of masculinities and the history of men *qua* men. Although, as Nancy Cott has argued, there is no dearth of information about men, it has now become possible and necessary to analyze their history from the perspective of gender: "Since we know so little about men as gendered beings, 'men's history' must be about the social construction of masculinity and manhood rather than simply about men as a group." The delineations between the public and private sphere, the relationship between individual and society, and other leitmotifs of U.S. history and Western civilization could then be identified as being grounded in a specifically male discourse. . . .

Difference and Dominance

Most critically, historians of minority groups often perceive themselves to be marginalized within these debates; once again, women's history's dominant paradigm seems to ignore their theoretical and empirical contributions to women's history as well as fail to explain their history to women of color. From the perspective of historians of race and ethnicity, it has been obvious that Marxist categories of analysis were not only "sex-blind," but also deficient to explain why certain racial and ethnic groups were the most discriminated against within a class-based hierarchy. . . . The propagation of a woman's culture historically and ideologically rooted in middle-class domesticity, and frequently claimed to be morally superior to men's, was hardly convincing to African-American women, given their specific history of slavery, physical and psychological violence, urban poverty, and their oppression at the hands of white women as well as white men. Similarly, many perceived the poststructuralist concept of gender, with its emphasis on race, class, and gender as metalanguages of difference, to be equally inadequate to grasp their specific experiences of oppression and resistance. . . .

Amidst recent debates about multiculturalism, this renewed emphasis on difference *among* women is especially pertinent to and propagated by historians of ethnic minorities. Analogous to women's history's original agenda to dethrone the "universal man of American history," it is now seen as necessary to topple the "uniracial universal woman" from the pedestal she has come to occupy in historical scholarship—thus the avowed motivation behind the first *Multicultural Reader in U.S. Women's History.* Also seconding the effort to move marginal subjects center-stage, lesbian theorists and historians are increasingly being heard again in their attempt "to bring the lesbian subject out of the closet of feminist history." . . .

While these critiques and perspectives promise a host of new insights and major revisions of traditional concepts and paradigms of U.S. historiography, the question of how to conceptualize such inquiries is again at the forefront of scholars' debates. How is one to do justice to the coexistence, collaboration, or confrontation of different groups within a certain historical and geographical context and to the complexity of individual lives? Historians wonder how the manifold stories of "race/class/sex/sexual/regional/generational/national/religious subgroups[s]"—thus the certainly incomplete list compiled by Nancy Hewitt—can be brought together into one narrative, how these parts can be put together to form a new whole. How is one to determine, especially in hindsight, whether a married Cuban-born tobacco field worker and mother of two in Florida or a single, bisexual, WASP female lawyer in Massachusetts have acted and reacted in certain contexts because of their skin color, ethnic identification, sexual orientation, economic positioning, religious convictions, marital or life-cycle status, or any mixture of the above? How is one to write history, if the subject of history—be it the nation-state or the individual—is, so to speak, falling into pieces? . . .

Conclusion

It seems to me that two caveats are in order at this point. First, one would do well to remember that the theoretical debates among feminist historians, prone to develop a dynamic of their own, can hardly do justice to the heterogeneity and diversity of approaches employed by historians when they embark upon their empirical studies. While the focus of this, as of any, article is necessarily exclusionary and limited, I would venture to justify my choice of themes by arguing that they, more than any other paradigms and positions, have constituted the pivots of extremely far-reaching and fundamental debates among women's historians; as such, their significance lies as much in the criticism and commentary they have sparked as in the insights they have produced. Second, if my attempt to summarize the debates within women's history has created the impression that I have argued for a progressive evolution within the discipline, which permits new formulations and explanations to discard their predecessors as outdated or obsolete, this impression would be very unfortunate. Not only has a critique of the notion of progressive evolution been one of the earliest and central insights of women's history; more important, the three paradigms I have chosen as organizing principles cannot be separated as neatly—both for their chronological sequence as well as their contents—as I have done here for analytical and presentational reasons. (This probably goes to show how difficult it is to adopt a presentational mode that does justice to the complexity and simultaneity of the dialogue among women's historians.) . . .

If one were to try to find a common theme among the debates presented here, it could be the issue of who and what constitutes the appropriate subject of (feminist) history. Initially, the agenda was to retrieve women, individually and collectively, as historical agents and subjects. Yet if women's historians were writing about women, which women were we going to talk about and what were we going to call them? While historians of feminism and lesbian historians debated definitions, historians of women of color argued that one, after all, was not simply woman and thus questioned the usefulness of a subject identified exclusively through her sex or gender. The post-structuralist insight that the very "notion of what a woman is" changes historically and cross-culturally and that "woman" was thus a discursive construct led to a focus on the production of categories and discourse as a subject for historical analysis. And with feminist theory voluminously debating the issue of "difference," there is a feeling that "a debate about difference seems to have replaced the debate about women." Yet I would argue that there has been not so much a shift as a multiplication of subjects that allows feminist history not only to reach a broader constituency both within and outside the academy, but also makes for a more complex, colorful, and thus credible picture of the past. . . .

. . . [I]t seems to me that a "grand theory" cannot be a realistic option nor should it be the ultimate goal of women's history, even if such holistic stringency and logic can, in theory, be achieved. Instead of every approach claiming to be more feminist and more effective than the one it criticizes yet builds upon, one should keep in mind that the more varied the theories and tactics, the better the chance eventually to bring about a lasting transformation of academic and social structures. Rather than signifying a dissipation or even paralysis of its radical potential or energies, the diversity of approaches and subjects of U.S. women's history bespeaks its vigor and strength. This becomes especially apparent when one looks to and out from countries where women's history has not yet achieved the degree of prominence and acceptance it now takes for granted in the United States. Thus, amidst their internal squabbles, U.S. women's historians might do well to look abroad, not in order to export their paradigms and insights wholesale to other countries and cultures, but in order for all sides to profit from a dialogue that will enrich U.S. theoretical debates as much as it might empower those struggling to write and institutionalize women's history elsewhere.

Challenging Dichotomies in Women's History

GISELA BOCK

Women's history has come a long way. Some twenty years ago, Gerda Lerner wrote that "the striking fact about the historiography of women is the general neglect of the subject by historians." Historical scholarship was far from "objective" or "universal," because it was based on male experience, placed men at the centre and as a measure of all things human, thereby leaving out half of humankind. In the past two decades, the situation has changed considerably. In an enormous (and enormously growing) body of scholarship women have been rendered visible. They have been placed at the centre, and what women do, have to do, and want to do has been re-evaluated in view of social, political and cultural change, of an improvement in women's situations and, more generally, in terms of a change towards more freedom and justice. More precisely, what has been rendered historically visible by making women a subject of research was, in the first place, their subjection. In the second place, however, it was their subjectivity—because women are not only victims, but also actively shape their own lives, society and history.

Much of this research was carried out in the context of three conceptual or theoretical frameworks that have been used by many feminist scholars, particularly historians, in the past two decades and which will be outlined in the first section of this paper. These frameworks point to three dichotomies in traditional thought on gender relations, and all of them have been not only used, but also profoundly challenged. The second section will illustrate three further dichotomies which, in the

Gisela Bock, "Challenging Dichotomies: Perspectives on Women's History, in *Writing Women's History: International Perspectives,* ed. Karen Offen et al. 1991, pp. 1–12, 15–17. Reprinted by permission of Gisela Bock.

development of modern women's history, have emerged more recently and which presently seem to dominate and direct women's studies. . . .

1. Nature versus culture.   It was mainly in the United States in the early 1970s that the relation of the sexes was discussed in terms of the relation, or rather dichotomy, between "nature and nurture" or "nature and culture." Men and their activities had been seen as culture and of cultural value, whereas women and their activities had been seen as natural, outside of history and society, always the same and therefore not worthy of scholarly, political or theoretical interest and inquiry. Moreover, it was the relations between the sexes, and most particularly their relations of power and subjection, that had been attributed to nature. "Nature," in this context, most often meant sexuality between men and women, women's bodies and their capacity for pregnancy and motherhood. Fatherhood, however, was usually seen not as natural but as "social." Female scholars challenged this traditional dichotomy. They argued that what "nature" really meant in this discourse was a devaluation of everything that women stood for, that "'nature' always has a social meaning," that both "nature" and "culture" meant different things at different times, in different places and to the different sexes, and that women's bodies and bodily capacities were not always and everywhere seen as disabilities, but also as a basis for certain kinds of informal power and public activities. The nature/culture dichotomy was recognised as a specific and perhaps specifically Western way of expressing the hierarchies between the sexes. The binary terms of this dichotomy only apparently refer to antagonistic and independent terms; but in fact, they refer to a hierarchy of social realities and cultural meanings, between strongly interdependent terms. In other words: no such nature without such culture, and no such culture without such nature. One of the linguistic results of such insights in women's history is that the term "nature" is now almost always placed in quotation marks. . . .

2. Work versus family.   A second theoretical framework for rendering women visible, and for dismantling their identification with the merely natural, unchanging and therefore uninteresting, was the issue of their distinctive patterns of work. The discussion around it had its origins more in the European than in the American context, particularly in Italy, Britain, Germany and France. What had been seen as nature was now seen as work: bearing, rearing and caring for children, looking after the breadwinner-husband and after other family members. To call this activity "work" meant to challenge the dichotomy "work and family" (because the family may mean work to women), but also "work and leisure" (because men's leisure may be women's work), and "working men and supported wives" (because wives support men through their work). It meant questioning the view that work is only that which is done for pay. Women have always worked, and unpaid work was and is women's work. Obviously, men's work is valued more highly than women's work. In theoretical and economic terms, it has been demonstrated that women's work was overlooked by male theoreticians of work and the economy and why this happened; accordingly the value or "productivity" of domestic work came to be discussed. . . .

    The sexual division of labour was found to be not just a division, but a hierarchy of labour; and not just one of labour but, primarily, a sexual division of value and rewards. The lower value of women's work continues—through economic and cultural mediation—in employment outside the home. Here, where women have always worked, they earned only 50 per cent to 80 per cent of men's earnings in the nineteenth and twentieth centuries in western countries, with variations over time and space. . . .

The apparent dichotomy between "work and family," between men as workers and women as "non-workers," turns out to be one between paid and unpaid work, between underpaid and decently paid work, between the superior and inferior value of men's and women's work respectively. The underlying assumption of mutually exclusive superiority and inferiority seems to be another common feature of such gender-linked dichotomies. The challenge posed by women's studies to this opposition is obviously linked to political and economic challenges to pay women's as yet unpaid work, to raise their earnings in low-pay jobs, and to admit more women to well-paid professions. It has also led to some linguistic changes. Even though, in the English language, the terms "working women" and "working mothers" are still reserved for employed women only, and non-employed women are still often called "non-working," the terms "work and family" are now often replaced by "paid and unpaid work." . . .

3. Public versus private.   A third conceptual framework of women's history has been the relation between the public and the private, or the political and the personal, or the sphere of power and the domestic sphere. Traditional political theory has seen them, again, as a dichotomy of mutually exclusive terms, identified with women's "sphere" and men's "world." Women's studies have profoundly challenged this view, pointing out its inadequacy for understanding politics and society. The slogan "the personal is political" indicated that the issue of power is not confined to "high politics," but also appears in sexual relations. Men inhabit, and rule within both spheres, whereas women's proper place was seen to be only in the domestic sphere and in her subjection to father or husband. This means, on the one hand, the dichotomy is not one between two autonomous, symmetrical and equivalent spheres, but rather a complex relation between domination and subordination, between power and powerlessness. On the other hand, women's studies have shown that the public "world" was essentially based on the domestic "sphere." Male workers, male politicians and male scholars perform their tasks only because they are born, reared and cared for by women's labour. The boundaries between public and private shift significantly over time and cross-culturally, as in the historical transition between private charity and public assistance, in both of which women played important roles. . . .

Women's history has also discovered that what is perceived as "private" by some may be seen as "public" by others. The domestic tasks of bearing and rearing children, for instance, were proclaimed as being of public importance by many women in the early women's movement. They requested that it be re-evaluated, and many of them based their demand for equal political citizenship precisely on this vision of the "separate sphere," understood not as a dichotomy of mutually exclusive and hierarchical terms, but as a source of equal rights and responsibilities of the female sex in respect to civil society. On this basis, they did not so much challenge the sexual division of labour, as the sexual division of power. . . .

These three dichotomies seem to have some important characteristics in common. They are eminently gender-linked, and as such they have distant roots in European and western traditions of gender perception. They have been taken up and used as crucial conceptual frameworks in the newly emerging women's history of the past decades, and simultaneously their long-standing apparent validity for the perception of gender relations has been thoroughly challenged. This challenge concerned the analysis, historicisation and deconstruction of the character and meaning of these three dual categories, as well as the links between them, and it questioned the traditional assumption that these dichotomies were expressions—natural and necessary expressions—of sexual difference.

The question has been raised as to whether these dichotomies are just a few examples among many similar binary oppositions and dualistic modes of western thought in general, or whether their gender-linked character makes them very special. . . . But it seems that, whenever they are used for describing gender relations, they do not refer so much to separate, autonomous, independent, equivalent dual spheres, as to relations of hierarchy: hierarchies of spheres, meanings, values, of inferiority and superiority, of subordination and power; in other words, to relations where "culture" subjects "nature," the world of "work" reigns over that of the "family," the "political" dominates the "private." . . .

Somehow, ironically, the same process by which women became historically (and not only historically) visible through the critique of these contradictories has also led to a number of new dichotomies of which little or nothing was heard during the first phase of women's studies, and which later came to the fore within the context of feminist scholarship itself. In part, they are the result of past attempts to resolve the earlier binary modes with the help of new concepts and theoretical frameworks. It seems that future strategies for women's history lie precisely, and once more, in the possibility and necessity of challenging these newer dichotomies.

1. Sex versus gender. The concept "gender" has been introduced into women's history and women's studies in the 1970s as a social, cultural, political and historical category, in order to express the insight that women's subordination, inferiority and powerlessness are not dictated by nature, but are social, cultural, political and historical constructions. Whereas "gender" had previously referred mainly to linguistic-grammatical constructions, it now became a major theoretical framework. One of the reasons for its success in replacing the word "sex" has been the insistence that the study of women does not only deal with sexuality, wifehood and motherhood, but with women in all walks of life. Women's studies do not only concern half of humankind, but all of it, because it is not only women who are gendered beings, but also men who are therefore far from representing universal humanity. Consequently, "men's history" and "men's studies" which analyse men as "men" have emerged. The concept of "gender" radicalised and universalized the efforts to make women visible, and the insight that gender is a basic, though flexible structure of society meant that women's and gender studies concern, in principle, any field or object of historical (and non-historical) scholarship.

But the new terminology has also brought to the fore major problems. They result from the fact that the concept of gender has been introduced in the form of a dichotomy. It distinguishes categorically between gender and sex, "sex" to be understood as "biological" and "gender" as "social" or cultural, and both are seen as

Problem w/ gender

combined in a "sex/gender system" where "raw biological sex" is somehow transformed into "social gender." The dichotomous structure of the pair had been evident since the late 1950s when, even before being taken up by feminist scholarship,
it came to be theorised by male scholars who studied intersexuals and transsexuals.
But this dichotomy between the "biological" and the "social" does not resolve but
only restates the old nature versus culture quarrel. Again, it relegates the dimension
of women's body, sexuality, motherhood and physiological sexual difference to a
supposedly pre-social sphere, and it resolves even less the question of precisely
what part of women's experience and activity is "biological" and what part "social"
or "cultural." . . .

In this situation, it is not the concept of gender that should be challenged—as
some feminist historians seem to prefer at present—but the linguistic and theoretical dichotomy of sex and gender. Particularly in history, the humanities and social
sciences, it might be challenged through using "gender" in a comprehensive sense
which may include both the physiological and the cultural dimension, and using
"sex" in the same sense as "gender," thus leaving space for continuities instead of
polarities of meaning.

2. Equality versus difference.   The problems of the sex/gender dichotomy are
closely related to those of another dichotomy with which we are faced today in a
new way and in an international debate which has taken on different shapes and
phases in different countries: that of "equality versus difference." Women's studies
have largely relied on the concept of "sexual" or "gender equality" as an analytical
tool, and physiological "difference" has been played down as insignificant because
it has so often been used to justify discriminatory treatment of women. In this perspective, it has been demanded that women be treated in the same way as men, as
if they were men, and that new laws and reforms be formulated in gender-neutral
terms . . . , thus eliminating sexual difference and rendering masculinity and femininity politically irrelevant. Other feminist scholars, however, argue that burning
issues such as rape, abortion or wife-battering cannot be dealt with adequately in
gender-neutral terms; that female "difference," physiological as well as social,
should not be erased but recognised, in historical, philosophical and legal terms;
that it has never had a chance to develop autonomous political and cultural forms
other than in social niches and in opposition to dominant cultures; that emphasis
should be laid on a critical evaluation of men's distinctive needs and activities and
that women's distinctive needs and activities should be valued, thus opening alternatives both to female inferiority and to women's assimilation to men. . . .

Some scholars tend to believe that the dichotomy "equality versus difference" is
simply a false dichotomy, more the result of misunderstandings than of insight. But
others insist on the mutually exclusive character of the relation between "equality"
and "difference," and therefore on the necessity of an either/or choice. The historian
Joan Hoff-Wilson urges that a decision be made, particularly by feminist leaders,
between either "equality between the sexes based on prevailing masculine societal
norms" or "justice between the sexes based on a recognition of equal, but different
socialised patterns of behavior." On the other hand, the historian Joan Scott considers
this to be "an impossible choice," and she questions precisely the dichotomy itself. I
also believe that it is unacceptable, among other reasons because both the "difference

dilemma" ("difference" being used, overtly or implicitly, to confirm women's inferiority in relation to men) and the "equality dilemma" ("equality" being used, overtly or implicitly, to erase gender difference in view of women's assimilation to male societal norms) are far from being sufficiently explored. Such an exploration should be put on the agenda for future women's history. Why is it, for instance, that "equality" and "justice" seem to complement each other in the case of men, but be opposed to each other in the case of women? Why is it that "difference" is only attributed to one half of humankind and not to the other? Why is it that "equality" is so intimately bound up with "fraternity," but not with sisterhood, since the French Revolution but also in earlier political thought?

Again the only way forward seems to be to challenge the dichotomy itself, and to do so by analysing and dismantling the sexist construction of difference as well as of equality. . . .

3. Integration versus autonomy.   An analogous argument may be appropriate in regard to the problems of the "integration" or "autonomy" of women's studies in respect to scholarship at large, and of women in respect to academic institutions. Despite the expansion of women's studies, and even though it is now occasionally admitted as a "sub-disciplinary specialisation," its impact on and integration in the academic disciplines have remained minimal, and what has been called "mainstreaming" is still far from being implemented, even though there are important differences here as to countries and disciplines. . . .

Clearly, women's studies need to be recognised as an integral part of scholarship at large. But such "mainstreaming" may also risk being drawn into a dynamic that makes women invisible again. There are now a number of cases where "gender history" is being opposed, in a dichotomous way, to "women's history," and where chairs in "women's history" are strongly opposed, but chairs in "gender history" are welcome. As an institutional problem, the latter situation may be dealt with according to institutional circumstances, but the theoretical problem remains, largely due to a specific definition of "gender" which excludes sexual "difference," meaning women, by classifying it as "biological" and therefore as socially and historically irrelevant. In such a view, the radical promise of gender history as an extension of women's history risks being subverted by the reduction of the history of women, once again, to a mere appendix of an allegedly more "generic" gender history. Again, women are not considered to be an equally universal subject as are other, and male-centred subjects.

Therefore, women's history also requires autonomy from male-dominated scholarship, in institutional and particularly in intellectual terms, in order to develop its full potential. But "autonomy," another virtue central to the heritage of the Renaissance and the Enlightenment, also needs to be redefined. In practice, the difficult question is to recognize the fine line, which is also a profound divide, between autonomy and segregation, the ghetto in which women's studies often find themselves. It seems that the problem "autonomy versus integration" cannot be adequately dealt with through terminological distinctions, between women's history, feminist history, and gender history. . . .

Challenging dichotomies seems to be a major issue on the scholarly as well as the political agenda of women's and gender history, and of women's studies more broadly. The act of challenging requires, of course, further study of the precise character of the opposing categories, of the particularities and dynamics of the dichotomous relationship, and of the form and character of the challenge itself.

As to the nature of gender-based dichotomies, there is obviously a significant difference between the first set of three which have been mentioned in the earlier section of this paper, and the latter set of three. This difference reflects, among other things, the increasingly complex character of the categories under which gender relations are being considered and studied. The dichotomies nature/culture, paid/unpaid work, public/private were constructed in alignment with a fixed divide between women and men, the ostensibly internally homogeneous categories on each side of which pointing either to women or to men. In the case of sex/gender, equality/difference, integration/autonomy, however, both (apparently) opposing terms refer to both sexes. We are therefore not dealing just with relations between the sexes, but with relations between relational categories; and not just with (apparent) contradictories between women and men, but with opposing or apparently opposing conceptualisations and practices of gender relations. Hence, women's studies and the search for new visions of gender has led us—despite, or rather because of sometimes profoundly different approaches—to at least one common ground: gender issues are issues which concern complex human relations, relations both between the sexes and within the sexes.

And what could or should be the character of the challenge? It requires continuous work on the dismantling, historicisation, and deconstruction of the apparently given meanings of the various categories. I believe that it also implies the rejection of mutually exclusive hierarchies, and especially of either/or solutions, in favour of as-well-as solutions. . . . In the case of the two latter dilemmas, we may particularly need to challenge their mutual exclusiveness and claim "equality in difference" and "difference in equality," "autonomy in integration" and "integration in autonomy." For both of them one might object, and it has been objected, that women cannot have their cake and eat it too. But for too long, women have baked the cake and taken only the smallest slice to eat for themselves.

African American Women in History

EVELYN BROOKS HIGGINBOTHAM

"Ah wanted to preach a great sermon about colored women sittin' on high, but they wasn't no pulpit for me." This line from Zora Neale Hurston's *Their Eyes Were Watching God* expresses the frustration of Nanny, the black grandmother who never realized the fulfillment of her dreams of "whut a woman oughta be and to do." Racism and poverty had silenced her and left her no opportunity or means to voice, much less realize, her message to the world. Like Nanny, the story of black American womanhood has been denied a "pulpit" for far too long. It was not until the mid-1970s that scholars began to notice the omission of black women in historical

Evelyn Brooks Higginbotham, "Beyond the Sound of Silence: African-American Women in History," from *Gender and History*, I, no. 1 (spring 1989), pp. 50–63. Reprinted by permission of Basil Blackwell Publishers.

literature. Even today, with the plethora of publications in Afro-American and women's history, the black woman's voice goes largely unheard. The sound of silence, which resonates throughout much of the scholarship on Afro-Americans and women, reflects the failure to recognize black women's history as not only an identifiable field of inquiry in its own right, but as an integral part of Afro-American, American, and women's history.

Writing black women into history is critical in illuminating the relation of both Afro-American and women's history to American history. Both Afro-Americans and women reflect the complicated dialectic of being integrally part of the larger American story, while also being quite distinguishable and apart from it. Both Afro-Americans and women find meaning and self-identity in the American past and in American culture, and yet they each claim a cultural uniqueness and separate consciousness. Afro-American history and women's history have shared similar historiographic trends throughout the twentieth century. Each has depended heavily upon the conventional sub-disciplines, e.g., political, economic, and social history, for periodization, conceptual frameworks, and methodologies. Yet each has made its own unique methodological contributions as well. Both have suffered from the weakness of omission. Afro-American history has failed to address gender issues adequately, while women's history has similarly failed to address questions of race. . . .

Women's history, like black history, came to life during the early twentieth century, but it came of age during the politically charged 1960s and early 1970s. In certain respects, the study of women has followed a historiographic course similar to that of black history. It has striven to fill the female gaps in the American story by integrating women into political and social histories. It has devoted entire textbooks to the subject of women's achievements. It has revised misconceptions and chronicled woman's struggle for equality. Women's history has benefited especially from social history's focus on the invisible and anonymous masses in society and has exploited its quantitative and interdisciplinary methods in examining female life cycles, labour force participation rates, and household and family structures.

Influenced by the concept of "cultural separatism" especially as utilized in studies of slave culture—historians of women have sought to identify a female culture and consciousness divorced from male points of reference and have explored hitherto uninvestigated, even unimagined, topics and sources related to the private world of women. Most important, in their formulation of the gender system as a set of social relations that interact and intersect with class and race relations, historians of women have made a valuable and unique methodological contribution. These varied historiographic trends notwithstanding, women's history has suffered from a racial bias. Criticized for its white, middle-class, and northeastern emphasis, it has just begun to write black women into its blossoming field of literature.

Although published work on black women remains sparse, articles and books increase yearly and now exist in sufficient number to reveal the different and conflicting voices of the black female experience. The conflicting voices usher from the paradoxical nature of the black woman's identity—of being simultaneously black and female, black and American, and American and female. By focusing on black women within the Afro-American context and including them in studies on American womanhood, historians will discover the importance of black women to both black and women's history. It is in addressing the conflicting voices of black womanhood that historians will ultimately unveil the too-often obscured dialectical relationship between women's and American history and between Afro-American and American history.

The theme of double jeopardy marks the starting point for all literature on black women. To be black and female carries the dual burden of racial and sexual oppression. Most historians assert the primacy of race as opposed to gender when identifying the objective context for the black female experience and black women's subjective perceptions of it. . . .

Historians of black women call into question the concept of a universal womanhood by understanding the unity of white men and women in determining American racial thought and policy. The white suffragists' vision of representative government excluded black women and black men alike. Their discrimination against black suffragists, along with their vacillation between silence and vocal support for the southern states' disfranchisement of black male voters, exposed their goal as being equality with white men only. In this regard, the white suffragists remained an integral part of the dominant American culture.

Social histories focusing on women's lives provide another source for observing racial differences. Again, black women defy dominant American patterns. Such studies employ an arsenal of statistics to disclose racial disparities in household structures, workforce participation rates, and types of occupation. The more sophisticated social histories place black women against the backdrop of contrasting patterns among various white ethnic groups and introduce cultural factors to explain these differences. . . . Proponents of cultural difference deny that any one culture embraces both black and white women, while they simultaneously question a racial identity that does not account for gender differences. Shaped by African traditions and American socio-economic forces, black women are described as perceiving and experiencing their lives in ways distinguishable from both white women and black men. . . .

Research on slave women . . . highlights cultural difference and finds the existence of a black female culture and consciousness to be anchored in the reality of daily work for black women. Black women worked, for the most part, either in gender-specific employment or in female-segregated groups within types of employment that engaged both sexes. Except for harvesting time, when male and female worked side by side, male gangs commonly plowed and female ones hoed. However, a noticeable number of women plowed and performed other physically arduous tasks associated with masculine strength. On the other hand, the positions of cook, mid-wife, and seamstress—all female jobs—commanded respect in the quarters. Since slave women worked largely in sexually segregated groups during the course of the day, they shared a world in which they developed their own criteria and value system for ranking and ordering themselves. The private world of slave women afforded, too, a sense of interdependence and cooperation that encouraged female self-esteem both individually and collectively and helped mitigate the dehumanizing aspects of slavery. . . .

The preponderant emphasis on differences between black and white women testifies to the overarching historical reality of racist oppression and the exclusion of blacks from a large part of American life. Yet, the acknowledgement of this reality does not negate the bicultural voice that also articulates the values of the dominant society. A singular focus on racial difference misses the bicultural aspects of the black woman's existence. It avoids understanding her as both black and American.

Black women have historically lived in a community whose collective behaviour derived not only from Afro-American traditions, but also from the values and social behaviour of the dominant American society. The case for cultural difference is strongest, although not beyond challenge, for the slave period, as slave narratives themselves reveal. . . .

The bicultural tensions heightened dramatically after emancipation. . . . Although slavery prescribed the black community to a "cultural world whose dictates and values were accepted with a minimum of ambivalence and questioning, or inhibiting self-consciousness," freedom introduced new and alternate standards, namely those of the dominant American society. The new standards, promoted by Yankee missionaries, black schools and colleges, and black churches, set the process of biculturation in motion. Schools, churches, and many black leaders taught that individual advancement, as well as the advancement of the entire black community demanded a lifestyle that stood at odds with many of the older black cultural traditions. Gaining respect, even justice, from white America required changes in religious beliefs, speech patterns, and also in gender roles and relations.

In the self-conscious as well as sub-conscious acceptance of dominant American values, many blacks increasingly linked the new values with upward mobility and the old with backwardness. Even the masses, held down by poverty and racial oppression, deemed certain mainstream values and behaviour as proper and correct, despite their inability to manifest them in practice. [This] is the same "double consciousness" of which [W.E.B.] Du Bois wrote so eloquently at the dawn of the twentieth century: "One ever feels his twoness,—an American, a Negro; two souls, two thoughts, two unreconciled strivings; two warring ideals in one dark body, whose dogged strength alone keeps it from being torn asunder."

My own work on the women's movement in the black Baptist church between 1880 and 1920 exposes the class dimension of biculturation and the decisive participation of women missionaries in the dissemination and internalization of middle-class values among and by countless poor and uneducated blacks. Despite the racial segregation, disfranchisement, and violence of the late nineteenth-century South, women's societies—called conventions by black Baptists—influenced some blacks to aspire to and even achieve upward mobility, but they influenced many more to make financial sacrifices, limit personal consumption, and channel their meager resources to the support of the educational and other self-help institutions of their race. . . .

If the concept of biculturation informs the black woman's identity as a black American, it simultaneously shapes her identity as an American woman. In the immediate post–Civil War South, black families sought the withdrawal of mothers and wives from the workforce in order to attend to their own households. The attempt on the part of blacks to practice gender roles prevalent among white Americans met with a hostile response from white Union army officers, planters, and Freedmen's Bureau agents, who viewed black women's domesticity not as an ideal but as an "evil of female loaferism." Economic necessity soon returned these women to the fields and kitchens of the South, but this reversal does not imply a rejection of their preference for domesticity. . . .

Ex-slaves were quick to idealize the role of man as provider and woman as homemaker, even though both were forced to work. . . . Indeed, Afro-Americans protested the racist reality that forced so many of their women into the full-time jobs of cleaning and caring for white women's homes and children. This reality served as a constant reminder of the inability of black men to earn a "man's" wage. Racial restrictions and job ceilings denied them the same "breadwinner" self-image that white husbands enjoyed. Implicit in their idealization of domesticity seemed to be the reinstatement of dignity to black manhood and womanhood.

The visible assimilation or, at least, psychological allegiance to the sexual be-haviour and attitudes of white middle-class America conveys the class-specific con-text of gender relations within the black community. Unquestioningly, discussions of class differences among blacks become inherently problematic, because of the difficulty in establishing objective definitions that are useful beyond the slavery period. Until recently racism and poverty skewed income and occupational levels so drastically that sociologists relied heavily upon values and behaviour as additional criteria for discerning blacks who maintained or aspired to middle-class status from those who practiced alternative lifestyles. Thus social scientists as well as members of the black community, in general, focused on adherence to bourgeois standards of respectability and morality in designating classes.

Gender relations constitute one of the important variables, although not the only one, traditionally used to establish attitudinal and behavioural criteria for class differences among blacks. Nineteenth and early twentieth century leaders rarely al-luded to income or occupation when referring, as they frequently did, to the "better class of Negroes." Domestic servants could be included, and some were cited in this category, for it comprised all who were hardworking, religious, clean, and, so far as sex was concerned, respectful of the dominant society's manners and morals.

The club movement among middle-class black women during the late nine-teenth century constituted an effort to win greater respectability for black woman-hood through the uplift of black working women. "Lifting as we climb," the motto of the National Association of Colored Women, reveals the black middle-class woman's commitment to her working-class sister, but also to dominant American assumptions regarding the benefits of upward mobility. . . . Given the economic realities, many black women sought to emulate mainstream female roles, codes of dress, and public behaviour as best they could, for they linked assimilation with self-respect and racial progress. It is not uncommon for oppressed peoples to adopt the values of their oppressors for reasons of their own. The shared acceptance of the dominant society's normative gender roles forged the link between black and white missionary women and permitted their cooperative work through religious and educational institutions. . . .

. . . At specific historical moments, black women have borne discrimination that was peculiar to their gender. The ratification of the Fifteenth Amendment, for instance, accentuated discrimination against the black woman as woman. During Reconstruction black women shared their men's ecstasy and optimism, but not their right to wield the ballot. Like all American women, they stood as spectators, not as recipients of an expanding democracy. Black women rejoiced to hear the voices of their men resound from the lowest local offices in the South to the halls of the United States Congress, and yet they, as women, remained on the margins of representative government. Sojourner Truth, an outspoken critic of the unequal political rights of black men and women, expressed her displeasure with the limitations of the Fifteenth Amendment: "There is a great stir about the colored men getting their rights, but not a word about the colored women; and if colored men get their rights, and not colored women theirs, you see the colored men will be masters over the women, and it will be just as bad as it was before."

Black clubwomen and countless numbers in church societies championed woman's suffrage in the early twentieth century. Studies . . . clearly exhibit the importance of the vote to black women. Divisions in women's political and reform work reflected the very real barrier of white racism; however, parallels and cooperative efforts, which also existed between black and white women's organizations, reflected commonalities and shared interests among women regardless of race. . . .

Writing black women into history carries scholarship beyond the silence of the past, while ultimately weaving a more intricate, yet more honest narrative of women, Afro-Americans, and this nation as a whole. Studies of Afro-American women, when taken together, tell a story of gender and racial oppression, but also one of new dimensions of cultural autonomy, cooperation, supportive bonding, and survival strategies. The inclusion of black women holds the key to recognizing and analyzing American social systems and social relations in all their permutations of race, class, and gender. Attention is thereby called to the interaction and intersection of gender, race, and class, and their roles—as sets of social relations—in both determining and being determined by power relations.

The relation of gender to power is at the core of women's history; yet factors of class and race make any generalization regarding womanhood's common oppression impossible. The relation of race to power remains central to Afro-American history, but gender and class preclude a monolithic black community as well. Studies of black women help to dispel the silence and correct imbalances in both Afro-American and women's history. By so doing, they also help to explain the contradictory relationship of women and blacks to the American experience.

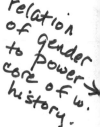

relation of gender to power, core of w. history.

⬥ F U R T H E R   R E A D I N G

DuBois, Ellen, and Vicki Ruiz, eds. *Unequal Sisters: A Multicultural Reader in American Women's History* (3d ed., 2000).

Evans, Sara. *Born for Liberty* (1997).

Giddings, Paula. *When and Where I Enter: The Impact of Black Women on Race and Sex in America* (1984).

Hewitt, Nancy A. "Beyond the Search for Sisterhood: American Women's History in the 1980s," *Social History* 10, no. 3 (October 1985): 299–321.

Higginbotham, Evelyn Brooks. "African-American Women's History and the Metalanguage of Race," *Signs* 17 (1991–1992): 254–274.

Hoff, Joan. "Gender as a Postmodern Category of Paralysis," *Women's History Review* 3, no. 2 (1994): 149–168.

Kelly, Joan. *Women, History, and Theory* (1984).

Kerber, Linda. "Separate Spheres, Female Worlds, Women's Place: The Rhetoric of Women's History," *Journal of American History* 75 (1988–1989): 3–39.

Lerner, Gerda. *The Majority Finds Its Past* (1979).

Melosh, Barbara, ed. *Gender and American History Since 1890* (1993).

Riley, Denise. *"Am I That Name?" Feminism and the Category of "Women" in History* (1988).

Scott, Joan W. *Gender and the Politics of History* (1988).

Woloch, Nancy. *Women and the American Experience* (1984).

Zinsser, Judith P. *Feminism and History: A Glass Half Full* (1993).

CHAPTER
2

Colonial Women
in New Worlds

Until recently, historians wrote about the three groups resident in colonial North America—Indians, Europeans, and Africans—as though they lived entirely separate lives. That is, studies of "the colonies" rarely examined colonists' interactions with "the Indians" except when warfare was at issue; works on "Indians" and their lives primarily sought to reconstruct native peoples' existence before the arrival of the colonizers, or at least to minimize attention to Europeans, again with the exception of times of war; and examinations of early African residents focused on their lives in or out of slavery, but within the confines of a black—or at most, a black-and-white—community.

Now, however, scholars have come to understand that the societies coexisting in colonial North America were not sealed off from one another. Indeed, complex inter-relationships, for women as well as for men, were far more common than historians once realized. Recent essays, like those reprinted in this chapter, accordingly have begun to look at the wide variety of ways in which Indians, settlers, and enslaved Africans—and the offspring of racially mixed unions—interacted in a colonial setting. Scholars are thus demonstrating that North America was "multicultural" from the earliest days of European settlement.

◆ *D O C U M E N T S*

The documents in this chapter detail a few of the myriad ways in which women and men of different races interacted in the North American colonies. During the first decades of English settlement in Georgia, an Anglo-Creek woman named Mary Musgrove served as an important intermediary between the Indians and the settlers. Document 1 is a letter she addressed to James Oglethorpe, founder of the colony, in 1734, describing current relationships with the Choctaws. Thirteen years later (Document 2), she petitioned an English officer for compensation for her many services to Georgia. In other colonies during the middle years of the eighteenth century, Indians regularly raided European settlements, seeking plunder and captives. Document 3, a priest's report of such a raid in New Mexico in 1747, outlines the fates of several captives and complains about the inability of the religious authorities to defend their communities against such attacks. Another priest's account in 1761, Document 4, offers information about the other side of the story—the treatment of Indian captives by the Spaniards and their Christian Indian charges. In 1771, Israel and Mary Wilkinson of Rhode Island testified in a lawsuit about the relationship of Sarah Muckamugg, an Indian woman, and Aaron, an African American man (Document 5). Somewhat more than two decades later, by enacting the marriage law provision found in Document 6, Rhode Island ensured that such intimate relationships between Indians and African Americans would continue, for it prohibited members of either group from marrying whites.

1. Mary Musgrove Assists the Georgians in Dealing with the Choctaws, 1734

Savannah, July 17, 1734

Honoured Sir

I make bold to acquaint You that Thomas Jones is returned from the Choctaws and according to your Honours Desire he has brought the Choctaws down and they have received great favours from Col. Bull and Mr. Causton and all the rest of the Colony, and a great deal of Respect shewed them which they are wonderfully pleased at. And when they came down Mr. Jones brought with him some of the Heads of the Tallooposes which is called the Upper Creeks; The Dog King of Uphalais Chauaway by name went with Mr. Jones up to the Choctaws to make peace, and he is mighty glad that he and Mr. Jones did persuade them to come down which is more than ever Carolina could do to get them down before. And the Choctaws are so glad that some white People whom they called their Masters had taken such Care of them as to send for them and they was very glad of the opportunity to come for they lived very poor before and now they are in good hopes to live as well as the other Indians do, for they had nor have no Trade with the French and their Skins lye by them and rot. When Mr. Thomas Jones came to them at first there was thirty Towns only that had the notice. Before Mr. Jones came away all they gave their Consents for their Coming, but Notice was still sent on farther. And they say that they like the English better than the French, and that they will stand by the English as long as they have one left alive. There was some of the Caupahauches and the Hulbaumors came with them. The Choctaws are all amazed to see the Creeks drink as they do, and they think the Creeks are saucy to the white People. The Choctaw King thinks they are obliged to the white People and thinks they cannot do enough for the white People especially the English. And since they have been here there has not one of them been disguised in Liquor or any ways saucy upon any Account. They have been here 21 Days for Mr. Causton thought it proper to send for Col. Bull and that was the Reason of their being Detained so long here. Governor Johnson has sent for them to come to Carolina but Thomas Jones was not willing they should go to Carolina for fear of disobliging your Honour, and as he was sent for them for the Colony he did not Care

---

Colonial Records of Georgia, 20: 63–64. This document can also be found in John T. Juricek, ed., *Georgia Treaties 1733–1763*, vol. 11 of *Early American Indian Documents: Treaties and Laws, 1607–1789* (Frederick, Md.: University Publications of America, 1989), 38–39.

they should go any where else. You Honour's Name is spread very much amongst them and they say that when your Honour comes back to Georgia they will be bound to raise a thousand or two at your Honour's Command if desired, and they design to leave the French entirely and then they will come down and pay their Respects to You, and to Governor Johnson if your Honour desires they should go to Carolina but not without your Honour's Consent. Mr. Thomas Jones does insist of the Trade amongst the Choctaws as your Honour did promise him, and the Choctaws have so very great Respect and Value for Mr. Jones that they had rather have him to trade among them than any body else because he ventured his Life to bring them down to the English.

2. Mary Musgrove Seeks Aid from Georgia in Return for Past Service and Losses, 1747

August 10, 1747

TO The Honourable Lieutenant Collonel Alexander Heron Commander in Chief of his Majestys Forces in the Province of Georgia the Memorial and Representation of Mary Bosomworth of the Said Province.

HUMBLY SHEWETH.

That your Memorialist was born at the Cowetaw Town on the Oakmulgee River which is a Branch of the Alatamaha and the Chief Town of the Creek Indian Nation.

That She is by Descent on the Mothers Side, (who was Sister to the Old Emperor) of the Same Blood of the Present Mico's and Chief's now in that Nation, and by their Laws, and the Voice of the Whole Nation is esteemed their Rightfull and Natural Princess.

That her Ancestors, Tho under the Appellation of Savages, or Barbarions, were a brave and free born people, who never owed Allegiance, to or Acknowledged the sovereignty of any Crowned Head whatever, but have always maintained their own Possessions and Independency, Against all Opposers by Warr, at the Expence of their Blood; as they Can shew by the many Troophies of Victory, and Relicts of their Enimies slain in Defence of their Natural Rights.

That they have entered into Several Treaties of Peace, Friendship and Commerce, with Persons properly impowered, in behalf of the Crown of Great Britain.

That they Have made Concessions of Several Portions of Land, (their Natural Right by Ancient Possession) in behalf of his Majesty; and have for several Years past on their parts, Strictly and faithfully Observed the Treaty of Friendship and Alliance entered into with the Honourable Major General Oglethorpe in behalf of his Brittannick Majesty. And have on all Occasions been ready to fight Against his Majestys Enimies which they Have very much Annoyed.

That both the french and Spaniards well know by Dear Experience how terrible they are to their Enemies in War. They are so highly Sensible of the Vast Importance of the Friendship and Alliance of the Creek Nation to the British Interest; (and the

---

Colonial Records of Georgia, 36: 256–273. This document can also be found in John T. Juricek, ed., *Georgia Treaties 1733–1763*, vol. 11 of *Early American Indian Documents: Treaties and Laws, 1607–1789* (Frederick, Md.: University Publications of America, 1989), 140–147.

only Barrier to hinder them from gaining the utmost of their Wishes upon the Continent of America) That they Have for some time past, and are at this Juncture, Labouring by all the Artifices Imaginable to seduce that Nation from their Alliance with his Majestys Subjects, which will certainly be a great Addition and Increase of Territory Strength and Power to his Majestys Enimies; and the Dangerous Consequence May be the Utmost Hazard of the safety of his Majestys Southern Frontiers Carolina and Georgia.

That your Memorialist hath by her Intrest since the First Settlement of the Colony of Georgia for the Space of 14 Years continued that Important Nation Steady and Steadfast in their Friendship and Alliance with his Majestys subjects at the Expence of her own private Fortune to the Utter Ruin of her self and Famely as will evidently Appear by a plain Narrative of Incontestable Matters of Fact. . . .

THAT whereas His Majesty in the Preamble of his Royal Charter to the Honourable the Trustees for Establishing the Colony of the Georgia, bearing Date the 9th Day of June 1732 has been graciously pleased to Declare that the Intention of the Settlement of the Said Colony was partly as a Protection to his Majestys Subjects of South Carolina, whose Southern Frontiers continued unsettled and Lay exposed to the frequent Ravages of Enimy Indians etc. which Signal Instance of his Majestys peculiar Care for the Protection of that Province, is Most gratefully Acknowledged by a Memorial sent to his Majesty from the Governor and Council of the Said Province Dated the 9th April 1734.

And whereas his Majestys Gracious Intentions in the Settlement of the Colony of Georgia, have been so far Answered; that no out Settlements have been cutt off; Boats taken; nor men killed; since that time (which used before frequently to happen,) your Memorialist therefore humbly hopes that upon a Representation of her Case to his Majestys Governor and Council of the Province of South Carolina; How far his Majestys Subjects of that Province have been enabled to Improve the southern parts of that Province (which Before Lay Waste) by your Memorialist's Interest in Continuing the Indians in friendship and Alliance with his Majestys Subjects: THAT, That Government would be induced to make her some Restitution for her past services and Losses sustained in his Majestys service as she is Now indebted several Considerable sums of Money to Merchants in Charles Town, and Other Persons in south Carolina: and Destitute of Credit to Carry on her Affairs (which takes away the Very Means of her having it in her Power to Do Justice to her Creditors in that Province) and Whatever the Government shall think her Worthy off, she Desires may be Applyed to that end.

AND Lastly your Memorialist cannot Help repeating with an equal Mixture of a Real Grief of Heart, and Indignation; that her Injuries and Oppressions have been such, as she believes; have been scarce paralleled under a British Government. Language is too Weak to Represent her present Deplorable Case; She at present Labours under every sence of Injury; and Circumstances of Distress; Destitute of even the Common Necessaries of Life, being Insulted, Abused, contemned and Dispised by those ungratefull People who are indebted to her for the Blessings they Injoy.

The Only Returns she has met with for her past Services, Generosity, and Maternal Affection (she has at all times shewn for the whole Colony) has been injust Loads of Infamy and Reproach; Branded and Stigmatized with the Odious Name of Traytor, for Making any Pretentions to those Rights she is Justly entitled to by the

Laws of God and Nature (as her ancestors were the Natural born Heirs Sole Owners and Proprietors of every Foot of Land which is now his Majestys Colony of
Georgia,) tho she has in Vain made Application for a Grant from the Crown, and is
Desireous and Willing to hold What Posesions she is there entitled to by the Laws
of Nature and Nations, as a Subject of great Britain.

It is with the greatest Reluctancy, that your Memorialist is Drove to the Neces-
sity to declare; That the Collony of Georgia was settled by her Interest with the
Creek Indians: that it has in a Great Measure been supported by it, (as she can
make Appeare by Authentick Letters and Testimonies,) and that she has at this Day
Interest enough to command a Thousand fighting men to stand in the face of his
Majestys Enemies; and to Countermine every intended Design of both the french
and spaniards in alienating the Creeks Nation of Indians from the British Interest; If
Suitable Encouragements are given her, to prevent her being Drove to the Necessity
of Flying to her Indian Friends for Bread which will Greatly Confirm the Jealousies
and uneasinesses which his Majesty's Enimies have so Industriously fomented and
Spirited up Amongst them. . . .

THAT Whereas your Memorialist is highly sensible that its not in your Power
to Redress her Grievances, and of the Great Difficulties you Labour under at this
Juncture, in not being allowed any fund for continuing the Creek Indians in Friendship and Alliance with his Majestys Subjects and how far his Majestys service and
Interest may Suffer thereby, she therefore Humbly begs that you would be Pleased
to Lay this Memorial before his Grace the Duke of Newcastle one of His Majestys
Principal Secretarys of State for His Graces Consideration with this Assurance, that if
the Government should think proper to allow a Certain Sum per Annum to be applyed
for maintaining his Majestys Peace and Authority Amongst the Indians that she on her
Part would engage by her Interest Amongst them, to Doe every Duty that ever was
Done by Rangers etc. in Georgia which have Cost the Government so many Thous-
sands, of Pounds, and With the Regiment under your Honours Command, and her Interest with the Creek Indians she believes that every Foot of his Majestys Possessions,
and this Important Frontier could be maintained Against all his Majestys Enemies.

All Which is Humbly Submitted to your Consideration by your Memorialist
this 10th Day August 1747.

MARY [MUSGROVE] BOSOMWORTH

3. Father Juan Sanz de Lezaún Reports a Comanche Raid in New Mexico, 1747

The fathers receive no credit whatever for their service to God or to our king. Evidence of this is the invasion of the enemy into the town of Habiquiú in August,
1747, when they carried off twenty-three women and children, besides killing a girl
and an old woman for having defended themselves. Reverend Mirabal, who was cus-
todian and lived in the mission of San Juan, immediately reported this to the governor, who at the time was Don Joaquín Codallos. The governor paid no attention until

Juan Sanz de Lezaún, "An Account of Lamentable Happenings in New Mexico. . . ," in Charles Wilson
Hackett et al., eds., *Historical Documents Relating to New Mexico, Nueva Viscaya and Approaches
Thereto* (Washington, D.C.: Carnegie Institution, 1923), 476–477.

the reverend father, moved by the unrest of all his neighbors, again wrote, and, as the affair was now public knowledge in the entire kingdom, the governor gave orders after four days, and they went out in pursuit of the enemy, but accomplished nothing because the latter had had plenty of time to get ahead of them. A few settlers went out to follow their trail and found three women dead and a new-born child; the rest had all been carried off. One of them was brought back at the end of seven years by the Comanches, they having been the ones responsible for this misdeed, while the poor heathen Yutas paid for it. At the time when they brought this woman the governor was Don Tomás Vélez Cachupín. This being the situation, what can the poor religious do about it all, burdened as they are with sorrows, unable to defend any one, and seeing so many souls lost without being able to find a means of proving all these things?

4. Father Pedro Serrano Describes the Treatment of Captive Indian Women in New Mexico, 1761

Here, in short, is gathered everything possible for trade and barter with these barbarians in exchange for deer and buffalo hides, and, what is saddest, in exchange for Indian slaves, men and women, small and large, a great multitude of both sexes, for they are gold and silver and the richest treasure for the governors, who gorge themselves first with the largest mouthfuls from this table, while the rest eat the crumbs. Here only God can so confuse this innumerable multitude of Indians—barbarians, cannibals, armed, and mixed with numerous apostates from our holy faith—that they do not ally themselves and unite in secret treason with the Christian Indians, oppressed and tyrannized over in the manner that I have already described, and make a general attack upon the entire kingdom, especially when the blindness and greed displayed in these markets or fairs reaches such extremes that, heedless of the trading, or of God, or the king, or the law, or the kingdom, or even of themselves, these men with their wrongs and injustices stir up these barbarous nations, and lead them to conspire. There has already been such an occasion when they attempted to begin hostilities, and they had already announced war and taken up arms, when it was by our Lord God alone that they were appeased, in this instance through the medium of a religious who is still living. Among many other infamies there is one of such a nature that if I did not so desire a remedy I would remain silent, since it is so obscene and unfit for chaste ears. It is the truth that when these barbarians bring a certain number of Indian women to sell, among them many young maidens and girls, before delivering them to the Christians who buy them, if they are ten years old or over, they deflower and corrupt them in the sight of innumerable assemblies of barbarians and Catholics (neither more nor less, as I say), without considering anything but their unbridled lust and brutal shamelessness, and saying to those who buy them, with heathen impudence: "Now you can take her—now she is good." The laws that are broken in this hellish ceremony or exhibition alone I have already cited in number 38, but the consequences that follow from it can only be wept for, for it is impossible to fathom them and much less to tell them.

Pedro Serrano to the Marquis of Cruillas, 1761, in Charles Wilson Hackett et al., eds., *Historical Documents Relating to New Mexico, Nueva Viscaya and Approaches Thereto* (Washington, D.C.: Carnegie Institution, 1923), 487.

5. Israel and Mary Wilkinson Describe the Relationship of Sarah Muckamugg and Aaron, an African American Man, 1771

Israel Wilkinson deposes, 25 July 1771

"I have heard her say that she was not married to the said Negro Man."

Mary Wilkinson deposes, 24 and 25 July 1771

"She then [about 1741] built a small hut and lived there some time, during which one Aaron a negro man came to said hut and as I understand by said Sarah had been Quariling with her and she complained of his abuse to her I then asked if he was her Husband she answered he was none of her Husband Nither had she any thing to Do with him and I think She told he She was never married to him but of this I am not Certain.

"She said that Aaron Sayeth that he never would Live with me any more neither would he help maintain the Children & I asked her wether they was ever marryed & she Said no & I asked was the Reason was & she Said that he promised to do well by me & further Said that She would then be marrd but he wuld not & further Sayeth that he had got another Squaw that he Lovd better."

6. Rhode Island Prohibits Whites from Marrying People of Color, 1798

Sec. 5. *And be it further enacted,* That no person, by this act authorized to join persons in marriage, shall join in marriage any white person with any Negro, Indian or mulatto, on the penalty of two hundred dollars, to be recovered by action of debt, one moiety thereof to be paid to and for the use of the State, and the other moiety to and for the use of him who shall prosecute for the same; and all such marriages shall be absolutely null and void.

◆ E S S A Y S

James F. Brooks (who was recently appointed to Research Faculty and Director of SAR Press at the School of American Research in Santa Fe, New Mexico) examines captivities in eighteenth-century New Mexico, contending that Indian women and children captured by the Spaniards and their Indian allies, and Spanish women and children taken by such Indian tribes as the Comanches and the Navajos, all served as important "cultural brokers," bridging the disparate worlds of colonizer and colonized. Michele Gillespie, of Wake Forest University, describes the role of the remarkable Anglo-Creek woman Mary Musgrove, who for several decades worked as an intermediary between

Box 1, folder 4, John Milton Earle Papers, American Antiquarian Society, Worcester, Mass. Thanks to Daniel Mandell for supplying transcripts of these documents.

Section 5, "An Act to Prevent Clandestine Marriages," *The Public Laws of the State of Rhode Island and Providence Plantations, 1798.*

Georgia settlers and her Creek relatives. The life of the New England Nipmuc Sarah Muckamugg, primary subject of the third essay, exemplified trends among her contemporaries, Daniel R. Mandell argues. The Truman State University historian points out that, like many other Indian women, she sought intimacy in a relationship with an African American man who for other—but related—reasons had difficulty finding a sexual partner from among his own people.

Captivity in the New Mexico Borderlands

JAMES F. BROOKS

Late in the summer of 1760, a large Comanche raiding party besieged the fortified home of Pablo Villalpando in the village of Ranchos de Taos, New Mexico. After a daylong fight, the Comanches breached the walls and killed most of the male defenders. They then seized fifty-seven women and children, among whom was twenty-one-year-old María Rosa Villalpando, Pablo's second daughter, and carried them into captivity on the Great Plains. María's young husband, Juan José Xacques, was slain in the assault, but her infant son, José Juliano Xacques, somehow escaped both death and captivity.

[margin handwriting: Value of women in trade as Commodity.]

The Comanches apparently traded María shortly thereafter to the Pawnees, for by 1767 she lived in a Pawnee village on the Platte River and had borne another son, who would come to be known as Antoine. In that year, the French trader and co-founder of St. Louis, Jean Salé dit Lerole, visited the Pawnees and began cohabiting with María. About one year later, she bore Salé a son, whom they named Lambert. Perhaps this arrangement suited Salé's trading goals, for it wasn't until 1770 that he ended María's Indian captivity and brought her to St. Louis, where they married.

Jean and María (now Marie Rose Salé) had three more children, when, for unknown reasons, Jean returned to France, where he remained the rest of his life. María stayed in St. Louis to become the matriarch of an increasingly prominent family. Her New Mexican son, José Juliano, would visit her there, although we will see that the reunion proved bittersweet. María finally died at the home of her daughter, Hélène, in 1830, at well over ninety years of age. For María Rosa Villalpando, captivity yielded a painful, yet paradoxically successful, passage across cultures into security and longevity. . . .

Whatever the large-scale antagonisms between Spanish colonists and Native Americans, problems of day-to-day survival required methods of cross-cultural negotiation. Prolonged, intensive interaction between New Mexican *pobladores* (village settlers) and nomadic or pastoral Indian societies required some mutually intelligible symbols through which cultural values, interests, and needs could be defined. Horses, guns, and animal hides spring immediately to mind as customary symbols of exchange, but women and children proved even more valuable (and valorized) as agents (and objects) of cultural negotiations. In New Mexico, as elsewhere in North America,

---

James F. Brooks, " 'This Evil Extends Especially . . . to the Feminine Sex': Negotiating Captivity in the New Mexico Borderlands," *Feminist Studies* 22, no. 2 (summer 1996): 279–309. Reprinted by permission of the publisher, Feminist Studies, Inc.

the "exchange of women" through systems of captivity, adoption, and marriage seem to have provided European and Native men with mutually understood symbols of power with which to bridge cultural barriers.

Rival men had seized captives and exchanged women long before European colonialism in North America. The exogamous exchange of women between "pre-capitalist" societies appears to represent a phenomenon by which mutual obligations of reciprocity are established between kindreds, bands, and societies, serving both to reinforce male dominance and to extend the reproductive (social and biological) vigor of communities. This article approaches the issue from a variety of sources and perspectives. Combining Spanish archival research with some of the classics of North American Indian ethnology, and viewing both through the lens of feminist critiques and extensions, I suggest that the capture and integration of women and children represented the most violent expression along a continuum of such exchange traditions. The patriarchal subordination of women and children, it has been argued, served as a foundation upon which other structures of power and inequality were erected. Gerda Lerner contends that the assertion of male control over captive women's sexual and reproductive services provided a model for patriarchal owner-ship of women in "monogamous" marriages by which patrilineal bloodlines remained "pure." From this sense of proprietorship grew other notions of property, including the enslavement of human beings as chattels.

In New Spain, under the *Recopilación* of 1680 (a compendium of laws govern-ing colonial/Indian relations), Spanish subjects had been encouraged to redeem indigenous captives from their captors, baptize them into the Catholic faith, and acculturate them as new "detribalized" colonial subjects. These redemptions oc-curred in roughly two forms—either through formal "ransoming" at annual trade fairs *(ferias* or *rescates)* or small-scale bartering *(cambalaches)* in local villages or at trading places on the Great Plains. Trade fairs at Taos, Pecos, and Picuris Pueblos had long fostered the exchange of bison meat for corn, beans, and squash between Plains Indians and the Río Grande Pueblos and had probably included some ex-changes of people as well. . . .

Judging from extant New Mexican parochial registers, between 1700 and 1850, nearly 3,000 members of nomadic or pastoral Indian groups entered New Mexican society as *indios de rescate* (ransomed Indians), *indios genízaros* ("slaves"), *criados* (servants), or *huerfanos* (orphans), primarily through the artifice of "ransom" by colonial purchasers. Ostensibly, the cost of ransom would be retired by ten to twenty years of service to the redeemers, after which time these individuals would become *vecinos* (tithes-paying citizens). In practice, these people appear to have experienced their bondage on a continuum that ranged from near-slavery to familial incorpora-tion, an issue that will be addressed at length in this article.

Ransomed captives comprised an important component in colonial society, averaging about 10 to 15 percent of the colonial population, and especially in periph-eral villages where they may have represented as much as 40 percent of the "Span-ish" residents. Girls and boys under the age of fifteen composed approximately two-thirds of these captives, and about two-thirds of all captives were women "of serviceable age" or prepubescent girls.

This commerce in women and children proved more than a one-way traffic, how-ever. Throughout the period under consideration, nomadic groups like Comanches and Navajos made regular raids on the scattered *poblaciones* (settlements), at times

fictive kin → fictitious

seizing as many as fifty women and children. In 1780, Spanish authorities estimated that the *Naciones del Norte* (Plains tribes of the northern frontier) alone held more than 150 Spanish citizens captive, and by 1830 the figure for the Comanches alone may have exceeded 500. Among the Navajos, as late as 1883 U.S. Indian agent Dennis M. Riordan estimated that there were "300 slaves in the hands of the tribe," many of whom were "Mexicans captured in infancy." Like their Indian counterparts, these women and children found themselves most often incorporated into their host society through indigenous systems of adoption. As fictive kin, they too experienced a range of treatment. Although impossible to arrive at precise numbers of New Mexican captives in Indian societies, their representation becomes increasingly significant in a discussion of the workings of the captive system and the personal experience of captives themselves.

The captive-exchange system appears overwhelmingly complex when examined through particular cases, but certain overall patterns seem consistent. First, captive taking and trading represented the most violent and exploitative component of a long-term pattern of militarized socioeconomic exchange between Indian and Spanish societies. Second, it seems that New Mexican captives and *indios de rescate* generally remained in their "host" societies throughout their lifetimes. Third, female captives often established families within the host society, and their descendants usually became full culture-group members. Male captives, on the other hand, suffered either a quick retributive death or, if young, grew to become semiautonomous auxiliary warriors within their new society. Finally, it appears that many captives found ways to transcend their subordinate status by exercising skills developed during their "cross-cultural" experience. In doing so, they negotiated profound changes in the cultural identity of the societies within which they resided, changes which continue to reverberate in the borderlands today.

captive-exchange system

Torn from their natal societies in "slave" raids, treated like *piezas* ("coins," a common term in New Spain for slaves, both Indian and African) in a volatile system of intercultural exchange, and finally the "property" of strangers, captive and ransomed women seem unlikely subjects as historical actors. But the experiences recounted henceforth show these women and children negotiating narrow fields of agency with noteworthy skill. From positions of virtual powerlessness, captive women learned quickly the range of movement allowed by the host culture, especially in regard to adoption and *compadrazgo* (god-parenthood) practices. This first phase of integration gave them "kin" to whom they could turn for protection and guidance. But this security remained limited, and many faced coercive conjugal relationships, if not outright sexual exploitation by their new masters.

quality of life

Whether of Spanish or Indian origin, two factors are essential to our understanding of the captive experience in greater New Mexico and perhaps to similar cases in other periods and regions. First, captives' status and treatment within the host society would establish the structural constraints (culturally specific customs and laws governing rights and obligations) within which individuals might pursue their goals. Second, sheer luck and the individual captive's personal resources determined much of her actual lived experience, ranging from terror and exploitation to a few remarkable cases of deft negotiation and good fortune, into which María Rosa Villalpando's story certainly falls. Overall, the interplay of structural constraints, contingency, and skills can be seen in most captives' lives. . . .

. . . Because one side of the captive system originates in indigenous, precontact exogamous exchange traditions, we need to look at gender and social hierarchies within Native American societies to begin to understand the structural constraints that . . . captives might have experienced. Although they display variation, women's and captives' status within Indian societies of the borderlands (Navajo, Apache, Ute, and Comanche) may be generally described as subordinate to men and holders of the "cultural franchise" but enhanced by traditions of matrilineality and social mobility.

Navajo patterns of gender and social hierarchies show a blending of southern Athabascan systems and cultural adaptations to Spanish colonialism near their homelands. Navajo women owned the flocks of sheep and wove the textiles that formed the core of their pastoral economy. Matrilineal descent, therefore, conferred important productive resources as well as kin-reckoning through women. Navajo men, however, prevailed in "public" decisions involving warfare and diplomacy.

Captives taken in warfare with other tribes or raids on Spanish settlements again experienced a range of treatment. If not killed in vengeance satisfaction, the captive invariably suffered a period of harsh and terrifying ritual abuse. This "taming" process probably formed the first phase in adoption ritual. After "taming," most captives became inducted into the clan of their captor, or the "rich man" who purchased them from the successful warrior. Once a clan member, it seems few barriers stood in the way of social advancement. . . . Captive women usually became clan members and married exogenously. Even if not inducted into clan membership, their children by Navajo men were considered members of the father's clan. . . .

Captives seem to have fared less well among the Jicarilla Apaches, a semisedentary people who practiced a seasonal economy that balanced hunting and collecting with extensive horticulture. Apache women, however, benefited from matrilineality and ownership of fields and crops which "were planted, weeded, and harvested by the joint labors of the entire family." This gender-integrated labor diverged when men hunted or raided and women engaged in the life-cycle labor of family reproduction. Although subordinate to men, women made important ritual contributions to the success of hunters: "a man and his wife pray together and smoke ceremonially before the husband leaves for the hunt. After his departure the woman continues a series of ritual duties." Similarly, before men departed for warfare or raiding, "a woman [was] chosen to represent each man to serve as proxy in group decisions, [and she] obeyed many restrictions in matters of dress, food, and behavior to ensure his safe return."

Warfare among the Jicarillas often involved the seizure of captives, either for vengeance satisfaction or cultural integration. Adult male captives "were tied to posts and slain by women with lances," but captive women and children found themselves incorporated into the band. A captive woman "could not be molested until she had been brought back and a ceremony . . . performed over her," probably some form of adoption that established her subordination within the Apachean levirate. Even with this adoption, captive women "were not considered fit wives. They were sexually used, and sent from camp to camp to do the heavy work. Their children by Apache men, however, were recognized as Jicarilla" and "accepted into Apache life." We shall see that this second-generation integration appears nearly universal among the indigenous groups in question and provides another constraining structure in captive women's decisions to remain within the host society even when offered their "freedom."

These patterns of gender and social subordination, mitigated by adoption and generational enfranchisement, are reiterated in an examination of Comanche society. . . . No other Plains society engaged in captive raiding as vigorously as did the Comanches. This seems a result of both individual status competition and the need to replace a population ravaged by warfare and epidemic disease. Comanche society offered several social locations into which captives could be integrated, ranging from chattels to kinsmen and women. . . .

Captive women often found themselves under the protection of Comanche women. Rosita Rodrigues, writing in 1846, reported she "remained a prisoner among the Comanche Indians about one year, during which time I was obliged to work very hard, but was not otherwise badly treated as I became the property of an old squaw who became much attached to me." Similarly, Sarah Ann Horn, taken captive in 1837, reported that she was taken in "by an old widow woman . . . a merciful exception to the general character of these merciless beings." Although she was "set to work to dress buffalo hides," she did not suffer sexual abuse. It appears that at least some captive women were informally adopted by older women, by which action they received the protection of the Comanche incest taboo. By extension, it bears consideration that in some cases, Comanche women may have identified and acted upon interests counter to those of Comanche men, protecting captive women either for their value as "chore sisters" or through basic empathy.

Rodrigues and Horn are among the very few women who, when repatriated, wrote of their experiences among the Comanche. Most captive women seem to have remained with their captors, marrying and establishing families in the host society. Rodrigues herself left a son behind among the Comanche, reporting that she "heard from him a short time ago—he is well and hearty but he is pure Indian now." . . .

These women had good reason to fear social opprobrium if they returned to Spanish society. When authorities introduced an alms-gathering plan in 1780 to raise funds for the ransom of Spanish captives, Teodoro de Croix declared with alarm that "this evil [captivity] extends especially . . . to the feminine sex . . . on account of the lascivious vice of sensuality in which they are now afforded the greatest liberty to indulge themselves." This may have been a rhetorical flourish to heighten interest in the plan, but it suggests that the conjugal arrangements of Comanche women might entail certain attractions to captive Spanish women as well.

Spanish concerns about the influence of Indian lifeways on their subjects went beyond anxieties about the behavior of "their" women in captivity. The simple fact that thousands of Indian captives and their descendants now resided in "Spanish" society stimulated a growing polemic of caste-conscious distancing by elite *españoles* vis-à-vis the culturally mixed people in the border villages. Elite anxieties were provoked by evidence that border villagers often exhibited behavior and pursued interests more in tune with their Indian neighbors than those contained in policy directives from Santa Fe or Mexico City. Gradual movement toward "borderlands communities of interest" linking New Mexico villagers with contiguous Indian groups emerged as one consequence of the presence of captive Indian women in colonial New Mexico. . . .

The seeds of these linkages were both cultural and biological, which we see revealed in a village-level intermingling of status groups. In Ranchos de Taos, for example, the Spanish census of 1750 reported nine Spanish households of fifty-seven persons, six *coyote* households of fifty-five persons, and eight *genízaro* households of twenty-five persons. Even the Spanish households showed a blurring of caste category; the house of Antonio Atiensa include his *coyota* wife, María Romero; their *castizo (español* and *coyota)* son, Domingo Romero; and the widow, Juana, with her daughter, Manuela, no doubt *criadas.* Similarly, the house of Juan Rosalio Villalpando, an important *español,* included his wife, Maria Valdes, and their six children, all of whom are termed *coyote,* suggesting that Maria may have been an *india de rescate.* Pablo Francisco Villalpando's household, from which María Rosa would be seized ten years later, contained three female and two male *servientes,* two of whom carry the family name. Mixing may have crossed class as well as caste lines in some village families.

The fact that the census arranged households by caste category reveals a conscious concern about caste status on the part of Spanish administrators, but the data also demonstrate how informally these categories might be arranged at the village level. Census findings from a cluster of Plazas at Belén show a somewhat different, yet consistent, pattern. In 1790 the third Plaza, "Nuestra Señora de los Dolores de los Genízaros," contained thirty-three households, all designated as *genízaro,* a strong indication that in some cases true communities developed among some *indios de rescate.* But the adjacent second Plaza of Jarales held thirty Spanish, twelve *mestizo,* four *coyote,* and two *genízaro* households. The marriage patterns from these communities reveal little caste-anxious endogamy; of the twenty-eight unions, only one is *español-española.* Six marriages involved *genízaro-genízara,* and five *mestizo-mestiza.* The remaining sixteen show a crossing of caste lines. In most of these, hypogamy seems the rule, with women marrying men of "lower" status. Children of these unions, for example, *genízaro-coyota,* follow the father's status and are later enumerated as *genízaros.* . . .

Although the creation of kinship seems the primary avenue by which captive women sought security and identity, we may also discern other facets of their lives from within the historical record. In addition to the life-cycle labor of family reproduction, these women engaged in subsistence and market production. The eighteenth and nineteenth centuries saw dramatic shifts in the status and work of Plains Indian women as peoples like the Comanches, Kiowas, and Cheyennes began participating in the European fur and hide trade. With the horse and gun, one Indian man could procure fifty to sixty buffalo hides per season, twice as many as one Indian woman could tan for use or exchange. An increase in polygamy, and raiding for captive women, served to counteract this labor shortage. The captivity narratives quoted earlier make it clear that captive women were "set to work to tan hides" almost immediately. The appearance of polygamous households probably made this work more efficient, for "cowives" might process hides while the "first-wife" performed higher-status production and distribution like cooking, clothing manufacture, and ceremonial activities.

Indias de rescate appear most often as household servants, but to consider their work entirely "domestic" is probably misleading. Because both Apache and Navajo captive women came from societies in which women were the principal horticulturists, they may have found themselves gardening and even tending flocks in New Mexican villages. . . . Navajo and Apache women held captive in New Mexican households also worked as weavers, both of basketry and textiles. . . . Captive women and children played important roles in one last area, that of Spanish-Indian diplomacy. Their cross-cultural experience made them valuable as interpreters, translators, and envoys for Spanish military leaders. . . .

Often deemed invisible commodities in the "slave trade" of the Spanish borderlands, the captive women and children discussed here emerge as human actors engaged in a deeply ambivalent dialectic between exploitation and negotiation. Their stories begin in a moment of abject powerlessness, where subordination serves as a substitute for violent death. But from that moment forward, we see them taking tentative steps toward autonomy and security. Captive women worked within the limits set by their captors, yet through the creation of kinship, their daily labors, and their diplomatic usefulness, they managed to carve out a future for themselves and their lineages. . . . In New Mexico, Spanish and Indian men found that even more than horses, guns, or hides, their counterparts valued women and children; and they established some nominal agreement that these would serve as objects and agents of intersocietal exchange. Conflict and accommodation patterns, therefore, between these rival societies may represent attempts by differing forms of patriarchal power to achieve external economic and military objectives while reinforcing the stability of internal social and gender hierarchies.

Of course, the social consequences of exchanging women and children across ethnic boundaries proved difficult to contain, and both New Mexicans and their Indian neighbors found customary relations unsettled by cultural hybridity. In time, mixed-blood descendants of captive women and children exhibited new collective interests that influenced their choice of cultural identification. The collective interests of second- (and subsequent-) generation descendants blurred the boundaries between New Mexican villagers and their Indian neighbors. . . .

Although the American conquest of 1846–48 resulted in the erosion of shared values and interests between New Mexicans and southwestern Indians, vestiges of the borderlands communities of interest still survive. Miguel Montoya, historian of the village of Mora, defines the historical identity of his neighbors in this way: "We were Spanish by law, but Indian by thought-world and custom. We respected *los viejos* (the elders), who looked after our spiritual health. We have relatives in the Pueblos, and out there, in Oklahoma (pointing east, to the reservations of the Comanches, Kiowas, and Southern Cheyenne)."

Mary Musgrove and the Sexual Politics of Race and Gender in Georgia

MICHELE GILLESPIE

Early Saturday evening on August 12, 1749 the white residents of Savannah learned that several dozen Lower Creek warriors and their chiefs, accompanied by Mary Musgrove, her third husband Reverend Thomas Bosomworth, and his brother Abraham, were nearing town. "Alarmed by the beat of the drum" and fearing an Indian attack, the residents called out the militia, who prepared to fire on the visitors as they approached the Upper Square. The colony's leaders wisely chose this moment to intervene, inviting the chiefs and Reverend Bosomworth to engage in wine and talk rather than combat. Mary Musgrove, once the most respected arbiter of Anglo-Creek relations in the colony, was excluded from this session.

As James Oglethorpe's princip[al] interpreter between 1733 and 1743, negotiator for many thorny problems between the Creeks and the white colonists, and the most popular Indian trader south of Augusta, Mary Musgrove, the adult daughter of a Tuckabachee Creek woman and a white Carolina trader, was insulted at her exclusion. So great was her anger at the white leaders' blatant snub and her concern that her authority over both the Lower Creeks and the English settlers had been sabotaged, that after several hours of waiting, she entered the meeting room unbidden and proceeded to berate the leaders and their "white town" for the successive abuses she and the Creek people had endured at their hands. The white men responded to her outburst by treating the nearly fifty-year-old woman like a child, admonishing her "to go home, go to Bed and not expose herself." To the astonishment of all in attendance, Musgrove not only refused to leave but rebuked those present for not recognizing her status as leader of the Creek Nation. The Creeks in the room, she stated, were "her People." She added that all who resided on Creek lands, including the English settlers, were subject to her sovereignty.

Mary Musgrove found herself in these circumstances because she was the progeny of an interracial sexual relationship between a Creek woman and an English man. Such interracial unions aided the exchange of cultures that hastened both English colonization and Native American acculturation in southeastern North America in the eighteenth century. No wonder then that some English authorities sanctioned interracial marriage between Native American women and Englishmen. Through these unions, colonizers sought more than the fostering of peaceful relations with Native Americans—they sought their conquest. History and myth have linked famous Native American women from Pocahontas to Sacagawea to virtually every so-called successful encounter, from the European point of view, between Europeans and Native Americans in the New World. But the scores of anonymous Native American women who engaged in sexual liaisons with European men, and the children these liaisons produced, acted as mediators between these two cultures and played an equally significant and enduring role in colonial history. . . .

Unlike native peoples to the north, the southeastern indigenous groups had adapted their reduced populations, political organizations and cultural practices in response to the Spanish presence over several generations of time and prior to settlement by the English in Carolina. Thus English merchants and their traders, eager to procure furs and deerskins from these Indians, discovered in the late seventeenth century that the native peoples of the southeast were already familiar with Europeans, their ways, and their goods. This familiarity, along with native customs that sanctioned premarital intercourse and exogamous marriage, made sexual relationships and marriages between Native American women and white traders acceptable practice in most southeastern native societies in the late seventeenth and early eighteenth centuries.

exogamous marriages

Although acceptable practice, neither sex or marriage between Native American women and European men ensured that Native American women's subsequent lives, or the lives of their children, would be ordinary by Native American standards.

Instead, these women and their bicultural children were forced to assume the mantle of "cultural broker." Caught between two worlds, they found themselves occupying the contested terrain between distinctly different cultures. Both of these worlds, moreover, anticipated not only that cultural brokers understood the differences that separated them, but could "broker" some measure of understanding between them.

Despite their significance to the history of British settlement in the colonial southeast, the voices of these women and their progeny are virtually absent from the historical record with a few exceptions—almost always "half-breed" sons such as Alexander McGillivray of the Creeks and John Ross of the Cherokees who came to assume important leadership positions in their societies in the last half of the eighteenth and early nineteenth centuries. Mary Musgrove, however, the daughter of an interracial union herself, achieved significant standing among both the white settlers and the Lower Creeks in the first half of the eighteenth century. Though she is probably the most frequently cited woman in the history of colonial Georgia, Mary Musgrove remains an enigmatic figure. She has alternately been celebrated for her critical role as Oglethorpe's interpreter, vilified by those who view as extortion her demand for prime coastal lands given her by the Lower Creeks, and pitied by those who see her as the unwitting dupe of her conniving husbands and their grandiose schemes.

While very few extant records document Musgrove's own words, the texts that describe her prove as revealing as those she penned herself. These documents indicate that Musgrove's status as a "mixed-blood" woman proved useful, at least at times, as she moved back and forth across two different cultures for some five decades. The privileges Musgrove garnered as well as the drawbacks she endured by virtue of her perceived racial and gendered status, however, were not unique to her alone. We simply know more about Musgrove because her life experiences and their impact on the colonial enterprise assured their inclusion in the official record. Musgrove was exceptional in that she wielded substantial power as a cultural broker for the settlers and the Lower Creeks alike during the first two decades of white settlement in Georgia. Yet her circumstances, because they are relatively well documented, can also help us begin to understand how scores of other women in colonial Georgia, also the daughters of intercultural unions, negotiated the same changing boundaries of race, gender, sex, and culture. . . .

Mary Musgrove carefully cultivated her identity in response to the racial and gendered boundaries she encountered in the colonial culture of Georgia. As a "subjugated body," her choices were shaped by each successive phase of English settlement. Like all bicultural women, her body literally and figuratively linked these two distinct societies. Musgrove's life, then, can be used to exemplify the process of colonization and the importance of shifting racial and gendered boundaries in that process. Through Musgrove's experiences we see how and on what terms the English colonizers dominated and excluded from the increasingly hierarchical world they were constructing those individuals and social groups who proved most threatening to the establishment of their authority.

Little about Mary Musgrove's youth can be fully documented since original accounts about her and by her differ greatly. She was probably born between 1700 and 1708 to a Lower Creek woman and a South Carolina trader who lived together in the Creek town of Tuckabachee, near the Chatahoochee River. Though many historians dispute her version of her lineage, she claimed late in life that her mother was the sister of two important Creek leaders, Brim and his brother and successor Chigelli, thereby entitling her to call herself "Princess Coosaponakeesa." Musgrove also related that, at the age of seven, she "was brought Down by her Father from the Indian Nation, to Pomponne in South Carolina; There baptized, Educated and bred up in the principles of Christianity." She returned to her Creek town shortly after the Yamasees and their allies attacked the Carolina frontier in the Yamasee War of 1715, living with her relatives for as many as ten years before marrying Johnny Musgrove.

Johnny Musgrove was also the child of an interracial liaison. His mother was either a Tuckesaw or Apalachicola Creek woman, whose identity is unrecorded; his father, John Musgrove, was a wealthy South Carolina planter. Mary and Johnny probably married in 1725 and lived in South Carolina for seven years before moving to the Yamacraw settlement in 1732, near the future site of Savannah. The Yamacraws, perhaps a hundred in number, were a mixed group of Creeks and Yamasees who had settled on this coastal site only a few years before Oglethorpe's arrival. The Musgroves had been invited to establish a trading post at this settlement at the request of the Governor of Carolina and Tomomichichi, the Yamacraw leader.

By the 1720s, Creek leaders had concluded that the best strategy for contending with the influx of European colonizers was to maintain respectful but removed relations with all three: the Spanish, French, and English. But from the vantage point of the English, relations with the Creeks needed to be far more cordial if the colony of Carolina and the proposed colony of Georgia were to succeed. The Musgroves came to the aid of the English by negotiating peaceful relations between the settlers and the Creeks and Yamacraws. Shortly after the official founding of Georgia in 1732, Mary Musgrove quickly became Oglethorpe's favorite interpreter, helping him secure two treaties and two land cessions before his final departure from Georgia in 1743. . . .

Because Mary Musgrove was especially influential with the Creeks, due as much to her savvy as her alleged royal relations, Oglethorpe took great advantage of her willingness to aid him. When war with the Spanish loomed on the horizon, Musgrove successfully urged the Creeks to stand by the English, much to Oglethorpe's relief. Worried about the colony's weak borders, Oglethorpe subsequently convinced the Musgroves to establish a trading establishment sixty miles up the Altamaha River, where Mary Musgrove could watch the Spanish and monitor Creek loyalties. Oglethorpe consistently relied on Mary Musgrove as translator, fact gatherer and mediator during almost all his negotiations with the Creek leaders during his decade in Georgia. Nor did Mary Musgrove's influence falter with the death of her husband in 1735.

Shortly after John Musgrove's demise, Mary wed Jacob Matthews, her former indentured servant and the current commander of twenty rangers stationed at her Altamaha trading house, Mount Venture. She continued to assist Oglethorpe, who secured a substantial land cession from the Creeks in 1737–1738 with her aid. Although some Savannah residents felt she had married beneath her—while Matthews was an Englishman, he was also her former servant—no one could contest her continued influence with Oglethorpe and the Creeks and the benefits this relationship reaped for the colonists.

In the fall of 1738, the leaders of four Lower Creek towns invited Oglethorpe to meet them, with Mary Musgrove acting as interpreter. At this meeting the chiefs informed Oglethorpe that they were bestowing on Mary Musgrove some 300 prime coastal acres south of Savannah (on the old Yamacraw tract). A surprised Oglethorpe found himself forced to acknowledge this exchange, though he had no legal right under English law to approve it. Yet by witnessing this event, Oglethorpe had in fact sanctioned it, at least in the eyes of the Creek leaders and Mary Musgrove. All three parties clearly understood that for Oglethorpe to challenge Musgrove's right to this land would threaten far more than his relationship with his trusted interpreter; it would threaten the hitherto cordial relationship between the Creeks and the English, since the Creeks had bestowed gifts of land to the English under similar circumstances. Oglethorpe's unfortunate but calculated presence at this event would not only cost him much of his credibility with the other trustees but would generate a host of problems for the colonists in years to come.

Respect for Oglethorpe's leadership skills waned from this date forward. Two years later, England's war with Spain and the tensions between the Cherokees and the Creeks that ensued meant that relations between the Creeks and the English were at their weakest in nearly a decade. Oglethorpe's increasing ineffectualness compelled the Georgia Trustees to assess his negotiations in a more critical light. One of their first decisions was to condemn his spending habits, which had included many gifts for the Native Americans, and to take over the financial reins of the colony for themselves. This action had serious repercussions for Creek relations; Mary Musgrove and her new husband Jacob Matthews now had far fewer presents to dispense at their trading post, which exacerbated bad will between the Creeks and the English. Meanwhile Mary Musgrove, because she had been providing food and supplies to needy colonists and Creeks alike and had frequently been forced to leave her store unattended to assist Oglethorpe, lost money and business.

Despite her legitimate disgruntlement with the English leaders, Musgrove continued to act as an intermediary for Oglethorpe. Yet the new colonial government refused to pay not only for the costs encumbered by hosting Creeks, Yamacraws, and traders at her trading post but for her services as interpreter as well. The leaders also refused to recognize her stake in the coastal property awarded her by the Creeks. Still, the colony's leaders did not want to alienate her completely, for she remained an influential ally and diplomat. The trustees, therefore, chose to stall her request for legal recognition of her lands by initiating a Trustee's Grant that required lengthy legal procedures on the other side of the Atlantic.

In June 1742, Jacob Matthews died, which compelled Musgrove to leave their home, the Mount Venture post on the Altamaha. Most of the Creeks who had settled with her in the area departed as well. In their absence, the Spanish and their new allies the Yamacraws destroyed the place, straining Musgrove's declining resources even more. Then in the spring of 1743, Oglethorpe was ordered to depart the colony just as relations between the Creeks and the English soured anew in the wake of England's successful repulsion of the Spanish. Before leaving Georgia, Oglethorpe gave Musgrove 100 pounds and a diamond ring from his own hand as payment for her services and the losses she suffered at Mount Venture. He also promised her an annual salary of 100 pounds.

Despite these gifts, Oglethorpe left Mary Musgrove in a precarious situation. The leadership that had replaced him encouraged further deterioration of Creek-English relations. The new governor would honor neither the gift-giving traditions that had smoothed these relations in the past nor the concessions Oglethorpe had reached with the Creeks in 1738–1739. Meanwhile, Musgrove's appeals to the colony for legal recognition of her Yamacraw tract lands were denied.

Especially vulnerable at this time of her life given her reduced resources, Oglethorpe's departure, and her widowed status, Mary Musgrove chose to marry a third time to Thomas Bosomworth, an Anglican minister in the town of Savannah. The two had met during a boat voyage in June 1743 and were wed shortly thereafter. Bosomworth retained his title as minister but moved with Mary to her plantation where the two of them renewed her battle for legal right to the Yamacraw tract. Over the next four years, the trustees summarily rejected Musgrove's successive requests despite the passionate memorials she and her husband penned. . . .

. . . War in Europe . . . ended in 1748. The peace treaty that ensued vanquished fear of Spanish invasion in Georgia. At the same time, some two thousand settlers, largely self-sufficient landholders, now resided in the colony which was experiencing slow but steady economic growth. These changing diplomatic and economic realities turned the historic relationship between the Creeks and the colonists on its head. Previously courted by the English, the Creeks suddenly found themselves scrambling for their suitor's favor. The tensions between the Creeks, Mary Musgrove and the colony that accompanied this transformation culminated in the fateful visit of Mary Musgrove, her husband Thomas Bosomworth, and several dozen Creek men to Savannah on a steamy summer evening in 1749.

Once the arbiter for all significant Anglo-Creek discussions, Mary Musgrove was pointedly excluded by white leaders from the session that followed the delegation's arrival. Distraught at the larger significance of this action, she broke into the meeting without invitation to deliver her extraordinary speech before the Creek chiefs and the colonial leaders. An unsympathetic white male eyewitness described Mary Musgrove's entrance and words as follows:

> [She] rushed into the Room, in the most violent and outrageous manner, that a Woman spirited up with Liquor, Drunk with passion, and disappointed in her Views could be guilty of. . . . She then, if possible, grew more outrageous, and in the most insulting manner declared, She was Empress of the Upper and Lower Creeks, Yea, went so far in her imaginary Sovereignty, as to call herself King, and that she should command every Man in these Nations to follow her, and We should soon know it our cost. It is needless to repeat, the threatening and irritating language used by this woman, indicating both her and [her] husband's wicked designs.

The white male officials present responded to Mary Bosomworth's impassioned speech by putting her under temporary custody. They were convinced that she was out of her mind or at the very least in a drunken rage. While we can never truly know her actual state, it seems likely that her accusers were attempting to justify their punitive actions against her by identifying her behavior as flagrantly inappropriate in accordance with their expectations about racial and gendered behavior. By labeling her either crazy or "just another drunken Indian," the colonial authorities could dismiss the deeper meanings behind her actions. Although too little evidence exists to assess Mary Musgrove's condition, it seems highly likely that she was both sane and sober and that her speech was a heroic act to preserve her authority in a society that was shifting the terms of colonization and settlement to suit itself.

Thomas Bosomworth himself was clearly aware that his wife's relationship to the colonists had been dramatically altered by her speech and her subsequent imprisonment. He responded to this turn of events by asserting his authority as a white man and a husband within this marriage. The day after his wife's impromptu oration, he publicly apologized to the colony's leaders for her behavior, stating that henceforth he would speak on behalf of the couple and that any and all utterances made by his wife should be ignored. Mary Musgrove herself later claimed that from that day forward she was "no longer countenanced by the White People," despite her significant record of diplomacy and trade that had contributed so enormously to the colony's successful venture.

Mary Musgrove's verbal assault on the officials was a desperate measure by a desperate woman. She had come to understand that the colony no longer appreciated either her skillful negotiations with the Creeks or her right to lay claim to lands she had earned. She also had come to recognize that the role she had carved out for herself as Christian helpmeet to the colonists was no longer tenable.

By renouncing the colonial leaders and their "white Town," by reclaiming her Creek identity, Mary Musgrove not only lost the respect of the white male European leaders but was subsequently silenced by them. It did not help her cause that she had chosen such an inappropriate way for a woman in this society, particularly a Christian woman born of a Creek mother, to convey her anger. In the eyes of the colony's stewards, she had transformed herself overnight, reduced to the status of outcast and heathen. Even her spouse understood the implications of her debacle when he publicly declared himself her spokesman. While Mary Musgrove and her third husband would continue to seek legal right to the Creek lands awarded her for another decade, eventually securing a compromise deal that allowed her to claim St. Catherine's Island as her own, along with the money made from the public sale of Ossabaw and Sapelo Islands, she never regained her former status as cultural broker to the colony.

This denouement should not be too surprising. Mary Musgrove's speech in essence had denigrated every Anglo-American premise on which the white leaders had erected their colony and on which she had allegedly acted, with the understandable effect of turning the entire white colony against her. Although Mary Musgrove had supposedly been negotiating on behalf of the colonial leaders' best interests for years, her speech indicated that her allegiance now clearly lay with the Creeks. She had turned her back in a most deliberate and spectacular fashion on the white officials who believed she had embraced them as her own. Despite the serious consequences of her actions, one suspects that after years of negotiating the sexual, racial, and gendered boundaries of the Anglo-American male world as a woman of "mixed blood," she breathed a long sigh of relief at being able to shed the conflicting identities she had carefully negotiated for so long. . . .

Oglethorpe and his men had not considered Mary Musgrove a particularly worthy woman on making her acquaintance in 1732. Knowing little of her background, they used English notions about fashion and status as well as race and gender to mark her among the lower sort in social rank, observing that "she appeared to be in mean and low circumstances, being only cloathed with a red stroud petticoat and

Osnabrig Shift." Yet Mary Musgrove soon earned their respect despite their initial assessment, proving her worth to Oglethorpe and the colony as a whole. These Englishmen discovered that the social codes embedded in notions of gender and race as well as dress and behavior, which structured their views of both Old World and New, were far from accurate in the early days of English settlement in Georgia.

Over time Mary Musgrove's authority as a cultural mediator was legitimated in English eyes more by her status as a good Christian helpmeet than by her rough attire or Creek background. Thus, while an earlier generation of historians pinned Musgrove's willingness to remarry so quickly following on the deaths of her husbands on her lusty nature, an assumption with unsavory undertones about status and sexual desire, another interpretation is well worth considering. Musgrove may have known that prolonged widowhood would have made her vulnerable to scandal as a single woman on a remote frontier working with men of all races. Marriage, especially to an Englishman, offered her reputation some measure of protection, especially since the institution was sanctified by the Church. Taken in that light, Musgrove may have held her third and final marriage to the minister Thomas Bosomworth as the most significant. In a society in which she remained in most ways an outsider, marriage to someone as venerable as a minister raised her social standing and protected her reputation. Widowed white women were legally permitted to retain their property in colonial Georgia, and Mary Musgrove was one of the largest women landholders in a colony where land afforded its owners status and independence as well as subsistence. Yet Musgrove may have chosen not to remain single, despite her relative wealth and influence, because of her marginal status as a mixed-blood woman.

Although Musgrove spent most of her adult life as a married woman, she bore children only with her first husband and none of them lived to adulthood. Yet she knew the significance that the English settlers tied to their prescribed gender roles. Childless by the 1740s, she publically upheld maternal feelings and used the term "Maternal Affection" to describe her relationship with "the Infant Colony" of Georgia. Musgrove's claim to be the Mother of the Colony, despite its grandiosity, remained grounded in Christian notions about a woman's special calling. Musgrove used this metaphor in her memorial to the trustees in 1747 since its meaning was understood by the white leaders. Through it she inferred that she was not a greedy powermonger, bent on shaping the colony to her will, but a Christian woman fulfilling her female duty as best she could. . . .

The complexities and contradictions that surrounded Mary Musgrove throughout her life were manifold. The daughter of a white father and a Creek mother, raised among whites, and the recipient of a Christian education, she aided both the Creeks and the English settlers as an interpreter and a trader, accruing substantial property, servants, and slaves throughout the 1730s and early 1740s. As the colonial leaders perceived that Musgrove's usefulness to the maturing colony was on the wane, however, and as Musgrove sought formal recognition of the lands the Creeks had bestowed on her, the English authorities who dealt with Musgrove reassessed her value to the colony. As they did so, they also reconceptualized her racial and gendered identity to suit their changing needs. Musgrove's influence with the Lower Creeks, along with her knowledge of English and Creek cultures, had made her an invaluable ally to the Georgia Trustees during the earliest stages of settlement. Her careful negotiations had in fact assured the relative success of the colonial venture. But by 1749 she was forced to contend with a new series of ordeals and confrontations at the hands of the latest colonial government. These challenges to her authority reflected the leadership's lowered opinion of her value to the Georgia colony. Colonial leaders had shifted the terms, demanding that she adhere to their conceptions of race and gender difference in order to diminish her authority and power. Henceforth she would be expected to observe a whole new set of boundaries to fit into their world.

Certainly Mary Musgrove was a product of, as well as a contributor to, the evolution of the triracial cultural encounter in Georgia and therefore defies easy analysis. After all, the limited nature of the sources makes it difficult to determine with absolute certainty where her allegiances really lay and how they changed over time. Nor can it be determined precisely how the shifting boundaries of race, class, gender, and sex in early Georgia influenced the kinds of choices she made, though again the sources seem suggestive. Was Mary Musgrove struggling to survive the personal circumstance of the cultural encounter? Or was she struggling for more power and influence given her special authority and status? The latter seems far more likely.

At the very least, Mary Musgrove clearly understood the cultural differences that separated the Creeks and the English. Moreover, she used that knowledge to wage a fierce contest, to triumph, however briefly, in this new society. Her life story demonstrates that colonial mix in Georgia was far more complicated than any simple depiction of violent conquest. Mary Musgrove's words, actions, and authority defy any essentialist interpretations that hinge on the good Indian woman's loss of status and respect in the evil Christian world of the white colonialists. Far more complex interactions were at play here.

A Case Study of Indian and African Intermarriage in Colonial New England

DANIEL R. MANDELL

In 1728, at the home of William Page in Providence, Rhode Island, Sarah Muckamugg, a Nipmuc from Hassanamisco in Massachusetts, "solemnized" her union with Aaron, a slave of African ancestry. The two had at least one child, Joseph Aaron, before their union dissolved twelve years later. Sarah then returned to Hassanamisco (which had, during her absence, become the mostly Anglo-American town of Grafton) and became involved with another African, Fortune Burnee. In 1744 she bore a child from that union, also named Sarah. But her new relationship was also ill-fated: she became sick, was abandoned by Burnee, and died at the home of a white man in the summer of 1751.

Sarah Muckamugg, her spouses, their relationships, and their "mixed" children represent the emerging trend of Indian-African intermarriage in late colonial New England. When we carefully place these few bits of direct evidence into the broader picture of Indians and African Americans in colonial New England, a penetrating view emerges of the causes and effects of the little-noted but increasingly common

Daniel R. Mandell, "The Saga of Sarah Muckamugg: Indian and African Intermarriage in Colonial New England," in Martha Hodes, ed., *Sex, Love, Race: Crossing Boundaries in North American History* (New York: New York University Press, 1999), 72–79, 85–86. Reprinted by permission.

love and marriage across the line separating Natives from involuntary African immigrants. Sarah's relationships with Aaron and Fortune show how intermarriages developed out of the needs of Indians and blacks, who shared a marginal social status in New England. Her two marriages also highlight the two worlds in which Indians and Africans met and married: urban seaports where poor laborers of all races came together, and farm villages that had once been entirely Indian. At the same time, Sarah's problems with both of her husbands show how the different needs of individuals from the two groups, as well as the pressures generated by their shared condition, could shatter their marriages. . . .

Sarah Muckamugg may herself have been the product of a mixed marriage. Her father, Peter Muckamugg, was either a Narragansett or grew up among Narragansetts, having lived as a boy in or near Providence, Rhode Island. Her mother, Sarah Robbins, was a Nipmuc, the people who occupied central, inland Massachusetts. In the wake of King Philip's War in 1675–76, Hassanamisco lay within a frontier where no English dared live, due to continuing conflicts with Abenakis and their French allies. Of approximately eight thousand Indians who remained in southern New England after the war, about five hundred, mostly Christianized Natives from "praying towns" who had been incarcerated by the English, resettled a few interior villages after the war, including Hassanamisco, Sarah Robbins's community. They fished, hunted, and grew crops—as had their aboriginal ancestors—but also traveled to work for English farmers or to trade furs, deerskins, and other produce with the colonists. And Natives no doubt visited with some of the Indians who were servants or slaves in the growing port towns. Hassanamisco lay where the path between Boston and Connecticut intersected with the Blackstone River, which ran down a wide valley to Providence and the Narragansett Bay, making an easy highway. While we do not know where or when Peter Muckamugg and Sarah Robbins met and married, or when or where their daughter Sarah was born, they apparently traveled back and forth between Hassanamisco and Providence.

The 1713 Treaty of Utrecht ended British hostilities with the French and their Native allies, and reopened Nipmuc territory to eager colonists. Fifteen years later, colonists purchased the Hassanamisco reserve from the seven Indian families living there, including the Muckamuggs, in exchange for money, shares in the schoolhouse and church to be built by the colonists, and large allotments in the new town of Grafton. When Peter and Sarah Muckamugg returned to claim their allotments in May 1728, they left their daughter Sarah living in the Providence household of John Whipple, the eldest son of one of the most prestigious families in the town, apparently working as a domestic. Like Sarah, a growing number of Indians were moving to New England port towns to find work as laborers, mariners, tavern help, and in other unskilled occupations. There they lived and worked alongside poor whites and freed and enslaved Africans, whom they often loved and married. One such relationship was "solemnized" about 1728, when "an Indian woman known by name of Indian Sarah, also called the daughter of Sarah Muckamugg was married to a Negro man named Aaron the servant of Col. Joseph Whipple of Providence."

Only about a thousand Africans and their descendants—mostly enslaved but a few free—lived in New England in 1700, but their number rapidly increased to about eleven thousand by midcentury. Slaves in New England experienced a very different life than their contemporaries in the South and the West Indies. Most lived in port towns and performed tasks for which free labor was scarce: they worked as artisans' assistants, house servants, seamen, and in construction. The few slaves in rural villages usually served as status symbols as well as providing relatively inexpensive menial labor for the local elites, particularly ministers.

Like indentured servants and apprentices, slaves were considered part of the extended household, a situation that held both benefits and drawbacks. Individuals experienced a considerable lack of autonomy, and were expected to adopt the dominant culture quickly. On the other hand, blacks were allowed to participate in the larger community and its culture. Many were taught to read, for it was a Puritan duty to see that all could read and understand the Bible. They could hire themselves out to work for other employers, and even buy their own and their family's freedom. And slaves in New England port towns worked alongside free, apprenticed, and indentured laborers, and often caroused with them in pubs after work.

Few Africans lived in Providence: only 7 of the 1,500 residents (0.5 percent) in 1708, rising to 225 of 3,177 (7 percent) in 1748. Even fewer Indians resided in that town: only fifty at midcentury. Aaron, Sarah, and other African Americans and Indians in Providence were set apart as the lowest social class in New England, and were subject to special laws designed to exert an extra measure of control over the potentially dangerous minority. . . . Africans and Indians were also barred, by law and custom, from joining with whites in socially sanctioned sex—that is, in marriage. . . . These measures clearly limited potential partners for both Indians and African Americans and, considering their small numbers, helped bring Aaron and Sarah Muckamugg together in the Anglo-American town of Providence. . . .

But was their union recognized as a marriage by others? The son and daughter of John Whipple, who claimed to have known both Sarah and Aaron quite well, were adamant that "we never understood that the said Aaron and Sarah were married together but on the contrary are almost certain that they never were married." The Providence town clerk testified that he could find no record of their marriage. Years later, several Anglo-American acquaintances claimed to know nothing of their being married. In fact, the ceremony that joined Sarah and Aaron lay outside the scope of state-sanctioned marriages in New England. The midwife Hallelujah Olney, who assisted at the births of Sarah's children, first described "Sarah Aaron" as "the wife of a Negro man Aaron," and then three years later testified that she never knew that Aaron was married to Sarah "but frequently heard that they Cohabited together."

Such common-law marriages remained normal for Indians and African Americans, dwellers on New England's margins, even as more whites sought the legal protection and legitimation of unions set in law. A two-tiered system of marriages emerged during the late colonial period, as legal forms and rituals became more prominent and prevalent in Anglo-American society, while folk customs continued among Indians, blacks, and poorer whites. Such marriages were, as an Anglo-American minister noted, "performed by mutual consent without the blessings of the church," and the two partners could easily agree to break "by mutual consent their negro marriage." And such marriages were rarely recorded—unfortunately for historians, for estimates of the number of Indian–African American unions are impossible.

Like most nonliterate individuals and laboring families, Sarah and Aaron left no traces except when social problems or tragedy drew the attention of the authorities or the lettered elite. We know from others that Sarah had at least four children while in Providence. The couple's circumstances were hardly conducive, however, to a long and happy marriage: not only did they live with the ongoing pressure of social and legal subordination, but they were unable even to live together under one roof as husband and wife, for Aaron remained Joseph Whipple's slave and Sarah remained in John Whipple's household. Around 1740 something snapped the fragile threads that bound them together—perhaps the birth of their last child, Joseph Aaron. Sarah probably had hoped that Aaron would be able to live with her and help support their children, and perhaps Aaron's reaction when Joseph arrived made the finality of their situation clear to her. Their relationship soured: they were frequently quarreling, and Aaron may have become abusive.

Approximately a year after Joseph's birth, Sarah Muckamugg left Providence with several of her children, seemingly headed for Hassanamisco, now Grafton. Probably her relationship with Aaron had become unbearable, and she may have missed her aging parents. Her ability (and willingness) to leave Aaron and Providence on her own also points to the different customs of Indian women, who, since they traditionally held and worked land, could readily leave husbands. Sarah's route north through the Blackstone River valley took her past the Smithfield farm of a family named Wilkinson. There she stopped and obtained the Wilkinsons' permission to build a wigwam and live on their land. Their detailed recollections of Sarah hint that she may have helped around the Wilkinson home, as she did for the Whipples.

Aaron, who, like other bound Africans, could obtain his owner's permission to travel independently for short visits or other personal matters, soon made the short trip to the Wilkinson farm. Their reunion only widened the rupture between the African man and the Nipmuc woman, and generated an explosion that was noticed even by the master of the farm. Three decades later, Israel Wilkinson remembered that Aaron "had some Difference with her and I have heard her say that she was not married to the said Negro Man." Sarah was far more forthcoming with Israel's wife, Mary (or perhaps Mary paid more attention to Sarah's words); the bond between these two women may have been deeper than their ethnic or racial divide. One day, when returning to the house—perhaps from the orchard or barn—Mary found Sarah crying bitterly. When asked, the Nipmuc woman sobbed out the bitter state of her relationship with her visitor. "She said that Aaron Sayeth that he never would Live with me any more neither would he help maintain the Children & I asked her wether they was ever marryed & she Said no & I asked what the Reason was & she Said that he promised to do well by me & further Said that She would then by [be] marr[ie]d but he w[o]uld not & further Sayeth that he had got another Squaw that he Lovd better."

Sarah's words hint at a relationship that was split by gradually widening expectations that were impossible to reconcile. She had been happy, back in 1729, to bear his children after he had "promised to do well by me" when they formalized their union. But by 1740 Sarah wanted or needed more, for "She would then be married," perhaps because the legal status and future welfare of their children were in doubt, or more likely because she was weary of her dependence and near-servitude at the Whipples and wanted her family to live together. Unfortunately, Sarah lacked the money to buy her husband's freedom, as many Indian women would do for their African American spouses. Perhaps this was the wedge that had split Aaron from Sarah: he desperately wanted his freedom and abandoned her for another when it became clear that she could not fulfill that desire. And their conflict may have had a deeper complexity that reflected their different backgrounds. Did "Indian Sarah" (as some documents call her) want her children raised as Hassanamisco Nipmucs, with roots in her clan and community? Aaron, on the other hand, would have seen far more opportunity, for himself as well as for their free children, in the expanding maritime town of Providence. Different customs in postmarital residence—Nipmuc matrilocality versus Anglo-American (and perhaps African) patrilocality—may also have underlain the friction between Sarah and Aaron.

On the other hand, the fate of their children points to different concerns in their relationship and the observance of customs that were quite different from Anglo-American ways. Apparently during her relationship with Aaron, Sarah bound three of her children—Abraham, Rhode, and Abigail—to a white family named Brown. Richard Brown and his son Richard were amazed to find that "Aaron had no concern about this," and saw the African man's failure to exercise patriarchal authority as casting doubt on Sarah and Aaron's marriage. The Browns could not have been surprised that Sarah and Aaron's children were indentured; such arrangements were not unusual for Anglo-American children, particularly from poorer families, and were quite common for African American children. What surprised them was that, when Sarah took responsibility for her children's future, she displayed the familial authority that was exercised by the husband in the dominant culture and legal system. Sarah's actions, Aaron's apparent lack of "concern," and the Browns' surprise point to the different levels of authority that women and men held in Indian, African, and Anglo-American cultures. And while Sarah clearly claimed the authority due her within the matrilineal Nipmuc culture, and Aaron voiced no objections to observers, the two must have had conflicts that arose from their very different roots.

Sarah Muckamugg did not remain long at her wigwam on the Wilkinson farm, but soon returned to her family in Grafton. By midcentury Grafton had become a typical New England farming village, with excellent pasture and cropland, not far from the growing regional center of Worcester. Few Nipmucs remained in the town, and few Anglo-American residents owned African slaves: a provincial census in 1764–65 found 7 Negroes, 14 Indians, and 742 whites. Sarah may have arrived in Grafton as early as January 1741, for town records show Thomas English, an Indian, marrying a Sarah Muckamugg on that date, but records do not make clear whether this was mother or daughter. Sarah Muckamugg had certainly returned by November 1744, when she bore a daughter, Sarah, to Fortune Burnee, a "free Negro."

Burnee's background remains a mystery; nor do we know where and how they met. Perhaps they met while Sarah was living at the Wilkinson's farm. Gideon Hawley, the white minister of the Indian enclave of Mashpee, noted to his dismay that "many of our women have found negroe husbands, as they were stroling in the country and bro't them home." If Sarah had not been the Muckamugg who married English, perhaps she brought Fortune home to Hassanamisco. Or perhaps he was already living in or near Grafton. But clearly they were united by Sarah Burnee's birth in 1744. Tragically, neither their relationship nor Sarah Muckamugg's life lasted long. She fell ill in late 1750 or early 1751. Fortune either abandoned Sarah or was physically unable to care for her, for she was placed by the town's select-men in the home of an Anglo-American, Hezekiah Ward, where she died in the summer of 1751.

By the time of Sarah Muckamugg's death, marriages between Indian women and African American men were becoming increasingly common in New England. Native enclaves suffered from a precipitous decline in the number of their men between 1740 and 1780. Many enthusiastically volunteered for and died in the militia during King George's War (1744–48) and the Seven Years' War (1754–60). Censuses from Massachusetts, Rhode Island, and Connecticut, taken between 1765 and 1774, show about 60 percent more women than men. Men were needed to father the next generation and to work the fields or to bring home income from the dominant world of the Anglo-American economy. Anglo-American prejudice against Indians meant that Native women were often able to meet their emotional, demographic, economic, and social needs only by marrying African American men—which also served to adopt the newcomers into family and community.

Advantages to African / Indian marriages

   Sarah Muckamugg's saga helps us translate these regional demographic trends into the experiences of individuals. Few Indians, but a growing number of blacks, lived in the small but vital port town of Providence, so while Sarah lived there she was far more likely to meet men of African descent. Upon her return to Grafton, Sarah found only eight adult Hassanamisco men, most of whom were already married; six soon died in the war. . . . Sarah may have had another reason, far more personal, elusive, and impossible to quantify, for seeking out and marrying African American men: a preference for a man from another culture, with different values, who would be willing and able to support her and her children in their changing world. . . . [C]onsidering that so many Indian women married outsiders, perhaps [they] were indeed convinced that marrying black men provided the best opportunities in the changing world for themselves and their families.

   During the colonial period, African American men married Indian women for many of the same reasons. The two peoples in fact experienced complementary demographic imbalances, for New England's demand for semiskilled laborers meant that most of the black slaves brought to the region were men. Although the percentage of native-born blacks grew throughout the eighteenth century, at midcentury the 2,700 adult African Americans in Massachusetts included 1.75 men for each woman. For men like Aaron in Providence in the 1720s or Fortune Burnee in Grafton in the 1740s, an Indian may have been their only possible mate, given the lack of black women, their frequent isolation in otherwise all-white households and villages, and Anglo-American prejudices.

   African men also gained social and economic benefits from an Indian wife. Even if she could not purchase his freedom, their children would be born free. The husbands of Indian women like Sarah Muckamugg gained access to Native land and other resources. Last, but not least, an African man could gain a community with an Indian wife, for Native enclaves generally welcomed newcomers. Sarah's second husband, the appropriately named Fortune Burnee, is one of the best examples of the advantages that a man of African descent could gain. He obtained access to the Muckamugg land and annual interest receipts by marrying Sarah. After her death in 1751 he became the guardian of their young daughter, seemingly the only heir to the family property. But since much of Sarah's property was sold in May 1752 to pay her medical bills, six years later he married another Hassanamisco, Abigail Printer. After Abigail died in 1776, Fortune continued to use and profit from her land and annual interest income until his death in 1795. While Burnee was barred by Massachusetts law from selling his wife's lands without the General Court's permission, he held her property in all but title. . . .

Indians and African Americans brought similar needs but different expectations and desires to marriages across their ethnic boundaries—boundaries that widened at the end of the colonial period. The two peoples shared a marginal position in New England society and complementary demographic imbalances. Many Indians, like Sarah Muckamugg of Hassanamisco, had no choice but to marry outsiders[;] the men they married, like Aaron of Providence or Fortune Burnee of Grafton, faced similar constraints. In many cases Indians and African Americans were each other's only potential spouses, offering the sole opportunity for companionship, support, and the perpetuation of their families and community. . . .

Their relationships, unfortunately, would suffer from a host of problems, including, as with Sarah and Aaron, prolonged separations. Wives as well as husbands were often forced to find work far from home. Couples who remained in or moved to Native enclaves found that Indian traditions of female independence and authority and community management of property clashed with the patriarchal, market-oriented values adopted by African Americans. Indian groups were initially willing and able to accept the newcomers and to raise their children. But as more Indian women married black men, Indian men became resentful, and conflicts arose over rights to communal resources. While groups with valuable resources adopted new rules to manage immigrants, the boundaries of small enclaves such as Hassanamisco became more permeable.

The children of intermarriages were faced with difficult choices of identity and community, particularly when an African American community emerged in the region and embraced very different values. . . . [A]s time went on, a growing number of "mixed" children . . . followed their fathers and found more opportunities in the outside world. At the same time, New England whites became less willing and able to distinguish Indians from African Americans. In these ways, intermarriage both literally and symbolically reshaped Native communities.

FURTHER READING

Anderson, Karen. *Chain Her by One Foot: The Subjugation of Native Women in Seventeenth-Century New France* (1991).

Axtell, James. *The Invasion Within: The Contest of Cultures in Colonial North America* (1985).

Bragdon, Kathleen. "Gender as a Social Category in Native Southern New England," *Ethnohistory* 43 (1996): 573–592.

Brooks, James F. *Captives and Cousins: Slavery, Kinship, and Community in Southwest Borderlands* (2002).

Brown, Kathleen M. "Brave New Worlds: Women's and Gender History," *William and Mary Quarterly,* 3d ser, 50 (1993): 311–328.

Clinton, Catherine, and Michele Gillespie, eds. *The Devil's Lane: Sex and Race in the Early South* (1997).

Demos, John. *The Unredeemed Captive: A Family Story from Early America* (1994).

Devens, Carol. *Countering Colonization: Native American Women and Great Lakes Missions* (1992).

Gutiérrez, Ramón. *When Jesus Came, the Corn Mothers Went Away: Marriage, Sexuality, and Power in New Mexico, 1500–1846* (1991).

Namias, June. *White Captives: Gender and Ethnicity on the American Frontier* (1993).

Plane, Ann Marie. *Colonial Intimacies: Indian Marriage in Early New England* (2000).

Smith-Rosenberg, Carroll. "Captured Subjects/Savage Others: Violently Engendering the New American," *Gender and History* 5 (1993): 177–195.

CHAPTER
3

The Economic Roles of Women
in the Northern Colonies

When scholars first began investigating American women's history, they assumed
that from the beginnings of settlement colonial women primarily assisted their
husbands on farms or engaged in spinning and weaving to produce the family's
clothing. Women, the narrative ran, worked as parts of a household economy and
were respected for their economic contributions to the family's welfare, achieving
near equality with men as a result. Echoing early-twentieth-century authors who
compiled advertisements from newspapers, some historians also contended that in
colonial cities women freely participated in many artisanal and other occupations
closed to them after the nation industrialized.

   After several historians challenged this rosy picture, which is sometimes known
as the "golden age" theory of colonial women's history, others set out to uncover the
true parameters of women's work in early America. What they found has both refined and rendered more complex what once seemed obvious. In addition to unpaid
labor in the home (encompassing such tasks as caring for children and cooking for
families), women did engage in paid labor, but only of particular sorts. Furthermore,
their activities changed over time. Most notably, they did little spinning and even
less weaving in the early seventeenth century, adopting those occupations only after
the 1670s. The documents and essays in this chapter explore the range—and the
limitations—of women's employment in preindustrial America.

◈ D O C U M E N T S

Document 1 consists of randomly selected excerpts from the diary of the Philadelphia
Quaker Elizabeth Sandwith Drinker over a nearly forty-year period, from 1758 to 1794.
Before her marriage to the merchant Henry Drinker in 1761, when she was twenty-six,
the young woman kept a list of the needlework projects she had completed, occasionally
writing as well about other tasks in which she engaged. After 1761, she more commonly
wrote about the labor of other women she encountered; many of them came to her house
to work for her in various capacities. Likewise, Ruth Henshaw, a resident of Leicester,
Massachusetts, kept a diary for many years, focusing primarily on her work with textiles,

her schoolteaching , and her familial and social life. Document 2 comprises the entries pertinent to her work in the year 1792, when she was nineteen.

1. Elizabeth Sandwith Drinker, a Wealthy Philadelphian, Describes Her Work and That of Other Women, 1758–1794

Work done in part of the Years: 175[7,] 1758: 1759: 1760.
Work'd a Irish stitch Pocket Book for Catn. Morgan.
A Double Pocket Book in Irish Stitch for Peggy Parr.
A Irish stich Purse Pincushon for Ditto.
Plated a Watch String for Saml. Wharton.
A Watch String for John Hunt.
Knit a round Pincushon for R. Drinker.
Knit a round Pincushon for R. Coleman. . . .
Crown'd a Boys cap, for R. Rawle.
Help'd to make Baby Cloaths, for Betty Smith at Point.
Work'd a Irishstitch Tea Kittle holder for M. Parr.
Work'd a large silk Needle Book, in several stitches, for self.
A pair of silk Sleve-strings for Ditto.
A pair of Irishstitch Garters for Ditto. . . .
Novr. the 1. 1758. Finish'd a pair of White Wosted Stockings for self.
Finish'd 7 shifts for self.
Finish'd Kniting a pair of blue yarn Stockings, for Susey Georges youngest Child.
Finish'd Kniting a pair of White wosted Stockings for Polly. . . .
1759 Plated 2 Horse-Whip-strings for B. Moode.
July the 19 Plated a Watch-string for Henry Drinker.
Augt. the 31: 1759: Finish'd Kniting a pair of fine thread Stockings for Self.
Septr. the 14 Finish'd 2 Tea Kittle-Holders, in Irish Stitch for. . . .
May the 9. 1760 Finish'd working a Screen, in Irishstitch Flowers.
May the 21, Finish'd Knitting a pair of thread Stockings for self. . . .
Decemr. the 31. Finish'd knitting a pair white thread Stockings for self.
1761. Janry. the 2. Plated a Watch-string for Henry Drinker.
Janry. the 8, Finish'd Knitting a pair of Silk Mittins for Self. . . .
27 [April 1759] Went in the Afternoon with M Parr, to M. Burrows and R[ebecca] Steels, and several other Shops; she came home and drank Tea with us. . . .
13 [July 1759] went to R Steels to buy Silk. . . .
14 Stay'd at home all Day; Nancy Mitchell, call'd in the After-noon to Borrow a Pocket-Book, for a Patren. . . .
12 [February 1760] Peggy, Polly & Self, busy kniting. . . .
6 [October 1760] Becky Rawle, and Caty Howel, spent this Afternoon with us— up stairs helping to Quilt. . . .
[She marries Henry Drinker, 1761.]
7 [September 1762] Sister and self very busy Ironing &c. . . .

Diary of Elizabeth Drinker, Historical Society of Pennsylvania. This document can also be found in Elaine Forman Crane, ed., *The Diary of Elizabeth Drinker*, 3 vols. (Boston: Northeastern University Press, 1991).

26 [August 1763] put a Gown skirt in the Frame, to Quilt this Afternoon. . . .

30 Sister and self finish'd my Quilt this Afternoon. . . .

1 [July 1765] Phebe Morris . . . came to fit a Body Linning for me. . . .

15 Phebe Morris here this Afternoon fitting a Gown for me, Molly Worrel with Sitgreaves's Baby who she Nurses, were also here. . . .

1 December [1766] Sally Gardner came to live with us, at 2/6 p Week. . . .

22 June 1771 George Baker drove up Polly Campbell, whome I have hir'd this day to tind my little Henry. . . .

13 [July 1771] Dr. D. says I must wean my little Henry or get a nurse for him, either seems hard—but I must submitt. . . .

18 agree'd with [Sally Oats] to take my Sweet little Henry to Nurse. . . .

29 [August 1771] we set forward to David Levans 18 Miles from Reding, a Tavern in Manatawny, to this place we got about Dusk. . . . This Evening our Landlady, a dirty old Dutch Woman, refused Changing very dirty, for Clean Sheets, tho after much intreaty, she pretend'd to comply, but to our mortification found she had taken the same sheets, sprinkled them, then Iron'd and hung 'em by the fire and placed them again on the Bed; so that we were necessitated to use our cloaks &c & this Night slepp'd without sheets.—with the assistance of our two Servants cooking, we sup'd pretty Well and slep'd better than we had any Reason to expect, all in one Room. . . .

30 from this place to the Widdow Albrights at Macungee we proceeded about 8 miles, and then Breakfasted tolerably for a Dutch House. . . .

29 [September 1771] [on a second journey] about Dusk we got to the Widdow Jemmisons, here sup'd and lodg'd. . . .

23 January 1779 our Maid Elizabeth, has been in Bed all day, with the ague and Fiver, Sister is very much taken up in the Kitchen, having none but little John to help, Molly Brookhouse occasionly. . . .

20 [February 1779] Wid. Rusel [here] to measure the Girls for Stays. . . .

28 June [1779] I took Molly [her daughter] to School to Betsy Devonshire. . . .

9 [August 1779] we have had no Maid Servant for some weeks past but Molly Brookhouse who comes before dinner and goes away in the afternoon. . . .

10 [February 1780] I dismist my maid Caty Paterson this afternoon, on her return home after 2 or 3 days frolicking, our old maid Molly Hensel is to Supply her place tomorrow. . . .

23 [August 1784] a little before 7 before I was up, S Heartshorn sent for me;—she was deliver'd about 8 of a fine Girl,—who they call Susanna; I breakfasted there, came home about 9. . . .

30 [May 1792] Betsy Fordham at work here. . . .

19 [November 1793] Caty Mullen here to day, in great trouble; she came over from Irland a poor widdow, when her 2 Sons were small, she work'd industreously for their and her own maintannance, put them apprentice, took great care of them during that term, they have been some years free, and have work'd at their trades with reputation; she hop'd that they would be her support in the decline of Life, but how uncertain are all human prospects? they were both taken this fall with the prevailing desease [yellow fever], and died, one the day after the other, the poor mother 'tho very ill at the same time surviv'd them, and may be truly call'd a 'lone woman. . . .

11 April [1794] S S[wett] spent the day try'd on a gown for me. . . .

26 Betsy Fordham left us this afternoon, she has been near 2 weeks at work
   for us. . . .
20 October [1794] S Swett fitted a mantua gown on me, which I had provided
   [ordered] in the Summer, she is so kind to do what little I want in that way for
   me, I beleive I never had a gown better made in my life, and she is now within
   about seven weeks of 73 years of age, to work so neatly at such an age is the
   cause of my making the memorandum.

2. Ruth Henshaw, a Massachusetts
Teenager, Records Her Work in 1792

January 1 1792 I wish you a happy new year. Sunday rainy afternoon . . . tarried at
   uncle Wheeler's all night. rainy night. . . .
12 I wound the gown we [torn]. . . .
24 Extreamly cold. I spun filling for my gown &c
25 Ditto. washed. . . .
28 Cloudy. Weather moderate. I made Ma'am [her mother] a bonnet. . . .
2 [February] Fair Mrs Hawkins here to warp. . . .
4 Very Pleasent indeed. George Bruce & Hannah set off for Fraimingham.
   Patty Bruce assisted me in making a gown for myself. . . .
11 Fair. I finish'd making my coates. . . .
13 Pleasent. Daddy and Ma'am went to the cloathers carried cloath for Gowns to
   be dressed. . . .
21 Very cold & windy: Daddy went to Widow Gross's, alias Mrs. Adam's, upon
business for uncle Joseph Maam's cloath came from mill for gown. . . . I spun
   cotton for stockings.
22 Fair. Mrs Hawkins here to warp a web. I made Ma'am woolen gown. . . .
28 Very Pleasent. Trees glistening with ice make a beautiful appearance. Phebe went
   to aunt Wheeler to have her gown made &c. I made my red wool gown &c. . . .
12 [March] Fair cloudy aftrnoon. Dabby Cornish here washing. . . .
27 Miss Patty Eddy spent the day at D^r's making Lucy a gown. . . .
17 [April] Went up to aunt Wheeler's at night to spin a little. Daddy went to town,
   bought cotton of Harr[is]. . . .
19 Pleasent. Spun Cotton for Stockings &c. . . .
23 Very Pleasent, Daddy to Worcester, Maam & Phebe at mr Lynd's visiting,
   while I am at home alone Singing away my precious hour! Which time ought
   to be better employed, but thoughtless youth how swift do the moments years
   hours & days roll away unregarded by thee, whose Days are spent in jollity &
   mirth, but a little while to have, with those gay scenes of false happiness (for no
   other[wise] can I state it) and every other earthly enjoyment, May reflections
   of this kind often remind us, & serve to prepare us, for our approaching
   dissolution. . . .

Diary of Ruth Henshaw (later Bascom), American Antiquarian Society, Worcester, Mass. This document
can also be found on microfilm in the collection *American Women's Diaries, New England, from the
Collections of the American Antiquarian Society* (New Canaan, Conn.: Readex, 1984).

25 very Pleasant. Spun Cotton. . . .

26 Very rainy day indeed. Went to Mr Hawkins . . . to help Mrs Eddy Quilt.
Phebe went [and] a number of other ladies went out there for the same
purpose. . . .

30 Pleasant, afternoon Ma[am] went up to help Mrs Eddy sew. . . .

19 [May] Pleasant. in evening went over to Mrs Whitney's store with Daddy &
Aunt Sally. Bought me 10 yards of fine Muslin for a gown. . . .

21 Patty Bruce & I made my gown & coat. . . .

6 [June] I engaged to teach a school at Spencer. . . .

12 Cold for the season. Betsy Baird came here to live. At night Betsy & I went
of[f] to Mr Waite's on an errand.

18 Fair and Warm. Went to Spencer to teach a school. ariv'd at David Wilsons
about tea. . . . In afternoon open my school, which consisted of 17 scholars.
Patty Wilson in here.

19 Very warm—dismissed my school half past 6. 40 scholars

20 Warm, something windy. fine shower PM. 9 new scholars

21 Fine. 5 new scholars

22 Ditto. Dr Hirst called to see me. This day had 45 scholars. kept all day
Saturday. . . .

25 8 new schollars. . . .

27 Fair & windy. 5 new scholars. After school Went to Major Whites

28 Fair windyish coolish. This day had 45 scholars. Afternoon . . . I went up to
David Wilson's. B. Lynd calld to visit.

29 Warm. had 47 scholars to-day.

30 Warm & windyish—kept school all day Saturday. . . .

2 [July] Daddy came to see me at noon. brought me a book call'd the fathers'
Legacy to his Daughter. . . .

3 Had 45 schoolers. had 15 new scholars. After school went down to Major Whites,
drank Coffee. . . .

12 sew'd on mrs Wilson's cape. . . .

14 Warm. kept school all day. after school went with Becca White to mr James
Watson's. spent very agreeable afternoon &c. . . .

16 I made mrs Wilson's cape, muslin. . . .

18 Fair, after school took a ride to Leceister. . . .

19 Fair kept school for half day. . . .

21 Rain some in forenoon, fair afternoon—yesterday & to-day made Mrs Wilson's
Bonnet. kept school all Day saturday. . . .

24 Cold. N.E. Storm. had 24 scholars. . . .

31 Widow Whittimore from Leicester brought her fifth Daughter to live with
Mrs Wilson

4 [August] Fair. Saturday kept school all day. . . .

10 I made mr Wilson a shirt. . . .

16 Coldish . . . had 40 [scholars]. . . .

21 Fair, warm. Had 52 scholars, &c.

22 Cooler—had 48 Scholars. . . .

25 yesterday and to-day made mrs Wilson a callico gown. . . .

26 towards night went blackburying with Patty Watson. . . .

5 [September] after school went down to mr Joseph Bishop's and engaged
   Jerusha Atkens for 2 or 3 months to spin. to come in 3 weeks. . . .

[Her teaching ended, she returns to Leicester.]
18 afternoon went to work upon the wool
19 Fair. I carded for Phebe. . . .
20 Ditto, carding spining weaving. maam got web out. . . .
21 Ditto Ditto Ditto
22 Ditto Ditto Ditto. . . .
24 Polly Wheeler here to warp. . . .
28 Borrow'd mr Fowler's horse & went to . . . Jerusha Atkins, who came to our
   house to spin a while. . . .
2 [October] in evening Jerusha, Phebe & I went to Phiny Earle's & . . . took cards
3 Fair. P Wheeler and Abigail Earle here to warp webs. . . .
4 Jerusha began to weave on Web. . . .
10 Maam bought two & thirty stays of a pedlar . . . also combs &c. . . .
11 Phebe came . . . from uncle Wheeler's, been spining today for aunt. . . .
4 [November] Jerusha came here from mr sergents to weave. . . .
7 Jerusha got the web out & went home. . . .
8 deliver me from much to spin. . . .
2 [December] Jerusha came up here from mr sergeant's to spin tomorrow. . . .
3 Jerusha went away PM. . . .
15 This day I am 20 years old. spun 3 skains Lining wove 3 years all wool. . . .
17 mrs Hawkins came after her cape. . . .
18 Billy & Daniel went to Uncle Denny's & got 24 wool card, sat too. . . .
20 P Wheeler came here, wound & warped a web—staid all night.

◆ E S S A Y S

The first essay, by Gloria L. Main of the University of Colorado, Boulder, surveys
women's paid labor in colonial New England from the earliest days of settlement until
the American Revolution. The patterns Main identifies in this article add detail and
nuance to historians' understanding of both the variety of women's occupations and
the ways they changed over time. The second essay, by the young scholar Karin Wulf
of American University, examines women's occupations in late-eighteenth-century
Philadelphia. Urban women, she finds, had several opportunities to earn money largely
denied to the rural women studied by Main.

Gender, Work, and Wages in Colonial New England

GLORIA L. MAIN

Present-day demands for equal pay for equal work have awakened scholars' interests
in the determination of labor compensation in other societies. In the preindustrial
economies of western European countries and their colonies in the New World, the
household constituted the basic unit of production and consumption. Individual

Gloria L. Main, "Gender, Work, and Wages in Colonial New England," *William and Mary Quarterly,* 3d
ser, 51 (1994): 39–66. Reprinted by permission.

members did not wield exclusive control over either their labor or their income. Rather, the household's head, who was usually the oldest resident male, supervised the assignment of tasks and distributed the rewards among members. Depending on his temperament, his decisions could be crudely authoritarian and arbitrary, or he might routinely consult his family in the process of managing their resources for the benefit of all. For household heads of either disposition, the sex and age of members helped clarify everyone's particular responsibilities and just desserts. The continual reassociation of particular tasks with gender and age groups, in turn, reinforced members' distinctive social roles.

The division of labor within the family reflected and abetted the culturally sanctioned division of labor and rewards in society as a whole. Recruitment and compensation for labor services took place within a matrix of role expectations and family obligations. Religion, custom, and law combined to reinforce patriarchal authority over the household, but all three also supported separate spheres of responsibility for husband and wife. This division helped maintain respect between spouses by giving wives an area of clear authority over resources, children, and servants. Perhaps keeping out of each other's way also promoted harmony in cultures, such as in colonial New England's, that afforded little scope to self-assertiveness for females. . . .

Historians of colonial women . . . tend to ignore economic issues when debating trends in women's status and conditions. Most believe that white women were more highly regarded in the colonies than at home, because of the higher value of their labor and their relative scarcity, at least in the seventeenth century in regions such as the Chesapeake. Others posit that economic opportunities for women narrowed as colonial society developed beyond primitive conditions in which women shouldered burdens customarily borne by men. Data presented below lend support to the first proposition but dispute the second.

This article examines the types of work women in early New England did compared to men, weighs relative pay scales, and explores trends in the wages of both sexes. Evidence comes from two types of sources: wage ceilings discussed or imposed by governments in 1670 and 1777 and pay rates found in account books, diaries, and probate records. These sources also supply the basis for estimating women's rates of participation in the paid labor force and for tabulating the types of work women performed for pay. All of this material can be conveniently summarized by dividing the colonial period into four phases: initial growth (1620–1674), crisis and recovery (1675–1714), stability (1715–1754), and expansion (1755–1774). The sequence, however, defies simple linear interpretations of progression, either from good conditions to bad, declension, or from bad conditions to good, progress. Both the status of women and the region's economy experienced cycles of good and bad times, but the closing decades of the period saw real improvement for both. Perhaps the most important lesson of this investigation is that even relatively modest economic changes can, by their cumulative actions, significantly alter family relations and living standards.

We begin by looking at several governmental attempts to fix wages. Town and provincial governments in colonial New England undertook at various times to impose ceilings on wage rates, usually as part of a program to control inflation. Two such attempts in Massachusetts, one at the beginning of the American Revolution and the other a hundred years earlier, are interesting because they fixed rates for different kinds of workers and jobs. . . . Comparison of maximum wages prescribed a hundred years apart suggests three things: first, time spent in farming was worth two-thirds more in 1777 than in 1670; second, [by 1777] women had joined the paid labor force in numbers sufficient to warrant placing ceilings on their wage rates; and third, women earned about 37–42 percent of what men did. A reasonable interpretation of these findings is that demand for labor had risen sometime prior to 1777, pulling women into the labor force, and that women were replacing men in lower-paying jobs such as tailoring. If these ceiling rates, and the inferences drawn from them, represent the economic realities of their time and region, then labor productivity was far higher in New England on the eve of the Revolution than historians previously thought.

To test these findings, we turn to actual wages and work assignments inscribed in account books, diaries, and probate documents. Together, these sources supply a basis for estimating trends in the level of wages and for comparing the worth of male and female labor, as measured by employers. The sources also illuminate the bases of the division of labor by providing invaluable vignettes of gender relations. . . .

With the single exception of Elizabeth Newberry, a widow who managed her deceased husband's store, account keepers in the sample were all male. This situation is not surprising—most rural women born before 1730 could not write, read others' writing, or do arithmetic above the simplest level. Moreover, the legal restrictions on married women's property rights meant that wives could not normally sue or be sued for debt. Thus, when Joshua Hempstead bought twenty bushels of corn from his neighbor's wife in November 1721, it was "on Condition her husband will allow it."

Since the account books of farmers and artisans show them dealing almost exclusively with other men, one might conclude that women seldom stirred from home for any purposes other than those sanctioned by Christian prescription: errands of piety, charity, and neighborliness. Such inferences mesh neatly with the dark image of Puritan New England as a rigid, male-dominated society that tightly imprisoned women's personalities. Yet reasoning from the absence of written evidence is always dangerous, especially for members of a culture that, even in comparatively literate New England, continued to depend heavily on oral agreements. Informal borrowing and lending probably constituted the bulk of local exchanges in most rural communities, among men as well as women, even after the arrival of storekeepers. Women, therefore, may well have engaged in frequent, petty trade with other women without recording the transactions. The rare diaries kept by women later in the century occasionally mention just such bargains.

It remains true that few women in rural New England engaged in business on a scale or of a nature that required them to record their transactions in a systematic way. The inherently male-biased data that survive are nonetheless useful. . . . [W]age data from account books, probate records, and diaries confirm the implications of the Massachusetts wage maximums of 1777: farm labor productivity had risen by about two-thirds over the course of more than a century, and significant numbers of women worked for pay yet received appreciably less than male farm laborers. . . .

We can derive two important findings from these sources. First, the exchange value of women's economic activities varied considerably during the colonial period, and second, New England's economy flourished in the three decades before the Revolution. . . . Examining wage differentials among men, women, and boys in New England . . . we find that boys earned about two-thirds of the prevailing farm wage for men, and women averaged less than half. While the percentages of men's rates received by women in this period appear low to modern eyes, they compare favorably with levels prevailing in Massachusetts factories of the 1830s, when women's earnings averaged about 42–45 percent of men's earnings. . . . The gender gap in New England wages widened over time, but the trend reversed sharply after the Seven Years' War. . . . Women's wages continued to rise when men's wages did not, narrowing the gap between them. This improvement in women's pay is particularly surprising given the relative surplus in the number of women in older settlements. . . .

The changing level of monetary reward for women's work relative to men's work can be explained in part by the changing content of that work, the subject to which this article now turns. Later, sources of the demand for labor in New England, including the Seven Years' War, are explored to explain the forces shaping the changing contours of the gender division of labor. Finally, some of the material and social consequences of the changing relationships between men's and women's work and wages are considered.

Settlers in a new land must find ways to acquire the goods they want and cannot make for themselves. For New Englanders, this proved a major challenge. Probably the most notable characteristic of the economy that is evident in probate inventories was the economy's dependence on England for manufactures of all sorts, including textiles. In the first generation after settlement, few women could have engaged in spinning, weaving, or dyeing simply because unprocessed textile fibers were in short supply. . . . Flax production was labor intensive, and sheep did not thrive under pioneering conditions: wolves found them easy prey, and the woodland underbrush tore away their wool. By the 1670s these conditions had changed. An aggressive bounty system and the spread of settlements into the interior gradually exterminated the wolves and cleared enough pastureland so that sheep became a more familiar sight on mainland farms. . . . Nor did many early households possess the tools for such women's tasks as brewing, baking, or dairying. . . .

Most of New England's people were farmers. Women who were not tied down by young children probably spent their time outdoors working in gardens or with their men in the fields. Although English women did not customarily do heavy field work, they did garden with hoes, and in the colonies the hoe played a major role wherever families could use existing Indian fields. . . .

. . . [T]he ratio of women's pay to men's pay was at its highest point in this early period when the division of labor between men and women was less clearly defined than in contemporary England or as it later came to be in New England. Women could hoe in already-cleared Indian fields, and meadows and salt marshes supplied their small herds of animals with forage. When these sites filled up and the numbers of livestock expanded, newcomers had to break new ground and create meadows planted with English grasses. Inventories record the gradual advent of a more English farming style using heavy plows drawn by teams of oxen, while tax lists and town genealogies trace the growing supply of sturdy young sons. Similarly, the appearance of spinning wheels, firkins, brewing vats, and dye pots attests to the kinds of activities that came to employ women. The division of labor between the sexes widened and, as it did so, separated them physically.

The use of ox teams, restricted to older men, effectively segregated family members into field and home workers. Men and older boys also did the sowing and harrowing at the beginning of the farm year and the reaping and mowing at harvest. In early spring they planted and pruned orchards and carted and spread dung. In June they washed and sheared sheep. In fall they pressed cider and slaughtered hogs. In the slack seasons men cut and dragged timber, built and maintained fences, cleared underbrush, ditched bogs, and dug out stones. In most of these activities, handling draft animals was essential and was work for males only. The men used oxen to remove stumps and boulders, drag timber, cart dung, and haul hay and horses to drive cider presses. Only men and older boys paddled canoes, steered scows, piloted "gundalows" (gondolas), or rowed boats.

Women participated in none of these activities except at harvest time, when their help was welcomed. . . . [But] many farm tasks fell more or less exclusively to the female members of the household. Girls and women tended the fowl and small animals. They milked the cows at dawn and dusk, separated the cream, churned the butter, and made the cheese. They planted and hoed kitchen gardens in plots men had prepared by plowing and harrowing. Women boiled the offal for such by-products as sausage casings, head cheese, calf's foot jelly, and rennet after men killed, cleaned, and butchered animals. Gender-based assignment of many farm chores centered on objective differences in body height and strength rather than on what was deemed culturally appropriate to one sex or the other. Females carried out some of the same tasks as younger boys—they helped hay, hoe, weed, harvest crops, and husk corn.

Yet gender ordered male and female spheres in ways that went beyond obvious physical distinctions. . . . [Girls did not] drive cattle or carry grain on horseback to the mill, as boys did. Women did not thresh grain, even though boys of thirteen or fourteen did so. Although men and boys traveled abroad freely in their duties, women's work more often kept them inside or near their own home or those kinsmen or employers. In and around the home they earned income from tasks that males assiduously avoided: cleaning, cooking, sewing, spinning, washing clothes, nursing, and caring for children.

Thus, people allocated work among themselves based on physical capacity but also on gender. The advent of English-style agriculture, involving large draft animals and deep plowing, helped fix many boundaries between the sexes. . . . Those boundaries, however, were permeable. Men could and did cross into women's domain when the size of the market justified a larger scale of operations than the home could provide. For example, baking and brewing were normally women's work, but men in port towns also made their living by these activities. Men in New England did not lose self-respect if they milked cows, but they did not normally make cheese or churn cream into butter. If, however, the family began to specialize in dairying for sale, the men might take part. . . .

[S]ome male-dominated occupations were always open to women. Retail trade was perhaps the most common, although before 1740 such opportunities arose in only a few commercial areas. Most women in retailing were widows who had taken over a deceased husband's shop. . . . Though women had always acted as midwives, nursed the sick, and disbursed homemade remedies, a few also "doctored." . . . Women taught school, as did men. Generally speaking, women taught young pupils of both sexes to read and spell, and men instructed more advanced classes in writing and arithmetic. Seventeenth-century records occasionally identify "school dames" who took students for fees, but they do not seem to have been common outside the largest settlements. In the eighteenth century, women usually taught the younger children and girls during the summer, often for only half the wages of the young male college graduates who took the older children the rest of the year. . . . There was also a two-tier system in making apparel. Men normally tailored coats and breeches, and women sewed shirts and gowns; however, women in the eighteenth century also engaged in tailoring to a limited extent. . . .

Gender distinctions were very clear in the processing of textiles. Females did not comb worsted or hackle flax, which was men's work, although women, along with boys, pulled flax, carded wool, and picked seeds out of cotton. Girls and women spun, dyed, and knitted yarn, but few engaged in weaving, traditionally a male occupation in England. Women did take up the craft in the eighteenth century, doing simple weaves while men concentrated on more complex patterns. . . .

Weaving may be the only occupation in the colonial period for which there is sufficient documentation to compare men's and women's pay for the same type of work. . . . Of those for whom pay rates are available, comparisons with contemporary male weavers show that the sexes earned similar rates per yard for common kinds of cloth. . . . We can conclude that, in this instance, women did earn equal pay for equal work. . . . Although the sources do not reveal great numbers of women working at looms, women's growing presence in the late colonial period signals a trend that accelerated during the Revolution.

The history of weaving and tailoring in New England illustrates the flexibility inherent in the region's gender-based work roles. The further removed the activity was from hard-core masculine tasks associated with oxen, plows, and heavy equipment, the more likely that respectable women did it. The history of work and gender in New England during the colonial years divides readily into four periods of unequal duration. In the earliest period, before the 1670s, the economy simplified compared to England's economy, and the variety of occupations open to either sex contracted sharply. Women spent more time outdoors and working alongside men. The second period came with the proliferation of activities by which men habitually and strictly segregated themselves from women, and women undertook domestic manufacturing tasks with which historians have so often associated them: brewing beer, baking bread, churning butter, making cheese, spinning yarn, and knitting stockings and mittens. Not every housewife practiced all these arts, and specialization encouraged exchange between them.

The third period, beginning about 1715, constituted the farm maintenance stage in older settlements during which demand for unskilled labor declined relative to skilled labor. Increasing population densities created exchange opportunities that encouraged both men and women to specialize and invest more time in nonfarm occupations. This stage might have continued indefinitely, with population growth putting continuous downward pressure on wages, but outside forces intervened, creating the fourth and final phase of New England's colonial development. Beginning in 1739, wars and their aftermaths administered a succession of shocks to the system, creating sudden demands for men and provisions and putting large amounts of money into circulation. The conclusion to the Seven Years' War opened up northern New England and Nova Scotia to British settlement, and the treaty that ended the War for Independence swung open the gates to Iroquoia in New York, as did the Battle of Fallen Timbers (1794) for the Ohio Valley. Much of the labor supply that might have depressed wage rates emigrated instead; in New England, it was not replaced by immigrants.

Despite New England's limited resources and the absence of technological change, demand generated by war and export markets drove the region's economy at a faster rate than its population grew. Evidence for economic expansion appears in both account books and probate inventories. . . .

When farmers endeavored to raise more livestock and the grass to feed them, and when farm wives found themselves milking more cows, churning more butter, and making more cheese, men and women were putting pressure on a labor force that in the short run could expand only by crossing the gender division of labor. Every attempt by the colonial governments during the Seven Years' War to recruit soldiers for the summer campaigns further reduced the available pool of young men, and farmers found themselves engaged in a bidding war that raised wages and bounties. . . . The rise in wages beginning in the 1740s at first touched only men but in the long term affected everyone by loosening the bonds between parents and their grown children as daughters found work outside the home and sons joined the military or emigrated. The account books show that men abruptly began employing greater numbers of women in the final two decades of the colonial period. . . . Rising wages and expanding employment meant higher incomes for those who did not emigrate. The probate inventories of the late colonial period show that most New England families were prospering. . . .

. . . The growing proportion of young women working outside the home in the final decades of the colonial period accompanied a rise in their wages, which no doubt helped attract them. When combined with evidence that increasing numbers of country girls were attending school and learning how to write, the growing ability of women to earn money and conduct business at the local store can be viewed as a positive good, giving them greater control over their own lives. Furthermore, the addition of tea, sugar, and spices to their diets, painted earthenware to their tables, featherbeds to sleep on, and greater privacy, all surely added pleasures to generally hard lives. Although marriage still meant coverture, more women chose to remain single and access to divorce became easier. There is also a demographic indicator that women's lot was improving: life expectancy of married women rose. Mean age at death increased from sixty-two to sixty-six for women marrying between 1760 and 1774 and to sixty-eight for those marrying between 1775 and 1800. On balance, these changes appear beneficial. Women would not gain politically or legally from American Independence, and equality was never even a prospect, but in the decades before 1776 they had won a little liberty, and comfort is no mean thing.

Women's Work in Colonial Philadelphia

KARIN WULF

Even in a city as large as Philadelphia, with a transient population and a seaport buzzing with daily arrivals and departures, dense webs of relationships underlay urban neighborhoods. Thus, when John Barker, the constable of Philadelphia's High Street Ward, set out to enumerate the residents of his district in 1775, he encountered familiar faces and families of long residence. Among the householders he greeted while making these rounds was the widow Rachel Draper, a tavernkeeper. Rachel Draper had lived in High Street Ward for over twenty years by the time Barker came to make his Constable's Return. Her husband, James, a tailor who had earned a modest living, had died relatively young. . . . Rachel Draper was the sole executor of her husband's estate, a common phenomenon among Philadelphia's lower sort. The larger and more complex an estate was, the less likely it was that the widow was named as the sole executor, or even as a co-executor. After administering the settlement of her husband's estate, Rachel Draper set about making a living for herself and her two young daughters. She held onto the house, but her financial status was precarious. She was considered too poor and too burdened by the costs of supporting her young children to pay any taxes.

Like many others among Philadelphia's working poor, Draper used a variety of economic strategies to meet her family's needs. She was granted successive city licenses to operate a "dram shop," or small tavern, probably right in her home on Chancery Lane. She was a tavernkeeper from at least 1767 through 1773, and perhaps for much longer. To help with the annual rent of £14 on a house and lot that served as both residence and place of business, Draper took in boarders: Jacob Potts was boarding there in 1770, and Thomas Draper, no doubt a relation, was boarding there in 1775.

By 1775 Rachel Draper had lived in her neighborhood for at least two decades, the last twelve years of which she had headed her household. Although clearly economically marginal, Draper was in some ways a success story. She never fell into the transiency that marked the lives of so many among Philadelphia's laboring population. She not only kept her family fed and clothed, but she also made sure that her two daughters received an education. . . .

Rachel Draper's circumstances as a working, unmarried woman were far from unique. She lived and worked alongside such women as upholsterer Elizabeth Lawrence, tavernkeeper Susannah Harditch, and tallow chandler Ann Wishart. Each of these women was a neighbor of Draper's and a resident of long tenure. Each had extensive ties to the community. These women, and others like them, helped to shape urban community and urban culture in the eighteenth-century city. As independent women, they could act legally and economically in ways that their married sisters, bound by coverture, could not. Although historians have emphasized the importance of all women in creating social networks, unmarried women not only

Karin Wulf, "Rachel Draper's Neighborhood: Work and Community," *Not All Wives: Women of Colonial Philadelphia* (Ithaca, N.Y.: Cornell University Press, 2000), 119–121, 130–148. Copyright © 1999 by Cornell University. Used by permission of the publisher, Cornell University Press.

maintained existing ties of kinship and friendship but also created community ties that facilitated their independence. They exchanged credit and debt, rented property to and from their neighbors, served drinks, bought and sold goods, and engaged in friendly, practical, or even hostile conversation. Neighbors often worshipped together. Some were related by blood or marriage. Unmarried women were central actors in the creation and maintenance of the economic, religious, familial, and broadly political networks of association that defined urban life. . . .

Women's work was vital to Philadelphia's economy, but the extent and range of this work has been particularly hard to uncover. Scholars who study the occupational structure of early American cities have had to rely on sources that mask the work of women and other economically marginal groups, including laboring men, servants, and slaves. . . . The city was dependent on goods and services provided by laboring men and women. But the remaining inventories of merchants' goods, the records of indenture, and even tax records that nominally recorded occupations paid little attention to recording women's work in any systematic way. Thus sources have in some measure "hidden" women's work.

In addition, eighteenth-century culture was ambivalent about the meaning of women's work in general and about the economic contributions of domestic work in particular. *Present for an Apprentice: or, a Sure Guide to Gain both Esteem and Estate* circulated widely in the Anglo-American world. In Philadelphia, Benjamin Franklin printed the fourth edition of this book of advice for young, working men embarking on life's journey in 1749. The author cautioned that young men of the laboring sort should consider marriage an expense, rather than a financial gain. . . . Of the economic benefit of women's labor, there was no mention.

Although some source materials reflect the eighteenth-century elision of the significance of women's economic contributions, it is clear that women's work was both ubiquitous and necessary. A common assumption is that widows, who were the majority of unmarried women, were reliant on their inheritances. A husband's estate formed the bulk of a widow's wealth, and thus her own economic condition was utterly dependent on the state of his estate at his death and then on the provisions of his will. There are two problems with this assumption. The first is that it portrays widows as peculiarly financially dependent. In fact, economic interdependence, not independence, was the rule in this period. Men as well as women relied on inheritance and on transfers of wealth rather than strictly on accumulation through income. If anything, women aided men in this respect; the laws of coverture guaranteed men access to any property their wives possessed at marriage and gave them rights to their wives' earnings during the marriage. Men from George Washington to the famously "self-made" Benjamin Franklin prospered through the legally mandated transfer of wealth. The second problem with assuming that inheritance was widows' sole source of income is that it casts women as only passive recipients of wealth, rather than generators of wealth. A widow's inheritance, after all, was the product of her own as well as her husband's capital and labor. In addition, many widows who inherited subsequently increased their holdings through investment or through income-producing occupations.

The urban economy gave women more options for producing income or supplementing their capital than did strictly agricultural regions. Although widowhood often meant a difficult economic predicament, some female entrepreneurs flowered financially after they were widowed. Their experiences suggest that, as for men, familial, friendship, and economic connections helped them establish small businesses. Born in 1707, Hannah Breintnall was a little like Deborah Franklin. Mrs. Franklin often kept shop and accounts for her husband, but while Benjamin Franklin lived a long life during which Deborah was the distinctly subordinate partner in his ventures, Hannah Breintnall's husband died, leaving her to make her own way financially. She took up the most common occupations for female entrepreneurs: keeping a shop and tavern. During the early 1750s, Hannah Breintnall was the proprietor of the Hen and Chickens Tavern on Chestnut Street, and by the mid-1750s, she was making a fairly good living. Then she decided to change her occupation and opened an optician's shop, where she sold spectacles "of the finest Crystal . . . set in Temple, Steel, Leather or other Frames" and other optical aids, such as magnifying glasses and telescopes. This business, along with significant rental income, strengthened Breintnall's financial condition considerably. . . .

Hannah Breintnall was not unusual. She married, bore children, became widowed, managed businesses and finances, and provided for her family. The typical picture of the colonial entrepreneur and provider assumes his masculine gender. But many women like Hannah Breintnall, some more and some less successfully, acted independently to support themselves and their families. Widows could rarely afford to be passive guardians of their portion of a husband's estate, and many did not remarry. It was clear to many widows that they would have to take on the financial responsibility of their own and their family's care.

Women who never married—even those from middling or wealthy families—often had to generate more wealth than they inherited because fathers most often passed real property to sons but gave cash or other personalty, often in the form of marriage settlements, to daughters. Spinsters' work was usually directly related to their lack of inherited resources and their need to support themselves. . . .

Women's occupational opportunities were more restricted than men's for several reasons. Women were less likely to get specialized training in a craft or skill than were men. Female servants, for example, usually were trained only in "housewifery." Strictly limited access to capital prevented most women from creating businesses on their own, with the exception of some retail establishments headed by wealthier women. Widows of tradesmen were sometimes able to continue in their husbands' work, but other women had a hard time entering trades. Perhaps most importantly, the close association of domestic labor with women made it difficult for them to do other kinds of work, simply because whatever the size or economic status of their household, they were responsible for child care and housework. This labor, which was so critical to the functioning of the household economy, left women little time and energy to apply to another occupation. Thus, women who needed income— that is, the majority of married women as well as the vast majority of unmarried women—looked to work that could be fitted around other obligations and used their domestic skills.

Women's work in the eighteenth-century city can be divided into two broad categories: gender-specific work, primarily domestic labor, and nongender-specific work that both men and women performed. Shopkeeping and other mercantile activity, trades, and unskilled labor were all primarily male preserves in which some women could find employment. A degree of gender segregation appeared, however, even within such occupations as retailing or artisanal work.

Among gender-segregated occupations, domestic service was the most significant and visible source of employment for women. Cleaning houses; growing, butchering, preserving, and cooking food; making, repairing, and laundering clothes; caring for children—all of these were tasks that kept women moving in and out of the house and at close quarters with their neighbors. For poorer families, it was deemed both more appropriate and more economical for women to perform such tasks themselves at home. The work required long hours and a strong back. Water for laundry and cooking had to be fetched from a pump. Although urban women did not have to go very far to get water, they still had to haul many gallons a day. Caring for apprentices, servants and slaves, or boarders was also part of women's domestic labor in families of tradesmen or artisans. Even for merchants or others whose work brought income to the family without requiring extensive household labor, the value and extent of domestic labor was enormous.

Female servants performed a large portion of this work. In colonial American cities, as in Europe, domestic service was an increasingly important part of the changing urban economy and reflected the growth of middling classes. In the American South, where domestic work was performed largely by enslaved women, white servants were rare. In the North, however, particularly in mid-Atlantic cities, a variant of the European pattern prevailed. Domestic household servants were not simply the preserve of the rich and titled but became a critical part of the household economy of the middling classes. Whereas in a merchant's home servants would perform purely household tasks, in the home of an artisan a "maid of all work" would lend a hand in the workshop, then contribute to the household tasks of cooking, cleaning, and sewing. . . .

Servants could be either indentured or hired for a day, a week, or a year. Female indentured servants came primarily from three groups. The first were adult women who signed indentures before departing Europe or upon arrival in America in order to pay for their passage. . . . The second type of indentured women were poor girls bound out by the city or by their parents. Indentures could provide some training as well as bed and board. . . . A third category of indentures was made privately, apprenticing girls and boys to specific trades. It is not possible to estimate the size and character of this population, although more boys than girls were trained for trades. Families also sent children to relatives' households in exchange for their care and training in a marketable skill. . . .

The kinds of domestic work that servants did depended on the type of household in which they worked. Female servants in elite households often worked alongside their mistresses, who undertook burdensome domestic labor themselves. Hannah Callender, for example, regularly hired women to do washing and nursing, but did a great deal of sewing, ironing and gardening herself. According to the diary of her sister Elizabeth Drinker, Mary Sandwith ironed, a tedious chore. Hired servants could be expected to perform any range of tasks and to be flexible about accepting different assignments. Housework, then as now, encompassed a diverse set of tasks, and servants' contributions to the household naturally depended on the means, needs, and occupations of their employer. In many cases servants were not a luxury but an economic necessity. . . .

Work that was seen as feminine was often linked to domestic skills, specifically to providing care and personal services for others. Chief among these were nursing, midwifery, and mortuary work. Nursing seems to have been a specialized skill, but it also commingled with midwifery and laying out the dead. In an era when doctors were just beginning to acquire formal training, medicine was often administered by lay persons. Nurses were not simply women who happened to care for the sick, however. They were addressed as "Nurse," and some specialized in infant care, others in infectious diseases. . . . Despite increasing use of schooled physicians, midwives seem to have found regular, constant employment. . . . Even women who, later in the century, chose to have doctors rather than midwives deliver their babies hired nurses for their newborns. Breastfeeding was a matter of choice for elite women; Elizabeth Drinker nursed her own children until her doctor insisted that she quit, whereas her friend and school-fellow Hannah Callender Sansom sent her children out to a wet nurse. After nursing her son Henry for almost eight months, Drinker reported that she turned him over to "S. Oats, whose Breast he willingly suck'd." Wet-nursing supplied poorer households with some extra income, perhaps at a critical moment when a woman was prevented from income-earning activities by virtue of recent childbirth. . . .

Women's responsibility for the attending the dead was both social custom and economic opportunity. Women regularly stayed with women friends who were either sick or in labor, and with friends' children who were sick. Once a person had died, however, professional services were engaged. Some women, like Precilla Cowley, both nursed the ill and prepared the dead body for burial, while other women provided specialized mortuary and funerary services. . . .

. . . [W]omen and men had differential employment opportunities, with more skilled work available primarily to men, and . . . women were paid from one-quarter to one-half of the wages that men could command for similar work. In urban areas, the greater demand for more specialized skills and trades benefited males more than females, especially because domestic service was women's primary employment. But it appears that when specialized work was called for, wage differentials shrank so that women earned perhaps one-half to two-thirds of the wages that men commanded. . . .

Unmarried women faced economic pressures particular to their situation. They needed to work, but remunerative employment was scarce. A handful of cases of bawdy house brought before the Philadelphia Mayor's Court in the 1760s and 1770s attest to the unsurprising existence of prostitution in the seaport, but prostitution must have been a last resort. Reported instances of prostitution among poor women increased sharply only after the Revolution.

Domestic service did have some economic advantages, in particular the security of room and board. Unmarried female domestic servants who lived with their employers were provided with food and sometimes with clothing. A regular annual salary of £10 might have compared favorably, at least in economic terms, with the situation of a mistress of a laboring household.

Retailing goods or food and drink provided the next largest group of occupations for women after domestic service. Women accounted for perhaps as many as half of all retailers in the eighteenth-century city, although women's retailing was generally conducted on a smaller scale than men's and was less likely to be combined with wholesaling. . . . Over the eighteenth century, retailing became an increasingly viable economic option for women. Retailing increased in importance as imported consumer goods washed over the colonies, a process that intensified at mid-century. Benjamin Franklin commented on the replacement of his plain earthenware bowl and pewter spoon with china dishes and silver cutlery; his famous remark is emblematic of the transition that was occurring within middling households. Not only were these goods available in newly enlarged quantity and variety, but they were in demand by a new clientele. . . . This increase in the availability and variety of consumer goods prompted the elaboration of retail establishments, and of the activity of shopping itself. . . .

Women were well positioned to take advantage of both the retailing and the consumption of goods. Provisioning the household (or "marketing") was long thought to be a feminine responsibility, but the new dynamics of class and status competition were specifically gendered. . . . Both men and women shopped, but the increasing attention of retail advertisements to their female clientele and to items of female apparel testifies both to women's importance as consumers and to the importance of feminine attire to class aspirations. As retailers, women could tap the very market they helped comprise. Female shopkeepers among the middling or elite whose customers came from the same networks of association could help determine fashions. . . .

Retailing varied widely. At the lower end of the scale, hucksters purchased cast-off, second-quality, damaged, or otherwise less desirable merchandise, which they then hawked through the streets. Peddlers who moved from the city out into the countryside with imported or finished goods were regulated and licensed, and were almost exclusively male. Hucksters who carried goods through the city were usually female. Hucksters could acquire goods for their baskets from a variety of sources. Fresh food was brought into the city from the hinterlands on market days, when the city's famously extensive markets could be overwhelmed with meat, cheese, butter, and produce, along with homespun cloth and other hand-made goods. Any goods left by the end of the day, unsold or of inferior quality, were sold to hucksters, who might make a tiny profit by reselling them. Walking outward from the city center, hucksters might find customers among those who could not get to the market—for example, housewives confined at home who had no servants to make their purchases, and laboring families for whom a trip to the market or first-quality fresh goods were a rare luxury. One step up from hucksters were those women who operated tiny shops within a corner of a room, sometimes buying only small lots of goods to sell at a time. . . .

A handful of elite women shopkeepers operating during the third quarter of the eighteenth century, including Mary Coates, Magdalena Devine, Elizabeth Paschall, and Mary and Rebecca Steel, were very prosperous and carried extensive inventory. For these women, as for many successful male entrepreneurs, economic, social, kinship, and religious circles all overlapped; shopkeeping mixed easily with their other social obligations. They shopped in each others' stores, bought wholesale goods together, and circulated within the same group of friends. Coates, Paschall, and Rebecca Steel bought goods together at vendue for sale in their respective shops. They purchased goods from each other when these items were not available from their own inventories, or when one happened on a better wholesale price. . . .

Retailing was an increasingly viable option for women in the colonial city, as consumer demand increased and could support specialization as well as a wide range of retailing venues. Related employments, such as millinery, which combined both craft work and retailing and which also depended on both availability of fine imports and consumer demand for fashionable items, expanded as well.

Opportunities in tavernkeeping also increased as the city grew. A few gathering spots, such as the London Coffee House on Market Street, catered to a new clientele of merchants who wanted not just to exchange business talk but to engage in the whole realm of discussions that were beginning to constitute public discourse. The only women welcomed there were servers. Most taverns, however, remained gathering spots for neighbors or work-fellows, providing modest provisions and drink at a low price. For many women like Rachel Draper, tavernkeeping was a reasonably good prospect. . . . In some areas of the city there were as many or more female as male publicans. Tavernkeeping could also be combined with shopkeeping in a single establishment, which may have made it especially appealing to women.

A few women worked in the specialized trades supported by the urban economy, especially after mid-century. Most probably had husbands or fathers who had worked in these trades and perhaps already established workshops that they could assume. Among those who made their living supplying the many seaport industries, Sarah Jewell continued the ropewalk her husband had founded, making ropes and rigging so necessary for shipbuilding, while Hannah Beales continued her father's fishnet-making business. No guilds kept women in Philadelphia from pursuing trades, as they did in early modern Europe, but the complications of acquiring apprentices and gaining master status were enough to discourage most women. Informal pressure from loose organizations of artisans may also have had a hand in discouraging women's participation in such trades.

Almost all urban women worked either within or outside the home, and most probably worked for pay. Economic connections that women made while working could be a critical outgrowth of other relationships, particularly among family members, but the formation of economic networks was also a fundamental opportunity provided by neighborhood. Unmarried women were in a unique position to take advantage of such opportunities, and they did so largely out of economic necessity. The better-developed a woman's personal networks of association were, the better her chances were of surviving economically in the city. Women, like men, accessed credit and debt networks by exercising familial and economic resources, including personal relationships. Because women had much less access to trans-Atlantic credit, however, wholesale merchant work was an unlikely pursuit, whereas local credit networks such as those employed by small retailers were much more readily available. Women such as the shopkeepers Mary Coates, Elizabeth Paschall, and Rebecca Steel, who purchased wholesale goods together, used their familial and neighborhood connections to further their economic goals.

By forming economic connections and networks, work also became an important source of personal and community identity. Although not all workers identified with their work, many did, especially those whose work enmeshed them in networks of obligation and association. Contributing to the association of work and identity was the way that work became bound up with the community's needs and one's place in the community.

◈ *F U R T H E R   R E A D I N G*

Cleary, Patricia. "'She Will Be in the Shop': Women's Sphere of Trade in Eighteenth-Century Philadelphia and New York," *Pennsylvania Magazine of History and Biography* 119 (1995): 181–202.

Goldin, Claudia. "The Economic Status of Women in the Early Republic," *Journal of Interdisciplinary History* 16 (1985–1986): 375–404.

Hood, Adrienne. "The Gender Division of Labor in the Production of Textiles in Eighteenth-Century Pennsylvania (Rethinking the New England Model)," *Journal of Social History* 26, no. 3 (March 1994): 537–561.

Nash, Gary B. "The Failure of Female Factory Labor in Colonial Boston," *Labor History* 20 (1979): 165–188.

Norton, Mary Beth. *Founding Mothers & Fathers: Gendered Power and the Forming of American Society* (1996).

————. "'The Ablest Midwife That Wee Knowe in the Land': Mistress Alice Tilly and the Women of Boston and Dorchester, 1649–1650," *William and Mary Quarterly,* 3d ser, 55 (1998): 105–134.

Salinger, Sharon. "'Send No More Women': Female Servants in Eighteenth-Century Philadelphia," *Pennsylvania Magazine of History and Biography* 107 (1983): 29–48.

Sklar, Kathryn K. "The Schooling of Girls and Changing Communities Values in Massachusetts Towns, 1750–1820," *History of Education Quarterly* 33 (1993): 511–542.

Tannenbaum, Rebecca. *The Healer's Calling: Women and Medicine in Early New England* (2002).

Ulrich, Laurel Thatcher. "Wheels, Looms, and the Gender Division of Labor in Eighteenth-Century New England," *William and Mary Quarterly,* 3d ser, 55 (1998): 3–38.

CHAPTER 4

The Impact of the
American Revolution

In many ways, the American Revolution changed the course of history for the
residents of what had been Britain's mainland North American colonies. In 1774,
the settlers were colonials—subjects of a monarchy based thousands of miles across
the Atlantic and participants in a traditional political system. Less than a decade
later, these successful revolutionaries, now Americans, were the founders of an
independent republic and the first colonists in history to win their freedom and
establish their own nation.

Such dramatic events, it could be argued, impinged primarily on men, not
women. After all, men alone fought in the armies, voted in the new republic's
elections, drafted state and national constitutions, and served in legislative bodies.
Women traditionally did not take part in politics, their domain was the household,
whereas the public world was defined exclusively as the men's arena. Did the revolu-
tion, then, affect women? If so, did it have different effects on black women than it
did on white women? Or can the revolution be safely ignored by historians of women
because it held so little meaning for their subjects?

◆ D O C U M E N T S

In March 1776, recognizing that the American colonies, which had already been at war
with Britain for nearly a year, would soon declare independence, Abigail Adams wrote
to her congressman husband, John, in Philadelphia, reminding him to "remember the
ladies" in the nation's "new code of laws." She thus initiated the first known exchange in
American history on the subject of women's rights. The Adamses' comments on the matter make up Document 1. Document 2 dates from 1780: after the Americans had suffered
one of their worst defeats of the war at Charleston, South Carolina, a Pennsylvanian
named Esther DeBerdt Reed published a broadside, "The Sentiments of an American
Woman," proposing a nationwide ladies association to contribute to the welfare of
the troops. Document 3 is a laconic description of what happened to the slaves from
Thomas Jefferson's plantations who ran off to join the invading British forces in 1781.
In Document 4, dated many years after the Revolution, Sarah Osborn, who had traveled

with her husband and the American army, recalled those experiences as she applied for a government pension in 1837.

1. Abigail and John Adams Discuss "Remembering the Ladies," 1776

Abigail Adams to John Adams

Braintree March 31 1776

I long to hear that you have declared an independancy—and by the way in the new Code of Laws which I suppose it will be necessary for you to make I desire you would Remember the Ladies, and be more generous and favourable to them than your ancestors. Do not put such unlimited power in the hands of the Husbands. Remember all Men would be tyrants if they could. If perticuliar care and attention is not paid to the Laidies we are determined to foment a Rebelion, and will not hold ourselves bound by any Laws in which we have no voice, or Representation.

That your Sex are Naturally Tyrannical is a Truth so thoroughly established as to admit of no dispute, but such of you as wish to be happy willingly give up the harsh title of Master for the more tender and endearing one of Friend. Why then, not put it out of the power of the vicious and the Lawless to use us with cruelty and indignity with impunity. Men of Sense in all Ages abhor those customs which treat us only as the vassals of your Sex. Regard us then as Beings placed by providence under your protection and in immitation of the Supreem Being make use of that power only for our happiness.

John to Abigail

Ap. 14. 1776

As to Declarations of Independency, be patient. Read our Privateering Laws, and our Commercial Laws. What signifies a Word.

As to your extraordinary Code of Laws, I cannot but laugh. We have been told that our Struggle has loosened the bands of Government every where. That Children and Apprentices were disobedient—that schools and Colledges were grown turbulent—that Indians slighted their Guardians and Negroes grew insolent to their Masters. But your Letter was the first Intimation that another Tribe more numerous and powerful than all the rest were grown discontented.—This is rather too coarse a Compliment but you are so saucy, I wont blot it out.

Depend upon it, We know better than to repeal our Masculine systems. Altho they are in full Force, you know they are little more than Theory. We dare not exert our Power in its full Latitude. We are obliged to go fair, and softly, and in Practice you know We are the subjects. We have only the Name of Masters, and rather than give up this, which would compleatly subject Us to the Despotism of the Peticoat, I

Adams Papers, Massachusetts Historical Society, Boston, Mass. This document can also be found in Lyman H. Butterfield et al., eds., *The Book of Abigail and John: Selected Letters of the Adams Family, 1762–1784* (Cambridge, Mass.: Harvard University Press, 1975).

hope General Washington, and all our brave Heroes would fight. I am sure every good Politician would plot, as long as he would against Despotism, Empire, Monarchy, Aristocracy, Oligarchy, or Ochlocracy—A fine Story indeed. I begin to think the Ministry as deep as they are wicked. After stirring up Tories, Landjobbers, Trimmers, Bigots, Canadians, Indians, Negroes, Hanoverians, Hessians, Russians, Irish Roman Catholicks, Scotch Renegadoes, at last they have stimulated the   to demand new Priviledges and threaten to rebell.

Abigail to John

B[raintre]e May 7 1776

I can not say that I think you very generous to the Ladies, for whilst you are proclaiming peace and good will to Men, Emancipating all Nations, you insist upon retaining an absolute power over Wives. But you must remember that Arbitrary power is like most other things which are very hard, very liable to be broken—and notwithstanding all your wise Laws and Maxims we have it in our power not only to free our selves but to subdue our Masters, and without violence throw both your natural and legal authority at our feet—

> "Charm by accepting, by submitting sway
> Yet have our Humour most when we obey."

2. The Patriot Esther DeBerdt Reed Describes the "Sentiments of an American Woman," 1780

On the commencement of actual war, the Women of America manifested a firm resolution to contribute as much as could depend on them, to the deliverance of their country. Animated by the purest patriotism, they are sensible of sorrow at this day, in not offering more than barren wishes for the success of so glorious a Revolution. They aspire to render themselves more really useful; and this sentiment is universal from the north to the south of the Thirteen United States. Our ambition is kindled by the fame of those heroines of antiquity, who have rendered their sex illustrious, and have proved to the universe, that, if the weakness of our Constitution, if opinion and manners did not forbid us to march to glory by the same paths as the Men, we should at least equal, and sometimes surpass them in our love for the public good. I glory in all that which my sex has done great and commendable. I call to mind with enthusiasm and with admiration, all those acts of courage, of constancy and patriotism, which history has transmitted to us: The people favoured by Heaven, preserved from destruction by the virtues, the zeal and the revolution of Deborah, of Judith, of Esther! The fortitude of the mother of the Macchabees, in giving up her sons to die before her eyes: Rome saved from the fury of a victorious enemy by the efforts of Volumnia, and other Roman Ladies: So many famous sieges where the Women have been seen forgeting the weakness of their sex, building new walls, digging trenches with their feeble hands, furnishing arms to their defenders, they themselves darting the missile weapons on the enemy, resigning the ornaments of their apparel, and their fortune,

A broadside. Historical Society of Pennsylvania, Philadelphia.

to fill the public treasury, and to hasten the deliverance of their country; burying themselves under its ruins; throwing themselves into the flames rather than submit to the disgrace of humiliation before a proud enemy.

Born for liberty, disdaining to bear the irons of a tyrannic Government, we associate ourselves to the grandeur of those Sovereigns, cherished and revered, who have held with so much splendour the scepter of the greatest States, The Batildas, the Elizabeths, the Maries, the Catharines, who have extended the empire of liberty, and contented to reign by sweetness and justice, have broken the chains of slavery, forged by tyrants in the times of ignorance and barbarity. The Spanish Women, do they not make, at this moment, the most patriotic sacrifices, to encrease the means of victory in the hands of their Sovereign. He is a friend to the French Nation. They are our allies. We call to mind, doubly interested, that it was a French Maid who kindled up amongst her fellow-citizens, the flame of patriotism buried under long misfortunes: It was the Maid of Orleans who drove from the kingdom of France the ancestors of those same British, whose odious yoke we have just shaken off; and whom it is necessary that we drive from this Continent.

But I must limit myself to the recollection of this small number of atchievements. Who knows if persons disposed to censure, and sometimes too severely with regard to us, may not disapprove our appearing acquainted even with the actions of which our sex boasts? We are at least certain, that he cannot be a good citizen who will not applaud our efforts for the relief of the armies which defend our lives, our possessions, our liberty? The situation of our soldiery has been represented to me; the evils inseparable from war, and the firm and generous spirit which has enabled them to support these. But it has been said, that they may apprehend, that, in the course of a long war, the view of their distresses may be lost, and their services be forgotten. Forgotten! never; I can answer in the name of all my sex. Brave Americans, your disinterestedness, your courage, and your constancy will always be dear to America, as long as she shall preserve her virtue.

We know that at a distance from the theatre of war, if we enjoy any tranquility, it is the fruit of your watchings, your labours, your dangers. If I live happy in the midst of my family; if my husband cultivates his field, and reaps his harvest in peace; if, surrounded with my children, I myself nourish the youngest, and press it to my bosom, without being affraid of seeing myself separated from it, by a ferocious enemy; if the house in which we dwell; if our barns, our orchards are safe at the present time from the hands of those incendiaries, it is to you that we owe it. And shall we hesitate to evidence to you our gratitude? Shall we hesitate to wear a cloathing more simple; hair dressed less elegant, while at the price of this small privation, we shall deserve your benedictions, Who, amongst us, will not renounce with the highest pleasure, those vain ornaments, when she shall consider that the valiant defenders of America will be able to draw some advantage from the money which she may have laid out in these, that they will be better defended from the rigours of the seasons, that after their painful toils, they will receive some extraordinary and unexpected relief; that these presents will perhaps be valued by them at a greater price, when they will have it in their power to say: *This is the offering of the Ladies.* The time is arrived to display the same sentiments which animated us at the beginning of the Revolution, when we renounced the use of teas, however agreeable to our taste, rather than receive them from our persecutors; when we made it appear to them that we placed former necessaries in the rank of superfluities, when our

early example of women organized to promote cause

liberty was interested; when our republican and laborious hands spun the flax, prepared the linen intended for the use of our soldiers; when exiles and fugitives we supported with courage all the evils which are the concomitants of war. Let us not lose a moment; let us be engaged to offer the homage of our gratitude at the altar of military valour, and you, our brave deliverers, while mercenary slaves combat to cause you to share with them, the irons with which they are loaded, receive with a free hand our offering, the purest which can be presented to your virtue,

BY AN AMERICAN WOMAN

[Esther DeBerdt Reed]

3. Thomas Jefferson's Slaves Join the British, 1781

DEATHS ETC.

1781.
Elkhill

Hannibal.
Patty
Sam.
Sally.
Nanny
Fanny
Prince
Nancy

} fled to the enemy & died.

Elkhill

Flora. (Black Sall's)
Quomina (Black Sall's) } joined enemy & died.

Black Sall
Jame. (Bl. Sall's)
Joe. (Sue's.) } joined enemy, returned & died

Cumbl^d.

Lucy
[erasure]
[erasure]
Sam.
Jenny
[erasure]
Harry

} joined enemy.

Elk-hill
Shadwell.

Monticello.

Barnaby. run away. returned & died.

Elkhill.

York.
Isabel.
Jack
Hanah's child.
Phoebe's child

} caught small pox from enemy & died.

[note Judy & Nat of Elkhill, Will & Robin of Shadwell joined the enemy, but came back again & lived. so did Isabel, Hannibal's daughter. aftwds given to A.S. Jefferson.]

Elk-hill

Branford
sue. Sue's daur.

} caught the camp fever from the negroes who returned: & died

Monticello
Elk-hill

Old Jenny
Phoebe (Sue's)
Nanny (Tom's) } 1782

Edwin M. Betts, ed., *Thomas Jefferson's Farm Book* (Princeton, N.J.: Princeton University Press, 1953), 29.

sexual connotations

4. Sarah Osborn, a Camp Follower, Recalls the Revolution, 1837

applying for your pension

(She came for economic reasons)

poor women were camp followers

Culture (wives owning property)

That she was married to Aaron Osborn, who was a soldier during the Revolution-ary War. That her first aquaintance with said Osborn commenced in Albany, in the state of New York, during the hard winter of 1780. That deponent then resided at the house of one John Willis, a blacksmith in said city. That said Osborn came down there from Fort Stanwix and went to work at the business of blacksmithing for said Willis and continued working at intervals for a period of perhaps two months. Said Osborn then informed deponent that he had first enlisted at Goshen in Orange County, New York. That he had been in the service for three years, depo-nent thinks, about one year of that time at Fort Stanwix, and that his time was out. And, under an assurance that he would go to Goshen with her, she married him at the house of said Willis during the time he was there as above mentioned, to wit, in January 1780. . . .

That after deponent had married said Osborn, he informed her that he was re-turned during the war, and that he desired deponent to go with him. Deponent de-clined until she was informed by Captain Gregg that her husband should be put on the commissary guard, and that she should have the means of conveyance either in a wagon or on horseback. That deponent then in the same winter season in sleighs accompanied her husband and the forces under command of Captain Gregg on the east side of the Hudson river to Fishkill, then crossed the river and went down to West Point. . . .

Deponent further says that she and her husband remained at West Point till the departure of the army for the South, a term of perhaps one year and a half, but she cannot be positive as to the length of time. While at West Point, deponent lived at Lieutenant Foot's, who kept a boardinghouse. Deponent was employed in washing and sewing for the soldiers. Her said husband was employed about the camp. . . .

When the army were about to leave West Point and go south, they crossed over the river to Robinson's Farms and remained there for a length of time to induce the belief, as deponent understood, that they were going to take up quarters there, whereas they recrossed the river in the nighttime into the Jerseys and traveled all night in a direct course for Philadelphia. Deponent was part of the time on horse-back and part of the time in a wagon. Deponent's said husband was still serving as one of the commissary's guard. . . .

They continued their march to Philadelphia, deponent on horseback through the streets, and arrived at a place towards the Schuylkill where the British had burnt some houses, where they encamped for the afternoon and night. Being out of bread, deponent was employed in baking the afternoon and evening. Deponent recollects no females but Sergeant Lamberson's and Lieutenant Forman's wives and a colored woman by the name of Letta. The Quaker ladies who came round urged deponent to stay, but her husband said, "No, he could not leave her behind." Accordingly, next day they continued their march from day to day till they arrived at Baltimore, where

---

Revolutionary War Pension Files, National Archives. This document can also be found in John Dann, ed., *The Revolution Remembered* (Chicago: University of Chicago Press, 1980), 241–246.

deponent and her said husband and the forces under command of General Clinton. Captain Gregg, and several other officers, all of whom she does not recollect, embarked on board a vessel and sailed down the Chesapeake. There were several vessels along, and deponent was in the foremost. . . . They continued sail until they had got up the St. James River as far as the tide would carry them, about twelve miles from the mouth, and then landed, and the tide being spent, they had a fine time catching sea lobsters, which they ate.

They, however, marched immediately for a place called Williamsburg, as she thinks, deponent alternately on horseback and on foot. There arrived, they remained two days till the army all came in by land and then marched for Yorktown, or Little York as it was then called. The York troops were posted at the right, the Connecticut troops next, and the French to the left. In about one day or less than a day, they reached the place of encampment about one mile from Yorktown. Deponent was on foot and the other females above named and her said husband still on the commissary's guard. Deponent's attention was arrested by the appearance of a large plain between them and Yorktown and an entrenchment thrown up. She also saw a number of dead Negroes lying round their encampment, whom she understood the British had driven out of the town and left to starve, or were first starved and then thrown out. Deponent took her stand just back of the American tents, say about a mile from the town, and busied herself washing, mending, and cooking for the soldiers, in which she was assisted by the other females; some men washed their own clothing. She heard the roar of the artillery for a number of days, and the last night the Americans threw up entrenchments, it was a misty, foggy night, rather wet but not rainy. Every soldier threw up for himself, as she understood, and she afterwards saw and went into the entrenchments. Deponent's said husband was there throwing up entrenchments, and deponent cooked and carried in beef, and bread, and coffee (in a gallon pot) to the soldiers in the entrenchment.

On one occasion when deponent was thus employed carrying in provisions, she met General Washington, who asked her if she "was not afraid of the cannonballs?"

She replied, "No, the bullets would not cheat the gallows," that "It would not do for the men to fight and starve too."

They dug entrenchments nearer and nearer to Yorktown every night or two till the last. While digging that, the enemy fired very heavy till about nine o'clock next morning, then stopped, and the drums from the enemy beat excessively. . . .

All at once the officers hurrahed and swung their hats, and deponent asked them, "What is the matter now?"

One of them replied, "Are not you soldier enough to know what it means?"

Deponent replied, "No."

They then replied, "The British have surrendered."

Deponent, having provisions ready, carried the same down to the entrenchments that morning, and four of the soldiers whom she was in the habit of cooking for ate their breakfasts.

Deponent stood on one side of the road and the American officers upon the other side when the British officers came out of the town and rode up to the American officers and delivered up [their swords, which the deponent] thinks were returned again, and the British officers rode right on before the army, who marched out beating and playing a melancholy tune, their drums covered with black handkerchiefs and their fifes with black ribbands tied around them, into an old field and there grounded their arms and then returned into town again to await their destiny. . . .

On going into town, she noticed two dead Negroes lying by the market house. She had the curiosity to go into a large building that stood nearby, and there she noticed the cupboards smashed to pieces and china dishes and other ware strewed around upon the floor, and among the rest a pewter cover to a hot basin that had a handle on it. She picked it up, supposing it to belong to the British, but the governor came in and claimed it as his, but said he would have the name of giving it away as it was the last one of twelve that he could see, and accordingly presented it to deponent, and she afterwards brought it home with her to Orange County and sold it for old pewter, which she has a hundred times regretted.

E S S A Y S

Joan Hoff of Ohio University has posited that the effect of the American Revolution on white women, if there could be said to be an effect, was chiefly negative. The war, she argues, brought few or no benefits to women, whose prewar situation was so circumscribed that they could not take advantage of the opportunities that had opened up for their male contemporaries. After reading hundreds of women's and men's letters and diaries from the period, however, Mary Beth Norton of Cornell University has reached the opposite conclusion, contending in her book *Liberty's Daughters* that the Revolution was, to a limited extent, "liberating" for white women and for some black men and women as well. Jacqueline Jones, who teaches history at Brandeis University, has focused her attention on enslaved women and concluded that for them the revolution had decidedly mixed results.

The Negative Impact of the American Revolution on White Women

JOAN HOFF

I will argue that certain types of female functions, leading either to the well-known exploitation of working women or to the ornamental middle-class housewife of the nineteenth century, were abetted by the American Revolution, although not caused by it.

This occurred because the functional opportunities open to women between 1700 and 1800 were too limited to allow them to make the transition in attitudes necessary to insure high status performance in the newly emerging nation. In other words, before 1776 women did not participate enough in conflicts over land, religion, taxes, local politics, or commercial transactions. They simply had not come into contact with enough worldly diversity to be prepared for a changing, pluralistic, modern society. Women of the postrevolutionary generation had little choice but to

Excerpts from Joan Hoff-Wilson, "The Illusion of Change: Women and the American Revolution," in Alfred Young, ed., *The American Revolution: Explorations in the History of American Radicalism,* 386–401, 419–431. Copyright 1976 by Northern Illinois University Press. Used by permission of the publisher.

fill those low status functions prescribed by the small minority of American males who *were* prepared for modernization by enough diverse activities and experiences.

As a result, the American Revolution produced no significant benefits for American women. This same generalization can be made for other powerless groups in the colonies—native Americans, blacks, probably most propertyless white males, and indentured servants. Although these people together with women made up the vast majority of colonial population, they could not take advantage of the overthrow of British rule to better their own positions, as did the white, propertied males who controlled economics, politics, and culture. By no means did all members of these subordinate groups support the patriot cause, and those who did, even among whites, were not automatically accorded personal liberation when national liberation was won. This is a common phenomenon of revolution within subcultures which, because of sex, race, or other forms of discrimination or deprivation of the members, are not far enough along in the process toward modernization to express their dissatisfaction or frustration through effectively organized action.

Given the political and socioeconomic limitations of the American Revolution, this lack of positive societal change in the lives of women and other deprived colonials is to be expected. It is also not surprising that until recently most historians of the period have been content to concentrate their research efforts on the increased benefits of Lockean liberalism that accrued to a relatively small percent of all Americans and to ignore the increased sexism and racism exhibited by this privileged group both during and after the Revolution. They have also tended to ignore the various ways in which the experience of the Revolution either hastened or retarded certain long-term eighteenth-century trends already affecting women.

What has been called in England and Europe "the transformation of the female in bourgeois culture" also took place in America between 1700 and 1800. This process would have occurred with or without a declaration of independence from England. It produced a class of American bourgeoises who clearly resembled the group of middle-class women evident in England a century earlier. However, the changing societal conditions leading up to this transformation in American women were much more complex than they had been for seventeenth-century British women because of the unique roles, that is, functions, that colonial women had originally played in the settlement and development of the New World. The American Revolution was simply one event among many in this century-long process of change. It was a process that ultimately produced two distinct classes of women in the United States—those who worked to varying degrees exclusively in their homes and those who worked both inside and outside of their homes. . . .

It is true, however, for most of the period up to 1750 that conditions *out of necessity* increased the functional independence and importance of all women. By this I mean that much of the alleged freedom from sexism of colonial women was due to their initial numerical scarcity and the critical labor shortage in the New World throughout the seventeenth and eighteenth centuries. Such increased reproductive roles (economic as well as biological) reflected the logic of necessity and *not any fundamental change* in the sexist, patriarchal attitudes that had been transplanted from Europe. Based on two types of scarcity (sex and labor), which were not to last, these enhanced functions of colonial women diminished as the commercial and agricultural economy became more specialized and the population grew.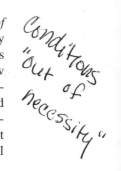

A gradual "embourgeoisement" of colonial culture accompanied this prein-dustrial trend toward modern capitalism. It limited the number of high status roles for eighteenth-century American women just as it had for seventeenth-century English and European women. Alice Clark, Margaret George, Natalie Zemon Davis, and Jane Abray have all argued convincingly that as socioeconomic capitalist orga-nization takes place, it closes many opportunities normally open to women both inside and outside of the family unit in precapitalist times. The decline in the status of women that accompanied the appearance of bourgeois modernity in England, ac-cording to Margaret George, "was not merely a relative decline. Precapitalist woman was not simply relatively eclipsed by the great leap forward of the male achiever; she suffered rather, an absolute setback."

In the New World this process took longer but was no less debilitating. Before 1800 it was both complicated and hindered by the existence of a severe labor short-age and religious as well as secular exhortations against the sins of idleness and vanity. Thus, colonial conditions demanded that all able-bodied men, women, and children work, and so the ornamental, middle-class woman existed more in theory than in practice.

The labor shortage that plagued colonial America placed a premium on women's work inside and outside the home, particularly during the war-related periods of economic dislocation between 1750 and 1815. And there is no doubt that home industry was basic to American development both before and after 1776. It is also true that there was no sharp delineation between the economic needs of the com-munity and the work carried on within the preindustrial family until after the middle of the eighteenth century. Women's role as a household manager was a basic and integral part of the early political economy of the colonies. Hence she occupied a position of unprecedented importance and equality within the socioeconomic unit of the family.

As important as this function of women in the home was, from earliest colonial times, it nonetheless represented a division of labor based on sex-role stereotyping carried over from England. Men normally engaged in agricultural production; women engaged in domestic gardening and home manufacturing—only slave women worked in the fields. Even in those areas of Massachusetts and Pennsylvania that originally granted females allotments of land, the vestiges of this practice soon disappeared, and subsequent public divisions "simply denied the independent economic existence of women." While equality never extended outside the home in the colonial era, there was little likelihood that women felt useless or alienated because of the importance and demanding nature of their domestic responsibilities.

In the seventeenth and eighteenth centuries spinning and weaving were the primary types of home production for women and children (of both sexes). This economic function was considered so important that legal and moral sanctions were developed to insure it. For example, labor laws were passed, compulsory spinning schools were established "for the education of children of the poor," and women were told that their virtue could be measured in yards of yarn. So from the beginning there was a sex, and to a lesser degree a class and educational, bias built into colonial production of cloth, since no formal apprenticeship was required for learning the trade of spinning and weaving.

lack of genuine feminine consciousness

1776
"*Putting out system*"

1775–1815 Depression living standards

It has also been recognized that prerevolutionary boycotts of English goods after 1763 and later during the war increased the importance of female production of textiles both in the home and in the early piecework factory system. By mid-1776 in Philadelphia, for example, 4,000 women and children reportedly were spinning under the "putting out system" for local textile plants. . . .

American living standards fluctuated with the unequal prosperity that was especially related to wars. Those engaging in craft production and commerce were particularly hard hit after 1750, first by the deflation and depression following the French and Indian War (1754–1763), and then by the War for Independence. In fact, not only were the decades immediately preceding and following the American Revolution ones of economic dislocation, but the entire period between 1775 and 1815 has been characterized as one of "arrested social and economic development." These trends, combined with increased specialization, particularly with the appearance of a nascent factory system, "initiated a decline in the economic and social position of many sections of the artisan class." Thus with the exception of the innkeeping and tavern business, all of the other primary economic occupations of city women were negatively affected by the periodic fluctuations in the commercial economy between 1763 and 1812.

Women artisans and shopkeepers probably suffered most during times of economic crisis because of their greater difficulty in obtaining credit from merchants. Although research into their plight has been neglected, the documents are there—in the records of merchant houses showing women entrepreneurs paying their debts for goods and craft materials by transferring their own records of indebtedness, and in court records showing an increased number of single women, especially widows sued for their debts, or in public records of the increased number of bankrupt women who ended up on poor relief lists or in debtors' prisons or who were forced to become indentured servants or earn an independent living during hard times.

It was also a difficult time for household spinners and weavers, about whom a few more facts are known. First, this all-important economic function increasingly reflected class distinctions. In 1763 one British governor estimated that only the poor wore homespun clothes, while more affluent Americans bought English imports. Second, it was primarily poor women of the northern and middle colonies who engaged in spinning and weaving for pay (often in the form of credit rather than cash), while black slave women and white female indentured servants performed the same function in the South. Naturally women in all frontier areas had no recourse but to make their own clothing. Beginning with the first boycotts of British goods in the 1760s, women of all classes were urged to make and wear homespun. Several additional "manufactory houses" were established as early as 1764 in major cities specifically for the employment of poor women. Direct appeals to patriotism and virtue were used very successfully to get wealthier women to engage in arduous home-spinning drives, but probably only for short periods of time.

In the name of Patriotism women of all classes recruited for home textile manuf.

Thus all classes of women were actively recruited into domestic textile production by male patriots with such pleas as, "In this time of public distress you have each of you an opportunity not only to help to sustain your families, but likewise to call your mite into the treasury of the public good." They were further urged to "cease trifling their time away [and] prudently employ it in learning the use of the spinning wheel." Beyond any doubt the most well-known appeal was the widely reprinted 9 November 1767 statement of advice to the "Daughters of Liberty" which first appeared in the *Massachusetts Gazette.* It read in part:

> First then throw aside your high top knots of pride
> Wear none but your own country linen.
> Of economy boast. Let your pride be the most
> To show cloaths of your make and spinning.

Peak periods in prerevolutionary spinning and weaving were reached during every major boycott from 1765 to 1777. But the war and inflation proved disruptive. For example, we know that the United Company of Philadelphia for Promoting American Manufacturers, which employed 500 of the City's 4,000 women and children spinning at home, expired between 1777 and 1787, when it was revived. The record of similar organizations elsewhere was equally erratic.

It is common for developing countries with a labor shortage to utilize technological means to meet production demands. After the war, the new republic proved no exception, as the inefficiency and insufficiency of household spinners became apparent. Ultimately the "putting out" system was replaced entirely by the factory that employed the same women and children who had formerly been household spinners. It took the entire first half of the nineteenth century before this process was completed, and when it was, it turned out to be at the expense of the social and economic status of female workers. . . .

Why didn't the experiences of the Revolution result in changing the political consciousness of women? Part of the answer lies in the socialized attitudes among female members of the revolutionary generation that set them apart from their male contemporaries. Their attitudes had been molded by the modernization trends encountered by most women in the course of the eighteenth century. Out of the necessity wrought by the struggle with England, women performed certain tasks that appeared revolutionary in nature, just as they had performed nonfamilial tasks out of necessity throughout the colonial period. But this seemingly revolutionary behavior is not necessarily proof of the acceptance of abstract revolutionary principles.

Despite their participation in greater economic specialization, despite their experiences with a slightly smaller conjugal household where power relations were changing, despite a limited expansion of the legal rights and somewhat improved educational opportunities for free, white women, the revolutionary generation of females were less prepared than most men for the modern implications of independence. Their distinctly different experiential level, combined with the intellectually and psychologically limiting impact of the Great Awakening and the Enlightenment on women, literally made it impossible for even the best educated females to understand the political intent or principles behind the inflated rhetoric of the revolutionary era. Words like virtue, veracity, morality, tyranny, and corruption were ultimately given public political meanings by male revolutionary leaders that were incomprehensible or, more likely, misunderstood by most women.

As the rhetoric of the revolution began to assume dynamic, emotional proportions, its obsession with "virtue" versus "corruption" struck a particularly responsive chord among literate women, as evidenced for example, in their patriotic statements as individuals and in groups when supporting the boycott of English goods between

1765 and 1774. While these statements are impressive both in number and intensity of feeling, it can be questioned whether the idea of taking "their country back on the path of virtue" and away from "the oppression of corrupt outside forces" was understood in the same way by female and male patriots, when even men of varying Whig persuasions could not agree on them. Virtue and morality for the vast majority of Americans, but particularly women, do not appear to have had the modernizing implications of pluralistic individualism, that is, of the "acceptance of diversity, the commitment to individual action in pursuit of individual goals, the conception of politics as an arena where these goals contest and the awareness of a national government which is at once the course of political power and the framework for an orderly clash of interest." These are characteristics of "modern man."

lost opportunities ↓
Characteristics of modern man.

How does one prove such a generalization about attitudes behind the behavior of women during the Revolution? Few poor white and black women left records revealing how they felt about the war. Such women, whether Loyalists or patriots, conveyed their sentiments silently with their physical labor. Among the more articulate and educated women there is written testimony to at least an initial sense of pride and importance involved in their participation in the war effort. Thus a young Connecticut woman named Abigail Foote wrote in her diary in 1775 that carding two pounds of whole wool had made her feel "Nationly," while others recorded their contributions in similarly patriotic terms.

Patriotism

But the question remains: did their supportive actions prepare them to accept a vision of society anywhere near the version ultimately conveyed by James Madison's Federalist Number Ten in the fight over the Constitution of 1787? To date there is little evidence that this type of sophisticated political thought was present, either in the writings of women about the Revolution and its results or in the appeals made to them during or immediately following the war. From the popular 1767 statement of advice to the Daughters of Liberty to the 1787 one urging women to use "their influence over their husbands, brothers and sons to draw them from those dreams of liberty under a simple democratical form of government, which are so unfriendly to . . . order and decency," it is difficult to conclude that women were being prepared to understand the political ramifications of the Revolution.

1767 — Daughters of Amer Rev. →
women "use your influence"

The same lack of political astuteness appears to underlie even the least traditional and most overtly political activities of women, such as the fifty-one who signed the anti-tea declaration in Edenton, North Carolina, on 25 October 1774 (later immortalized in a London cartoon). The same could be said of the more than 500 Boston women who agreed on 31 January 1770 to support the radical male boycott of tea; of the Daughters of Liberty in general; and of the 1,600 Philadelphia women who raised 7,500 dollars in gold for the Continental Army. Even Mercy Otis Warren never perceived the modern political system that evolved from the Revolution. Instead she viewed the war and its aftermath as the "instrument of Providence that sparked a world movement, changing thought and habit of men to complete the divine plan for human happiness" largely through the practice of virtue.

Perhaps the most important aspect of the supportive activities among women for the patriot cause was the increase in class and social distinctions they symbolized. For example, it appears unlikely that poor white or black women joined Daughters of Liberty groups, actively boycotted English goods, or participated in any significant numbers in those associations of "Ladies of the highest rank and influence,"

club work and social divisions

who raised money and supplies for the Continental Army. On the contrary, it may well have been primarily "young female spinsters" from prominent families and well-to-do widows and wives who could afford the time or the luxury of such highly publicized activities. The vast majority, however, of middle-class female patriots (and, for that matter, Loyalists), whether single or married, performed such necessary volunteer roles as seamstresses, nurses, hostesses, and sometime spies, whenever the fighting shifted to their locales, without any undue fanfare or praise.

The same is true of poorer women, with one important difference: they had no choice. They had all they could do to survive, and although this did lead a few of them to become military heroines, they could not afford the luxury of either "disinterested patriotism" or the detached self-interest and indulgences that some of the richer women exhibited. The very poorest, particularly those in urban areas, had no resources to fall back on when confronted with the personal or economic traumas caused by the War for Independence. As noted above, this was especially evident in the case of women wage earners who, regardless of race or class, had apparently always received lower pay than free men or hired-out male slaves, and who had suffered severely from runaway inflation during the war. Women's services were more likely to be paid for in Continental currency than with specie. Fees for male "doctors," for example, according to one Maryland family account book, were made in specie payment after the middle of 1780, while midwives had to accept the depreciated Continental currency for a longer period of time. Thus, the American Revolution hastened the appearance of greater class-based activities among "daughters of the new republic," with poor women undertaking the least desirable tasks and suffering most from the inflationary spiral that plagued the whole country. It is easy to imagine the impact that inflation had on the rural and urban poor, but it even affected those middle- and upper middle-class women who were left at home to manage businesses, estates, plantations, or farms. Their activities often meant the difference between bankruptcy and solvency for male revolutionary leaders.

Probably the classic example of housewifely efficiency and economic shrewdness is found in Abigail's management of the Adams's family and farm during John's long absences. But in this respect Abigail Adams stands in direct contrast to the women in the lives of other leading revolutionaries like Jefferson, Madison, and Monroe—all of whom were bankrupt by public service in part because their wives were not as capable at land management as she was. This even proved true of the most outspoken of all revolutionary wives, Mercy Otis Warren. Numerous lesser well-known women, however, proved equal to the increased domestic responsibilities placed upon them. Only the utterly impoverished could not resort to the traditional colonial task of household manager.

As the months of fighting lengthened into years, more and more poverty-stricken women left home to join their husbands, lovers, fathers, or other male relatives in the army encampments. Once there, distinctions between traditional male and female roles broke down. While a certain number of free white and black slave women were needed to mend, wash, and cook for officers and care for the sick and wounded, most enlisted men and their women took care of themselves and fought beside each other on many occasions. Moreover, unlike the English, German, and French commanders, American military leaders were often morally offended or embarrassed by the presence of these unfortunate and destitute women, "their hair flying, their brows beady with the heat, their belongings slung over one sholder [*sic*], chattering and yelling in sluttish shrills as they went and spitting in the gutters."

This puritanical, hostile attitude on the part of patriot army officers toward such a common military phenomenon insured that camp followers of the American forces were less systematically provided for than those of foreign troops. Aside from its class overtones (after all Martha Washington, Catherine Greene, and Lucy Knox were accepted as respectable camp followers), it is difficult to explain this American attitude, except that in the prevailing righteous rhetoric of the Revolution and of later historians these women were misrepresented as little better than prostitutes. In reality they were the inarticulate, invisible poor whose story remains to be told from existing pension records based on oral testimony. At any rate there is pathos and irony in the well-preserved image of Martha Washington, who visited her husband at Valley Forge during the disastrous winter of 1777–1778, copying routine military communiques and presiding over a sewing circle of other officers' wives, while the scores of combat-hardened women, who died along with their enlisted men, have been conveniently forgotten.

These camp followers, as well as the women who stayed at home, complained about their plight privately and publicly, and on occasion they rioted and looted for foodstuffs. Women rioting for bread or other staples never became a significant or even a particularly common revolutionary act in the New World as it did in Europe, largely because of the absence of any long-term, abject poverty on the part of even the poorest colonials. The most likely exception to this generalization came during the extreme inflation that accompanied the war. Then there is indeed some evidence of what can be called popular price control activity by groups of women who had a definite sense of what were fair or legitimate marketing practices. At the moment we have concrete evidence of only a half-dozen seemingly spontaneous instances of "a corps of female infantry" attacking merchants. Other examples will probably be discovered as more serious research into the "moral economy of the crowd" is undertaken by American historians.

What is interesting about the few known cases is that the women involved in some of them did not simply appear to be destitute camp followers passing through towns stripping the dead and looting at random for food. A few at least were women "with Silk gownes on," who were offering to buy sugar, salt, flour, or coffee for a reasonable price with Continental currency. When a certain merchant insisted on payment with specie or with an unreasonable amount of paper money, the women then, and only then, insisted on "taking" his goods at their price. These appear, therefore, to be isolated examples of collective behavior by women where there was, at the least, a very strongly held cultural notion of a moral economy.

Nevertheless, there is still no clear indication of an appreciable change in the political consciousness of such women. Perhaps it was because even the poorest who took part in popular price control actions primarily did so, like the Citoyennes Républicaines Révolutionnaires during the French Revolution, out of an immediate concern for feeding themselves and their children and not for feminist reasons growing out of their age-old economic plight as women in a patriarchal society. In addition, except for camp followers and female vagabonds, the principal concern of most members of this generation of primarily rural women remained the home and their functions there. During the home-spinning drives and during the war when their

[handwritten marginal notes: "Class lines separated opinions of Camp Followers" and "moral economy enforced by women"]

men were away, their domestic and agricultural duties became all the more demanding, but not consciousness-raising. . . .

Lastly, in explaining the failure of the equalitarian ideals of the Revolution to bear even limited fruit for women, one must analyze the narrow ideological parameters of even those few who advocated women's rights, persons such as Abigail Adams, Judith Sargent Murray, Elizabeth Southgate Bowne, Elizabeth Drinker, and Mercy Otis Warren.

These women . . . were not feminists. Like most of the better organized, but no less successful Républicaines of France, they seldom, if ever, aspired to complete equality with men except in terms of education. Moreover, none challenged the institution of marriage or defined themselves "as other than mothers and potential mothers." They simply could not conceive of a society whose standards were not set by male, patriarchal institutions, nor should they be expected to have done so. Instead of demanding equal rights, the most articulate and politically conscious American women of this generation asked at most for privileges and at least for favors—not for an absolute expansion of their legal or political functions, which they considered beyond their proper womanly sphere. Man was indeed the measure of equality to these women, and given their societal conditioning, such status was beyond their conception of themselves as individuals.

Ironically it is this same sense of their "proper sphere" that explains why the most educated female patriots did not feel obliged to organize to demand more from the Founding Fathers. It is usually overlooked that in the famous letter of 31 March 1776 where Abigail asks John Adams to "Remember the Ladies," she justified this mild request for "more generous and favourable" treatment on the grounds that married women were then subjected to the "unlimited power" of their husbands. She was not asking him for the right to vote, only for some legal protection of wives from abuses under common law practices. "Regard us then," she pleaded with her husband, "as Beings placed by providence under your protection and in imitation of the Supreme Being make use of that power only for our happiness." Despite an earlier statement in this letter about the "Ladies" being "determined to foment a Rebellion" and refusing to be "bound by any Laws in which we have no voice, or Representation," Abigail Adams was not in any sense demanding legal, let alone political or individual, equality with men at the beginning of the American Revolution. If anything, her concept of the separateness of the two different spheres in which men and women operated was accentuated by the war and the subsequent trials of the new republic between 1776 and 1800.

This idea that men and women existed in two separate spheres or orbits was commonly accepted in the last half of the eighteenth century as one of the natural laws of the universe. While European Enlightenment theories adhered strictly to the inferiority of the natural sphere that women occupied, in colonial America they were tacitly challenged and modified by experience—as were so many other aspects of natural law doctrines. On the other hand, the degree to which educated, upper-class women in particular thought that their sphere of activity was in fact equal, and the degree to which it actually was accorded such status by the male-dominated culture, is all important. Historians have tended to place greater emphasis on the former rather than the latter, with misleading results about the importance of the roles played by both colonial and revolutionary women.

It is true that Abigail Adams was an extremely independent-minded person who firmly criticized books by foreign authors who subordinated the female sphere to that of the male. Writing to her sister Elizabeth Shaw Peabody in 1799, she said that "I will never consent to have our sex considered in an inferior point of light. Let each planet shine in their own orbit, God and nature designed it so—if man is Lord, woman is *Lordess*—that is what I contend for." Thus, when her husband was away she deemed it was within her proper sphere to act as head of the household on all matters, including the decision to have her children inoculated against smallpox without his permission. At the same time, however, she always deferred to his ambitions and his inherent superiority, because the equality of their two separate orbits did not make them equal as individuals. In general Abigail Adams and other women of her class accepted the notion that while they were mentally equal to men their sphere of activity was entirely private in nature, except on those occasions when they substituted for their absent husbands. "Government of States and Kingdoms, tho' God knows badly enough managed," she asserted in 1796, "I am willing should be solely administered by the lords of creation. I should contend for Domestic Government, and think that best administered by the female." Such a strong belief in equal, but separate, spheres is indeed admirable for the times, but it should not be confused with feminism. . . .

Only unusual male feminists like Thomas Paine asked that women be accorded "the sweets of public esteem" and "an equal right to praise." It was Paine—not the female patriots—who also took advantage of American revolutionary conditions to attack the institution of marriage. Later, in the 1790s, only a few isolated women in the United States supported Mary Wollstonecraft's demand for the right to public as well as private fulfillment on the grounds that "private duties are never properly fulfilled unless the understanding enlarges the heart and that public virtue is only an aggregate of private. . . ." Her criticisms of marital bondage were never seriously considered by American women in this postrevolutionary decade.

The reasons for this unresponsiveness to the feminism of both Paine and Wollstonecraft are complex, for it was not only opposed by the sexist Founding Fathers, but by most women. Again we must ask—why?

The physical and mental hardships that most women had endured during the war continued to varying degrees in the economic dislocation that followed in its wake. Sheer personal survival, not rising social or material expectations, dominated the thinking and activities of lower and even some middle- and upper-class women. Probably more important, the few well-educated American women, fortunate to have the leisure to reflect, clearly realized the discrepancy that had occurred between the theory and practice of virtue in the course of the war and its aftermath. While it was discouraging for them to view the corruption of morals of the society at large and particularly among men in public life, they could take some satisfaction in the greater consistency between the theory and practice of virtue in their own private lives. Such postrevolutionary women found their familial duties and homosocial relationships untainted by the corruption of public life. They considered themselves most fortunate and they *were*, compared to their nineteenth-century descendants, who had to pay a much higher price for similar virtuous consistency and spiritual purity.

It was natural, therefore, for the educated among this generation to express disillusionment with politics, as they saw republican principles corrupted or distorted, and then to enter a stage of relative quiescence that marked the beginning of the transitional period between their war-related activities and a later generation of female reformers who emerged in the 1830s. They cannot be held responsible for not realizing the full extent of the potentially debilitating features of their withdrawal to the safety of modern domesticity—where virtue becomes its own punishment instead of reward.

A final factor that helps to explain the absence of feminism in the behavior of women during the Revolution and in their attitudes afterward is related to the demographic changes that were taking place within the family unit between 1760 and 1800. Middle- and upper-class women were increasingly subjected to foreign and domestic literature stressing standards of femininity that had not inhibited the conduct of their colonial ancestors. While the rhetoric of this new literature was that of the Enlightenment, its message was that of romantic love, glamorized dependence, idealized motherhood, and sentimentalized children within the ever-narrowing realm of family life. At poorer levels of society a new family pattern was emerging as parental control broke down, and ultimately these two trends would merge, leaving all women in lower status domestic roles than they had once occupied.

In general it appears that the American Revolution retarded those societal conditions that had given colonial women their unique function and status in society, while it promoted those that were leading toward the gradual "embourgeoisement" of late eighteenth-century women. By 1800 their economic and legal privileges were curtailed; their recent revolutionary activity minimized or simply ignored; their future interest in politics discouraged; and their domestic roles extolled, but increasingly limited.

Moreover, at the highest *and* lowest levels of society this revolutionary generation of women was left with misleading assumptions: certain educated women believing strongly in the hope that immediate improvement for themselves and their children would come with educational reform, and some lower-class women believing that improvement would come through work in the "manufactories." Both admitted, according to Mercy Otis Warren, that their "appointed subordination" to men was natural, if for no other reason than "for the sake of Order in Families." Neither could be expected to anticipate that this notion would limit their participation in, and understanding of, an emerging modern nation because the actual (as opposed to idealized) value accorded their postrevolutionary activities was not yet apparent.

A few, like Priscilla Mason, the valedictorian of the 1793 graduating class of the Young Ladies' Academy of Philadelphia, might demand an equal education with men and exhort women to break out of their traditional sphere, but most ended up agreeing with Eliza Southgate Bowne when she concluded her defense of education for women by saying: "I believe I must give up all pretension to *profundity*, for I am much more at home in my female character." And the dominant male leadership of the 1790s could not have agreed more.

For women, the American Revolution was over before it ever began. Their "disinterested" patriotism (or disloyalty, as the case may be) was accorded identical treatment by male revolutionaries following the war: conscious neglect of female rights combined with subtle educational and economic exploitation. The end result was increased loss of function and authentic status for all women whether they were on or under the proverbial pedestal.

The Positive Impact of the American Revolution on White Women

MARY BETH NORTON

Women could hardly have remained aloof from the events of the 1760s and early 1770s even had they so desired, for, like male Americans, they witnessed the escalating violence of the prerevolutionary decade. Into their letters and diary entries—which had previously been devoted exclusively to private affairs—crept descriptions of Stamp Act riots and "Rejoicings" at the law's repeal, accounts of solemn fast-day observances, and reports of crowd actions aimed at silencing dissidents. The young Boston shopkeeper Betsy Cuming, for instance, was visiting a sick friend one day in 1769 when she heard "a voilint Skreeming Kill him Kill him" and looked out the window to see John Mein, a printer whose publications had enraged the radicals, being chased by a large crowd armed with sticks and guns. Later that evening Betsy watched "ful a thousand Man & boys" dragging around the city "a Kart [on which] a Man was Exibited as . . . in a Gore of Blod." At first Betsy believed Mein had been caught, but she then learned that the victim was an unfortunate customs informer who had fallen into the crowd's hands after Mein made a successful escape.

Betsy herself confronted an angry group of Bostonians only a few weeks later. She and her sister Anne had just unpacked a new shipment of English goods when "the Comitey wated" on them, accusing them of violating the nonimportation agreement. "I told them we have never antred into eney agreement not to import for it was verry trifling owr Business," Betsy explained to her friend and financial backer Elizabeth Murray Smith. She charged the committeemen with trying "to inger two industrious Girls who ware Striving in an honest way to Git there Bread," resolutely ignoring their threat to publish her name in the newspaper as an enemy to America. In the end, Betsy and Anne discovered, the publicity "Spirits up our Friends to Purchess from us," and they informed Mrs. Smith that they ended the year with "mor custom then before."

Despite their bravado the Cuming sisters had learned an important political lesson: persons with their conservative beliefs were no longer welcome in Massachusetts. As a result, they emigrated to Nova Scotia when the British army evacuated Boston in 1776. Patriot women, too, learned lessons of partisanship. Instead of being the targets of crowds, they actively participated in them. They marched in ritual processions, harassed female loyalists, and, during the war, seized essential supplies from merchants whom they believed to be monopolistic hoarders. In addition, when they prepared food for militia musters and, in the early days of September 1774—when the New England militia gathered in Cambridge in response to a false rumor that British troops were mounting an attack on the populace—they were reported by one observer to have "surpassed the Men for Eagerness & Spirit in the Defense of Liberty by Arms." As he rode along the road to Boston, he recounted later, he saw "at every house Women & Children making Cartridges, running Bullets, making

Mary Beth Norton, *Liberty's Daughters: The Revolutionary Experience of American Women, 1750–1800* (Ithaca, N.Y.: Cornell University Press, 1996), 156–163, 166–169, 212–214, 216–222, 225–227. Reprinted by permission of the author.

Wallets, baking Biscuit, crying & bemoaning & at the same time animating their Husbands & Sons to fight for their Liberties, tho' not knowing whether they should ever see them again."

The activism of female patriots found particular expression in their support of the colonial boycott of tea and other items taxed by the Townshend Act of 1767. Male leaders recognized that they needed women's cooperation to ensure that Americans would comply with the request to forgo the use of tea and luxury goods until the act was repealed. Accordingly, newspaper essays urged women to participate in the boycott, and American editors frequently praised those females who refused to drink foreign Bohea tea, substituting instead coffee or local herbal teas. . . .

In a marked departure from the tradition of feminine noninvolvement in public affairs, women occasionally formalized their agreements not to purchase or consume imported tea. Most notably, the *Boston Evening Post* reported in February 1770 that more than three hundred "Mistresses of Families" had promised to "totally abstain" from the use of tea, "Sickness excepted." Their statement showed that they understood the meaning of their acts: the women spoke of their desire to "save this abused Country from Ruin and Slavery" at a time when their "invaluable Rights and Privileges are attacked in an unconstitutional and most alarming Manner." In the South, groups of women went even further by associating themselves generally with nonimportation policies, not confining their attention to the tea issue alone. The meeting satirized in the famous British cartoon of the so called Edenton Ladies' Tea Party fell into this category. The agreement signed in October 1774 by fifty-one female North Carolinians—among them two sisters and a cousin of Hannah Johnston Iredell—did not mention tea. Instead, the women declared their "sincere adherence" to the resolves of the provincial congress and proclaimed it their "duty" to do "every thing as far as lies in our power" to support the "publick good."

This apparently simple statement had unprecedented implications. The Edenton women were not only asserting their right to acquiesce in political measures, but they were also taking upon themselves a "duty" to work for the common good. Never before had female Americans formally shouldered the responsibility of a public role, never before had they claimed a voice—even a compliant one—in public policy. Accordingly, the Edenton statement marked an important turning point in American women's political perceptions, signaling the start of a process through which they would eventually come to regard themselves as participants in the polity rather than as females with purely private concerns.

Yet the North Carolina meeting and the change it embodied aroused amusement among men. The same tongue-in-cheek attitude evident in the satirical drawing of the grotesque "Ladies" was voiced by the Englishman Arthur Iredell in a letter to his emigrant brother James. He had read about the Edenton agreement in the newspapers, Arthur wrote, inquiring whether his sister-in-law Hannah's relatives were involved in the protest. "Is there a Female Congress at Edenton too?" he continued. "I hope not," for "Ladies . . . have ever, since the Amazonian Era, been esteemed the most formidable Enemies." If they choose to attack men, "each wound They give is Mortal. . . . The more we strive to conquer them, the more are Conquerd!"

Iredell thus transformed a serious political gesture that must have been full of meaning for the participants into an occasion for a traditional reference to women's covert power over men. Like many of his male contemporaries, he dismissed the first stirrings of political awareness among American women as a joke, refusing to recog- *Stirrings of political awareness* nize the ways in which their concept of their role was changing. In an Englishman, such blindness was understandable, but the similar failure of perception among American men must be attributed to a resolute insistence that females remain in their proper place. The male leaders of the boycott movement needed feminine co-operation, but they wanted to set the limits of women's activism. They did not expect, or approve, signs of feminine autonomy.

Nowhere was this made clearer than in a well-known exchange between Abigail and John Adams. . . . Abigail asked her husband in March 1776 to ensure that the new nation's legal code included protection for wives against the "Naturally Tyran- *Abigail & John Adams* nical" tendencies of their spouses. In reply John declared, "I cannot but laugh" at "your extraordinary Code of Laws." Falling back upon the same cliché employed by Arthur Iredell, he commented, "[O]ur Masculine systems . . . are little more than Theory. . . . In Practice you know We are the subjects. We have only the Name of Masters." Adams, like Iredell, failed to come to terms with the implications of the is-sues raised by the growing interests in politics among colonial women. He could deal with his wife's display of independent thought only by refusing to take it seriously.

American men's inability to perceive the alterations that were occurring in their womenfolk's self-conceptions was undoubtedly heightened by the superfi-cially conventional character of feminine contributions to the protest movement. Women participating in the boycott simply made different decisions about what items to purchase and consume; they did not move beyond the boundaries of the feminine sphere. Likewise, when colonial leaders began to emphasize the impor-tance of producing homespun as a substitute for English cloth, they did not ask women to take on an "unfeminine" task: quite the contrary, for spinning was the very role symbolic of femininity itself. But once the context had changed, so too did women's understanding of the meaning of their traditional tasks. . . .

The first months of 1769 brought an explosion in the newspaper coverage of women's activities, especially in New England. Stories about spinning bees, which had been both rare and relegated to back pages, suddenly became numerous and prominently featured. The *Boston Evening Post*, which carried only one previous account of female domestic industry, printed twenty-eight articles on the subject between May and December 1769, and devoted most of its front page on May 29 to an enumeration of these examples of female patriotism. The editor prefaced his extensive treatment of women's endeavors with an enthusiastic assessment of their significance: "[T]he industry and frugality of American ladies must exalt their char-acter in the Eyes of the World and serve to show how greatly they are contributing to bring about the political salvation of a whole Continent."

It is impossible to know whether the increased coverage of spinning bees in 1769 indicated that women's activities expanded at precisely that time, or whether the more lengthy, detailed, and numerous stories merely represented the printers' new interest in such efforts. But one fact is unquestionable: the ritualized gatherings attended by women often termed Daughters of Liberty carried vital symbolic mean- *Daughters of Liberty* ing both to the participants and to the editors who reported their accomplishments.

The meetings, or at least the descriptions of then, fell into a uniform pattern. Early in the morning, a group of eminently respectable young ladies (sometimes as many as one hundred, but normally twenty to forty), all of them dressed in homespun, would meet at the home of the local minister. There they would spend the day at their wheels, all the while engaging in enlightening conversation. When they stopped to eat, they had "American produce prepared which was more agreeable to them than any foreign Dainties and Delicacies," and, of course, they drank local herbal tea. At nightfall, they would present their output to the clergyman, who might then deliver a sermon on an appropriate theme. For example, the Reverend Jedidiah Jewell, of Rowley, Massachusetts, preached from Romans 12:2, "Not slothful in business, fervent in spirit, serving the Lord," and the Reverend John Cleaveland of Ipswich told the seventy-seven spinners gathered at his house, "[T]he women might recover to this country the full and free enjoyment of all our rights, properties and privileges (which is more than the men have been able to do)" by consuming only American produce and manufacturing their own clothes.

The entire community became involved in the women's activities. Large numbers of spectators—Ezra Stiles estimated that six hundred persons watched the bee held at his house in 1769—encouraged the spinners in their work, supplied them with appropriate American foodstuffs, and sometimes provided entertainment. The occasional adoption of a match format, in which the women competed against each other in quality and quantity, must have further spurred their industry. And they must have glorified in being the center of attention, if only for the day. In reporting a Long Island spinning bee, the *Boston Evening Post* captured the spirit of the occasion with an expression of hope that "the ladies, while they vie with each other in skill and industry in their profitable employment, may vie with the men in contributing to the preservation and prosperity of their country and equally share in the honor of it."

"Equally share in the honor of it": the idea must have been exceedingly attractive to any eighteenth-century American woman raised in an environment that had previously devalued both her and her domestic sphere. Those involved in the home manufacture movement therefore took great pride in their newfound status, demonstrating that fact unequivocally when satirical essayists cast aspersions on their character.

Late in 1767, "Mr. Squibo" of Boston joked that the spinners were so patriotic they consumed only "New-England Rum . . . the principal and almost only manufacture of this country." Shortly thereafter, "A Young American" hinted that women discussed only "such triffling subjects as Dress, Scandal and Detraction" during their spinning bees. Three female Bostonians responded angrily to both letters, which they declared had "scandalously insulted" American women. Denying that gossip engrossed their thoughts or that rum filled their glasses, they pronounced themselves so committed to the patriot cause that they would even endure the unmerited ridicule of "the little wits and foplings of the present day" in order to continue their efforts. "Inferior in abusive sarcasm, in personal invective, in low wit, we glory to be," they concluded; "but inferior in veracity, honesty, sincerity, love of virtue, of liberty and of our country, we would not willingly be to any." Significantly, the Bostonians made a special point of noting that women had been "addressed as persons of consequence, in the present economical regulations." They thereby revealed the novelty and importance of that designation in their own minds. Having become established as "persons of consequence" in American society, women would not relinquish that position without a fight.

The formal spinning groups had a value more symbolic than real. They do not seem to have met regularly, and in most cases their output appears to have been donated to the clergyman for his personal use. The women might not even have consistently called themselves Daughters of Liberty, for many newspaper accounts did not employ that phrase at all. But if the actual production of homespun did not motivate the meetings, they were nonetheless purposeful. The public attention focused on organized spinning bees helped to dramatize the pleas for industry and frugality in colonial households, making a political statement comparable to men's ostentatious wearing of homespun on public occasions during the same years. The spinning bees were ideological showcases: they were intended to convince American women that they could render essential contributions to the struggle against Britain, and to encourage them to engage in increased cloth production in the privacy of their own homes. Sometimes the newspaper accounts made this instructional function quite explicit. The fact that many of the participants came from "as *good families as any in town*," one editor remarked, showed that "it was no longer a disgrace for one of our fair sex to be caught at a spinning wheel." . . .

Wives of ardent patriots and loyalists alike were left alone for varying lengths of time while their spouses served in the army or, in the case of loyalists, took refuge behind the British lines. Although women could stay with their soldier husbands and earn their own keep by serving as army cooks, nurses, or laundresses, most did not find this an attractive alternative. Life in the military camps was hard, and army commanders, while recognizing that female laborers did essential work, tended to regard them as a hindrance rather than as asset. Only in rare cases—such as the time when the laundresses attached to General Anthony Wayne's regiment staged a strike in order to ensure that they would be adequately paid—were camp followers able to ameliorate their living and working conditions. Consequently, most women who joined the army probably did so from necessity, lacking any other means of support during their husbands' absence.

At least, though, patriot women had a choice. For the most part, loyalists were not so fortunate. From the day they and their spouses revealed their loyalty to the Crown, their fate was sealed. Like other eighteenth century women, their lives had focused on their homes, but because of their political beliefs they lost not only those homes but also most of their possessions, and they had to flee to alien lands as well. Understandably, they often had difficulty coping with their problems. Only those women who had had some experience beyond the household prior to the war were able to manage their affairs in exile in England, Canada, or the West Indies with more than a modicum of success.

Female loyalists' claims petitions are particularly notable because the women frequently commented on their lack of a network of friends and relatives. The laments convey a sense of an entire familiar world that had been irretrievably lost. Many women submitted claims after the deadline, each giving a similar reason in her request for special consideration: there had been "no person to advise her how to proceed," she "was destitute of advice and Assistance," or "she had nobody to advise with & that she did not know how to do it." Even when some of a woman loyalist's friends were also exiles her situation was little better; as one southerner pointed out to the claims commission, "[T]hose Friends and Acquaintances to whom under other circumstances she could look up to for comfort and Assistance are equally involved in the Calamities which overwhelm" her. . . .

The importance of friendship networks and a familiar environment for women left alone is further confirmed when the focus shifts from widowed loyalists to the patriots who called themselves temporary widows—those women whose husbands had joined the American army. In contrast to the distressed, disconsolate refugee loyalists, who often complained of their inability to deal effectively with their difficulties, patriot women who managed the family property in the absence of their menfolk tended to find the experience a positive one. Although they had to shoulder a myriad of new responsibilities, they did so within a well-known and fully understood context: that of their own households. Accordingly, aided by friends and relatives, they gained a new sense of confidence in themselves and their abilities as they learned to handle aspects of the family affairs that had previously fallen solely within their husbands' purview. And the men, in turn, developed a new appreciation of their wives' contributions to the family's welfare. . . .

Patriot men found it difficult to avoid service in the militia or the Continental Army. They accordingly had to leave their wives behind to take charge of their affairs for months or years at a time. Most sets of wartime correspondence that survive today come from the families of officers or congressmen—in other words, from those patriots of some wealth or prominence who also tended to experience the longest separations—but the scattered evidence available for couples of lesser standing suggests that the same process was at work in poor, middling, and well-to-do households alike. As the months and years passed, women became more expert in their handling of business matters and their husbands simultaneously more accustomed to relying on their judgment.

A standard pattern emerges from the sequences of letters, some of which will shortly be examined in greater detail. Initially, the absent husband instructed his wife to depend upon male friends and relatives for advice and assistance. In 1776, for example, Edward Hand, a Pennsylvania officer, told his wife, Kitty, to have one neighbor invest money for her and to ask another to estimate the value of two horses he had sent home for sale. Women, for their part, hesitated to venture into new areas. "In some particulars I have been really puzzled how to act," a South Carolinian informed her spouse, a private soldier; and in 1777 Esther Reed, asking Joseph whether she should plant some flax, explained, "[A]s I am not famous for making good Bargains in things out of my Sphere I shall put it off as long as possible, in hopes you may be at home before it is too late."

But as time went on, women learned more about the family's finances while at the same time their husbands' knowledge became increasingly outdated and remote. Accordingly, whereas men's letters early in the war were filled with specific orders, later correspondence typically contained statements like these: "I Can't give any Other Directions About Home more than what I have Done but must Leave all to your good Management" (1779); "Apply [the money] to such as you think proper" (1780); draw on a neighbor for "any Sums you may choose, for providing things necessary & comfortable for yourself & the little Folks & Family for the approaching Season, in doing which I am sure you will use the greatest discretion" (1779). By the same token, women's letters showed their increasing familiarity with business and their willingness to act independently of their husbands' directions. . . .

letters change in tone

The diary of the Philadelphian Sally Logan Fisher provides an especially illuminating example of this process. Thomas Fisher was among the Quakers arrested and sent into exile in Virginia by the patriots just prior to the British conquest of Philadelphia in September 1777. Then nearly eight months pregnant with her daughter Hannah, Sally at first found "this fiery triall" almost more than she could bear. Nine days after the men had been forcibly carried off, she commented, "I feel forlorn & desolate, & the World appears like a dreary Desart, almost without any visible protecting Hand to gaurd us from the ravenous Wolves & Lions that prowl about for prey." Sally became so depressed that she failed to write in her diary for several weeks, and when she resumed her daily entries in mid-October she observed, "[N]o future Days however calm & tranquil they may prove, can ever make me forget my misery at this time."

Soon thereafter, though, Mrs. Fisher became too busy to be able to allow herself the luxury of debilitating depression. A long entry on November 1 reflected her changed role in its detailed attention to household financial affairs and at the same time signaled the end of her period of incapacitating despair. "I have to think & provide every thing for my Family, at a time when it is so difficult to provide anything, at almost any price, & cares of many kinds to engage my attention," she wrote revealingly. After Hannah's birth six days later Sally remarked, "[I have] been enabled to bear up thro' every triall & difficulty far beyond what I could have expected." Although in succeeding months she continued to lament Tommy's absence, her later reflections differed significantly from her first reaction to her situation. Instead of dwelling upon her despondency, Sally wrote of "the fond, the delightfull Hope" that her husband would return to love her as before. "Oh my beloved, how Ardently, how tenderly how Affectionately, I feel myself thine," she effused in February 1778, describing "the anxiety I feel for thee, the longing desire to be with thee, & the impatience I feel to tell thee I am all thy own"—but not indicating any sense of an inability to cope with problems in his absence. When Tommy returned in late April 1778, she welcomed him gladly, but she did not revert completely to her former role of ignorance about monetary matters. Her diary subsequently noted several consultations with him about household finances, a subject they had not discussed before his exile.

Although Mary Bartlett, the wife of a New Hampshire congressman, left no similar record of her feelings about her husband's extended stays in Philadelphia during the war, she nevertheless subtly disclosed the fact that her role had undergone a comparable change. When Josiah Bartlett first went to Congress in the fall of 1775, he told Mary he hoped she would have "no Great trouble about my out Door affairs," and he continued to write to her about "my farming Business." In 1776 she accepted his terminology, reporting on "Your farming business," but during Josiah's second stint in Congress in 1778 that phrase became "our farming business" in her letters. No longer was the farm simply "his": she had now invested too much effort in it for that. The distinction between male and female spheres she had once accepted without question had been blurred by her own experience.

blurring of male female spheres

Although Josiah Bartlett's persistent use of "my farm" implies that he did not recognize the way in which his wife's role had altered, other patriot men separated from their spouses for long periods revealed changing attitudes toward their womenfolk in their correspondence. The differences are especially apparent in the case of a New Englander, Timothy Pickering, because he began with a severely limited conception of his wife's capability. . . .

Pickering adopted a patronizing tone in his early letters to his wife, Rebecca White. In November 1775, before their marriage, he told her he wanted to "instruct" her and went on to quote the same poem other Americans cited in discussions of children's education: "'Tis a 'Delightful task to rear the tender thought, / To teach the fair idea how to shoot.'" Like a father teaching a daughter, he encouraged her to write to him, saying, "[F]requent writing will improve your hand." Unremarkably, Pickering's condescension continued during the early years of their marriage, after he had joined the Continental Army's quartermaster corps. When he sent home a lame horse in June 1777, he told her to consult male friends "for advice and direction" in caring for it, then apologized for asking her to undertake a task that was "entirely out of [her] sphere." Even his praise contained an evident patronizing note. "Your conduct in domestic affairs gives me the highest satisfaction," he told her in July 1778, spoiling it by adding, "even if you had done wrong I could not find fault; because I know in every action you aim at the best good of our little family: and knowing this: it would be cruel and unreasonable to blame you." In other words, he was telling her she would be judged on the basis of her intentions, not her actual performance, because he feared she could not meet the higher standard.

For the Pickerings matters changed in October 1780 after Rebecca acted as Timothy's agent in a complex arrangement for the repayment of a debt. "I am very glad you made me fully acquainted with it," she told him. "It is a satisfaction to me to pa[r]take of any thing that gives you Concern. I know my Dear you would make me happy in telling me any thing that had a tendency to make you so." After the successful resolution of the debt problem and her verbalization of her desire to assist him with their financial affairs, Timothy began to rely more heavily upon her. When the family rented a farm in 1782, she ably shouldered the responsibility for managing it despite her fears of "not being acquainted with farming business." Five years later, after they had moved to the frontier community of Wilkes-Barre, Pennsylvania, and Timothy's post required him to be in Philadelphia, she not only supervised the building of their new house but also oversaw the harvest, all the while nursing their newest baby. Timothy continued to apologize for the burdens he was placing on her (as well he should have), but he no longer mentioned her "sphere." Rebecca Pickering, like Mary Bartlett before her, began to speak in her letters of "our business" and "our crops." Timothy had already revealed his new attitude as early as August 1783: "This war which has so often & long separated us, has taught me how to value you," he told her then. . . .

The war dissolved some of the distinctions between masculine and feminine traits. Women who would previously have risked criticism if they abandoned their "natural" feminine timidity now found themselves praised for doing just that. The line between male and female behavior, once apparently so impenetrable, became less well defined. It by no means disappeared, but requisite adjustments to wartime conditions brought a new recognition of the fact that traditional sex roles did not provide adequate guidelines for conduct under all circumstances. When

Betsy Ambler Brent looked back on her youth from the perspective of 1810, she observed, "[N]ecessity taught us to use exertions which our girls of the present day know nothing of. We Were forced to industry to appear genteely, to study Manners to supply the place of Education, and to endeavor by amiable and agreeable conduct to make amends for the loss of fortune."

The realization that they had been equally affected by the war led some women to expect equal treatment thereafter and, on occasion, to apply to their own circumstances the general principles promulgated by the revolutionaries. "I have Don as much to Carrey on the warr as meney that Sett Now at ye healm of government & No Notice taken of me," complained the New Jersey widow Rachel Wells as she protested to the Continental Congress in 1786 about a technicality that deprived her of interest payments on the money she had invested in state bonds during the war. "If she did not fight She throw in all her mite which brought ye Sogers food & Clothing & Let them have Blankets," she explained, asking only for the "justice" due her. "Others gits their Intrust & why then a poor old widow be put of[f]?" Mrs. Wells asked. "Now gentelmen is this Liberty?"

Mary Willing Byrd's social standing was much higher than that of Rachel Wells, but she advanced a similar argument when she contended in 1781 that Virginia had treated her unfairly. She claimed the right to redress of grievances "as a female, as the parent of eight children, as a virtuous citizen, as a friend to my Country, and as a person, who never violated the laws of her Country." Byrd's recital of her qualifications was peculiarly feminine in its attention to her sex and her role as a parent (no man would have included such items on a list describing himself), but it was also sexless in its references to her patriotism and her character as a "virtuous citizen." In developing the implications of the latter term, Byrd arrived at her most important point. "I have paid my taxes and have not been Personally, or Virtually represented," she observed. "My property is taken from me and I have no redress."

Mary Byrd

The echoes of revolutionary ideology were deliberate. Mary Byrd wanted the men she addressed to think about the issue of her status as a woman, and she adopted the revolutionaries' own language in order to make her point. The same tactic was employed by Abigail Adams in her most famous exchange with her husband.

In March 1776, after admonishing John to "Remember the Ladies" and to offer them legal protection from "the unlimited power" of their husbands, Abigail issued a warning in terms that John must have found exceedingly familiar. "If perticular care and attention is not paid to the Laidies," Abigail declared, "we are determined to foment a Rebelion, and will not hold ourselves bound by any Laws in which we have no voice, or Representation." On one level, she was speaking tongue-in-cheek; she did not mean her husband to take the threat seriously. Yet she chose to make a significant observation about women's inferior legal status by putting a standard argument to new use and by applying to the position of women striking phraseology previously employed only in the male world of politics. Like Mary Willing Byrd, Abigail Adams thus demonstrated an unusual sensitivity to the possible egalitarian resonances of revolutionary ideology and showed an awareness of implications that seem to have escaped the notice of American men.

The Mixed Legacy of the American
Revolution for Black Women

JACQUELINE JONES

For the historian, race, as a socially defined category of human relationships, should constitute a central consideration in exploring the self-evident truths of this country's past. More specifically, during the era of the American Revolution, the status of all black women differed in fundamental ways from the status of all white women. Together, slave women and men endured the agony of bondage, and together blacks, both enslaved and free, struggled to form families that eventually served as the foundation of a distinctive Afro-American culture. The military conflict between loyalists and rebels intensified physical hardship among blacks, while the ensuing social and economic turmoil afforded some of their race the opportunities for a basic kind of freedom that white women and men—for all their rhetoric about the evils of tyranny—already enjoyed. Therefore, any discussion of the war's impact on American women must first highlight racial factors before dealing with issues related to class, regional, ethnic, and religious diversity in the late eighteenth-century population.

Yet within the confines of the slave system, and within the boundaries of their own households and communities, black women shouldered burdens that set them apart from their menfolk. In the period from 1750 to 1800, the nature and extent of these burdens varied according to whether a woman was African- or American-born; whether she lived in the North or South, in a town or rural area; whether she toiled in the swampy South Carolina lowcountry or on a Virginia wheat farm. This is not to suggest that black women suffered more than black men under the oppressive weight of the racial caste system, only that gender considerations played a significant role in shaping the task assignments parceled out to blacks by slaveholders, and in shaping the way blacks structured relationships among themselves. . . .

The ordeal of black women as wives, mothers, and workers encapsulates all the ironies and tensions that marked the history of slavery during the era of the American Revolution. In their efforts to create and preserve a viable family life, these women sought to balance caution and daring, fear and hope, as they reacted to the peculiar matrix of individual circumstances. Regardless of their work and family status in Boston, on a small farm in Pennsylvania, on George Washington's plantation, or in the South Carolina lowcountry, they saw freedom through the prism of family life. Consequently they perceived this revolutionary idea in ways fundamentally different from the white men who tried to claim the War for Independence as their own, and from the white women who remained so awkwardly suspended between their racial prerogatives on the one hand and gender and class liabilities on the other. Caught in the crossfire of sexual and racial oppression, black women contributed to the definition of liberation in these turbulent times. Indeed, through

Jacqueline Jones, "Race, Sex, and Self-Evident Truths: The Status of Slave Women During the Era of the American Revolution," in Ronald Hoffman and Peter J. Albert, eds. *Women in the Age of the American Revolution* (Charlottesville, Va.: University Press of Virginia, 1989), 296–298, 324–334. Reprinted with permission of the University Press of Virginia.

their modest everyday struggles, these wives and mothers offered a vision of freedom that was, by virtue of its consistency and fairness, more enduring than the one
articulated so eloquently by the Founding Fathers. . . .

The political unrest and wartime devastation that marked the Revolutionary era
brought into focus all the contradictions implicit in the emerging democratic republic of slaveholders and their allies. Masters found themselves confronted by their
own demands for liberty and reacted accordingly, either by manumitting their
slaves or by fighting ever more tenaciously to enforce black subordination. These
conflicting impulses among the white elite helped to shape the experiences of
black women during this period of upheaval, but so too did the economic transformations wrought by armed conflict and incipient nation-building. For their part,
slaves seized the initiative whenever an opportune moment presented itself and
fought their own battles for self-determination as field hands, refugees, and libera-
tors of their own kin. Finally, black women's family responsibilities as wives and
mothers remained constant even as the Revolution gave their productive abilities a
new political significance. . . .

For the bulk of slave women located on southern plantations, the war entailed
both physical suffering and great latitude for personal action. Forced to make do with
less in the way of food, clothing, and other basic supplies, white southerners considered the daily needs of their slaves to be a low priority (especially after 1778, when
fighting engulfed the region). At least some whites fulfilled the prediction of the
patriot who railed against runaway slave men seeking protection from the British:
"The aged, the infirm, the women and children, are still to remain the property of the
masters, masters who will be provoked to severity, should part of their slaves desert
them." Untold numbers of slave women felt the wrath of "an enraged and injured
people" desperate to keep the upper hand at home as well as on the battlefield.

The women who remained with their masters gave whites cause enough for
alarm. Thomas Pinckney's depleted South Carolina plantation consisted primarily
of mothers and children in 1779, but they proved no more tractable than the male
slaves who had already deserted; according to the white man, the slave women "pay
no attention" to the overseer. Residing on another estate, Pinckney's mother com-
miserated with him, noting that she had lost control over her servants, "for they all
do now as they please everywhere." As the war raged near her North Carolina estate
in 1781, another mistress complained bitterly about the insolent Sarah: "She never
came near me till after repeated messages yesterday to come and Iron a few clothes.
. . . She made shift to creep here and then was very impudent." Such recalcitrance
could provoke some whites to violence, others to reluctant indulgence. A Baltimore
slaveholder urged his overseer not to upset the slave Ruth, or "she will run off, for
she is an arch bitch."

Slaveholders might try to brutalize, cajole, or bribe black women into submission, but they could not escape the fact that they needed every available worker.
The estimated 55,000 slaves who absconded, and many others pressed into service
by the colonists and British alike, left some areas of the South bereft of field hands
and thus devastated by food shortages. Planters who sought to institute a system of
household cloth production reserved the positions of spinners and weavers for
black women and girls, a sexual division of labor shaped in part by the now critical

lack of male laborers. The rebels were not about to let gender considerations interfere with their exploitation of black labor in this time of crisis, and southern states often sought to buy, hire, or impress slaves of both sexes for use on public works projects. For example, in 1780 the Board of Trade of Virginia purchased twenty-six blacks (among them three women) to work in its tanneries, ironworks, boatyards, and army hospitals. The intense demand for unskilled labor during the war, exacerbated by a temporary halt in the foreign slave trade, endangered the well-being of free blacks, as well as slave women. In 1778 Ann Driggus of North Carolina suffered a beating at the hands of two men who then kidnapped four of her children in order to sell them.

Increased demands on their productive energies, combined with the confusion produced by wartime, prompted slave women to seek safety with the enemies of their master, whether rebel or loyalist. According to Gerald W. Mullin and other historians, family ties assumed even greater significance as a source of motivation among runaways, compared to the colonial period, perhaps reflecting more favorable conditions for flight and for beginning a new life elsewhere with kinfolk. Moreover, Mary Beth Norton has suggested that "although a majority of runaways were male, women apparently sought freedom in greater numbers [that is, proportion] during the war than in peacetime." Evidence from scattered sources reveals that up to a third of all wartime refugees were female, compared to the 10 percent or so of runaways listed in colonial newspapers who were female. Panic-stricken, patriot law-enforcement officials condemned to hard labor, executed, or sold to the West Indies those women and men who failed in their bid for freedom.

Benjamin Quarles has estimated that 5,000 black men served in the patriot armed forces, including the Continental army and navy, and state militias. This figure includes slaves who deserted their loyalist owners to fight with the rebels, and free blacks (almost all in the North) who volunteered for duty. But a far larger number of blacks perceived their best interests to lie with the British, a conviction no doubt encouraged early on by Virginia's royal governor Lord Dunmore, who in 1775 promised to liberate all the slaves of patriots who joined his army. As a slaveholder, Dunmore promoted policies that reflected the opportunistic attitude of the British toward blacks in general; they were considered worthy of decent treatment only insofar as they furthered the king's cause as soldiers, manual laborers, or insurgents who deprived the colonists of much needed labor. According to Sylvia Frey, British authorities showed little inclination to offer refuge to the slaves of loyalists. Dunmore himself refused sanctuary to runaways whom he could not readily use in his current military campaigns.

As might be expected, few slave women found a haven behind British lines. Army camps along the coast of Virginia were crowded and disease-ridden, with black people of both sexes and all ages suffering from exposure, hunger, and smallpox. The grisly image of a child seeking nourishment from the breast of its dead mother on Gwynne Island in 1776 conveys the bitter reality of black life—and death—in refugee camps. The image itself is also a reminder of the unique forms of oppression that impelled slave women to flee their owners' plantations and the lack of concern for their plight among officials on either side of the conflict. Few white women had cause to risk so much during the war. . . .

The black people evacuated with British troops after the war faced an uncertain future indeed. At least 15,000 black women and men left the country aboard British ships that sailed from Savannah, Charleston, and New York; some were self-defined loyalists, others served loyalist masters, and still others hoped to benefit from British efforts to deprive their conquerors of personal property. The wide range of experiences that awaited individual women—a lifetime of slavery in the West Indies; a struggle to survive in the fledgling British colony of Sierra Leone; or a new beginning of health, safety, and freedom in Nova Scotia—mirrored the crosscurrents of hardship and liberation that characterized the status of slave women during the Revolutionary War.

Thus the black fight for independence proceeded apace, whenever formerly compliant slave women suddenly turned "sassy" and defiant or abandoned their master's household, either to cast their lot with the British or slip as self-freed persons into the anonymity of urban life. A more formal (though no less difficult) route to freedom lay through the state courts and legislatures and through the efforts of free blacks to buy and then emancipate their own kin. . . .

Within three decades of the war's end, all of the northern states had provided for emancipation, although some enacted gradual provisions that left thousands of blacks in slavery for years to come. For example, according to New York's law of 1799, the daughters born to slave women after that date were to be bound (like indentured servants or apprentices) to the mother's master for twenty-five years, sons for twenty-eight years. . . . Two points are relevant to this issue: first, the most far-reaching antislavery legislation was enacted by northerners, who had the least to lose financially from their altruism; and second, the burden of transition from a slave to free black population fell most heavily on mothers whose offspring perpetuated the system of bondage. . . .

NY law of 1799 slave + children indentured 25/28 yrs.

Regardless of how they obtained their freedom, black women shared common goals: to consolidate family members, keep their households intact, and provide for the material welfare of dependents. . . . Many newly freed blacks (and runaways) from the upper South and rural areas migrated to northern towns. This movement gradually produced an unbalanced urban sex ratio in favor of women (the reverse of the colonial pattern), probably because single women found it easier to support a family in the city than on the countryside. . . . Although they might now labor for wages, the vast majority continued to perform the same services they had for whites under slavery—cooking, washing clothes, cleaning, serving, and tending white children. The fact of freedom did not affect the racial caste system as it related to the social division of labor.

Racial caste system → social division of labor

In the 1780s and 1790s, free and slave women together actively participated in the creation of an "institutional core" for Afro-American life—the formation of churches, schools, and benevolent societies separate and distinct from those of whites, blending an African heritage with American political realities. Although several historians have described in detail the emergence of black organized religion after the war, the role of women in that story remains untold. . . .

During these years the exhilaration of freedom experienced by some black women contrasted mightily with the plight of many more who remained condemned to slavery. . . . Masters fully appreciated a self-replenishing labor force, but their efforts each year to grow as much cotton as humanly possible worked to the detriment of childbearing females. Most white men did not fully comprehend the connection between overwork and high miscarriage and infant mortality rates; the result was untold pain and grief for slave mothers. As the institution of bondage renewed

Overworked to miscarriage

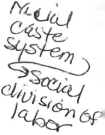

itself, so too did the drive for hegemony among ambitious men on the make as well as among the sons of Revolutionary-era slaveholders—a drive that held sacred the tenet of private property(no matter what its form) and eventually provoked a war far bloodier than the rebellion of 1776. While their free sisters kept alive the spirit of Afro-American community autonomy, black mothers and wives in the Cotton South would continue to eat the bitter fruit borne of a white man's political and economic revolution.

F U R T H E R   R E A D I N G

Bloch, Ruth H. "The Gendered Meanings of Virtue in Revolutionary America," *Signs* 13 (1987–1988): 37–58.

Buel, Richard, and Joy Buel. *The Way of Duty: A Woman and Her Family in Revolutionary America* (1984).

Gelles, Edith. *Portia: The World of Abigail Adams* (1992).

Gundersen, Joan R. "Independence, Citizenship, and the American Revolution," *Signs* 13 (1987–1988): 59–77.

———. *To Be Useful to the World: Women in Eighteenth-Century America* (1996).

Hoffman, Ronald, and Peter Albert, eds. *Women in the Age of the American Revolution* (1989).

Kerber, Linda K. *Women of the Republic: Intellect and Ideology in Revolutionary America* (1980).

——— et al. "Beyond Roles, Beyond Spheres: Thinking About Gender in the Early Republic," *William and Mary Quarterly,* 3d ser, 46 (1989): 565–585.

Klinghoffer, Judith, and Lois Elkins. "'The Petticoat Electors': Women's Suffrage in New Jersey, 1776–1807," *Journal of the Early Republic* 12 (1992): 159–193.

Lacey, Barbara E. "Women in the Era of the American Revolution: The Case of Norwich, Connecticut," *New England Quarterly* 53 (1980): 527–543.

Lewis, Jan. "The Republican Wife: Virtue and Seduction in the Early Republic," *William and Mary Quarterly,* 3d ser, 44 (1987): 689–721.

Nash, Margaret A. "Rethinking Republican Womanhood: Benjamin Rush and the Young Ladies' Academy of Philadelphia," *Journal of the Early Republic* 17 (1997): 171–191.

Norton, Mary Beth. "Eighteenth-Century American Women in Peace and War: The Case of the Loyalists," *William and Mary Quarterly,* 3d ser, 33 (1976): 386–409.

Skemp, Sheila. *Judith Sargent Murray: A Brief Biography with Documents* (1998).

Zagarri, Rosemarie. "Morals, Manners, and the Republican Mother," *American Quarterly* 44 (1992): 192–215.

———. *A Woman's Dilemma: Mercy Otis Warren and the American Revolution* (1995).

———. "The Rights of Man and Woman in Post-Revolutionary America," *William and Mary Quarterly,* 3d ser, 55 (1998): 203–230.

CHAPTER
5

White Women and Politics
in the Antebellum Years

◆

Women's historians' treatment of politics appears, in some respects, to be coming full circle. Before the field of women's history was launched in the late 1960s and early 1970s, one of the few aspects of women's past that attracted much scholarly attention was the study of women's role in politics generally and in the women's rights movement in particular. Early practitioners of the new style of women's history rejected such an emphasis, arguing that it privileged men's priorities over women's. Accordingly, they devoted their primary energies to delineating women's familial and domestic ("private") roles and distinguishing them from men's "public" responsibilities. With respect to the antebellum period, scholars explored and analyzed what has become known as the doctrine of "separate spheres"—the then prevalent notion that women and men had different, mutually exclusive, but complementary roles in life.

Eventually, historians came to realize that the women who stressed their commitment to "domestic" ideals and "separate spheres" often did not practice what they preached; some of the most popular purveyors of such ideas, for example, were women who supported themselves and their families by writing novels or editing magazines, belying their words by their actions. Other antebellum women used "woman's special role" as an argument for the employment of female teachers or the establishment of reformist benevolent societies, both involving activity outside the household. Such "public" functions, scholars soon recognized, necessarily brought antebellum women into the realm of politics.

Current work has gone beyond that initial insight to break down the once-distinct categories of "public" and "private." Scholars are now exploring a wide variety of new questions about women's involvement in antebellum politics, both in conjunction with men (through the party system) and on their own (through the independent women's rights movement).

◆ D O C U M E N T S

During the presidential campaign of 1840, Virginia Whigs did their best to enlist female supporters. When the famous Whig orator Daniel Webster visited Richmond in October, he and three prominent Virginia Whigs formally addressed "the ladies." Document 1, by an

101

anonymous male observer, satirically commented on that event. Four years later, Virginia Whig women began a campaign to raise money to erect a statue of their recently defeated presidential candidate, Henry Clay. Two negative responses, both undoubtedly by men, constitute Document 2. When the participants in the first women's rights convention were publicly criticized in 1848, two of their number, Elizabeth McClintock and Elizabeth Cady Stanton, vigorously defended their actions (Document 3). Yet their approach did not easily or quickly carry the day. Sarah Josepha Hale, editor of the important women's magazine, *Godey's Lady's Book,* rejected woman suffrage in 1852 (Document 4). Two men, Henry Mills Alden (the editor of *Harper's New Monthly Magazine)* and Anson Bingham (a women's rights supporter), debate the issue, in Document 5, in 1853 and 1854.

1. A Correspondent of the *Richmond Enquirer* Satirizes the Political Role of "the Ladies of Richmond," 1840

To the Editor of the Enquirer.

During the last week I have been a "looker on" here in Richmond; and, Sir, I must confess, that I have been not a little amused at some of the prodigies. Of all the entertaining spectacles, however, that at the Log Cabin, or rather "between the logs" on Wednesday, was surpassingly exhilirating. There, Sir, from four of the "intellects" of the age, we had, in a very short space, Tragedy, Comedy, Interlude and Farce. The ostensible purpose of the "gathering" was to improve the morals and to mend the heart; and, that "generations yet unborn" might be profited, (*not to say,* the present,) the ladies of Richmond, representing Virginia, were to be addressed by Messrs. Webster, Barbour, Leigh, and Lyons!!

Upon reading the report of the "proceedings," in a certain paper of Friday last, the following thoughts rose uppermost in my mind:

1. The meeting was not opened with prayer. A venerable clergyman was present, (as I learn) but no petition for divine assistance was offered up, as at the *political* assemblages. But Mr. Webster's address was professedly a moral one. Either then, the ladies are not in need of grace—or a moral essay, unlike a political one, may be ushered in without the acknowledgment of a superintending Providence. . . .

3. Mr. W. seemed to suppose that the ladies, one and all expected a *call* from him. Now, this was certainly a very "amiable" feeling, but it is somewhat remarkable that he should apologize to Virginia ladies for not paying his individual respects, when it is well known that the ladies of Virginia are accustomed generally to select their individual visitors.

4. Are the ladies of Virginia so destitute of religious and moral instruction, that they need a thorough politician to enlighten them on the subject of the training of the children?

5. Mr. Leigh ascribed the victory at Yorktown to the ladies, because two naked Yankee Regiments were clothed by the ladies of Baltimore. Why did not the Orator go back to earlier days and make some reflections on the "fruit of that forbidden tree which brought death into the world with all our woe!" . . .

NO QUIZ, *alias* NEQUIS.

October 12, 1840.

Richmond Enquirer, October 13, 1840.

2. Two Commentators Deride
Virginia Whig Women's Plan to Erect
a Statue to Henry Clay, 1844

For the Enquirer.

Harry of Navarre

It seems this great hero, who has figured in some of the great events of this country, is no longer able to wield a lance in his own defence. He who, his friends would have us believe has ever stood foremost to carry out Federal measures, (they call them their measures,) has been defeated, in fair and open conflict; and if we are to believe Whig authority, their Orators have been totally annihilated, for the Ladies of Richmond are called upon "to step forth to shield the statesman of the age from the slanders of the day, and vindicate his name from foul aspersion."—Has it come to this, that the "gallant Harry" has been turned over to the tender mercies of the ladies—that the "thrice defeated" is now in his old age, to be taken under their especial patronage?—Well, be it so. The gallantry of the Democrats has never been called in question; and the fair sex, in "these piping times of peace," have had and will have their assistance, to keep him in the retired shades of Ashland, ministering to his own comforts, and removed from the cause of contention. And if hereafter it should be found that justice was not rendered him in this election, impartial history will right the wrong, without the assistance of the ladies.

CLINTON.

The True View! *(Instead of the Tower of Babel!)*

"Incognita" in Saturday's Whig thus gives her opinion as to the propriety of a *public meeting* of the Whig ladies of Richmond "to perpetuate our (their) respect and gratitude to Mr. Clay." We entirely accord with her sentiments as to the meeting, and we would add, that we have heard many zealous Whig ladies express the same feelings.

As to the honor proposed to be paid to Mr. Clay—an honor never rendered to our own immortal Washington or pure Marshall—we have nothing to say. If the thing is to be done, we think "Incognita" points out the proper *mode* of achieving it:

"To decide upon some plan of proceeding in this matter, a meeting of the Whig ladies of Richmond and Manchester, has been called—*a public meeting of political amazons! Mercy on us! Was such an event ever recorded, or before heard of, in the annals of time?* Defend us from it, Mr. Pleasants!—or instead of erecting a statue, you may anticipate results like those which followed the building of a certain tower of old, that never was finished. Ladies are unaccustomed to such assemblies, and unacquainted with the rules and method necessary to maintain order, and carry resolutions into effect. I, therefore, with many others, am opposed to such a useless appropriation of time . . .

Richmond Enquirer, November 29 and December 2, 1844.

Thomas
Jefferson
W.R. movement

3. Elizabeth McClintock and
Elizabeth Cady Stanton Defend the
Seneca Falls Women's Rights Convention, 1848

For the National Reformer.

Woman's Rights.

Messrs. Editors:—As you announce Mr. Sulley, (the author of the article headed "Woman's Rights Convention," published in your paper of last week) as a man who seeks to know the truth, and one who will do justice to any subject he examines, and as he declares himself to be a great lover of his race, and one who has thought deeply on the subject of human improvement, I humbly ask *him* what are these other means to which he refers, by which the present social, civil and religious condition of woman can be improved. It is evident, aside from his own assertion, that Mr. Sulley has thought much on this subject, for he says, "I am not one of those who think that no improvement can be made in the condition of woman, even in this favored land." He is interested, too, in our movement, and has been kind enough to tell us what means will not effect what we desire. He says those recommended and presented by the convention will not do. He thinks legislative action cannot alter the laws of nature. Does Mr. Sulley assume that our present degradation is in accordance with the laws of God? Mr. Sulley having been announced as a lover of truth, we rejoiced in the belief that at length we had found one opponent who would meet us in fair argument, one who though not agreeing with us fully in our measures, was yet sufficiently interested in this subject to give us some plan by which the elevation of woman might be effected. But alas! we have the same old story over again—ridicule, ridicule, ridicule. We have hints of great arguments that could be produced—profound philosophy, fully convincing and satisfactory to all thinking minds, but he gives us nothing tangible, not even the end of the tail of any of these truths, by which could we get a fair hold, we might draw out all the rest. Mr. Sulley thinks our convention was a mere pompous outward show; because, forsooth, we could not give on the spot, a panacea for all the ills of life—because we could not answer Mr. Sulley's silly questions in a manner to satisfy him, though the audience thought him fully answered. We did not assemble to discuss the details of social life—we did not propose to petition the legislature to make our husbands just, generous and courteous; no, we assembled to protest against an unjust form of government, existing without the consent of the governed; to declare our right to be free as man is free: to claim our right to the elective franchise, our right to be represented in a government which we are taxed to support; to have such laws as give to man the right to chastise and imprison his wife, to take the wages which she earns—the property which she inherits, and in case of separation the children of her love; laws which make her the more dependant on his bounty: it was to protect against such disgraceful laws, and to have them, if possible, forever erased from

What they want
end to coverture

Elizabeth McClintock and Elizabeth Cady Stanton, "Women's Rights," *Rochester National Reformer,* September 21, 1848. This document can also be found in Patricia Holland and Ann D. Gordon, eds., *The Papers of Elizabeth Cady Stanton and Susan B. Anthony* (Wilmington, Del.: Scholarly Resources, 1991).

our statute books, as a shame and reproach to a republican, christian people in the enlightened nineteenth century. We did not meet to decide home questions—to say who should be the ruling spirit, the presiding genius of every household—who should be the umpire to settle the many differences in domestic life. . . .

Mr. S. expressed a wish to quote the Bible on this subject, but found it would have no authority with us. We affirm that we believe in the Bible. We consider that Book to be the great charter of human rights, and we are willing, yes, desirous to go into the Bible argument on this subject, for its spirit is wholly with the side of Freedom. . . .

> *brought us Mothers Day*

E. W. MCCLINTOCK,
E. C. STANTON.

spinster

4. Sarah Josepha Hale, editor of *Godey's Lady's Book,* Praises Women's Indirect Political Influence, 1852

HOW AMERICAN WOMEN SHOULD VOTE.—"I control seven votes; why should I desire to cast one myself?" said a lady who, if women went to the polls, would be acknowledged as a leader. This lady is a devoted, beloved wife, a faithful, tender mother; she has six sons. She *knows* her influence is paramount over the minds she has carefully trained. She *feels* her interests are safe confided to those her affection has made happy. She *trusts* her country will be nobly served by those whom her example has taught to believe in goodness, therefore she is proud to vote by her proxies. This is the way American women should vote, namely, by influencing rightly the votes of men.

5. Two Men Debate Women's Proper Role, 1853–1854

Henry Mills Alden, the Editor of Harper's New Monthly Magazine, *Attacks Women's Rights, 1853*

Anson Bingham Responds in The Lily, *1854*

[T]he claim of "woman's rights" presents not only the common radical notion which underlies the whole class, but also a peculiar enormity of its own; in some respects more boldly infidel, or defiant both of nature and revelation, than that which characterizes any kindred measure. It is avowedly opposed to the most time-honored proprieties of social life; it is opposed to nature; it is opposed to revelation. . . .

. . . There is an inner and an outer sphere. The first is as honorable as the second; it is even more intimately connected with the essential life, while the latter stands to it more in the position of a means to a higher ultimate good. Woman was meant to be the main influence in the one, man in the other. To this all civilization tends. Its recognition and establishment is ever in proportion to the advance of a pure Christianity. Destroy this dual life, and the merely physical or sexual distinction becomes a source of immeasurable mischief. Preserve the former, and the latter, instead of a

---

Godey's Lady's Book 44 (April 1852), 293.

Harper's Magazine, November 4, 1853, 838–841; *The Lily,* April 1, 1854.

hot-bed of sensualism, is converted into a fountain of the purest and most sacred affections of which our earthly nature is capable.

To denote this inner life of which woman is the guardian angel, no term could be better adapted than the one in most common use, and which must be etymologically the same in every cultivated language. It is the *domestic* life—the *res domi* in distinction from the *res foras.* The latter is the out-door life, the life abroad, the *forensic* life, or life of the *forum,* including in that term all political as well as judicial employment. Now we know that to a superficial thinker, the former may present the idea of the narrower sphere; and hence those logomachies about personal rights, and rank, and "equality and subjugation," which such a one would present as the real issues. If, however, there be any question of rank at all, the domestic is certainly the higher sphere; because, as we have said, it is more closely connected with the essential life, or the end for which humanity exists, and to which all that is outward or *forensic,* with all its imagined importance, is but a subordinate means. Men may *act* abroad, but they *live,* if they live at all, at home. The *State* is for the *Family,* the *forum* for the *domus.* The former would have but little value except as it is found in the protection, the refinement, and the elevation of the latter. And so we may say of the reciprocal influence. The best service that woman can confer upon the State, (and thus, through it, obtain the best security for her own personal rights and dignity) is by making the home what it ought to be. In the right education of her children, she exerts a far purer and more effectual political power, than she could ever wield through the freest admission to the ballot-box or the caucus. . . .

. . . [W]e may say that in this country, and in every other in which there is a representative system based on popular suffrage, married women *do* vote—they *are* represented—they have a part in the political action, and just the part which is most conservative of their true interests, while it is least subversive of those ideas on which the family, and through it the whole social structure, must ultimately rest. The wife does exercise the right of suffrage. Through the husband, as the family representative, she casts a vote, and the only vote which is consistent with the oneness of that elementary political organism we may call the family State. . . .

. . . [I]t is the Family, the household, which should be immediately represented in the State, rather than the individual. It is the family that votes, and not the individual. Whoever deposits that vote, deposits it as the agent of the whole domestic community, just as the Member of Assembly represents the town from which he is sent, and the Senator the State by which he is delegated. Since, then, such voting can only be done by one member, the husband and the father is certainly the most proper person for that purpose. In fact, if we are to preserve at all the idea of the domestic and forensic spheres, this is a matter of absolute necessity. He represents this outward life, and is, therefore, the natural embassador of the little organism in its outward relations to other and similar communities.

But the husband may cast a ballot different from that which would be acceptable to the wife. What then? Shall there be separate voting? If so, the family is at an end. The domestic community is sundered, and the organic life expires. No evils arising from separate property would be so terrible, or so completely subversive of the marriage idea, as the separate voting of the husband and wife, the father and the mother, the outward and inner representatives of the family unity. . . .

. . . The Church as well as the State, is composed of families, or may be regarded as having the family for its unit. It is the *"Church in the house"* with its altar, its service, its sacred instruction. Here, as in the other case, the interior religious life is especially intrusted to woman. The outward or embassadorial relations involved in the preaching and episcopal office belong to the other sphere. Any confusion here would destroy, not only that essential idea of harmony involved in the construction of the Christian Ecclesia, but also that sacred similitude through which the Apostle traces the bridal relation of the Church herself to her Spiritual Lord and Head. But what care these platform brawlers for sacred similitudes and spiritual analogies? It is not at all, as they would make it, a question of "equality and subjugation." A true spiritual equality, as we have seen, is best promoted by the Apostle's notion of keeping each sex within its allotted sphere. It is the only way of avoiding that un-natural mixture of habits, of office, of employments, of dress, which would soon bring on a moral degradation, and, through this, as abject a slavery of one to the other as has ever been witnessed in savage life. No fallacy could be greater than that which confounds *subordination* with inequality. The first exists in the co-equal and co-essential tri-unity of the Divine Persons, and there could be, strictly, no oneness without it. So also may we say of the demand for perfect uniformity, or identity of pursuit. No mathematical proposition is more certain than the seeming paradox, that *sameness* here is separation, incoherence, dissolution—*diversity* is union, attraction, strength. The doctrine we condemn is essentially inorganic. Instead of that exquisitely harmonized instrument which comes from the right temperament of the sexual relations, it would make human life, at the best, a tuneless monochord, if not, in the end, a chaos of all harsh and savage dissonance. . . .

. . . [T]he Editor in defending woman's enslavement as it exists the world over, repeats the often repeated dogma, "Society has framed her laws and usages in obe-dience to the Divine and physical ordinance. Every attempt to break through them, therefore, must be pronounced as unnatural as it is irreligious and profane."

This is the dogma of the aristocracies, the oligarchies, the hierarchies, the tyran-nies and despotisms of the old world. It is the dogma of classes and castes, and of master and slave, every where. . . .

. . . [H]e says, "There is an inner and an outer sphere." Where? Among the Turks, or the Christians? The civilized, or the uncivilized? The Jew, or the Gentile? The married, or the unmarried? The denizen of the city, or the sojourner in the wilderness? This world of ours is considerable of a place, and its men and women are not all fenced in alike, and when he talks of spheres, curiosity, if nothing else, prompts the question, where?

But supposing there is, what of that? Recollect, he is denying to woman not only an equality of social and political rights, but the right of any. Now what bear-ing can his doctrine of spheres have upon that? Do we grant, or withhold political franchises to male citizens by occupational standard, or the spheres they move in? The President of the United States has no greater personal political prerogatives than the man who cooks his dinner, or grooms his horses. Yet here are the two spheres, according to the Editor's definition—the inner and the outer—his forensic and his domestic—his *res domi* and his *res foras*—and all in the possession of the like political prerogatives. Is it claimed that there is anything wrong in this? What then have spheres to do with the right of suffrage, or any other franchise?

And if the sphere in which the individual moves is to determine that individual's personal and political rights, what has the sex of the individual to do with it? If the

woman who cooks, or darns the stockings, is to be disfranchised because she does so, what saves the man who is similarly employed? And if she is to be disfranchised because of her sex, then it is all twaddle to talk about spheres. There is no logical connection between the two positions, and it therefore ill becomes reverend and editorial seniors to be playing the sneak between them.

E S S A Y S

An influential synthetic essay by Paula Baker of the University of Pittsburgh argues that historians have not fully recognized women's political role in the years before they gained the right to vote, in part because scholars' definition of "politics" has been too narrow. Although acting within a so-called separate sphere, she contends, women still affected political decisionmaking. The Wellesley College historian Elizabeth R. Varon modifies Baker's premise by contending that even in the conservative pre–Civil War South (specifically Virginia), female Whig sympathizers and, later, female Democrats became deeply involved in partisan politics, not merely in the benevolent activities on which Baker focuses. Nancy Isenberg (a historian at the University of Northern Iowa) expands Baker's definition of "politics" in another direction by including Protestant church structures and beliefs in her study. Women's rights advocates, she asserts, correctly understood the intertwining of church and state in the antebellum years when they developed simultaneous challenges to the authority of both.

White Women's "Separate Sphere" and Their Political Role, 1780–1860

PAULA BAKER

[F]rom the time of the Revolution, women used, and sometimes pioneered, methods for influencing government from outside electoral channels. They participated in crowd actions in colonial America and filled quasi-governmental positions in the nineteenth century; they circulated and presented petitions, founded reform organizations, and lobbied legislatures. Aiming their efforts at matters connected with the well-being of women, children, the home, and the community, women fashioned significant public roles by working from the private sphere.

. . . Historians have told us much about the lives of nineteenth-century women. They have explained how women gained political skills, a sense of consciousness as women, and feelings of competence and self-worth through their involvement in women's organizations. But as important as these activities were, women were also shaped by—and in turn affected—American government and politics. Attention to the interaction between women's political activities and the political system itself can tell us much about the position of women in the nineteenth century. In addition, it can provide a new understanding of the political society in which women worked—and which they helped change.

Paula Baker, "The Domestication of Politics: Women and American Political Society, 1780–1920," *American Historical Review* 89 (June 1984): 621–632. Reprinted by permission of the author.

Politics

In order to bring together the histories of women and of politics, we need a more inclusive definition of politics than is usually offered. "Politics" is used here in a relatively broad sense to include any action, formal or informal, taken to affect the course or behavior of government or the community. Throughout the nineteenth century, gender was an important division in American politics. Men and women operated, for the most part, in distinct political subcultures, each with its own bases of power, modes of participation, and goals. In providing an intellectual and cultural interpretation of women and politics, this essay focuses on the experiences of middle-class women. There is much more we need to learn about the political involvement of women of all classes in the years prior to suffrage; this essay must, therefore, be speculative. Its purpose is to suggest a framework for analyzing women and politics and to outline the shape that a narrative history of the subject could take.

The basis and rationale for women's political involvement already existed by the time of the Revolution. For both men and women in colonial America, geographically bounded communities provided the fundamental structures of social organization. The most important social ties, economic relationships, and political concerns of individuals were contained within spatially limited areas. Distinctions between the family and community were often vague; in many ways, the home and community were one. There were, to be sure, marked variations from place to place; community ties were weaker, for example, in colonial cities and in communities and regions with extensive commercial and market connections, such as parts of the South. Still, clear separations existed between men and women in their work and standards of behavior, and most women probably saw their part in the life of the community as the less important. A little-changing round of household tasks dominated women's lives and created a routine that they found stifling. Women had limited opportunities for social contact, and those they had were almost exclusively with other women. They turned work into social occasions, and they passed the milestones of their lives in the supportive company of female friends and relatives. But, however confining, separation provided a basis for a female culture—though not yet for female politics.

Differences between men's and women's political behavior were muted in the colonial period, compared with what they later became. In many places, men who did not own land could not vote because governments placed property restrictions on suffrage. Both men and women petitioned legislatures to gain specific privileges or legal changes. Citizens held deferential attitudes toward authority; elections were often community rituals embodying codes of social deference. A community's "best" men stood for election and were returned to office year after year, and voters expected candidates to "treat" potential supporters by providing food and drink before and on election day. Deferential politics, however, weakened by the middle of the eighteenth century. Economic hardship caused some men to question the reality of a harmony of interests among classes, and the Great Awakening taught others to question traditional authorities. Facing a growing scarcity of land, fathers could no longer promise to provide for their sons, which weakened parental control. This new willingness to question authority of all sorts was a precondition for the Revolution and was, in turn, given expression by republican thought.

Republicanism [handwritten annotation]

Republicanism stressed the dangers posed to liberty by power and extolled the advantages of mixed and balanced constitutions. In a successful republic, an independent, virtuous, watchful, and dispassionate citizenry guarded against the weakness and corruption that threatened liberty. Although interpreted by Americans in different ways, republicanism provided a framework and a rationale for the Revolution. It furnished prescriptions for citizenship and for the relationship between citizens and the state. And it helped unify a collection of local communities racked by internal divisions and pressures.

While the ideology and process of the Revolution forced a rethinking of fundamental political concepts, this re-evaluation did not extend to the role of women. As Linda K. Kerber persuasively argued, writers and thinkers in the republican tradition were concerned more with criticizing a particular political administration than with examining traditional assumptions about the political role of all inhabitants. Given their narrow intentions, they were not obliged to reconsider the position of women in the state. The language of republicanism also tended to make less likely the inclusion of women. Good republicans were, after all, self-reliant, given to simple needs and tastes, decisive, and committed first to the public interest. These were all "masculine" qualities; indeed, "feminine" attributes—attraction to luxury, self-indulgence, timidity, dependence, passion—were linked to corruption and posed a threat to republicanism. Moreover, women did not usually own land—the basis for an independent citizenry and republican government.

feminist qualities a threat to republicanism [handwritten annotation]

Despite their formal prepolitical status, women participated in the Revolution. They were central to the success of boycotts of imported products and, later, to the production of household manufactures. Their work on farms and in business in their husbands' absences was a vital and obvious contribution. Women's participation also took less conventional forms. Edward Countryman recounted instances in which groups of women, angered at what they saw as wartime price-gouging, forced storekeepers to charge just prices. During and after the war, women also took part in urban crowd actions, organized petition campaigns, and formed groups to help soldiers and widows. Some even met with legislatures to press for individual demands. Whatever their purposes, all of these activities were congruent with women's identification with the home, family, and community. In boycotts of foreign products and in domestic manufacture during the Revolution, women only expanded traditional activities. In operating farms and businesses, they stepped out of their sphere temporarily for the well-being of their families. Because separations between the home and community were ill defined in early America, women's participation in crowd actions can also be seen as a defense of the home. As Countryman and others pointed out, a communalist philosophy motivated the crowd actions of both men and women. Crowds aimed to redress the grievances of the whole community. Women and men acted not as individuals but as members of a community— and with the community's consent.

women in the Revolution [handwritten annotation]

Women's political participation took place in the context of the home, but the important point is that the home was a basis for political action. As Kerber and Mary Beth Norton have shown, the political involvement of women through the private sphere took new forms by the beginning of the nineteenth century. Women combined political activity, domesticity, and republican thought through motherhood. Although outside of formal politics, mothering was crucial: by raising civic-minded,

19th C [handwritten annotation]

"republican motherhood" [handwritten annotation]

virtuous sons, they insured the survival of the republic. On the basis of this important task, women argued for wider access to education and justified interest and
involvement in public affairs. As mothers women were republicans; they possessed
civic virtue and a concern for the public good. Their exclusion from traditionally
defined politics and economics guaranteed their lack of interest in personal gain.
Through motherhood, women attempted to compensate for their exclusion from the
formal political world by translating moral authority into political influence. Their
political demands, couched in these terms, did not violate the canons of domesticity
to which many men and women held.

During the nineteenth century, women expanded their ascribed sphere into community service and care of dependents, areas not fully within men's or women's
politics. These tasks combined public roles and administration with nurturance and
compassion. They were not fully part of either male electoral politics and formal
governmental institutions or the female world of the home and family. Women
made their most visible public contributions as founders, workers, and volunteers
in social service organizations. Together with the social separation of the sexes and
women's informal methods of influencing politics, political domesticity provided
the basis for a distinct nineteenth-century women's political culture.

  Although the tradition, tactics, and ideology for the political involvement of
women existed by the first decades of the nineteenth century, a separate political culture had not yet taken shape. Women's style of participation and their relationship to
authority were not yet greatly different from those of many men. Until the 1820s—
and in some states even later—property restrictions on suffrage disfranchised many
men. Even for those granted the ballot, political interest and electoral turnout usually
remained low. During the early years of the republic, deferential political behavior
was again commonplace. Retreating from the demands of the Revolutionary period,
most citizens once again seemed content to accept the political decisions made by
the community's most distinguished men. This pattern persisted until new divisions
split communities and competing elites vied for voters' support.

  Changes in the form of male political participation were part of a larger transformation of social, economic, and political relationships in the early nineteenth
century. The rise of parties and the re-emergence of citizen interest in politics had a
variety of specific sources. In some places, ethnic and religious tensions contributed
to a new interest in politics and shaped partisan loyalties. Recently formed evangelical Protestant groups hoped to use government to impose their convictions about
proper moral behavior on the community, a goal opposed by older Protestant groups
and Catholics. Other kinds of issues—especially questions about the direction of
the American political economy—led to political divisions. Citizens were deeply
divided about the direction the economy ought to take and the roles government
ought to play. They thought attempts to tie localities to new networks and markets in
commerce and agriculture could lead to greater prosperity, but such endeavors also
meant that economic decisions were no longer made locally and that both the social
order and the values of republicanism could be in danger. Local party leaders linked
these debates to national parties and leaders, and the rise of working men's parties
in urban areas seemed to spring from a similar set of questions and sense of unease
about nineteenth-century capitalism.

party strength

Whatever their origin, parties also served other less explicitly "political" purposes. The strength of antebellum parties lay in their ability to fuse communal and national loyalties. The major parties were national organizations, but they were locally based: local people organized rallies, printed ballots, worked to gain the votes of their friends and neighbors. Through political activities in towns and cities, parties gained the support of men and translated their feelings into national allegiances. Political organization provided a set pattern of responses to divisive questions, which raised problems to the national level and served to defuse potential community divisions. Indeed, by linking local concerns to national institutions and leaders, parties took national political questions out of the local context. The local base of the Democrats and Whigs allowed them to take contradictory positions on issues in different places. Major party leaders searched for issues that enabled them to distinguish their own party from the opposition, while keeping their fragile constituencies intact. At the same time, local politics returned in most places to a search for consensual, nonpartisan solutions to community questions.

rise of the 2 party system

The rise of a national two-party system in the 1820s and 1830s inaugurated a period of party government and strong partisan loyalties among voters that lasted until after the turn of the twentieth century. Parties, through the national and state governments, distributed resources to individuals and corporations, and patronage to loyal partisans. Throughout most of the nineteenth century, roughly three-quarters of the eligible electorate cast their ballots in presidential elections. The organization and identity of the parties changed, but the pre-eminence of partisanship and government-by-party remained. Party identifications and the idea of partisanship passed from fathers to sons.

male political involvement

Partisan politics characterized male political involvement, and its social elements help explain voters' enthusiastic participation. Parties and electoral politics united all white men, regardless of class or other differences, and provided entertainment, a definition of manhood, and the basis for a male ritual. Universal white manhood suffrage implied that, since all men shared the chance to participate in electoral politics, they possessed political equality. The right to vote was something important that men held in common. And, as class, geography, kinship, and community supplied less reliable sources of identification than they had at an earlier time, men could at least define themselves in reference to women. Parties were fraternal organizations that tied men together with others like themselves in their communities, and they brought men together as participants in the same partisan culture.

symbols to appeal to manhood

Election campaigns celebrated old symbols of the republic and, indeed, manhood. Beginning as early as William Henry Harrison's log cabin campaign in 1840, parties conducted entertaining extravaganzas. Employing symbols that recalled glorious old causes (first, the Jacksonian period and, later, the Civil War), men advertised their partisanship. They took part in rallies, joined local organizations, placed wagers on election results, read partisan newspapers, and wore campaign paraphernalia. In large and small cities military-style marching companies paraded in support of their party's candidates, while in rural areas picnics and pole raisings served to express and foster partisan enthusiasm.

Party leaders commonly used imagery drawn from the experience of war: parties were competing armies, elections were battles, and party workers were soldiers. They commented approvingly on candidates who waged manly campaigns, and they disparaged nonpartisan reformers as effeminate. This language and the campaigns themselves gathered new intensity in the decades following the Civil War. The men who marched in torchlight parades recalled memories of the war and demonstrated loyalty to the nation and to their party. Women participated, too, by illuminating their windows and cheering on the men; sometimes the women marched alongside the men, dressed as patriotic figures like Miss Liberty. The masculine character of electoral politics was reinforced on election day. Campaigns culminated in elections held in saloons, barber shops, and other places largely associated with men. Parties and electoral politics, in short, served private, sociable purposes.

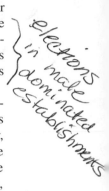

elections in male dominated establishments

Just as the practice and meaning of electoral politics changed in the early nineteenth century, so did the function of government. State and local governments gradually relinquished to the marketplace the tasks of regulating economic activity, setting fair prices, and determining product standards. State governments limited the practice of granting corporate charters on an individual basis and, instead, wrote uniform procedures that applied to all applicants. These governments also reduced, and finally halted, public control of businesses and private ventures in which state money had been invested. A spate of state constitutional revisions undertaken from the 1820s through the 1840s codified these changes in the role of government in economic life. In state after state, new constitutions limited the power of the legislatures. Some of this power was granted to the courts, but most authority passed to the entrepreneurs. This transformation in governance is just beginning to be re-evaluated by political historians. For our purposes, the important point is that governments largely gave up the tasks of regulating the economic and social behavior of the citizenry.

The rise of mass parties and characteristic forms of male political participation separated male and female politics. When states eliminated property qualifications for suffrage, women saw that their disfranchisement was based solely on sex. The idea of separate spheres had a venerable past, but it emerged in the early nineteenth century with a vengeance. Etiquette manuals written by both men and women prescribed more insistently the proper behavior for middle class ladies. Woman's attributes—physical weakness, sentimentality, purity, meekness, piousness—were said to disqualify her for traditional public life. Motherhood was now described as woman's special calling—a "vocation," in Nancy Cott's term—that, if performed knowledgeably and faithfully, represented the culmination of a woman's life. While a handicap for traditional politics, her emotional and guileless nature provided strengths in pursuing the important tasks of binding community divisions and upholding moral norms.

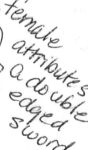

female attributes a double edged sword

At the same time, political activity expanded in scope and form. New organizations for women proliferated in small and large cities and became forums for political action. These organizations took on some of the tasks—the care of dependents and the enforcement of moral norms—that governments had abandoned. If not maintained by church, government, and community, the social order would be preserved by woman and the home. Women's positions outside traditionally defined politics and their elevated moral authority took on new importance and may have allowed men to pursue individual economic and social ends with less conflict. Through selfless activities in the home and community, women could provide stability.

women offer stability to social order

As historians of women have pointed out, one of the ironies of Jacksonian democracy was the simultaneous development of the "cult of true womanhood"

Irony of Jacksonian democ.

and rhetoric celebrating the equality of men. These developments were related and carried ramifications for both male politics and woman's political role. The notion of womanhood served as a sort of negative referent that united all white men. It might, indeed, have allowed partisan politics to function as a ritual, for it made gender, rather than other social or economic distinctions, the most salient political division. Men could see past other differences and find common ground with other men.

"Womanhood" was more than just a negative referent, for it assigned the continued safety of the republic to the hands of disinterested, selfless, moral women. In the vision of the framers of the Constitution, government was a self-regulating mechanism that required good institutions to run properly—not, as in classical republicanism, virtuous citizens. Men's baser instincts were more dependable than their better ones; hence, the framers made self-interest the basis for government. While politics and public life expressed selfish motives, private life—the home—maintained virtue. The republican vocabulary lingered into the nineteenth century, but key words gained new meanings that were related to private behavior. "Liberty," "independence," and "freedom" had economic as much as political connotations, while "virtue" and "selflessness" became attributes of women and the home. Because order was thought to be maintained by virtuous women, men could be partisans and could admit that community divisions existed. At the same time, male electoral participation defined politics. As the idea of parties gained citizens' acceptance and other modes of participation were closed or discouraged, electoral participation stood as the condoned means of political expression.

Women's political demands and actions that too closely approached male prerogatives met with resistance. Women fought hard—and sometimes successfully—in state legislatures to end legal discrimination. But even their victories had as much to do with male self-interest as with women's calls for justice. Still, they slowly gained legal rights in many states. And since male politics determined what was public and political, most of those demands by women that fell short of suffrage were seen as private and apolitical. The political activities of women in clubs and in public institutions achieved a considerable degree of male support. Women reformers not only drew little visible opposition from men but often received male financial support. Women's moral nature gave them a reason for public action, and, since they did not have the vote, such action was considered "above" politics.

Ideas about womanhood and separate spheres, as well as forces as diverse as urbanization and the resurgence of revival religion, gave women's political activity a new prominence. But that female sphere had now grown. Men and women would probably have agreed that the "home" in a balanced social order was the place for women and children. But this definition became an expansive doctrine: home was anywhere women and children were. Influential women writers such as Catherine Beecher described a "domestic economy" in which women combined nurturance and some of the organizational methods of the new factory system to run loving, yet efficient, homes. Others expanded the profession of motherhood to include all of society, an argument that stressed the beneficial results that an application of feminine qualities had on society as a whole. This perspective on motherhood and the home included not only individual households but all women and children and the forces that affected their lives. And it had a lasting appeal. As late as 1910, feminist and journalist Retha Childe Dorr asserted: "Woman's place is Home. . . . But Home

Home = Community

is not contained within the four walls of an individual house. Home is the community. The city full of people is the Family. The public school is the real Nursery. And
badly do the Home and Family need their mother." Many nineteenth-century women
found this vision of the home congenial: it encouraged a sense of community and responsibility toward all women, and it furnished a basis for political action.

White Women and Party Politics
in Antebellum Virginia

ELIZABETH R. VARON

urban phenom.

The nineteenth-century ideology of "separate spheres," which prescribed that men
occupy the public sphere of business and politics and women the domestic sphere of
home and family, has exercised a powerful hold over historians of the antebellum
United States. As a result, the fields of antebellum political history and women's
history have used separate sources and focused on separate issues. . . .

Women's historians . . . have shown little interest in the subject of party politics.
Drawing primarily on personal papers, on legal records such as wills, and on the
organizational records of female associations, they have illuminated women's domestic lives, their moral reform activities, and the emergence of the woman's rights
movement. Those few scholars—Paula C. Baker, Mary P. Ryan, and Michael E.
McGerr—who have tried to integrate political history and women's history have not
challenged the historiographical impression that the realm of antebellum party politics was a male preserve. While these scholars note that women took part in political
campaigns, they stress the theme of female exclusion from male political culture. As
McGerr has written, women were let into the political sphere only "to cook, sew, and
cheer for men and to symbolize virtue and beauty." They were denied "not only the
ballot but also the experience of mass mobilization."

The distance between antebellum political history and women's history is
perhaps nowhere so great as in the historiography on the Old South. While northern feminist abolitionists who demanded political enfranchisement have begun to
receive their due from historians of northern politics, no such radical vanguard existed in the South to command the attention of political historians. Both the major
historians of antebellum southern politics and the major practitioners of southern
women's history have neglected the subject of female partisanship. The current
historiographical consensus holds that southern women, in keeping with the conservatism of their region, by and large eschewed politics even as northern women
were fighting for access to the political sphere.

This essay attempts to close the gap between women's history and political
history. Focusing on the Commonwealth of Virginia, it argues that historians have
underestimated the extent and significance of women's partisanship in the antebellum period. . . . Historians generally agree that the Whigs' 1840 campaign marks
the first time a political party systematically included women in its public rituals.

1840 1st time Political Party included women

Elizabeth R. Varon, "Tippecanoe and the Ladies, Too: White Women and Party Politics in Antebellum
Virginia," *Journal of American History* 82 (September 1995): 494–521. Reprinted by permission of the
Organization of American Historians.

All around the country, women turned out at Whig rallies; on occasion they even made speeches, conducted political meetings, and wrote pamphlets on behalf of the Whigs. And yet, while many scholarly studies note these developments, none draw out their implications. Historians have relegated women's partisanship to a few pages of description here and there; and they generally present women, not as political actors, but as "audience and symbol." The pioneering treatment of Whig women, Robert Gray Gunderson's *The Log-Cabin Campaign,* characterizes women's role at rallies as "conspicuous, but passive." A recent study by Ryan makes a similar case: women who attended Whig political events in 1840 did so "not in public deliberation but as symbols," as "passive and respectable representatives of femininity."

The Virginia evidence suggests that to characterize women's partisanship as passive is to obscure the transformation in women's civic roles that the election of 1840 set in motion. Newspapers, pamphlets, and speeches, taken together with women's diaries, letters, and reminiscences, chart that transformation. The function of antebellum newspapers, which were the organs of political parties, was to make partisanship seem essential to men's identities. With the campaign of 1840, Whig newspapers took on the additional task of making partisanship seem essential to women's identities.

Whig newspapers in Virginia, in lockstep with the party's national organ, the *Washington National Intelligencer,* featured invitations to women to attend the speeches and rallies of "Tippecanoe and Tyler, Too," clubs and provided glowing reports of such events. The *Staunton Spectator* noted, for example, that the women of Mt. Solon favored its "Tipp and Ty" club with their attendance and "enjoyed very highly the display of eloquence" by the speakers. Whig rhetoric argued that the presence of women at such events bespoke not only their admiration for Harrison but also their opposition to the policies of the Democrats. In an article in the *Washington National Intelligencer,* one Whig correspondent, commenting on the high turnout of women at Whig rallies, declared that women supported the Whigs because the "selfless schemings" of the Van Buren administration had "made themselves felt in the very sanctum sanctorum of domestic life." . . .

According to the Whig press, women could contribute to the campaign not only by listening to speeches and by exerting influence over men but also by making public presentations. On October 1, 1840, the "Whig Ladies of Alexandria" presented a banner with the motto "Gen. Wm. H. Harrison, the Glory and Hope of our Nation" to the local Tippecanoe club; male delegates of the club carried the banner in a Whig procession that took place four days later in Richmond. Whig newspapers also occasionally published Harrison songs and poems by women. One Virginian wrote a song in honor of her party's candidate that ended with the refrain "Down with the Locos / dark hocus-pocus / The Banner of Liberty floats through the sky."

The single most vocal female contributor to the Tippecanoe campaign was [Lucy] Kenney. She published two pamphlets, *A History of the Present Cabinet* and *An Address to the People of the United States,* in support of Harrison's 1840 campaign. He was an honorable statesman who had earned the "blessings of thousands of women and children" in his career as an Indian fighter. In keeping with a favorite Whig theme, Kenney asserted that Harrison's private character was as unassailable as his public record. He was an "honest and upright" and "chivalric" man who would restore the United States to "peace, plenty and prosperity." "Let the present party leaders remember that in November next we will shout the harvest home," she declared, sure of Harrison's triumph.

The personal papers of Virginia women confirm that the 1840 campaign was different from its predecessors. "Fashionable topics seem to turn on politics more than anything else at present," Whig Judith Rives wrote her son in February 1840, from the family plantation in Albermarle County. "I never saw anything like the excitement here," Sarah Pendleton Dandridge of Essex County informed her sister; "we hear of nothing but Gen. Harrison." . . . Private residences and businesses became sites for the consumption and production of partisan material culture. Women not only bought a vast array of Whig paraphernalia (such as stationery, songbooks, plates, buttons, glassware, and quilts bearing Harrison's name) but also made their own. . . . In the age of mass politics, even women's housekeeping could serve partisanship. Party conventions, rallies, and processions might bring thousands of visitors who had to be lodged, fed, and cared for. Naturally, women played a key role in providing these services and so facilitated the political process. . . .

For Whig women in Virginia, the crowning event of the 1840 campaign was Whig luminary Daniel Webster's visit to Richmond. . . . After giving two speeches to huge crowds of enthusiastic Whig men and women, Webster yielded to the "particular request of the ladies of Richmond" and agreed to present a special address on women's political role to them at the Whig campaign headquarters. On October 7, some twelve hundred women turned out for the event. Webster took issue with the popular maxim that "there is one morality for politics and another morality for other things," and he looked forward to the day when the standards of private life would govern public conduct. It was women's special duty, he suggested, to bring that day about.

Because their moral perceptions were "both quicker and juster than those of the other sex," Webster continued, women could infuse society with the "pure morality" on which sound government depended. Mothers had to teach their children that

> the exercise of the elective franchise is a social duty, of as solemn a nature as man can be called on to perform; that a man may not innocently trifle with his vote; that every free elector is a trustee as well for others as himself, and that every man and every measure he supports has an important bearing on the interests of others as well as on his own.

Webster refrained from analyzing specific political issues, not because he feared the women would not be interested, but because, he said, "You read enough—you hear quite enough on those subjects."

Webster's views were echoed by two of Virginia's leading Whigs, former governor James Barbour and Richmond lawyer James Lyons, who spoke to the crowd after Webster had finished. They made explicit what Webster had implied: women's civic duty was to create Whig families, and their public participation in Whig events empowered them to fulfill that role. . . . Webster and his fellow speakers were in effect articulating a new theory of women's civic duty. That theory, Whig womanhood, attempted to reconcile women's partisanship as Whigs with the ideology of domesticity or "true womanhood." The canon of domesticity, like the revolutionary-era theory of republican motherhood, celebrated woman's power and duty to mold the character of her sons, to instill in them civic virtue and a love for the Republic. At the same time, domestic doctrine held that the "true woman" was nonpartisan. Men

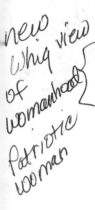

embodied the "baser instincts"—selfishness, passion, and ambition—which partisanship expressed. By contrast, women were selfless, disinterested, and virtuous. Men pursued their self-interest in the public sphere; women maintained harmony, morality, and discipline in the domestic one.

What was new about Whig womanhood was its equation of female patriotism with partisanship and its assumption that women had the duty to bring their moral beneficence into the public sphere. Whig rhetoric held that women were partisans, who shared with men an intense interest and stake in electoral contests. No longer was patriotism a matter of teaching sons to love the Republic. A patriotic woman would teach her family to love the Whig party; she, after all, understood that the Whigs alone could ensure the health and safety of the Republic.

That very understanding was forged in public. Rather than affirm a cherished tenet of the ideal of domesticity, that women must avoid the contentious political arena in order to safeguard their virtue, Whig speakers argued that by attending campaign events, women could transform the public sphere, fostering "domestic" virtues such as fairness, harmony, and self-control in a larger setting. Women's "countenance" sanctified the Whig cause: their presence bespoke the party's moral rectitude. Not only did women legitimize partisan behavior, they helped set limits on it—they guarded men with a "shield of purity" and made them understand the moral consequences of their actions. In a sense, Whig womanhood was the ultimate testament of faith in true womanhood. Its expositors held that *even* participation in party politics could not corrupt women or erase the fundamental differences between them and men.

How well did Whig rhetoric about women conform to reality? The Whigs' claim that the "ladies are all Whigs" was, of course, a fanciful fabrication. Even though expressions of partisanship by Whig women outnumber those by Democratic women in extant writings from 1840, it seems unlikely that a majority, let alone the entirety, of Virginia women supported the Whigs. Despite Harrison's vigorous campaign, the Democrats still had the support of a majority of voters in Virginia in 1840; women's private papers simply do not bear out the Whig connection that many of these Democratic voters had Whig wives. Since women did not cast ballots, the Whigs' assertion that there was a gender gap in politics cannot be empirically proven or refuted— therein, no doubt, lay some of its viability as propaganda. But the Whig party clearly did much more than its rival to encourage and celebrate female partisanship, and Whig women, most likely as a result, outdid their Democratic counterparts in displays of partisan zeal.

Judging by the campaign reports of Democratic newspapers, the Democrats were deeply ambivalent about women's partisanship. Jackson, the grand old hero of the Democratic party, drew admiring crowds of men and women when he toured the South, but such Democratic newspapers as the party's national organ, the *Washington Globe,* did not make a concerted effort to publicize or encourage women's presence at Democratic rallies. The leading Democrats in Virginia did little to contest the Whig party's assertion that it alone had the blessing of women. Some Democrats openly expressed their contempt for Whig tactics. . . .

Why was the Whig and not the Democratic party the first to seize the opportunity to make, as one Democrat put it, "politicians of their women"? Answers to the question must be speculative, for neither Whig nor Democratic commentators

explicitly accounted for this difference in the political tactics of the two parties. Stud- ~~Stable~~ *Stable*
ies of Whig ideology argue that women were central to the Whigs' world view. Al- *Amer.*
though the Democrats sought to maintain a strict boundary between the private and *Character*
public spheres and resented attempts to politicize domestic life, the Whigs invested
the family—and women in particular—with the distinct political function of forming
the "stable American character" on which national well-being depended. While the
Democrats acknowledged the reality of social conflict, the Whigs preferred speaking
of a society in which harmony prevailed; women's "special moral and spiritual qualities," Whigs maintained, fitted them for the task of promoting such harmony. . . .

As many recent studies show, by 1840, women had long been active in the
sphere of benevolent reform. They had proved that they were effective organizers,
skilled at mobilizing public support for their projects. In Virginia, men had enthusiastically enlisted female support in the temperance and African colonization causes,
arguing that the participation of "disinterested" and virtuous females would legitimate those causes. In short, when reform-minded Whig leaders such as Barbour
encouraged women to join in the party's glorious crusade, they were not inventing or
advancing new arguments to justify public activism by women, but rather recasting
old ones, adapting the ideology of benevolent femininity to the new realities of
mass party politics. . . . Women's role at political rallies . . . was more to contain
passions than to give in to them. Political passion, according to nineteenth-century
rhetoric, was a sort of "blindness"; critiques of "blind party spirit" float through
the campaign rhetoric of the 1840s. Whig rhetoric implied that women, by virtue of
their moral superiority, could resist this blindness. Whig men occasionally praised
female enthusiasm, but they more often stressed Whig women's disinterestedness,
dignity, and decorum.

*

In other words, the participation of women helped to relieve men's anxieties *Campaign*
about changes in electoral behavior. Even though men likened partisan competition *plan?*
to warfare, they were intensely concerned with constraining the behavior of partisans. This concern, it might be argued, ran especially high among Whigs in 1840,
when they began their appeals to women. The Whigs wanted to have it both ways: to
steal the Jacksonians' democratic thunder and to claim that the Whigs were a breed
apart from the Democrats—and a superior one at that. The Whigs' 1840 campaign
was masterminded by a new cadre of professional politicians who sought to beat the
Jacksonians at their own game of rousing the common man. They hoped that the din
produced by Harrison's Log Cabin campaign of 1840 would drown out the Democratic charge that the Whigs had no platform and no policies. Even as they stressed
the humble origins of their candidate and claimed to be more democratic than the
Democrats, the Whigs also sought to retain the mantle of patrician dignity. . . . The
Democrats naturally asserted that the Whigs' efforts to unleash voter enthusiasm
were immoral and destructive to the public peace; particularly disturbing, Democrats
charged, was the way the dispensing of hard cider by Harrison campaign workers *women*
encouraged intemperance. But the Whigs had the perfect counterargument—the *as a*
very presence of women at Whig events insured decorum and sobriety. With women *screen?*
on their side, Whigs could lay claim both to popular democracy and to dignity.

The Whig party's victory in the 1840 presidential contest proved to be short-lived.
The death of Harrison within a month after his inauguration exposed the fault lines

in the Whigs' fragile coalition. Seeking a consensus candidate in 1844, the Whigs chose [Henry] Clay, whom their northern and southern wings could agree on. Clay, a southerner, opposed the annexation of Texas unless on terms acceptable to the North. And he championed an "American System" of internal development that would bind the country together through commercial ties.

The years between Harrison's victory in 1840 and Clay's campaign in 1844 afforded women and men alike fewer opportunities to display partisanship than the presidential campaign season had. Women did attend political speeches and debates in nonelection years. But they were not generally included in the year-round succession of meetings, held behind closed doors, in which the state business of the Whig party, such as the selection of delegates to state conventions, was conducted. Women's function in partisan life had clear limits: their role was not to choose Whig candidates but to affirm the choices of Whig men, particularly in high-stakes presidential campaigns; to help maintain party discipline; and to bring new members into the Whig fold.

As soon as the presidential canvass of 1844 got underway, the tide of female partisanship rose again, to new heights. The Whig party in Virginia flooded women with a virtual torrent of invitations to Whig events. . . . Women attended Whig events in towns, villages, county courthouses, and rural settings around the state. . . . The Whig party's campaign rhetoric conjured up an <u>image of the ideal Whig woman</u>: a chaste, honorable lady who attended political rallies to sanction the party, to dignify its proceedings, to affirm her loyalty, and to gather information that would allow her to transmit Whig culture to her family, friends, and acquaintances. Although often spoken of, Whig women rarely got the chance to "speak" for themselves before partisan audiences in1844. . . .

On November 19, 1844, the *Richmond Whig* published a seemingly innocuous letter that would touch off months of debate in the Virginia press. The letter, from Lucy Barbour of Barboursville, Orange County, proposed that the "Whig women of Virginia" give some "token of respect" to Clay, who had just lost his third bid for the presidency of the United States. Barbour was a member of Virginia's social elite. Her husband James, who had died in 1842, had been one of the most prominent Whigs in Virginia. He had served as governor of the commonwealth, United States senator, and the secretary of war under John Quincy Adams. The Barbours counted Clay among their close friends.

Barbour anticipated that her call to action would raise eyebrows. "I know our sex are thought by many unstable as water," her letter continued, "but after crowding the Whig festivals, and manifesting so much enthusiasm, few will be found so hollow-hearted as to refuse a small sum to so good—I had almost said, so holy a cause": the tribute to Clay. The editors of the *Richmond Whig* agreed to adopt Barbour's scheme as their own. The editors of the *Richmond Enquirer* wasted no time in ridiculing the plan to honor Clay: "Has it come to this, that the 'gallant Harry' has been turned over to the tender mercies of the ladies . . . ?" The *Enquirer* also printed a letter from one "Incognita," who thoroughly disapproved of the notion that Whig women should hold a meeting to decide on a strategy for honoring Clay: "a public meeting of political amazons! . . . Was such an event ever recorded, or before heard of, in the annals of time?"

Barbour vigorously defended her project. In a December 4 letter to the *Richmond Whig,* she stated that women deserved "freedom of thought even on political subjects; and the power of performing an act of justice to an injured statesman; when, doing so, we neglect no duty assigned to us by the most rigid." "We are the nursing mothers of heroes, statesmen, and divines," she continued, "and while we perform a task so important, we mean to be counted something in the muster-roll of man."

Inspired by Barbour's appeal, a group of Whig women met on December 9 at the First Presbyterian Church in Richmond and formed the Virginia Association of Ladies for Erecting a Statue to Henry Clay; they elected Barbour as president. The statue was to be funded by membership subscriptions, costing no more than one dollar each. Men could make donations but not become members. Auxiliaries to the association, with women as officers and collectors, were organized all around the state and began the work of soliciting donations to pay for the cost of commissioning the statue.

Thanks to the survival of a subscription book from around 1845–1846 that lists contributors to the Clay Association by county, we can get a sense of the breadth and nature of the organization. The book lists the names of 2,563 subscribers, covering counties from Accomac on the Eastern Shore to Nelson on the Blue Ridge; at least 2,236 of the subscribers were women. The association, which received national publicity in the *National Intelligencer,* also had auxiliaries in Alexandria (204 subscribers) and in Boston (215 subscribers). Additional contributions came from families in Vermont, Mississippi, and Georgia.

The list of subscribers confirms that there was a strong connection between Whiggery and female benevolence in Virginia. . . . [But] the social prominence of the Clay Association's leaders did not insulate them from criticism. As auxiliaries sprang up around the state, so, too, did debate over the propriety of the association. On December 22, 1844, for example, two days after the Whig women of Lynchburg formed an auxiliary, the editors of the Democratic *Lynchburg Republican* attacked the Clay Association, suggesting with derision that "the name of every lady who mingles in this great work of generosity and patriotism will be handed down to posterity as a *partisan* lady." "Is not this whole movement conceived in a spirit of rebellion?" the editors asked. The Democrats mocked the notion that partisanship was appropriate for women—that partisanship and patriotism were synonymous. . . .

Whig women themselves came forward on their own and Clay's behalf. In December 1844 a female correspondent to the *Richmond Whig* wrote that women had a duty to honor Clay since he had been "shamefully neglected by his countrymen." She had nothing good to say about the newly elected president, James K. Polk: "The more insignificant a man is, the greater are his chances, with the Democracy, for attaining exalted honors." . . . [Such] women who spoke for the association tapped into two currents in Whig political culture: the party's social elitism and its emphasis on "statesmanship." The Whigs considered themselves the party of "property and talents." . . .

One of the central issues in the 1844 campaign was Clay's stature as a gentleman and statesman. The Democrats assailed Clay's character, charging him with the unchristian practices of dueling, gambling, and womanizing. The Whigs countered that Clay was the epitome of a southern gentleman, a model of gallantry and social grace. Just as women's support had helped Harrison establish a virtuous reputation, so, too, did it help, in Clay's case, to defuse the "character issue." Women around the country flocked to Clay's speeches and showered him with gifts. . . .

On April 12, 1860, the eighty-third anniversary of Clay's birth, the Clay statue was inaugurated in Richmond, amid great public celebration. Business in the city had been virtually suspended so that the entire community could participate in the inaugural ceremonies; an estimated twenty thousand spectators witnessed the unveiling. The Clay statue, which stood in an iron pavilion in Capitol Square until 1930, now stands in the Old Hall of the Virginia House of Delegates.

The 1844–1845 debates over the Clay Association, though short-lived, are significant for revealing the tensions inherent in Whig womanhood, a new variation on the timeworn and resilient doctrine of "indirect influence." This doctrine, which eventually emerged as a key argument against woman suffrage, held that women's civic duty lay, not in casting a ballot, but rather in influencing men's opinions and behavior. The Whig innovation was to suggest that in the era of mass party politics, women could not fulfill this mandate properly unless they were integrated into the culture of political parties. For all its homages to female influence, the concept of Whig womanhood still ultimately vested women's power in male proxies. An unanswered question at the heart of Whig womanhood was implicitly posed by Lucy Barbour. What if men, despite the benign efforts of women, simply failed to do the right thing? What if they elected the wrong man? What were women to do then?

In the wake of Clay's 1844 defeat, Barbour and her supporters offered an answer: women had the duty to restore the reputation of their party's rejected hero. Barbour conceived of women as opinion makers. They were not simply to affirm the choices of men, but to advance their own ideas of what constituted political worth in men—before, during, and after campaign season. In attacking the association, Democrats worried out loud about the potentially radical implications of this view and paid backhanded tribute to women's influence. When Whig men rushed to defend Barbour, they reminded Democrats that Whig women's partisanship came with the full approbation of Whig men; the women of the Clay Association were not challenging the authority of all men, only of Democratic ones. Rather than symbolizing female rebelliousness, the Clay Association came to symbolize the efficacy and propriety of political collaboration between men and women.

By the time the Clay statue was inaugurated in 1860, both Clay and the Whig party were long gone. Clay had died in 1852, the same year that the Whig party—its fragile coalition of supporters torn apart by sectionalism—ran its last presidential campaign. But in at least one respect, Whig political culture, like the Clay statue that symbolized it, proved more enduring than the party itself. For even as the Whigs disintegrated, their policy of making "politicians of their women" became standard practice in Virginia politics.

In the presidential campaigns of 1848, 1852, and 1856, each of the parties competing for voters in Virginia actively appealed to women to join its ranks. In 1848 and again in 1852, the Whigs sounded familiar themes with respect to female partisanship. One feature that distinguished the 1852 campaign from earlier ones was the frequency with which women made public presentations of campaign decorations, occasionally accompanied by brief addresses. . . . The Democrats seem to have finally come around by the campaigns of 1848, 1852, and 1856. Virginia

Democrats nearly matched their opponents' zeal for female support and partici- pation. The rhetoric of Democratic women and men reveals how fully they had appropriated Whig ideas about female partisanship. . . . The Whig argument that women both legitimized and purified partisan activities was now enthusiastically advanced by Democrats. Describing an October [1852] rally in Norfolk, a Democratic correspondent wrote: "There was no *fuss*—no disturbance. The ladies—guardian angels that control our natures—were around us with their illuminating smiles to cheer, and their bright countenances to encourage us on to victory." . . .

. . . The kind of evidence presented here has far-reaching implications for the fields of political history and women's history. On the one hand, my findings underscore what political historians have been saying for years. Partisanship was indeed a con- suming passion and pastime for antebellum Americans. On the other hand, the Vir- ginia evidence calls into question a common assumption in the historiography of antebellum politics: participation in campaign activities was a highly significant form of political expression for men, but not for women. . . .

A recognition of the extent of women's involvement in campaigns may hold the key to understanding another issue of great interest to political historians: polit- ical socialization. Party loyalty was notoriously strong during the era of the second party system. Scholars have explored the importance of families and kin groups in transmitting partisan loyalties; Whig discourse, along with women's own testimony, shows that women played a key role in the socialization of young voters. . . .

If evidence on antebellum women's partisanship serves both to deepen our un- derstanding of party politics and to suggest avenues for further inquiry, so, too, does it shed light on fundamental issues in women's history. Whig womanhood represents a distinct stage in the historical evolution of women's civic role. Linda K. Kerber's pathbreaking study has established that in the early republic, republican motherhood, the notion that women should serve the state by raising civic-minded sons, was the dominant theory of women's civic duty. Numerous studies have shown that in the first three decades of the antebellum period, republican motherhood was transformed into benevolent femininity—the idea that women had the duty to promote virtue not only within their families but also in the surrounding community by supporting benevolent enterprises.

Whig womanhood took the assumption of female moral superiority embedded in these existing concepts of female duty and adapted it to the realities of mass party politics. Women's moral virtue, their influence within the home, and their proven benevolence fitted them, the Whigs held, to play a distinct role in the new political order. They could exert a civilizing influence on partisan competition, even as they fostered partisan loyalties in their families and communities. Whigs wedded the doctrine of indirect influence to the notion of women's incorruptibility—women who assumed a public identity as Whigs did not, so the party asserted, lose their claim to special virtue.

Baker has rightly argued that the "cultural assignment of republican virtues and moral authority to womanhood helped men embrace partisanship" by relieving their anxieties about electoral competition; what she and others have failed to appreciate is the extent to which women themselves embraced partisanship in the antebellum era and were embraced by parties. . . .

trans. to Confederate womanhood

As the antebellum period drew to its explosive close, Whig womanhood was transmuted in Virginia into Confederate womanhood. Male and female secessionists argued that women should be Confederate partisans and should play a public role in promoting the cause of southern independence. Sectional identities had come to eclipse partisan affiliations. . . . In Virginia, and, I venture to suggest, in the South as a whole, the political mobilization of white women that began in 1840 culminated, not in the formation of a woman suffrage movement, but in active support of the Confederacy by most women and active support of the Union by some.

diverted from issue of suffrage

Women's Rights and the Politics of Church and State in Antebellum America

NANCY ISENBERG

In 1853 the editor of *Harper's Magazine* condemned "Woman's Rights—or the movement that goes by that name." No other movement was "so decidedly infidel," he claimed, opposed as it was to divine revelation, time-honored proprieties, and biblical authority. At stake was a fragile but socially vital alliance between church and state, because, the editor contended, the "Christian ecclesia" bound civil society together by preserving sexual differences. . . .

woman's place according to the church

The editor's charges did not go unanswered. In three sequential articles— "Harper's Editor and the Women"—published in the *Lily,* the first significant period- ical to herald the woman's movement, the New York lawyer and woman's rights supporter Anson Bingham challenged what he claimed was an absurd view of the Christian ecclesia. The term itself, like the dispute in which it figured, linked the political and religious realms. Originally, the Greek work *ekklēsia* referred to an assembly of free citizens of a town. The early Christians borrowed it to name their religious assemblies, suggesting that the church constituted a social order. By the nineteenth century, Protestants had grown comfortable with the idea that the church and state had similar ways to legitimate masculine authority in public forums. Bingham thus rejected the contention that by "divine appointment" man acquired "domination" as his "prerogative," while woman acquired a place of "subordina- tion." If married couples commingled in the temple of the home, then man and woman likewise could establish a "co-equality in all that concerns their common interests" in the *res foras* or the life of the forum. . . .

A similar debate had occurred in 1848, in a public exchange of letters, published in newspapers in Seneca Falls and Rochester, New York, between a clergyman and Elizabeth Cady Stanton and Elizabeth McClintock. The dispute had been sparked by the first woman's rights convention, held in July, in Seneca Falls, in which Stanton and McClintock had assumed prominent public roles. In the aftermath of the Seneca Falls convention and during a meeting in Rochester the following month, Stanton and McClintock felt obliged to defend their gatherings against the combined charges of religious and political infidelity made by religious opponents—particularly Protestant

Nancy Isenberg, "'Pillars in the Same Temple and Priests of the Same Worship': Woman's Rights and the Politics of Church and State in Antebellum America," *Journal of American History* 85 (June 1998): 98–122, 128. Reprinted by permission of the Organization of American Historians.

ministers. They responded to a vociferous attack from a Seneca Falls minister who asserted that the existing government was "established by God" and that woman's rights mocked both Christianity and democracy. McClintock and Stanton claimed that woman's rights were founded on a religious liberty that rejected "fetters that bind the spirit of woman." They also called for ministers to engage in open and public debate on woman's rights. . . .

. . . I argue that the church must be viewed as a political institution and that when scholarship treats religion as purely a moral activity, it obscures key historical developments. Religion involves not only moral values but also theories about caste hierarchy, ecclesiastical power, and disciplinary practices that define behavior and reinforce political ideologies. The debates between the *Harper's* editor and Bingham and between Stanton and McClintock and the local minister demonstrated that the church could not be reduced to a moral terrain separate and distinct from the *res foras* or the political sphere; on the contrary, the model of the church, or *ecclesia,* provided guidelines for gender relations appropriated by the state. An alliance between church and state, then, contributed significantly to cultural and legal perceptions of women's civil status. . . . Because nineteenth-century woman's rights advocates and their opponents used a political and legal vocabulary infused with religious meaning, modern distinctions between religious and private morality, on the one hand, and political and public representation, on the other, distort our understanding of how religion shaped gendered notions of constitutional and political rights. . . .

Antebellum woman's rights activists believed that the older tradition of *ecclesia,* which celebrated religious liberty, had suffered as a result of what Antoinette Brown in 1851 saw as an "unholy alliance" between church and state. Public opinion required open debate and discussion, gatherings among equals. In 1843 Lucretia Mott urged that the "partition walls of prejudice" that divided men and women into different castes be surmounted. The "Christian ecclesia" had to return to its primitive, New Testament model of being "called forth," which antebellum reformers translated to mean being "called out" of conventional society. At the heart of this notion of the church was dissent—a critical posture that led many woman's rights activists to leave their churches, to form new religious organizations, or in the case of prominent activists such as Mott, to act as vocal critics and provocateurs within their well-established religious institutions. . . .

Recognition of the strong connection between church and state reveals the need for a reexamination of two themes important in women's history—the separation of private and public and the feminization or domestication of religion. . . .

. . . Antebellum Americans conceived of public opinion and representation much as the adherents of classical and Enlightenment traditions did, highlighting speech as essential to defining a public gathering, equality as a forum of peers, and representation as based upon public appearance, presence, and the capacity to embody the views of the people. The same conceptions allowed politicians and constitutional interpreters to legitimize the restrictions placed on women's political and legal standing. As the New York jurist Elisha Hurlbut argued in his 1845 *Essays on Human Rights, and Their Political Guaranties,* women lacked the capacity for self-representation; women's exclusion from the polls was justified by the rule that women voted by proxy through male relatives. Similarly, although women had to

appear before the court and stand trial, women did not exercise the right to judge others, as in jury service. From the beginning of the nineteenth century, jurors were "representatives" of the people, and women's exclusion from the jury box demonstrated that they were not considered the "peers" of men. Jurors were peers and "centinels and guardians of each other," language that reinforced the gendered assumptions about jury duty by comparing it to military service (sentinels) and legal guardianship. Consent and dissent—exercised by those able to voice public opinions and to renounce political decisions as equals in the halls of government—were fundamental rights denied women. At best, women had the right to petition, a right they had even before the American Revolution, or to request a hearing in the legislature. Such limitations, Mott remarked in 1849, made woman nothing more than a "cypher" in the state. . . .

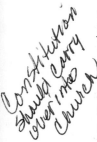

. . . [W]oman's rights activists eagerly and conscientiously applied the language of dissent to demand equal representation in both religious and political forums. In that language, two key terms of condemnation were *caste* and *sect.* Activists compared the clergy to "castes," groups whose authority came, not from current popular consent, but from inherited, vested privileges—especially the coveted monopoly over religious "truth" displayed through public speaking or preaching. Activists also challenged the existing church as a "sect," a narrow, exclusive, stultifying group. Their image of sect was revealed in the claim that the "ecclesiastical machinery" of most Protestant congregations had lost its public function as the embodiment of religious liberty and instead controlled the laity (and women, in particular) through rules, discipline, and creeds.

Woman's rights activists clearly believed that the antebellum debate over the Christian ecclesia was destined to shape representative democracy and American jurisprudence. Constitutional conventions and church secessions suggested that the 1840s were a time of political and ecclesiastical transformation. Activists argued that women's status as a "disabled caste" in the church or state constituted a violation of equal protection under the law, and they simultaneously promoted a revolutionary kind of public exchange between men and women that was premised on the ideal of "co-equal representation." By changing the public forum of the church, activists sought to enhance women's civil standing in government, thus reconstituting the meaning of representation for men and women in both religious and political assemblies.

Sacred Rights and Sectarian Wrongs

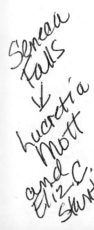

At the Seneca Falls convention on July 19–20, 1848, supporters gathered to discuss the "Social, Civil, and Religious condition of Woman." Most participants came from the town of Seneca Falls, New York, the neighboring village of Waterloo, and the nearby city of Rochester. Lucretia Mott, the only nationally known speaker at the meeting, acquired new notoriety as the "moving spirit of the occasion." The convention produced two major documents: a preamble and eleven resolutions, previously drafted and debated during the deliberations, and the Declaration of Sentiments, written a short time earlier by Elizabeth Cady Stanton, read and amended during the meeting.

Declar. of Sentiments ↓ Certain "fundamental rights"

In the Declaration of Sentiments, Stanton insisted that women should "have immediate admission to the rights and privileges which belong to them as citizens of the United States." Here Stanton imitated a strategy popular with antebellum legal reformers eager to revise state constitutions. They asserted that certain fundamental rights defined national citizenship and that states could not violate those basic inalienable rights. . . . In the Declaration of Sentiments Stanton also appealed to natural law, contending that women, contrary to their birthright, were "fraudulently deprived of their most scared rights." . . . [T]he burden of proof for women's exclusion from the rights and privileges of full citizenship now required a constitutional justification that explained this apparent disregard for the authority of natural law and the protection of women's "most sacred rights." . . .

Religion proved to be essential in helping women envision themselves as rights bearers, for the language of rights was closely intertwined with female activists' conception of religious liberty, accountability, and the exercise of conscience that, they believed, was necessary for forming public opinion. Consent had to be based on the "courthouse of conscience," as the members of the Worcester woman's rights convention were to proclaim in 1850, while dissent allowed women to demand the right to have rights, two exercises of liberty that antebellum woman's rights activists recognized as fundamental conditions for claiming and protecting sacred rights in the church and state. Conscience demanded respect for women's equality before God. . . .

Antebellum woman's rights advocates assumed that the church functioned as a bastion either of liberty or of censorship. The key issue was whether the church constituted a public forum. When ministers rewarded conformity and curbed public criticism and members kept silent for fear of reprisal, then . . . Christian liberty was sacrificed for church order and ecclesiastical rules were legitimated at the expense of the rights of the laity. As one reformer astutely noted in 1845, antebellum churches often sacrificed the life of the forum in the church to the ecclesiastical needs of the institution, especially when churches mobilized all their "ecclesiastical machinery" to make the "church itself into a state." To be a public forum, the church had to create an environment where members exercised consent and dissent, developing a critical perspective toward the abuses of state power. Absent such an environment, the greatest danger for the laity was spiritual paralysis or alienation, what McClintock and Stanton described as the "fetters that bind the spirit of woman."

"fetters that bind"

This kind of criticism of the church resonated among reformers. In 1848, Gerrit Smith gave voice to what many antebellum dissenters believed, namely, that most churches or religious societies had been reduced to "the soul-shrivelling enclosures of a sect." The term "sect" and the political and denominational development identified as "sectarianism" reflected an intellectually and emotionally charged understanding concerning church-state relations. Having adapted the eighteenth century's contempt for political factionalism, critics were newly claiming that sectarianism resulted in the corruption of the public sphere through self-interested competition. The ambitious efforts of Protestant denominations for building the "evangelical empire" and factional struggles within churches over policy and creeds indicated to dissenters a dangerous climate. A vast expanse of sects vied for members, institutional power, and public influence. Sectarian churches were portrayed by dissenters as exclusive enclaves, preoccupied with theological squabbles and petty rivalries, that carefully circumscribed members within their "respective circles of theology." Antebellum dissenters gave sectarianism a modern meaning when they focused on the control of information and the closing of the American mind. . . .

The public nature of the church had a direct bearing on women's capacity for political action. Lucretia Mott echoed Smith's allusion when she described the "sectarian enclosure on woman's mind." Activists believed that sectarianism constrained women's knowledge, undermining and "dwarfing" women's mental capabilities by preempting their ability to make independent decisions. . . .

For antebellum dissenters, the solution to sectarianism was what they called a "free church" or "people-church." As in the Congregational Friends or the Religious Union of Associationists, membership was open to anyone in the community, and the goal was to attract men and women from a wide range of religious faiths to discuss moral and political questions. . . . These radical new assemblies all experimented with a more democratic church polity and blended the constitutional fiction of popular sovereignty or rule by the people with their notion of a religious public forum. . . .

Woman's rights advocates believed that the conception of a church as a "simple democracy" raised the question of whether women had an equal place in such assemblies. As Elizabeth Wilson, an orthodox Presbyterian turned dissenter and woman's rights supporter, asked in her comprehensive study, *A Scriptural View of Woman's Rights and Duties* (1849): "If women were collected together to hear the word of God, would they constitute a church?" Wilson's query went to the heart of the issue. Could women as "two or three gathered together" constitute a public assembly for worship?

The answer was "no" for most denominations because incorporation required that trustees and elders possess the legal status of property holders. . . . Wilson had her own explanation for the absence of all-woman churches. A church as a public body required the presence of men, which Wilson sardonically acknowledged. She wrote that for a typical congregation, the ideal church required a "fine" meetinghouse and a male minister in the pulpit addressing a "large assembly of people ornamented with *beards*." . . .

. . . Distinction and presence presupposed the marks of masculinity—the shared ornament of beards—which for Wilson connoted adulthood, civil standing, and, of course, manhood. The beard distinguished men from women; it also placed women in the same category as young male children incapable of self-representation, who had not yet achieved independence and public standing. In political parlance, women and children shared their status as dependents, which was why fathers and husbands represented their interests at the polls. Presence thus equated physical appearance with the capacity for representation and the symbolic marks of masculinity.

Antebellum activists saw that standing in the church and state was derived from the relationship forged between public appearance and investiture, in which the masculine coding of presence clothed men with certain rights and privileges. Women could not constitute a public assembly for worship, because, as Wilson implied, they lacked presence—the vested symbols of social and public power. Women also lacked the presence to stand in the place of another, particularly as the proxy for men. For antebellum Americans, the right of public representation meant the capacity to act as a peer of, and proxy for, the people. And as woman's rights advocates understood only too well, in the words of Abby Price, women were doomed to "stand without a temple," as long as they lacked the right of "co-equal representation."

Co-equality and Castes

In 1850, woman's rights activists decided to turn their convention at Salem, Ohio, into public theater by closing their proceedings to men. As a powerful symbolic gesture, the men were asked to retreat to the gallery, forced to watch the deliberations voicelessly. For the first time, women constituted the public assembly, debating and discussing resolutions, while the men were denied the right of public standing, assuming women's traditional role as silent spectators.

That year activists highlighted the theme of co-equality during the Salem and Worcester conventions, calling for women's "co-sovereignty" and shared administration in the church and state. Abby Price cleverly used the word "co-equal" to redefine the "self-evident" phrase—*"life, liberty, and the pursuit of happiness"*—from the Declaration of Independence, and she, like Wilson and Mott, offered poignant biblical interpretations using the creation story as a metaphor for the first covenant and social contract. Price, Wilson, and Mott all rejected the traditional biblical prescription of the ordained subordination of woman as the helpmeet of man, instead arguing that man and woman were created simultaneously as "co-equals." As Mott explained in her "Discourse on Woman," read at the Salem convention: "In the beginning, man and woman were created equal. 'Male and female created he them, and blessed them, and called their name Adam.' He gave dominion to both over the lower animals, but not to one over the other." By rewriting the social contract, woman's rights advocates did far more than argue for individual rights. Through co-equality, they carved a theoretical space for women within the imaginary script of the "original contract" in the state of nature, and they challenged the vested superiority of man—as the "first" and privileged creation of God—over all creatures, including woman. . . .

Co-equality was a counterpoint to what Paulina Wright Davis described as women's current political and legal status as a "disabled caste." In her presidential address at the 1850 national woman's rights convention held in Worcester, Davis called for the "emancipation of a class," predicated on the constitutional principle of equal protection and due process of the law. A year earlier she had observed that the sexual double standard flouted the principle of equality under the law. She had reason for concern. In 1849, Chief Justice Lemuel Shaw of Massachusetts reinforced the idea of unequal vested rights, ruling in *Roberts v. City of Boston* that men and women were not "legally clothed with the same civil and political powers." Shaw reaffirmed the argument that women and children were subject to "paternal consideration" but not vested with the same rights as adult men. He assumed that the courts acted as a surrogate father or guardian for legal dependents, an approach that mirrored the standard approach to female representation—proxy. As Davis understood, women's status as a "disabled caste" sealed their political disenfranchisement. The state divested women of political rights such as suffrage, because government had a prior obligation to protect the vote as a vested right of men.

Arguments about vested rights, the sexual order of creation, and public presence introduced by woman's rights activists contributed to the antebellum controversy over women's right to represent themselves in the church and the state. As activists realized, establishing a public presence was difficult for women, because distinction implied literally and figuratively commanding respect and the attention of a public audience. Drawing on an eighteenth-century critique of fashionable or aristocratic women, antebellum critics associated public women with "spectacles," that is, false women who treated the public domain as a stage, wore disguises, and, like actresses, recited lines rather than voicing their actual opinions. Women who commanded an audience inverted the order of creation, daring to preach or teach to men, as one minister argued at the New York woman's rights convention in 1853. By demanding "awe and reverence" from male spectators, women appeared "unnatural," and they were accused of imitating men, or arrogantly asserting their independence from the supervision of male guardians, husbands, or ministers. . . .

. . . In the 1850s, "female politicians" and woman's rights activists were commonly lampooned in the newspapers either for stealing the breeches from duped husbands or pirating the petticoats of unsuspecting wives. Such images satirized apolitical men and public women as cross-dressing freaks and social misfits. The "battle for the pants" continued a much older motif of sexual inversion that had its origins during the Protestant Reformation in Germany. The power of its message persisted in attacks against those women seeking equality in "Christian, public, religious assemblies," as Elizabeth Wilson noted, who were labeled women "putting on the pantaloons." The fear of sexual confusion mimicked the more subtle reasoning used to restrict women's constitutional equality. Indeed, vested rights depended on political dress, and the idea of women "putting on the pants" indicated their unnatural attempts to usurp the civic power of male citizens.

Such charges surfaced in the *Harper's* editorial of 1853. The woman's rights movement was ridiculed for its "hybrid conventions," and the editor accused women of hiding behind their "Quaker bonnets." One particular bonnet—that of Lucretia Mott—probably inspired this angry harangue. During the previous decade, Mott had emerged as a highly visible public woman by traveling thousands of miles, attending hundreds of meetings, and speaking before large and small crowds on such topics as woman's rights, antislavery, sectarianism, peace reform, and land monopoly. She was considered the "principal speaker" at the Seneca Falls convention in 1848, and Mott either presided or gave keynote addresses at later conventions. . . .

To satisfy woman's rights advocates, the church had to eliminate all caste privileges, particularly the exclusive monopoly that men had over clerical offices, which elevated public speaking as the preeminent symbol of their vested authority. . . . Accordingly, the most telling sign of priestcraft for Mott was the "appropriation of the pulpit by one sex." Apostolic authority offered the most telling source of women's exclusion from teaching and preaching, borne in the biblical verse dictating that women remain silent in church and ask their husbands for instruction. Elizabeth Wilson summed up this credo by noting that ministers called for "woman always to be a learner" and "novice." Sarah Owen made a similar comment at the 1848 Rochester woman's rights convention, sarcastically remarking that priests and husbands shared the same faith that a woman's opinion must always echo their own.

Co-equality, then, required that the church create a public forum that vested men and women equally with the right to preach, that both encompassed and represented the opinions of the congregation. Dissenters promoted this idealized forum, encouraging a deliberative meeting of "so many different minds," where the public mind "presents itself without waiting to be re-presented." In this environment one was neither ruler nor ruled, men were not masters and women were certainly not novices, because there were "fewer orators, but more speakers; fewer speeches, but more talk; less spoken, but more said." By engaging in what Abby Price described as "an intercourse purified by a forgetfulness of sex," women and men could now recognize each other as co-equal sources of the truth. Indeed, men and women could view each other as two corresponding parts of the whole, each contributing a partial understanding of the truth. . . .

Antebellum feminists had seen the contradiction between abstract rights and the dominant political discourse that defined representation as a masculine enterprise. Gender was never peripheral to the meaning of representation; it was vital in explaining the masculine marks of presence and speech that remained crucial to a nineteenth-century understanding of the public forum. It was the "fetters of the law, both sacred and secular," as Antoinette Brown claimed, that had placed a "thorny crown" on the brow and a "leaden scepter" in the hands of woman. To untangle this unholy alliance between church and state, women had to be welcomed onto the same public platform as men and vested with the right of co-equal representation. As the president of the West Chester woman's rights convention, Mary Ann Johnson, declared in 1852, only then would the day arrive when "woman and her brother are pillars in the same temple and priests of the same worship."

F U R T H E R   R E A D I N G

Boydston, Jeanne, et al. *The Limits of Sisterhood: The Beecher Sisters on Women's Rights and Woman's Sphere* (1988).

Bunker, Gary. "Antebellum Caricature and Woman's Sphere," *Journal of Women's History* 5, no. 3 (1992): 6–43.

DuBois, Ellen C. *Feminism and Suffrage: The Emergence of an Independent Women's Movement in America, 1848–1869* (1978).

Epstein, Barbara. *The Politics of Domesticity: Women, Evangelism, and Temperance in Nineteenth-Century America* (1980).

Ginzberg, Lori. *Women and the Work of Benevolence: Morality, Politics, and Class in the Nineteenth-Century United States* (1990).

Hewitt, Nancy. *Women's Activism and Social Change: Rochester, New York, 1822–1872* (1984).

Hoffert, Sylvia. *When Hens Crow: The Women's Rights Movement in Antebellum America* (1995).

Kelley, Mary. *Private Woman, Public Stage: Literary Domesticity in Nineteenth-Century America* (1984).

Kellow, Margaret. "'For the Sake of Suffering Kansas': Lydia Maria Child, Gender, and Politics of the 1850's," *Journal of Women's History* 5, no. 2 (1993): 32–49.

Matthews, Jean V. *Women's Struggle for Equality: The First Phase, 1828–1878* (1997).

Munson, Elizabeth, and Greg Dickinson. "Hearing Women Speak: Antoinette Brown Blackwell and the Dilemma of Authority," *Journal of Women's History* 10, no. 1 (1998): 108–126.

Smith-Rosenberg, Carroll. *Disorderly Conduct: Visions of Gender in Victorian America* (1985).

Zboray, Ronald, and Mary Zboray. "Whig Women, Politics, and Culture in the Campaign of 1840: Three Perspectives from Massachusetts," *Journal of the Early Republic* 17 (1997): 277–315.

CHAPTER
6

Women and Slavery

Historians once wrote about slavery as though only men were involved in perpetuating as well as challenging that inhumane system. White men, after all, owned the vast majority of slaves (because of married women's dependent legal status); most prominent opponents of slavery, black and white, appeared to be men; and men debated in state and national legislatures about maintaining or abolishing the legal structures that sustained this system of perpetual bondage. Moreover, the study of slaves themselves focused on men—their work, their day-to-day resistance, their leadership of rebellions. Even slave families were examined primarily from a male perspective; historians, for example, concerned themselves with such issues as whether men were able to exert paternal or husbandly authority over their wives and children in the absence of legal marriage and in light of masters' ability to intrude on black family lives in various ways (such as separating or selling family members).

All that has now changed dramatically, for women's historians have started to investigate the many facets of women's involvement in the slave system. Many new questions have come to the fore. How common was the sexual abuse of female slaves by masters or their sons? How did enslaved women subsist within the slave community and their own families? What did plantation mistresses think about their slaves, male and female, and did they act to perpetuate or to subvert the system? What roles did women, black and white, play in the abolitionist movement, and did their gender have a significant effect on those roles? The documents and essays in this chapter address some of these important inquiries.

DOCUMENTS

The documents in this chapter reveal some of the complex ways in which American women experienced and interacted with the slave system. In the early 1830s, a Philadelphia shopkeeper, Lydia White, decided to oppose slavery by refusing to sell textiles made from slave-grown cotton (Document 1). About the same time, in Document 2, a teenaged New Englander vigorously called on other females to join the antislavery movement. In 1858, the freeborn black Frances Ellen Watkins (later Harper) published an emotional poem attacking slavery (Document 3). Document 4, a brief extract from the diary of Ella Gertrude Clanton Thomas written that same year, offers one plantation mistress's opinion on the subject of slave masters' sexual liaisons with their female chattel. The Female Publication Society of Philadelphia, an organization of black women, in 1861 wrote Document 5 to explain their decision to contribute to the support of racially uplifting publications. Finally, Document 6, the oral history of a rape preserved in the memory of one African American family for more than a century, was recounted in the 1956 autobiography of Pauli Murray, a prominent leader of the twentieth-century women's rights movement.

1. Lydia White, a Philadelphia Shopkeeper, Refuses to Carry the Products of Slave Labor in Her Dry Goods Store, 1831

Free Cotton

Among the females who are interesting themselves in behalf of the poor slaves, Lydia White of Philadelphia, a member of the Society of Friends, deserves high commendation. She has been very zealous in procuring the manufacture of domestic goods from cotton raised by free labor, and during the past year has kept a Free Dry Goods Store at No. 86, North Fifth-street. Those who wish to examine patterns of her goods are requested to call at this office. We have lately received a letter from her, from which we take the following extracts:

> I am glad to hear that the people of Boston and New-Hampshire are becoming uneasy with using the produce of slave labor, which I have long had to view as the main staple of slavery. Much do I regret that we have not a full supply and a better assortment of domestic cotton goods manufactured of the material which is cultivated by free labor; for I believe if this was the case, and stores were opened in different sections of the Union by conscientious persons, whose concern would be more to promote justice and accommodate the necessary wants of their fellow creatures, than to accumulate wealth for themselves, they would have a tendency to greatly increase the demand for the produce of remunerated labor.
>
> I think I may safely say, that the concern to bear a testimony against African slavery by abstinence is gaining and spreading far and wide over our country. Orders are repeatedly sent to me for free goods from different parts of several States, viz. Vermont, Rhode-Island, New-York, Ohio, Indiana, Delaware, and I think Maryland and Virginia; and frequently new customers call on me for the same from Pennsylvania and New-Jersey.
>
> Two days since, I purchased a small lot of free Cotton from North Carolina, which I shall endeavor to have manufactured to the best attainable advantage, in quality, variety and price. I am increasingly desirous to do what I can in this way, to encourage the conscientious in abstinence from the products of the slaves' labor: to me it seems very important for us (the advocates of liberty and justice) to be steadfast in this particular.
>
> When I meditate on the subject, the query arises, what avails the abundant profession of religion which is made in this day, if it do not lead us practically to bear testimony against this greatest of evils, cruelly oppressing and degrading our fellow-creatures? Surely the truth leads out of all this.

The Liberator, May 28, 1831.

2. "A. F. M.," a Young Rhode Island Girl, Exhorts "the Daughters of New England" to Oppose Slavery, 1832

The writer of the following Appeal is a young lady only 13 years old, residing in North Providence. In intelligence and philanthropy, she is in advance of a large number of her sex.

For the Liberator.

An Address to the Daughters of New-England

Awake, ye multitude, that have slumbered so long! Awake! in behalf of the injured children of Africa. And think not because ye are women, that ye can take no part in the glorious cause of emancipation. You have influence—exert it. Arm your fathers and brothers with the patriotic feelings of liberty and equal rights. Although the inhabitants of New-England are an exception in the vast multitude denominated slaveholders, shut not your hearts against the cries of the oppressed, which go up from the sister states. Woman's voice, though weak, may be heard; for it is hers, in a peculiar manner, to plead the cause of suffering innocence. And let not posterity have cause to say that you remained inactive, while two millions of your fellow mortals were oppressed with the yoke of bondage. Your land is the boasted land of liberty! But how much like vain mockery must this name appear to other nations! and what a discord does it make with those tones of the oppressed, which rise in condemnation from the centre of the nation! Had that Congress which declared the independence and freedom of these United States, allowed it to have its influence over all, as it should have done, it would have presented a brighter era in the chronicles of liberty than has ever been presented to the world, or probably ever will be. Your land is the one that makes the greatest pretensions to freedom, and yet holds slaves in as much degradation as any spot on earth. In many cases, it is not only the body is enslaved, but the *mind* is also held in chains; to be riven only by death when it shall leave its frail tenement of suffering, and soar to those regions where it is destined to rove in freedom. Let not the ignorance of the blacks plead as an excuse for continuing them in servitude; for is not their being so, entirely the fault of the whites? Was not Egypt the birth-place of the arts and sciences? and did she not long remain the proud mistress of knowledge, and long wield the sceptre of literature? And now that Egypt has fallen, and nought remains of her glory but what is recorded in the pages of history, or what meets the eye of the traveller, in his wanderings amid the wreck of grandeur which he finds every where in this once flourishing country; let us not forget that it is a country in Africa, that degraded Africa, whose sons and daughters are bought and sold and enslaved! And the soil of Africa covers the remains of many a noble patriarch, whose heart may have glowed with the generous feelings of freedom, and the archives of whose nation hold up as possessing intellects equal, if not superior to many who now flourish in

The Liberator, March 3, 1832.

our own country, as the supporters of slavery. Daughters of Columbia! ye that live in the far-famed land of Liberty! ye that have so often heard it extolled as the seat of independence and freedom! arise, throw off the veil which now obscures your reason, and let your names be enrolled as the defenders of liberty.

A. F. M.

[handwritten: born free — lives in N.]

3. Frances Ellen Watkins (Harper), a Freeborn Black Poet, Pleads, "Bury Me in a Free Land," 1858

You may make my grave wherever you will,
In a lowly vale or a lofty hill;
You may make it among earth's humblest graves,
But not in a land where men are slaves.

I could not sleep if around my grave
I heard the steps of a trembling slave;
His shadow above my silent tomb
Would make it a place of fearful gloom.

I could not rest if I heard the tread
Of a coffle-gang to the shambles led,
And the mother's shriek of wild despair
Rise like a curse on the trembling air.

I could not rest if I heard the lash
Drinking her blood at each fearful gash,
And I saw her babes torn from her breast
Like trembling doves from their parent nest.

I'd shudder and start, if I heard the bay
Of the bloodhounds seizing their human prey;
If I heard the captive plead in vain
As they tightened afresh his galling chain.

[handwritten left margin: forced to stand naked / slavery / notified to / notified / women]

If I saw young girls, from their mothers' arms
Bartered and sold for their youthful charms
My eye would flash with a mournful flame,
My death-paled cheek grow red with shame.

[handwritten right margin: rape to propagate the slave population]

I would sleep, dear friends, where bloated might
Can rob no man of his dearest right;
My rest shall be calm in any grave,
Where none calls his brother a slave.

Anti-Slavery Bugle, November 20, 1858. This document can also be found in Peter Ripley, ed., *The Black Abolitionist Papers* (Chapel Hill: University of North Carolina Press, 1985–1992), 4:403, 405.

> I ask no monument proud and high
> To arrest the gaze of passers by;
> All that my spirit yearning craves,
> Is—bury me not in the land of slaves.

4. Ella Gertrude Clanton Thomas, a Plantation Mistress, Discusses Interracial Sexual Relationships, 1858

I know that this is a view of the subject that it is thought best for women to ignore but when we see so many cases of mulattoes commanding higher prices, advertised as "Fancy girls," oh is it not enough to make us shudder for the standard of moral-ity in our Southern homes? A most striking illustration of general feeling on the subject is to be found in the case of George Eve, who carried on with him a woman to the North under the name of wife—She was a mulatto slave, and although it was well known that he lived constantly with her violating one of God's ten command-ments, yet nothing was thought of it. There was no one without sin "to cast the first stone at him," but when *public opinion* was outraged by the report that the ceremony of marriage had been passed between them—then his father was terribly mortified and has since attempted to prove that he is a lunatic—with what success I do not know. He preferred having him living in a constant state of sin   to having him pass the boundary of Caste. I can well understand his horror of that kind of marriage. I can appreciate his feeling perfect antipathy to having negro blood mingle in the veins of his descendants but I cannot understand his feeling of indifference to having that same blood flowing through the veins of a race of descendants held in perpetual slavery—perhaps by other men—

I once heard Susan (Ma's nurse) speaking of her reported father in a most con-temptuous manner. Laughingly I said to her, "Why Susan, was not he your father?" "What if he was," she said. "I don't care anything for him and he don't for me. If he had, he would have bought me when I was sold. Instead of that he was the auc-tioner when I was sold for 75 dollars." She was sold for debt, separated from her mother and has lived in the yard ever since she was three years old. What a moral! It speaks for itself— And these "white children of slavery" as Miss Bremer calls them lower the tone of the South. They are not to blame. Oh No! They know no in-centive for doing well and often if they wished they could not. The happiness of homes are destroyed but what is to be done— There is an inborn earnestness in woman's nature to teach her to do right, but this is a mystery I find I cannot solve— Southern women are I believe all at heart abolitionists but there I expect I have made a very broad assertion but I *will stand* to the opinion that the institution of slavery degrades the white man more than the Negro and oh exerts a most deleterious effect upon our children.

[handwritten marginalia: degrades white man more than the negro ??.]

Virginia I. Burr, ed., *The Secret Eye: The Journal of Ella Gertrude Clanton Thomas* (Chapel Hill: University of North Carolina Press, 1990), 168–169.

5. Mary Still, a Prominent Black Abolitionist, and Other Free Women in Philadelphia Form the "Female Publication Society" to Promote the Moral Uplift of Free and Enslaved African Americans, 1861

Rev Elisha Weaver, Editor of the *Christian Recorder:*

Dear Brother:—The members of the Female Union Publication Society present to you a small donation ($20) to aid you in keeping the *Christian Recorder* in circulation. This we do with no ordinary degree of pleasure, as we are quite sure the high moral sentiments which it takes will prove an effectual means to the improvement and elevation of our people. There are thousands, this moment, of our helpless race, who are perishing from the want of moral and religious culture. The press has ever proved a powerful and an efficient means in producing a moral and religious element in a community. We therefore feel bound, as a society, to do all that we can to sustain you in your present position. The means which you have to work with are but limited, and your labor arduous, but your cause is most noble. Every week's issue may be regarded as so many sparks flying through the atmosphere, that will inevitably kindle ere long to a flame, and then our moral horizon will be lighted up with the glorious effects of its refulgent rays. Never was there a time in the history of our race, that required a more uncompromising and indefatigable effort to promote general literature than the present. A time when we, as an oppressed people, should rally to the standard, and concentrate an influence that will prove more than equivalent to the present state of ignorance, darkness, and spiritual wickedness. Come, friends of our common cause, let us be up and doing. These, truly, are perilous times, and they call for a concert of action. And then, there are four millions and a half of our countrymen who groan in abject slavery; they, too, call upon our sympathies. Humanity in general calls upon us. And He who holds the destiny of nations in his hand, is calling upon us. The issue of this political struggle, will decide an important question in our favor. The issue will clearly demonstrate the startling fact, that the people of color are to become citizens of these United States, and that the fields which they have reaped down without wages, will yet become the habitations for them and their children. It must be so. We can see it no other way. Then the thumb screw, stock, and lash shall be felt and feared no more. But over them will wave majestically the banner of peace, liberty, and equal rights. The propriety of religious and moral publications was considered by many of us a matter of great importance. It was our earnest conviction, that an effort like the present would help to sustain the object. We then called a meeting of our female friends, to take into consideration the propriety of forming a society, whose object should be to promote moral and religious publications, under the guidance and direction of the General Conference of the A. M. E. Church. It was thought best to form a society. It is now in existence, and bears the name of the Female Union Publication Society of Philadelphia. Its object is as above stated. Having all things in readiness, we laid it before our church, hoping to meet with their hearty co-operation. But like many other good efforts, it

---

The Christian Recorder, May 11, 1861. This document can also be found in *Black Abolitionist Papers,* microfilm, reel 13, frame 526.

was sadly repulsed by the cold indifference manifested by the major part of the members. But, nothing daunted, we persevered, by asking the guidance of our Heavenly Father, who has promised to give wisdom to those who ask him and then patiently wait his answer. Our prayers have been graciously answered; and to-day finds that noble little band vigorously engaged in the dissemination of religion, morality, literature, and science. We humbly invite all who are friendly to this noble enterprise, to join with us.

MARY STILL,
On behalf of the Female Publication Society

6. Pauli Murray Recounts the Rape of her Enslaved Great-Grandmother in 1844

"Child, you listen to your grandmother," she told me. "Hold your head high and don't take a back seat to nobody. You got good blood in you—folks that counted for something—doctors, lawyers, judges, legislators. Aristocrats, that's what they were, going back seven generations right in this state." . . .

Years later when I looked up the records I found Grandmother's family history to be remarkably accurate. But there was one haunting story she told me about the Smiths and Great-grandmother Harriet which did not appear in the records. I don't think she realized it but she repeated this story again and again with such passionate single-mindedness it was like the recounting of a long-buried wrong which had refused to die and which she expected me to right somehow. . . . When Grandmother spoke of Great-Grandmother Harriet her face saddened and she shook her head sorrowfully. . . . After a long while she would say, "My mother was a good woman and did the best she could, but she couldn't help herself." . . .

Grandmother referred to the three Smiths of her story as "Miss Mary Ruffin," "Dr. Frank," and "my father, Lawyer Sidney Smith." They belonged to a leading Orange County family which lived first in Hillsboro and later near Chapel Hill. . . . Folks thought it was a shame that none of the three Smiths married, considering their talents and the fine family they came from. . . . Of course some folks said that Harriet was at the bottom of all the trouble, as if she were to blame, although she was the one person who never had any choice at all. Folks claimed that if she just hadn't come to the Smith home, Frank and Sid might have settled down to solid respectable married lives. Nobody would have condemned them too harshly for doing what many southern men of high standing had done—bred two lines of children simultaneously and on the same place, one by their lawful white wives and the other by a slave concubine. . . .

It was to Dr. James Smith's credit that he had kept free of this sort of thing. Until he bought Harriet [in 1834] the slaves he owned were listed as Blacks and there were no mulatto children on his place. . . . Even then Harriet was known to be one of the most beautiful girls in the county, white or black. She was small and shapely, had richly colored skin like the warm inner bark of a white birch, delicate

Pauli Murray, *Proud Shoes: The Story of an American Family* (New York: Harper, 1956), 33–44.

[handwritten marginalia: "Queeth white" "plantation became chapel hill"]

features, flashing dark eyes and luxuriant wavy black hair which fell below her knees. She was shy and reticent but her eyes talked. I never knew whether she had any Negro blood. Grandmother always said she was three-fourths white and one-fourth Cherokee Indian. . . .

Harriet was around twenty when she expressed the desire to marry young Reuben Day, a free-born mulatto who lived and worked around Hillsboro. Dr. Smith readily gave his permission. . . . It was good business. He had no obligation to the husband, and every child by the marriage would be his slave and worth several hundred dollars at birth. . . . Reuben and Harriet could not even live together. They had to share brief visits in a little cabin on the Smith lot when Reuben was given permission to see her. When their son Julius was born around 1842, he was a Smith slave like his mother. . . .

That was the way things stood when Francis and Sid came home from school and began practicing their professions around Hillsboro. They had not seen much of Harriet during their school days, but now they found a mature woman just a little younger than themselves and good to look at. Each had the same thought when he saw her and each read the look in the other's eyes. . . .

Before long everybody in the house knew that a storm was brewing between the brothers and that Harriet was the cause of it. Francis watched her furtively from a distance, but Sidney was open with it. From the moment he returned home he could not leave her alone. . . .

. . . Harriet felt like a hunted creature. When Sidney wasn't following her around, Francis' eyes were on her with an unmistakable look in them. Each brother was biding his time. She grew thin and haggard and Miss Mary frequently caught her weeping. Miss Mary was nobody's fool. She had watched her brothers and seen what was coming. Her mother was a meek, delicate little woman who had never taken a strong hand in her sons' affairs and only wrung her hands about it. She spoke to her father, but Dr. Smith seemed strangely unconcerned. He said the boys had to sow a few wild oats and they'd get over it. . . .

. . . The brothers beat Reuben with the butt end of a carriage whip and when they finally let him go they told him if he ever came back on the Smith lot they'd shoot him on sight. He disappeared from the county and nothing was heard of him again. . . .

. . . It happened right after Reuben was run off the place. Harriet had nailed up the door as usual and put barricades against it. Later that night, after everyone had gone to bed, the other slaves heard Marse Sid break open Harriet's door. Ear-splitting shrieks tore the night, although he stuffed rags in the door and window cracks to muffle Harriet's cries. They heard little Julius screaming and Harriet's violent struggle before Sidney had his way with her. Nobody interfered, of course.

That was only the beginning. After that first night, Harriet went into fits of hysterical screaming whenever Sidney came near her. The more she reviled him the better he seemed to like it. He raped her again and again in the weeks that followed. Night after night he would force open her cabin door and nail it up again on the inside so that she could not get out. Then he would beat her into submission. She would cry out sharply, moan like a wounded animal and beg for mercy. The other slaves, hearing her cries, trembled in their beds and prayed silently for her deliverance.

It came one night when Francis laid for Sidney and caught him just as he was coming out of Harriet's cabin. The brothers had it out once and for all, and there was a terrible fight. Early the next morning one of the slaves found Marse Sid lying unconscious in the yard, his clothes soaked with blood and an ugly hole in his head. He got over it but it was a long time before he was up and about again. The Smiths never talked about what happened that night; they hushed it up and told some cock-and-bull story about Marse Sid falling off his horse. The slaves knew, however, that Marse Frank had carried out his threat.

Sidney was only twenty-four at the time and had a bright political future ahead of him, but he was never quite the same after that beating. He took to drinking and brooded his life away. He went down to Raleigh for one term in the legislature and there were flashes of brilliant success here and there when he was sober, but in the end he turned out to be one of the worst drunkards in the county.

He learned his lesson. He never touched Harriet again after that night. She was at last free to come and go unmolested, but for months afterward there was a wild look in her eyes as she carried Sidney's child and she went about with a silent smoldering hatred against him to the end of her days.

" *grandmother* "

◈ E S S A Y S

Catherine Clinton, an independent scholar, briefly examines the important question of sexual relationships within the plantation household, investigating the incidence of sexual abuse of female slaves and the responses of plantation mistresses to their husbands' and sons' sexual misdeeds. Her essay, she would be the first to admit, is suggestive rather than definitive, but it raises numerous issues that students and scholars should consider. The University of Washington's Shirley J. Yee studies the small group of freeborn black women who became prominent promoters of abolition through their public lectures and writings. What points did they stress, and what special hurdles did they have to surmount because they were both black and female? she asks. Julie Roy Jeffrey, a professor at Goucher College, looks at "ordinary" women who supported abolition. Who were these unknown women who enlisted in such a radical cause? she seeks to learn. Jeffrey reads the letters and diaries of hundreds of women in her attempt to find out.

Sexuality in Black and White

CATHERINE CLINTON

The various strands of intimacies and blood which wove together black and white in the Old South created a tangle of issues that is enormously difficult to unravel. Even the passage of time does not give us enough distance from these explosive topics. Nevertheless, it is essential for our understanding of women's lives and especially for exploring sexuality in the Old South that we address these important topics.

Many complexities and myriad contradictions were apparent at the time. A survey of antebellum southern travel literature reveals references to relationships

---

Catherine Clinton, "Caught in the Web of the Big House: Women and Slavery," in Walter Fraser et al., eds., *The Web of Southern Social Relations: Women, Family, and Education* (Athens: University of Georgia Press, 1985), 19–34. Copyright © 1985 by the University of Georgia Press. Reprinted by permission.

between masters and their female slaves. Not only did observers mention these illicit liaisons, but several commented on the hypocrisy such connections reveal. Fanny Kemble, the famed English actress, who married a wealthy Georgia slave-owner, provides sharp commentary about her months on her husband's sea island plantation:

> Nobody pretends to deny that, throughout the South, a large proportion of the population is the offspring of white men and colored women. . . . Mr——(and many others) speaks as if there were a natural repugnance in all whites to any alliance with the black race; and yet it is notorious, that almost every Southern planter has a family more or less numerous of illegitimate colored children. . . . If we are to admit the theory that the mixing of the races is a monstrosity, it seems almost as curious that laws should be enacted to prevent men marrying women toward whom they have an invincible natural repugnance.

Kemble criticizes southerners who make racist claims about the inferiority and repulsiveness of blacks, observing tartly that despite owners' complaints that their slaves were foul-smelling, many still managed to share the beds of female chattel. She does not imagine slaves would smell any worse if they were freed. Kemble, like other British critics of slavery, harps on the theme of hypocrisy.

Members of the southern planter class who recorded their critiques of slavery did not often attack the immorality of owners. Most bemoaned the immorality of slaves. The few who acknowledged that male planters could and did fall from grace treat the matter casually, offering a variety of lame excuses ranging from black female promiscuity to protection of white women from sexual licentiousness. . . .

Sexual abuse manifested itself in various ways. "Slave breeding" was an indignity of which many slaves complained. Slaves bitterly resented masters' attempt to control mating by matching up couples. In addition to manipulating pair bonding, some masters might rent or borrow men for stud service, subjecting their female slaves to forced breeding or rape. These inseminators appear in the slave narratives in the guise of "stockmen," "travelin' niggers," or "breedin' niggers." Casual references and the slang terms used to describe these men give credence to the commonality of such practices. One former slave recalled that stockmen were "weighed and tested." On the other extreme, a former slave recalled castrations and that "runty niggers" were operated on like hogs, "so dat dey can't have no little runty chilluns." Although Paul Escott, discussing his research on the slave narratives, warns that evidence of such incidents was rare, he argues that "mere numbers cannot suggest the suffering and degradation they caused, and it is likely that reticence caused some underreporting."

Masters attempted to control reproduction in other ways. Slave women were expected to bear children as frequently as possible. If they failed to give birth, they might be sold. Barren women were shunned by their communities and punished by their owners. All of these factors impaired slave sexuality and crippled the stability of traditional family structure.

Evidence from both blacks and whites indicates that forced interracial sex was more common than slave breeding. Blacks often were coaxed before they would reveal sexual exploitation. One exchange with a former slave from Alabama reflects this syndrome: "'Granny,' I said, 'did your master harm you in another way?' She did not understand at once, then as she gained my meaning, she leaned over and answered, 'did you see dat girl in de house below here? Dat's my chile by him. I had five, but dat de only one livin' now. I didn't want him, but I couldn't do nothin'. I uster say 'What do yer want of a woman all cut ter pieces like I is?' But 'twant no use.'"

It is also important to note that blacks were reluctant to discuss such matters, especially with racial and sexual factors inhibiting responses. In fact, evidence from the appendixes of Escott's survey of the WPA interviews indicates that the sex and race of the interviewer influenced the frequency of former slaves' revelations concerning interracial sex. For example, more than 13 percent of the WPA interviewees confessed to having a white father when interviewed by a black female, although only 5.3 percent of those interviewed by white males responded yes to the question and only 4.4 percent of those questioned by a white woman. Concerning queries about forced sex, these ratios are even more dramatic: white female interviewers reported that only 6.1 percent of their respondents claimed slaves were sexually exploited and only 8.6 percent of those interviewed by white males. But 13 percent of those questioned by 65 black male interviewers reported forced sex and 18 percent of the former slaves interviewed by black females. If we assume that former slaves were more honest with interviewers of their own race—and indeed black women might have been more comfortable to reveal such practices to a woman than to a man—we might conclude that forced sex was a problem on roughly one out of five plantations.

An interview with former slave Harry McMillan was equally revealing. When asked about the morality of slave women, he confessed that although most were church members, girls were more likely to succumb to sexual temptation than were boys. McMillan reported, "Sometimes the Masters, where the Mistress was a pious woman, punished the girls for having children before they were married. As a general thing the Masters did not care, they like the colored women to have children." When an interviewer directly asked McMillan, "Suppose a son of the Master wanted to have intercourse with the colored women, was he at liberty?" the former slave demurred that white owners were "not at liberty" because it was considered a stain "on the family." But he admitted that "there was a good deal of it." McMillan remembered masters who kept "one girl steady," others who maintained "sometimes two on different places," regardless of whether they were married or unencumbered by white wives. His vivid recollection—"if they could get it on their own place it was easier, but they would go wherever they could get it"—demonstrates that, as a rule, white males in slave society were at liberty to exploit slave women, despite family or Christian obligations to the contrary.

McMillan was not depicting his own or his family's encounters with sexual exploitation. Many blacks discussed the abuse of other slaves on the plantation, perhaps unwilling to recount the indignities to which their own kin were subjected. Their revelations reflect genuine horror when they describe the practice of masters who auctioned off their own offspring. . . .

Perhaps most remarkable within the spectrum of interracial connection was the system of *plaçage,* which developed in New Orleans. This port city was renowned for its unique Franco-American culture, particularly the European influence on sexual and social mores. In addition, with the excessive ratio of free women of color to free men of color within this southern city (one hundred women to fifty-seven men in 1850), contractual concubinage flourished. The system that developed guaranteed

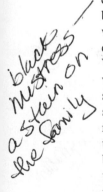

these women both male protectors and financial support for illegitimate children. The city was famous for its "quadroon" or "fancy girl" balls at which the refined, cultivated daughters of the *gens de couleur libres* were put on display for the dandies of Louisiana society. The balls, attended only by free mulatto women and white men, provided the means for matching up *placées* with protectors. After brief courtship, a formal contract between the girl's family and her protector was signed. <u>*Plaçage* guaranteed financial security for these women of color and perpetuated concubinage.</u> ✕ *guarantees*

A quadroon *placée* often groomed her octoroon daughter to follow her example; sons were encouraged to pursue artisanal trades. This elaborate system of codification was peculiar to New Orleans, although evidence of legal protection of concubines and their children appears in Charleston and Mobile as well, and owner-slave liaisons developed throughout the South.

The offspring of these interracial unions, slave or free, were referred to as "natural children." They appear in the wills of planters, often along with their mothers, as beneficiaries of their fathers' generosity. The fate of slave concubines and their natural children following an owner's death most often depended upon whether white relatives honored the will. A white widow or legitimate children were likely to ignore the wishes of the testator for their own financial advantage. . . . *family ignores the will?*

. . . [S]lavery reinforced the rule of white supremacy. Slave women involved in illicit relationships with white men were accorded more privilege than those who contracted regular unions with black men. Because both sets of relations were outside the law, the woman's status depended solely upon the rank of the man with whom she shared her bed and had no relation to any attempts to replicate traditional patterns of virtue and legitimacy. Evidence indicates that mulatto concubines might wield more influence than free women of color because of the complex perversities fostered by slavery. So slave women, given the limited options they faced within severely circumscribed spheres, might improve their lots by liaisons with owners. . . .

Many examples can be found of white women on plantations attempting to prevent interracial liaisons. The burdens of humiliation and responsibility seem to have fallen more heavily on women than men. One black woman described the rude awakening of her grandmother, Mathilda:

> She were near thirteen-year old, behind the house tee-teein when young marster came up behind her. She didn't see him, but he put his hand up her dress and said, "Lay down, Tildy." . . . And so this thing happened, and her stomach began to get big. One day, grandma and old mistress, they was putting up clean clothes. Old mistress had a pair of socks in her hand. She said, "Tildy, who been messin wit you down there?" Grandma say, "Young marster." Old mistress run to her and crammed these socks in her mouth and say, "[D]on't you ever tell nobody. If you do, I'll skin you alive."

The violent reaction of the mistress and her attempt to silence any testimony of a sexual connection are the most common responses within the records of plantation slavery. Wives as often as mothers agonized over illicit interracial affairs.

Owner-slave liaisons not only wreaked havoc within black families, they created violence and resentment among members of white families as well. Lacking the power to prevent sexual activities between male owners and slaves, white women on plantations struggled to discourage sons, shame brothers, and conceal marital infidelities. The jealousy and hatred many white women harbored for the slave women to whom their husbands were attached was legend within the Old South.

White southern women uniformly scorned black women's physical attributes. Mary Chestnut's diary illuminates her prejudices: "There will never be an interesting book with a negro heroine down here. We know them too well. In fact they are not picturesque—only in fiction do they shine. Those beastly negress beauties. Animals—tout et simple." In a later entry she describes a "beautiful mulatress" but qualifies her judgment: "that is, as good-looking as they ever are to me. I have never seen a mule as handsome as a horse—and I know I never will. Complaining about the "unattractiveness" of black women was perhaps an unconscious defense mechanism against the "attraction" many white men acted upon within southern society. An undertone of hysteria appears in many diaries of plantation mistresses when black women are discussed. Some women pathetically clung to the notion that owners slept with their slaves, as one woman claimed, "by no other desire or motive but that of adding to the number of their slaves," neglecting the reality that there was no shortage of black men available for this purpose.

Travelers, observers, court records, and slave narratives all testify to the hostility many white women felt toward black concubines. In these situations they may have felt equally at the mercy of white men. Harriet Jacobs's mistress, the slave confessed, "watched her husband with unceasing vigilance; but he was well practised in means to evade it." Southern masters, used to ruling unchallenged in sexual matters as single men, were loath to bridle their licentiousness after marriage, even to please their wives.

Plantation matrons had few options when confronted with their husbands' infidelities with a slave. Some might beg their husbands' fathers for assistance, and others might look to their own parents for comfort, but generally women were expected to turn a blind eye toward these dalliances. Under extreme circumstances, if a husband abused his privilege by flaunting an affair, a wife might demand that the slave be sold. If her husband refused, she could retaliate by petitioning for divorce, citing infidelity as legal grounds for dissolution. Although the very wealthiest of slaveowners were not often sued for divorce (the upper ranks of society rarely allowed their names to be soiled by scandal), many divorce petitions filed during the antebellum era demonstrate the humiliations to which white wives might be subjected.

Evidence from the county records of Virginia reveals the scope of the problem. An Augusta woman complained in 1814 that her husband took her slave Milly "in his own wife's bed." Milly gave birth to a mulatto shortly thereafter. A Henry County wife reported in 1820 that her husband took to bed with him, night after night for three months, a female slave—in the same bedroom with his wife. In an 1837 petition from King William County an abused wife revealed that not only was her spouse smitten with a hired female slave but he "suffered and even encouraged the said negro woman, Grace, to use not only the most insolent language, but even to inflict blows upon the said Elizabeth, his wife." . . .

The presence of a slave concubine and, secondarily, her bastard children promoted conflict within the plantation household. Such women's mere existence would cause pain for most wives, but their constant presence was a burden few women could tolerate. Most responded by lashing out at the helpless victims—the slave women. Evidence suggests that mistresses were free with the whip when dealing with women and children. It is futile to advance any single causal factor, but women's need to attack their rivals and their husbands' illegitimate offspring surely inspired some violence. Fears and suspicion played as large a role as fact in motivating many white women.

In the vast records of slavery, not just the papers of slaveowners and white institutions but also slave narratives, both whites and blacks confirm that mistresses attempted to enforce Christian principles and to deal morally with a very brutal and dehumanizing system. Yet how are we to explain the barbarity of white women torturing and even killing slaves? Former slave James Curry reported to his abolitionist audience: "I could relate many instances of extreme cruelty practised upon plantations in our neighborhood, instances of *woman* laying heaving stripes upon the back of *woman,* even under circumstances which should have removed every feeling but that of sympathy from the heart of *woman,* and, which was sometimes attended with effects most shocking." Curry might have been referring to the fact that the whipping of pregnant women could and did result in miscarriages. Murderous assaults might have been provoked by jealous rage. Appreciation of the dynamics at play can broaden our understanding of antebellum households. . . .

Historical records abound with senseless acts of cruelty. Elizabeth Sparks recounted that her mistress's mother beat her with a broom or a leather strap and that severe whippings were inflicted for such trifles as burning bread. Susan Merrit described being knocked in the head for trying to learn to read and being forced to walk barefoot through a bed of coals after being accused of carelessness. Several slaves reported that abusive mistresses administered daily whippings as morning rituals. Therefore, despite the general goodwill she supposedly maintained toward her charges and despite the positive impact the majority of slaves claimed she had on their lives, the plantation mistress could and did succumb to the cruelties fostered by southern slavery.

Although many cruelties may have been motivated by the existence of concubines and illegitimate mulattoes, it is also possible that white women, like white men, sometimes perpetrated violence without any rational cause. Scholars sensitive to the complexities of human motives realize that there are many events that can never be fully reconstructed and many facets of a given circumstance that may never be fathomed. Yet we must attempt to explore below the surface of historical records, to reveal the deeper meanings of people's experiences.

Perhaps we will never be able to determine causal factors for either individual or even group behavior within slave society. By looking at the "darker side" of the system of slavery, however, at the dynamics that have been obscured by modesty or distorted for numerous motives, we may discover some lost insights into this complex chapter of the southern past. It may be essential to place gender and sexuality in the foreground of our portrait of the Old South in order to sharpen our focus on some important areas of exploitation and suffering. The prolonged emphasis on slavery as an economic system has blurred our ability to understand the critical dynamics of slavery as a social system.

Women, both black and white, were ensnared within the confines of southern slave society. Color and class gave white women the privilege to exercise control over their lives, but evidence demonstrates that many were nevertheless victimized by a system that subjected them to prolonged humiliation and severe psychological stress. The problems of white women pale in comparison to those that plagued slave women in white households and black women within southern society. In some cases the anguish and frustration of white women compounded black women's difficulties, resulting in the physical and emotional abuse of slave mothers and children. Even though they were pitted against one another by a racist sexual ideology, black and white women were often trapped in similar situations: both were at the mercy of male will. Southern women have rarely been able to identify their common interests, to recognize that they were "sisters under the skin," until the modern era.

Free Black Women in the Abolitionist Movement

SHIRLEY J. YEE

For a number of black women, commitment to the movement for racial equality led to participation in activities that challenged nineteenth-century notions of acceptable behavior for women and blacks. When women wrote antislavery poetry and prose, spoke from public platforms, or signed and circulated petitions condemning slavery and northern racism, they defied customary codes of behavior. In the process, they, as individuals and as a group, reconstructed notions of respectability within the free black community regarding black female activism. . . .

With the exception of Sojourner Truth and Ellen Craft, many of the leading black women who engaged in public speaking and writing shared a common background. Margaretta Forten, Sarah Forten, Maria Miller Stewart, Frances Harper, Mary Ann Shadd Cary, and Sarah P. Remond had all been born into free black families in which they enjoyed some measure of economic privilege and formal education. Their background of education, relative economic comfort, and family activism set them apart from both slaves and the majority of free blacks. Their personal and professional connections with abolitionist friends, in addition to their own talents, undoubtedly helped them gain access to abolitionist newspapers and the public platform.

Public speaking and writing had long been acceptable ways for men to engage in intellectual self-expression, but not until the 1840s had women, white or black, begun in any numbers to break the custom barring them from such activities. . . . Proclaiming the evils of slavery and the possibility of racial equality, on the antislavery lecture circuit, was risky for anyone. Like abolitionist writers and editors, who faced the destruction of their presses and physical violence at the hands of anti-abolitionist mobs, antislavery lecturers risked their personal safety in their travels. Black women speakers, like other abolitionist men and women, were often at the mercy of hostile audiences who harassed them physically as well as verbally. . . . Violence on the lecture tours was an even greater threat for black women than for black men and white abolitionists. Physical and verbal attacks against black women activists could originate at any time or place from crowds motivated by three sources of hostility: anti-black feelings, anti-abolitionist sentiments, and hatred of "public" women. Unlike male abolitionists, women who spoke in public invited criticism from audiences who believed they had violated basic ideals of "proper" behavior for women.

Shirley J. Yee, "Breaking Customs," in *Black Women Abolitionists: A Study in Activism, 1828–1860* (Knoxville: University of Tennessee Press, 1992), 112–135. Reprinted by permission of the University of Tennessee Press.

Although black women enjoyed support from the men of their race for their writings and, eventually, for their speeches, they still found themselves bound by codes of proper behavior for women. As in the white community, social custom in the free black community still required women to act like "ladies." Black male leaders applauded black women speakers only so long as they did not criticize black men directly or assume a position of authority in gatherings where men were present. The period between 1830 and the 1860s was one in which female public speakers gradually gained acceptance from both abolitionist leaders and their audiences. . . .

Public speaking, more than any other abolitionist activity, seemed to spark the greatest conflict between the sexes. Public opinion was slow to accept female lecturers, regardless of race, because public speaking was an activity in which an individual assumed a role of authority long the domain of political leaders and a predominantly male clergy and forbidden to women by social and religious custom. Much of the criticism of women who spoke in public came from clergymen, who consistently condemned this form of activism as not only improper for respectable women but also in violation of St. Paul's biblical order for women to "keep silent." . . .

Public Speaking greatest conflict between sexes.

During the 1820s and 1830s, a number of influential black men also made strong objections to female lecturers. . . . Black male audiences were especially hostile when women speakers publicly criticized the behavior of black men. In 1831 in Boston, an audience of black men jeered and threw rotten tomatoes at Maria Miller Stewart when she delivered an address to black men that criticized them for failing to follow basic Christian principles of thrift, sobriety, and hard work. . . .

Abolitionists such as Frederick Douglass and Charles Lenox Remond, who gave wholehearted support to female lecturers, perceived the situation a bit differently. They put aside such notions of sex roles for the moment and saw these women as assets to the campaign to promote race pride, as well as a source of public opposition to slavery and racism. By the 1840s and 1850s, many male leaders argued that black women speakers . . . occupied an important place in the abolitionist movement. . . . The appeal to race pride, in particular, helped to justify black women's participation in public activities and made it more acceptable for black women than for white women to engage in non-traditional activities such as public speaking. Mary Ann Shadd Cary, for example received praise from black colleagues for her speaking efforts. Her coeditors of the *Provincial Freeman* portrayed her in 1856 as a positive representative of the free black community: "Remember, that they [blacks] belong to a class denied all social and political rights, and after they had been listened to, will the people say they are inferior to ANY of the lecturers among white fellow citizens? O' why will the people not be just?"

acceptability of black women speakers

The fact that many black female speakers delivered effective lectures also helped make them more acceptable to their audiences. Black and white observers could not deny that many of the black women who gained prominence as speakers were actually talented orators who often expressed ideas that intrigued their audiences. . . . Finally, the fact that black women speakers exuded "feminine qualities" when they spoke from the public platform undoubtedly helped make them more acceptable to their audiences. William Still once described Frances Harper as "gentle," as well as an "earnest, eloquent, and talented heroine." When Shadd Cary delivered an address at Elkhorn, Indiana, in 1856, one observer praised not only the content of her speech, but the manner of its delivery, which was termed "modest, and in strict keeping with the popular notions of the 'sphere of women.'" . . .

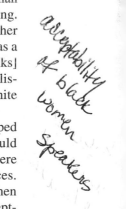

Both black and white women also challenged contemporary codes of appropriate behavior for women through the act of writing. White women writers found themselves limited primarily by gender expectations: they found a large, receptive audience only when they wrote on "feminine" subjects, such as female piety and domesticity, and only so long as they were not aggressive or political. Even within these bounds, however, the success of white women writers such as Catharine Maria Sedgewick and Lydia H. Sigourney led competition with male writers in the already crowded literary marketplace. To defend such obvious intrusion into a male domain, many white women writers felt obliged to argue that their writing would not lead them away from their homes and domestic duties.

Black women writers struggled not only with contemporary views on women's "sphere" but with barriers of race. For them, the act of writing challenged prevailing stereotypes of black female intellectual inferiority, even though they were following in a tradition first charted by writers such as Lucy Terry and Phillis Wheatley, who had established writing as a form of black female expression during the mid-eighteenth century. Between 1830 and 1865, Sarah Forten, Margaretta Forten, Frances Harper, and Mary Ann Shadd Cary all continued to write, within the context of protest.

Race prejudice usually prevented black women from getting their works published. Lucy Terry's poem, "Bar's Fight," for example, was not published until 1895, though it had been written in 1746. During the antebellum period, black women poets and essayists were able to publish their works only with the aid of prominent abolitionists, and they gained the most public attention when they wrote for abolitionist audiences. Lydia Maria Child, Garrison, and Still, for example, helped several black women writers publish collections of poetry and essays.

Readers often praised the women and their works as shining examples of black progress, which refuted racist stereotypes. . . . Mary Ann Shadd Cary, the first black female newspaper editor, also received praise for providing a vehicle for black voices and for expanding the role of black women in the movement. Shadd was well aware of the significance her position held for black women, and even congratulated herself for setting a precedent: "To colored women, we have a work—we have 'broken the Editorial ice' . . . for your class in America; so go on editing, as you are ready." H. T. Williams, a black male abolitionist, commended Shadd for breaking the gender barrier in publishing: "Although this routine of business for a female looks masculine, in the eyes of some, and is sneered at by the same class . . . yet it is creditable and praiseworthy, and never fails to produce a salutary effect. If Miss Shadd has gained any new plumes to her wreath, she is fully deserving of them, for her intrinsic value is not half known, nor appreciated by the people she has so faithfully served."

Several common themes emerge from Black women's oral and written work: the sexual exploitation of slave women by white men and the impact of slavery on slave mothers, the hope for creating an alliance between black and white women, and the need for black community improvement. An examination of their speeches and writings reveals the particular contribution they made to abolitionist thought and rhetoric. Sarah Forten, Frances Harper, Sarah Remond, and Sojourner Truth described the harshness of slavery; though only Truth had actually been a slave, even the free-born women related vivid descriptions of the black woman's experience under slavery. They probably gained their knowledge of slavery from contacts with fugitive slaves that can be traced to their families' involvement in the Underground Railroad and their connections with prominent abolitionists. In Sarah Forten's poem. "Grave of the Slave," she suggests that death might be preferable to life in bondage:

> Poor slave! shall we sorrow that death was thy friend!
> The last and the kindest that Heaven could send:—
> The grave to the weary is welcome and blest;
> And death to the captive is freedom and rest.

Harper, Remond, and Truth argued that slavery was especially difficult for slave mothers, who often saw their children sold away from them, and their writings examined the breakup of the slave family and the sexual exploitation of slave women. . . . By emphasizing the experience of motherhood, perhaps Harper and Truth hoped to appeal to white women and to create a common bond between all women abolitionists and slave women. Black women writers and speakers, when addressing the public, often promoted the idea of a cross-racial "sisterhood," even though they knew that racism existed openly within the movement as well as in society at large. The writings of Sarah Forten reflect this effort to emphasize the shared experiences of women of both races. . . .

Another topic of much concern to black women writers and speakers was the encouragement of free black men and women to participate in community-improvement activities. Not all audiences, of course, appreciated this advice, as Maria Stewart discovered more than twenty years earlier when she attempted to advise black men on "proper" conduct. Like other reformers of her generation, Stewart promoted middle-class values of thrift, sobriety, and hard work, and argued against gambling and dancing, which she believed undermined efforts to achieve black self-sufficiency: "I would implore our men, and especially our rising youth, to flee from the gambling board and the dance-hall; for we are poor, and have no money to throw away." Contemporary newspapers note that her advice met with hostility.

Stewart also argued that improved education in the free black community would help end racial prejudice by convincing whites of the "moral worth and intellectual improvement" of blacks. During the early 1830s, Stewart predicted that "prejudice would gradually diminish, and the whites would be compelled to say— Unloose those fetters! Though Black their skins as shades of night, Their hearts are—pure—their souls are white." Using widely accepted Christian imagery in her arguments, Stewart, like most thinkers of her time, referred to sin as black and righteousness as white.

Nearly a generation later, Frances Harper maintained that education in "virtue and morality" as well as in practical skills was necessary for improving the condition of free blacks and would result in their reception "as citizens, not worse than strangers." She added that material wealth among free blacks, though important for improving the community, entailed a special responsibility to the slave. In an essay submitted to the *Anglo-African Magazine* in May 1859, Harper urged blacks to use their time and money to support the movement to end slavery: "We have money among us, but how much of it is spent to bring deliverance to our captive brethren? Are our wealthiest men the most liberal sustainers of the Anti-slavery enterprise? Or does the bare fact of our having money, really help mould public opinion and reverse its sentiments?"

Although these writers and lecturers often received praise from black male abolitionists, social custom within the black community still required them to act like "respectable ladies." The career of Mary Ann Shadd and her tumultuous relationship with Henry Bibb suggests that as late as the 1850s such ideas prevailed, even when black male leadership supported female public activism. The feud between Shadd and Henry Bibb over "caste" schools and the Refugee Home Society contributed to Shadd's decision to establish her own abolitionist newspaper, symbolic of the rift between them. Her newspaper, the *Provincial Freeman,* published articles on a variety of subjects, including anti-colonization, emigration, slavery, self-help, and moral improvement. The project, however, was more than simply a vehicle for opposing the Bibbs; it was intended in part to open the way for black women who desired careers in editing and publishing. White abolitionist women, such as Elizabeth Chandler and Lydia Maria Child, already had broken the white gender barrier in newspaper editing. Shadd's claim that she had "broken the Editorial Ice" for the women of her race reveals that she clearly identified herself with her female readers, whom she urged to pursue careers in writing and publishing.

Shadd's plainspoken and direct style contrasted markedly with the eloquent poetry and prose of Sarah Forten and Frances Harper. Shadd never hesitated to criticize persons and institutions she considered harmful to herself, to the antislavery cause, or to the progress of the free black community. For example, she attacked churches in Canada and the United States for allegedly supporting slavery, arguing that the "American church is the pillar of American slavery." In 1856, she expressed disdain for Frederick Douglass in an article for the *Provincial Freeman:* "Having been permitted so long to remain in our tub, we would rather that the great Frederick Douglass, for whose public career we have the most profound pity, would stay out of our sunlight." In the same issue, she despaired that a number of leading white and black abolitionists (including, in her opinion, Douglass) could still support colonization. . . .

Black women abolitionists' use of the pen and the public platform to articulate their opinions demonstrated an individual independence and a willingness to challenge prevailing expectations of gender and race. The act of public speaking and writing among black women, by defying racist expectations of black docility and intellectual inferiority, led black male leaders as well as many white abolitionists to accept black women writers and speakers as symbols of black success and resistance. Unlike white women, they could be perceived as assets to both the black community and the abolitionist movement. Their writings and speeches, as explicit forms of black protest and self-expression, provided fuel for abolitionist propaganda even as they continued a tradition of writing established by black female authors a century earlier. For black women, public speaking gradually became socially acceptable, as long as they stopped short of direct criticism of black men or challenges to male authority.

Male and female abolitionists of both races had frequently used the petition as a way to protest slavery and race discrimination in the "nominally free states." They flooded Congress and their state legislatures with antislavery petitions throughout the antebellum period, demanding the end of slavery and race discrimination in the District of Columbia and the United States. The onslaught of petitions so incensed

*gag rule
on Slavery
Issue*

Petition

southern congressmen that they succeeded in passing a gag rule, which, until its repeal in December 1844, tabled any discussion of slavery on the floor of the House. For women and black men, however, the petition was more than an abolitionist tactic. Political disfranchisement was a condition they shared until 1869, when the passage of the Fifteenth Amendment left women as the only adult group without the right to vote. Although anyone could circulate and sign a petition, this form of political expression reflected their exclusion from the American political system. For disfranchised groups—but not, of course, for white men, who had the right to vote— the petition was the only legal means to make their voices heard and seek changes in the law. In 1840, several white male abolitionists formed an antislavery political party in hopes of overthrowing the "Slave Power" in Congress. For women and most black men, who could not vote, the formation of political parties held little meaning. A contributor to the *Colored American,* known only as "A Friend," expressed support for women's involvement in petition drives: "I think as they are identified with us in our sufferings. . . . [T]hey are the aggrieved with us, and being aggrieved with us certainly ought to have the right to petition also to have these grievances removed."

Many male observers considered women's participation in petitioning campaigns an improper intrusion into a traditionally male domain. One defender of female petitioners described some of these criticisms: "The New York Sun is very severe upon the 'Eastern women' who are getting up petitions against the admission of Texas [as a slave state], and thinks they had better be shaking bed ticks rather than politics." Supporters of women petitioners combined ideas of women's "nature" and patriotism as justification for participation in a political activity. . . . Supporters also argued that these women were merely following in the patriotic traditions of their foremothers in the War for Independence. . . .

Female antislavery societies and activist groups within the black community provided black women with opportunities to participate in abolitionist petition drives. Between 1834 and 1850, for example, the members of the Philadelphia Female Anti-Slavery Society sent petitions to the state legislature of Pennsylvania and to Congress, demanding the end of slavery. To Congress, they wrote: "The undersigned respectfully ask that you will . . . abolish everything in the Constitution or Laws of the U.S. which in any manner sanctions or sustains slavery." In the society's 1836 annual report, members wrote of their commitment to petitioning:

> Since the year 1834, we have annually memorialized Congress, praying for the abolition of slavery in the District of Columbia and the Territories of the United States. We are frequently asked what good have petitions done: The full amount of good produced by them, is yet to be revealed. . . . We knew that our petitions were not ineffectual, when the wise men of the South, sent back to us the cry, "Impertinent intermeddlers! incorrect devils! &c."

Black women members of the society frequently served on committees to coordinate petition drives in the Philadelphia area. Committee members drew up detailed maps of the city and assigned individuals and groups of women to cover specific neighborhoods. In 1835, for example, Sarah Forten and Hetty Burr were the two black members appointed to a committee to "obtain signatures to a petition to Congress."

In Boston, members of the Female Anti-Slavery Society also signed and circulated petitions. In 1837, Maria Weston Chapman, representing the society, coordinated women's petitions protesting the annexation of Texas as a slave state. In addition to petitioning against slavery, members also circulated petitions protesting race discrimination against free blacks. Black and white abolitionists petitioned, in particular, against discrimination on railroads, racial segregation in public schools, and the state marriage law, which outlawed interracial marriages.

In 1839, black members Susan Paul, Eunice R. Davis, Lavinia Hilton, Chloe Lee, Jane Putnam, and Julia Williams joined with the other "undersigned women of Boston," in submitting a petition to the Massachusetts legislature denouncing the law that forbade interracial marriage. This protest revealed a radical side to the predominantly white, middle-class group. It has been argued that the movement to abolish the marriage law, which was repealed in 1843, was primarily the result of white initiative, because blacks, recognizing the sensitivity of the issue, approached it cautiously. Additional evidence, however, indicates that although the movement for repeal had been a pet project for white abolitionists since the emergence of Garrison, the black community may also have felt strongly; in February 1843, a group of "Colored Citizens of Boston" met to draw up resolutions supporting *The Liberator,* and denouncing the state marriage laws and race discrimination on railroads. The group agreed to circulate these resolutions within the black community in Boston, and antislavery-society member Eunice R. Davis was one of three black women appointed to a committee to obtain signatures for the petitions. . . .

Although they failed to convince Congress to abolish slavery and prevent its extension into the territories of the Southwest, black and white petitioners did succeed in obtaining repeal of some discriminatory laws on the state and local levels. For black women, petitioning served as a way both to protest slavery and race discrimination and to participate in a political system that excluded them from full citizenship on the basis of race and sex.

Petitioning provided black women with their only opportunity to appear to the state and federal governments for the end of slavery and race discrimination. Like writing and speaking, it was a way to make their voices heard in a society in which they, as blacks and as women, had been expected to keep silent. The public work that many women performed for the sake of abolition, however, quickly raised questions about the "proper" role of women in public reform. For black women abolitionists, this "woman question" held important implications for the black abolitionist agenda, because women's rights would, in some ways, directly contradict black goals for the creation of a truly free community.

Ordinary Women in the Antislavery Movement

JULIE ROY JEFFREY

In 1847, William Lloyd Garrison's abolitionist newspaper, the *Liberator,* declared that "the Anti-Slavery cause cannot stop to estimate where the greatest indebtedness lies, but whenever the account is made up, there can be no doubt that the efforts and sacrifices of the WOMEN, who helped it, will hold a most honorable and conspicuous position." Garrison's certainty that participants in the great crusade would ultimately

Julie Roy Jeffrey, "Introduction" to *The Great Silent Army of Abolitionism: Ordinary Women in the Antislavery Movement* (Chapel Hill: University of North Carolina Press, 1998), 1–11. Copyright © 1998 by the University of North Carolina Press. Used by permission of the publisher.

recognize the contributions of women to abolitionism was not shared by his son. While acknowledging the importance of women to the movement to free the slave, William Lloyd Garrison Jr. seems to have accepted the fact of abolitionist women's historical invisibility when he referred to that "great army of silent workers, unknown to fame, and yet without whom the generals were powerless."

Scholars studying the most important reform movement before the Civil War have also tended until quite recently to overlook the army of silent workers. Although historians have offered differing interpretations of the significance of abolitionism, the motives and achievements of its leaders, and the relationship of abolitionism to historical processes and events, they have traditionally focused on male leaders and male activities like third-party politics. While the birth of women's history helped to remedy the neglect of abolitionist women, attention tended to center on the small number of radical women who became feminists. The majority of women who shied away from feminism still remained in the shadows. . . .

Frederick Douglass, who had ample reason to acknowledge the important role black and white abolitionist women played in sustaining his own activities, tried to describe why women were important to abolitionism. He pointed to the "skill, industry, patience and perseverance" shown at "every trial hour," the willingness to "do the work which in large degree supplied the sinews of war," and the "deep moral convictions" that helped to give abolitionism its character. As Douglass knew, it was white middle-class and some black women who did much of the day-to-day work of reform. For more than three decades, they raised money, created and distributed propaganda, circulated and signed petitions, and lobbied legislators. During the 1840s and 1850s, they helped to keep the moral content of abolitionism alive when a diluted political form of antislavery emerged.

Women important to Abolitionism

Women formed the backbone of the movement, and without their involvement, as William Lloyd Garrison Jr. recognized, the leaders would have been powerless. Observers acknowledged at the time that individual women and women's groups often sustained abolitionism when men became dispirited. In 1850, a resident of Portland, Maine, admitted the "mortifying" fact that, in a period of darkness and discouragement, men had allowed the antislavery society to die, while the women of the Portland Anti-Slavery Sewing Society had "kept up their meetings" and work for the cause. The same year, when the English abolitionist lecturer George Thompson visited Salem, Massachusetts, he noted the advances abolitionism had made since his earlier visit in 1835: "A few faithful women," members of the Salem Female Anti-Slavery Society, had been "scattering anti-slavery seed," for fifteen difficult years and had changed "almost the entire sentiment" of the community. Women, Thompson knew, did not play a peripheral role in abolitionism but a central one.

Abolitionism was never a popular cause before the Civil War. Although it is impossible to know how many people either supported or worked for immediate emancipation between 1830 and 1865, one historian has estimated that, out of a population of over 20 million in 1860, only around 20,000, or 1 percent of all American men and women, were abolitionists. Not only was the reform unpopular, but it also generated hostility and even violence, as George Thompson learned when mobs accosted him during his first American tour in the 1830s. Women abolitionists belonged to a minority movement that many Americans distrusted and even despised.

Despite the "social ostracism, persecution, slander, [and] insult" that Rhode Island abolitionist Elizabeth Chace recalled abolitionist women encountering,

open to attacern Illinois 1837 — Elijah Lovejoy

evidence suggests that some, like Elizabeth herself and those women belonging to the Portland and Salem female societies, maintained their interest over long periods of time. Others, including members of Rochester's Female Anti-Slavery Society, took up and then abandoned abolitionism, and then sometimes became interested again years later. Although public hostility, lack of progress, and dissension among abolitionists caused attrition, more continuous interest in the cause may have existed than it is possible to document. At the end of the 1830s, disagreements within abolitionist ranks over the place of women in antislavery organizations, the relationship of abolitionism to other reforms, and the advisability of pursuing antislavery through politics rather than through moral suasion led to noisy and rancorous divisions that some scholars have suggested reduced women's involvement in antislavery. Most abolitionist women disagreed with Garrisonian radicalism, to be sure, but they did not necessarily reject the necessity of working for immediate emancipation. Dover, New Hampshire, women reorganized their antislavery society as a non-Garrisonian sewing society in 1840 and kept up associational records for decades, but more informal groupings like church sewing circles usually left no written evidence of their involvement at all. Letters written by abolitionist women of one faction often bemoaned the fact that they were almost alone in their support for the cause even as they acknowledged that other women in their communities were pursuing antislavery in secular or church societies. The emphasis on division, then, possibly obscures the extent of female commitment.

The collapse of a unified national antislavery effort in 1840 actually created a variety of individual and collective opportunities to work for the slave and encouraged different styles of activism. As Nancy Hewitt has shown in her study of Rochester, middle-class women from different social, economic, and religious backgrounds did not approach reform in similar ways.

While women differed in their expression of abolitionism over the decades, common convictions undergirded their activities. They agreed that slavery was a sin that, as women, they had a moral and religious duty to eradicate. Despite the scope of the change they were seeking, they were confident that, in the end, their cause would triumph, that moral activism would be efficacious. What might happen to former slaves once slavery had ended was not a question that troubled most of them. Yet they were not indifferent to racism that permeated American life in both the North and South. Although few women were interested in racial equality as understood in the late twentieth century, they did believe that abolitionists should work to improve the situation of free blacks in the North. The 1835 constitution for the first female antislavery organization in Dover, New Hampshire, like those of many other societies, proclaimed the importance of elevating the character and condition of blacks, correcting the "wicked prejudices" of the majority of northern whites, and striving for civil and religious equality.

Some groups and individuals, however, stressed certain of these ideas more than others. Black abolitionists, aware of the serious problems in their communities, became far more interested in improving the status of free blacks than most white abolitionists, and they felt the demands of moral duty far less keenly than the demands of racial responsibility. The egalitarian tradition of the Society of Friends led Quaker women abolitionists to minimize the idea of women's particular responsibility for moral causes that evangelical women stressed so strongly. But substantial ideological agreements undergirded abolitionist women's activism.

. . . [F]emale activism changed over time as abolitionism responded to outside events and internal realities. In the 1830s, for example, most abolitionist women expected that the church would support and further their cause. They joined secular antislavery societies and used them as their base for work like petitioning. When the reluctance of church leaders to take a stand against slavery became clear in the 1840s, however, strategies to expose and pressure Protestant denominations became more central, and the locus for activity often changed. For the abolitionists who established individual abolitionist congregations, the church became the main institutional home for antislavery work. . . .

Despite the changing rhythms of activism as time passed, women from different abolitionist camps relied on similar tactics to pursue their goals. Securing financial support for abolitionist work consumed countless hours and energy. Although women devised numerous ways to collect money, one of their most successful measures was the antislavery fair. When the black women of New York State who determined to raise money for the *Impartial Citizen,* a black Liberty Party newspaper, decided to hold a fair, they were in good company. Women from all camps of abolitionism mounted fairs and bazaars. While a major purpose of the fair was to generate income, fair managers also used the occasion as an opportunity to make powerful symbolic statements about the nature of their cause and to connect abolitionists to one another. They relied upon fairs as a means of energizing and linking local antislavery groups and individuals who produced the goods to be sold at the fair.

Despite disagreements on issues like the relevance of political action to abolitionism, abolitionist women undertook similar projects, ranging from collecting signatures on petitions to sewing. Although the greatest petitioning effort of the antebellum period occurred in the 1830s, women mounted petition drives throughout the 1840s and 1850s, culminating in a spectacular campaign during the Civil War. The work of creating and circulating antislavery propaganda and sponsoring lectures, as the Salem Female Anti-Slavery Society did for so many years, was also ubiquitous.

Sewing for fairs, fugitives, poor northern blacks, or for freedpeople during the war united abolitionist women of all stripes. The modest and tangible character of such work helped keep women involved in abolitionism. One Georgetown, Massachusetts, woman explained that the humble sewing circle had the power to "augment our numbers and cause a more punctual attendance." The exposure that members had to abolitionist conversation and literature during meetings meant that antislavery's "influence may be diffused into all the families where our members reside and thus the whole community be *abolitionised.*" While she may have overestimated the impact of the local sewing circle, the concrete tasks women undertook seem to have kept many of them attached to the cause for long periods of time. That women had something tangible in which to root their loyalty may be one reason that women, not men, constituted the great silent army of abolitionism. Continuing and often humble labors bound women together and provided milestones on the way to a distant goal.

. . . Most of the women who wrote the letters and diaries I read and who left the few surviving organizational records were busy women with substantial family and domestic commitments. Many came from modest backgrounds and did most of their own housework. Unmarried white women and married black women often also worked outside of the home. Written sources reveal some of the difficulties women experienced as they tried to mesh their abolitionist convictions with day-to-day responsibilities and suggest both the emotional costs and rewards involved in supporting the cause. They give brief but revealing glimpses of lives that are otherwise lost to the historical record. . . .

. . . The tendency to classify some women abolitionists as radical and others as conservative, usually based upon their attitude toward feminism, misses an essential truth about abolitionism and the ways in which it led its adherents to transgress ideological norms. No matter what one's attitude might be toward women's rights, to embrace abolitionism was to embrace radicalism. The commitment to immediate emancipation challenged the political, economic, religious, and social status quo. It also became a challenge to gender arrangements. The latter challenge was ironic, for, with the exception of Quaker women, most women who adopted abolitionism did so because they accepted a gendered view of the world and women's unique religious and moral responsibilities. Their positive response to the call of duty, however, led them in unexpected directions. In the early 1830s, when the parameters of women's participation were unclear, the prevailing expectation was that white middle-class women would quietly pursue abolitionism in the privacy of their own homes. But it soon became apparent that the beleaguered movement needed more from women than home life would allow.

Abolitionist women, more directly than other women reformers who enjoyed greater community approval than did antislavery advocates, gradually and often in a piecemeal fashion, contested many of the norms that supposedly governed their behavior and woman's sphere. Moral commitments demanded public expressions. Abolitionists could neither be silent nor inconspicuous. The struggle against slavery led them to speak out in a variety of settings, ranging from their parlors to the public streets and meetinghouses. They confronted authority even when it claimed sacred prerogatives, and they broke the law when it was unjust. Even the women who formed church circles to sew for fugitive slaves and supply their settlements in Canada were acting out their repudiation of the law of the land. The crisis in gender relations that some scholars have explored in terms of early feminism and the Civil War began as ordinary abolitionist women followed the dictates of duty. It affected not only women's relations with men but also their self-perception and self-image.

For women, whose sphere was supposedly private and domestic, in whom innate qualities of sympathy and intuition sufficed, abolitionism proved a demanding taskmaster. Home life proved to be an inadequate preparation for new responsibilities. To advocate immediate emancipation successfully, women had to learn to reason and to argue, to appeal to the mind as well as to the heart and emotions. Routine projects led them to transgress the usual norms for female behavior in public places and to participate alongside men in political events. While they did not vote, some assumed a more visible and meaningful political presence than the symbolic ceremonial role Mary Ryan describes in *Women in Public*. Indeed, some women went so far as to distribute third-party propaganda to voters. Their activities suggest that they understood that political activities encompassed far more than going to the polls. Far from being shielded from the vagaries of a market economy, their interest in raising money enmeshed them in the marketplace and the consumer economy. They acquired and used an array of managerial and financial skills. As time passed, they more frequently entered the public debate about slavery, and, when a second generation of abolitionists emerged, they felt an ease in their public identity as abolitionists that had been rare in the 1830s.

. . . In the decades during which abolitionists were active, a middle class, different from both the middling sort of the eighteenth century and the new industrial working class, was taking shape. Middle-class American men increasingly held nonmanual, "white collar" jobs that provided their families with the means for a respectable and genteel way of life. Because the process of class formation was incomplete and its membership and identity not yet set, there was room to contest class definitions and boundaries. The activities of abolitionist women defied emerging middle-class norms and helped to broaden the arena of action for white middle-class women, even though it did not lead most of them to feminism. The powerful conviction that women's moral duty demanded an abolitionist commitment limited the challenge to gender arrangements. Only a few women were willing to abandon woman's moral voice for feminist egalitarianism. . . .

Most of the women leaving a record of their involvement in abolitionism were white evangelical Protestant or Quaker women living in rural and small-town communities. . . . Several profiles suggest the nature of these ordinary women's lives and hint at the meaning abolitionism had for them.

[handwritten marginalia: Protestant or Quaker.]

Mary White (1778–1860), daughter of a minister, wife of a farmer and shopkeeper, and mother of ten children, lived in an old homestead, a "good specimen of New England domestic comfort," in Boylston, Massachusetts. Like most farm wives, she had varied responsibilities and chores, and her life was a busy one. Despite all her domestic commitments, she became active in antislavery in the mid-1830s. Mary joined a female antislavery society, circulated petitions, attended many antislavery lectures, and sewed for the Boston fair and for fugitives. In addition to her abolitionist activities, she also supported temperance and taught Sunday school. Her diary records the way in which she integrated her reformism into her day-to-day routine and shows the antislavery involvement of other members of her family and her community.

Lucy Colman was perhaps as much as forty years younger than Mary White and never enjoyed the settled life that Mary took for granted. One of her early memories was of her mother singing an antislavery song to her before her early death, when Lucy was only six. Lucy married twice and found herself a widow for the second time when she was not yet forty. Although her determination to work for emancipation predated the accidental death of her second husband, the work took on another meaning with her widowhood. Lucy became an antislavery lecturer during the 1850s, first earning her own expenses and salary as an agent of the Western Anti-Slavery Society of New York and then winning a paid position from the American Anti-Slavery Society. Primitive traveling conditions, frequently unsympathetic audiences, and constant self-denial made her tours through the Midwest taxing. "I never allowed myself the luxury of more than one meal a day, nor a fire in my room," she later recalled. Although eventually a young black woman shared speaking responsibilities, Lucy found life as an agent exhausting. When the war broke out, she left lecturing to become a teacher at a school for black children in

Georgetown, New York. There, as she struggled to teach her students middle-class values, she concluded that "generations of the most debasing, abject slavery, is not productive of a high order of morals."

For decades, Frances Drake, probably the wife of Jonathan Drake, was a tireless worker for abolitionism in central Massachusetts. In the 1840s and 1850s, she organized local women to work for the great Boston fairs, gathered and sent greens to decorate the halls, and helped to plan and mount local fairs in Fitchburg and Worcester. She arranged for antislavery lectures and, in 1856, nursed Bernardo, a black boy, during his final illness. She regarded her nursing as a privilege, and, when Bernardo died, she acknowledged that it had been a "great . . . blessing . . . to me, to pillow his dying head on my bosom." An 1862 issue of the *Liberator* provides the last view of Frances in her role serving as secretary for an antislavery convention in Leominister, Massachusetts.

In Salem, New Jersey, Abigail Goodwin had kept her antislavery convictions alive for decades with little support from her immediate community. A Quaker and a friend of Esther Moore, first president of the Philadelphia Female Anti-Slavery Society, Abigail joined the society in its petition work during the 1830s. Determined to collect signatures and not to become discouraged, she found New Jersey weak in "the abolitionist faith." Local women did not even have enough enthusiasm "to form a society just yet." Twenty years later, Abigail, now a poor widow, again entered the historical record. A friend explained her new focus: "Giving to the colored people was a perfect *passion* with her." Abigail's correspondence with the Philadelphia Vigilance Committee reveals some of the details of this passion to assist fugitive slaves. Without the ability to dip into her own pocket for funds, Abigail either earned or solicited money to support her interests. In the 1860s she was still active, collecting dollars and clothing for contrabands. She died in 1867.

Like many abolitionists, Andrew and Sarah Ernst carried their commitments with them when they moved west in 1841. Originally from Boston, Sarah Otis Ernst was a strong Garrisonian. When she arrived in Cincinnati, she found that the city did not have one antislavery society, although African Americans had established the Educational Society for the Colored. Like many white abolitionists, Sarah was less interested in free blacks than in slaves and dismissed the Educational Society because it did "nothing at all for the slave." When political and Christian abolitionists became active in the city, she rejected their approaches as misguided. Yet, although she worked hard to generate a "new . . . spirit," she ultimately found it expedient to cooperate with other abolitionist groups. She made a major contribution to antislavery in the Midwest through her work for the Cincinnati fair and inclusive antislavery conventions. Her commitment had personal and familial costs. She found organizing the fair a "physical drudgery" and feared her work might be harmful to her newborn baby, whom she was nursing. "Sleepless nights and anxious distressed days are not calculated to give a healthy constitution to my baby," she worried. Moreover, the storage of fair items in her home disrupted domestic life and was contrary to her husband's "*wishes—his pride.*" As Sarah discovered, stress was part and parcel of abolitionism.

Mary Still (1808–1889), an African American who left traces of her abolitionist activities, was the daughter of a former slave from Maryland and his fugitive wife. She grew up in New Jersey and, like four of her siblings, moved to Philadelphia. In the late 1840s, she kept a school for black children there and became involved in the life of Philadelphia's black community. As a member of the Female Union Publication Society of Philadelphia, an organization affiliated with the African Methodist Episcopal Church, she helped raise money for publications that contributed "to the improvement and elevation of our people." Her professional and organizational commitments, like her abolitionism, helped to establish her place in the city's black middle class. During the war, she volunteered to teach freed slaves. Heading south, she found her "heart . . . very sad" and realized that "I have desided hastily about going so far from home alone." Although the climate in South Carolina proved problematic for her health, the enthusiasm of her pupils lifted her spirits. She adapted so well to her important work that in 1869 she moved to another American Missionary Association school in Florida, where she remained until 1872.

The contributions of these and countless other women to abolitionism reveal the varied and important part they played in the most significant reform before the Civil War. Herbert Aptheker points out that abolitionism was the first major social movement to involve women in all aspects of the work. What he does not emphasize enough, however, is what many of the leaders realized: without women, abolitionism would have been far more marginal a movement for change than it was.

F U R T H E R   R E A D I N G

Bynum, Victoria. *Unruly Women: The Politics of Social and Sexual Control in the Old South* (1992).

Clinton, Catherine. *The Plantation Mistress: Woman's World in the Old South* (1983).

Fox-Genovese, Elizabeth. *Within the Plantation Household: Black and White Women of the Old South* (1988).

Hansen, Debra G. *Strained Sisterhood: Gender and Class in the Boston Female Anti-Slavery Society* (1993).

Hersh, Blanche. *The Slavery of Sex: Feminist-Abolitionists in Nineteenth-Century America* (1978).

Hodes, Martha. *White Women, Black Men: Illicit Sex in the Nineteenth-Century South* (1997).

Jennings, Thelma. "'Us Colored Women Had to Go Through a Plenty': Sexual Exploitation of African-American Slave Women," *Journal of Women's History* 1, no. 3 (1989–1990): 45–74.

Lebsock, Suzanne. *The Free Women of Petersburg: Status and Culture in a Southern Town, 1784–1860* (1984).

McMillen, Sally. *Southern Women: Black and White in the Old South* (1991).

Morton, Patricia, ed. *Discovering the Women in Slavery: Emancipating Perspectives on the American Past* (1996).

Murray, Gail S. "Charity Within the Bounds of Race and Class: Female Benevolence in the Old South," *South Carolina Historical Magazine* 96 (1995): 54–70.

Schaefer, Judith K. "'Open and Notorious Concubinage': The Emancipation of Slave Mistresses by Will and the Supreme Court in Antebellum Louisiana," *Louisiana History* 28 (1987): 165–182.

Sklar, Kathryn K. "'Women Who Speak for an Entire Nation': American and British Women Compared at the World Anti-Slavery Convention, London, 1840," *Pacific Historical Review* 59 (1990): 454–499.

Weiner, Marli. *Mistresses and Slaves: Plantation Women in South Carolina, 1830–1880* (1998).

White, Deborah Gray. *Arn't I a Woman? Female Slaves in the Plantation South* (1985).

Yellin, Jean Fagan. *Women and Sisters: The Antislavery Feminists in American Culture* (1990).

Yellin, Jean Fagan, and John C. Van Horne, eds. *The Abolitionist Sisterhood: Women's Political Culture in Antebellum America* (1994).

CHAPTER 7

White Women in the

Civil War Crisis

In the United States, the Civil War is frequently described as a conflict of "brother against brother." Recent scholarship and the publication of many women's wartime diaries and letters in the last decade suggest that it might also be called a struggle of "sister against sister." Union and Confederate women recorded in their private and public writings their attachment to the causes of their respective sections and their contempt for each other.

After years of surprising neglect, the experience of women in the Civil War has finally become the subject of intense scholarly study. Historians have begun the process of exploring the impact of the war on the women of both sides, and they have found significant differences. Whereas wartime privations and the ultimate Confederate defeat helped to leave southern white women in conditions that emphasized resistance to change after the war, the Union victory and northern white women's pride in their role therein gave them confidence in their organizational abilities and inspired lasting patriotic sentiments. The differences were so profound that some have argued that the disparate impact of the war on northern and southern women was still evident as recently as the 1950s, prior to the development of the civil rights movement in the South.

◆ *D O C U M E N T S*

In 1862, Maria Daly, a New Yorker, recorded observations on southern women and on her war-relief-worker friends in her diary; some selected entries make up Document 1. Sarah Morgan, a resident of Louisiana, the following year penned an entry in her diary confessing herself a rebel (Document 2). When some northern men accused Union women of being less attached to their cause than their Confederate counterparts were, Caroline Kirkland indignantly wrote and published Document 3, "A Few Words in Behalf of the Loyal Women of the United States" (1863). As the war drew to a close in 1865, Ella Gertrude Clanton Thomas, a Georgia slave mistress whose remarks are also included in Chapter 6, contemplated Sherman's March to the Sea, General William T. Sherman himself, and his wife (Document 4). Nearly four decades after the war had begun, Mary Livermore, a Union partisan, recalled with pride women's role in the first days of northern mobilization (Document 5).

1. Maria Daly, a New Yorker, Criticizes Southern Women and Records the War Work of Her Acquaintances, 1862

June 26, 1862

In the paper this morning, there is an incendiary appeal of the women of New Orleans to the Southern soldiers, the burden of which is that they would rather be buried beneath the ruins of their homes than be left to the mercy of the barbarous Yankees—these barbarous creatures who have done nothing but feed their hungry and clothe their naked since they took their pestilent city. . . .

July 3, 1862

Mrs. Hilton told me that a lady who knew [A. T.] Stewart's head-man, Fairchild, walked up to him and asked him to look at her brooch. He said it seemed to be nothing very remarkable.

"No?" said she, "No? It is made from the skull of a Federal soldier!"

Now such a demon in female form as that, I think, should have been arrested. I lose all patience when I think of these demoniac Southern women, whose pride and arrogance have had so much to do with this fearful state of things. Southern ladies and gentlemen . . . are very agreeable people with very finished and courtly manners, but they are a class utterly unsuited and antagonistic to the principles of our government. We do not want a nobility here of any kind, except intellect; no millionaires with miles of territory belonging to them and an army of retainers. So they must go down, like the old feudal keeps, etc., which were very picturesque but dangerous from their strength to the public weal. . . .

August 14, 1862

Ellen Naudain, spending the evening here a few nights since, told us much about the hospitals where she attends two days in the week. She had been attending a sick soldier who told her that he and two brothers and their father had all enlisted the same day and that he was anxious to get well to rejoin them. She thinks the army very patriotic from what she has seen. . . .

September 13, 1862

. . . Harriet Whetten stopped this morning, dear old soul, to see us. She has seen hard service this summer, and says that the rank and file of the army are splendid. She says little for the officers. The soldiers bear all with unmurmuring patience,

Maria Daly, *Diary of a Union Lady,* ed. Harold E. Hammond (New York: Funk & Wagnalls, 1962), 155, 158–159, 164, 172–173.

but she is disgusted by the coldness and delay and want of feeling in the government officers. She related that the day after the last battle of Fair Oaks, the *Spalding* came near enough for them to go and try to feed some of the men on the battlefield. The cargo was taken out and five hundred of the most badly wounded were to be taken aboard. Orders came to replace the cargo and move to Harrison's Landing (seven miles), where the poor fellows were left.

Harriet has met Arabella, who has been living, it seems, very comfortably at government expense at the hospital at Harrison's Landing near her husband's regiment. She has done nothing, comparatively, but lounge on a sofa, for the men told her that there had not been a lady near them to sit beside them a moment for ten days. The hospital, too, is small. Harriet was asked, although she was a stranger, for a night only to give out the linens whilst Mrs. Barlow was sprawling out on the couch. My instincts are right about her. Barlow, they say, is very cruel to his men. He may, however, be only a stern disciplinarian.

Whilst waiting for the return prisoners from Richmond, the rebel officers came on board, drank with Captain Harris and his officers, and to Harriet's disgust dined on board. After dinner, the Captain asked her if she would not give these men some tea. Harriet said she wished she had authority to say no, but she answered that she only distributed things to the sick. He must ask the quartermaster, who she was vexed to see give it. The rebels said it was $16 a pound, and it would be a great comfort. How contemptible to take it! I would not, it seems to me, have touched a leaf. Harriet said the utmost cordiality seemed to exist between them, and the surgeon said: "Our officers told all they knew. The rebels were not quite so bad."

Charles advised Harriet to leave the boat, as so much is said about the nurses who have gone. Some of the men say that they are closeted for hours with the surgeons in pantries and all kinds of disorders go on. The surgeons dislike, as a body, the Sisters of Charity because they are obliged to be respectful of them.

2. The Louisianian Sarah Morgan Proudly Proclaims Herself a Rebel, 1863

January 23, 1863

I confess my self a rebel, body and soul. *Confess?* I glory in it! Am proud of being one, would not forego the title for any other earthly one! Though none could regret the dismemberment of our old Union more than I did at the time, though I acknowledge that there never was a more unnecessary war than this in the beginning, yet once in ernest, from the secession of Louisiana I date my change of sentiment. I have never since then looked back; forward, forward! is the cry; and as the Federal States sink each day in more appalling folly and disgrace, I grow prouder still of my own country and rejoice that we can no longer be confounded with a nation which shows so little fortitude in calamity, so little magnanimity in its hour of triumph.

Charles East, ed., *The Civil War Diary of Sarah Morgan* (Athens: University of Georgia Press, 1991), 410–411.

Yes! I am glad we are two distinct tribes! I am proud of my country; only wish I could fight in the ranks with our brave soldiers, to prove my enthusiasm; would think death, mutilation, glorious in such a cause; cry "war to all eternity before we submit!" But if I cant fight, being unfortunately a woman, which I now regret for the first time in my life, at least I can help in other ways. What fingers could do in knitting and sewing for them, I have done with the most intense delight; what words of encouragement and praise could accomplish, I have tried on more than one bold soldier boy, and not altogether in vain; I have lost my home and all its dear contents for our Southern Rights, have stood on its deserted hearth stone and looked at the ruin of all I loved without a murmur, almost glad of the sacrifice, if it would contribute its mite towards the salvation of the Confederacy. . . .

Well! I boast myself Rebel, sing Dixie, shout Southern Rights, pray for God's blessing on our cause, without ceasing, and would not live in this country if by any possible calamity we should be conquered; I am only a woman, and that is the way I feel.

3. Caroline Kirkland Offers "a Few Words in Behalf of the Loyal Women of the United States," 1863

It has lately become the fashion to say that, with regard to their interest in the present most unhappy war, the women of the North have not equalled those of the South in patriotic interest, labors, and sacrifices. The first utterer of this opinion probably aimed at nothing more than a sensational paragraph; for had there been any more serious or earnest intent, some specifications would have been given, that those accused might have had either the opportunity to defend themselves, or valuable hints for their future guidance and incitement to duty. One writer says—and this is as distinct a form of the accusation as any we remember to have met with: "But for the courage and energy of the women of the South, we believe the Rebellion would not have survived to this time. Had the women of the North with like zeal addressed themselves to the work of encouraging a loyal and devoted spirit among us, the copperhead conspiracy in behalf of the enemy would have been strangled at its birth, and the rebels would have learned, long ago, the futility of expecting aid and comfort from such a source." . . .

The gist of all that has been said of our deficiency in the present crisis, so far as we understand it, is that we have not shown *passion* enough; that we have acted naturally, in short. . . .

It can hardly be expected that the great body of loyal women should quietly accept the derogatory comparison alluded to. . . . Soldiers! you can speak for us. Have we been indifferent to your wants and sufferings; have we chilled your noble devotion by our faint-hearted words; have our letters to you breathed a spirit of discontent and repining, or failed to hail your enthusiasm and give the full measure of praise and joy to your heroic achievements? You who have lately, in a time of need, spoken so nobly for your country and its government, to the confusion of

---

Caroline Matilda Kirkland, *A Few Words in Behalf of the Loyal Women of the United States,* Loyal Publication Society, no. 10 (New York: Bryant and Co., 1863).

blatant traitors, lift your voices once more, in behalf of the loyal women who await you at home! . . .

As to the "sacrifices" said to have been made by the women of the South, and which are insisted upon by their Northern sympathizers as proofs of heroic resolution, their merit must depend upon circumstances. It is no virtue to wear a coarse dress if you can obtain no other, or to live poorly when good living is too costly for your means. It is very probable that the sacrifices of the women have been greater than those of the men, if we exclude from the calculation the hardships which all soldiers in all wars must necessarily endure. But we cannot class such sacrifices with those voluntarily borne by our revolutionary mothers, for they suffered gladly in the cause of LIBERTY, while the women of the South have no higher incentive than the determination to uphold their husbands in the attempt to perpetuate SLAVERY. The sacrifices required by a war which the South voluntarily commenced should have been counted beforehand. A rebellion against just and lawful, kind and beneficent authority; a war which pretends to no high or holy motive, and can allege in its justification no public wrong or injury, can claim no general sympathy for the sufferings and sacrifices it compels a consenting people to bear, nor can sacrifices in a bad cause take the rank which belongs to those endured for a principle sanctioned alike by God and man. We know that women usually adopt the political views of their husbands, and we profess no surprise that Southern women should have done so. We see it among ourselves, and have felt it in the refusal of women whose husbands sympathize with the South to do anything for the country or the army in this crisis, but we must regret that their sacrifices should not have been made in a more worthy cause, and hope for their own sakes that they will never glory in them. To suffer for liberty is glorious; to deprive ourselves of the comforts and necessaries of life in behalf of slavery, can never be anything but ignominious, though human sympathy views with pity the sufferings of those so desperately mistaken.

It is true that we of the North have seen as yet little occasion for these personal sacrifices which, doubtless, press heavily upon our belligerent neighbors. Our industry has known no interruption, and our prosperity has been ample, so far as material things are concerned. We weep for our losses by this cruel war, but not for any lack experienced in the ordinary comforts of our firesides. . . .

. . . [W]e advance no claim to *superiority* in zeal and devotedness, over the women of the South. It is to vindicate loyal women from a charge of *deficiency*, as compared with the other side, that we venture to speak. . . .

If we interpret aright the attempt to contrast us unfavorably with Southern women in devotion to the public service, the meaning is that *they* have sustained their men in fiery hate and contempt for their countrymen of the North, and done everything possible to incite and encourage them in the determination to found an empire, whose corner-stone should be human slavery. They, having seen slavery, felt it, known its horrors, suffered under its attendant evils, and learned, so far as they have learned Christianity, its incompatibility with God's benign law of love, have deliberately lent themselves and those dearer than life to them, to the perpetuation of so awful an evil, for the sake of an idea, however futile, of worldly prosperity! The separation of families, the lashing of women, brutal tortures of young girls from the most atrocious motives—all these and long list of crimes and outrages upon humanity, of which these are but specimens, excite no repugnance, it seems, in the minds of Southern women? They are willing to go on and on, and to uphold the whole abomination just as it is, and the reward for which they submit to this fearful self-degradation is the pleasure of a triumph over the hated "Yankees!" . . .

. . . We are told of the sacrifices they have made in the cause of War—have they ever made a sacrifice in the cause of Truth? If all the women in the rebellious States who disapprove of slavery, and believe it to be an evil and a sin, had, as with one voice, remonstrated against this war for its extension and perpetuity, instead of weakly allowing passion to influence them, without regard to principle or conscience, there would have been no war. If every Southern wife had done her whole duty by her husband, using the "still, small voice" to which God has given such power, in persuading him to listen to reason and duty, rather than to the trumpet-blare of a wicked and heartless ambition, what misery might have been saved! But not only failing to prevent, she has, so we are told, used all her power, and most successfully, to add fuel to the cruel flame, and to stifle, as far as possible, the whisper of conscience, which might at some happy moment have become audible.

4. Ella Gertrude Clanton Thomas Describes Conditions in the Confederacy and Criticizes Northern Women, 1865

Tuesday, January 3, 1865

Mr Thomas has gone up stairs and I have just finished reading an interesting letter giving an account of the movements of the state line troops during Sherman's march through Georgia. Alluding to the evacuation of Savannah he mentions that after our troops left the city he could hear the shrieks of women caused by the stragglers—the skullers of our army who had commenced to pillage and destroy. Some of them were shot by the citizens and others captured by the Yankees. "Wither are we drifting?" is the pertinent question asked by the Editor of the Charleston *Mercury* in commenting upon the increase of crime and lawlessness in that city— and this enquiry comes with startling energy from others when the time appears rapidly approaching when we have almost as much to dread from our own demoralized mob as from the public enemy.

. . . [I]n God's name what are we doing? Striving to defend ourselves against our brethren who would butcher us—annihilate us if they could— War is a terrible demon. It does not elevate—it debases. It does not lift heavenward—it crushes into the dust. I lose faith in humanity when I see such efforts to sink the nobler better part of man's nature in an effort to exterminate the white race at the South in order to elevate the Negro race to a position which I doubt their ability to fill—

The time will come when Southern women will be avenged— Let this war cease with the abolition of slavery and I wish for the women of the North no worse fate than will befall them. Their husbands already prepare for them the bitter cup of humiliation which they will be compelled to drink to the dregs— General Kilpatrick

Virginia Ingraham Burr, ed., *The Secret Eye: The Journal of Ella Gertrude Clanton Thomas* (Chapel Hill: University of North Carolina Press, 1990), 252–254.

spent a night in Waynesboro. [H]is headquarters were at Mrs Dr Carter's. He demanded that the best bed room in the house should be prepared for himself and a good looking mulatto girl whom he had traveling with him. A seat at the table was furnished her— The officers deferential in their manner to her while thus publicly insulting Mrs Carter in her own house. Lolling indolently in a rocking chair the girl awaits the entrance of the Gen. "What not retired yet Nellie?" is his salutation. "Not until your majesty returns" is her reply— Take *that scene* Mrs Kilpatrick as a reward for encouraging your husband to come amongst us. . . .

I don't know why it is but that man Sherman has interested me very much— perhaps it is upon the principle that all women admire successful courage and that Gen Sherman has proven himself to be a very brave man there can be no doubt. Our enemy as he is I can imagine that his wife loves him. A short time ago I read that his baby six months old had died— I could not be glad of it altho his men in their eager search after hidden treasure opened the graves of babys that had just been buried and left the coffins on the brink of the grave. At one time just after Sherman passed through Burke I wrote Mrs Sherman a letter which I intended having published under the head of Personal in one of the Richmond papers— I did not send it and now that I have read of the recent death of her baby I am glad that I did not. Woman's nature is the same the world over. She brooks no rival near the throne (except amongst the [illegible] that strange anamoly of nature). Northern women are colder in their temperature than our warm hearted children of the sun but I know that amongst the jubilee attendant upon her husband's "Christmas present" to Lincoln [Savannah] I could send Mrs Sherman "a New Year's gift" which would dim and make hollow and empty the mirth by which she is surrounded— I do feel very very sorry for her and will not send this letter if I could—

Mrs Gen Sherman—A few days since I read your husband's farewell telegram to you dated Atlanta. Will you believe it? *for a moment* I felt sorry for you. Forgetting who you were and for what purpose he was coming among us my heart went out in womanly sympathy for you. He bids you expect to hear from him only through rebel sources and urged by the same womanly intuition which prompted me to sympathise with you, I a rebel lady will give you some information with regard to Gen Sherman's movements. Last week your husband's army found me in the possession of wealth. Tonight our plantations are a scene of ruin and desolation. *You* bad him "God speed" on his fiendish errand, did you not? You thought it a gallant deed to come amongst us where by his own confession he expected to find "only the shadow of an army." A brave act to frighten women and children! desolate homes, violate the sanctity of firesides and cause the "widow and orphan to curse the Sherman for the cause" and this you did for what? to elevate the Negro race. Be satisfied Madam your wish has been accomplished. Enquire of Gen Sherman when next you see him who has been elevated to fill your place? You doubtless read with a smile of approbation of the delightfully fragrant ball at which he made his debut in Atlanta? Did he tell you of the Mulatto girl for whose safety he was so much concerned that she was returned to Nashville when he commenced his vandal march? This girl was spoken of by the Negroes whom you are willing to trust so implicitly as "Sherman's wife." Rest satisfied Mrs Sherman and quiet the apprehension of your Northern sisters with regard to the elevation of the Negros— Your husbands are amongst a coloured race whose reputation for morality has never been of the highest order—and these gallant cavaliers are most of them provided with "a companion du voyage"— As your brave husband considers a southern lady a fair object to wage war against and as I do not yet feel fully satisfied that there is no danger of a clutch from his heavy hand upon my shoulders, I will only add that intensely Southern woman as I am *I pity you.*

5. Mary Livermore Recalls Northern Women's Response to the Beginning of the Civil War, 1890

If men faltered not, and went gayly to death, that slavery might be exterminated, and that the United States might remain intact and undivided, women strengthened them by accepting the policy of the government uncomplainingly. When the telegraph recorded for the country, "defeat" instead of "victory," and for their beloved, "death" instead of "life," women continued to give the government their faith, and patiently worked and waited.

It is easy to understand how men catch the contagion of war, especially when they feel their quarrel to be just. One can comprehend how, fired with enthusiasm, and inspired by martial music, they march to the cannon's mouth, where the iron hail rains heaviest, and the ranks are mowed down like grain in harvest. But for women to send forth their husbands, sons, brothers and lovers to the fearful chances of the battle-field, knowing well the risks they run,—this involves exquisite suffering, and calls for another kind of heroism. This women did throughout the country, forcing their white lips to utter a cheerful "good-bye," when their hearts were nigh breaking with the fierce struggle.

The transition of the country from peace to the tumult and waste of war, was appalling and swift—but the regeneration of its women kept pace with it. They lopped off superfluities, retrenched in expenditures, became deaf to the calls of pleasure, and heeded not the mandates of fashion. The incoming patriotism of the hour swept them to the loftiest height of devotion, and they were eager to do, to bear, or to suffer, for the beloved country. The fetters of caste and conventionalism dropped at their feet, and they sat together, patrician and plebeian, Protestant and Catholic, and scraped lint, and rolled bandages, or made garments for the poorly clad soldiery.

An order was sent to Boston for five thousand shirts for the Massachusetts troops at the South. Every church in the city sent a delegation of needle-women to "Union Hall," heretofore used as a ballroom. The Catholic priests detailed five hundred sewing-girls to the pious work. Suburban towns rang the bells of the town hall to muster the seamstresses. The plebeian Irish Catholic of South Boston ran the sewing-machine, while the patrician Protestant of Beacon Street basted,—and the shirts were made at the rate of a thousand a day. On Thursday, Dorothea Dix sent an order for five hundred shirts for her hospital in Washington. On Friday, they were cut, made, and packed—and were sent on their way that night. Similar events were of constant occurrence in every other city. The zeal and devotion of women no more flagged through the war than did that of the army in the field. They rose

Mary A. R. Livermore, *My Story of the War* (A. D. Worthing and Co., 1890), 110–112, 120–122.

to the height of every emergency, and through all discouragements and reverses maintained a sympathetic unity between the soldiers and themselves, that gave to the former a marvellous heroism.

At a meeting in Washington during the war, called in the interest of the Sanitary Commission, President Lincoln said: "I am not accustomed to use the language of eulogy. I have never studied the art of paying compliments to women. But I must say that if all that has been said by orators and poets since the creation of the world in praise of women, was applied to the women of America, it would not do them justice for their conduct during this war. I will close by saying, God bless the women of America!" . . .

. . . It is better to heal a wound than to make one. And it is to the honor of American women, not that they led hosts to the deadly charge, and battled amid contending armies, but that they confronted the horrid aspects of war with mighty love and earnestness. They kept up their own courage and that of their households. They became ministering angels to their countrymen who perilled health and life for the nation. They sent the love and impulses of home into the extended ranks of the army, through the unceasing correspondence they maintained with "the boys in blue." They planned largely, and toiled untiringly, and with steady persistence to the end, that the horrors of the battle-field might be mitigated, and the hospitals abound in needed comforts. The men at the front were sure of sympathy from the homes and knew that the women remembered them with sleepless interest. "This put heroic fibre into their souls," said Dr. Bellows, "and restored us our soldiers with their citizen hearts beating normally under their uniforms, as they dropped them off at the last drum-tap." . . .

So determined were the people that their citizen soldiers should be well cared for, that "Relief Societies" were frequently organized in the interest of regiments, as soon as they were mustered into the service. They proposed to follow the volunteers of their neighborhoods with their benefactions—"to provide them with home comforts when well, and with hospital supplies and nurses when wounded or sick." It would have been an admirable plan if it could have been carried out. But numerous difficulties and failures soon brought these methods into disrepute. The accumulation of perishable freight for the soldiers became fearful. It demanded instant transportation, and the managers of freight trains and expresses were in despair.

Women rifled their store-rooms and preserve-closets of canned fruits and pots of jam and marmalade, which they packed with clothing and blankets, books and stationery, photographs and "comfort-bags." Baggage cars were soon flooded with fermenting sweetmeats, and broken pots of jelly, that ought never to have been sent. Decaying fruit and vegetables, pastry and cake in a demoralized condition, badly canned meats and soups, whose fragrance was not that of "Araby the blest," were necessarily thrown away *en route.* And with them went the clothing and stationery saturated with the effervescing and putrefying compounds which they enfolded.

E S S A Y S

The contrasting experiences of northern and southern white women during the Civil War are treated in two recent publications. LeeAnn Whites of the University of Missouri, Columbia, goes behind the fervent Confederate rhetoric to examine a region that was, she declares, "teetering on the edge of a critical racial and gender imbalance, pushed to the brink by changes in the sectional social and economic structure." Jeanie Attie, a historian at the C. W. Post campus of Long Island University, focuses on northern women's patriotism and involvement in the war effort. She concludes that the war offered them many new opportunities and raised their expectations about advances in the future.

Southern White Women and the Burdens of War

LEEANN WHITES

It was a cold winter's day and greenish ice flows clogged the turbulent river. Across its vast expanse, Eliza could see the far shore of Ohio and freedom. Behind her, coming ever closer, she could hear the baying dogs of the slavetrader, Haley. What could she do? On the one side was slavery and the certain loss of her child to the slavetrader. On the other was an impassable river and probable death. Looking down at her small son, Eliza knew only that she could not bear to lose him. And with one desperate burst of courage, she jumped onto the nearest ice flow. Scrambling and leaping from one teetering piece of ice to another, she struggled across the mighty Ohio and gained the far shore of freedom for herself and her child.

Laying down the collection of antislavery tracts she was reading, Harriet Beecher Stowe was deeply moved. In Eliza's desperate act of undaunted mother love, Stowe heard an almost irresistible call to action. She would tell the world Eliza's story, for herein lay the true sin of slavery—the way in which it thwarted and repressed the maternal bond, separating mother and child, brother and sister, husband and wife, eroding the emotional fabric of the black family in the name of the vested property rights of white slaveowners. The emergence of the family as a separate sphere in the North, freed from the sordid economic concerns of men, had constituted the domestic realm of the mother as a sphere in its own right, allowing her older sister, Catharine Beecher, to claim a new and boldly autonomous role for women as the moral arbiters of social life. Now Harriet Beecher Stowe would shine this newly emancipated light of the family and of the moral mother as the spokesperson of its interests upon what increasingly appeared to be a domestically retrograde southern slave system.

The rest is history. *Uncle Tom's Cabin,* the novel that Harriet Beecher Stowe wrote as if driven to it, swept the nation by storm to become the most popular novel of the entire century. Its claim for the domestic rights of slaves popularized the antislavery cause in the North in a manner that no abstract calls to the inherent equality of all mankind had ever succeeded in doing in the past. As Abraham Lincoln commented upon first meeting Harriet Beecher Stowe in the midst of the Civil War, "So you are the little woman who wrote the book that made this great war."

If, however, popular antislavery sentiment in the North, and the war that followed from it, was grounded upon a new understanding of the domestic rights of the family, and in particular in the expansion of the private and public authority of the mother as the bearer and rearer of life, then we must ask, what did this war of

LeeAnn Whites, "The Civil War as a Crisis in Gender," in Catherine Clinton and Nina Silber, eds., *Divided Houses: Gender and the Civil War* (New York: Oxford University Press, 1992), 3–9, 13–21. Copyright © 1992 by Catherine Clinton and Nina Silber. Used by permission of Oxford University Press, Inc.

domestic liberation mean for women of the South? How are we to understand the widespread support for the war among Confederate women, support for a War of Southern Independence that was understood by at least some of their northern sisters to be nothing less than the defense of the independence of Confederate men from the dictates of reproduction and the moral authority of motherhood? An independence that so subordinated the interests of reproduction and the family as a whole to the particular economic and productive interests of the individual planter that it gave him the right not only to own the child of some woman's heart and body but to dispose of it as *his* material interests would dictate.

While the readership of *Uncle Tom's Cabin* in the South was not as widespread as in the North, those who did read it were undoubtedly at least equally consumed by the critique of the southern slave household structure that it presented. Mary Boykin Chesnut, daughter of a prominent planter-class family and wife of a member of Jefferson Davis's staff, was haunted by the novel and returned to it time and again in her Civil War diary. She took particular umbrage at Stowe's claim for the moral superiority of northern women. "What self-denial," queried Chesnut, did northerners like Stowe practice while sitting in their "nice New England homes—clean, clear, sweet smelling?" She contrasted this picture of the northern household, pristine in its isolation, with the experience of her female relations, living in households enmeshed in the institution of slavery. These women of the planter elite were, according to Chesnut, educated in the same northern schools as their abolitionist critics. They read the same Bible and had the "same ideas of right and wrong," yet they were not so fortunate as to be safely ensconced in a separate familiar sphere dedicated to the domestic interests of their families alone. Instead they lived in "negro villages" where they struggled to "ameliorate the condition of these Africans in every particular."

> They set them the example of a perfect life—a life of utter self-abnegation. . . . Think of these holy New Englanders, forced to have a negro village walk through their houses whenever they saw fit. . . . [These women] have a swarm of blacks about them as children under their care—not as Mrs. Stowe paints them, but the hard, unpleasant, unromantic, undeveloped savage Africans. And they hate slavery worse than Mrs. Stowe.

Here the ultimate figure of domestic self-sacrifice and thus *the* "true woman" was not those abolitionist spokeswomen for the "cult of domesticity" and the family as a separate sphere, but rather the planter-class woman, who precisely *because* of the presence of slavery within the southern household was placed in a position to act as the mother of not only her own children but of her slave dependents as well. Of course, in Harriet Beecher's account, the most militant defender of motherhood was not in fact the northern abolitionist woman like herself, who risked only her good reputation in taking a public stance against slavery. Domesticity at its most insurgent was represented by those slave mothers, like Eliza, who in the very act of mothering their children could be called upon to subvert the institution of slavery itself. Chesnut's defense of the motherhood of the plantation mistress, on the other hand, spoke from within the confines of the institution of slavery. For it was the very same slave system that worked to deny Eliza her motherhood that gave Chesnut the basis for claiming it as the slave mistresses' own. Ownership in slaves not only made the planters the wealthiest men in the country through their appropriation of the productive labor of their slaves, but it also served to make their women into "ladies" by virtue of their own ability not only to "mother" their slaves but more fundamentally to appropriate their domestic labor. It was this ownership in slaves that empowered the white mistress, like Mary Boykin Chesnut, to define the slave woman not as a mother in her own right but as one of the many "children" under her own maternal care.

As slavery was an organic part of the southern household, it became organic to the slaveowners' very conception of themselves as men and as women, as mothers and as fathers. It both served to expand their own domestic claims as *individual* mothers and fathers, while it served to subordinate, literally to enslave, the sphere of reproduction and of domestic life as a whole to the class interests of this same planter elite. Ultimately the extent to which motherhood was rendered unfree within the southern slave system served to undermine the domestic position of even those women of the planter class who benefited from it most in class terms. For whatever power they gained for their own domestic position by having slave dependents, they lost by the manner in which slaveownership further empowered their own men. So while women of the planter class could claim to "mother" their slaves, at least some of their husbands were literally fathers of slaves. The outcome, concluded Chesnut, was often far more devastating than even Harriet Beecher Stowe envisioned, She recorded the conversation among one group of elite Confederate women. ". . . I knew the dissolute half of Legree well," asserted one of these women,

> He was high and mighty. But the kindest creature to his slaves—and the unfortunate results of his bad ways were not sold, had not to jump over ice blocks. They were kept in full view and provided for handsomely in his will. His wife and daughters in the might of their purity and innocence are supposed never to dream of what is as plain before their eyes as the sunlight, and they play their parts of unsuspecting angels to the letter.

"Southern women," wrote Ella Gertrude Clanton Thomas, in her antebellum journal, "are I believe all at heart abolitionists." When she made this claim, she in fact meant that all women of *her* class and race were abolitionists. Had she actually meant to refer to all southern women, her case would have been a stronger one. For to the extent that planter-class women were abolitionists, it was not in the first instance the consequence of their recognition of a common likeness among all women. It reflected instead their desire to be full-fledged members of their class, empowered like their men to dictate the cultural norms of their society. Planter-class women burned, admittedly in private or in the company of other women, at the power that the ownership of slaves gave their men to create a double standard of sexual behavior within the planter class itself. As Rebecca Latimer Felton, a Georgia planter-class woman, wrote in her memoirs many years after the war, for the "abuses" that made "mulattoes as common as blackberries," the planters deserved to have their entire system collapse.

> In this one particular slavery doomed itself. When white men put their own offspring in the kitchen and the cornfield and allowed them to be sold into bondage as slaves and degraded them as another man's slave, the retribution of wrath was hanging over this country and the South paid penance in four years of bloody war.

Hindsight is twenty-twenty, but where was this voice for the larger interests of southern motherhood in 1860? Jumping across ice flows? Not, certainly, coming from the likes of Rebecca Felton, who asserted in her memoirs that upon the outbreak of the Civil War, a war that she perceived to be a "battle to defend our rights in owner-ship of African slaves," there was "never a more loyal woman" than herself. "I could not," she wrote, "fight against my kindred." Besides, she concluded, she was "only a woman and nobody asked me for opinion." The political voice of domesticity was silenced even among these most powerful of southern women, if only by the force of their own class interests. For at bottom was the undeniable fact that the slave plantation economy promoted their own material well-being. Therefore, no matter how frustrated they may have been in their own efforts to claim an enlarged sphere of authority in relation to the men of their class, they could not ignore the benefits that their own position as members of this class, however subordinated, gave them. If only out of their concern for their own children, women of the planter class were forced to recognize that the same planter who "defied the marriage law of the state by keeping up two households on the same plantation," as Rebecca Latimer Felton wrote, was also, as Mary Chesnut concluded, "the fountain from whom all blessings flow." . . .

The mid-nineteenth-century South presents the picture of a society teetering on the edge of a critical racial and gender imbalance, pushed to the brink by changes in the sectional social and economic structure. The incredible demand generated for cotton by the industrial revolution taking place in Britain and in the North made cot-ton the King of plantation staple crops and made the planter King as well—a King empowered by the profitability of this crop to buy the reproductive capacity of ever larger numbers of slave women as well as to turn the domestic voice of the women of his own class to his own self-empowerment. Almost perversely, however, the very same industrial revolution which served to fuel the expansion of the patriarchal power of southern planter-class men also created the basis for the emergence of the family as a separate sphere in the North. Therefore while reproduction remained en-slaved within the plantation household economy and the voice of domestic politics was muted, it burst forth with equally dazzling clarity in the North. Northern feminist and abolitionist women formed organizations and petitioned for fundamental changes within households and in the society at large. Some of these women even claimed the right to demand a single sexual standard of behavior from their men. . . .

As the fiction of slave servility and childlike dependence upon the patriarchal planter dissolved in the crucible of war, it left only the subordination of southern white women—as the only dependents on whose loyalty the planter could continue to rely. As the racial and class basis for dependence slipped away, gender thus emerged as an ever more critical basis for the persistence of southern white men as "free men." Not surprisingly, Confederate men at the time and for years afterward have written in self-congratulatory tones of the loyalty that their women demon-strated during the conflict. Confederate women, we are repeatedly told, constituted the "very soul of the war," offering up that which they did possess, their domestic at-tachments to those nearest and dearest to them, for that which they as individuals could never hope to obtain, the liberties of free men. This was the discipline that the patriarchal slave system had reared them up to, to deny the interests of domesticity in the face of the interests of their class. Now, however, the necessity of placing class prerogatives over the interests of domestic life had come to their own families, rather than to those of their slaves. But they did not flinch. At least, not in public. . . .

Some historians have gone so far as to argue that the women of the Confederacy were even more intensely committed to the war than were their men, packing the galleries of secessionist congresses, hissing at the delegates who opposed secession and cheering on its advocates. One Selma belle was reputed to have broken off her engagement when her fiancé failed to enlist. She sent him a skirt and female under-garments with the message, "wear these or volunteer." A letter of one young woman to her local newspaper upon the outbreak of war certainly reflected an intense identi-fication with the cause:

> You will pardon the liberty I have taken to address you, when I tell you that my great inclination to do so assails me so constantly that I can only find relief in writing to you. . . . My father and family have always been the strongest of Whigs, and of course not in favor of immediate secession; but as that has been the irrevocable act of the South I submit to it, and say "as goes Georgia, so go I." But at the same time I am conscious that that very act has increased our responsibilities tenfold. We have outwardly assumed the garb of independence and now let us walk in the path our state has chosen. And shall man tread it alone? . . . No, no a thousand times no.

Urging other Confederate women to join her in the cause, she suggested that they "hurl the destructive novel in the fire and turn our poodles out of doors, and convert our pianos into spinning wheels." Not only would this return to home man-ufacturing make a critical contribution to their male relation's pursuit of political autonomy, the drive for political independence would make Confederate women more independent as well. As she concluded, "I feel a new life within me, and my ambition aims at nothing higher than to become an ingenious, economical, indus-trious housekeeper, and an independent Southern woman."

The demands of the war effort offered Confederate women a rare opportunity. Through their contributions to the cause they could enter into the heart of the struggle and like their men define themselves as "independent" southern women. Women who were independent because their privatized domestic pursuits were now thrust onto the center stage of southern life were not in violation of their sub-ordinated domestic status. Confederate women in their role as mothers found themselves in a particularly critical position. It was after all their children who were the very stuff of the war machine. If men, especially young men, were to participate in the war effort, women, especially their mothers, would have to acquiesce in their departure. As one newspaper noted, "The man who does not love his mother and yield to her influence is not the right stuff to make a patriot of, and has no business in a patriot army."

With such influence came a newfound responsibility for southern women. Let-ters in southern papers therefore urged women to consider the long-range impact the war might have on their sons. "Let them not, in future years . . . be forced in sadness of heart and reproaches of conscience, to say that in all this they took no part." Mothers should, according to this writer, consider with what "humiliation" sons would be forced to recognize that they were "unworthy of the liberty and home secured for them by the valor of others." Motherhood should exert a public and political presence.

Not only did the war serve to intensify the centrality of reproduction in southern society, it also gave public, political significance to the domestic manufacturing of women. For not only did the war demand the contribution of women's reproductive product, their children, but critical economic problems now revolved around essen-tially domestic questions of how the troops were to be clothed, fed, and nursed. Cotton proved to be virtually useless in this regard as it could not be eaten, made poor shoes, coats and blankets, and could hardly be shot. Local newspapers urged planters to turn their production toward subsistence crops instead and promoted the public organization of women into local Ladies Aid Societies dedicated to organizing their previously privatized labor in order to more efficiently clothe, feed, and nurse the troops. . . .

While Confederate men may have gone to war in defense of what they perceived to be their prerogatives as free men and in rejection of the threatened domination of a "horde of agrarians, abolitionists and free lovers," the actual demands of fighting the war made them increasingly conscious of their own dependence upon women's love and labor. As a result the southern soldier had to recognize, if only unconsciously, the extent to which his manhood and independence was relational—a social construction built upon the foundation of women's service and love, out of the fabric of his women's "dependence." For the more the war called forth women's domestic labor into the public arena, making public those "small gifts of service," the more the war itself was transformed from a struggle of men in defense of their individual prerogatives into a battle for the "firesides of our noble countrywomen." Confederate women seized this opportunity to lay claim to an increased reciprocity in gender relations. As one woman wrote to the newspaper, ". . . Do impress upon the soldiers, that they are constantly in our thoughts, that we are *working* for them, while they are *fighting* for us—and that their wants shall be supplied, as long as there is a *woman* or a *dollar* in the 'Southern Confederacy.'"

Confederate women found that the war might support a newly independent stature on their part. As Rebecca Latimer Felton wrote, "Nobody chided me then as unwomanly, when I went into a crowd and waited on suffering men. No one said I was unladylike to climb into cattle cars and box cars to feed those who could not feed themselves." Nor did the press find Amy Clark to be "unwomanly" when it was discovered that not only had she enlisted with her husband, but after he was killed she fought on alone in the ranks as a common soldier. She was described as "heroic *and* self-sacrificing" (emphasis added). But then as Sarah Morgan recorded in her diary upon hiding a pistol and a carving knife on her person in order to defend herself against the invading Union soldiers in Baton Rouge, "Pshaw! There are *no* women here! We are *all* men!"

As their women became more independent and, hence, more "male," Confederate men increasingly had to recognize their own dependence upon women, whether in managing their households in their absence, outfitting them in the field, or nursing them when wounded. Such men, in fact, became increasingly feminized. The male world of the camps was enough in and of itself to make many men think longingly of their lost domestic comforts. As Will Deloney wrote home to his wife, "Don't imagine that I have forgotten you—for I think of nobody else—and if you could see the discomfort my life held now you would conclude I could never forget. . . ."

William Deloney was shot from his horse while leading a cavalry charge in the fall of 1863. He died a hero to the cause, but he was lost to his family. He left his wife, Rosa, with four young children to carry on as best she might. In a letter written shortly after his death, a cousin urged Rosa to "take care of yourself for your dear children. Who can fill a *Mother's* place?" Who indeed? Here was the expansion of the domestic autonomy of planter-class women with a vengeance, as impoverished widows. For those Confederate men like Frank Coker, who were so fortunate as to survive the war and return to their homes, being a father and a husband was also at once more and less than it was before the War. For despite his wife's clever management and hard efforts at retrenchment during the war, the Cokers' finances were in great disarray. The economy was devastated, their section was defeated, and their slaves were emancipated. Frank Coker was no longer the same "lord of creation" that he once was: no longer a veritable "fountain from whom all blessings flow."

The Cokers' economic loss was mirrored in their slaves' domestic gain. For the ultimate *structural* rebalancing of southern domestic relations began when the southern household was sheared apart with the emancipation of the slaves. As the freedmen departed en masse from the households of their ex-masters in search of members of their own families lost to them under slavery, they moved toward a new domestic integrity for *all* southern families. They established themselves as heads of their own households, fathers and husbands in their own right. As freedwomen turned their labor toward the needs of their own kin, withdrawing from the kitchens and the fields of the master class insofar as they were able, they laid claim to a common status with their white counterparts as wives and mothers. In so doing they began to carve out what might have become a common ground for a future unity among southern women.

At the time, however, this newfound integrity of the southern family structure and the increased gender commonality of all women that it portended presented itself to planter-class women not as a victory for their gender interests but rather as the defeat of their men and of their class. For if the war served to intensify Confederate women's commitment to their men's class interests, their defeat served to set that commitment in concrete. "It was as though," in the words of one southern newspaper editor, "the mighty oak" was "hit by lightning" and only the "clinging vine" now kept it erect. Planter-class women urged their men to take solace in their own family circle, a family circle which should be more valued for that which had been lost. "Your wives and children are around you," wrote one woman, "sharing your sorrows as well as your joys. Though you may not have as many luxuries as in former days, you still have enough to eat and wear and can repose in security."

A retreat to familial life could make the sting of defeat more palatable, but it could not erase the necessity of subordination for defeated Confederate men. The "proud Southron" wrote one planter-class woman, Susan Cornwall, must now learn to "obey those laws which neither you nor yours had any hand in framing and those men who you fought four long years to be free from." It was defeat at the hands of other men that would finally force these men to adopt a world view more like that of their dependents. For as both slaves and women of the planter class had recognized before the war, the way to accept such subordination to another man's will and yet retain some sense of self-respect was to acknowledge a master above the master—to believe that subordination on this earth was but a prelude to some ultimate self-realization in another. "Teach us Oh, Father," wrote Cornwall, "those lessons of patience and resignation which hitherto we have refused to learn and grant that once more we may lift our hearts to thee and cry *Our* father." . . .

This lesson of victory in defeat—the proper place and power of the virtuous sufferers—was the lesson that Harriet Beecher Stowe meant to convey in the closing scene of her novel, through the story of Uncle Tom's fateful struggle with his rapacious owner, Simon Legree. For Harriet Beecher Stowe, Simon Legree represented the potentially devastating consequences of a male domination untempered by a recognition of the domestic claims of either his own family or that of his slaves. Running away to sea as a young man and abandoning his poor mother to die of a broken heart, Legree had eventually ended up in the South. There he acquired a plantation and many slaves, but never a home and a loving wife. Living in domestic squalor, he sexually exploited his female slaves while he worked all his field hands to exhaustion. Uncle Tom in fact sacrificed his own life to protect one of the slave women on the plantation from Legree's sexual abuse.

In the character of Uncle Tom, Harriet Beecher Stowe presented what she considered to be the highest exemplar of moral social behavior among men; men who, motivated by a keen sense of their own humility, turned their energies to upholding the human rights of those who were even more subordinated in the world than themselves. From this feminized vantage point, the defeat of the Confederacy and the economic difficulties of the region that followed upon it were perhaps not an unmitigated loss. The possibility of some gain ensued from the expanded significance and integrity that domestic life achieved. By sacrificing his own life, Uncle Tom had succeeded in forcing Simon Legree to recognize some limits to his power to dominate others. For although Legree won the battle and killed Uncle Tom, he was forced to acknowledge that he had lost the war for his soul. Through the moral power of his ultimate sacrifice, Tom found a better home, one in which he would be freed from the defeats and oppression he had endured in this world. "I'm right in the door," he gasped with his final breath, "I've got the victory."

For one brief moment in the course of the war itself, as advancing Union forces intensified the erosion of slavery that was already occurring from within, it had appeared that the defeat of the Confederate war effort would underwrite the earthly victory of the enslaved southern black population. The land would be redistributed and freedmen would acquire their forty acres and a mule and thereby their status as "free men" as it had been constructed in the antebellum social order. At the same time, it appeared that the subordinated status of motherhood would also be at least mitigated as the abolition of slavery promised to ratify the increased public status and significance that domestic concerns had gained during the war. The collapse of the slave plantation household in war and reconstruction did indeed fundamentally limit the extent to which some men could define their own status as free men by the measure of the limits of freedom on others. It did set certain structural limits to the subordination of reproduction and the family to the interests of the market. Families could no longer be bought or sold. It did not, however, create the basis for racial or gender equality in this country. For although the planter class was defeated, it was not vanquished. They lost their ownership in slaves, but not their control of the land. As a result, the war left white southern men feeling like less than men. It left black men with a manhood that frequently continued to cost them their lives. It left white southern women clinging to what was left of white southern men's ability to provide, and, all too often, it left black southern women with no alternative but to work in some white woman's kitchen. All men were not created equal and few women found themselves even comparatively free.

Northern White Women and the Mobilization for War

JEANIE ATTIE

On April 22, 1861, as southern troops shelled the federal base at Fort Sumter, igniting the American Civil War, Mary Livermore, an abolitionist and temperance lecturer, became swept up by the war fervor that suddenly engrossed Boston. For Livermore, those "never-to-be-forgotten days of Sumter's bombardment" were days of deep ambivalence, marked by apprehension about the possibility of a long and calamitous war but, at the same time, by elation about the prospect of slavery's demise. More than anything else, she remembered the exhilarating outbursts of patriotism and civic unity. On the following Sunday, pulpits in Boston "thundered with denunciations of the rebellion," recalled Livermore, who was surprised by the radical sermons offered by antislavery clergy. Amid this "blaze of belligerent excitement" came Lincoln's call for 75,000 troops to protect Washington and federal property; in what seemed like no time, recruiting offices opened in "every city, town, and village." In her memoir, Livermore wrote admiringly about military volunteers who were escorted through Boston by throngs of supporters. "Merchants and clerks rushed out from stores, bareheaded, saluting them as they passed. Windows were flung up; and women leaned out into the rain waving flags and handkerchiefs." By the time she returned to Chicago a few days later, Livermore was deeply impressed by the popular demonstrations that she had witnessed across the northern landscape; the "war spirit was rampant," she wrote, and "engrossed everybody."

Livermore's account echoed those of other northerners, who were astonished by the precipitous shift in public sentiment and the spirit of cohesiveness that characterized the first days and weeks of the war. In what became a familiar refrain among contemporaries, the North suddenly coalesced into a patriotic whole. Even in a society with a strong voluntarist tradition, and despite frequent evocations of comparable behavior during the Revolutionary War, the scope of civilian initiative during the Civil War seemed unprecedented. Given the contentious partisanship that had characterized the antebellum decades and the divisiveness generated by the secession of the southern states, the sudden disappearance of political differences elicited frequent comment. . . .

"It is easy to understand how men catch the contagion of war," Livermore conjectured; what required explanation was why women, "who send forth their husbands, sons, brothers and lovers to the fearful chances of the battle-field," were willing to endure such "exquisite suffering." The answer, she believed, lay in "another kind of patriotism," a love for their men and their country that diverged from male loyalties and masculine combativeness and provided women with a special strength to maintain "their own courage and that of their households."

Jeanie Attie, "'We All Have Views Now': Tapping Female Patriotism," in *Patriotic Toil: Northern Women and the Civil War* (Ithaca, N.Y.: Cornell University Press, 1998), 19–47. Used by permission of the publisher, Cornell University Press.

Implicit in Livermore's commentary on female loyalty was not only the idea that men's patriotism was something ingrained but also the idea that women's support of the war represented a conscious decision to make unique sacrifices in defense of the nation. Many women took on soldier aid work out of concern for husbands, sons, and neighbors leaving for war. Others were propelled by the excitement and urgency that marked mobilization drives. Yet the war's appeal to northern women went deeper than personal attachments or susceptibility to popular passions. Although the ferment surrounding the outbreak of military conflict seemed to cut across all social categories, troop mobilization presented distinct opportunities for many northern women. In a nation with a weak central government and a long tradition of political obligations performed at the local level, the urgent need for civilian support furnished women, especially white women of the middle class, with an occasion for presenting themselves as skilled members of the polity whose contributions were essential to the government's defense, a chance to enact their political beliefs on terms that both they and men appreciated and held to be legitimate. In the emergency conditions generated by war, women welcomed the sudden expansion of the emotional and physical spaces in which they could perform their citizenship. Although the antebellum gender divisions of labor and power meant that women would not be able to dictate either the extent of their political contributions or the measure of their sacrifices, many women nonetheless perceived that the military crisis might erase some of the boundaries that separated them from male preserves of power. . . . .

Mary Livermore was struck by the ways in which the war created arenas for men and women to join together as a newly constituted public, which was sanctioned to support the military on the battlefield whatever the cost. When, at Boston's Faneuil Hall, men filed in military-like columns to answer Lincoln's first call for volunteers, Livermore observed that "men, women, and children seethed in a fervid excitement." Amid the seemingly universal approbation for combat, women felt free to vent a belligerency toward the Confederacy and a fondness for military regalia that contravened the bourgeois socialization of women. Maria Lydig Daly was surprised to hear upper-class New York City women "admiring swords, pistols, etc., and seeming to wish to hear of the death of Southerners." Many women coveted masculine emblems of militarism. In Skowhegan, Maine, one group of women appropriated local artillery to stage "a salute of thirty-four guns." And then there were the famous cases—estimated at a minimum of four hundred—of women who disguised themselves as men and joined the Union army.

But the historic identification of militarism with masculinity also pointed to the disadvantages women faced in enacting their politics. When the ultimate gesture of political obligation was military service, offering one's life for the preservation of the state, more than a few women chafed at the legal constraints imposed on their sex. As soon as the war began, Louisa May Alcott confided in her diary: "I long to be a man; but as I can't fight, I will content myself with working for those who can." Another woman who devoted herself to war relief work reasoned, "[F]or . . . what else can we women do, at such a time as this? We cannot fight ourselves, but we can help those who can."

Although legal and social codes prevented women from performing their loyalties in the same manner as men, war mobilization nonetheless presented women with ways of exploiting the very structures of gender inequality to demonstrate their politics and loyalties. In acts of production and self-denial, many women discovered distinctly feminine methods for increasing their visibility as members of the polity. "They lopped off superfluities, retrenched in expenditures, became deaf to the calls of pleasure, and heeded not the mandates of fashion," Livermore wrote of her middle-class peers. In the production of uniforms and supplies for departing soldiers, women applied their mastery of domestic arts to political uses. Through military rallies, village parades, charity bazaars, and the household production of patriotic artifacts, they devised creative means to express their inclusion in the national crisis, while simultaneously underscoring their identities as women.

The symbol women chose most often to signify their patriotism was the United States flag. This choice of symbol was not surprising; northerners everywhere embraced the flag as an expression of their loyalty to the Union. . . . "Love for the old flag became a passion," Livermore recalled, as women "crocheted it prettily in silk, and wore it as a decoration on their bonnets and in their bosoms." Household reproductions of the flag motif proliferated as women incorporated its design and colors in a variety of crafted items. . . . Along with declaring one's nationalism, the flag could also embody more particular political content. For Livermore, the flag came to represent her antislavery sentiments. . . .

In spite of the poignant emotions they voiced about the purposes of the war and the passion they displayed for political affairs, most northern women were depicted by the popular culture of the war years as personifying a special "female" patriotism. Though women believed they had responded to the war emergency as members of communities and citizens of a nation alongside men, their support of the military was frequently characterized as gender-specific behavior, the manifestation of an apolitical and charitable nature. Whether women expressed their patriotism through their domesticity or as a result of the gendered modes of thought that permeated midcentury American culture, wartime invocations of political cohesion went hand in hand with an intensely gendered nationalist rhetoric. Throughout the war, northern women worked in a context that cast their patriotism as reflecting "feminine" rather than universal political concerns.

The Civil War notion of female patriotism stressed the naturalness of female loyalty, implying that women engaged in mobilization drives and soldier relief out of moral instincts, not political reason. When northern women threw themselves into the war effort, male contemporaries had a readymade intellectual framework through which to comprehend such activities, and few were surprised or unduly impressed. In his account of northern war charity, the Sanitary Commission's chronicler noted that the "earliest movement that was made for army relief [was] begun, as it is hardly necessary to say, by the women of the country." What appeared, rhetorically, to be a single patriotism was, in fact, a dichotomous concept, calling men to patriotic obligation as citizens who offered services to the state through their own free will and summoning women as citizens who were guided by apolitical and irrepressible propensities.

Wartime references to women's distinct political nature were plentiful. In 1863, the conservative *Godey's Lady's Book and Magazine* intoned that, although women could not "grasp all the subjects relating to the world," it was unimportant, for "moral sense is superior to mental power." An 1862 article in *Arthur's Home*

Magazine declared that while men dominated as statesmen, patriots, and conquerors, women were invisible but all-important heroines at home. Extolling the female heroism of "self-sacrifice [and] self-denial" the article explained that the "heroisms of the home" were in fact undertaken unconsciously. "They are *only natural*. They are nothing more than the spontaneous impulses and instincts of the heart. Those who perform them could do no less."

The idea of female patriotism repackaged domestic ideology for the war emergency, placing voluntarism and moral purity at the heart of women's political obligations to the state. Just as the antebellum ideology of separate spheres mystified the economic contributions of housework during the expansion of waged labor, so female patriotism veiled women's domestic labor in service to the Union with an aura of sentiment. Because the rhetoric of female patriotism was about love and not work, about sacrifices driven by nature rather than by calculation, women's wartime benevolence was assumed to be limitless. This dichotomous reading of patriotic loyalty elevated men's capacity to control women's unpaid domestic labor, moving from appropriating ownership of such labor in individual households to claiming authority over it for the nation. While men were never asked to perform labor for free, whether as soldiers or agents of benevolent organizations, women were expected to demonstrate their loyalty through donating labor.

One measure of the dominance of this gendered construction of northern patriotism was the effort many women made to distance themselves from it. As if to deflect the repercussions of their unequal access to military service and to question the double standard applied to their patriotic activities, women who wrote about the war frequently stressed the inherent parity of their political passions with those of men. In her autobiography, the feminist Elizabeth Cady Stanton made a point of noting that the "patriotism of woman shone forth as fervently and spontaneously as did that of man." . . .

The sense of possibility that attended women's voluntary support of the Union grew out of the particular conditions of northern mobilization, predicated on the voluntary enlistment of soldiers and the freely offered support of their communities. As a consequence of the customary American reliance on volunteer troops and citizen militia, and of the absence of mandatory conscription policies, the Union army was largely constructed through individual acts of voluntarism. Even after the federal government instituted conscription in 1863, the draft functioned primarily as an incentive to voluntarism (and the bounty systems functioned more as revenue-raising devices), rather than as compulsory means of raising troops. The numerous permissible exemptions to the draft and the prerogative, until the middle of 1864, to pay for substitutes greatly weakened the force of Union draft rules. Throughout the course of the war, the vast majority of men joined the Union forces as volunteers. . . .

In the context of a highly decentralized and voluntaristic mobilization of human and economic resources, middle-class women constituted a wellspring of needed labor and supplies. Anxious to convey loyalty to the Union cause and accustomed to handling the welfare needs of others, thousands of northern middle-class women reacted to the war emergency both by refocusing existing charitable organizations to meet the increased demands of military mobilization and by creating new societies devoted solely to the needs of soldiers.

Many of the initiatives undertaken by women during the first weeks of the war drew on the social networks they had developed in antebellum sewing groups, church associations, and moral reform societies. They also drew on women's extensive domestic skills. It is probable that nearly every nineteenth-century northern woman had some ability to sew and, at the outbreak of the war, most were still responsible for the production of their households' clothing. While the burgeoning textile industry increasingly relieved women from the spinning of yarn and manufacture of cloth, few could afford to rely solely on ready-made clothing. Indeed, most women were regularly occupied with the cutting, sewing, and repairing of clothing. Even genteel women, who could hire the services of seamstresses (and whose husbands and fathers purchased ready-made suits), were expected to be able to sew and do needlework. Women often sewed together, gathering to share each other's company while engaged in the time-consuming task of stitching personal garments. Farm women, with less available time, came together for quilting bees, combining their labor to produce large items, sharing techniques and camaraderie. In smaller towns and villages, women formed sewing circles and "Dorcas" societies, merging work and social interaction in quasi-institutional formats.

Though it was easy to modify the object of a local sewing group to serve the needs of mobilization, the war prompted women in many locales to create organizations specifically charged with aiding the federal war effort and, through a process of renaming, provided women with another means of making their patriotism visible to a larger public. The first recorded soldiers' aid society was constituted on April 15, 1861, in Bridgeport, Connecticut. In many cases, organized relief was instigated by the elite—"leading"—women in the community, such as those in Peekskill, New York, who arranged to receive contributions and prepare supplies before the first volunteers departed from town. The women of Rockdale, Pennsylvania, began war relief within days of the South's insurrection, soon extending their labors to the military hospital in nearby Philadelphia.

The historical record is inherently skewed to reflect the activities of those with the resources and self-consciousness to keep accounts of their doings, or those with sufficient social stature to merit attention in contemporary narratives and regional histories. But working-class women also participated in soldier relief work: some, like their propertied counterparts, as members of local aid societies, and others as laborers hired to work in improvised workshops to produce garments from materials purchased by wealthier neighbors. Mary Marsh reported that at Henry Ward Beecher's Brooklyn church "a dozen sewing machines [were] hard at work ever since Sumter," allowing the wealthier women to boast that they had accomplished "heaps of work." . . .

A few women sought more direct means of providing needed supplies and assistance to the men they gave up to the Union army. Learning of horrid camp conditions, a dearth of nursing services, and inadequate cooking, these women took it upon themselves to carry food and clothing directly to men at the warfront. For many, the line separating the war from the homefront was blurred by the improvisational means through which the army itself was constituted, as well as the realities of a civil war fought on familiar territory at close proximity. While most women paid only brief visits, a few remained at camp, some donning uniforms and traveling with their husbands to battle. The most famous military wife to join her husband at the front was Julia Grant. Coming at General Grant's request, Julia brought their children as well. . . .

As women in remote villages and small cities mobilized themselves to outfit troops and provide supplies, believing that their labors translated into real assistance to the war effort, stories began to surface that their energies were in fact producing an opposite effect. By rumor and hearsay, accounts of useless clothing, ill-fitting uniforms, spoiled food, and overstocked hospital supplies flowed from army camps and military hospitals back to the homefront. Despite the efforts of women who, according to Livermore, "rifled their store-rooms and preserve-closets of canned fruits and pots of jams" and packed all these together with clothing, blankets, and books, the results were dispiriting. "Baggage cars were soon flooded with fermenting sweetmeats, and broken pots of jelly. . . . Decaying fruit and vegetables, pastry and cake in a demoralized condition, badly canned meats and soups . . . were nec essarily thrown away *en route.*"

More than the cakes stood to become demoralized. Even before such reports surfaced, the prospect that women's labors for the army might be viewed as well-meaning but feeble attempts to augment military strength worried a group of professional and upper-class New York City women. Barely a week after the firing on Fort Sumter, these women anticipated the criticisms that would be leveled at female volunteers. The absence of some system of coordination threatened to efface the considerable labors northern women had undertaken. They concluded that the "uprising of the women of the land" was in need of "information, direction, and guidance." . . .

Only two weeks into the war, [Dr. Elizabeth] Blackwell announced . . . a review of the voluntary activities already under way on behalf of Union recruits. Blackwell invited women from many of New York's leading upper-class and Unitarian families, including Mrs. William Cullen Bryant, Mrs. Peter Cooper, and Mrs. George Schuyler and her daughter, Louisa Lee Schuyler. She also extended an invitation to the Unitarian minister Henry Whitney Bellows, who led the city's prominent All Soul's Church.

The meeting's organizers published a letter the next day in the New York newspapers addressed to the women of New York, "especially . . . those already engaged in preparing against the time of wounds and sickness in the Army." Signed by "Ninety-Two of the Most Respected Ladies," the announcement offered to coordinate the efforts of existing charities and soldiers' aid societies through one organization and warned women that their lack of direct communication with government authorities about the needs of the army would cause problems. Anticipating what indeed was about to happen, the letter predicted that women engaged in voluntary war relief "are liable to waste their enthusiasm, to overlook some claims and overdo others, while they give unnecessary trouble in official quarters." The plan emphasized the collaborative nature of the work; to avoid competition among voluntary associations, no single group would be elevated above any other. The chief goal was to facilitate and intensify what the meeting had identified as the two predominant forms of female war relief contributions: the donation of "labor, skill and money," and the "offer of personal service as nurses." Henceforth both activities would be managed by a single administrative structure. To consolidate the proposals and gain citywide support for the idea, the women's letter called for a second public meeting to be held the next day at Cooper Union.

On April 26, the Great Hall at Cooper Union was filled to capacity. On the platform, according to the *Tribune,* were the "wives and daughters of many of our most distinguished citizens." Among those who addressed the crowd of four thousand were Henry Bellows, Vice President Hannibal Hamlin, and a number of noted physicians. Before adjourning the meeting, a committee of women and men announced the formation of the Woman's Central Association of Relief. The new organization would meet the needs outlined the day before: "give organization and efficiency to the scattered efforts" already in progress; gather information on the wants of the army; establish relations with the Medical Staff of the army; create a central depot for hospital stores; and open a bureau for the examination and registration of nursing candidates. The women's association would be run with the voluntary labor of elite women, but it was to some degree a women's organization in name only. Its board of managers was composed of twelve women and twelve men, and was responsible for the selection of officers. Dr. Valentine Mott was named President and Rev. Henry Bellows Vice President of the Board of Management. Though men were given overriding authority, the association's structure provided a number of well-known, upper-class women with important positions as well. Two women, Mrs. Eliza L. Schuyler and Miss Ellen Collins, were included on the eight-member executive committee. Dr. Elizabeth Blackwell was made chair of the registration committee, which was charged with examining and registering women volunteering as nurses. Louisa Lee Schuyler was appointed corresponding secretary of the WCRA.

Of all the women appointed to the new association, none would have more influence than the young Louisa Lee Schuyler. The daughter of George Schuyler and Eliza Schuyler—one of the "Ninety-Two . . . Most Respected Ladies" and herself a well-known figure in New York's reform circles—Louisa Schuyler was a member of the Dutch Hudson Valley family that traced its lineage to Alexander Hamilton and Philip Schuyler. The Schuylers were also important members of Bellow's All Soul's Church. Then twenty-four years old, Louisa Schuyler was already active in one of the philanthropic enterprises that emerged in prewar New York City, working under the auspices of the Children's Aid Society as a sewing instructor in an industrial school for immigrant children. Louisa Schuyler's appointment as corresponding secretary accorded with her mother's view that the day-to-day running of the office was best left to the "younger ladies." Schuyler worked closely with Ellen Collins, herself a daughter of a wealthy New York merchant family that was prominent in New York philanthropic circles. At the outset of the war, Collins was thirty-two and like Schuyler, unmarried.

As the volume of women's voluntary work grew, Schuyler assumed an increasingly important role in the coordination of homefront relief to the army. Handling the correspondence between the WCRA headquarters and regional societies, she possessed a unique vantage point from which to observe female voluntarism and apprehend the homefront's approach to war relief. "She is certainly a most intelligent & energetic diligent young damsel," George Templeton Strong observed in his diary, "though not pretty at all," he felt compelled to add. . . .

. . . Able to exploit an established network of women's organizations, the women who led the WCRA expected that these groups would be sufficient to meet the demands of warwork. The association promoted greater participation in war re-lief and pushed for a coordinated handling of supplies, but it refrained from dictating the ways in which localities were to organize themselves and from calling for the creation of new societies. Aware that thousands of women had already rededicated their prewar benevolent and church groups to warwork and that some had even cre-ated new aid societies, the WCRA felt confident that these organizations could meet the army's demands. The association emphasized providing accurate information about army needs and assuring the efficient transport of donations from the home-front to the warfront.

The strategy worked; in response to WCRA announcements, hundreds of women mobilized neighbors, collected donations, and forwarded them to the asso-ciation's office at Cooper Union. For small-town and rural women, the initiative taken by elite urban women provided an example they were anxious to emulate. "On the same day of the monster meeting of ladies at the Cooper Institute in New York," the women of the Dorcas Society of Cornwall, New York, resolved to organ-ize themselves into the Cornwall Soldiers Aid Society and work for the duration of the war. "The response made to our appeals is grand," wrote Louisa Lee Schuyler in August 1861, "and it is a privilege to know and feel the noble spirit that animates the women of the loyal states."

The preliminary work of the Woman's Central Relief Association revealed more than the potential for a mass voluntary participation for the war effort; it also hinted at the possibility of revising popular notions of female sacrifice. Suddenly, women were being flattered and appreciated by national institutions and men of power, who paid tribute to women's supposedly unique contributions and the vital part they played in supplementing the limited, and sometimes shoddy, provisions of the federal government. Here was a scenario in which unpaid female labor might be judged as expressing unqualified political commitment and producing real economic value. The exigencies of war would test the ability of the antebellum ideology of gender to dictate how women's labors were comprehended, whether they would be reviewed as mere emanations of female nature or as the results of human exertion and skill.

Historically, wars have offered the politically disadvantaged opportunities to con-tribute to the defense of the state in return for expanded rights. African Americans, both slave and free, understood the Civil War to represent just such possibilities; by sacrificing lives and livelihoods to protect the Union, people could "earn" political and civil rights. For women, wars likewise have presented occasions to demonstrate their right to political inclusion by means of economic and personal sacrifices. While women have supported wars for immediate reasons, including the assistance of local regiments and defense of the military cause, the quid-pro-quo formula invariably emerges at war's end. During the American Revolution, colonial women organized consumers' organizations, anti-tea leagues and soldier relief societies. But despite some agitation for their inclusion in the apportionment of political rights during the writing of the Constitution, there was no reciprocity. The gendering of republican concepts of public virtue and liberty positioned women not as active citizens but as mothers of citizens, who possessed the morality necessary for producing virtuous free male citizens but were unsuited for participation in the political realm.

The Civil War portended something different. As a result of decades of agitation for women's rights, the feminist critique of women's secondary status hovered over northern society as an unanswered challenge. Wartime expectations for gains in women's status drew not only on the woman's rights movement but also on the experiences of those women who tried to enact the gender compromise through reform work. . . . With war mobilization so dependent on voluntary civilian support, the time seemed ripe for translating women's assistance to the state into an exchange of support for full inclusion in the body politic. Though women's patriotic sentiments were cast as the natural expression of moral beings, the changing conditions of women's lives and the need for their contributions opened the way for a different reading of their wartime activities. Soon after the fighting began, a number of northerners suggested that this war might permanently alter women's status. The movement for woman's rights was effectively put on hold for the duration of the conflict, as feminists decided it was incumbent on them to demonstrate their loyalty to a state to which they were making bids for greater political access. But expressions of raised expectations came from sectors beyond the woman's rights camp. In fact, it is probable that the American Civil War was the first modern war in which masses of women participated with expectations that their homefront contributions would translate into expanded political rights.

From the outset of the military conflict, the question of political compensation for women's assistance was in the air, palpable, alluded to in public as well as in private statements, by men as well as women. The idea that the war offered women unusual opportunities for advancement was voiced across the political and cultural spectrum. Just as the larger society cohered politically in the face of disunion, so too northern women put aside differences over feminist demands for equality in order to advance the war. In all the expressions of raised expectations lay assumptions that women would make some sort of political gain as result of their wartime sacrifices.

FURTHER READING

Campbell, Edward, and Kym Rice, eds. *A Woman's War: Southern Women, Civil War, and The Confederate Legacy* (1997).
Clinton, Catherine. *Civil War Stories* (1998).
Douglas (Wood), Ann. "The War Within a War: Women Nurses in the Union Army," *Civil War History* 18 (1972): 197–212.
Edwards, Laura. *Scarlett Doesn't Live Here Anymore: Southern Women in the Civil War Era* (2000).
Endres, Kathleen. "The Women's Press in the Civil War: A Portrait of Patriotism, Propaganda, and Prodding," *Civil War History* 30 (1984): 31–53.
Faust, Drew Gilpin. *Mothers of Invention: Women of the Slaveholding South in the American Civil War* (1996).
Frankel, Noralee. *Freedom's Women: Black Women and Families in Civil War Era Mississippi* (2000).
Giesberg, Judith Ann. *Civil War Sisterhood: The U.S. Sanitary Commission and Women's Politics in Transition* (2000).
Hamand, Wendy F. "The Woman's National Loyal League: Feminist Abolitionists and the Civil War," *Civil War History* 35 (1989): 39–58.
Leonard, Elizabeth. *Yankee Women: Gender Battles in the Civil War* (1994).
———. *All the Daring of the Soldier: Women of the Civil War Armies* (1999).

McClintock, Megan. "Civil War Pensions and the Reconstruction of Union Families,"
    Journal of American History 83 (1996–1997): 456–480.
Rable, George C. *Civil Wars: Women and the Crisis of Southern Nationalism* (1989).
Schultz, Jane. "The Inhospitable Hospital: Gender and Professionalism in Civil War
    Medicine," *Signs* 17 (1992): 363–392.
——. "Race, Gender, and Bureaucracy: Civil War Army Nurses and the Pension Bureau,"
    Journal of Women's History 6, no. 2 (1994): 45–69.
Sizer, Lyde C. *The Political Work of Northern Women Writers and the Civil War, 1850–1872*
    (2000).
Venet, Wendy H. *Neither Ballots nor Bullets: Women Abolitionists and Emancipation During
    the Civil War* (1992).
Whites, LeeAnn. *The Civil War as a Crisis in Gender: Augusta, Georgia, 1860–1890*
    (1995).

CHAPTER 8

Women in the Trans-Mississippi Frontier West

During the nineteenth century, the American West became a place of discord and violence as Anglos, Native Americans, Hispanics, and Asians competed—on highly unequal terms—for access to western lands, resources, and jobs. Disparate cultural communities struggled to coexist in the "frontier" West as straightforward instances of Anglo "conquest" mixed with patterns of exploitation, dependency, negotiation, and exchange. In the multicultural American West, women's experience was shaped simultaneously by gender and ethnicity. Thus, while thousands of nineteenth-century Indian women and girls witnessed the destruction of their traditional cultures and struggled to negotiate encounters with arrogant whites who believed them to be less than "true women," countless Anglo women experienced the loneliness and hardship that came with trying to transplant, in unfamiliar soil, the ideals and social practices of eastern or midwestern communities. As this example suggests, the West was a place where women of diverse backgrounds encountered tragedy, deprivation, and loss of status or identity. Yet it was also a place where women attempted both to retain cherished cultural traditions and to prosper amid persistent disadvantage and rapid change. How well did they succeed? What does the historical record tell us about the impact of continental migration and cross-cultural contact on the roles, status, and self-perceptions of Indian, Hispanic, Anglo, and Asian women in the nineteenth- and twentieth-century West? Under what circumstances did women of different racial or ethnic communities sustain injury to or a diminution of social standing and power? And when were they able to advance their interests by negotiating across cultural or gender boundaries?

◆ D O C U M E N T S

In Document 1, an anonymous individual pens a letter to a small California newspaper denouncing the rape of elderly Indian women in Tehama County by a party of U.S. soldiers who had been sent to that locale to protect white settlers. A Hispanic woman (Document 2) recollects, in 1877, her life in a California mission when that region was still under Mexican control. In Document 3, a young Indian girl describes her eagerness to attend a white-run school for Indian children and the profound disorientation she felt once her journey to the school had begun. Document 4 describes the self-pity and desolation felt by Mrs. A. M. Green, a white native of Pennsylvania, on moving to Colorado's Union Colony with her ambitious young husband and two small children in 1870. By way of contrast, Sadie Martin, another white migrant, describes in Document 5 her cheerful adjustment to the rigors of life on the Arizona desert in the late 1880s. Notable, too, are Sadie's affable yet belittling comments about her Indian neighbors. In Document 6, Leong Shee, a Chinese woman of the merchant class, provides testimony to an immigration official upon her arrival in San Francisco. She had lived in San Francisco before but had returned to China. In 1893 she sought reentry to the United States. U.S. law sought to prevent Chinese people from immigrating to America, and Leong Shee had to convince the skeptical official who questioned her that she was one of the exceptional few who should be permitted entry.

1. A Citizen Protests the Rape of Indian Women in California, 1862

Editor *Beacon:*—It is well known that there is, or has been, a body of soldiers in this county for several weeks past, for the avowed object of defending and protecting the citizens of the county against Indian depredations. . . .

On Friday night a party of these soldiers visited the ranch of Col. Washington, and made themselves annoying to the Indians in the rancheria. This party was small, only three, as reported.

Saturday night, the 4th of October, 1862, was made memorable by the visit of a portion of this command, headed, aided and abetted by the commanding officer, Lieut. ———, (or some one assuming his title,) to the farm of Col. Washington, and to the rancheria of peaceful and domesticated Indians resident thereon. Not one of the soldiers, private or Lieutenant, (or pretended Lieutenant, if such he was,) called at the farm house, but rode by and entered the Indian rancheria, with demands for Indian women, for the purpose of prostitution! They were requested to leave and ordered off the place. They answered they would do as they pleased, as they had the power. They were then told that it was true they were the strongest, and no force at hand was sufficient to contend with them, and they were left in the Indian rancheria. Most of the young squaws in the rancheria had by this time ran off and concealed themselves, and were beyond the reach and brutal grasp of the ravishers. They, however, were to be satiated, and like brutes dragged the old, decrepit "tar-heads" forth, and as many as three of the soldiers, in rapid succession, had forced intercourse with old squaws. Such was the conduct of the portion of the command of Co. E, on the night of the 4th of October, 1862, who visited the Indian rancheria at the Old Mill Place, about 3 miles from N. L. headquarters.

It is but proper, after consulting with those who are acquainted with the outrage, to say that the Lieut. (or pretended Lieut., if such he was,) did not arrive at the scene of action until after the larger portion of his men were on the ground—But it is absolutely certain that he was there—that he put his horse in the stable to hay, and

Beacon (Red Bluff), October 9, 1862. This document can also be found in Robert Hezier, ed., *The Destruction of California Indians* (Santa Barbara, Calif.: Peregrine Smith, 1974), 281–283.

then prowled around and through the Indian rancherias in quest of some squaw. Whether he found a fit subject upon which to practice his virtuous and civilizing purposes, the writer is not informed. He, however, saddled up and left the scene of moral exploit about daylight.

In justice to decency, humanity and civilization, these brutes should be punished. It is due to the honor, the reputation, the chivalry of the army of the United States, that the insignia of rank and position should be torn from the person of the Lieutenant (if it was he who was there,) as an officer unworthy its trust and confidence.

2. An Old Woman Recalls Her Life in Hispanic California in the Early Nineteenth Century, 1877

I, Eulalia Pérez, was born in the Presidio of Loreto in Baja California.

My father's name was Diego Pérez, and he was employed in the Navy Department of said presidio; my mother's name was Antonia Rosalia Cota. Both were pure white.

I do not remember the date of my birth, but I do know that I was fifteen years old when I married Miguel Antonio Guillén, a soldier of the garrison at Loreto Presidio. . . . I lived eight years in San Diego with my husband, who continued his service in the garrison of the presidio, and I attended women in childbirth. . . . In San Diego everyone seemed to like me very much, and in the most important homes they treated me affectionately. Although I had my own house, they arranged for me to be with those families almost all the time, even including my children. . . .

After being in San Diego eight years, we came to the Mission of San Gabriel, where my husband had been serving in the guard. . . . My last trip to San Diego would have been in the year 1818, when my daughter María del Rosario was four years old. I seem to remember that I was there when the revolutionaries came to California. . . .

Some three years later I came back to San Gabriel. . . . When we arrived here Father José Sánchez lodged me and my family temporarily in a small house until work could be found for me. There I was with my five daughters—my son Isidoro Guillén was taken into service as a soldier in the mission guard.

. . . Father Sánchez was between sixty and seventy years of age—a white Spaniard, heavy set, of medium stature—a very good, kind, charitable man. He, as well as his companion Father José María Zalvidea, treated the Indians very well, and the two were much loved by the Spanish-speaking people and by the neophytes and other Indians. . . .

Father Zalvidea was very much attached to his children at the mission, as he called the Indians that he himself had converted to Christianity. He traveled personally, sometimes on horseback and at other times on foot, and crossed mountains until he came to remote Indian settlements, in order to bring them to our religion.

Father Zalvidea introduced many improvements in the Mission of San Gabriel and made it progress a very great deal in every way. Not content with providing

Eulalia Pérez, "An Old Woman Remembers," in Harold Augenbaum and Marguerite Fernández Olmos, eds., *The Latino Reader: An American Literary Tradition from 1542 to the Present* (Boston: Houghton Mifflin, 1997), 71–80.

abundantly for the neophytes, he planted [fruit] trees in the mountains, far away from the mission, in order that the untamed Indians might have food when they passed by those spots. . . .

The priests wanted to help me out because I was a widow burdened with a family. . . . Because of . . . this, employment was provided for me at the mission. At first they assigned me two Indians so that I could show them how to cook, the one named Tomás and the other called "The Gentile." I taught them so well that I had the satisfaction of seeing them turn out to be very good cooks, perhaps the best in all this part of the country.

After this, the missionaries conferred among themselves and agreed to hand over the mission keys to me. . . . The duties of the housekeeper were many. In the first place, every day she handed out the rations for the mess hut. To do this she had to count the unmarried women, bachelors, day-laborers, vaqueros—both those with saddles and those who rode bareback. Besides that, she had to hand out daily rations to the heads of households. In short, she was responsible for the distribution of supplies to the Indian population and to the missionaries' kitchen. She was in charge of the key to the clothing storehouse where materials were given out for dresses for the unmarried and married women and children. Then she also had to take care of cutting and making clothes for the men.

Furthermore, she was in charge of cutting and making the vaqueros' outfits, from head to foot—that is, for the vaqueros who rode in saddles. Those who rode bareback received nothing more than their cotton blanket and loin-cloth, while those who rode in saddles were dressed the same way as the Spanish-speaking inhabitants; that is, they were given shirt, vest, jacket, trousers, hat, cowboy boots, shoes and spurs; and a saddle, bridle and lariat for the horse. . . .

Besides this, I had to attend to the soap-house, which was very large, to the wine-presses, and to the olive-crushers that produced oil, which I worked in myself. . . . When it was necessary, some of my daughters did what I could not find the time to do. Generally, the one who was always at my side was my daughter María del Rosario.

After all my daughters were married—the last one was Rita, about 1832 or 1833—Father Sánchez undertook to persuade me to marry First Lieutenant Juan Mariné, a Spaniard from Catalonia, a widower with family who had served in the artillery. I did not want to get married, but the father told me that Mariné was a very good man—as, in fact, he turned out to be—besides, he had some money, although he never turned his cash-box over to me. I gave in to the father's wishes because I did not have the heart to deny him anything when he had been father and mother to me and to all my family.

I served as housekeeper of the mission for twelve or fourteen years, until about two years after the death of Father José Sánchez, which occurred in this same mission.

A short while before Father Sánchez died, he seemed robust and in good health, in spite of his advanced age. When Captain Barroso came and excited the Indians in all the missions to rebel, telling them that they were no longer neophytes but free men, Indians arrived from San Luis, San Juan and the rest of the missions. They pushed their way into the college, carrying their arms, because it was raining very hard. Outside the mission, guards and patrols made up of the Indians themselves were stationed. . . .

The father left for the pueblo, and in front of the guard some Indians surged forward and cut the traces of his coach. He jumped out of the coach, and then the Indians, pushing him rudely, forced him toward his room. He was sad and filled with sorrow because of what the Indians had done and remained in his room for about a week without leaving it. He became ill and never again was his previous self. Blood flowed from his ears, and his head never stopped paining him until he died. He lived perhaps a little more than a month after the affair with the Indians, dying in the month of January, I think it was, of 1833. . . .

In the Mission of San Gabriel there was a large number of neophytes. The married ones lived on their rancherías with their small children. There were two divisions for the unmarried ones: one for the women, called the nunnery, and another for the men. They brought girls from the ages of seven, eight or nine years to the nunnery, and they were brought up there. They left to get married. They were under the care of a mother in the nunnery, an Indian. During the time I was at the mission this matron was named Polonia—they called her "Mother Superior." The alcalde was in charge of the unmarried men's division. Every night both divisions were locked up, the keys were delivered to me, and I handed them over to the missionaries. . . .

In the morning the girls were let out. First they went to Father Zalvidea's Mass, for he spoke the Indian language; afterwards they went to the mess hut to have breakfast, which sometimes consisted of corn gruel with chocolate, and on holidays with sweets and bread. On other days, ordinarily they had boiled barley and beans and meat. After eating breakfast each girl began the task that had been assigned to her beforehand—sometimes it was at the looms, or unloading, or sewing, or whatever there was to be done. . . .

The Indians were taught the various jobs for which they showed an aptitude. Others worked in the fields, or took care of the horses, cattle, etc. Still others were carters, oxherds, etc.

At the mission, coarse cloth, serapes, and blankets were woven, and saddles, bridles, boots, shoes, and similar things were made. There was a soap-house, and a big carpenter shop as well as a small one, where those who were just beginning to learn carpentry worked; when they had mastered enough they were transferred to the big shop.

Wine and oil, bricks and adobe bricks were also made. Chocolate was manufactured from cocoa, brought in from the outside; and sweets were made. Many of these sweets, made by my own hands, were sent to Spain by Father Sánchez.

There was a teacher in every department, an instructed Indian who was Christianized. A white man headed the looms, but when the Indians were finally skilled, he withdrew. . . .

The Indians also were taught to pray. A few of the more intelligent ones were taught to read and write. Father Zalvidea taught the Indians to pray in their Indian tongue; some Indians learned music and played instruments and sang at Mass. The sextons and pages who helped with Mass were Indians of the mission.

The punishments that were meted out were the stocks and confinement. When the misdemeanor was serious, the delinquent was taken to the guard, where they tied him up to a pipe or a post and gave him twenty-five or more lashes, depending on his crime. Sometimes they put them in the head-stocks; other times they passed a musket from one leg to the other and fastened it there, and also they tied their hands. That punishment, called "The Law of Bayona," was very painful.

But Fathers Sánchez and Zalvidea were always very considerate with the Indians. I would not want to say what others did because they did not live in the mission.

3. Zitkala-Ša Travels to the Land of the Big Red Apples, 1884

The first turning away from the easy, natural flow of my life occurred in an early spring. It was in my eighth year; in the month of March, I afterward learned. At this age I knew but one language, and that was my mother's native tongue.

From some of my playmates I heard that two paleface missionaries were in our village. They were from that class of white men who wore big hats and carried large hearts, they said. Running direct to my mother, I began to question her why these two strangers were among us. She told me, after I had teased much, that they had come to take away Indian boys and girls to the East. My mother did not seem to want me to talk about them. But in a day or two, I gleaned many wonderful stories from my playfellows concerning the strangers.

"Mother, my friend Judéwin is going home with the missionaries. She is going to a more beautiful country than ours; the palefaces told her so!" I said wistfully, wishing in my heart that I too might go.

Mother sat in a chair, and I was hanging on her knee. Within the last two seasons my big brother Dawée had returned from a three years' education in the East, and his coming back influenced my mother to take a farther step from her native way of living. First it was a change from the buffalo skin to the white man's canvas that covered our wigwam. Now she had given up her wigwam of slender poles, to live, a foreigner, in a home of clumsy logs.

"Yes, my child, several others besides Judéwin are going away with the palefaces. Your brother said the missionaries had inquired about his little sister," she said, watching my face very closely.

My heart thumped so hard against my breast, I wondered if she could hear it.

"Did he tell them to take me, mother?" I asked, fearing lest Dawée had forbidden the palefaces to see me, and that my hope of going to the Wonderland would be entirely blighted.

With a sad, slow smile, she answered: "There! I knew you were wishing to go, because Judéwin has filled your ears with the white man's lies. Don't believe a word they say! Their words are sweet, but, my child, their deeds are bitter. You will cry for me, but they will not even soothe you. Stay with me, my little one! Your brother Dawée says that going East, away from your mother, is too hard an experience for his baby sister."

Thus my mother discouraged my curiosity about the lands beyond our eastern horizon; for it was not yet an ambition for Letters that was stirring me. But on the following day the missionaries did come to our very house. I spied them coming up the footpath leading to our cottage. A third man was with them, but he was not my brother Dawée. It was another, a young interpreter, a paleface who had a smattering of the Indian language. I was ready to run out to meet them, but I did not dare to

Zitkala-Ša, *American Indian Stories* (1921; reprint, Lincoln: University of Nebraska Press, 1985), 39–45.

displease my mother. With great glee, I jumped up and down on our ground floor. I begged my mother to open the door, that they would be sure to come to us. Alas! They came, they saw, and they conquered!

Judéwin had told me of the great tree where grew red, red apples; and how we could reach out our hands and pick all the red apples we could eat. I had never seen apple trees. I had never tasted more than a dozen red apples in my life; and when I heard of the orchards of the East, I was eager to roam among them. The missionaries smiled into my eyes and patted my head. I wondered how mother could say such hard words against him.

"Mother, ask them if little girls may have all the red apples they want, when they go East," I whispered aloud, in my excitement.

The interpreter heard me, and answered: "Yes, little girl, the nice red apples are for those who pick them; and you will have a ride on the iron horse if you go with these good people."

I had never seen a train, and he knew it.

"Mother, I am going East! I like big red apples, and I want to ride on the iron horse! Mother, say yes!" I pleaded.

My mother said nothing. The missionaries waited in silence; and my eyes began to blur with tears, though I struggled to choke them back. The corners of my mouth twitched, and my mother saw me.

"I am not ready to give you any word," she said to them. "Tomorrow I shall send you my answer by my son."

With this they left us. Alone with my mother, I yielded to my tears, and cried aloud, shaking my head so as not to hear what she was saying to me. This was the first time I had ever been so unwilling to give up my own desire that I refused to hearken to my mother's voice.

There was a solemn silence in our home that night. Before I went to bed I begged the Great Spirit to make my mother willing I should go with the missionaries.

The next morning came, and my mother called me to her side. "My daughter, do you still persist in wishing to leave your mother?" she asked.

"Oh, mother, it is not that I wish to leave you, but I want to see the wonderful Eastern land," I answered.

My dear old aunt came to our house that morning, and I heard her say, "Let her try it."

I hoped that, as usual, my aunt was pleading on my side. My brother Dawée came for mother's decision. I dropped my play, and crept close to my aunt.

"Yes, Dawée, my daughter, though she does not understand what it all means, is anxious to go. She will need an education when she is grown, for then there will be fewer real Dakotas, and many more palefaces. This tearing her away, so young, from her mother is necessary, if I would have her an educated woman. The pale-faces, who owe us a large debt for stolen lands, have begun to pay a tardy justice in offering some education to our children. But I know my daughter must suffer keenly in this experiment. For her sake, I dread to tell you my reply to the mission-aries. Go, tell them that they may take my little daughter, and that the Great Spirit shall not fail to reward them according to their hearts."

Wrapped in my heavy blanket, I walked with my mother to the carriage that was soon to take us to the iron horse. I was happy. I met my playmates, who were also wearing their best thick blankets. We showed one another our new beaded moccasins, and the width of the belts that girdled our new dresses. Soon we were being drawn rapidly away by the white man's horses. When I saw the lonely figure of my mother vanish in the distance, a sense of regret settled heavily upon me. I felt suddenly weak, as if I might fall limp to the ground. I was in the hands of strangers whom my mother did not fully trust. I no longer felt free to be myself, or to voice my own feelings. The tears trickled down my cheeks, and I buried my face in the folds of my blanket. Now the first step, parting me from my mother, was taken, and all my belated tears availed nothing.

Having driven thirty miles to the ferryboat, we crossed the Missouri in the evening. Then riding again a few miles eastward, we stopped before a massive brick building. I looked at it in amazement, and with a vague misgiving, for in our village I had never seen so large a house. Trembling with fear and distrust of the palefaces, my teeth chattering from the chilly ride, I crept noiselessly in my soft moccasins along the narrow hall, keeping very close to the bare wall. I was as frightened and bewildered as the captured young of a wild creature.

4. Mrs. A. M. Green's Account of Frontier Life, 1887

Of the founder of this place I have nothing to say except that I regret the sad manner in which he came to his death, for I really believe he was a very pure minded man, and one who sought the good of his fellow beings. After securing several lots in the new town, we pitched our tent, which was almost daily blown to the ground. To say that I was homesick, discouraged and lonely, is but a faint description of my feelings.

It was one of those terrible gloomy days that I sat in my lonely tent with my baby, Frank, in my arms, who was crying from the effects produced by the sands of the American desert, while beside my knee stood my little Sisy, (as we called her) trying to comfort her brother by saying: "Don't cry, F'ankie, we is all going back to grandpa's pitty soon, ain't we, mamma?" Not receiving an immediate answer from me, she raised her eyes to mine, from which gushed a fountain of burning tears. "Don't cry, mamma," said she; "sing to F'ank like you always does, and he will stop crying." I obeyed the child's request. . . .

As I closed my song the curtain raised and my husband entered, sank wearily on a three-legged stool and took up our little five-year-old, placed her upon his tired knee and then addressed me thus: "Well, dear, how do you get along to-day? I see the tent hasn't blown down." I attempted to answer in the negative, but failed, the meaning of which he comprehended in a moment. Notwithstanding any vain attempts to conceal my emotion, he pressed to his sad heart the little charge which he held in his arms, saying in a low voice: "Darling little one, you and your poor mamma have hard times, don't you?" Then turning to me, he said: "Annie, I am very sorry for you. If I had compelled you to come to this country I could never forgive myself; as it is, I feel that you reflect on me." By this time I had regained

Mrs. A. M. Green, *Sixteen Years on the Great American Desert; or, the Trials and Triumphs of a Frontier Life* (Titusville, Pa.: Frank Truedell, Printer, 1887), 8–31. This document can also be found in Ruth Moynihan, Susan Armitage, and Christiane Fischer Dichamp, eds., *So Much to Be Done: Women Settlers on the Mining and Ranching Frontier* (Lincoln: University of Nebraska Press, 1990), 123–146.

my speech and endeavored with all my might, mind and strength to convince him to the contrary. Whether I succeeded or not I never knew, but I resolved there and then to cultivate a cheerful disposition, which I believe has prolonged my life, for, at the rate I was going into despair at that time, I could not have retained my reason six months' longer, and doubtless the brittle thread of life would have been snapped long ere this. O how thankful I am that I still live to love, work and care for those whom to me are dearer than life itself! If I have one wish above another in this world, it is that I may live a long and useful life. . . .

The 7th of July was Sabbath, and in those days I was usually found under the droppings of the sanctuary, for, though there was not a church in the town, we had regular services every Sabbath in the Union Colony Hall; but this morning I felt so depressed in spirits that I dispensed with going, and busied myself in writing to those for whom my heart panted continually. I had finished my third letter, closing up with a fervent prayer to Him whom I had been taught to believe would hear and answer the prayer of faith, for the preservation of my life, and also for those to whom I had been writing, until we should meet again (?) when the word *never, never,* sounded in my ear, and penetrated my aching heart with an arrow, the effect of which I feel to this day. At that moment my little girl approached me bearing in her hand the picture of her who loved me first and best on earth. I took it from the child, pressed it to my quivering lips, and cried: Oh, God, bereave me not of her! Until this time I had not ventured to open our album, but now that the ice was broken, I looked it through while tears gushed from my eyes. During this terrible emotion my husband returned from church, and again found me in tears and deep sorrow. This added pain to his already desponding heart. "Annie," said he, with a self-reproaching look, and in a pathetic tone which I shall never forget, "do you know you are killing me?" "I thought," he continued, "you had resolved to cultivate a more cheerful disposition; this will not do; it is cruel in the extreme for me to compel you to remain where you are so unhappy." My heart bounded for joy; and then, my pulse stood still to listen for the much longed for sentence,—we will go home; but, alas! it came in the singular number; "you must go home." "What!" I cried, "go without you, no, never," and I repeat those words to-day; and ever shall, so long as circumstances control my husband's freedom. Again I resolved to try and be cheerful, but, my resolution and promise were but to be broken in less than twenty-four hours. On this occasion the physician was summoned and my disease pronounced mountain fever, from which I recovered, after an illness of six weeks. During all my affliction I had answered each letter from home without intimating that I was out of health, until the shortness of my communications excited their attention, and they demanded an explanation, which I was obliged to give.

It was now August, but oh! how different from any one which I had ever witnessed. Not a tree, plant nor shrub on which to rest my weary eye, to break the monotony of the sand beds and cactus of the Great American Desert. My attention was often called to the grandeur of the snow capped Rocky Mountains, towering toward the skies; and although I sometimes feigned an appreciation of their beauty in order to coincide with my other half, who displayed much anxiety to have me admire something in Colorado, I speak the truth when I say that the sun, moon, or stars never put on that brilliant appearance in my western home as they did in the land of my nativity.

5. Sadie Martin's Memories of Desert Life, 1888

It was early on the morning of the 22nd of August, 1888, when my train rolled into the most desolate little town I had ever seen or ever expected to see. Nevertheless my heart was beating high as I was to meet my husband, who had preceded me to Arizona five months before. As I stepped from the train I could hardly realize that the young man coming toward me was my John. He was as dark as an Indian and only his height, eagerness, and familiar smile made me recognize him. . . .

We reached the ranch about sundown, tired, warm and hungry and were met by the members of the family who had preceded us. My! What a sight I was—my face burned to a deep and unbecoming red and down my left arm were three rows of blisters in the design of the lace in my sleeve. It was so good to have that sun go down and to take a long cool drink of delicious water from the great Mexican olla—a porous clay vessel, which was kept cool by a covering of wet gunny sacks. There was no ice on the desert, but I was soon to find that we could keep our milk and butter cool and sweet, by wrapping damp cloths around the receptacles that held them and setting them in the air. And as we were everlastingly thirsty it was a relief to find there would be no dearth of cooling drinks.

The family consisted of John's father, mother and brother and four or five Indian helpers. These were the first Indians I had ever seen and I must say I was greatly disappointed. Of course, I was not exactly expecting to see war paint and feathers, but I was hardly prepared for such harmless looking creatures in overalls. One of them had a light blue handkerchief draped around his neck in picturesque fashion and was grinning in an embarrassed way. They told me afterwards that he had been to school at the Yuma reservation, that his experience there had rather dissatisfied him with life among his own people and he was the laziest one of the lazy bunch.

I found that the family was living in the tents Father had used at the Toltec camp and were quite comfortable while the cabin of cottonwood logs (cut from the river bottom) was being built for a permanent home. . . .

Our great interest was the building of this log house. The Indians of the Yuma Apache tribe were there for the purpose of "chinking" and "mudding," as they called it, and for making adobes for the fire-places. The one in charge was named Steve and he had been a scout in one of the Indian wars and was mentioned in some of Captain King's novels. His father was one of the old timers—no overalls for him—nothing but a "gee string." His skin was like wrinkled leather. I was quite pleased to find him, as he more nearly typified what I was expecting to see in the way of an Indian. . . .

And now, after I had been there only three days, I was to experience my first sand storm. When the desert does things, it seems to do them in a great big way. It may only have been doing what it conceived to be its duty, but sometimes I have felt that back of it all there was a sort of resentment toward human beings who dared to come in there and meddle around in a puny way, to make things more

Sadie Martin, "My Desert Memories," typed manuscript, Arizona Historical Society Library, Tucson, Ariz., 1939. This document can also be found in Ruth Moynihan, Susan Armitage, and Christiane Fischer Dichamp, eds., *So Much to Be Done: Women Settlers on the Mining and Ranching Frontier* (Lincoln: University of Nebraska Press, 1990), 289–320.

comfortable for themselves. The longer I lived there, the more I felt this Spirit of the desert, sometimes benign, but often the opposite, as though it must make up for those heavenly days of smiling sunshine by a tremendous blast which would show those humans their absurd insignificance. . . .

We were indeed glad when the house was finished and I think we were in it by October. It was such a comfortable, rambling house (if only a log one) with a dirt roof. . . . The folks had cots, tables, chairs, etc., which they had used at camp, and the boys made other things that we needed until we could have our furniture shipped out from Iowa. . . .

There were few settlers in the valley at that time and it would be two or three months at a time that Mother and I would not see another white woman. Men would stop in often and sometimes Indians would come around—the squaws appearing without a sound and put their faces against the window pane to peek in at us. It took me some time to get used to this, but they were quite friendly and meant no harm and really were just as curious about us and our methods of living as we were about them. After a few years, they moved their tepees nearer us, as the men worked on the ranches and the women washed for us. What a boon that was for the boys, who up to this time, had insisted on doing the rubbing for us, which John said was the hardest work a woman could do. He was always considerate and helpful, so that life was well worth living even under such conditions. I was extremely lonely at times, but through it all felt that I had much to be thankful for.

6. Leong Shee's Testimony to an Immigration Official in San Francisco, 1893

I was married in San Francisco on Dec. 15, 1885 to Chong [Chin] Lung of the firm of Sang Kee wholesale dealers in tea & rice #808 Sac. St. San Francisco. When I first came to this country I came with my father Leong Hoong Wum and my mother Lee Shee and lived at #613 Dupont St. My father was formerly connected with the firm of Sang Kee #808 Sac. St. My father died in this city Nov. 25, 1887. My mother died in this city 1883 so long ago I have forgotten the date. I went home to China with my brother-in-law Chun Gwun Dai and my daughter Ah Kum who was 4 years of age the time of departure. After I was married I lived on the 2nd floor over the store of Sang Kee #808 Sac. St where my daughter Ah Kum was born on the 28 day of December 1886. My daughter is 8 years old now. My brother-in-law Chun Gwun Dai returned to S.F. in the later part of year 1891. Lee Moon's wife went home in the same steamer with me. I do not know her name. There was also a woman named Sam Moy and a child Ah Yuck on board. I do not speak English and do not know the city excepting the names of a few streets as I have small feet and never went out.

Leong Shee, case 12017/37232, Chinese Departure Case Files, San Francisco District Office, Immigration and Naturalization Service, Record Group 85, National Archives, San Bruno, Calif. This document can also be found in Judy Young, ed., *Unbound Voices: A Documentary History of Chinese Women in San Francisco* (Berkeley and Los Angeles: University of California Press, 1999), 21–22.

Coll-Peter Thrush and Robert H. Keller Jr. examine the life and murder trial of Xwelas, a S'Klallam woman who lived along the northern coast of Washington's Olympic Penin-sula in an era of complex interactions between native peoples and Euro-American migrants. Xwelas married, and then killed, a white man. Thrush and Keller explore the probable causes of her resort to violence, as well as the reasons that a white jury concluded that she was not guilty of murder, convicting her of the lesser crime of manslaughter. Judy Yung of the University of California, Santa Cruz, examines the serious abuse that Chinese women faced in late-nineteenth-century San Francisco, as well as the new opportunities and identities that began to open up for them.

The Life and Murder Trial of a Native American Woman in the Pacific Northwest

COLL-PETER THRUSH AND ROBERT H. KELLER JR.

Christmas Day, 1878. George Phillips, a Welsh immigrant cooper at the Langdon Lime Works on Orcas Island in Washington Territory, trudges along a forest trail with his teenage stepson, Mason Fitzhugh. Suddenly a gun explodes, lead shot rip-ping through underbrush beside the path and tearing into Phillips, who staggers backwards and cries to Fitzhugh for help. The boy eases his stepfather to the ground, but within moments Phillips is dead. As Mason Fitzhugh runs for help, he sees the killer standing in the brush along the trail. Shotgun in hand, a baby strapped to her back, the assailant is his mother and Phillips's wife, a woman known as Mary, but whose true name is Xwelas. She had fired the gun; she would be indicted for mur-der and she would eventually be tried and convicted by a court of white men. As a nineteenth-century native woman, her life was both common and exceptional, and it offers insight into ethnic, gender, and legal relations in the Pacific Northwest. . . .

When Xwelas (pronounced hweh-LASS) was born in the 1830s, her people faced sudden and profound changes. She belonged to the S'Klallam, who lived along the northern coast of Washington's Olympic Peninsula, to the southwest of the San Juan Islands. Speakers of the Lkungen dialect of Straits Salish, and relatives of the nearby Lummi and Samish, the S'Klallam in the 1830s were only a few years away from meeting the first large waves of Euro-American settlers. The S'Klallam had first encountered white explorers in July of 1788, when British officer Robert Duffin and his crew explored south from Vancouver Island. Duffin reached the site of to-day's Port Townsend before being driven away by canoes manned by S'Klallam warriors. Spanish visitors were equally unwelcome during this early period of con-tact, but when George Vancouver sailed into S'Klallam territory in 1792, the tribe decided to ignore the whites altogether. Vancouver recorded in May of 1790 that the villagers showed "the utmost indifference and unconcern . . . as if such vessels had been familiar to them, and unworthy of their attention." A half-century later, new forces gave the S'Klallam, and surrounding native communities, little choice

Coll-Peter Thrush and Robert H. Keller Jr., "'I See What I Have Done': The Life and Murder Trial of Xwelas, a S'Klallam Woman," *Western Historical Quarterly* 26, no. 2 (summer 1995): 169–184.

but to pay attention. Diseases such as smallpox began to ravage the coastal peoples, and deadly epidemics—along with a new economy, European trade goods that included alcohol, and massive immigration of white settlers—eroded the North Coast's traditional lifeways. Thus, Xwelas reached adulthood in a period of rapid social change and emotional turmoil. Not only were the S'Klallam forced to contend with the Euro-American settlers, but intertribal raiding and violence in the region may have also increased during the first half of the nineteenth century. Attacks by Vancouver Island tribes and bands from the south, together with the threat of slavery, depopulation due to disease, and the breakdown of traditional ways, could have encouraged a young Indian woman to seek relative refuge in marriage with a white man, miles from her home.

Xwelas's marriage reveals an important dynamic. Her people and other Northwest native communities did not simply drown under a flood tide of immigrants, merchants, and missionaries. Rather, for several generations after Euro-American settlement, we find extensive cultural interdependence. Newcomers, whether British, Russian, Spanish, American, Hawaiian, or Asian, depended upon native knowledge for survival and for access to resources that fueled the new economies. Likewise, Indians came to depend upon immigrants for trade and protection. Alliances between Indians and whites proved necessary for both parties, one form of alliance being marriage. . . .

One such marriage took place in the 1850s between E-yow-alth and Edmund Clare Fitzhugh. E-yow-alth was herself the daughter of a marriage of alliance between Xwelas's S'Klallam brother, S'ya-whom, and Tsi-swat-oblista, a Samish noblewoman. . . .

Fitzhugh, a native of Virginia's Stafford County, had served in the Virginia legislature in 1846 and 1847 and had practiced law in California before coming to the Pacific Northwest in the early 1850s. . . . Fitzhugh . . . was an influential figure during the early years of Sehome. He became, among other things, superintendent of the Bellingham Bay Coal Company, Indian agent, county auditor, customs inspector, military aide to Governor Isaac I. Stevens, and territorial supreme court justice under President James Buchanan. His busy career did not escape scandal, however. According to one settler's diary, during Fitzhugh's tenure as judge, he allegedly shot and killed a man after a gambling dispute, then promptly tried and acquitted himself of the murder charge.

But perhaps Fitzhugh's most glaring escapades involved his relations with women. . . . In the early Northwest, eligible white brides were few and far between, encouraging the common practice of Caucasian men marrying Indian women, a pact often made for both sexual and economic reasons. In Sehome and surrounding Whatcom County, the Lummi Indians had provided so many brides or "kloochman" to white settlers that by the time E. C. Fitzhugh sought a partner, Lummi leader Chowitzit protested that too many young women had already married outside the tribe. Chowitzit referred Fitzhugh to the nearby Samish people to the south of Bellingham Bay. There, the Lummi presided over negotiations between Fitzhugh, "the tyee [chief] of Whatcom Falls," and S'ya-whom, the Samish headman. Following the traditions of his culture, in which romantic love played a lesser part in marriage than political diplomacy or social mobility, Chowitzit pointed out the advantages of a marriage alliance, while Fitzhugh spoke of his own wealth and how well he would be able to provide for a wife. In the end, S'ya-whom gave his sixteen-year-old daughter E-yow-alth to Fitzhugh, a man more than twenty years her senior. Throughout the nuptial negotiations, E-yow-alth's aunt, Xwelas, watched from the sidelines.

Years later, Xwelas would remember traveling to visit her married niece on Bellingham Bay. The trip required five or six hours by canoe, following the shoreline below the storm-sculpted sandstone cliffs of the Chuckanut Mountains. On arriving for a visit not long after E-yow-alth's wedding, Xwelas learned that all was not well in the white man's household. Fitzhugh had become discontent with E-yow-alth, who had borne him a daughter they named Julia, and he now began to entice his young wife's aunt. Eventually, Fitzhugh took Xwelas as his second wife. While multiple marriages would not have raised eyebrows among the Indian population, one might expect it to have done so among white society, particularly when involving a figure as public as Fitzhugh. Surprisingly, however, no recorded condemnation of his bigamy exists. And so Fitzhugh—the "example of chivalry"—took both E-yow-alth and Xwelas, now christened respectively as Julie and Mary, to form a single family. Xwelas soon gave birth to two sons named Mason and Julius.

Over time, even with two wives, Fitzhugh found that the appeal of domestic life waned. Sometime in the late 1850s, he suddenly left Sehome for Seattle, taking daughter Julia with him. She disappears from the historical record, but Fitzhugh reappears from time to time. We find him fighting as a Confederate major in the Civil War, representing his home state of Virginia. He formed another family after the war and apparently abandoned them as well, as he would yet a third family in Iowa. Fitzhugh returned briefly to Bellingham Bay in 1874, seeking out his son Mason, now seventeen. Mason, however, gave his father a cold shoulder, and the elder Fitzhugh soon left for San Francisco. On 24 November 1883, his body was found on the floor of a room in that city's What Cheer Hotel. Edmund Clare Fitzhugh's life and death in many ways typify the schism between frontier myth and historical reality: fondly remembered as a brave pioneer and community leader, he was also an irresponsible, transient womanizer.

While Fitzhugh roamed, E-yow-alth and Xwelas rebuilt their lives. For E-yow-alth, that meant starting again, her daughter having disappeared with Fitzhugh. Eventually, she would marry Henry Barkhousen, yet another county auditor, and would raise a new family on Fidalgo Island. Xwelas also would marry again, this time to a man with a colorful name, but about whom the historical record reveals little: William King Lear.

Lear, an immigrant from Alabama who had profited from the Fraser River gold rush of 1858, settled among the few houses and shops clinging to a spit called Semiahmoo, twenty miles to the north of Bellingham Bay. A land speculator, Lear dispensed titles to lots on the spit and also served his clients as a storekeeper. In the mid-1860s, he married Xwelas, now in her thirties. No details remain of their union, but sometime around 1866, Xwelas gave birth to William Jr., or "Billy." Not long after Billy's arrival, Lear abandoned his family. . . . Lear's later life is a mystery, but legend has it that he went down with his ship sometime around the turn of the century on another profit-driven passage to Alaska. So, by her early thirties, Xwelas had been twice abandoned by white husbands who pursued their dreams—and their deaths—elsewhere.

According to one report, Xwelas returned to her people near Port Townsend after King Lear left for the East. A single woman with children required support that the extended kinship systems of the S'Klallam community could provide. That she would marry yet a third time comes as no surprise; the S'Klallam allowed and even encouraged individuals to remarry, especially to continue useful alliances. The social standing of Xwelas's third spouse, however, does come as a surprise. Rather than choosing a prominent figure in politics or business such as Fitzhugh or King Lear, she wedded a common laborer. Why? Perhaps, as a forty-year-old woman with three children fathered by two different men, Xwelas may have been considered "used merchandise" by potential white suitors and by tribal leaders looking for strategic marriage alliances Or perhaps there may have been a romantic attraction between Xwelas and the Welsh cooper. For whatever reasons, Xwelas married George Phillips on 9 February 1873.

As a poor immigrant barrel-maker at a lime kiln in the rough-and-ready Orcas Island outpost of Langdon, George Phillips lacked any political or economic standing. Local histories cast him in a much less beneficient light than Xwelas's first two husbands, and by any standard, her life as Mary Phillips seems to have been the worst of the three marriages. Virtually every account of George Phillips mentions his alcoholism and his penchant for violent rages. His beatings of Xwelas often drew the attention of neighbors, although she was not incapable of defending herself. One account describes an argument between the couple in a canoe, in which Phillips hit Xwelas with a paddle. After a moment of silence, she asked if she could take over the rowing, and after a few strokes hit him with the same paddle. Such violence appears to have been a staple of their relationship.

Again, there were children. Two toddlers, young enough to remain unnamed in the records, were playing at the lime works in 1877, when one dropped a lighted match into an open powder keg. The resulting explosion, fire, and deaths may have struck a crippling blow to the already unhealthy marriage of George and Mary Phillips, even though another child named Maggie followed, and Xwelas was pregnant once again on Christmas, 1878.

What exactly provoked the yuletide killing of George Phillips? Some reports claimed that the family—George, the pregnant Xwelas, the infant Maggie, and Xwelas's eldest son Mason Fitzhugh—had attended a "squaw dance," where Phillips's flirtations with another Indian woman provoked Xwelas's anger. According to this theory, she later ambushed and shot her husband out of jealousy.

Xwelas herself described the events of that day during her trial. She and Phillips had gone to the house of a neighbor, William Shattuck, to drink and gamble. She recalled that both she and her husband drank considerably, with Phillips "in very high spirits, laughing & singing songs." Eventually, he became so intoxicated that she asked for help escorting him home after finally persuading him to leave the party:

> After we had gone some distance George said, "where were you last night, you old whore you, when I was hunting for you?" After some quarreling I called him a dog & he struck me with the oar on the cheek, then everything became dark and I fell forward. I then rose up & picked up the child when he punched me in the side with the oar. I then called him a dog & said, "don't you know I've got a child in my bowels?" He said he didn't care if he killed me; he'd get another woman, that I was whoring with Siwashes.

According to Xwelas's testimony, her husband repeatedly threatened to kill her after they reached the Langdon settlement and their house in the late afternoon. "George told me to get my things and leave, calling me a slut. He demanded the key to the house & ere I could give it to him, he took the axe & broke open the door." Phillips then grabbed two guns from above the mantle and began loading them. Although Mason Fitzhugh assured her that George would sober up, Xwelas decided to spend the night in the woods. Putting baby Maggie on her back, she took a double-barreled shotgun and walked to a neighbor's root house. As her husband and Mason approached the building along the trail a short time later, Xwelas hid in the nearby brush. Then Maggie cried out "Papa," alerting Phillips:

> I raised up from behind the brush. George then rushed forward & grasped the gun by the middle of the barrel. We each tried to pull the gun from the other, & while we were thus struggling the gun went off shooting George. He staggered back calling for Mason. . . . Mason came [and] said to me, "Do you see what you have done?" I answered, "I see what I have done."

. . . Immediately after Phillips was killed, Mason Fitzhugh, who was near enough that wadding from the shotgun blast flew past him, dragged his stepfather's body into a barnyard and enlisted neighbors to keep the hogs away from the corpse. After a hasty coroner's inquest, the next day Xwelas was indicted for murder. The Orcas Island sheriff immediately took her by boat across the water to Port Townsend, where she awaited a trial. . . .

. . . [During the trial,] the major contradiction in testimonies regarded Xwelas's claim that she and Phillips had struggled over the gun; witnesses reported that she had indeed fired from behind a screen of underbrush. Most of Xwelas's neighbors seemed sympathetic, inclined toward what modern courts would call an insanity defense. . . . Even Xwelas's son, Mason Fitzhugh, testified that she would at times act "as if she were not in her right mind and at other times she is all right."

Judge Roger Greene had instructed the jurors to weigh whether or not Xwelas understood the consequences of her action, and whether or not that action was justified in the light of her husband's violence. Judge Greene also reminded jurors to consider Phillips's character and that he had attacked Xwelas with "the intention of destroying her unborn child."

By common notions of frontier justice, Xwelas should have hung. The jury might have doubted whether she was sane or whether her actions were justified, but that she had in fact killed George Phillips was never in question. During this period in the American West, no legal precedents existed that took into account as justification for homicide domestic violence against women. Moreover, one would have expected the bias of white male jurisprudence to prevail over the interests of an Indian woman.

But Xwelas did not hang. When the two-day trial ended on 16 September 1879—almost ten months after the shooting—foreman Rufus Calhoun read the verdict: "We find the defendant guilty of manslaughter and not guilty of murder." The jury recommended Xwelas to the mercy of Judge Greene, who sentenced her to two years in prison, less the ten months spent awaiting trial. In the case of *Washington Territory v. Mary Phillips,* the territorial justice system and Xwelas's neighbors had spent over $1600 to maintain due process of law, to bond witnesses, and to care for Xwelas's children, including the infant Tom, born while she was in the Port Townsend jail. Finally, Xwelas herself was allowed to testify, as was her mixed-blood son Mason. Our conventional wisdom about intercultural relations, about the status of women, about the low value placed on Indian opinion, and about the whimsy of nineteenth-century justice, tells us that a jury of white men should have been less forgiving in a case such as this. So why the lenient treatment?

One explanation of the verdict may have been pangs of conscience over convicting a mother with five surviving children, including an infant born in prison. A burgeoning Northwest town with eager boosters, prolific newspapers, and a concern for its own image may have found a harsh sentence and the ensuing publicity to its detriment. But other factors emerge as well.

First, many local white men, perhaps even a majority at the time, had married or enjoyed liaisons with Indian women. Even Xwelas's defense attorney had once been a "squaw man." Very possibly some of the jurors had been as well. Thus, while notions of racial and cultural superiority were central to territorial society, white male familiarity with native women could have favored Xwelas in the eyes of the jury.

Second, the presence of Xwelas's S'Klallam kin in the community could have influenced the jury's decision. During the 1870s, Native Americans of the Chimacum, S'Klallam, Lushootseed, Twana, and other tribal groups remained a familiar sight in Port Townsend and other Northwest communities. Just as interracial marriages could provide alliances between racial groups, a fair trial and positive outcome for Xwelas could have been important in maintaining stable relations between whites and S'Klallams.

Third, George Phillips's reputation could have prejudiced the jury. Had Xwelas killed Edmund Clare Fitzhugh, William King Lear, or another prominent civic figure, she more likely would have suffered a harsher sentence. But to ambush Phillips, a poor, alcoholic, abusive Welsh laborer signified no great loss. Social class and national standing could be at least as important as race and gender in ordaining the relative value of human life in the West.

Ultimately, the legal decision probably rested on whether or not Xwelas understood her actions. Unfortunately, the most important psychological evidence, the opinions of doctors called to testify at her trial, has been lost. The foreman's note says nothing on this matter, but it may have been easier to dismiss Xwelas as a crazy Indian woman and to mete out a lesser sentence than to deal with the personal and political consequences of a more severe judgment.

Finally, the murder trial of Xwelas took place during a period in which legal and judicial standards, as they applied to Native Americans, were ill-defined and in a constant state of flux. For example, five years previously in 1874, a mixed-blood Indian named Henry, or Harry, Fisk stood trial in Olympia for the murder of a Squaxin Indian shaman called Doctor Jackson. Fisk's primary defense for killing Jackson was that the shaman had caused Fisk's wife to become ill, and that only Jackson's death could reverse the illness. While nineteenth-century American jurisprudence was not known for allowing shamanic self-defense as a justification for murder, the trial proceedings were marked by an attempt to understand native concepts of justice, and the all-white jury acquitted Fisk after only eight minutes of deliberation. Five years after Xwelas's trial, in 1884, the Sto:lo youth Louie Sam was abducted and lynched by a white mob near Sumas on the Canadian border for the murder of a prominent local shopkeeper named James Bell. According to at least one historian, another white settler named William Osterman was the more likely culprit. Nevertheless, local white thirst for vengeance was slaked when a mob strung up Louie Sam.

Considered alongside the trial of Xwelas, in which an Indian woman ironically benefited from a legal system largely created by and for white men, these cases illustrate the kaleidoscopic morass that was the legal status of nineteenth-century Native Americans.

After her conviction, Xwelas virtually disappears from the historical record. Her later life seems to have been removed from crisis or controversy, living with sons Billy Lear and Tom Phillips on the Lummi Reservation. She did not marry again, nor did she bear more children, and she seems to have withdrawn from the white world altogether. Sometime near the end of World War I, Mary Sehome Fitzhugh Lear Phillips—Xwelas—died in her tiny home on the reservation. . . .

The story of Xwelas sheds light on the realities of frontier experience in the Northwest, laying bare several assumptions about the region, its history, and its cultural legacy. First, Xwelas's tribal affiliations reveal the fluid nature of Native American societies on the Northwest Coast. Born among the S'Klallam, she lived with the Samish and with whites, returned for a time to the S'Klallam, and then died among the Lummi. In light of her life, we must question the concept of geographically and culturally distinct native tribes existing separate from each other. . . .

Second, the interdependence of white settlers and Indian residents also becomes clear through her story. Rather than a tide of immigrants erasing the native presence, on many levels—sexual, financial, political—Xwelas's life illustrates the continuing importance of Native Americans long after initial contact. In fact, it may have been the influential political and social presence of her S'Klallam kin that saved Xwelas from a murder conviction.

Finally, Xwelas's relationship to white men helps to shatter the myth of Christian pioneers such as Henry Spalding, Marcus and Narcissa Whitman, Cushing Eels, and Jason Lee bringing civilization and morality to a savage frontier. In many ways, the deserter Edmund Clare Fitzhugh, the profiteer William King Lear, the abusive George Phillips . . . *were* the savage frontier.

Chinese Women in Nineteenth-Century San Francisco

JUDY YUNG

Few women were in the first wave of Chinese immigrants to America in the mid-nineteenth century. Driven overseas by conditions of poverty at home, young Chinese men—peasants from the Pearl River delta of Guangdong Province (close to the ports of Canton and Hong Kong)—immigrated to Gold Mountain in search of a better livelihood to support their families. . . . Like other immigrants coming to California at this time, Guangdong men intended to strike it rich and return home. Thus, although more than half of them were married, most did not bring their wives and families. . . . [B]ecause of the high costs and harsh living conditions in California, the additional investment required to obtain passage for two or more,

Judy Yung, "Bound Feet: Chinese Women in the Nineteenth Century," in *Unbound Feet: A Social History of Chinese Women in San Francisco* (Berkeley and Los Angeles: University of California Press, 1995), 15–51. Copyright © 1995 Judy Yung. Reprinted by permission.

and the lack of job opportunities for women, it was cheaper and safer to keep the family in China and support it from across the sea. . . .

Although initially welcomed to California as valuable labor and investors in an expanding economy, Chinese immigrants quickly became the targets of white miners, workers, and politicians when the gold ran out and economic times turned sour. . . . Laws were also passed by the California legislature that denied Chinese basic civil rights, such as the right to immigrate, give testimony in court, be employed in public works, intermarry with whites, and own land. Negatively stereotyped as coolie labor, immoral and diseased heathens, and unassimilable aliens, the Chinese were driven out of the better-paying jobs in the mines, factories, fishing areas, and farmlands. They were generally not allowed to live outside Chinatown, and their children were barred from attending white schools. . . .

The most damaging blow to Chinese immigration and settlement proved to be the Chinese Exclusion Act of 1882, passed by a Congress under siege from white labor and politicians at the height of the anti-Chinese movement. The act suspended the immigration of Chinese laborers to the United States for ten years. It was renewed in 1892 for another ten years, and in 1904 extended indefinitely. The Exclusion Acts were strictly enforced until they were repealed in 1943. . . . Although the number of Chinese immigrants dropped sharply—only 92,411 entered during the Exclusion period (1882–1943), as compared to 258,210 prior to the 1882 act—Chinese immigration was not totally stopped. . . . Chinese immigrants who could pool enough money to become partners in import export businesses were able to attain merchant status and so send for their wives and children. Many others who had merchant or U.S. citizenship status would falsely report a number of sons (rarely daughters) in China, thereby creating "paper son" slots that were then sold to fellow villagers who desired to immigrate. . . . Wives of laborers, although not specifically mentioned in the act, were barred by implication. . . .

The Exclusion Act severely limited the number of Chinese women who could come to America, keeping a crack open mainly for the privileged few—the wives and daughters of merchants. But in fact, rigorous enforcement of the act, along with the implementation of anti-Chinese measures regulating prostitution such as the Page Law of 1875, kept even those Chinese immigrant women with legitimate claims out of the country and made immigration to America an ordeal for any woman who tried to enter. Immigration officials apparently operated on the premise that every Chinese woman was seeking admission on false pretenses and that each was a potential prostitute until proven otherwise. Only women . . . who had bound feet and a modest demeanor were considered upper-class women with "moral integrity." . . .

A good number of the Chinese women who came to the United States in the nineteenth century—despite the social, economic, and political barriers—settled in San Francisco: 654, or 37 percent of all Chinese women in the country, lived in San Francisco in 1860; 2,136, or 47 percent, in 1900. But they were still grossly outnumbered by men, who on the average made up 95 percent of the total Chinese population during these years. . . . Most had either been sold into prostitution or domestic slavery, or they were coming to join their husbands. . . .

As in China, Chinese women stayed close to home and appeared as little as possible in public. Indeed, the predominantly male and relatively lawless society of mid-nineteenth-century San Francisco contributed to their sheltered existence. Moreover, the Chinese kinship system, which formed the buttress for patriarchal control in Chinatown, successfully kept them outside the power structure: only men could be members of the clan and district associations that governed China-town, or of the trade guilds and tongs (secret societies) that regulated both legal and illicit businesses. Footbinding, practiced only among the merchant wives, was not necessary to stop Chinese women in San Francisco from "wandering"; their physical and social mobility was effectively bound by patriarchal control within Chinatown and racism as well as sexism outside. . . .

Whereas the majority of white prostitutes came to San Francisco as independent professionals and worked for wages in brothels, Chinese prostitutes were almost always imported as unfree labor, indentured or enslaved. Most were kidnapped, lured, or purchased from poor parents by procurers in China for as little as $50 and then resold in America for as much as $1,000 in the 1870s. One young woman testified in 1892:

> I was kidnapped in China and brought over here [eighteen months ago]. The man who kidnapped me sold me for four hundred dollars to a San Francisco slave-dealer; and he sold me here for seventeen hundred dollars. I have been a brothel slave ever since. I saw the money paid down and am telling the truth. I was deceived by the promise I was going to marry a rich and good husband, or I should never have come here.

. . . A selected number of young women were sold to wealthy Chinese in San Francisco or outlying rural areas as concubines or mistresses and sequestered in comfortable quarters. As long as they continued to please their owners, they were pampered and well cared for. But if they failed to meet their masters' expectations, they could be returned to the auction block for resale. The remainder of the women either were sold to parlor houses that served well-to-do Chinese or white gentlemen or ended up in cribs catering to a racially mixed, poorer clientele.

Parlor houses were luxurious rooms on the upper floors of Chinatown establishments that were furnished with teakwood and bamboo, Chinese paintings, and cushions of embroidered silk. Here, anywhere between four and twenty-five Chinese courtesans, all richly dressed and perfumed, were made available to a select clientele. The "exotic" atmosphere, the relatively cheap rates, and the rumor that Chinese women had vaginas that ran "east-west" instead of "north-south" attracted many white patrons. . . .

In contrast, the cribs—considered the end of the line—were shacks no larger than twelve by fourteen feet, often facing a dimly lit alley, where prostitutes hawked their wares to poor laborers, teenage boys, sailors, and drunkards for as little as twenty-five cents. The cribs were sparsely furnished with a washbowl, a bamboo chair or two, and a hard bed covered with matting. The women took turns enticing customers through a wicket window with plaintive cries of "Two bittee lookee, flo bittee feelee, six bittee dooee!" Harshly treated by both owners and customers and compelled to accept every man who sought their business, most women succumbed to venereal disease. Once hopelessly diseased, they were discarded on the street or locked in a room to die alone. Thus, Chinese prostitutes in San Francisco, exploited as they were for their bodies by men who had control over their fates and livelihoods, were the archetype of female bondage and degradation.

Various studies of the manuscript schedules of the U.S. population censuses indicate that a high percentage of the Chinese female population in San Francisco worked as prostitutes: from 85 to 97 percent in 1860; 71 to 72 percent in 1870; and 21 to 50 percent in 1880. There were reasons for these high percentages. . . . Chinese cultural values and American immigration policies that discouraged the immigration of women resulted in a skewed sex ratio that, when combined with anti-Chinese prejudice and antimiscegenation attitudes (institutionalized in 1880 when California's Civil Code was amended to prohibit the issuance of a marriage license to a white person and a "Negro, Mulatto, or Mongolian"), forced most Chinese immigrants to live a bachelor's existence. Stranded in America until they could save enough money to return home, both married and single Chinese men found it difficult to establish conjugal relations or find female companionship. Some married other women of color—black, Mexican, or Native American; a few cohabited with white women; but the majority sought sexual release in brothels. The demand for Chinese prostitutes by both Chinese and white men intersected with an available supply of young women sold into servitude by impoverished families in China. What resulted was the organized trafficking of Chinese women, which proved immensely profitable for the tongs that came to control the trade in San Francisco. . . .

As hopeless and pathetic as this picture of enslavement appeared, Chinese prostitutes found a number of escape avenues. As in China, they were sometimes redeemed and married, mostly to Chinese laborers who had saved enough money to afford a wife. A few successfully ran away with lovers despite the heavy bounty often placed on the man's head by the owner. Others escaped their sordid reality through insanity or suicide by swallowing raw opium or drowning themselves in the bay—an honorable act of protest and vengeance by Chinese cultural standards. But being in America accorded them additional avenues of resistance. A few went to the police for protection. Some women, like Mah Ah Wah and Yoke Qui, two women detained by the authorities upon arrival, were able to escape prostitution by refusing to accept bail, claiming that they had been imported for immoral purposes against their will. Both were remanded to China. . . .

The most viable option open to Chinese prostitutes was two Protestant mission homes that singled them out for rescue and rehabilitation beginning in the 1870s; for in their view, "Of all the darkened and enslaved ones, the Chinese woman's fate seems the most pitiful." Inspired by the Social Gospel Movement, missionary women were intent on establishing female moral authority in the American West and rescuing female victims of male abuse. They saw Chinese women as the ultimate symbol of female powerlessness, as exemplified in their domestic confinement, sexual exploitation, and treatment as chattel. Unable to work effectively among Chinatown bachelors and spurned by white prostitutes, they found their calling among Chinese prostitutes and *mui tsai*. In turn, some Chinese prostitutes, calculating their chances in an oppressive environment with few options for improvement, saw the mission homes as a way out of their problems. . . .

Many . . . Chinese women sought refuge at the Presbyterian Mission Home. . . . As superintendent of the home from 1877 to 1897, Margaret Culbertson devised the technique of rescue work, whereby brothels were raided with the assistance of the police whenever a Chinese girl or woman sent word for help. According to Donaldina Cameron, who succeeded Culbertson, approximately 1,500 girls were rescued in this way during the first thirty years of the home's existence. Because of the high value placed on prostitutes, owners went to great expense to recover their "property," hiring highbinders to retrieve the women or paying legal fees to file criminal charges against the women on trumped-up charges of larceny. Once rescued, the women often had to be guarded in the home and defended in court. As inmates, the women were subjected to strong doses of Christian doctrine and a regimented life of constant activity, the combination of which was meant to instill "virtue" in them. . . . Women were assigned household chores, taught Chinese and English, trained for industrial or domestic employment, and encouraged to work for wages either sewing in the Mission Home or serving as domestic workers outside the institution. Some—particularly those assigned to the home by the courts— resented the restrictions and austerity of the Mission Home and chose to return to their former status. Others opted to return to China. A significant number, however, agreed to marry Chinese Christians and begin life anew in America. . . .

. . . Chinese women who sought help from the mission homes were neither powerless victims nor entirely free agents, but women who lived in a world with many constraints and few opportunities. Recognizing that the Mission Home offered them a chance to change their circumstances, they went there with their own hidden agendas. A number of entrants to the Presbyterian Mission Home between 1874 and 1880 were prostitutes who wanted the protection of home officials in order to marry suitors of their choice. Other women used the Mission Home as a temporary refuge from male abuse, to escape arranged marriages, or to gain leverage in a polygynous marriage. Although they were genuinely grateful for the services of the Mission Home, many did not convert to Christianity or end up mirroring the Victorian ideals of womanhood. Rather, . . . Chinese wives came to shape a new set of gender relations in their Chinese American marriages.

Not far from the reaches of prostitution were *mui tsai*—girls who were brought from China to work as domestic servants in affluent Chinese homes or brothels, or young daughters of prostitutes who worked in this capacity in brothels. Although John W. Stephens, in his study of the manuscript censuses, estimates that only 2 percent of Chinese women were listed as "young servants" in the 1870 census, their presence and role were more significant than that. The *mui tsai* system, a cultural carryover from China, was generally regarded by the Chinese as a form of charity for impoverished girls. The term itself comes from the Cantonese dialect and means "little sister." Under this age-old system, poor parents would sell a young daughter into domestic service, usually stipulating in a deed of sale that she be freed through marriage when she turned eighteen. Meanwhile, the girl received no wages for her labor, was not at liberty to leave of her own free will, and had no legal recourse for complaint should she be mistreated, raped, or forced into an unhappy marriage. . . . There was no guarantee that their contracts would be honored—that they would obtain freedom through marriage when they came of age. Indeed, depending on the family's economic situation, a *mui tsai* could be resold into prostitution for a handsome sum. . . . Nevertheless, like organized prostitution, the *mui tsai* system had all but vanished by the 1920s thanks to the efforts of missionary women and Chinese social reformers intent on modernizing Chinatown—this in a country, it should be noted, where slavery had been abolished in 1865 and contract labor in 1885.

Between 1870 and 1880, the percentage of Chinese women in San Francisco who were prostitutes had declined from 71 to 50 percent, while the percentage of women who were married had increased from approximately 8 to 49 percent, most likely owing to the enforcement of antiprostitution measures, the arrival of wives from China, and the marriage of ex-prostitutes to Chinese laborers. The number of wives continued to rise after the passage of the Chinese Exclusion Act of 1882, when merchant wives became the prime category of female immigrants from China. By the turn of the century, married women made up 62 percent of the Chinese female population in San Francisco.

Within the patriarchal structure of San Francisco Chinatown, immigrant wives occupied a higher status than *mui tsai* and prostitutes, but they too were considered the property of men and constrained to lead bound lives. Members of the merchant class, capitalizing on miners' and labor crews' need for provisions and services, were among the first Chinese to come to California. They were also the only Chinese who were allowed to and who could afford to bring their wives and families, or to establish second families in America. In the absence of the scholar-gentry class, which chose not to emigrate, the merchant class became the ruling elite in China-town, and their families formed the basis for the growth of the Chinese American population and the formation of the middle class.

Referred to as "small-foot" or "lily-feet" women in nineteenth-century writings because of their bound feet, most merchant wives led the cloistered life of genteel women. They generally had servants and did not need to work for wages or be bur-dened by the daily household chores of cooking, laundering, and cleaning. . . . At least one merchant wife in San Francisco Chinatown did not view her life . . . posi-tively, though. "Poor me!" she told a white reporter. "In China I was shut up in the house since I was 10 years old, and only left my father's house to be shut up in my husband's house in this great country. For seventeen years I have been in this house without leaving it save on two evenings." To pass her time, she worshiped at the family altar, embroidered, looked after her son, played cards with her servant, or chatted with her Chinese neighbors. Periodically, her hairdresser would come to do her hair, or a female storyteller would come to entertain her. Her husband had also provided her with a European music box and a pet canary. Only through her husband, servant, hairdresser, and female neighbors was she able to maintain contact with the outside world.

Despite her wealth, she envied other women "who are richer than I, for they have big feet and can go everywhere, and every day have something new to fill their minds." This woman, however, as she was well aware, was still only a piece of property to her husband, always fearful of being sold "like cows" if her husband tired of her, or of having her son taken from her and sent back to China to the first wife. Also, as she herself pointed out, she had few avenues of escape. Chinatown was governed by the laws of China, and the Mission Home could provide her with only a temporary refuge. "I am too old for any man to desire in marriage, too help-less in the ways of making money to support myself, too used to the grand living my husband provides to be deprived of it."

In fact, however, such women of leisure were but a small proportion of immi-grant wives in the late nineteenth century. Most wives were married to Chinese laborers who, having decided to settle in America, had saved enough money to send for a wife or to marry a local Chinese woman—most likely a former prostitute or American-born. As it was for other working-class immigrant women, life for this group of wives was marked by constant toil, with little time for leisure. Undoubtedly, they were the seamstresses, shirtmakers, washerwomen, gardeners, fisherwomen, storekeepers, and laborers listed in the manuscript census. Even those listed as "keeping house" most likely also worked for wages at home or took in boarders to supplement their husbands' low wages. In addition to their paid work, they were burdened with child care and domestic chores, which they had to perform in crowded housing arrangements. According to the San Francisco Health Officer's Report for 1869–70, "Their mode of living is the most abject in which it is possible for human beings to exist. The great majority of them live crowded together in rickety, filthy and dilapidated tenement houses like so many cattle." . . .

Like peasant women in China, working-class wives in San Francisco could freely go out to work, worship at the temple, or shop in the Chinatown stores that provided for all their needs. But they did not travel far from home or mingle with men. Even when they spent an occasional evening at the Chinese opera, they would sit in a separate section from the men. Nor did they linger long in the streets, so threatened were they by the possibility of racial and sexual assaults. . . . As it became more difficult to import Chinese prostitutes, Chinese women found themselves the targets of kidnappers, sometimes in broad daylight, to be sold into prostitution. During one week in February 1898, eight such kidnappings occurred. . . .

One of the advantages for women who immigrated to America was the chance to remove themselves from the rule of the tyrannical mother-in-law, the one position that allowed women in China any power. Not only was the daughter-in-law freed from serving her in-laws, but she was also freed of competition for her husband's attention and loyalty and given full control over managing the household. Because of the small number of Chinese women, wives in America were valued and accorded more respect by their men (although there were still incidences of wife abuse). In addition, most Chinese men, because of their low socioeconomic status, could not afford a concubine or mistress, much less a wife. Thus, having a wife was a status symbol to be jealously guarded. . . .

Wives were also more valued in America because they were essential helpmates in the family's daily struggle for socioeconomic survival. As it was for European immigrants, the family's interest was paramount, and all members worked for its survival and well-being. A Chinese wife's earnings from sewing, washing, or taking in boarders could mean the difference between having pork or just bean paste with rice for dinner, or between life and death for starving relatives back in China. It was also her duty to cook and prepare the Chinese meals and special foods for certain celebrations, to maintain the family altar, to make Chinese clothing and slippers for the family, to raise the children to be "proper Chinese," and to provide a refuge for the husband from the hostile world outside. Thus, even while the family was a site of oppression for Chinese women in terms of the heavy housework and child care responsibilities and possibly wife abuse, it was also a source of empowerment. Wives ran the household and raised the children; they also played an important role in the family economy and in maintaining Chinese culture and family life as a way of resisting cultural onslaughts from the outside.

As Protestant women gained a foothold in bringing Christianity, Western ideas, and contact with the outside world into Chinatown homes, Chinese wives became more aware of their bound lives. They also became an important link between the Chinese family and the larger society and an influential factor in the education and socialization of Chinese American children. Convinced that there was little hope of redeeming the Chinese unless the women were converted to Christianity and Americanized, missionary women visited Chinese homes regularly to give lessons on the Bible and American domestic and sanitary practices, often while the women worked—"one woman making paper gods, another overalls, another binding shoes." . . .

These visits won few converts, but some mothers were persuaded to educate their daughters and discontinue the practice of binding their feet, and a small number of women also began to venture out of the home to attend church functions. Abused wives also found their way to the mission homes. Records of the Presbyterian Mission Home indicate that a number of "runaway wives" came asking for help when they were threatened with being sold, subjected to beatings, or just unhappy with their husbands. In one case, Lan Lee, who had continually been beaten by her husband and threatened with murder, was assisted by the Presbyterian mission in winning a divorce on the grounds of extreme cruelty in 1893. Slowly, Chinese women were becoming aware of legal rights in America, rights that European women already knew how to take advantage of. . . .

Even at this early stage of their history, Chinese women were adapting to life in Gold Mountain with mixed results. Although most of them lived bound lives, remaining confined to the domestic sphere and subordinate to men, their important roles as producers (wage earners) and reproducers (childbearers as well as homemakers) in a predominantly male and pervasively racist land elevated their value as scarce commodities and essential helpmates to their men. Others, most notably prostitutes and *mui tsai,* suffered considerable abuse in America but found new options opened to them, through the assistance of missionary women and what legal rights were available to them at the time. Nonetheless, . . . it took the additional influence of Chinese nationalism and its inherent feminist ideology, combined with increased economic opportunities and the continued support of Protestant women, before Chinese immigrant women could become "new women" in the modern era of the twentieth century.

FURTHER   READING

Armitage, Susan, and Betsy Jameson, eds. *The Women's West* (1987).

Babcock, Barbara, and Nancy J. Parezo. *Daughters of the Desert: Women Anthropologists and the Native American Southwest, 1880–1980: An Illustrated Catalogue* (1980).

Butler, Anne M. *Daughters of Joy, Sisters of Mercy: Prostitutes in the American West, 1865–1890* (1985).

Del Castillo, Adelaida R., ed. *Between Borders: Essays on Mexicana/Chicana History* (1990).

Fink Deborah. *Agrarian Women: Wives and Mothers in Rural Nebraska, 1880–1940* (1992).

Foote, Cheryl J. *Women of the New Mexico Frontier, 1846–1912* (1990).

Gonzaléz, Deena J. *Refusing the Favor: The Spanish-Mexican Women of Santa Fe, 1829–1880* (1999).

Gutiérrez, Ramón A. *When Jesus Came the Corn Mothers Went Away: Marriage, Sexuality, and Power in New Mexico, 1500–1846* (1991).

Hirata, Lucie Cheng. "Free, Indentured, Enslaved: Chinese Prostitutes in Nineteenth-Century America," *Signs* 5 (1979): 3–29.

Hoffert, Sylvia D. "Childbearing on the Trans-Mississippi Frontier, 1830–1900," *Western Historical Quarterly* 22, no. 3 (August 1991): 273–288.

Jensen, Joan M., and Darlis A. Miller. "The Gentle Tamers Revisited: New Approaches to the History of Women in the American West," *Pacific Historical Review* 49 (1980): 173–213.

Kolodny, Annette. *The Land Before Her: Fantasy and Experience of the American Frontiers, 1630–1860* (1984).

Ling, Huping. "Family and Marriage of Late-Nineteenth and Early-Twentieth-Century Chinese Immigrant Women," *Journal of American Ethnic History* 19 (2000): 43–63.

Lomawaima, K. Tsianina. *They Called It Prairie Light: The Story of Chilocco Indian School* (1994).

Martin, Patricia Preciado. *Songs My Mother Sang to Me: An Oral History of Mexican-American Women* (1992).

Matsumoto, Valerie J., and Blake Allmendinger, eds. *Over the Edge: Remapping the American West* (1999).

Mihesuah, Devon A. *Cultivating the Rosebuds: The Education of Women at the Cherokee Female Seminary* (1993).

Milner II, Clyde A., ed. *A New Significance: Re-envisioning the History of the American West* (1996).

Osburn, Katherine M. B. "'To Build Up the Morals of the Tribe': Southern Ute Women's Sexual Behavior and the Office of Indian Affairs, 1895–1932," *Journal of Women's History* 9, no. 3 (1997): 10–27.

Pascoe, Peggy. *Relations of Rescue: The Search for Moral Authority in the American West, 1874–1939* (1990).

Schlissel, Lillian, Vicki L. Ruiz, and Janice Monk, eds. *Western Women: Their Land, Their Lives* (1988).

Van Kirk, Sylvia. *Many Tender Ties: Women in Fur Trade Society, 1670–1870* (1980).

CHAPTER
9

Work and Work Cultures in the Era of the "New Woman," 1880–1920s

During the early twentieth century, women became a significant presence in the American labor force, accounting for nearly 22 percent of all wage earners by 1930. Though they were as yet unwelcome in the majority of occupations and professions, millions of women found employment as factory operatives, retail clerks, and clerical workers. Women workers had not always been so conspicuous. For most of the nineteenth century, the labor force was overwhelmingly male and women were limited to a handful of occupations, the most common being live-in domestic service. In the decades after the Civil War, however, industrialization created millions of new jobs in manufacturing and commerce. Many jobs required only modest skills or strength and were highly repetitive; employers quickly hired single women to fill them, reasoning that "working girls" would suffer low wages and monotony with fewer complaints than men. To some extent, the employers' assumptions proved correct. Since women were usually ignored by unions, most could ill afford to complain about their wages or conditions of work. Moreover, the majority planned to work only until they married and therefore thought it not in their interest to pursue formal changes in the workplace. With great advantage accruing to employers, the industrial work force thus became highly sex segregated.

Women in the work force were also divided by ethnicity, class, and race. Working-class and European immigrant women flocked to factory positions, while middle-class women with a high-school or advanced education favored white-collar employment or tried to gain professional status in fields such as teaching, nursing, and social work that were expanding in response to industrialization. A small number of educated and ambitious black, Hispanic, and Asian women entered the so-called feminized professions or the world of business, but most women of African American, Mexican, and Asian heritage (married or single) filled the domestic service jobs abandoned by their more fortunate sisters.

While historians recognize the disadvantages under which women labored in the early twentieth century, their attention has recently turned to evaluating what

paid employment actually meant to women and the society around them. Did con-
temporary observers consider women's growing presence in the industrial, clerical,
and professional sectors of the labor force a sign of meaningful and positive change
in gender roles or social relations? How did wage work alter women's sense of self
and their relations with family members and the wider community? Were women
able to challenge or subvert disagreeable features of their work even when they lacked
the formal authority to do so? Finally, despite the intentions of their employers, did
women discover in patterns of gender or racial segregation a foundation for work-
place or professional solidarity?

◆ D O C U M E N T S

In Document 1, Rose Cohen, a young Russian-Jewish immigrant, describes the exhaustion, exploitation, and loneliness she experienced in her first job in a New York City
sweatshop in 1892. Two years later, Gertrude Stuart Baillie examines (Document 2)
the controversy surrounding professional and business women's declining interest in
marriage and concludes that they had entirely legitimate reasons for choosing to remain
single. In Document 3, Fannie Barrier Williams comments on the employment difficulties facing black women in 1903, urging them to make the best of segregation and to
treat domestic service as a field open to "unlimited improvement." In Document 4,
Harriet Brunkhurst, writing for the *Ladies Home Journal* in 1910, sympathetically describes the new difficulties that young women were encountering at home as they joined
the work force. *The Survey* magazine reported in 1914 (Document 5) on the first organized protest of unemployed women ever held in New York City; these women refused to
submit passively to their plight and demanded that they be given jobs. In Document 6, a
wartime advisory council reports favorably on college women's patriotism and ability to
adapt to the rigors of agricultural work during World War I. Several years after the war,
in 1923, Elizabeth Jones (Document 7) offers high praise to black women nurses, finding
that these women were meeting the highest standards of professionalism while also
improving race relations. Marion Bonner reports in Document 8 on women who joined
the textile strikes going on in a number of southern states in 1929. Observing a group
of strikers who had gone to the Southern Summer School for Women Workers (in North
Carolina) to speak about their strike experience with other women wage earners, Bonner
emphasizes, on the one hand, the terrible working and living conditions of the strikers,
and, on the other, the indomitable spirit of these women.

1. Rose Cohen Describes Her First
Job in New York City, 1892

The next morning when I came into the shop at seven o'clock, I saw at once that all
the people were there and working as steadily as if they had been at work a long
while. I had just time to put away my coat and go over to the table, when the boss

Rose Cohen, *Out of the Shadow: A Russian Jewish Girlhood on the Lower East Side* (1918; reprint,
Ithaca, N.Y.: Cornell University Press, 1995), 112–114.

shouted gruffly, "Look here, girl, if you want to work here you better come in early. No office hours in my shop." . . .

From this hour a hard life began for me. He refused to employ me except by the week. He paid me three dollars and for this he hurried me from early until late. He gave me only two coats at a time to do. When I took them over and as he handed me the new work he would say quickly and sharply, "Hurry!" . . . I hurried but he was never satisfied. By looks and manner he made me feel that I was not doing enough. Late at night when the people would stand up and begin to fold their work away and I too would rise feeling stiff in every limb and thinking with dread of our cold empty little room and the uncooked rice, he would come over with still another coat.

"I need it the first thing in the morning," he would give as an excuse. I understood that he was taking advantage of me because I was a child. . . .

I did not soon complain to father. . . . But when I had been in the shop a few weeks I told him, "The boss is hurrying the life out of me." I know now that if I had put it less strongly he would have paid more attention to it. Father hated to hear things put strongly. Besides he himself worked very hard. He never came home before eleven and he left at five in the morning.

He said to me now, "Work a little longer until you have more experience; then you can be independent."

"But if I did piece work, father, I would not have to hurry so. And I could go home earlier when the other people go."

Father explained further, "It pays him better to employ you by the week. Don't you see if you did piece work he would have to pay you as much as he pays a woman piece worker? But this way he gets almost as much work out of you for half the amount a woman is paid."

I myself did not want to leave the shop for fear of losing a day or even more perhaps in finding other work. To lose half a dollar meant that it would take so much longer before mother and the children would come. And now I wanted them more than ever before. I longed for my mother and a home where it would be light and warm and she would be waiting when we came from work. Because I longed for them so I lived much in imagination. For so I could have them near me. Often as the hour for going home drew near I would sit stitching and making believe that mother and the children were home waiting. On leaving the shop I would hasten along through the street keeping my eyes on the ground so as to shut out everything but what I wanted to see. I pictured myself walking into the house. There was a delicious warm smell of cooked food. Mother greeted me near the door and the children gathered about me shouting and trying to pull me down. Mother scolded them saying, "Let her take her coat off, see how cold her hands are!" But they paid no attention and pulled me down to them. Their little arms were about my neck, their warm faces against my cold cheeks and we went tumbling all over each other. Soon mother called, "Supper is ready." There was a scampering and a rush to the table, followed by a scraping of chairs and a clattering of dishes. Finally we were all seated. There was browned meat and potatoes for supper.

I used to keep this up until I turned the key in the door and opened it and stood facing the dark, cold, silent room.

2. Gertrude Stuart Baillie
Asks, "Should Professional
Women Marry?" 1894

Among the various women's clubs no question has been so often asked, so much discussed, as that of marriage of those women who go to make up the great professional and business world. It has been discussed by men in every station of life from the minister, to the lawyer, doctor, philanthropist, moralist and novelist, the conservative and the radical. . . .

It is said by some, that the higher education of women, though they consider it an excellent and praiseworthy movement, has resulted in training them for functions which belong exclusively to the sterner sex, and that during this process they gradually become more or less womanly and lose those charms of person and sentimentality which are supposed to be the birthright of every woman. Not only this, but her higher development mentally, is purchased at the cost of her physical deterioration, inasmuch as her sexuality is enfeebled or destroyed, and sexuality, Dr. Edson and Mr. Grant Allen informs us, is the base of everything. . . .

. . . The purport of this paper is rather to show that women in professional or business life . . . possess the same natural instincts as their mothers before them, with the exception, that their liberal education has stored their minds with the fundamental truths of nature. They are not stunted ascetics by any means, but they have learned to make their bodies subservient to their wills.

The reasons for professional women preferring to remain single, are many and obvious, and are not always due, as the critics would have us believe, to a lack of physical impulse.

Of course, no one who has kept apace with the latter half of this nineteenth century, will attempt to deny, that a momentuous revolution is taking place in all the so-called spheres of women. Progression has largely destroyed the domestic character of former times, consequently, the old idea, that every woman should be a wife, is disappearing as rapidly as those customs which heretofore deprived them of the same pecuniary and educational advantages of men. . . .

. . . A woman of lofty ambitions, high ideals, endowed with great talent and capacity, is sure, sooner or later, to become a small power in her way. She may be artist, novelist, physician, anything, but she begins by courting her profession and ends in being wedded to it. Should she marry, she would be none the less an artist, but she would be surrounded by numerous other cares, which as must eventually come to every married woman, and either her work or her family will feel the neglect. . . .

Mrs. E. D. E. N. Southworth recently admitted, she never could have accomplished so much in literature, had she not been left a widow in early life.

Gertrude Stuart Baillie, "Should Professional Women Marry?" in Dawn Keetley and John Pettegrew, eds., *Public Women, Public Words: A Documentary History of American Feminism, Volume 1: Beginnings to 1900* (1894; reprint, Madison, Wis.: Madison House, 1997), 292–294.

Two of America's most famous women novelists have refused many offers of marriage, not because they advocated asceticism, but for the best of reasons, viz.: they could not conscientiously give their hand where their heart was not, for their heart was given to their work.

One of the most successful physicians in this country, whose contributions to medical journalism are read with avidity by the medical profession abroad, as well as at home, asserts that women physicians, least of all, should hesitate to enter the matrimonial state. She, whose office it is to launch upon the sea of life frail nameless barks, who has learned to soothe the cradle of reposing age, to heal the sick and combat dread pestilence, she least of all, cannot work well under the yoke of matrimony. She lives by and for the people and hence must ever be in readiness to answer their summons, which, should she be married, it might not always be propitious to do. Whether the advice of the physician referred to, has been followed, I am not prepared to say, but statistics show, that there are fewer marriages among women in medicine, than any other profession.

Another reason why women who are in daily contact with the world and its ways hesitate before they exchange their freedom for a wedding ring, is, that they have learned self-control and gained a balance which is of inestimable value to them in dealing with the practical affairs of life. They are no longer compelled to sacrifice themselves to their own emotions. Again, they are convinced of their ability to take care of themselves, and they have heard how men– husband of friends—do not always "come to time" in the role of provider. Thus, is it to be wondered at, that they prefer celibacy, with the title of "old maid," rather than to fly to matrimonial evils they know not of! . . .

In one of his tirades against women and higher education, Mr. Grant Allen alludes in a very caustic manner to the self-supporting spinster, usually a school teacher, whom he terms "a deplorable accident of the passing moment." And what, pray, would become of the school system of either this country or England, if it were not for these very "accidents," whose self-sacrifice, patient endurance, and especial fitness for the great responsibilities put upon them, to teach them how to lead and direct the young ideas of both nations? How many more children owe their success in life, rather to their school than home training!

To recapitulate, some of the formidable causes that are responsible for the celibacy of professional women, "We find," they say, "that intellectually, we are the equals of the majority of men whom we meet. That as we are able to support ourselves comfortably, and have a keen appreciation of freedom of *being*, as well as *seeming,* we have no desire to reject our newly-found liberty for what would handicap and hamper us in our individual vocations."

Women, to-day, occupy an important position in human development. That they stand upon a morally higher level than men, modern sociology has long conceded, and herein lies another stern fact that repels the educated woman contemplating marriage.

Until men reach the same plane of morality, have the same worthy aspirations, and thereby bridge the chasm that stands between them and women who are a distinct product of the best evolutionary forces, they should raise no dissenting voice if women are less interested in them as possible lovers.

3. Fannie Barrier Williams Describes the "Problem of Employment for Negro Women," 1903

It can be broadly said that colored women know how to work, and have done their full share of the paid and unpaid service rendered to the American people by the Negro race. This is a busy world; the world's work is large, complicated, and increasing. The demand for the competent in all kinds of work is never fully supplied. Woman is constantly receiving a larger share of the work to be done. The field for her skill, her endurance, her finer instincts and faithfulness is ever enlarging; and she has become impatient of limitations, except those imposed by her own physical condition. In this generalization, colored women, of course, are largely excepted. For reasons too well understood here to be repeated, ours is a narrow sphere. While the kinds and grades of occupation open to all women of white complexion are almost beyond enumeration, those open to our women are few in number and mostly menial in quality. The girl who is white and capable is in demand in a thousand places. The capable Negro girl is usually not in demand. This is one of the stubborn facts of to-day. . . .

In the city of Chicago domestic service is the one occupation in which the demand for colored women exceeds the supply. In one employment office during the past year there were 1,500 applications for colored women and only 1,000 of this number were supplied. Girls of other nationalities do not seem to compete with colored women as domestics. It is probably safe to say that every colored woman who is in any way competent can find good employment. Her wages for general housework range from four to seven dollars per week, while a good cook receives from seven to ten dollars. Now what is the condition of this service? The two most important things are that the wages paid are higher than those given for the same grade of intelligence in any other calling; and that colored women can command almost a monopoly of this employment.

It might be safe to presume that as our women are so much in demand for this service they give perfect satisfaction. In considering that it is important to bear in mind that there are two kinds of colored women who perform domestic service:— First, there are those who take to the work naturally and whose training and habits make them perfectly satisfied with it; and second, those who have had more or less education and who are ambitious to do something in the line of "polite occupations." The women of the latter class do not take to domestic service very kindly. They do not enter the service with any pride. They feel compelled to do this work because they can find nothing else to do. They are always sensitive as to how they may be regarded by their associates and friends, and shrink from the term servant as something degrading "per se." . . .

It is of course an easy thing to condemn our young women who have been fairly educated and have had good home training, because they prefer idleness to domestic service, but I am rather inclined to think we must share in that condemnation. If our girls work for wages in a nice home, rather than in a factory or over a

Fannie Barber Williams, "The Problem of Employment for Negro Women," *Southern Workman* 32 (1903): 432–437.

counter, they are ruthlessly scorned by their friends and acquaintances. Our young men, whose own occupations, by the way, will not always bear scrutiny, will also give them the cut direct, so that between the scorn of their associates and the petty tyranny of the housewife, the colored girls who enter domestic service are compelled to have more than ordinary strength of character.

But after all is said, I believe that it is largely in the power of the young woman herself to change and elevate the character of domestic service. She certainly cannot improve it by taking into it ignorance, contempt, and inefficiency. There is no reason why a woman of character, graciousness, and skill should not make her work as a domestic as respectable and as highly regarded as the work of the girl behind a department-store counter. For example, if by special training in domestic service, a girl can cook so well and do everything about a house so deftly and thoroughly that she will be called a real home helper and an invaluable assistant, it is in her power, with her intelligent grasp upon the possibilities of her position, to change the whole current of public opinion in its estimate of domestic service. . . .

When domestic service becomes a profession, as it surely will, by the proper training of those who follow it, what will be the condition of colored girls who would participate in its benefits? It is now time to prepare ourselves to answer this question. In my opinion, the training for this new profession should be elevated to the dignity and importance of the training in mathematics and grammar and other academic studies. Our girls must be made to feel that there is no stepping down when they become professional housekeepers. The relative dignity, respectability, and honor of this profession should first be taught in our schools. As it is now, the young woman in school or college knows that if she enters domestic service, she loses the relationships that she has formed. But schools of domestic science cannot do it all. The everyday man and woman who make society must change their foolish notions as to what is the polite thing for a young woman to do. The kind of stupidity that calls industrial education drudgery is the same kind of stupidity that looks upon the kitchen as a place for drudges. We must learn that the girl who cooks our meals and keeps our houses sweet and beautiful deserves just as high a place in our social economy as the girl who makes our gowns and hats, or the one who teaches our children. In what I have said on this particular phase of our industrial life, I do not wish to be understood as advocating the restriction of colored girls to house service, even when that service is elevated to the rank of a profession. My only plea is that we shall protect and respect our girls who honestly and intelligently enter this service, either from preference or necessity. . . .

There is still another consideration which suggests the importance to the colored people of taking the lead in helping to improve and elevate this service. Race prejudice is kept up and increased in thousands of instances by the incompetent and characterless women who are engaged in this work. While there are thousands of worthy and really noble women in domestic service who enjoy the confidence and affection of their employers, there is a large percentage of colored women who, by their general unworthiness, help to give the Negro race a bad name, for white people North and South are very apt to estimate the entire race from the standpoint of their own servant girls. When intelligence takes the place of ignorance, and good manners, efficiency, and self-respect take the place of shiftlessness and irresponsibility in American homes, one of the chief causes of race prejudice will be removed.

It should also be borne in mind that the colored girl who is trained in the arts of housekeeping is also better qualified for the high duties of wifehood and motherhood.

Let me say by the way of summary that I have dwelt mostly upon the opportunities of domestic service for the following reasons:—

1. It is the one field in which colored women meet with almost no opposition. It is ours almost by birthright.
2. The compensation for this service, in Northern communities at least, is higher than that paid for average clerkships in stores and offices.
3. The service is susceptible of almost unlimited improvement and elevation.
4. The nature of the work is largely what we make it.
5. White women of courage and large intelligence are lifting domestic service to a point where it will have the dignity of a profession, and colored women are in danger, through lack of foresight, of being relegated to the position of scrub women and dishwashers.
6. The colored girl who has no taste or talent for school teaching, dressmaking, or manicuring is in danger of being wasted in idleness, unless we can make domestic service worthy of her ambition and pride.
7. There can be no feature of our race problem more important than the saving of our young women; we can perhaps excuse their vanities, but idleness is the mildew on the garment of character.
8. Education has no value to human society unless it can add importance and respectability to the things we find to do.
9. Though all the factories and offices close their doors at our approach, this will be no calamity if we are strong enough to so transform the work we must do that it shall become an object of envy and emulation to those who now deny us their industrial fellowship.

4. Harriet Brunkhurst Laments the Home Problems of "Business Girls," 1910

That the girl who goes to business frequently faces home problems more difficult than those she meets in an office is a fact that comparatively few people recognize. The status of the girl in the home changes when she becomes a breadwinner, yet there are many homes where the new order not only is not accepted, but is also stoutly combated. Perhaps the main difficulty arises from the fact that although the girl is out in the world and may develop capabilities and breadth unattainable to the one whose life lies in a narrower groove, yet she is still a girl, shrinking, sensitive, possessed of all the whims, fancies and weaknesses that have marked her sex from the beginning of things.

The mother whose daughter goes to business, as do the husband and sons, finds it difficult to realize that anything is changed beyond the mere fact that the girl is away all day. When she returns she slips into her old place; not "all in a minute" can the mother bring herself to acknowledge that the daughter's position in the home is,

Harriet Brunkhurst, "The Home Trials of Business Girls," *Ladies Home Journal* (September 1910): 30.

in fact, precisely like that of her brother. If the mother is long in recognizing this so is the rest of the world. Meanwhile the daughter may be having a hard time.

A certain little woman whose daughter is the household provider has a grievance that seems to her almost insupportable. The daughter, Rose, is advertising manager in a big store; she has a private office, a stenographer, errand-boys and clerical workers to assist her; she employs no heavier implement than pen or scissors; her hours are from nine to five, six, seven—possibly ten at night, as the occasion may demand. She earns a comfortable salary, and she pays into the family exchequer whatever sum is necessary, with never a question as to where the money goes.

The mother is careful in her expenditure and an excellent housekeeper; she refuses to keep a maid because they have no room for her, but the rough work is done by outside hands. Her ideas of housekeeping demand rising at five-thirty A.M. She sleeps lightly, having a midday siesta, and she prefers to do her work in the early morning. She is ready for breakfast at six-thirty. There is no necessity for Rose to breakfast before eight, but the mother begins each day with a complaint at the late breakfast hour. This point of difference, trivial in itself, causes continual irritation.

Rose, capable executive head of a big department though she is, simply cannot fight the matter to a finish. The same girl who calmly gives orders right and left, once the office is reached, chokes with tears and has not a word to say when the little mother, who does not know even the rudiments of business, tells her that she is indolent and selfish. Rose knows that she herself is right—that she must have recreation and rest; deprivation of her morning sleep might be serious to the point of a breakdown—and she must not be ill, for she is the breadwinner. It is the principle of the thing, the mother avers, and she means just the best in the world, of course. But there is only one right way, and that is her way.

This mother is overlooking some very pertinent facts, even excluding the unhappiness she causes her daughter. Rose is actually, by right of her earnings, the head of the house; yet the mother, who would yield without question to husband or son occupying the same position, debates Rose's every movement simply because she is a girl. Were Rose to take her courage in her own hands and face her mother it would avail nothing. So she accepts an unnecessary unhappiness simply because she can see no solution. If the mother could see things in their true light she would be appalled.

There is another mother whose daughter, Cecil, carries a similar burden in the home. The latter finds that many little economies are necessary in order to conduct the home liberally. With fingers as nimble as her brain she finds a woman's innumerable tasks about her wardrobe—lace to be mended, fresh ribbons needed, a stitch here and there that she may be immaculate and insure the longest possible service from her clothing. When Cecil returns from her work, however, she is too weary to attempt any sewing. If she is to remain bright and alert, hold her position and not become ill, she must have relaxation in the evening. She goes to the theater, opera, concerts, has friends to see her, or spends a quiet evening with a book. At nine in the morning she is at her desk, bright-eyed and with a clear brain.

That their support is absolutely dependent upon Cecil's remaining "fit" the mother knows; but that recreation is necessary to maintain the condition she cannot grasp. Consequently, when Cecil takes Sunday morning for the little fussy tasks about her wardrobe the mother sees only sheer perversity, to say nothing of incipient depravity, about it. And there is the incontrovertible fact that Cecil "has all her evenings free." Moreover the mother wails: "She never has time to do anything for me!" It does not occur to her that she is asking of Cecil, whose strength already is fully taxed, more than she would ask from a man. She is the type of woman who would say of her husband: "John is so tired when he returns from work!" That Cecil may be tired she never considers. . . .

One of the most difficult phases of the situation appears with the subject of house-work. While going to business absolves the daughter, even as it does the husband and sons, it is a fact not so fully recognized as it might be. To the mother seven or eight hours of work followed by complete release appear so easy in comparison with her own lot that a few additional duties seem no more than fair. Moreover there is that family, its relations and friends, to make the contention should the mother take a different view of the matter.

Maud's mother, for instance, is criticised severely by her relatives for her care-ful fostering of her daughter's strength.

"It is perfectly ridiculous for you to iron Maud's shirtwaists," declared an elderly aunt. "She doesn't work half as hard as you do, and it wouldn't hurt her a bit to do her ironing in the evening. We used to do ours, and we were none the worse for it."

Maud's mother made no reply as she hung the sixth white blouse in a row with its mates. The years had gifted her with a sweet wisdom the other had not attained, and she knew well the futility of argument.

"I did my own fine ironing at home," she said afterward, "but there was never an afternoon or a morning when I could not go out if I chose. A task in the evening, unless it was for our pleasure, we never knew. Maud goes to the office in sun and in storm; she has never a day or an afternoon, except holidays, when she is free to do as she pleases. Days of headache or other slight indisposition, when I would have been on the sofa or comfortably in bed, she trudges bravely away. Often she is too tired even for recreation, to say nothing of work, when she returns in the evening."

"But six white shirtwaists!" exclaimed the listener.

"She works in an office where the furnishings are of mahogany, with rich rugs, polished brass and other things in harmony. How long could she hold her position were she to appear in a soiled blouse?"

Now that was only plain, practical good sense, clear-eyed recognition of perti-nent facts; but astonishingly few people can boast it.

Mabel's mother, for example, takes a different and a more usual view of a simi-lar situation. True, her work is far heavier than is that of Maud's mother, but Mabel works eight hours a day while Maud works seven. She is home in time to assist in preparing dinner, she helps with the dishes afterward, and there are innumerable little "odd jobs" that frequently keep her busy until nine o'clock. If she goes out there is a mad rush to finish the dinner work and be dressed sufficiently early. She does not go out very much, however, for she must rise at six-thirty, assist with the preparation of breakfast, and be at the office by eight-thirty o'clock.

That Mabel is fagged continually is inevitable. "I am so tired, Mother," she said once, when an additional bit of work was suggested.

"Aren't you ashamed to say that when you see how your mother works?" de-manded the father.

Mabel did the required work with no further comment, although the tears smarted in her eyes, her heart ached with the injustice of the taunt, and her weary little body seemed ready to fail her. She could earn her own living, but she could not fight her own battles. . . .

The problems these girls face are delicate, whichever way they are viewed. Perhaps part of the trouble arises from non-recognition of arrival at "years of discretion." We are all of us individuals first, and members of a family afterward. The family fosters and develops, but it may hamper freedom as well. There must be dependence upon one another, there must be community of interests; but in the successful home there must also be a clearly-defined recognition of individual existence. The girl attains her "majority" when she goes to business, and the home must learn when to "let go." It is not a question of independence—a word often misapplied and misunderstood—but simply one of self-reliance, and acknowledgment of the girl's right to it.

5. *The Survey* Reports on a Protest of Unemployed Women in New York City, 1914

The meeting in Cooper Union on January 28, under the auspices of the Woman's Trade Union League was the first organized protest of unemployed women and girls ever held in New York city, perhaps in America.

The speakers on the platform railed against capitalism and the present system of industry. In turn they laid unemployment at the door of child labor, excessive hours of work, and capitalist ownership. They could do nothing toward the alleviation of the "problem," and they declared as much.

The audience listened grimly. The simple stolid demand was for work—"We want work, not charity," was displayed on a placard over the platform where Lincoln spoke.

These unemployed women had drifted into the hall with the half-hearted hope that in a mysterious way the mayor or the governor or some other vague potentate would dole out jobs to each in turn. Whatever the causes, whatever the cure, the solid, immediate fact was this roomful of workless women.

Department store help, stenographers, garment workers, scrub women, widows with children, young, middle-aged and old women of all races, nationalities and creeds followed each other in describing heart-rending experiences of looking for work. They told stories of sordid misery, of hungry children, of cold and suffering, of ragged clothing and broken shoes, of ceaseless, agonizing search for the work that was not forthcoming, of the alternatives of suicide or prostitution.

A German woman, thin and stoop shouldered, but dressed in tidy black, told how she and her fifteen-year-old daughter had been living since Christmas on three dollars a week. At one time she made fifteen and eighteen dollars a week as a dressmaker, but since her husband's death she had barely been able to support her daughter.

"My girl," she cried brokenly, "she is as pure as gold and I must keep her so. Everywhere I go they say I am too old to work, and my daughter they say she is too

"Protest of the Working Women of New York," *The Survey,* February 17, 1914, 605–606.

young. If I am too old do I have to die? Does my daughter have to die? No work anywhere. What can I do? That's what I say."

A young girl who said she had been out of work since October told of her experiences in trying to get a job as a saleswoman. She repeated the insults heaped upon her by some employers who told her that so young and pretty a girl should not be looking for work.

Another woman, who speaks several languages, said that she was told in one place that if she did not want a $6-a-week job offered to her she could join the bread line as there were many girls anxious to get work at $4 and $5 a week.

"It is suicidal," declared a frail young girl. "In my shop, braid-making, they get a girl fifteen years old to tend ten machines. She don't last long. She soon breaks down and then they throw her out and get a fresh one."

And so they told their stories, one after another: a laundry worker who had not been able to get work since she was blacklisted in the laundry strike two years ago; a sickly girl who spoke for two or three minutes and then sat down, explaining in a weak voice that she was no longer able to stand on her feet; a machine operator who had made complete shirt waists for fifty cents a dozen until she could stand the place no longer; a stenographer who had been turned aside for a younger girl.

Two or three things reiterated by woman after woman emphasized certain discouragements in the search for work which were common to many present. One was the way in which newspaper "want ads" and the employment agencies, without any discrimination, sent hundreds of applications to one open position. Another was the time wasted by superintendents and managers in "taking a girl's pedigree" when there was absolutely no idea of hiring her.

A noticeable feature of the meeting was the fact that Christmas was the starting point of unemployment for most of the girls and that a large number of speakers were department store employes.

The number of women present was not so large as some had expected, but the meeting was in deadly earnest. It closed with a resolution, adopted by a rising vote, reciting that "Whereas thousands of working women and young girls who are dependent upon themselves for support," are idle; "we, the unemployed women and girls in mass meeting assembled, do hereby call upon the city and state authorities to provide us with work. . . .We emphatically protest against our enforced idleness."

One outcome of the Cooper Union meeting was a permanent conference on unemployment, which has established a free employment bureau for women and girls.

6. College Women Offer Patriotic Service in Agriculture During World War I

Vassar College owns and works a farm of 740 acres. Last spring there was great difficulty in getting farm hands to cultivate this land. Partly therefore to make the college independent of outside markets, partly as a patriotic service to test out untried women and see whether they could do farm work efficiently and without danger to their health, an appeal was made to the students. Out of 33 who volunteered 12 were

---

"Women on the Land" (New York: Advisory Council of the Woman's Land Army of America, 1918).

chosen. All but one of these were in excellent health; all but one were town-bred girls, with no previous agricultural experience. These girls worked on an average 8 hours a day for two months. Out of deference to the opinion of the men who claimed that the girls could not do the same work that they did, the girls received 17½ cents an hour. The men received 20 cents. The girls worked from 4:30 A.M. to 6:30 A.M., four hours after breakfast and from two to four hours in the afternoon. Each girl was granted two days off a month with pay and Saturday afternoons. They performed all the kinds of labor done on the farm. They did "ploughing, both with a traction and a two horse plough; harrowing; planting; cultivating; thinning; weeding; hoeing; potato planting; berry picking; mowing, with scythe and mowing machine; hay raking and pitching; reaping; shocking grain; making fences and milking." And these tasks they performed so satisfactorily that at the end of the season the men said that the girls should have received the same wage that they had.

Louis P. Gillespie, General Superintendent of the College, in a letter to Miss Alice Campbell, manager of the group, writes of these girl farmers:

"They took great interest in the work and did the work just as well as the average man and made good far beyond our most sanguine expectations."

The girls said they never had a healthier, happier summer and the health of all, of even the delicate girl, was better for the experience.

7. Elizabeth Jones Praises Negro Women in the Nursing Profession, 1923

Recalling the words of the great pioneer of the nursing profession and the world's greatest nurse, Florence Nightingale, when speaking of the profession as "God's Work—A True Vocation" one cannot forget the sacrifice, struggle and hardships which she endured for the sake of others, for the sake of God's Work, for the sake of her life's vocation. Nor did she lack those qualities which tend to develop the true nurse. Overcoming difficulties and hardships, she did not struggle in vain, but left an indelible impression upon the memories of all nationalities, races and creeds.

Many have grasped the opportunity to answer to the call. Among those we have our first Negro nurse in Miss Mary E. T. Mahoney, a graduate of the New England Hospital for Women and Children, Rothberry, Mass. She, like the other great pioneers, had her difficulties, which were even greater than those of her white sisters. But like a true soldier, she fought her battles bravely, and today is able to see the great reward that comes through perseverance. We may safely say that to this great Negro pioneer, the Negro Nursing profession owes its thanks. For today the race is the proud possessor of at least twelve large training schools for Negro women, as well as a number of small ones throughout the south. This number is being increased as the white training schools are opening their doors to the aspirant Negro woman.

Here we find her received kindly and yet with a doubt of her ability. Nothing is left undone to test the endurance of a young nurse. Ofttimes these tests have to be handled with tact so as not to become an imposition. Once the Negro nurse has

Elizabeth Jones, "The Negro Woman in the Nursing Profession," *The Messenger* 5 (July 1923): 764–765. This document can also be found in Darlene Clark Hine, ed., *Black Women in the Nursing Profession: A Documentary History* (New York: Garland, 1985), 123–124.

shown her ability, her aptness to grasp situations, she is no longer looked upon as an intruder in the profession, but she is received kindly and given the respect due her by both the patients, their families and the physicians.

Nor has the advancement ceased at bedside nursing (private duty) but has extended to public health nursing and social service work. In the public health service we find the Negro nurse in dental and tuberculosis clinics. We find her in public schools and preventoriums, giving instructions to those suffering from and in contact with infectious diseases, such as scarlet fever, diphtheria, and the venereal diseases. In social service we find her visiting homes and giving relief, where needed, to the poor, by referring their cases to a charity organization.

Daily the Negro woman has avenues opened up to her. She is no longer looked upon only as a servant. She is no longer held down as greatly as in the past by prejudice. She has been given the opportunity and has grasped it; not only aiding herself but her race by proving her efficiency in a field that was heretofore occupied exclusively by her white sister.

In 1908 New York City's Department of Health opened up its doors to the Negro nurse, and Miss Harris, a Lincoln Hospital graduate, was first to brave the civil service examination and the adversities which followed. Yet she attempted and succeeded. Today, following along in her footsteps smoothly, are many other determined young women of different countries and hospitals. Another, Miss Mae Clendenin (whom Lincoln Hospital also claims), was the first Negro nurse in Henry Street Settlement's Visiting Nurse Staff, and today she, like the others, is followed by many more.

Nor have these opportunities been only in New York City, but cities throughout the United States have accepted the Negro nurse. Not only has the advancement been in just the medical field but also in the social and educational as well.

Miss M. Franklin, a graduate of the Women's Hospital, Philadelphia, Pa., was the first to become active in bringing about the National Association of Colored Nurses. She realized fully the advantages of unity and today she is the leading spirit in one of the finest organizations in the United States, one that is recognized and respected by the entire medical profession.

Prior to the founding of the National Association of Colored Nurses no effort was made to influence the nurse to join the white organization. But with the founding of the Negro organization a decided effort to obtain the colored nurse has been made by the white association.

Then there is the educational unrest. The Negro nurse is restless. She is seeking, always seeking those things which tend to increase her efficiency. The well equipped nurse of today should be trained to some extent in business. She should have some knowledge of secretarial work, etc. This knowledge she will find useful in all parts of her profession: scientific knowledge of dietetics, pathology, bacteriology, a broader knowledge of psychology and some knowledge of more than one of the many languages spoken in a large American city. . . .

God created all men equal, and why should she, because of her dark skin, be brow-beaten? Why should she stand by and see her race looked upon in an attitude little better than one would look upon a snake or an insect? She realizes that merit counts a great deal toward achievement and, why, because of lack of education, should her race suffer? She realizes fully that it is a long and hard fight, but she does not forget the influence she has over those poor unfortunate ones with whom she comes in contact. She sees the life of an individual as it really is, and not as it seems to be, for she often has other problems besides that of helping to heal the diseased body. She often has the economical, spiritual and moral problems of the patient to solve. She has for her studies the many problems that are found at all ages among the different races of people. . . .

It is not the duties we have to perform that count, it is the way in which we do them that leaves an impression. The respect that the Negro nurse can win for her race through close professional contact is indeed surprising. Here she meets the masses of people; all ages, all races and creeds. It is up to her to leave a good impression on the minds of those with whom she comes in contact. She has for her material hundreds and hundreds of young minds; minds that can be shaped and impressed. It is through these that she must bring about better race relations. . . .

Through free discussion, she learns that, the Negro is, in the white man's mind, much inferior. . . . We have to educate him. We have to show him wherein he is wrong. To be what we are and what we want to be and not to submit to be what he would like us to be, will exact an immeasurable meed of respect. Thus when we unite and determine to take our place among people, then, and only then, will we be given a fair deal in all professions.

8. Marion Bonner Reports on the Women of the Southern Textile Strikes, 1929

"We're fightin' for our rights. We didn't want no strike. We went to the president and asked him to give us a ten-hour day without cuttin' our wages and to take back the fifteen men and women he fired for joinin' the union." . . .

A thin, wiry woman with a pinched face that looked at least ten years older than it was, was talking to a group of faculty and students of the Southern Summer School for Women Workers in Industry. On July 11 when the school began its session of six weeks at Burnsville, North Carolina, about six hundred and fifty men and women joined the United Textile Workers Union and went on strike against conditions in the Marion Manufacturing Company. Some of the strike leaders, knowing that the Southern Summer School was teaching economics, public speaking, and health, brought seven girls over the forty miles of beautiful mountain road to the school.

. . . Five girls from Elizabethton, Tennessee, who had been in the strikes in the Glanzstoff and Bemberg silk mills, mountain born, too, understood her and nodded approvingly. Girls from cities, in some cases making no more than ten dollars a week, but dressed in silk and speaking the language of cities, looked at her half in amusement, half in admiration. Some of the girls from Marion, seeing the amused glances, became self-conscious and whispered that they wished "J——— wasn't so talky." . . .

Gradually her intelligence, earnestness, intensity won the respect of most of the students. Other girls from Marion emerged from their protective shells and grew communicative. Sensitive, proud, feeling a chasm between themselves and some of the girls who had lived in the cities, they would often anticipate superiority and at first were on their guard. Girls who felt superior because they had toilets and bathrooms in their houses and did not have to draw their water from a street

Marion Bonner, "Behind the Southern Textile Strikes," *The Nation,* October 2, 1929, 351–352. Reprinted with permission.

pump, and who had gone through several years of high school and had heard of grammar became interested in the struggle of these women of Marion to get better conditions and began to listen attentively to their speeches. . . .

One of the Marion girls described her work on the farm. "We raised corn, potatoes, cane, and tobacco. We also had lots of hay to take care of. My two older sisters married, and my two older brothers got jobs and left home to make wages. That left just my sister and me out of a family of eight large enough to work. My mother's health failed her and so my sister and I had most of the house-work to do and to help father on the outside. We got up at four o'clock every morning to get the house-work done, the cows milked, the chickens fed to get to the fields early. We would hoe corn all day long; come home at night and help mother get supper. Very often she would have beans picked or apples gathered so we could string beans after supper or peel apples to be dried. I have helped father saw wood time after time and I have driven a team of horses day after day hauling rock, hay, corn. After we got our crop planted father would get a job somewhere and tell us what he wanted done on the farm."

Those who have known life back in the mountains, on poor hillside farms that furnished inadequate nourishment to the large families living on them, know too the inadequacy of the mental food. Interference of work at home, short terms, teachers not too well trained—it is amazing that they learned to read, write, and figure. The following experience related by one of the girls from Marion is representative.

"I started to school at the age of seven. The first three or four years I attended regularly but after I got large enough to work and after my sisters married and my older brothers left home, I was in school a day or two and out a day or two. I was kept out of school to help take fodder, gather corn, hand tobacco, and take care of all the crops. We had only six months school the first five years of my school days. Our school building had only one room. There were two teachers and about eighty pupils. The room was very noisy. We had straight back benches with two or three students on each bench, and the students talked more than they studied. I went to school until I finished the eighth grade. I couldn't go any farther in school at home in the country. I told my parents I had a desire to go to high school, that if they would buy my clothes I would work my way through school, but they would not consent. They told me they needed me to help at home. I went off badly discouraged.

"Two years ago I told father and mother I would get a job in a factory and work and get enough money to go to school. I went to work in the cotton mill. I made $9.35 a week. I paid $5 a week for board and I also had my laundry bill and insurance, so after all I didn't get the money to go on to school."

Of course, some girls are glad enough to stop school and go to work as soon as possible with the hope of getting clothes and beaus, but the girls who are sent to the Southern Summer School for the most part are almost pathetic in their desire for an education.

In the hope of bettering their conditions the girls left the farm and went to live in the mill village of East Marion. Here is a description given by one of the students. "There are families of eight and ten living in three-room houses. Roofs on many of the houses leak. Most of the houses need repairing and painting. There are dry-pit toilets strung up at the back door of all these houses. The water the people use is drawn from pumps. There are but two or three pumps on each street and on part of the mill village there are sixteen families that use water from two pumps. The company recently built a Y.M.C.A. It has a swimming pool, a ten-pin alley, library, sewing and cooking department, shower baths, and a basket-ball court. The people of the village pay ten cents for a shower bath, ten cents for bathing in the pool, and ten cents for a game of ten pins. The only store that most of the working class ever trade in is the company store, for most of them eat up today what they work out tomorrow."

Conditions that would make many of us shudder were related by the thirty-five students; the girls from Marion could tell a story of the longest working day and of the most unsanitary conditions. . . .

One of the girls gave this account:

"I work twelve hours and twenty minutes a day and I am completely worn out at stopping time. Men and women who work in the mill are weak and sallow looking, some of them just dragging along half dead and overworked until they don't know what it is to take a rest and feel good. The average workingman or woman makes from $1.60 to $2.70 a day, and some have families of from three to seven and sometimes more depending on them for a living. The employees of the mill walked out on a strike on July 11 for shorter hours and for the same pay they were getting for longer hours. Do you blame us for striking?"

. . . To some of the young strikers the strike meant excitement, a chance for the spectacular; to some of the older ones it meant a chance to rest; to most of them it was a reaching out for more tolerable conditions of life and work not only for themselves but for their families and neighbors.

E S S A Y S

Elizabeth Clark-Lewis of Howard University examines the experience of black women who moved from the rural South to become domestic workers in Washington, D.C., in the early twentieth century. Despite constraints imposed by race, gender, and class, Clark-Lewis finds that domestic workers discovered novel ways to enhance their autonomy. University of Washington historian Susan A. Glenn contends that young Jewish immigrant women employed in garment workshops and factories created a subculture that subverted the strict rules and harsh discipline of employers, while generally avoiding direct confrontation. Through workplace subcultures, young immigrant women also expressed their interest in social change and personal growth.

Community Life and Work Culture Among African American Domestic Workers in Washington, D.C., 1910–1940

ELIZABETH CLARK-LEWIS

When African-American women migrated from the rural South to the urban centers of the North to work as live-in servants, few imagined they were beginning an escape from restraints imposed by race, gender, and class. But escape they did, and this essay examines the transition of twenty-three such women as they moved beyond live-in household servitude to self-employment during the first three decades of this century. It also demonstrates that as their roles changed, they experienced a new freedom to exercise control over their own lives, and their perceptions about themselves and their relationships to others underwent a significant change. It is important to recognize, however, that these changes occurred within a restrictive cultural environment.

. . . When foreign immigration slowed to a trickle after World War I, an important source of new white servants was eliminated. Within the first two decades of the twentieth century, household work lost its importance as an occupation for white women. By contrast, the number of African-American female household workers *increased* by 43 percent. Nationally, during the 1900–1930 period, the southern exploitive system triumphed: African-American women were forced into a "servant caste."

Surveys of specific northern urban centers found that the sharp rise in the number of African-American household workers had three sources: the new, large-scale migration of African-Americans to urban centers outside the South; the fact that African-American women were twice as likely as white women to be employed; and discriminatory policies that barred African-American women from 86 percent of employment categories. By 1926 the predominance of African-American migrant women in household service in Washington, D.C., was well established. . . . In 1900, 54 percent of the employed African-American women in the District were working in domestic service; by 1930, that figure had risen to 78 percent.

Expanded employment opportunities lured a stream of migrants to the urban North, where they moved into segregated communities that coalesced around churches, schools, philanthropic institutions, and businesses. But because of anti-migrant biases in the established African-American communities, only rarely could the newcomers find work in businesses owned by African-Americans or in the segregated schools of the communities where they settled. Disproportionately young, female, and poorly educated, they found themselves in urban centers where the pattern of racial segregation combined with class and gender restrictions to limit the jobs available to them. In overwhelming numbers the female migrants became household workers. . . .

Fourteen of the twenty-three women I interviewed grew up on farms owned by their parents; nine lived on share-tenant farms. Nearly all were reared in extended family households consisting of mothers, fathers, grandparents, siblings, and other relatives. They were all born between 1884 and 1911. Each household included at least one former slave; thus every woman in the study vividly recalled hearing first-hand descriptions of the degrading conditions of slavery. Further, the women were able to cite beliefs held by those former slaves regarding patterns and practices that enabled slave families to survive under the harshest of circumstances.

Family support, according to all of the women interviewed, was a focal point of rural churches. In addition to religious instruction, churches provided the only mutual aid, educational, and recreational activities available to African-American families in the rural South. After the family, the church was the most important means of individual and community expression.

The education of all of the women in the study had been severely limited by the need to help support the family, which they recognized as their primary responsibility by the age of seven. They worked first on the family farm, caring for the youngest children and serving as apprentices to older girls and women. Each of the twenty-three women recalled her mother's leaving home for residential (live-in) employment in white households in the surrounding area and recognized that independently employed children were an important part of the family's survival strategy. "Like everybody, by eight years old I went in to work with Mama," said Bernice Reeder in discussing the short period of outside tutelage which preceded a girl's first employment as live-in servant to a white family. She was alone on her first job, "at just nine years old! I was so scared," she continued. "Nobody cared you were a child. . . . You was a worker to them." The economic constraints faced by African-Americans in the rural South in the late nineteenth and early twentieth centuries made such early labor an unavoidable and accepted part of family and community life.

. . . By the age of ten, the women in this study told me, they also had to show clearly that they had the maturity to take another step: to travel to Washington, D.C., where sisters and aunts who worked as live-in servants (and sent money home) needed support in the form of child care and housekeeping by younger family members. These girls made the journey north by train. None had ever been out of her home state before. Twenty were taken to the train station by a male relative; all left their places of birth in the early morning, traveled alone, and were met by other relatives upon arrival in Washington.

When sharing reminiscences of their northbound journey, the women always described the feeling of freedom they experienced. "When you got on the train," Velma Davis exclaimed, "you felt different! Seem like you'd been bound up, but now this train untied you. It's funny . . . like being untied and tickled at the same time!" The girls understood that their first obligation was to carry on the rural-based family survival strategy in the homes of kin who served Washington's white households as live-in workers. The only significant change in their lives, initially, was the move to the North. . . .

Urban kin gave support to the migrant in several ways, if we may judge from information provided by the women interviewed. They paid all of her travel expenses to Washington, helped her adjust to urban life, and found employment for her within twelve months. In all the cases studied, the women were hired where their kin had contacts; in twenty-one of twenty-three cases, the coresident kin acquired employment for the migrants in households where they themselves were currently living. The girls migrated originally to provide support only to their urban kin; once they themselves became employed, however (after an average of one year), they were expected to assume responsibility for meeting the needs of both the urban and rural segments of the family.

As newly hired live-in servants, these female migrants learned that their primary role was to serve the mistress of the house, not just to complete the assigned tasks—a departure from the way they had worked in southern households. In the South, these African-American household workers had received daily task assignments from the white male head of the household. Migrants stressed that in Washington they slowly learned a new employment reality. Through trial and error, and with the advice of the more experienced earlier migrants, they learned to act in response to the needs of the wife rather than the husband.

Each of the twenty-three women was dismayed to learn that uniforms were mandatory in the District of Columbia. The wearing of uniforms was perceived by all as the major difference between their servant *work* in the South and their servant *role* in Washington. For these women, the uniform objectified the live-in servant and determined her fate in the workplace. The home was the white mistress's stage and major realm of influence, and the uniform legitimized her power. Ophilia Simpson recalled that "them uniforms just seemed to make them know you was theirs. Some say you wore them to show different jobs you was doing. Time in grey. Other times serving in black. But mostly them things just showed you was always at their beck and call. Really that's all them things means!" . . .

Despite the fact that each woman (and her family in the rural South) desperately needed the income her labor generated, within seven years these women were actively trying to leave the "servant life." There were several aspects of live-in employment that they all disliked. The uniform formalized the serving of the family for long hours, which they could not control. The wife as the authority figure had little respect for their needs. Worse still, they were forced to live in small quarters completely isolated from the African-American community.

But it was the question of church participation that first stimulated more than half of those interviewed to seek a change. Not being able to attend regular services on Sundays and generally feeling left out of the continuing life of their churches became for these women a potent symbol of the restrictions of live-in labor. "Even working-out down home, you'd go to church," Costella Harris explained, bedridden at eighty-six after a lifetime of household employment in Georgetown. "Everybody did," she continued slowly. "Now, most came just to hear the Word. But some came to keep from being in a kitchen somewhere. . . . Church gave you six, not seven days of work. But up here you never saw inside any church on Sunday, living-in."

Painful as all these restrictions were, however, they were probably not sufficient by themselves to lead the women to reject live-in servant work. The *ability* to make the change emanated from the phenomenon known as "penny savers clubs." Twenty-one of the twenty-three women actively associated themselves with such mutual benefit associations, which sponsored social gatherings and provided sickness and death benefits to members. . . . Although rarely mentioned in the literature, the penny savers clubs served as a vital economic base for the female migrant. After an average of six years of saving, the women were able to develop the important economic leverage they needed to leave servant life.

The role of the church and of the penny savers clubs in first awakening the desire for change and then facilitating the process of that change cannot be overestimated. The clubs permitted the women, during the transition from live-in service to household day work, to maintain financial security for themselves and their kin in the rural South. No woman left live-in work until she had saved enough money to maintain herself and send money monthly to rural kin. . . . They sought to find a less circumscribed economic and employment environment without abandoning one of the original motivations for leaving their rural families—relief of the family's economic distress.

The women soon identified laundresses as critical figures in their search for autonomy. Laundresses served as role models: unlike the other staff members, they did not belittle the migrant woman's desire to gain household work on a nonresidential basis, and they alone knew the categories and rules related to operating within several households simultaneously. The laundress also brought information about households that were seeking the services of women on a live-out basis for one or two days a week. . . .

The women saw six major benefits to the shift from live-in servant to household day worker. First, as indicated by the language they used to describe their experiences, their work seemed more their own. They spoke of their earlier jobs in depersonalized language because they sought detachment from their employers and a buffer against the employers' insensitivity to them as workers and African-Americans. . . . Velma Davis recalled, "When I say 'my job,' I mean a job I got and I'd keep if they acted decent. 'They job' is for them; a job that you did and did, more and more— from one thing to another, early to late, and you worked!" . . .

Second, the previously isolated African-American women began to make contact with one another amid their newly flexible working conditions, encountering many others like themselves. The structure that had created social marginality among African-Americans in Washington was slowly being dismantled; the women's isolated and restrictive living circumstances were relegated to an oppressive past. . . .

Third, as the women changed jobs, they moved to rooms in boardinghouses and began to adopt a sharply different lifestyle. The other girls in the house where Velma Davis became a boarder "was all doing day-work, too," and "soon I was doing just about everything with them. I just liked being with these girls [who] was single, nice." After the move from live-in servant work, Velma Davis said that she did not see her family for long periods of time. She said that it was when she moved to the boardinghouse that she began to feel she had finally left home. . . .

Fourth, their places of work changed. Employers usually hired someone other than their former live-in servants to work as daily household employees. The women acknowledged this policy; thus, in communicating their new plans to their employers, they understood that future employment in that household would not be considered. . . .

Fifth, each woman indicated that turning to day work produced a subtle change in her relationship to the white women for whom she worked. Virginia Lacey described the new experience with an employer this way: "She'd meet you at the door, tell you how she wanted her house done, and she'd be gone. You did the work without her in the way, slowing you up. On a day job we all knew how to get everything done—but, in your own way. Having anybody around will make you work slower." . . .

Finally, all of the women stressed that as they moved out of live-in work, they shed their uniforms and other symbols of their identities as live-in servants. Each had felt locked into a narrow and constricted role by the need to wear uniforms of "black for this" and "gray for that." Discarding that badge of their station in life clearly disaffiliated them from their previous work. . . .

Virginia Lacey agreed: "I'd go to whatever house I'd have to be to work at. I change to my work clothes and then clean the house. . . . I never liked to be in the uniform. I guess serving in a uniform made you be back on staff. And you wasn't, so you'd just not want to wear that uniform." She paused for a moment, reflecting. "Wearing your own clothes—that's like you being your own boss! You was on your own job for a day and pay, then go home."

Some scholars and artists who are sensitive to the problems of domestic service have tended to view negatively the bags in which day workers carried their clothes. But these women took pride in the fact that they "carried work clothes" to their jobs; they felt that the bags were symbols of personal freedom and in that sense were positive. In fact, Marie Davis reported that workers often called them "freedom bags"; she observed, "When I got to carry clothes, I was finally working in what I wanted to. No black or gray uniforms or castoffs from the whites down home. I was proud to put my stuff in a bag at home. I guess I wanted to finally show I didn't wear a uniform. I wasn't a servant." . . .

A new identity was gained. Gone was the identity to which they were born or which had been ascribed to them; this new one they had *achieved* on their own, and their newly acquired friends and associates validated their achieved status. As Bernice Reeder explained, "Once you got some work by the day and got around people who did it, you'd see how you could get ahead, get better things. You'd see how to get more and more days, some party work, extra sewing, stuff like that." Velma Davis agreed: "When I started working days, other people [other household day workers] would show you how to get a few extra dollars. In this town you could make more money, and they'd sure show you how."

The women's transformed identities and modified employment modes led to several other changes in the African-American community. For one, the women's interest in the penny savers clubs waned. . . . Although the associations continued to exist . . . household day workers perceived them as institutions serving the needs of live-in servants. The day workers transferred their money to banks, in part because their new jobs gave them the opportunity to do so. As Eula Montgomery remarked, "I'd have used them [banks] earlier, but with that woman you never got time to go to a place like that. I know I didn't." Minnie Barnes verified this point: "I used a bank as a day worker because it was on my streetcar line home." . . .

The waning of the mutual benefit associations did not, however, mean the decline of support for rural kin. On the contrary, economic assistance typically increased after the transition to household day work. In speaking of the support she provided her relatives still living in the South, Velma Davis said, "I didn't miss a month. . . . That's why I got myself set before I left live-in. I never missed sending my share home." If anything, the women adhered even more strongly to their premigration beliefs concerning kinship obligations. . . .

The level of these women's participation in the African-American churches of Washington also changed significantly. Live-in servant work had greatly restricted their attendance and involvement in church activities. Velma Davis recalled, "Living in? You never dreamed of going to day service. Sundays, you'd be out of there [the live-in household], if you was good, by four or five." Regular participation in daytime church services was also an indication of status. "Big people, like government messengers, or people working in a colored business office, that's who'd be regular at Sunday day services," Eula Montgomery said. Individuals who worked in those types of jobs, she pointed out, had their Sundays free; they could also, therefore, "be on the church's special committees."

Live-in service had limited all aspects of interactions with other church members. Eula Montgomery went on: "If you lived in a room in the attic, how could you be in any of them clubs? You couldn't bring nobody over there. . . . You never got to be in a fellowship. That was for people who got off on Saturday and Sunday. They had a nice place to have people over to—not no kitchen." . . .

Regular church attendance, achieved through less confining employment, was accompanied by more leisure-time activity. A married couple could go to morning church services, and in summer they could go out for picnics, Dolethia Otis pointed out.

Participation in church and leisure activities was viewed, not surprisingly, as representative of the attainment of *better* work; according to Nellie Willoughby, a migrant from Virginia, "it showed you had work you didn't live at." It did not mean that these women did *easier* work. The point was that the work they did—even if more strenuous—permitted some previously unavailable free time. . . .

All of the women interviewed asserted that household day work was directly responsible for their ability to participate in the churches. The result of this change was wider church membership. Previously, working-class women had not been well represented in the African-American churches. "Most women down at Mason Street Baptist who were real active," said Helen Venable. "were educated good and had jobs like teaching. As people got more away from live-in you saw a lotta different people in all the things that church has. Then more and more people got in the church's clubs or work."

The growth of African-American churches in Washington, then, was a direct consequence of the steady influx of these working-class (former live-in) women. They strongly supported church expansion because their participation in the church activities further separated them from the stigma of servitude. . . .

Live-in servant work imposed countless burdens upon African-American female migrants to the District of Columbia before the Depression, yet "service-class" women developed and controlled philanthropic organizations that allowed them eventually to escape the boundaries of live-in servant employment. Although the African-American women quoted here remained in household service work all their lives, they restructured its salient features and created more freedom for themselves.

Reformers who rely only on archival records may view household service work as "a dead end." Scholars all too often see household workers as merely products of change, never as its causes; as objects of events, not as their subjects; as passive reactors, not as active forces in history. The words and lives of these women refute such views. Orra Fisher's response sums up best what the women expressed when asked about the progress and the success they have seen in their lives:

> I worked hard to serve God and to see that my three girls didn't have to serve nobody else like I did except God. I satisfied to know I came a long way. From a kitchen down home to a kitchen up here, and then able to earn money, but live with my children and grands. Now Jesus took me every step—that's real.
>
> But look at me, with more than I ever dreamed I'd have. And my three, with houses, and jobs. My girls in an office, and the baby—my son—over twenty years in the Army. I get full thinking about it. I had it bad, but look at them.

The Working Lives of Jewish Immigrant Daughters in Urban America, 1900–1920

SUSAN A. GLENN

The working lives of Jewish immigrant daughters profoundly affected their social and cultural understandings. Going to work meant confronting a world of conflicting messages and sensibilities, a world that both assaulted women's dignity and introduced them to the liberating potential of new ideas and social patterns. In its negative as well as its positive associations, working life served as a powerful incubator for young women's emerging identities.

Even before Jewish daughters left their homes in eastern Europe, many of them shared an orientation toward social and cultural change. Although they did not necessarily eschew traditional customs and values, growing numbers of Jewish women (and many men as well) were striving to make a place for themselves in the modern world. In their longing for new and better educational opportunities, in their appreciation for modern conceptions of womanhood and marriage, in their growing faith in the redeeming power of socialism, Jewish women looked to the possibilities of the future while still respecting and practicing traditions of the past. "While we did miss the *shtetl*," one immigrant woman insisted, "it was not in the sense to go back" to an earlier way of life.

The attitudes of these women toward the workroom environment were no exception. In contrast to the attitudes historians have often associated with new immigrant workers—namely a tendency to cling stubbornly to older patterns of work and social relations—many Jewish women disdained the traditional workroom environment common to small neighborhood shops run by immigrant contractors, preferring instead to labor in larger, more modern factories. Even as these women sought to preserve some features of traditional shop life and work customs, they also displayed a range of social concerns about the workplace that reflected their curiosity about, and interest in, change. In the shops and factories where they spent most of their waking hours young, first-generation immigrant women expected to find more than the means of earning a living. They also sought a social environment that would open up new possibilities for personal growth and learning.

The garment factory, with its strict rules, arbitrary discipline, and sometimes extensive subdivisions of labor, hardly seems an inviting place for recently arrived immigrants. But many daughters preferred it over the small neighborhood shop. . . .

Immigrant novelist Sholem Asch captured the essence of the social environment and the interactions between workers and bosses in the tiny neighborhood garment shops in New York when he described the dynamics as "not purely industrial, but rather personal—almost in the nature of a family relationship." . . . Here everyone, including the boss, addressed others on a first-name basis, knew most of the details of one another's personal lives, and labored together almost as if they were a family. . . . Coming from the same town or region of Russia, Poland, or

Galicia as his workers, a contractor . . . knew who was struggling to procure a *shiftscarte* (steamship ticket) for a relative. He knew about the pogroms and the poverty. In short, he shared a past as well as a present with his immigrant laborers. And he knew how to encourage their loyalty by expressing a fatherly concern for their welfare: lending money to impoverished greenhorns, helping underwrite ship passage for a relative, and otherwise offering advice and consolation and, of course, providing a job. . . .

The informal authority of the boss, the small size of the shop, and the shared ethnic background of the work force created a relatively unstructured work environment. Few rules governed shop life. Hard work was expected, but any form of social behavior that encouraged it was usually tolerated. As a result, singing, talking, smoking, drinking, eating, and other "merry makings" were a regular part of the routine in these shops. . . . While they appreciated some of the freedoms associated with the traditional artisan work culture of these tiny neighborhood shops, young immigrant workers found other aspects of the environment less attractive, even oppressive. The cramped and unsanitary quarters of these sweatshops posed a health threat to employers and laborers alike. Conviviality and informality did not mask these conditions, nor did they mitigate the grueling pace of work in a sweatshop or the downward pressure on wages. As every immigrant who labored in this type of setting knew, "to squeeze his own profit out the contractor must squeeze his workmen's wages down." Moreover, the familial intimacy of the immigrant sweatshop sometimes had a dark underside, as the boss overstepped the bounds of patriarchal authority and, like some of the master tailors in the Pale, used verbal or physical violence to intimidate his workers.

. . . Although immigrant women found the factories inhospitable in some respects, they knew that factories offered important opportunities absent in the shops. Often work was steadier in the factories, and larger manufacturers often paid better wages than what one Jewish writer referred to as "the small boss with his 'one-cent' soul." Moreover, inside factories such as those in New York's shirtwaist and dress industries and Chicago's modern tailoring establishments tended to provide women with a greater range of jobs and more potential for occupational and wage mobility than the contractors could.

Beyond the chance to make more money, always a priority of young wage earners, other considerations made the factory an enticing place. Women discovered in the factory the social benefits of a young female work group, a peer culture that offered opportunities for social and cultural experimentation. For many foreign-born women, working in a factory also signified a kind of cultural mobility: they were moving out of the ghetto and into a more Americanized environment. . . .

. . . Differences between the physical conditions of work in the factories and shops were at times more apparent than real. In some factories, posh front offices and beautiful showrooms concealed behind-the-scenes working conditions that rivaled tenement shops: littered floors, dark and dangerous stairways and halls, filthy and broken-down toilets, an absence of drinking water and dressing rooms, blocked exits, inaccessible fire escapes, stifling heat in the summer and chilly drafts during winter. . . . Still, the idea of working in a modern factory rather than a small shop seemed to have an intangible appeal for many immigrants. The threadbare contractor's shop reminded them of the material deprivation of the shtetl, whereas the inside factory suggested the prosperity of America. . . .

To disdain the Old World work environment of the contractors' shops and go to work in a modern garment factory did not, however, mean to forsake all connection to traditional Jewish culture. Many young immigrants who wished to take advantage of factory jobs did so at some emotional cost. The factory environment that women were entering left little room for religious Orthodoxy. To work in a factory usually required that Jews abdicate a central component of their religion—keeping the Saturday Sabbath. Rarely did the factories accommodate immigrants' religious needs. Contractors rather than factory bosses were more likely to share a concern for the Sabbath and close their doors on Saturdays. By 1912 the estimated 25 percent of Jewish workers living on New York's Lower East Side who continued to observe the Sabbath probably worked in contracting shops run by their landsleit. In growing numbers contractors also remained open on Saturdays, but nearly all factories operated on that day.

The attitudes of immigrant women toward the Sabbath issue suggests the diversity among them. For some it posed little conflict, for others it created a moral dilemma, and for still others it represented a full-fledged crisis. Ella Wolff was among the many immigrants who felt very keenly the conflict between opportunity and religious commitment. She remained in the same neighborhood shop throughout her working life because of her strict Orthodox upbringing. "I had to stop [work] Friday at four because of my father's religion," she explained. Although she periodically sought employment elsewhere in the garment industry, once hired she would soon be fired for absenteeism on Saturday. "Nobody else would have me," she said. "If I stopped Friday at four o'clock and didn't come in Saturday . . . I was given notice that I'm not wanted." . . .

Not everyone shared this young woman's quandary. By the first decade of this century strict Orthodoxy was declining in Jewish immigrant communities, especially among the younger generation. In pre-migration Russia and Poland young people, especially those in sympathy with radical political movements, had already begun to question and sometimes reject the religious Orthodoxy of their parents and grandparents. . . . Immigration, with its new challenges and opportunities and the ethos of modernity that many Jews associated with becoming American, eroded Orthodoxy still further. The vast majority of Jewish immigrants were not openly defiant about "discarding" the Sabbath, yet feelings of doubt and even indifference toward strict Orthodox practices were growing. . . . Overall, . . . circumstances and necessity contributed to a pattern of religious neglect, if not a decline in faith. Even those who felt committed to keeping the Sabbath often resigned themselves to working because they had little choice in the matter and because the need to earn a living took precedence over all else. As one New York garment worker recalled: "It was either you take it or leave it and you wouldn't leave it because in those years it wasn't easy to get a job, the industry was a seasonal thing." . . .

Even as they grappled with the religious dilemmas of factory work, many daughters . . . found that factory work, in addition to providing a living, exposed them to new sources of sociability and new kinds of information. The demographics of the inside factory were an essential element of its appeal. In contrast to the small contractors' shops, where the work force was usually dominated by men, the factories in the shirtwaist, dress, and undergarment industries employed large numbers not only of young Jewish women but of female workers of other nationalities as well.

In these industries women vastly outnumbered men, comprising between 80 and 90 percent of the work force. Even in the men's clothing industry, in cities like Chicago, women made up as much as 50 percent of the workers in the inside factories. Here, then, was an opportunity to participate in a female world, a world of young people that provided an array of possibilities for socializing, informal education, emotional and moral support, and challenging the more degrading aspects of industrial wage work.

Even in Russia young women had displayed a certain excitement about going off to work in urban factories. . . . Factory work . . . offered a certain amount of freedom from familial authority and gave Jewish girls novel opportunities for social life. . . . So too, in big cities of the United States, many Jewish immigrants viewed the factory setting as an important source of social life. "I confess, that I go to work with much pleasure," a recent immigrant wrote to the *Jewish Daily Forward* in 1906. "Often I can hardly await the minute" when work begins. "Do not think, that boys play a part here. At our place only girls are working, not a single boy. . . . I very much love to sit with the other girls at work and I work with much zeal."

Few immigrant women found this degree of exhilaration in the male-dominated workrooms of the contractors' shops. The masculine work environment of the small shops instead left young women feeling insecure and socially isolated. . . . [T]he most humiliating aspect of this male work group was its vulgarity. Some men found release in joking, storytelling, and casual banter, which might be heavily spiced with sexual innuendo and outright obscenity. Young women, preoccupied with their own self-respect, felt repulsed and humiliated by the behavior of their male coworkers in these tiny shops. . . . Not uncommonly, young immigrant women were pinched, fondled, patted, or grabbed by a boss or foreman, either in full sight of the other workers or in a hall, corridor, or office. In rare cases a woman might even be forced to sleep with the boss in order to keep her job. Most often, sexual harassment took the form of more superficial but no less infuriating acts of physical aggression. . . .

. . . In contrast to the male-dominated environment of the small shop, . . . the factory, though not a female-controlled world, often allowed women to exert a mediating social influence. Men were still present and invariably in charge of the workroom; verbal and physical harassment continued to be a problem. But female work groups provided a degree of emotional and psychological support less available to those who worked in small contractors' shops. . . . When a foreman came in and called Chicago dressworkers "vile nicknames," the women might at least gain some degree of satisfaction in criticizing him among themselves. A raised eyebrow as a signal of disgust and camaraderie as a foreman or a boss made a pass at one of the workers must have provided an important and reassuring gesture of sympathy. And the moral support of a predominantly female work group occasionally enabled women to fend off an aggressor. At the very least the surrounding presence of other sympathetic workers might deter a potential seducer or embarrass a boss or foreman who was caught in the act. . . .

Factory life provided women with important social resources, but as in any work situation these were partly shaped by the structure of their jobs. Sewing, especially at a machine, required intense concentration and attention to speed. Unlike workers in industries such as textiles, who moved about freely on the shop floor as they tended their machines, garment workers had little physical mobility, spending the workday seated at their machines or sewing tables. Thus conversations were usually limited to women who sat nearby or else took place during the lunch break. Moreover, the method of payment—by the piece or by the week—affected the degree to which a worker might socialize on the job. . . . Many pieceworkers in the factories enjoyed the privilege of coming and going at their own discretion. Not only did pieceworkers make their own hours, but bosses and foreman felt little compulsion to impose standards of workroom demeanor on them. . . . Of course, pieceworkers always felt some tension between the desire to socialize and the compulsion to maintain a high level of production. Anne Marion MacLean, who observed women workers in New York's garment factories, noted that many girls "talked as freely as they could above the noise of the machines," but "on the whole the work was too serious to be coupled with much conversation." . . .

. . . In the absence of the self-imposed discipline of pieceworkers, week workers were more heavily subjected to the watchful eye of the boss or supervisor. Week workers, though paid at different rates according to the bargains they struck with employers, received a weekly sum that did not vary with the hours they worked or the amount they produced. Although most had to meet a production quota they had little incentive to exert themselves beyond the minimum required by the employer. Consequently, bosses and supervisors took pains to speed their work and to insure their time on the job was well spent.

. . . They were told when to be at work and when they could leave, and the bosses used stern measures to enforce their rules. Requirements for working over-time were among the most hated features of the factory regimen for week workers who, unlike pieceworkers, had no financial motivation for extending their hours. Thus every Saturday during the busy season at the Triangle Shirtwaist Company, where Newman worked as a child, the supervisor put up a sign near the elevator that read: "If You Don't Come In On Sunday, Don't Come In On Monday."

Not only did week workers have little choice about the time they worked, they were continually subjected to what Rose Pesotta called "the whip of the foreman." . . . Too much talking, singing, or visiting the restroom or the drinking fountain cut into production time and thus had to be controlled. One former week worker described the discipline in her factory as a kind of bondage. "We were like slaves," she said. "You couldn't pick your head up. You couldn't talk. We used to go to the bathroom. The forelady used to go after us, we shouldn't stay too long." . . .

Factory discipline was part of a common set of grievances that bound women together in opposition to their employers and supervisors. To argue, as one historian has, that industrial discipline served only to exacerbate women's feelings of impotence and inferiority as workers is to oversimplify its impact. Jewish women probably did feel powerless as individuals to redefine their relationship with their employers, but the frustration that resulted ultimately intensified their commitment to industrial reform and their tendency toward labor militance. Not only did the oppressive behavior of bosses and supervisors threaten to interfere with the social pleasures of their jobs, but it also clashed with Jewish immigrants' image of America as a land of freedom. Those who imposed the excessive discipline and rules became the enemy against whom women could unite.

On a daily basis, however, immigrant women found ways of compensating for the limitations of their work environment. When the factory imposed rules against singing and conversing on the job, women communicated in more subtle ways.

Sometimes their interaction consisted of little more than an exchange of friendly glances and smiles to the girl at the next machine or a word or two spoken in haste after the forelady left the room or turned her back. At other times women would talk and sing quietly "when the boss didn't see." But even in the best of circumstances most shopfloor interaction took place during the lunch period, usually thirty to forty minutes. Lunch time constituted the most important arena for social life. Whether a woman sat at her machine or work table, or gathered with others in a special lunch area or cheap restaurant, that time gave women an opportunity to converse freely, joke, sing, and even dance with their coworkers.

The factory work group served as an important source of emotional support for young immigrant women. It also provided a new kind of social life and functioned as an informal school—indeed, that was part of its attraction to women who were interested in cultural experimentation. Like the classroom, the work group provided information and an exchange of ideas about a range of topics and problems of interest to young immigrants. The whole idea of broadening their cultural horizons was centrally important to Jewish immigrant daughters and had been even before they left their homes in eastern Europe. Hungry for new forms of knowledge, they had viewed the journey to America as an avenue not only for formal schooling but for learning in general. . . .

Young women who had dropped out of day school to go to work, and those who had gone directly to the factory upon their arrival, continued to cherish the possibility of an education. Of particular concern to Jewish women was their ability to converse in English, because it represented their progress toward Americanization. . . . But hardworking immigrants did not always have the energy to attend or keep up in evening school and, like Pauline Newman and her coworkers, tried to educate themselves in more informal ways: "I recall on Saturday nights we'd gather in each other's apartments and try to read English. We were limited, naturally enough, because none of us went to school. We tried to go to school and then overtime would interfere. Evening classes, when they were available, were useless because it was a question of attending school or keeping a job." . . .

Given these concerns, it is not surprising that Jewish daughters sought new kinds of knowledge wherever they could. The female work group partly served that function. If individual women lacked the time for evening school or other forms of outside education, they might try to learn from more worldly and enlightened coworkers. Socializing at work with their contemporaries—some of whom had the benefit of American schooling, spoke some English, and knew more about American culture than greenhorns—provided immigrant women with important sources of information about life outside the shop. Sometimes newcomers practiced speaking English with each other at work, struggling with conversation, or rehearsing the latest American songs. . . . Just the opportunity to spend time with other young people of the same age and sex allowed immigrants, whatever their background, the freedom to explore new ideas and values in an atmosphere of comfortable feminine sociability. . . .

No subject was more important than men and the intriguing business of dating and courtship. Given the attraction of the female work groups, this was something of an irony. Immigrant daughters valued the sisterhood they found among young women at work, but not because they sought out an exclusively "homosocial" or same-sex environment so valued by many middle-class American women. For working-class daughters, the female gang at work served as a mediating force to funnel them into the still somewhat unfamiliar territory of mixed-sex socializing. As Kathy Peiss has argued, the workroom served as an arena in which young female wage earners "articulated their sexual feelings and shared their acquired wisdom about negotiating the attentions of men, both on the job and in their leisure time." Just as female work groups might serve as a buffer against the unwanted attentions of bosses and supervisors, so they provided a safe harbor for rehearsing one's entrance into the world of dating and courtship. . . .

Conversations with other young women at work strengthened the emerging belief that what mattered in marriage was love, not whether the groom brought *yichus* (prestige) to her family. . . . Jewish daughters debated whether marriage, romantic or pragmatic, promised economic salvation. A good many immigrant wage earners fantasized that being married would solve all of their problems, whereas others took a more realistic approach, insisting that matrimony, though desirable, would not put an end to either poverty or drudgery. . . . Critical of the growing assumption that marriage was "the remedy of the working girl," socialist women in the factories tried to convince others that they should marry for love, not convenience. Marriage could not be the working woman's "remedy," Elizabeth Hasanovitz told her friends at work, because "the kind of man I shall marry is likely to be a poor wage-earner, also exploited as we all are, and our lives would be miserable under the present conditions. As for marrying money—you know what I think of marriage without love." Change the working conditions, the socialists argued, and women would not have to be "driven from the shop" either to a life of prostitution or, equally tragic, to a loveless and confining marriage. The unsettled debate about the goals of marriage suggests the complex process by which Old World daughters were redefining the meanings of Jewish womanhood. But whether they married for romantic love or opted for less idealistic unions, most immigrant daughters made marriage a central social preoccupation.

At the same time that young garment workers were learning more about romance and modern marriage from others at work, they were also exploring the related world of leisure and consumption. During the long working day women shared with each other the details of last night's fancy dress ball, the plot of the movie or play they had seen, or the expensive hat they had spied while walking down Grand Street after work. New tastes in dress and adornment, along with the seductive lure of new commercial amusements, were cultivated in the social world of the work group. Encouraged by the interests of fellow workers and enticed by the bright lights of the street and the seduction of the music or matinee, immigrant girls both talked about and participated in the excitement of modern American urban culture. . . .

Movies, dances, rides at the amusement park, the Yiddish theater, the ice-cream parlor, the downtown cafés, even the shop windows on big city streets gave young working women new outlets for pleasure and fantasy. . . . Those women who indulged in American amusements enthusiastically reported their activities to others at work, and the less fortunate women listened to their stories in awe and anticipation. . . . Even more central to the factory social world was an interest in American styles of dress and personal attire. For new immigrants, buying American clothing was the first symbolic step in the long, complex process of adaptation. . . . Ida Richter remembered the fascination she and other Jewish working women had for American styles. "We used to love the American people, to copy them. I wanted to be American very much. I saw people who looked better and dressed better and I wanted to be like that kind." For these women, and for countless others, clothing remained a powerful cultural symbol—a signal to others that one was no longer a "greener"; a way of communicating one's identification with America and Americans; and even more, an attempt to appear more prosperous or middle-class than one's living conditions or working life would have suggested.

The meaning of these preoccupations with leisure, consumption, and romantic fantasy for working daughters' identity was multifold. Historians have discussed these issues in terms of generational conflict, noting the tensions that arose between financially and socially conservative parent and adventurous working-class youth. . . .

Less frequently discussed is the evidence that leisure and consumption were not the exclusive preoccupations of immigrant daughters. Mothers also shared an interest in the world of urban products and pleasures. The movies are a good example. An especially potent medium for introducing new attitudes about dress and sex roles as well as a vehicle for exploring generational and cultural tensions over these issues, movies were a family entertainment in the immigrant ghettos, a cultural and consumer experience shared by parents and children alike. Some Jewish immigrant mothers also shared their daughters' fascination with consumer goods, including store-bought clothing. . . .

. . . Nevertheless, as household managers mothers had to carefully scrutinize children's spending habits. The meager household budgets of most immigrant families limited the amount of money daughters could squander on dances and personal adornment. . . . Most Jewish daughters continued to turn their pay envelopes over to their parents in exchange for a weekly allowance averaging about 11 percent of their wage. . . .

Working daughters in pursuit of consumer pleasures found ways of getting around tight household budgets. Young wage earners learned to use the American installment system to pay for clothing they could not afford to purchase in one lump payment. And once a girl began "keeping company" with a boyfriend, she could sometimes persuade him to help her with the payments. Moreover, much of the time dating meant treating. "I want a good time," one Russian-born clothing operator who was helping to support her family told an investigator. "And there is no . . . way a girl can get it on $8 a week. I guess if anyone wants to take me to a dance he won't have to ask me twice." Thus like other working girls in American cities, many immigrant daughters relied upon young men to treat them to movies, dances, and other city pleasures. . . .

The interest in consumerism had dual implications. It offered an escape from working-class drudgery. Paradoxically, however, it also added an incentive to work-related ambitions and ultimately helped fuel workplace militance. Not surprisingly, the rising interest in consumer goods and the more general aspiration for a better standard of living heightened Jewish women's concerns about low wages and added complicating expectations to the relationship between immigrants and their employers. Although wages were usually better in the inside factories than in the contractors' shops, they were still insufficient to satisfy appetites for new clothing and commercial amusements. Moreover, the dirt, the overcrowding, and the absence of the most basic amenities in many factories were hardly conducive to workers' efforts to look and feel like respectable young ladies. It was not unusual, then, for young women who took such pains to look presentable to be angered not only by low wages but by employers' failure to provide decent dressing rooms to protect the cheap clothing they *could* afford to purchase. As Russian-born Clara Lemlich, a leader in the 1909 shirtwaist strike, told a reporter, shirtwaist workers "have to hang up their hats and coats—such as they are—on hooks along the walls. Sometimes a girl has a new hat. It is never much to look at because it never costs more than fifty cents, but it's pretty sure spoiled after it's been at the shop." Protested Lemlich, "We're human, all of us girls, and we're young. We like new hats as well as any other young women. Why shouldn't we?" . . .

. . . The fantasy world that many women created as they discussed the latest style in hats, swooned over movie or stage actors, or dreamed of leaving the factory for the arms of a rich suitor provided comfort from the pressures of their jobs. But that escapist interest did not define women's lives: it was merely one of several influences that shaped their identities as females, as workers, and as Jewish immigrants. For along with their fantasies about romance, marriage, or clothing, eastern European Jewish women shared with one another their dreams about the possibilities for social justice and economic equality—possibilities that many had imagined would be fulfilled in America. . . .

Female work groups would prove to be extremely elastic in their preoccupations and concerns, focusing sometimes on the latest fashion in hats or petticoats but in other instances on the problem of labor organization. Depending on the influences they absorbed, and on the force of circumstance, work groups could either function as an outlet for romantic fantasy or become a vital mechanism for focused and purposeful labor protest.

◈ *F U R T H E R   R E A D I N G*

Benson, Susan Porter. *Counter Cultures: Saleswomen, Managers, and Customers in American Department Stores, 1890–1940* (1986).

Cobble, Dorothy Sue. *Dishing It Out: Waitresses and Their Unions in the Twentieth Century* (1991).

Cohen, Lizabeth. *Making a New Deal: Industrial Workers in Chicago, 1919–1939* (1990).

Cohen, Miriam. *Workshop to Office: Two Generations of Italian Women in New York City, 1900–1950* (1993).

DeVault, Ileen A. *Sons and Daughters of Labor: Class and Clerical Work in Turn-of-the-Century Pittsburgh* (1990).

Dudden, Faye. *Serving Women: Household Service in Nineteenth-Century America* (1983).

Dye, Nancy Schrom. *As Equals and as Sisters: Feminism, the Labor Movement, and the Women's Trade Union League of New York* (1981).

Einsenstein, Sarah. *Give Us Bread but Give Us Roses* (1983).

Enstad, Nan. *Ladies of Labor, Girls of Adventure: Working Women, Popular Culture, and Labor Politics at the Turn of the Twentieth Century* (1999).

Ewen, Elizabeth. *Immigrant Women in the Land of Dollars: Life and Culture on the Lower East Side* (1985).

Faue, Elizabeth. *Community of Suffering and Struggle: Women, Men, and the Labor Movement in Minneapolis, 1915–1945* (1991).

Fine, Lisa. *The Souls of the Skyscraper: Female Clerical Workers in Chicago, 1870–1930* (1990).

Frank, Dana. *Purchasing Power: Consumer Organizing, Gender, and the Seattle Labor Movement, 1919–1992* (1994).

Fraundorf, Martha. "The Labor Force Participation of Turn-of-the-Century Married Women," *Journal of Economic History* 39 (1979): 401–418.

Gamber, Wendy. *The Female Economy: The Millinery and Dressmaking Trades, 1860–1930* (1997).

Garrison, Dee. *Apostles of Culture: The Public Librarian and American Society, 1876–1920* (1979).

Glenn, Evelyn Nakanno. *Issei, Nisei, War Bride: Three Generations of Japanese American Women in Domestic Service* (1986).

Glenn, Susan A. *Daughters of the Shtetl: Life and Labor in the Immigrant Generation* (1990).

Goldin, Claudia. "The Work and Wages of Single Women, 1870–1920," *Journal of Economic History* 40 (1980): 81–88.

Hall, Jacquelyn Dowd. "Disorderly Women: Gender and Labor Militancy in the Appalachian South," *Journal of American History* 73, no. 2 (September 1986): 354–382.

Hareven, Tamara. *Family Time and Industrial Time* (1982).

Harris, Barbara. *Beyond Her Sphere: Women and the Professions in American History* (1978).

Hine, Darlene Clark. *Black Women in White: Racial Conflict and Cooperation in the Nursing Profession, 1890–1950* (1989).

Horowitz, Helen Lefkowitz. *The Power and Passion of M. Cary Thomas* (1994).

Hummer, Patrice M. *The Decade of the Elusive Promise: Professional Women in the United States, 1920–1930* (1981).

Jensen, Joan, and Sue Davidson, eds. *A Needle, a Bobbin, a Strike* (1984).

Jones, Jacqueline. *Labor of Love, Labor of Sorrow: Black Women, Work, and the Family from Slavery to the Present* (1985).

Katzman, David. *Seven Days a Week: Women and Domestic Service in Industrializing America* (1978).

Kessler-Harris, Alice. *Out to Work: A History of Wage-Earning Women in the United States* (1982).

———. *In Pursuit of Equity: Women, Men, and the Quest for Economic Citizenship in Twentieth-Century America* (2001).

Meyerowitz, Joanne. *Women Adrift: Independent Wage Earners in Chicago, 1880–1930* (1988).

Moldow, Gloria. *Women Doctors in Gilded Age Washington: Race, Gender, and Professionalization* (1987).

Norwood, Stephen. *Labor's Flaming Youth: Telephone Operators and Worker Militancy, 1878–1923* (1990).

Orleck, Annelise. *Common Sense and a Little Fire: Women and Working-Class Politics in the United States, 1900–1965* (1995).

Peiss, Kathy. *Cheap Amusements: Working Women and Leisure in Turn-of-the-Century New York* (1986).

Reitano, Joanne. "Working Girls Unite," *American Quarterly* 36 (1984): 112–134.

Rose, Elizabeth. *A Mother's Job: The History of Day Care, 1890–1960* (1999).

Rossiter, Margaret W. *Women Scientists in America: Struggles and Strategies to 1940* (1982).

Rotella, Elyce. *From Home to Office: United States Women at Work, 1870–1930* (1981).

Ruiz, Vicki L. *From Out of the Shadows: Mexican Women in Twentieth-Century America* (1998).

Shakir, Evelyn. *Bint Arab: Arab and Arab American Women in the United States* (1997).

Shaw, Stephanie J. *What a Woman Ought to Be and to Do: Black Professional Women Workers During the Jim Crow Era* (1996).

Soloman, Barbara Miller. *In the Company of Educated Women* (1985).

Stricker, Frank. "Cookbooks and Law Books: The Hidden History of Career Women in Twentieth-Century America," *Journal of Social History* 10, no. 1 (fall 1976–1977): 1–19.

Strom, Sharon Hartmann. *Beyond the Typewriter: Gender, Class, and the Origins of Modern American Office Work, 1900–1930* (1992).

Tax, Meredith. *The Rising of the Women: Feminist Solidarity and Class Conflict, 1880–1917* (1981).

Walsh, Mary Roth. *Doctors Wanted: No Women Need Apply* (1977).

Wandersee, Winifred. *Women's Work and Family Values, 1920–1940* (1981).

CHAPTER
10

The "New Woman" in Public Life and Politics, 1900–1930

In the early decades of the twentieth century, American women joined a myriad of women's organizations, thereby trying to expand opportunities for their sex, to remove obstacles to women's advancement, and to "uplift" the nation's culture, government, and politics. Often referred to as "new women," this generation of organized women became important players in crafting the agendas and tactics of Progressive reform at the local, state, and national levels, and they sought both to expand their own civil rights and to create a liberal welfare state. Women's long campaign for suffrage was finally victorious when Congress ratified the Nineteenth Amendment to the Constitution in 1920. Other reform campaigns spearheaded by women produced a federal children's bureau, protective labor legislation, pure food and drug acts, juvenile courts, public kindergartens, city beautification projects, and a wide array of public health and social welfare programs for mothers and children.

Organized women did not always act in concert; indeed, they were often divided by values, strategies, and differences in social background. For example, while black women's collective experience taught them that race and sex oppression had to be challenged simultaneously, the majority of white women refused to participate in efforts to combat racist ideology, segregation, disfranchisement, or lynching. Similarly, after suffrage was won, Florence Kelley and other advocates of women's protective labor legislation became entangled in a bitter debate with members of the National Woman's Party over the party's fight for an equal rights amendment. And yet, though organized women experienced disunity and disagreement, they also struggled with a common problem: how to claim rights or authority in public life in the face of persistent discrimination and patterns of marginalization. What were some of the ways in which organized women tried to combine a belief in sexual difference with the pursuit of gender or racial equality? In what circumstances did women downplay gender differences? What were the benefits and limitations of their varied approaches to reform?

◉ D O C U M E N T S

Mary Church Terrell, the president of the National Federation of Colored Women's Clubs, in 1901 praised the reform efforts of organizations composed entirely of black women (Document 1). In Document 2, Terrell calls on white women, especially those of the South, to join in the fight against lynching. Mary B. Dixon, in Document 3, reacts with indignation in 1908 to the refusal of a nurses' association to support the suffrage movement and explains why nurses ought to give the campaign for woman suffrage vigorous support. The following year (Document 4), Margaret Dreier Robins urges women, especially privileged members of the middle class, to consider the plight of young women wage earners and lend support to the goals of the Women's Trade Union League. Document 5, written in 1912, offers the rationale of the California Supreme Court in upholding an eight-hour-workday law for women. Relying on the argument that there were fundamental differences between the sexes and that women were more vulnerable to harm in the workplace than men, the court supported the claim that the state had a compelling interest in protecting women from the excessive demands of employers. In October 1920, in an effort at interracial cooperation, the Women's Council of the Methodist Episcopal Church, South, issued a statement supporting a number of reforms desired by black women. Conspicuously absent from this list, however, was suffrage—a right long denied black men in the South and now likely to be withheld from black women as well. The omission was not lost on the Southeastern Federation of Colored Women's Clubs, which pointedly responded to the white women's statement in June 1921 (both in Document 6). In Document 7, published in 1922 in *The Nation* magazine, Elsie Hill of the National Woman's Party called for the elimination of all legal distinctions between men and women. Florence Kelley of the National Consumers' League presented a rejoinder to Hill (also included), arguing that the National Woman's Party misunderstood women's legal interests and seemed intent on undermining hard-won labor laws that protected and benefited women wage earners. These documents reveal the widely held view that societal constructions of gender, race, and class made women different from men, while also demonstrating women's desire for equality of rights; the documents also indicate the numerous programs and strategies women devised to advance their rights and promote social reform in the early decades of the twentieth century.

1. Mary Church Terrell Praises the Club Work of Colored Women, 1901

Should anyone ask me what special phase of the Negro's development makes me most hopeful of his ultimate triumph over present obstacles, I should answer unhesitatingly, it is the magnificent work the women are doing to regenerate and uplift the race. Though there are many things in the Negro's present condition to discourage him, he has some blessings for which to be thankful: not the least of these is the progress of our women in everything which makes for the culture of the individual and the elevation of the race.

 For years, either banding themselves into small companies or struggling alone, colored women have worked with might and main to improve the condition of their people. The necessity of systematizing their efforts and working on a larger scale

---

Mary Church Terrell, "Club Work of Colored Women," 1901. This document may also be found in *Southern Workman* 30 (1901): 435–438.

became apparent not many years ago, and they decided to unite their forces. Thus it happened that in the summer of 1896 the National Association of Colored Women was formed by the union of two large organizations, from which the advantage of concerted action had been learned. From its birth till the present time its growth has been steady. Interest in the purposes and plans of the National Association has spread so rapidly that it has already been represented in twenty-six states. Handicapped though its members have been, because they lacked both money and experience, their efforts have for the most part been crowned with success.

Kindergartens have been established by some of its organizations, from which encouraging reports have come. A sanitarium with a training school for nurses has been set on such a firm foundation by the Phyllis Wheatley Club of New Orleans, Louisiana, and has proved itself to be such a blessing to the entire community, that the municipal government of that Southern city has voted it an annual appropriation of several hundred dollars. By the members of the Tuskegee branch of the association the work of bringing the light of knowledge and the gospel of cleanliness to their poor benighted sisters on the plantations in Alabama has been conducted with signal success. Their efforts have thus far been confined to four estates, comprising thousands of acres of land, on which live hundreds of colored people yet in the darkness of ignorance and in the grip of sin, and living miles away from churches and schools.

Plans for aiding the indigent orphaned and aged have been projected, and in some instances have been carried into successful execution. One club in Memphis, Tenn., has purchased a large tract of land on which it intends to erect an Old Folks' Home, part of the money for which has already been raised. Splendid service has been rendered by the Illinois Federation of Colored Women's Clubs, through whose instrumentality schools have been visited, truant children looked after, parents and teachers urged to cooperate with each other, rescue and reform work engaged in, so as to reclaim unfortunate women and tempted girls, public institutions investigated, and garments cut, made and distributed to the needy poor.

Questions affecting our legal status as a race are sometimes agitated by our women. In Tennessee and Louisiana colored women have several times petitioned the legislature of their respective states to repeal the obnoxious Jim Crow car laws. . . .

Homes, more homes, better homes, purer homes, is the text upon which our sermons have been and will be preached. There has been a determined effort to have heart-to-heart talks with our women, that we may strike at the root of evils, many of which lie at the fireside. If the women of the dominant race, with all the centuries of education, culture and refinement back of them, with all the wealth of opportunity ever present with them, feel the need of a Mothers' Congress, that they may be enlightened upon the best methods of rearing their children and conducting their homes, how much more do our women, from whom shackles were stricken but yesterday, need information on the same vital subjects! And so the Association is working vigorously to establish mothers' congresses on a small scale, wherever our women can be reached.

From this brief and meagre account of the work which has been and is still being accomplished by colored women through the medium of clubs, it is easy to observe how earnest and effective have been our efforts to elevate the race. No people need ever despair whose women are fully aroused to the duties which rest upon them, and are willing to shoulder responsibilities which they alone can successfully assume. The scope of our endeavors is constantly widening. Into the various channels of generosity and beneficence the National Association is entering more and more every day.

Some of our women are urging their clubs to establish day nurseries, a charity of which there is an imperative need. The infants of wage earning mothers are frequently locked alone in a room from the time the mother leaves in the morning until she returns at night. Not long ago I read in a Southern newspaper that an infant thus locked alone in the room all day had cried itself to death. When one reflects on the slaughter of the innocents which is occurring with pitiless persistency every day, and thinks of the multitudes who are maimed for life or are rendered imbecile, because of the treatment received during their helpless infancy, it is evident that by establishing day nurseries colored women will render one of the greatest services possible to humanity and to the race. . . .

Nothing lies nearer the heart of colored women than the cause of the children. We feel keenly the need of kindergartens, and are putting forth earnest efforts to honeycomb this country with them from one extreme to the other. The more unfavorable the environments of children the more necessary is it that steps be taken to counteract blameful influences upon innocent victims. How imperative is it then, that, as colored women, we inculcate correct principles and set good examples for our own youth, whose little feet will have so many thorny paths of prejudice, temptation and injustice to tread. . . .

And so, lifting as we climb, onward and upward we go, struggling, striving and hoping that the buds and blossoms of our desires will burst into glorious fruition ere long. With courage born of success achieved in the past, we look forward to a future large with promise and hope. Seeking no favors because of our color, nor patronage because of our needs, we knock at the bar of Justice and ask for an equal chance.

2. Mary Church Terrell Describes Lynching from a Negro's Point of View, 1904

Before 1904 was three months old, thirty-one negroes had been lynched. Of this number, fifteen were murdered within one week in Arkansas, and one was shot to death in Springfield, Ohio, by a mob composed of men who did not take the trouble to wear masks. Hanging, shooting and burning black men, women and children in the United States have become so common that such occurrences create but little sensation and evoke but slight comment now. . . . In the discussion of this subject, four mistakes are commonly made.

In the first place, it is a great mistake to suppose that rape is the real cause of lynching in the South. Beginning with the Ku Klux Klan the negro has been constantly subjected to some form of organized violence ever since he became free. It is easy to prove that rape is simply the pretext and not the cause of lynching. Statistics show that, out of every 100 negroes who are lynched, from 75–85 are not even accused of this crime, and many who are accused of it are innocent. . . .

Mary Church Terrell, "Lynching from a Negro's Point of View," *North American Review* 178 (June 1904): 853–868. This document may also be found in Gerda Lerner, ed., *Black Women in White America: A Documentary History* (New York: Pantheon Books, 1972), 205–211.

In the second place, it is a mistake to suppose that the negro's desire for social equality sustains any relation whatsoever to the crime of rape. . . . It is safe to assert that, among the negroes who have been guilty of ravishing white women, not one had been taught that he was the equal of white people or had ever heard of social equality. . . .

The third error on the subject of lynching consists of the widely circulated statement that the moral sensibilities of the best negroes in the United States are so stunted and dull, and the standard of morality among even the leaders of the race is so low, that they do not appreciate the enormity and heinousness of rape. . . . Only those who are densely ignorant of the standards and sentiments of the best negroes, or who wish wilfully to misrepresent and maliciously slander a race already resting under burdens greater than it can bear, would accuse its thousands of reputable men and women of sympathizing with rapists, either black or white, or of condoning their crime. . . .

What, then, is the cause of lynching? At the last analysis, it will be discovered that there are just two causes of lynching. In the first place, it is due to race hatred, the hatred of a stronger people toward a weaker who were once held as slaves. In the second place, it is due to the lawlessness so prevalent in the section where nine-tenths of the lynchings occur. . . .

Lynching is the aftermath of slavery. The white men who shoot negroes to death and flay them alive, and the white women who apply flaming torches to their oil-soaked bodies today, are the sons and daughters of women who had but little, if any, compassion on the race when it was enslaved. The men who lynch negroes to-day are, as a rule, the children of women who sat by their firesides happy and proud in the possession and affection of their own children, while they looked with unpity-ing eye and adamantine heart upon the anguish of slave mothers whose children had been sold away, when not overtaken by a sadder fate. . . . It is too much to expect, perhaps, that the children of women who for generations looked upon the hardships and the degradation of their sisters of a darker hue with few if any protests, should have mercy and compassion upon the children of that oppressed race now. But what a tremendous influence for law and order, and what a mighty foe to mob violence Southern white women might be, if they would arise in the purity and power of their womanhood to implore their fathers, husbands and sons no longer to stain their hands with the black man's blood!

3. Mary B. Dixon, R.N., Endorses
Votes for Women, 1908

The Nurses' Associated Alumnæ of the United States, at its recent convention in San Francisco, refused to indorse the following resolution:

"WHEREAS, the thinking women of America are striving more earnestly than ever before to be a helpful part of the people, in the firm belief that men and women together compose a democracy, and that until men and women have equal political rights they cannot do their best work, therefore be it

Mary B. Dixon, R.N., "Votes for Women," *Nurses' Journal of the Pacific Coast* 4 (October 1908): 442–447.

"*Resolved,* That the Nurses' Associated Alumnæ of the United States, numbering fourteen thousand members, as a company of workers, heartily indorse every *well-directed* movement which tends to emancipate the women of our land and give them their rightful place in government."

I am told by our delegate it was the consensus of opinion "that nurses had affairs enough of their own to attend to without getting mixed up in politics." I claim that we were "mixed up in politics" before we were born, and that it is impossible to attend to the smallest part of our own affairs without taking politics into consideration.

Our "health, wealth, and happiness" are all involved, deeply involved. Our health: the quality and quantity of air in towns, homes, hospitals, stores, and factories; our water, milk, food, and drug supplies; the sewage and garbage questions, are all directly controlled by government. House and factory inspections, fire escapes, saloons, houses of prostitution, infectious diseases, preventable accidents, men, women, and children's labor, are all "in politics."

Our wealth: If it is not possible to procure good laws regulating the practice of nursing, we cannot expect the nursing profession to maintain, or improve its quality, or scope, and the public will not pay good salaries for inefficient work. Our salaries and the number of calls we receive are more or less controlled by the wealth of the country, and this in turn is controlled by government policies. Our investments, whether they be rides on street-railway cars or boats, or in food, clothes, pictures, books, bonds, or insurance, are all regulated by the government.

Our happiness: How can we be happy—deeply, thoughtfully happy—when we know, by actual experience as nurses, how much cruelty and injustice there is in the world, which might be prevented?

We are living in a country governed by law; these laws are made by men placed in authority by the voters of the country. What is the law in your state on this voting question? Maryland says, putting the clause in a few words, "All persons over twenty-one (21) years, having lived in a community one year, have the right to vote, *except women, children, idiots,* and *criminals.*"

We teach both boys and girls in public schools that the ideal of government in the United States of America is "of the people, by the people, and for the people."

Opponents of equal suffrage, your first mistake was in educating your girls. . . .

The Anti-Suffrage Association formed to oppose the "further extension of the ballot to women" believe with all their hearts (I am not so sure of their heads) that the silent influence is mighty and must prevail, that now, only the "good women" have an influence in policies; if the ballot were given, all women might have an influence.

I am sure that the "Anti's" have accomplished some splendid results along philanthropic lines through legislation, but I claim that they have accomplished these results not because they were fighting for "just measures," but because they were "specially privileged." History teaches that the "specially privileged," "silent influence" of woman in politics is capable of doing an infinite amount of harm as well as good.

. . . A great many women not only want the right to vote, but have it. In the last twenty-five years, full suffrage has been granted to women in Colorado, Utah, Idaho, New Zealand, Australia, Finland, and Norway. Russia has given them a proxy vote in the election of the Douma. Ireland has given them a vote for all officers, except members of Parliament. England and Scotland have given them county suffrage. Kansas, Nova Scotia, British Columbia, the Northwest Territory, Ontario, New Brunswick, and Quebec have given them municipal suffrage. Tax-paying women have been given a vote upon tax questions in Montana, Louisiana, Iowa, and in all the towns and villages of New York State. School suffrage has been granted by North and South Dakota, Arizona, Montana, New Jersey, Illinois, Connecticut, Ohio, Delaware, Wisconsin, and Oklahoma. Great Britain has made women eligible as mayors, aldermen and town and country councillors.

A majority of both men and women, now indifferent or opposed, would believe in woman suffrage if they had the opportunity of hearing the question discussed without prejudice. But why this prejudice? . . . If you want an interesting ten minutes, try to "draw out" the prejudiced type of man on the subject of woman suffrage—try to get his virile opinion.

The usual style is, "We don't interfere with the soup," etc. . . . Wouldn't he, if it wasn't flavored to suit his taste . . . ? Another gallant knight of the "Sunny South" will say, off his guard, "We made one mistake by giving the vote to the negro, and we are not going to make another, if we can help it." Another type of argument is that woman's enthusiasm for politics would result in "the baby being left comfortless, the husband ignored, the fireside deserted, and the food left uncooked," but this is pretty evenly balanced with the statement that "women wouldn't have sense enough to vote or care about it, if they had a chance." We shall have to include in this prejudiced type not only the average man, but men-presidents of women's colleges, doctors, ministers, and lawyers. I believe that man's superior physical strength, and the Adam-and-Eve theory, are prime factors in creating this prejudice. I am not finding fault with "by-gone" ideas; I am only trying to understand to-day's. Brute strength is important and plays its part, but history has taught us that the "race is not to the swift, nor the battle to the strong," but endurance, brains, and moral force are winners in the game.

I claim that the *mothers* of the race have *endurance;* science and our colleges have proved that women's brains are intrinsically equal to men's. As for moral force, it is futile to say "women are better than men"; their moral qualities are different, and it is because of this difference (not because she ought to be like men) she should have a voice directly—not indirectly—in the government under whose laws she must be born, live, and die. . . .

Another question: Are the states in which women have suffrage improved? The anti-suffragists claim conditions are not better; the suffragists claim that the laws applying to women and children are vastly improved, and better enforced, that women are leading infinitely more interesting, thoughtful lives, and that the men, babies, and homes are not only made happier by this fact, but receive more thoughtful, intelligent care and appreciation.

History tells us the countries that have reached the highest water-mark in all that pertains to higher civilization are those in which woman has been accorded the nearest approach to an equality with man.

Shall we not strive to place our country on the highest plane, and is not citizenship for women the next logical step onward and upward?

If I have been fortunate enough to create a desire in any one to "hitch her wagon to this star," please let me beseech her to be practical and put her "shoulder to the wheel."

4. Margaret Dreier Robins
Describes the Purposes of the
Women's Trade Union League, 1909

What is the Women's Trade Union League?

This question is asked of me daily, and, I think, my friends, that I can answer it best by asking you some questions in turn:

Do you know that the average wage of the women workers of our country is less than $270.00 a year? Do you know that one-half of the six million working women in the United States are under twenty-one years of age, and that the conditions of work in many of the trades into which women have entered put such a strain upon the physical organization that a brief service precludes motherhood?

We have tried to tell you very simply in the following pages what some of these conditions are; and we believe that the more you study these conditions the more convinced you will become that they are destructive, not only of all physical strength, but also of all mental and spiritual development—destructive alike of all expression of ideals in the life of the individual and in the nation.

What is to be done?

Many things; but it will be readily understood that the most important factor in the industrial problem is the worker herself, and that the most significant fact about the woman worker is her youth.

We are forcing young girls of fourteen and sixteen years of age into the industrial struggle, and are demanding of them the knowledge and wisdom of trained maturity. If in her need for work whereby to earn her daily bread, and in her ignorance of the cost, a girl of fourteen underbids her fellow-worker, how is she to know that in so doing she is competing against her own home; and that, in the years to come, as wife and mother she must bear the heaviest burden of the lesser wage? How is she to know that the division and sub-division of labor demands of her the joyless task of tending a machine; not only for today, but for tomorrow as well, and for all the succeeding tomorrows? Can you see her standing alone in the midst of her fellow-workers, alone and afraid, because she has discovered that even as she became the underbidder, so all may become "underbidders" or pace-makers? Where can she learn that "two are better than one, for if they fall the one will lift up his fellow"? Where can she find this fellowship?

Where, but in the great school of the Working People, the Trade Union, which is open to all and within the reach of all? In this school the members are taught that "An injury to one is the concern of all," and thus they enter into fellowship with one another, for they have found the way to work with each other and not against each other. Knowledge of the trade in all its aspects, judgment, decision, patience and fidelity are here called into action, for by seeking to establish trade agreements with her fellow-workers and with her employer, the duties and rights of each must be discussed, considered, and voted upon; and except in those states or cities where the initiative and referendum have been enacted into law I know of no training in

National Women's Trade Union League, *Handbook, Convention at Chicago, September 27–October 2, 1909* (Chicago: National Women's Trade Union League, 1909).

democratic self-government and citizenship that equals the training received in the School of the Trade Union. As the personal needs become increasingly protected by collective action, thoughts are turned into new channels, energies are directed towards other tasks, and with a wider horizon educational and social issues command attention. The child has grown into the woman; the untutored girl has grown into the intelligent, capable, clear-sighted leader and citizen, and under her direction social progress is written into the laws of our country. This opportunity for learning, for development, for character-building, has been given to her in the Trade Union School—the open sesame to fellowship and service.

5. The California Supreme Court Upholds an Eight-Hour Law for Women, 1912

In the Matter of the Application of F. A. Miller for a Writ of Habeas Corpus

. . . The petitioner applies for release from custody on a charge of violating the provisions of the act of March 22, 1911, forbidding the employment of women in certain establishments for more than eight hours in one day, or more than forty-eight hours in one week. (Stats. 1911, 437.) The specific charge is that on June 12, 1911, he employed and thereupon required Emma Hunt, a female, to work during that day for nine hours in the Glenwood Hotel, as an employee therein. His contention is that the act is unconstitutional and void.

. . . 1. That the restrictions imposed by the statute upon the freedom of contract are in violation of section 1, article I, and section 18 of article XX, of the constitution, and that it is consequently invalid; 2. That the act is special, that it is not uniform in its operation, and that it makes arbitrary discriminations between persons and classes of persons similarly situated contrary to the limitations of sections 11 and 21, article I, and section 25 of article IV of the constitution. . . .

The material parts of the statute are as follows:

"Section 1. No female shall be employed in any manufacturing, mechanical or mercantile establishment, laundry, hotel, or restaurant, or telegraph or telephone establishment or office, or by any express or transportation company in this state more than eight hours during any one day or more than forty-eight hours in one week. . . .

"Section 2. Every employer in any manufacturing, mechanical or mercantile establishment, laundry, hotel or restaurant, or other establishment employing any female, shall provide suitable seats for all female employees, and shall permit them to use such seats when they are not engaged in the active duties of their employment."

Section 3 declares it a misdemeanor, punishable by fine or imprisonment, or both, for any employer to require any female to work in any of the places mentioned

Supreme Court of the State of California, "Decision Upholding the Constitutionality of the Eight-Hour Law for Women" (Sacramento: Superintendent of State Printing, 1912), 1–7.

in section 1 more than the number of hours allowed by the act, during any one day of twenty-four hours. . . .

Recognizing the importance of personal liberty, our state constitution at the outset declares that all persons have an inalienable right to enjoy life and liberty and to acquire and possess property. (Art. I. sec. 1.) This, necessarily, includes liberty to work for the purpose of acquiring property, or to accomplish any desired lawful object, and liberty to continue that work each day a sufficient time to gain more than is required for the daily needs. Hence comes the right to make contracts to serve and contracts to employ such service. There can be no contract by the employee to serve without a corresponding contract by the employer to hire and receive such service. Therefore, although the act in question provides a punishment only for the employer, its prohibition applies to both and it clearly restricts the liberty of both the employer and the employed, in the specified establishments, to freely contract with each other as to the length of a day's service or to perform such contracts, when made. Consequently, it does, to that extent, take away the liberty guaranteed by this provision of the constitution.

Although this guaranty of the constitution is apparently absolute and unqualified, yet it is well established that it is subject to the exercise, by the legislature, of what are known as the police powers of the state.

Says the Supreme Court of the United States in *Holden* vs. *Hardy*. 169 U.S. 391: "This right of contract, however, is in itself subject to certain limitations which the state may lawfully impose in the exercise of its police powers," a power which "may lawfully be resorted to for the purpose of preserving public health, safety, or morals, and a large discretion is necessarily vested in the legislature to determine not only what the interests of the public require, but what measures are necessary for the protection of such interests." . . .

The means adopted to produce the public benefit intended, or to prevent the public injury, must be reasonably necessary to accomplish that purpose and not unduly oppressive upon individuals. The determination of the legislature as to these matters is not conclusive, but is subject to the supervision of the courts, and if the above qualities are wanting, a law arbitrarily interfering with the right of contract, or imposing restrictions upon lawful occupations, will be held void. . . . If this were not so, the constitutional guaranties of the personal right to liberty and property would be wholly subject to the will of the majority acting through the legislature.

It is settled, however, that some occupations may have a tendency to injure the health of those engaged therein, that this injury may be so general or extensive as to affect the public health and general welfare, and that in such cases the legislature may, in the exercise of the police power of the state, enact laws limiting the time of labor therein to eight hours a day. Thus, laws have been upheld restricting to eight hours the daily labor of persons working in underground mines, or in smelters and quartz mills, and the legislative judgment on the subject of the extent and effect of the injury was considered sufficiently supported to be beyond judicial interference. . . .

So, also, it has been recognized that some occupations followed by women, though less arduous than those generally followed by men, may have such a tendency to injure their health, if unduly prolonged, that laws may be enacted restricting their time of labor therein to ten hours a day. The application of these laws exclusively to women is justified on the ground that they are less robust in physical organization and structure than men, that they have the burden of child-bearing, and, consequently, that the health and strength of posterity and of the public in general is presumed to be enhanced by preserving and protecting women from exertion which men might bear without detriment to the general welfare. (See *Commonwealth* vs. *Hamilton Mfg. Co.,* 120 Mass. 383; *Wenham* vs. *State,* 65 Neb. 394; *State* vs. *Buchanan,* 29 Wash. 602; *State* vs. *Muller,* 49 Ore. 252; *Muller* vs. *Oregon,* 208 U.S. 412; *Whitey* vs. *Blæm,* 153 Mich. 419; *Ritchie* vs. *Wayman,* 244 Ill. 509; *State* vs. *Somerville,* 122 Pac. [Wash.] 324.) . . .

The question of the effect of the various occupations in which women engage, upon their health, is one upon which medical men differ and with respect to which the prevailing opinion changes from time to time. It has not been, and probably never will be, a settled question, either with respect to the deleterious effects of particular occupations, or the hours of labor which measure the limit of safety in each. Women who work for others usually have household or other domestic duties to perform which oblige them to continue at work each day for a much longer period than their time of service. Even those who live at their places of work generally have to make and mend their clothing and do other things for their personal welfare, in addition to the work done for their employers. In view of these circumstances affecting the generality of employed women, it could scarcely be claimed that a limitation to eight hours a day to the time of employment in many of the occupations mentioned in the act is unreasonable as a health regulation. The work in hotels may not be as severe as that in some of the other places covered by the law, but considering the delicate frame of women as compared with men, we can not perceive that the difference is so radical as to make it unreasonable to include employees in hotels among those protected by the law. . . .

The next objection is that the act is special because there are no reasons for making the restriction as to the particular employments mentioned in the act which do not apply with equal force to other similar occupations. There may be, and probably are, other occupations followed by women which are equally injurious to their health, and which should also be regulated. But if this be true it does not make the law invalid. If there are good grounds for the classification made by the act, it is not void because it does not include every other class needing similar protection or regulation. "The law is not rendered special by the mere fact that it does not cover every subject which the legislature might conceivably have included in it." (*Ex parte Martin,* 157 Cal. 57.) . . .

Let the petitioner be remanded to the custody of the sheriff of Riverside County.

SHAW, J.

We concur:
ANGELLOTTI, J.
SLOSS, J.
LORIGAN, J.
MELVIN, J.
BEATTY, C. J.

6. Two Statements on Race Relations

Women's Council of the Methodist Episcopal Church, South, 1920

We, a company of Southern white women, in conference assembled on the invitation of the Commission on Inter-Racial Cooperation, find ourselves with a deep sense of responsibility to the womanhood and childhood of the Negro race, and also with a great desire for a Christian settlement of the problems that overshadow the homes of both races. . . .

We recognize and deplore the fact that there is friction between the races, but we believe that this can be largely removed by the exercise of justice, consideration, and sympathetic cooperation.

In order that the results of this conference may be perpetuated and enlarged, we recommend:

That a Continuation Committee be appointed to devise ways and means for carrying out the work considered by this conference; that this committee be composed of one woman from each denomination and Christian agency here represented, and that it be empowered to add to its membership as may seem necessary; that each local community form a Woman's Inter-Racial Committee, which may include representatives from all religious, civil and social service bodies working in the community, and that this Continuation Committee recommend plans by which they may be accomplished.

Desiring that everything that hinders the establishment of confidence peace justice and righteousness in our land shall be removed in order that there shall be better understanding and good will in our midst, we call attention to the following points as possible causes of friction, which if corrected, may go far toward creating a better day.

Domestic Service.   We acknowledge our responsibility for the protection of the Negro women and girls in our homes and on the streets. We therefore recommend: That the domestic service be classed as an occupation and coordinated with other world service in order that better relations may be established by both employer and employee.

Child Welfare.   We are persuaded that the conservation of the life and health of Negro children is of the utmost importance to the community. We therefore urge: That day nurseries and kindergartens be established in local communities for the protection, care and training of children of Negro mothers who go out to work; that free baby clinics be established and that government leaflets on child welfare be distributed to expectant mothers, thus teaching the proper care of themselves and their children; that adequate playgrounds and recreational facilities be established for Negro children and young people.

Sanitation and Housing.   Since good housing and proper sanitation are necessary for both physical and moral life, we recommend: That a survey of housing and

---

"Statement of Women's Council of the M.E. Church, South," October 1920, and "Statement of the Southeastern Federation of Colored Women's Clubs," June 1921, *Negro Year Book* (Tuskegee, Ala.: 1922), 6–10.

sanitary conditions be made in the Negro section in each local community, followed by an appeal to the proper authorities for improvements when needed.

Education.   Since sacredness of personality is the basis for all civilization, we urge: That every agency touching the child life of the nation shall strive to create mutual respect in the hearts of the children of different races. We are convinced that the establishment of a single standard of morals for men and women, both black and white, is necessary for the life and safety of a nation. We therefore pledge ourselves to strive to secure respect and protection for womanhood everywhere, regardless of race or color. Since provision for the eduction of Negro children is still inadequate, we recommend: More equitable division of the school fund, suitable school buildings and equipment, longer school terms, higher standards and increased pay for teachers.

Travel.   Since colored people frequently do not receive fair treatment on street cars, on railroads and in railway stations and recognizing this as one of the chief causes of friction between the races, we urge: That immediate steps be taken to provide for them adequate accommodations and courteous treatment at the hands of street car and railway officials.

Lynching.   As women, we urge those who are charged with the administration of the law to prevent lynching at any cost. We are persuaded that the proper determination on the part of the constituted officials, upheld by public sentiment, would result in the detection and prosecution of those guilty of this crime. Therefore we pledge ourselves to endeavor to create a public sentiment which will uphold these officials in the execution of justice.

Justice in the Courts.   We recommend: That our women everywhere raise their voices against all acts of violence to property and person, wherever and for whatever cause occurring. We further recommend: That competent legal assistance be made available for colored people in the local communities in order to insure to them the protection of their rights in the courts.

Public Press.   Since the public press often gives undue prominence to the criminal element among Negroes, and neglects the worthy and constructive efforts of law-abiding citizens, we pledge ourselves to cooperate with the men's committees in endeavoring to correct this injustice, and to create a fair attitude to Negroes and Negro news. . . .

Southeastern Federation of Colored Women's Clubs, 1921

We desire to state our position on some matters relating to the welfare of colored people, and to enlist the sympathy and cooperation of Southern white women in the interest of better understandings and better conditions, as these affect the relations between white and colored people.

　　We take this opportunity to call to your attention certain conditions which affect colored women in their relations with white people and which if corrected will go far toward decreasing friction, removing distrust and suspicion and creating a better atmosphere in which to adjust the difficulties which always accompany human contacts.

Conditions in Domestic Service.   The most frequent and intimate contact of white and colored women is in domestic service. Every improvement made in the physical, moral and spiritual life of those so employed must react to increase the efficiency of their service to their employers.

We, therefore, direct your attention to: Long and Irregular Working Hours; (1) lack of provision for wholesome recreation; (2) undesirable housing conditions. We recommend, therefore, (1) definite regulation for hours and conditions of work; (2) sanitary, attractive and wholesome rooming facilities; (3) closer attention to personal appearance and deportment; (4) provision for and investigation of character of recreation.

Child Welfare.   The large burden of economic responsibility which falls upon many colored women results in their prolonged absence from home and the consequent neglect of the children of the homes. We direct your attention to: Child Welfare— (1) neglected homes (irregularity in food, clothing, conduct, training); (2) truancy; (3) juvenile delinquency. We therefore recommend—Welfare Activities—(1) day nurseries, play grounds, recreation centers; (2) home and school visitation; (3) probation officers and reform schools.

Conditions of Travel.   Race friction is perhaps more frequent in street cars and railroad trains than in any other public places. To reduce this friction and remove causes for just complaint from colored passengers we call your attention to: (1) seating accommodations on street cars; (2) unsanitary surroundings, at stations and on trains; (3) toilet facilities, at stations and on trains; (4) difficulty in securing tickets, Pullman accommodations and meals; (5) abuse of rights of colored passengers by train crew and white passengers occupying seats while colored passengers stand, smoking, profane language, overcrowding; (6) as corrective measures we suggest provision of equal accommodations in all public carriers and courteous treatment at the hands of street car and railway officials, for all passengers.

Education.   Without education for all the children of all the people we cannot sustain a democracy. Ignorance and crime are the twin children of neglect and poverty. We urge your increasing effort for better educational facilities so that there may be provided: adequate accommodations for all Negro children of school age, vocational training in all secondary schools, improved rural schools—longer terms, suitable buildings, training schools for teachers, adequate salaries for teachers.

Lynching.   We deplore and condemn any act on the part of any men which would tend to excite the mob spirit. We believe that any man who makes an assault upon any woman should have prompt punishment meted out to the limit of the law, but not without thorough investigation of the facts and trial by the courts. The continuance of lynching is the greatest menace to good will between the races, and a constant factor in undermining respect for all law and order. It is our opinion that mob violence incites to crime rather than deters it; and certainly it is less effective in discouraging crime than the watchful, thorough and deliberate processes of a fair and just trial.

Toward the suppression of this evil, we appeal to white women to: (1) raise their voices in immediate protest when lynchings or mob violence is threatened; (2) encourage every effort to detect and punish the leaders and participants in mobs and riots; (3) encourage the white pulpit and press in creating a sentiment among law-abiding citizens and urge outspoken condemnation of these forms of lawlessness.

The Public Press.   In the great majority of cases the white press of the South gives undue prominence to crime and the criminal element among Negroes to the neglect of the worthy and constructive efforts of law-abiding Negro citizens. We feel that a large part of friction and misunderstanding between the races is due to unjust, inflammatory and misleading headlines, and articles appearing in the daily papers. We suggest that white women include in their local community program a united effort to correct this evil and to secure greater attention to worthy efforts of Negro citizens.

Suffrage.   We regard the ballot as the democratic and orderly method of correcting abuses and protecting the rights of citizens; as the substitute of civilization for violence. As peace loving, law-abiding citizens we believe the ultimate and only guarantee of fair dealing and justice for the Negro, as well as the wholesome development of the whole community, lies in the peaceful, orderly exercise of the franchise by every qualified Negro citizen. We ask therefore, that white women, for the protection of their homes as well as ours indicate their sanction of the ballot for all citizens as representing government by the sober, reasoned and deliberate judgment of all the people.

In these articles offered at your request we are stating frankly and soberly what in our judgement, you as white women may do to correct the ills from which our race has so long suffered, and of which we as a race are perhaps more conscious now than ever. We recall how in the recent days of our nation's peril so many of us worked side by side for the safety of this land and defense of this flag which is ours as it is yours. In that same spirit of unselfishness and sacrifice we offer ourselves to serve again with you in any and every way that a courageous facing of duty may require as you undertake heroically this self-appointed yet God-given task. We deeply appreciate the difficulties that lie before you, but as you undertake these things which are destined to bless us all, we pledge you our faith and loyalty in consecration to God, home and country.

7. Elsie Hill and Florence Kelley Take Opposing Positions on a Proposed Woman's Equal Rights Bill, 1922

Elsie Hill Explains Why Women Should Have Full Legal Equality

The removal of all forms of the subjection of women is the purpose to which the National Woman's Party is dedicated. Its present campaign to remove the discriminations against women in the laws of the United States is but the beginning of its determined effort to secure the freedom of women, an integral part of the struggle

Elsie Hill and Florence Kelley, "Should Women Be Equal Before the Law?" *The Nation*, April 12, 1922, 415–421.

for human liberty for which women are first of all responsible. Its interest lies in the final release of woman from the class of a dependent, subservient being to which early civilization committed her.

The laws of various States at present hold her in that class. They deny her a control of her children equal to the father's; they deny her, if married, the right to her own earnings; they punish her for offences for which men go unpunished; they exclude her from public office and from public institutions to the support of which her taxes contribute. These laws are not the creation of this age, but the fact that they are still tolerated on our statute books and that in some States their removal is vigorously resisted shows the hold of old traditions upon us. Since the passage of the Suffrage Amendment the incongruity of these laws, dating back many centuries, has become more than ever marked. . . .

The National Woman's Party believes that it is a vital social need to do away with these discriminations against women and is devoting its energies to that end. The removal of the discriminations and not the method by which they are removed is the thing upon which the Woman's Party insists. It has under consideration an amendment to the Federal Constitution which, if adopted, would remove them at one stroke, but it is at present endeavoring to secure their removal in the individual States by a blanket bill, which is the most direct State method. For eighty-two years the piecemeal method has been tried, beginning with the married women's property act of 1839 in Mississippi, and no State, excepting Wisconsin, where the Woman's Party blanket bill was passed in June, 1921, has yet finished. . . .

The present program of the National Woman's Party is to introduce its Woman's Equal Rights Bill, or bills attaining the same purpose, in all State legislatures as they convene. It is building up in Washington a great headquarters from which this campaign can be conducted, and it is acting in the faith that the removal of these discriminations from our laws will benefit every group of women in the country, and through them all society

Florence Kelley Explains Her Opposition to Full Legal Equality

"The removal of all forms of subjection of women is the purpose to which the National Woman's Party is dedicated."

A few years ago the Woman's Party counted disfranchisement the form of subjection which must first be removed. Today millions of American women, educated and uneducated, are kept from the polls in bold defiance of the Suffrage Amendment. Every form of subjection suffered by their white sisters they also suffer. Deprivation of the vote is theirs alone among native women. Because of this discrimination all other forms of subjection weigh a hundred fold more heavily upon them. In the family, in the effort to rent or to buy homes, as wage-earners, before the courts, in getting education for their children, in every relation of life, their burden is greater because they are victims of political inequality. How literally are colored readers to understand the words quoted above?

Sex is a biological fact. The political rights of citizens are not properly dependent upon sex, but social and domestic relations and industrial activities are. All modern-minded people desire that women should have full political equality and like opportunity in business and the professions. No enlightened person desires that they should be excluded from jury duty or denied the equal guardianship of children, or that unjust inheritance laws or discriminations against wives should be perpetuated.

The inescapable facts are, however, that men do not bear children, are freed from the burdens of maternity, and are not susceptible, in the same measures as women, to poisons now increasingly characteristic of certain industries, and to the universal poison of fatigue. These are differences so far reaching, so fundamental, that it is grotesque to ignore them. Women cannot be made men by act of the legislature or by amendment of the Federal Constitution. This is no matter of today or tomorrow. The inherent differences are permanent. Women will always need many laws different from those needed by men.

The effort to enact the blanket bill in defiance of all biological differences recklessly imperils the special laws for women as such, for wives, for mothers, and for wage-earners. . . .

Why should wage-earning women be thus forbidden to get laws for their own health and welfare and that of their unborn children? Why should they be made subject to the preferences of wage-earning men? Is not this of great and growing importance when the number of women wage-earners, already counted by millions, increases by leaps and bounds from one census to the next? And when the industries involving exposure to poisons are increasing faster than ever? And when the over-work of mothers is one recognized cause of the high infant death rate? And when the rise in the mortality of mothers in childbirth continues?

If there were no other way of promoting more perfect equality for women, an argument could perhaps be sustained for taking these risks. But why take them when every desirable measure attainable through the blanket bill can be enacted in the ordinary way? . . .

Is the National Woman's Party for or against protective measures for wage-earning women? Will it publicly state whether it is for or against the eight-hour day and minimum-wage commissions for women? Yes or No?

✦ E S S A Y S

Kathryn Kish Sklar of Binghamton University compares the male-dominated American Association of Labor Legislation (AALL) and the (all-female) National Consumers' League (NCL). The NCL emphasized gender difference in seeking reforms beneficial to women and children and accomplished more than the AALL. Sklar is convinced that women were at the very center of the politics and policies that most characterized Progressive reform. Yale history professor Glenda Elizabeth Gilmore argues that by claiming a distinctly female moral authority and an identity as clients of the emerging welfare state, organized black women in North Carolina challenged the racism of the dominant culture. Specifically, they resisted the political disempowerment of blacks that southern whites hoped to achieve by disfranchising black men at the turn of the century, and they foiled plans by southern whites to reserve the benefits of Progressivism solely for their own race. Black women's subversion was masked by outward coopera-tion with whites, especially white women. Unable to claim full civil rights, black women nonetheless gained limited social services for the black community.

Differences in the Political Cultures of Men and Women Reformers During the Progressive Era

KATHRYN KISH SKLAR

The single most important center of reform activity during the Progressive Era could be found at the Charities Building at Twenty-second Street and Fourth Avenue in New York City. Behind a four-story stately exterior, the structure's spacious offices and corridors housed the national headquarters of many leading reform organizations, including the National Child Labor Committee, the National Consumers' League (NCL), and the staffs of *Survey* and *Outlook,* prominent reform periodicals. There men and women reformers constantly interacted, occasionally worked together as members of the same organization, but more often formed ad hoc coalitions across the boundaries of their gender-specific associations. "What's this bunch call itself today?" the editor of *Outlook* asked in March 1906, pausing by a meeting room filled with many familiar faces. The presence of Florence Kelley, head of the National Consumers' League and one of the era's most active coalition builders, may have prompted his affectionate gibe. Less well known in this New York setting was John R. Commons, who had come from the University of Wisconsin to introduce the newly founded American Association for Labor Legislation (AALL). The March 1906 meeting drew together men and women interested in joining the AALL's efforts.

If we had a snapshot of this gathering we might think that it depicted the growing equality of women and men reformers as they met on common ground to work toward shared goals. Yet if we take a longer view and compare the two chief organizations represented that day—the NCL and the AALL—we find a different story, one that locates more importance in their gender-specific differences than in their cross-gender similarities.

This essay explores those differences and what we can discover from them about the political consequences of the social construction of gender during a major watershed in American history between 1900 and 1920. . . . Fundamental social, political, and economic changes in American life between 1890 and 1930 laid the foundation for the modern nation that we know today, but these changes were anything but smooth. By 1890 massive immigration, rapid industrialization, and urbanization had generated the potential for widespread social disorder. Social relationships and values constructed in preindustrial America no longer met the needs of an increasingly diverse and stratified society. Pastoral landscape gave way to sprawling cities and towering smokestacks. Day laborers and an urban proletariat outnumbered the skilled artisans who previously had dominated working-class life. Great wealth accumulated in the hands of a few, their spacious mansions contrasting grotesquely with the crowded tenements of immigrant neighborhoods.

Kathryn Kish Sklar, "Two Political Cultures in the Progressive Era: The National Consumers' League and the American Association for Labor Legislation," in Linda Kerber, Alice Kessler-Harris, and Kathryn Kish Sklar, *U.S. History as Women's History: New Feminist Essays* (Chapel Hill: University of North Carolina Press, 1995), 36–62. Copyright © 1995 by the University of North Carolina Press. Used by permission of the publisher.

Native-born middle-class Americans benefited in many ways from the new entrepreneurial opportunities available within the expanding national economy. For example, they moved into the new white-collar jobs created by the managerial revolution that accompanied vertical economic integration, and they had access to a cornucopia of new consumer goods. But the same forces that enhanced middle-class life also threatened to topple middle-class dominance within American political and social institutions. Politically, they were displaced by urban bosses who drew much of their support from recent immigrants. Socially, their authority diminished when, due to the Catholic and Jewish identities of most "new" immigrants from Southern and Eastern Europe, Protestant churches and clergymen became less important arbiters of social and class relations. Clearly, a new America was emerging, but its connections with earlier patterns of life were unclear. Did the grinding poverty of vast numbers of working people imperil the comforts of middle-class life? What did the social classes owe one another? Was democracy compatible with capitalism? These questions grew in urgency during the 1890s, when struggles between capital and labor repeatedly erupted into bloody armed conflict, and a severe depression crippled the economy.

Out of this crucible a multitude of middle-class organizations emerged to address the nation's problems. Women's organizations were prominent among them. "Progressive reform" (as this movement came to be called) developed three basic thrusts—economic, political, and social. Economic reform, expressed in the Sherman Antitrust Act of 1890, sought to protect the competitiveness of small economic units and curb the growing might of large ones. Political reform, seeking changes in governmental structures and the electoral process, tried to increase governmental responsibility and responsiveness by instituting innovations like the referendum, the recall of public officials, and the popular election of U.S. senators. Political reform also sought to rationalize governmental decision making by creating new administrative units, especially city managers, whose decisions were based more on scientifically based expertise and less on purely political considerations. Last, but not least, social reform expressed concern for the nation's social fabric by focusing on the quality of life among working people.

The efforts of middle-class women were concentrated in political and social reform, but their chief impact lay with the latter. Were working-class children attending schools? Or did their families' economic circumstances require them to work? Were wage-earning women and children exploited through long hours and low wages? Did working-class families have adequate food, housing, and health care? Middle-class women, better educated than ever before, posed and answered these questions through expertise acquired in women's organizations. . . .

My own work . . . emphasizes a "strong state–weak state" paradigm to explain the broad strokes of women's activism and sees class relations as a prominent theme. In this view, women's activism was greater when the state's activism was weaker, and crucial dimensions of women's success were achieved because gendered policies acted as a surrogate for class policies. . . .

To highlight the effects of class and the impact of American traditions of limited government on women's activism, this essay compares two organizations with very similar goals in neighboring niches in the pantheon of Progressive reform, the National Consumers' League and the American Association for Labor Legislation. . . .

Both organizations were part of the remarkable surge of social reform in the Progressive Era that sought the passage and enforcement of laws promoting "the conservation of the human resources of the nation." Founded within a decade of one another, the NCL in 1898, the AALL in 1906, each was responding to the problematic qualities of industrial work in the context of the growing power of the American nation-state. Although both forged cross-class coalitions that embraced organized labor, the heart and soul of each was middle-class. Both claimed to speak for the welfare of the whole society, and to rise above "interest group" or "partisan" politics. Both maintained national offices with a paid staff, drew on professional expertise, lobbied for legislation, and forged coalitions with other reform organizations. While they chiefly worked at the state level, each also became involved in federal legislative campaigns. Their shared goal of creating nationwide minimum standards of labor legislation placed them among the progenitors of the American welfare state. These similarities meant that the two organizations frequently interacted and benefited from one another's activities.

More remarkably, perhaps, the two groups functioned relatively independently. By exploring their differences we learn about the gendered construction of American politics and public policies. This essay explores three dimensions of the differences between the National Consumers' League and the American Association for Labor Legislation: the origins of the two groups, their organizational structures, and their legislative agendas. These differences show that an analysis of women's experience sheds new light on fundamental themes in American history, especially the process by which knowledge and power translated into expanded state responsibility.

The National Consumers' League came into being in 1898, when local consumer leagues in New York, Massachusetts, Pennsylvania, Illinois, Minnesota, New Jersey, and Wisconsin decided to form a national office to coordinate their efforts. The movement began in New York City in 1888 in response to protests by wage-earning women against sweatshop working conditions. Leonora O'Reilly, [who was] a shirtmaker, . . . and others "made an eloquent appeal for help and sympathy from the wealthy and educated women of New-York for their toiling and down-trodden sisters." . . . Two years later, when wage-earning and middle-class women met again to discuss women's working conditions, an organization emerged. Imitating a group formed in London a few months earlier wherein consumers compiled a register similar to the list of "fair houses" published by trade unions, they hoped to enlist "the sympathy and interest of the shopping public" in a "White List" of retail stores that "treated their employees fairly." . . .

With Florence Kelley's appointment as general secretary of the national league in 1899, the NCL assumed leadership of a burgeoning Consumers' League movement. Her early annual reports urged new forms of knowledge and power on league members as a by-product of persisting gender distinctions. "The one great industrial function of women has been that of the purchaser," Kelley wrote in 1899. "All the foods used in private families," as well as furniture, books, and clothing, are "prepared with the direct object in view of being sold to women." To be effective consumers, women had to be organized. "What housewife can detect, alone and unaided, injurious chemicals in her supplies of milk, bread, meat, home remedies?" Goods that women used to make themselves were now produced in unregulated shops and factories. . . . By uniting in the Consumers' League, Kelley promised, women could safeguard their families and at the same time could drive out of the market-place articles produced under conditions "injurious to human life and health."

The NCL thus held out a dual hope of aiding both consumers and producers. This vital link between consumer and producer generated substantial social power for the NCL. It lent personal meaning to the commitment that members made to the organization and connected that meaning to the lives of working people. The NCL not only supplied its members with knowledge of the relationship between consumer and producer, it also sought to transform that knowledge into a moral force. Far from being passive purchasers, consumers actually constructed production, Kelley insisted. Daily choices "as to the bestowal of our means" determined how others "spend their time in making what we buy." Kelley and the NCL sought to politicize those choices by moralizing them: "It is *the* aim of the National Consumers' League to moralize this decision, to gather and make available information which may enable all to decide in the light of knowledge, and to appeal to the conscience, so that the decision when made shall be a righteous one." This old-fashioned word, "righteous," captured the league's stance as a moral arbiter anchored in an earlier era. . . .

. . . [I]n the first five years of the league's existence, Florence Kelley devoted herself to building a grassroots movement of righteously knowledgeable consumers. Between 1900 and 1907 she spent roughly a day on the road for every desk-bound day. Her efforts were rewarded by the spectacular expansion of NCL locals, both in number and location. The NCL's 1901 report mentioned thirty leagues in eleven states; by 1906 they numbered sixty-three in twenty states. . . . Local leagues sustained the national's existence, channeling money, ideas, and the support of other local organizations into the national office. At the same time locals served as vehicles for the implementation of the national's agenda at the state level. Most league members were white, urban, middle-class Protestants, but Jewish women held important positions of leadership. Catholic women became more visible after Cardinal James Gibbons of Baltimore consented to serve as a vice president of a Maryland league, and Bishop J. Regis Canevin of Pittsburgh encouraged members of that city's Ladies Catholic Benevolent Association to join. In 1903 the Massachusetts league undertook a systematic effort "to enlist the wives of farmers through the Farmers' Institutes, Granges, etc."

But "righteous" choices by a multitude of consumers were not in themselves strong enough to counter the economic and cultural forces against which they were arrayed. Women's knowledge could be translated into power only if women forced government to act. . . . The "Consumers' White Label," devised by Florence Kelley and adopted by the NCL as the chief activity during its first decade, became the tactic that wove together women's knowledge, women's power, and expanded state responsibility. It replaced the White List of stores with a strategy that sought to regulate the conditions under which goods were produced, not only the conditions under which they were sold. Both White List and White Label carefully avoided the appearance of blacklisting or secondary boycotts, which, as a tool tried by organized labor, the courts had declared illegal.

The NCL's White Label campaign focused on the manufacture of white muslin underwear. Seeking to affect the conditions under which these goods were produced throughout the country, the league awarded its White Label to manufacturers who shunned child labor and overtime work and abided by state factory regulations. By limiting its attention to "one narrow field of industry," the NCL shined an investigative spotlight on the production of garments that every middle-class consumer needed. . . .

The goods were intimate, but the goal was political. Throughout the Northeast, Midwest, and Pacific West, the White Label ineluctably carried middle-class women into the nitty-gritty of local factory conditions and law enforcement. Did the manufacturer subcontract to home workers in tenements? Were children employed? Was overtime required? Were working conditions safe and sanitary? Were state factory laws violated? How far below the standard set by the consumers' label were their own state laws? Even more technical questions arose when women's organizations came into contact with factory inspectors, bureaus of labor statistics, state legislatures, and courts. Should the state issue licenses for home workers? What was the relationship between illiteracy in child workers and the enforcement of effective child labor laws? . . . Questions recently quite alien to middle-class women held the interest of thousands of the most politically active among them. This was no small accomplishment. State leagues differed in the degree to which they worked with state officials, but wherever they existed they created new civic space in which women used their new knowledge and power to expand state responsibility.

To some degree the NCL's mobilization of middle-class women against the power of unregulated capitalism derived from Florence Kelley herself, . . . a warrior with formidable rhetorical and organizational skills. Yet Kelley's rage for social justice bore fruit because her vision of expanded state responsibility for the welfare of women and children took root within the ranks of "organized womanhood." Her chief means of carrying the NCL's vision to a larger constituency lay through the General Federation of Women's Clubs (GFWC). By 1900 the GFWC had grown to thirty-six state federations of 2,675 clubs with a membership of more than 115,000. At the GFWC biennial meeting that year in Milwaukee, Kelley and others introduced the federation to the work of the Consumers' League at a special evening program, and federation officers "asked the delegates to report favorably to their respective clubs and federations upon the work of the League." The results, Kelley said in 1901, "are still perceptible at our office in the form of invitations for speakers, requests for literature, and a vast increase in correspondence and in the demand for labeled goods in many diverse parts of the country."

Between 1900 and 1902 Kelley chaired the federation's standing committee on "The Industrial Problem as It Affects Women and Children." This committee and its state counterparts were expected "to influence and secure enforcement of labor ordinances and state laws." State federations were asked to "agitate for enforcement of laws, and for amendments to laws, if they were not up to the standard of the Massachusetts labor laws." . . . To individual clubs Kelley sent 2,000 copies of a circular offering a brief but cogent class-based explanation of "the industrial problem as it affects women and children." . . . Arguing that middle-class and working-class women were related to and affected by the same industrial process, one positively, one adversely, this analysis pricked the consciences of middle-class women about the material basis of their leisure and linked their destinies with working women and children.

. . . Where statewide Consumers' Leagues existed, they worked closely with state federations of women's clubs. . . . By 1903 both the National Congress of Mothers and the National American Woman Suffrage Association had created child labor committees, and Florence Kelley headed both. . . . Standing between capital and labor, a grassroots phalanx of consumers became thoroughly implicated in the conditions under which goods were produced.

Having built her constituency, Kelley in 1906 shifted away from the White Label into a campaign for the legal limitation of women's hours. . . . Throughout the industrializing world, reformers and trade unionists alike viewed shorter working hours as the key to the improvement of working-class standards of living; for trade unionists, shorter hours were second in importance only to the right to unionize. . . . Yet only a small, well-organized portion of the labor force, mostly skilled men, could achieve the benefits of shorter hours. Others, including most female and child workers and the vast majority of unskilled male workers, . . . endured twelve-hour, fourteen-hour, or even longer working days that imperiled their health and undercut their ability to rise above their impoverished circumstances. . . .

Despite the need that reformers saw for legislative regulation of hours or wages, such statutes were very difficult to achieve in the United States, primarily because American political institutions circumscribed the power of legislatures by investing courts with the power to rule legislative enactments unconstitutional. . . . [T]he harsh conditions of laissez-faire capitalism were preserved by political traditions that defended the freedom of employers to devise the terms on which they employed workers. Between 1900 and 1920 the National Consumers' League circumvented those traditions by invoking gender-specific justifications for legislation designed to benefit working women. The league and its supporters argued that gender-specific legislation was constitutional because it utilized the state's police powers to preserve health and morals. First, they asserted, since women workers tended to be young and unskilled and therefore did not have trade unions to represent them in negotiating better working conditions directly with their employers, they were unable to protect themselves, so it fell to the state to safeguard their health and morals through legislation. Second, they contended that because most women workers later became mothers, their injuries through overwork or low wages could produce birth defects or lead to prostitution, each of which affected the welfare of the whole community and should be prevented through legislation. These arguments embodied nineteenth-century notions of gender differences, which women reformers like Kelley shared when it was pragmatically effective for them to do so, but just as easily evaded when it helped their cause. Most important, these assertions earned them the support of constituencies beyond the reach of their own organizations, including judges and working men.

Responding to such arguments, nineteen states passed some form of hours laws for women by 1906. That year the NCL successfully defended an Oregon ten-hour law for women before the state supreme court. After the U.S. Supreme Court upheld the Oregon statute in 1908, the NCL led a campaign that established hours laws for women in twenty-one more states by 1919. . . .

The American Association for Labor Legislation offers a compelling contrast to the NCL's rallying of middle-class women. AALL leaders treated knowledge as professional, not personal. They exercised power through the prestige of their position and expertise, not through numbers. And, rather than seeing government as a democratic extension of the popular will, the AALL viewed the state as a vehicle of enlightened administration. This set the association on a different political path from the NCL and made it a frustrating ally.

The AALL grew . . . under the leadership of John Commons, Richard Ely, and other economists. . . . From the start, the AALL was an elite group, "composed of experts and officials as well as public spirited citizens." Article III of the constitution limited membership to those who were "elected by the Executive Committee."

In contrast to the NCL's mass mobilization for direct consumer action, the AALL's mandate was grander but more vague: "the conservation of the human resources of the nation." But for what purpose? An early AALL statement answered this question by declaring its commitment to both labor and capital, to the "conservation of human resources in the mutual interest of employer and employee by non-partisan legislation." Ever "objective," the AALL viewed partisanship as its antithesis. Yet without a political constituency and the partisanship that came with it, the AALL had much greater difficulty than the NCL in forging an effective political agenda.

Whereas the NCL treated local branches as its main arteries of power, the AALL tolerated local branches only briefly. . . . By 1916, . . . they had all lapsed. . . . The AALL, Commons concluded, "occupies the unique position of an organization to promote legislation by means of scientific investigation." Societies "equipped for the work of propaganda and political agitation . . . must necessarily look to us for the scientific basis that will make their agitation effective and keep it on solid ground." This "work of information" did not require local branches. . . .

. . . Yet at the same time that the AALL cleared its decks for "the work of information," Andrews and Commons recognized the need to engage in more substantive activities and pursue its secondary mandate of recommending particular forms of legislation. . . . [T]he AALL placed compensation for workplace injuries at the top of its agenda. . . . In 1911 ten states passed some form of compensation, and by 1915 the number had grown to thirty-three. Yet the AALL experience with workmen's compensation differed in one crucial respect from the NCL's contemporaneous campaign to reduce hours and raise wages for working women. Although it claimed a leadership position by virtue of its "scientific" superiority, in fact the AALL often took second place to a group that sought to represent the joint interests of workers and employers, the National Civic Federation (NCF). Founded in 1900 to pursue arbitration and mediation between capital and labor, the NCF began working on workmen's compensation in 1908. By 1910 its Department on Compensation attracted the participation of 600 representative employers, attorneys, labor leaders, insurance experts, economists, state officials, and members of state compensation commissions. The NCF's model laws on workmen's compensation, although they often favored employers, became the chief focal point for discussion among state legislatures, employers, and representatives of organized labor because they were seen as efforts to combine the interests of labor and employers. For example, the NCF's model compensation law of 1914 was sent to all the affiliated bodies of the AFL and to 25,000 employers. The AALL lacked this reach into grassroots constituencies and failed to dominate the issue on the basis of scientific expertise alone. . . .

The AALL's ability to shape public policy was severely limited by its failure to form an effective relationship with organized labor—the most obvious group capable of serving as its grassroots equivalent to the NCL's women's organizations. Whereas trade union organizing was an important secondary or indirect goal of the NCL—for example, Kelley thought that shorter hours and higher wages would increase the number of women who joined trade unions, and she worked closely with the WTUL [Women's Trade Union League]—this was never the case with the AALL. "The active support of organized labor would probably tend to strengthen the work of your association," Morris Hillquit wrote Andrews in 1911, but Andrews explained to an AALL member in 1913, "while I am a firm believer in the necessity for trade unions, yet my conclusion is that the greatest permanent social gains have come and will continue to come from remedial legislation, slow and conservative as this movement sometimes appears and is." He expressed special concern for "the cause of the unskilled worker," which seemed "particularly hopeless" through organization. . . .

Knowledge, power, and expanding state responsibility meant different things to the NCL and the AALL and flowed in different channels. One practical effect of those differences can be seen in the relationship of each organization to the nation's first minimum wage campaign, 1909–17. . . .

Viewed by one advocate as "the keystone of the arch in labor legislation," minimum wage laws were integrally related to other reform efforts aimed at the working poor, especially to hours legislation, and antisweatshop measures. More explicitly intended as a means of redistributing wealth than any previous labor laws, minimum wage legislation expressed a new form of social justice that aimed to establish a floor beneath which wages could not fall. Reformers hoped that such a floor would end the downward spiral of wages wherein sweatshop employers paid low wages to workers, who then required support from relief or charity, thereby indirectly providing employers with subsidies that enabled them to lower wages further. . . .

As early as 1899 Kelley hoped "to include a requirement as to minimal wages" in the NCL's White Label, . . . but the path to an American equivalent did not seem clear until she and other Consumers' League leaders in 1908 attended the First International Conference of Consumers' Leagues, in Geneva, where they learned about the proposed British wage boards. Almost immediately on her return Kelley established her leadership in what became an enormously successful campaign. First she raided the languishing AALL branches for male supporters. . . . In 1911 Kelley organized a "special Committee on Minimum Wage Boards" in the NCL. . . .

Also in 1911 the Massachusetts Consumers' League, the Women's Trade Union League, the United Textile Workers, and the Massachusetts Association for Labor Legislation all lobbied for the creation of a state commission to investigate minimum wage legislation. But the power to shape the proposal fell to the NCL when Mary Dewson, a Consumers' League activist, was appointed the commission's secretary, and Elizabeth Glendower, one of the commission's five members and a close friend of Kelley, . . . funded much of the commission's work. The high point of the campaign occurred in 1913, when eight additional states passed minimum wage laws for women: California, Colorado, Minnesota, Nebraska, Oregon, Utah, Washington, and Wisconsin.

Relying on grassroots support from women's organizations, the NCL's leadership in this campaign was augmented by organized labor and conscientious employers who sought to eliminate unscrupulous competition. Although the NCL could not count on universal backing from women or men trade unionists, cooperation with the Women's Trade Union League and with many state federations of labor produced a much smoother alliance than the relationship the AALL had forged with the national

American Federation of Labor. The political stance of organized labor varied from state to state, but whereas the AFL officially opposed wage legislation (arguing that the minimum could become the maximum), the NCL promoted minimum wage as an agent of both class and gender realignment. . . .

. . . In some respects the wage campaign reinforced the gendered status quo. . . . Reformers had to squeeze their arguments through the only constitutional loophole through which the courts might sustain wage laws—that low wages affected the health and morals of (young) women and therefore were properly subject to intervention under the police powers of the state. . . .

During this arduous campaign Kelley received almost no help from the AALL. . . . [T]he AALL . . . opposed minimum wage legislation as premature. . . .

Until the passage of the Fair Labor Standards Act (FLSA) of 1938, all state minimum wage laws and many state laws regulating working hours in the United States applied only to women. Not until 1942, when the U.S. Supreme Court approved the constitutionality of the FLSA, did the eight-hour day and the minimum wage become part of the social contract for most American workers. The class-bridging activism of middle-class women forged the way with these fundamental reforms. . . .

. . . [T]he activism of NCL members can best be seen as the culmination of nineteenth-century trends, many of which have not survived into the late twentieth century. Moral notions about public responsibility for the welfare of women and children rank high among these. Because they accentuated gender differences, today these notions seem outdated and ineffective. Yet as this comparison between the NCL and the AALL shows, through grassroots mobilization women's organizations succeeded in accomplishing reforms that male expertise and power could not initiate. Women did not reside at the margins of progressive social reform; they occupied its center.

The agency of women and the agency of men were shaped by the gendered definitions of their opportunities for political activism in the Progressive Era. Ultimately, this comparison suggests that no corner of American political life was unconnected to the system of gendered meanings that informed the ongoing process by which civic activity was molded. The more we understand about American women, the more we understand about American history.

Diplomats to the White Community: African American Women in Progressive-Era North Carolina

GLENDA ELIZABETH GILMORE

After disfranchisement, "the Negro," white supremacists were fond of saying, was removed from politics. But even as African American men lost their rights, the political underwent a transformation. As state and local governments began to provide social services, an embryonic welfare state emerged. Henceforth, securing teetertotters and playgrounds, fighting pellagra, or replacing a dusty neighborhood track with an oil-coated road would require political influence. Thus, at the same time that whites restricted the number of voters by excluding African Americans, the state created a new public role: that of the client who drew on its services. Contemporaries and historians named this paradoxical period the Progressive Era.

From the debris of disfranchisement, black women discovered fresh approaches to serving their communities and crafted new tactics designed to dull the blade of white supremacy. The result was a greater role for black women in the interracial public sphere. As long as they could vote, it was black men who had most often brokered official state power and made interracial political contacts. After disfranchisement, however, the political culture black women had created through thirty years of work in temperance organizations, Republican Party aid societies, and churches furnished both an ideological basis and an organizational structure from which black women could take on those tasks. After black men's banishment from politics, North Carolina's black women added a network of women's groups that crossed denominational—and later party—lines and took a multi-issue approach to civic action. In a nonpolitical guise, black women became the black community's diplomats to the white community.

In the first twenty years of the century, the state, counties, and municipalities began to intervene in affairs that had been private in the past. Now, government representatives killed rabid dogs and decided where traffic should stop. They forced bakers to put screens on their windows and made druggists stop selling morphine. They told parents when their children could work and when their children must go to school. As they regulated, they also dispensed. Public health departments were formed, welfare agencies turned charity into a science, and juvenile court systems began to separate youthful offenders of both sexes from seasoned criminals. Public education expanded exponentially and became increasingly uniform across the state. The intersection of government and individual expanded from the polling place to the street corner, from the party committee meeting to the sickbed.

Black women might not be voters, but they could be clients, and in that role they could become spokespeople for and motivators of black citizens. They could claim a distinctly female moral authority and pretend to eschew any political motivation. The deep camouflage of their leadership style—their womanhood—helped them remain invisible as they worked toward political ends. At the same time, they could deliver not votes but hands and hearts through community organization: willing workers in city cleanup campaigns, orderly children who complied with state educational requirements, and hookworm-infested people eager for treatment at public health fairs. . . .

. . . In comparing black women's progressivism to white women's progressivism, one must be cautious at every turn because black and white women had vastly different relationships to power. To cite just one example, white middle-class women lobbied to obtain services *from* their husbands, brothers, and sons; black women lobbied to obtain services *for* their husbands, brothers, and sons.

Black women's task was to try to force those white women who plunged into welfare efforts to recognize class and gender similarities across racial lines. To that end, they surveyed progressive white women's welfare initiatives and political style and found that both afforded black women a chance to enter the political. They had two purposes in mind. First, they would try to hold a place for African Americans in the ever-lengthening queue forming to garner state services. Second, they would begin to clear a path for the return of African Americans to the ballot box. . . .

Given the expansion of the public sphere and whites' attempts to exclude African Americans from new state and municipal programs, black women's religious work took on new meaning. In the wake of disfranchisement, African American men and women turned to their churches for solace and for political advice. Yet many black men now feared the potentially explosive mixture of politics and religion in turbulent times. Ministers of all denominations began to circumscribe their own discourse and to monitor their flocks' debate. A Baptist minister declared that such "perilous times" made even "preaching of the pure gospel embarrassing, if not dangerous."

Using women's church organizations to press for community improvement incurred less risk than preaching inflammatory sermons on civil rights. . . . While white political leaders kept their eyes on black men's electoral political presence and absence, black women organized and plotted an attack just outside of their field of vision. They began by transforming church missionary societies into social service agencies. . . .

. . . The tasks of black women's home missionary societies read like a Progressive Era primer. They organized mothers' clubs and community cleanup days. They built playgrounds and worked for public health and temperance. Marshaling arguments from the social purity and social hygiene movements, they spoke on sexual dangers outside of marriage. To achieve their goals, southern black women entered political space, appearing before local officials and interacting with white bureaucrats.

Even as they undertook this "peculiar work," black women knew that they must avoid charges of political interference. . . . Taking a lesson from the high price of black men's former public presence, capitalizing on the divisions among whites over the allocation of new services to African Americans, and concerned about gender politics among African Americans, black women reformers depended on not being seen at all by whites who would thwart their programs and not being seen as political by whites who would aid them. They used their invisibility to construct a web of social service and civic institutions that remained hidden from and therefore unthreatening to whites.

Women's organizations within religious bodies were not new, but they became more important, expanded, and reordered their priorities after disfranchisement. For example, the Women's Baptist Home Mission Convention of North Carolina began in 1884, primarily as an arm for evangelical work. At the turn of the century, the group employed [Sallie] Mial as a full-time missionary in the state. In this capacity, she organized local women's groups and founded Sunshine Bands and What-I-Can Circles for girls. Mial explained her work to the African American Baptist men this way: "We teach the women to love their husbands, to be better wives and mothers, to make the homes better." At the same time, church workers taught Baptist women lobbying and administrative skills. One woman remembered, "From this organization we learn[ed] what is meant to be united." Another observed, "Many of our women are being strengthened for the Master's use." Along the way, the organization began calling itself the Baptist State Educational Missionary Convention.

Making "the homes better" covered a wide range of community activities. Good homes rhetoric was, of course, promulgated by whites to justify white supremacy;

southern educational reformers used depictions of debasement, for example, to justify industrial education. Black women could use this discourse for their own purposes, and they grasped the opportunity it gave them to bargain for the state services that were beginning to improve whites' lives but were denied to African Americans. As Margaret Murray Washington put it, "Where the homes of colored people are comfortable and clean, there is less disease, less sickness, less death, and less danger to others [that is, whites]." Good homes, however, required good government. "We are not likely to [build good homes] if we know that the pavements will be built just within a door of ours and suddenly stop," Washington warned. Turning from the ballot box to the home as the hope of the future was canny political strategy that meshed nicely with the new welfare role of the state, and it explicitly increased women's importance at a time when women across the nation campaigned to extend their influence through volunteer activities and the professionalization of social work.

The elevation of the home to the centerpiece of African American life sprang from several sources. Certainly it resonated with a nationwide Progressive Era movement for better homes, particularly among immigrant enclaves in crowded northern cities. But among North Carolina's African Americans, the movement's roots reached closer to home. Religious convictions that had inspired nineteenth-century black women who did church work continued to serve as moral imperatives to bring families to godly lives. African American women tried to eliminate grist for the white supremacy mill by abolishing the images of the immoral black woman and the barbaric black home. Moreover, now that voting required literacy, education was political, and it began at home. Able to tap into the larger context of rhetoric on better homes and the importance of literacy, black women expanded their roles, first in the church, then in the community as a whole. . . .

. . . African American women's denominational groups created a vast network throughout the South, virtually invisible to whites. It is helpful to see the groups as cells through which information and ideas could pass quickly. The invisibility of black women's work suited them. They did not want to antagonize their husbands by making a power play within their denominations—the men in the church were already uneasy about their activities. They did not want to endanger their families by drawing attention to themselves. They did not want to risk interference from whites by being overtly political. Better to call social work "missionary work"; better to gather 100,000 Baptist women in a movement to produce good homes. If such activities resulted in organizing the community to lobby for better schools, swamp drainage, or tuberculosis control, no white could accuse them of meddling in politics.

From these bases, women forged interdenominational links. North Carolinian Anna Julia Cooper, by then living in Washington, D.C., was present at the creation of the National Association of Colored Women's Clubs in 1896. Delegates to that first meeting represented a wide range of women's denominational organizations, interdenominational unions such as the WCTU and the King's Daughters, and secular civic leagues. . . . North Carolina black women founded a statewide federation of clubs in 1909 and elected Marie Clinton president. . . .

Activist black women also met at frequent regional sociological conferences. The Progressive Era trend toward organization, discussion, and investigation blossomed in these huge confabulations. Mary Lynch went to the Negro Young People's

Christian and Educational Congress in Atlanta in 1902, where she delivered the address, "The Woman's Part in the Battle against Drink." There she met Charlotte Hawkins, a young Boston student who had just moved to Sedalia, North Carolina, and banker Maggie L. Walker of Richmond. She also renewed ties with Lucy Thurman of the national WCTU and Josephine Silone-Yates, president of the National Association of Colored Women's Clubs. The Woman's Day theme was "No race can rise higher than its women."

As women were building vast voluntary networks, public school teaching was becoming an increasingly feminized profession. In 1902, the number of black women teachers and black men teachers was almost the same: 1,325 women and 1,190 men. The percentage of black women teachers exactly matched that of white women teachers: 52 percent. By 1919, 78 percent of black teachers were women, and 83 percent of the white teachers were women. . . . The increasing number of black women teachers was a result . . . of declining wages. In addition to driving black men from the profession, low wages contributed to a difference in the marital status of white and black women teachers. White women teachers were almost always single. Many black women teachers were married women who remained partially dependent upon their husbands' income. . . .

   Even without their own progressive agenda, African American women teachers would have found schools to be an increasingly politicized setting. After 1900, the importance of literacy for voting and the movement toward industrial education commanded the attention of both the black and white community, and perennial battles over allocating taxes for education turned the black schoolhouse into a lightning rod, propelling female teachers into the political sphere, for better or for worse. . . .

   The racial inequities of school funding have been well documented, but the efforts of black students and teachers to keep their schools from starving cannot be celebrated enough. Even in the best black schools, for example, the Charlotte graded school, there were few desks and "two and sometimes three small pupils sat crowded in a wide seat." The state gave so little—inadequate furniture, a meager library—but teachers made so little go so far. "There was much blackboard space in a room which was a good thing," Rose Leary Love recalled. "At the time, blackboards were not termed visual aids, but they really were the most important available ones." The teachers used them to explain lessons; the pupils used them in lieu of paper. In the state's eyes, African Americans were not training to be full citizens; they needed no civics classes, no maps, no copy of the Constitution, no charts on "How a Bill Becomes a Law." That left teachers on their own to define citizenship. Somehow they did. Teachers chose talented students to "draw the National Flag or the State Flag on the blackboard," Love remembered. "These flags were assigned a place of honor on the board and they became a permanent fixture in the room for the year. Pupils were careful not to erase the flags when they cleaned the blackboards." Despite whites' efforts to rob African Americans of their country, black teachers taught each day under the flag.

   A centralized state bureaucracy grew to oversee the curriculum in African American schools. In 1905, Charles L. Coon, a white man who had recently been superintendent of Salisbury's schools and secretary of the General Education Board, accepted the newly created position of superintendent of the state colored normal schools. According to his boss, Coon's oversight would "send out into the counties each a larger number of negro teachers, equipped with the knowledge and the training, and filled with the right ideals necessary for the . . . most practical, sensible and useful education of the negro race." By putting African American normal schools under the control of a white man, the state hoped to produce teachers who embraced industrial education and to force the private African American normal schools out of business.

Ironically, state oversight created controversy rather than quelling it primarily because of Coon's independent personality. An amateur statistician who often challenged authority, Coon created a furor by proving that the state spent less on African American education than the taxes blacks paid in. In fact, Coon produced figures to prove that black tax dollars educated white children. Coon's boss, James Y. Joyner, distanced himself from Coon's argument and decried him to Josephus Daniels. But Aycock admitted that Coon spoke the truth. . . .

Whites quarreled a great deal more over funding black education than they did over its content, which white educators overwhelmingly agreed should be based on the Hampton model.* Very little industrial training could begin, however, without spending dollars on equipment and tools. Ironically, it proved more expensive to build a bookcase than to explain an algebra problem on a broken piece of slate. Outside help would be critical. As a few dollars began to trickle down, black women teachers learned to exploit whites' support of industrial education. The Negro State Teachers Association recognized in 1903 that "the industrial and manual idea . . . is a much felt need in our public and private schools, since the development of negro womanhood is one of its immediate results." At the same time that black women recognized the potential of industrial education to improve home life, they began to clamor for a greater voice in its administration. When officials from the Rockefeller-funded General Education Board and local white educators met with black teachers in 1913, Charlotte Hawkins Brown told the group flatly that since women made up the majority of rural teachers, industrial education would fail unless philanthropists and white educators listened more closely to black women's suggestions and rewarded them for their efforts. African American women's tilting of the industrial education ideology was slight but important. While paying lip service to the ideal of producing servants for white people, black women quietly turned the philosophy into a self-help endeavor and the public schools into institutions resembling social settlement houses. Cooking courses became not only vocational classes but also nutrition courses where students could eat hot meals. Sewing classes may have turned out some dressmakers and cobbling classes some cobblers, but they had the added advantage of clothing poor pupils so that they could attend school more regularly.

The Negro Rural School Fund, a philanthropy administered by the Rockefeller Foundation's General Education Board, gave the state's black women teachers the basic tools they needed to incorporate social work into the public school system. Begun in 1909 as the Anna T. Jeanes Fund, it paid more than half of the salary of one industrial supervising teacher on the county level. County boards of education

---

*The Hampton model was a type of school for blacks and Native Americans that emphasized industrial, manual, and agricultural education. Academic instruction was of secondary importance.

paid the rest. The Jeanes supervisor traveled to all of the African American schools in a county, ostensibly to teach industrial education. In 1913, the General Education Board offered to pay the salary of a state supervisor of rural elementary schools in North Carolina to oversee the thirteen Jeanes teachers already in place and to expand the work to other counties. In naming the supervisor, the board had a hidden agenda: northern philanthropists did not trust southern state administrators to allocate and spend their grants wisely. They wanted a white man loyal to them in state government, a professional who could walk the tightwire of interracial relations, placating obstreperous legislators at the same time that he kept a keen eye on black industrial curricula. They found their man in Nathan C. Newbold, who had been superintendent of public schools in Washington, North Carolina. . . .

Nonconfrontational and optimistic, as state agent for the Negro Rural School Fund Newbold became an extraordinary voice for African American education. He quickly persuaded more county boards of education to fund half of a Jeanes teacher's salary at the same time that he forged strong alliances with the incumbent Jeanes teachers. By the end of his first year, twenty-two counties employed Jeanes teachers, who found themselves in the often awkward position of having to report to both Newbold and the county superintendent. Newbold appointed a black woman, Annie Wealthy Holland, as his assistant. The Jeanes board's initial expenditure of $2,144 in the state in 1909 grew to $12,728 by 1921. . . .

Faced with local white administrators' neglect, Jeanes teachers had an enormous amount of responsibility. Sarah Delany, the Jeanes supervisor in Wake County, recalled, "I was just supposed to be in charge of domestic science, but they made me do the county superintendent's work. So, I ended up actually in charge of all the colored schools in Wake County, North Carolina, although they didn't pay me to do that or give me any credit." Delany, raised as a "child of privilege" on the Saint Augustine's College campus, stayed overnight with parents in rural areas, where she encountered not just a lack of indoor plumbing but a condition even more appalling to a citified house guest: no outhouse. Delany went to her pupils' homes to teach their parents how to "cook, clean, [and] eat properly," and when General Education Board officials visited North Carolina in 1913, she agreed to serve on the statewide committee to establish a cooking curriculum. She painted schoolrooms, taught children to bake cakes, raised money to improve buildings, and organized Parent Unions. Jeanes teachers also transformed their students into entrepreneurs. In 1915, their Home-Makers Clubs, Corn Clubs, and Pig Clubs involved over 4,000 boys and girls and 2,000 adults in 32 counties. The clubs were intended to teach farming, of course, but they also enabled poor rural African Americans to make money on their produce. The students raised more than $6,000 selling fruits and vegetables that year.

Jeanes teachers saw themselves as agents of progressivism, and they combined public health work with their visits to schools and homes. . . . Carrie Battle, the Jeanes supervisor in Edgecombe County, . . . visited the homes of pupils across the county to organize a Modern Health Crusade against tuberculosis in the schools. Moving from school to school with a set of scales, she would not weigh ill-groomed boys and girls, nor would she weigh anyone in a dirty schoolroom. She made the children promise to clean up the room, bathe, use individual drinking cups, and sleep with the windows open. . . . Soon Battle had established Modern Health Clubs in every school and a total of 4,029 children enrolled as Crusaders. Her work attracted attention from the white community, and she began to cooperate with the white Red Cross nurse to produce public health programs. Many of Battle's students had never been farther than ten miles from their homes. She brought the world to them through regularly scheduled visits of the "Moving Picture Car," a truck equipped with projection equipment used to screen films on health education.

Jeanes teachers also built schools across the state—schools for which the state took credit and of which the counties took possession. Weary of asking for their fair share of tax dollars, black communities simply built their own schools and gave them to the county. For example, in the academic year 1915–16, thirty-two black schools were built and thirty improved at a total cost of $29,000. African Americans contributed over $21,000 of the total: $15,293 in cash and the equivalent of $5,856 in labor. . . .

The next year, the Julius Rosenwald Committee, a Chicago-based philanthropy, appropriated $6,000 to stimulate public school building in rural areas of North Carolina. Although this amount was a great deal less than African Americans were already raising annually to build their own schools, Rosenwald grants often embarrassed state and county officials into contributing funds for building black schools. . . .

The unique role of the Jeanes teacher points up the distinctiveness of southern progressivism and provides clues to the reasons for historians' difficulties in finding and understanding it. The Jeanes teacher had no counterpart in the North. She did social work on the fly, leaving neither permanent settlement houses nor case files behind through which one might capture her experience. She understood the latest public health measures and passed them along even in the most remote areas. She fought to obtain Rosenwald school money to build schools that were airy and modern, then turned them into clubhouses in the evenings. By establishing Parent Unions, she provided a new organizational center for black communities. She lobbied school boards and county commissions for supplies and support. And she accomplished all of this while trying to remain invisible to the white community at large. To locate the progressive South, one must not just visit New South booster Henry Grady in Atlanta but find as well a schoolroom full of cleanly scrubbed Modern Health Crusaders, lined up for hot cereal cooked by the older girls in Rosenwald kitchens, each Crusader clutching the jelly jar that served as his or her very own glass.

By 1910, African American women in the state realized the need to create a united front to lobby local governmental officials and to improve civic life. Connected on the state level through the North Carolina Association of Colored Women's Clubs, these organizations would have to bring together on the local level denominational women's groups, interface with public school programs, and marshal all of the experience and resources that women had acquired in the past decade. The Salisbury Colored Women's Civic League exemplifies such an organization. . . .

Women from all walks of life joined the Civic League. As Rose Aggrey's daughter recalled, "There wasn't poor and rich . . . not a rigid difference between people. The difference between people was those who had training and those who didn't." Her mother, an active Civic Leaguer, had a knack for getting "women of all backgrounds together." The league's rolls included the wife of an AME Zion bishop, a dressmaker, a teacher, a laundress, a domestic worker, and a woman "from the other side of town—not trained, whose husband was in trouble, but a fine Christian woman." Members embraced a wide range of religious denominations— Mrs. A. Croom was a Baptist minister's wife, Lizzie Crittendon an Episcopalian, Lucy Spaulding a Presbyterian, and Mary Lynch and Victoria Richardson members of the AME Zion Church—and they put the agendas of their women's missionary societies into action in the Civic League. . . .

Many of the Civic League's projects involved interaction with white women. In fact, the impetus for the league's formation appears to have been an interracial community cleanup day, a project initiated by white club women throughout the state. Whites had tried to organize cleanup efforts before 1913, but "the most vigorous urging failed to stir the Negroes to action." It was not until they recruited Lula Kelsey to meet with a white male civic leader that plans for a joint cleanup day went forward. White Salisbury citizens finally realized that they could not coerce civic action among African Americans and that "without a Negro leader it is probable that the movement would have been a flat failure." The city donated twelve barrels of lime, a disinfectant, and the Civic League supervised its distribution. The city's two African American doctors spoke to the women on sanitation and disease.

Cleanup days evoked images of African Americans in the traditional role of servants, but they also put white people to work at servants' tasks: raking yards, whitewashing fences, carting trash, and improving housing. This made them a perfect place for black women to launch interracial forays. Moreover, on cleanup days, the entire community expected white landlords to improve their rental houses in black neighborhoods. As segregation rigidified, even the most prosperous black families found it difficult to buy decent housing, and they often had to tolerate living in neglected white-owned rental housing at close quarters. In the absence of building standards and housing laws, community cleanup days focused white attention on slumlords while also organizing black neighbors around a positive self-help project.

As knowledge of disease transmission grew, whites initiated cleanup days to protect themselves from the peril they imagined they were in due to their poor black neighbors' lack of sanitary measures. Typhoid spread by flies and tuberculosis by uncleanliness, and both represented public health emergencies in the South in the 1910s. It is difficult to imagine just how prevalent and problematic flies were in urban areas with poor sanitation or how thoroughly they invaded homes before screening. In a sketch entitled, "You better eat before you read this," Eula Dunlap recalled that people sold the contents of their privies for fertilizer, and it was spread on fields and gardens, with dire consequences. The flies were so thick inside homes that if someone was sick in the summer, a family member had to fan constantly. Babies wore fly netting draped around them as they played outdoors in the summertime. The death rate during "fly season" soared dramatically in the black community and increased modestly in the white community. In reality, germs traveled to both communities, but better health care for whites limited their mortality rate.

The fly carried more than disease; it also carried the germ of interracial cooperation. Since flies knew nothing about the color line, they flew back and forth across it with no regard for class standing or race. As white interracialist Lily Hammond put it in her essay, "The Democracy of the Microbe," "The [white] club women came upon Christian principles of racial adjustment without realizing that they were dealing with racial problems at all. They simply started out with common sense as their guide and cleanliness as their goal." In order to eradicate flies, one had to pick up garbage and extend sanitary sewage treatment to both the white and the black community. Such a cause fit perfectly into African American women's better homes movement. . . .

These efforts, begun through voluntary club work, aided the institutionalization of charity after 1910. In the following decade, large cities in North Carolina established Associated Charities branches to formalize and coordinate social service casework. In cities that were large enough, as in Charlotte, African Americans formed auxiliaries of the Associated Charities, presided over by leading black club women. In Salisbury, the relationship was more informal, and Lula Kelsey became an unpaid social worker for the Associated Charities. The Civic League joined the Associated Charities in 1917. Soon Civic Leaguers passed out pledge cards for the Associated Charities' annual fund-raising campaign throughout the African American community. Thereafter, when a needy case came to the attention of the Civic League, they referred it to the Associated Charities. The Associated Charities used the league to determine whether a person seeking help really needed it and asked Kelsey to perform home studies on applicants. Kelsey's son recalled that whenever an African American came for help to the Associated Charities office, the white social worker there would telephone Lula Kelsey before she acted.

With disfranchisement, African American women became diplomats to the white community, and contact with white women represented a vital, though difficult, part of that mission. As white women gained more power in social service organizations and public education during the first two decades of the century, they began to exercise growing influence in the public sector. Contact between black and white women came about not because the two groups felt gender solidarity but because white women controlled the resources that black women needed to improve their communities. What interracial contact meant to white club women is more confusing, as it must have been to the white club women themselves. Just as their mothers had met educated, middle-class black women for the first time in the 1880s in the Woman's Christian Temperance Union, after the white supremacy campaign, many white club women got their first glimpse of organized African American women when they planned cleanup days together. Such meetings may have been the first time a white woman had ever spoken to [a] black woman who was not a servant. From these contacts, a handful of white and black women formed cooperative working partnerships to further mutual goals, as did Lula Kelsey and the white Association Charities social worker. But those partnerships were rare. To some, they represented a necessary step toward accomplishing their own civic goals; to others, they offered some fulfillment of religious imperatives. Beyond that, most white women probably did not give much thought to the meaning of their contacts with black women.

Yet however sporadic and confusing women's interracial contacts were, they represented a crack in the mortar of the foundation of white supremacy. White club women came to know more about the black community and its women leaders and became less pliant in the hands of male politicians who attempted to manipulate them to further the gendered rhetoric of white supremacy. The same process had taken place in the 1880s when white temperance women ignored the dire warnings of men and planned local-option campaigns together with black women. But imperialist rhetoric, scientific racism, the Democrats' white supremacy campaign, and women's lack of direct access to the political process had ended those contacts. This time, things would be different. This time, the local contacts between black and white club women had a chance to take root and grow.

In addition to fostering useful contact between women of both races, community cleanup work earned certain black women power within their neighborhoods and brought them into contact with city officials. The Civic League did not just hold cleanup days; it inspected homes afterward, counseled residents who did not follow sanitary practices, and reported them to the city if they did not comply with sanitary guidelines. The membership card of the Civic League required the bearer to pledge to "improve the sanitary condition of the home in which I live" and to use "lime to disinfect and whitewash." Upon presentation, the bearer of the card could claim one gallon of lime, "Given by City; distributed by COLORED WOMEN'S CIVIC LEAGUE." This public/private partnership across racial lines was a shaky one, but organized African American women quickly capitalized on it.

White men in local government came to know Lula Kelsey, Rose Aggrey, Mary Lynch, and the other leaguers as spokespeople for the black community—as women who could get things done. The women proceeded as if the city owed them a fair hearing in return for their civic work. Shortly after the first cleanup day, the league voted to send a representative to speak with the city administration about "helping with the cemetery," and by the next month, Lula Kelsey announced to the group that she had met with the mayor and he had "promised that it would be taken care of better in the future." . . .

. . . The city lacked a public playground for its African American children, and the Civic League lobbied city officials to provide one. . . . Likewise, the women participated in "maternalist politics" by sponsoring "baby day," when mothers could bring their babies to a meeting for a doctor's advice. Civic League women centered much of their effort around the public schools. They held fairs and paper drives to raise money for the industrial department of the graded schools, and a teacher who was a member of the league organized a Junior Civic League at her school. The women visited the city jail regularly, ministered to a chain gang, and began an outreach program at the county home for the indigent.

By 1917, Salisbury's African American women had two mechanisms in place to gain a hearing before both private and public manifestations of the state. First, contacts with white club women provided entry into the growing private social welfare system. Since black club women had met the white club women involved in social service, the Civic League could join the Associated Charities and then use that membership to direct the flow of aid to the African American community. Second, with husbands and brothers virtually disfranchised, diplomatic women could go in their places to the mayor and county commissioners to lobby for city services and, once there, cast their mission in female-coded, and unthreatening, terms.

As much as southern whites plotted to reserve progressivism for themselves, and as much as they schemed to alter the ill-fitting northern version accordingly, they failed. African American women embraced southern white progressivism, reshaped it, and sent back a new model that included black power brokers and grass roots activists. Evidence of southern African American progressivism is not to be found in public laws, electoral politics, or the establishment of mothers' aid programs at the state level. It rarely appears in documents that white progressives, male or female, left behind. Since black men could not speak out in politics and black women did not want to be seen, it has remained invisible in virtually every discussion of southern progressivism. Nonetheless, southern black women initiated every progressive reform that southern white women initiated, a feat they accomplished without financial resources, without the civic protection of their husbands, and without publicity.

At the same time that black women used progressivism to reshape black life and race relations, an organizational approach slowly began to replace racial "paternalism." The black community in Salisbury would not listen to influential whites who told them to clean up their communities. Nothing happened until whites recognized black women leaders, met with them publicly, and gave them authority. Then the city was "completely transformed." Despite whites' extensive efforts to undermine black education by imposing a nineteenth-century version of industrial education, black women's progressive ideas made industrial education modern and useful by linking it to the sanitary science movement. Contacts between white and black women with progressive agendas set the groundwork for inclusion of African Americans in formal social service structures. Her desire to help solve civic problems gave Lula Kelsey the right to appear before city officials during a period when black men risked their lives if they registered to vote for those officials.

This is certainly not to argue that disfranchisement was a positive good or that African Americans were better off with limited social services than they would have been with full civil rights. It means that black women were given straw and they made bricks. Outward cooperation with an agenda designed to oppress them masked a subversive twist. Black women capitalized upon the new role of the state to capture a share of the meager resources and proceeded to effect real social change with tools designed to maintain the status quo.

◆ *F U R T H E R   R E A D I N G*

Antler, Joyce. "After College, What? New Graduates and the Family Claim," *American Quarterly* 32 (1980): 409–434.

Baker, Paula. "The Domestication of Politics: Women and American Political Society, 1780–1920," *American Historical Review* 89 (June 1984): 620–647.

Barker-Benfield, G. J. "Mother Emancipator: The Meaning of Jane Addams' Sickness and Cure," *Journal of Family History* 4 (1979): 395–420.

Becker, Susan D. *The Origins of the Equal Rights Amendment* (1981).

Blair, Karen. *The Clubwoman as Feminist: True Womanhood Redefined* (1980).

———. *The Torchbearers* (1994).

Blee, Kathleen, M. *Women of the Klan: Racism and Gender in the 1920s* (1991).

Chafe, William. *The Paradox of Change: American Women in the 20th Century* (1991).

Chesler, Ellen. *Woman of Valor: Margaret Sanger and the Birth Control Movement* (1992).

Conway, Jill K. "Women Reformers and American Culture, 1870–1930," *Journal of Social History* 5, no. 2 (winter 1971–1972): 164–177.

Cott, Nancy F. *The Grounding of Modern Feminism* (1987).

Davis, Allen. *Spearheads for Reform: The Social Settlements and the Progressive Movement, 1890–1914* (1967).

———. *American Heroine: The Life and Legend of Jane Addams* (1973).

Deutsch, Sarah. *Women and the City: Gender, Space, and Power in Boston, 1870–1940* (2000).

Drachman, Virginia G. *Sisters in Law: Women Lawyers in Modern American History* (2001).

DuBois, Ellen Carol. *Harriot Stanton Blatch and the Winning of Woman Suffrage* (1997).

Fitzpatrick, Ellen. *Endless Crusade: Women Social Scientists and Progressive Reform* (1990).

Frankel, Noralee, and Nancy S. Dye, eds. *Gender, Class, Race, and Reform in the Progressive Era* (1992).

Frankfort, Robert. *Collegiate Women: Domesticity and Career in Turn-of-the-Century America* (1977).

Freedman, Estelle. "Separatism as Strategy: Female Institution Building and American Feminism, 1870–1930," *Feminist Studies* 5, no. 3 (Fall 1979): 512–529.

————. *Maternal Justice: Miriam Van Waters and the Female Reform Tradition* (1996).

Giddings, Paula. *When and Where I Enter: The Impact of Black Women on Race and Sex in America* (1984).

Glenn, Susan A. *Female Spectacle: The Theatrical Roots of Modern Feminism* (2000).

Goodwin, Joanne. *Gender and the Politics of Welfare Reform: Mothers' Pensions in Chicago, 1911–1929* (1997).

Gordon, Linda. "Black and White Visions of Welfare: Women's Welfare Activism, 1890–1945," *Journal of American History* 78 (September 1991): 559–590.

————. *The Great Arizona Orphan Abduction* (1999).

Hall, Jacquelyn Dowd. *Revolt Against Chivalry: Jessie Daniel Ames and the Women's Campaign Against Lynching* (1979).

Hayden, Dolores. *The Grand Domestic Revolution: A History of Feminist Design for American Homes, Neighborhoods, and Cities* (1981).

Hewitt, Nancy A., and Suzanne Lebsock, eds. *Visible Women: New Essays on American Activism* (1993).

Higginbotham, Evelyn Brooks. *Righteous Discontent: The Women's Movement in the Black Baptist Church* (1993).

Koven, Seth, and Sonya Michel, eds. *Mothers of a New World: Maternalist Politics and the Origins of Welfare States* (1993).

Kraditor, Aileen. *The Ideas of the Woman Suffrage Movement* (1981).

Ladd-Taylor, Molly. *Mother-Work: Women, Child Welfare, and the State, 1890–1930* (1994).

Lageman, Ellen. *A Generation of Women: Education in the Lives of Progressive Reformers* (1979).

Lasch-Quinn, Elizabeth. *Black Neighbors: Race and the Limits of Reform in the American Settlement House Movement, 1890–1945* (1993).

Lemons, J. Stanley. *The Woman Citizen: Social Feminism in the 1920s* (1973).

Lerner, Gerda. "Early Community Work of Black Club Women," *Journal of Negro History* 59 (1974): 158–167.

Lissak, Rivka Shpak. *Pluralism and Progressives: Hull House and the New Immigrants, 1890–1919* (1989).

Lunardini, Christine. *From Equal Suffrage to Equal Rights: Alice Paul and the National Woman's Party, 1913–1928* (1986).

Morgan, David. *Suffragists and Democrats* (1972).

Muncy, Robyn. *Creating a Female Dominion in American Reform, 1890–1935* (1991).

Newman, Louise Michele. *White Women's Rights: The Racial Origins of Feminism in the United States* (1999).

Orleck, Annelise. *Common Sense and a Little Fire: Women and Working-Class Politics in the United States, 1900–1965* (1995).

Parker, Alison M. *Purifying America: Women, Cultural Reform, and Pro-Censorship Activism, 1873–1933* (1997).

Payne, Elizabeth Anne. *Reform, Labor, and Feminism: Margaret Drier Robins and the Women's Trade Union League* (1988).

Preito, Laura R. *At Home in the Studio: The Professionalization of Women Artists in America* (2001).

Rosenberg, Rosalind. *Beyond Separate Spheres: The Intellectual Roots of Modern Feminism* (1982).

Rothman, Sheila. *Woman's Proper Place* (1978).

Rousmaniere, John. "Cultural Hybrid in the Slums: The College Woman and the Settlement House, 1889–1914," *American Quarterly* 22 (1970): 45–66.

Ruiz, Vicki L. *From Out of the Shadows: Mexican Women in Twentieth-Century America* (1998).

Salem, Dorothy. *To Better Our World: Black Women in Organized Reform, 1890–1920* (1990).

Scharf, Lois, and Joan Jensen, eds. *Decades of Discontent: The Women's Movement, 1910–1940* (1983).

Scott, Anne Firor. *Natural Allies: Women's Associations in American History* (1992).

Sklar, Kathryn Kish. *Florence Kelley and the Nation's Work* (1995).

Skocpol, Theda. *Protecting Soldiers and Mothers: The Political Origins of Social Policy in the United States* (1992).

Tomes, Nancy. *The Gospel of Germs: Men, Women, and the Microbe in American Life* (1999).

Wheeler, Marjorie Spruill. *New Women of the New South: The Leaders of the Woman Suffrage Movement in the Southern States* (1993).

Wilson, Margaret Gibbons. *The American Woman in Transition: The Urban Influence, 1870–1920* (1979).

Wolfe, Allis R. "Women, Consumerism, and the National Consumer's League in the Progressive Era, 1900–1923," *Labor History* 16 (1975): 378–392.

Wortman, Marlene Stein. "Domesticating the Nineteenth-Century American City," *Prospects* 3 (1977): 531–572.

CHAPTER 11

Sexuality and Marriage
in Modern America

During the first half of the twentieth century, American sexual values and conduct changed in important ways, especially insofar as women were concerned. Women's increased presence in the workplace and public life helped to set the stage for changes in sexuality and marriage by providing compelling evidence of women's interest in self-definition and independence. Young wage-earning women were in the vanguard of changes in sexuality, for they seemed to believe that they had little to lose, and perhaps much to gain, in rejecting an ideal of female sexual purity that had been popular among Americans, especially those of the middle class, during the nineteenth century. Working-class young women embraced an identity that acknowledged the legitimacy of female sexual desire both inside and outside of marriage, and they began to construct with working-class young men new patterns of social interaction and extramarital sexual experimentation. An emerging consumer market gladly assisted the process by, for example, offering young people the chance to view films that starred women in eroticized roles. Entrepreneurs opened dance halls, amusement parks, and other places of entertainment where, for a fee, young men and women might explore the modern meanings of sexuality with little fear of adult surveillance.

Soon, middle-class young people on high-school and college campuses joined in giving new meaning to female heterosexual desire and heterosocial companionship, replacing chaperoned courtship with modern youth-directed "dating." At the same time, adult women and men participated in this era of sexual change, sometimes endorsing sexual expression outside of marriage, more often lending support to the notion that sex was important to the fulfillment of both partners in a marriage and should be separable from reproduction. Various reformers, most notably Margaret Sanger and Mary Ware Dennett, began campaigns to remove legal and cultural prohibitions against contraception and sex education. In some cities, men and women who were attracted to partners of the same sex gained sufficient autonomy to develop social and sexual identities that were altogether separate from heterosexual marriage and reproduction.

Importantly, as the essays and documents in this chapter show, changes in sexuality and marriage were uneven and never fully accepted by all Americans. Over time, some professionals in medicine, psychiatry, psychology, and social work came to support new notions of sexual fulfillment in marriage, but they also developed

*conceptions of "healthy" and "normal" sexual behavior that excluded and stigma-
tized homosexual men and lesbian women. So, too, as faith in female sexual purity
declined, young women often found it exceedingly difficult to put a stop to unwelcome
sexual advances at work or on the street. The criminal justice system, often with the
support of Progressive reformers (male and female), generally responded in a punitive, rather than permissive, way to sexually active young women, especially if they
were from working-class, immigrant, or African American homes. And not surprisingly, many other Americans resisted the trend toward sexual liberalization, including significant numbers of middle-class white and black women; these Americans
believed that women would lose moral authority in public life and the family if they
abandoned faith in women's essential sexual virtue. Finally, in important ways,
laws concerned with marriage and social welfare continued in the twentieth century
to treat women as the dependents of men, thus constraining women's social, economic,
and sexual autonomy. What, then, ought we to emphasize as we evaluate the history
of women, sexuality, and marriage in twentieth-century America? Women's agency
or the forces (and people) that resisted female autonomy? General trends and patterns
among women or divisions of background, belief, and practice?*

◈ D O C U M E N T S

In the 1890s, Clelia Duel Mosher, a California physician, began asking some of her
female patients about their sexual practices. Although she never formally analyzed her
findings, historians have come to rely heavily on her survey of forty-five women; four
extracts from longer questionnaires are included here as Document 1. In Document 2,
taken from a speech delivered in 1907, Dr. Carlton C. Frederick summarizes the opinions
he developed on female "nymphomania" over the course of a lengthy career in medicine.
His view that female sexual desire was unnatural, and that lesbianism was one of its
most degenerate forms, is representative of the medical orthodoxy of the early twentieth
century. Document 3 consists of excerpted letters to Margaret Sanger, the birth-control
reformer, written during the 1920s by working-class men and women who were desperate
for contraceptive information and products. In 1925, liberal medical physician Malcolm
Bissell described (Document 4) the difficulties that he and like-minded Americans faced
in seeking the legalization of contraception. Document 5 finds psychologists Phyllis
Blanchard and Carolyn Manasses examining (in 1930) from a liberal perspective the
ideals and problems of marriage in twentieth-century America.

1. Extracts from the Mosher Survey, 1892–1913

Number 1

*(Respondent Number 1 was twenty-five when interviewed in 1892. A former music
teacher, she had been married for two and one-half years and had one child, age
six months.)*

What knowledge of sexual physiology had you before marriage?
Knew process of ovulation & menstruation in fairly well-defined way. [Hence]
knew when conception was likely to take place & why. Very little about male sexual

Clelia Duel Mosher, *The Mosher Survey: Sexual Attitudes of 45 Victorian Women*, ed. James MaHood
and Kristine Wenburg (New York: Arno Press, 1980), questionnaires 1, 10, 35, 44.

physiology. Knew, in regard to intercourse, condition of man at time [hence] necessity also need of self-control; danger of its occurring too often; time when woman was supposed to desire intercourse, if ever; best time for conception, as regards health of mother & child; several means of preventing conception. Realized little how important it is to a man and how much self-control it may entail. Did not suppose it was often desired by women. Considered that it sh'd be regulated largely by the woman.

Did conception occur by choice or by accident?
Accident.

Habit of intercourse? Average number of times per month?
Two or three times. Before conception, once or at most twice per month.

Was intercourse held during pregnancy?
No.

    Did you desire it at this period?
    Occasionally during first months. Not at all, during last half—or more.

At other times have you any desire for intercourse?
Yes.

    How often?
    Once or twice a month.
    At what time in relation to your menses?
    Immediately after. Occasionally just before—and rarely at some other time. Except in 1st case, it is scarcely ever except when there is some outside exciting cause.

Is intercourse agreeable to you or not?
Usually.

Do you always have a venereal orgasm?
No.

What do you believe to be the purpose of intercourse?
    Necessity to the man?
    Yes.
    To the woman?
    No.
    Reproduction?
    Yes. Primarily.

Have you ever used any means to prevent conception? If so, what? What was the effect on your health?
Thin rubber covering for man. Depended on so-called "safety week" at first.
I have not perceived any effect on my health.

Number 10

(Respondent Number 10 was twenty-six, married for two and one-half years, when interviewed in 1894. She had two children.)

What knowledge of sexual physiology had you before marriage?
Very slight.

How did you obtain it?
Mostly from *Tokology* [a popular sexual guide].

Did conception occur by choice or accident?
First conception by choice. Second by accident.

Habit of intercourse, average number of times?
1st time 5 months after marriage. Then not until 7 mos. after our first child was born. After that twice a week usually.

Was intercourse held during pregnancy? If so, how often?
Not during first pregnancy. Yes during second pregnancy. Once or twice a week until 6th or 7th month. Not after that.
  Had you any desire for it during this period?
  Yes, at times.

At other times have you any desire for intercourse?
Yes.
  At what time in relation to your menses?
  Immediately after menstruation.

Is intercourse agreeable to you or not?
Yes.

Do you always have a venereal orgasm?
No, but usually.
  When you do, effect immediately afterwards?
  I think there is more exhaustion.

What do you believe to be the true purpose of intercourse?
  Necessity to the man? to woman?
  No. [The woman's single negative response applied to both sexes.]
  Pleasure?
  Not solely.
  Reproduction?
  What other reasons beside reproduction are sufficient to warrant intercourse?
  I think to the man and woman married from love, it may be used *temperately*, as one of the highest manifestations of love, granted us by our Creator.

Have you ever used any means to prevent conception?
Yes.
  If so, what?
  Sulphate of zinc. It is not infallible.
  Effect on your health?
  None.

What, to you, would be an ideal habit?
Occasional intercourse, with control over conception (?), everything to be absolutely mutual.

Number 35

(Respondent Number 35 was interviewed in 1897, when she was fifty-three. She had had six children and six miscarriages—twelve pregnancies in all—during more than twenty-eight years of marriage.)

What knowledge of sexual physiology had you before marriage?
Slight from girls. Mother taught her that such things were not only not talked about but also not thought of. School child at 14 told [her] what intercourse was. [She] was shocked and didn't believe it.

Habit of intercourse, average number of times per week?
[Average once a week,] sometimes oftener, sometimes less often.

Was intercourse held during pregnancy? If so, how often?
About average. Not so often during last 2 mo.
   Had you any desire for it during this period?
   [Often] more desire than at other times, and she needed it. "Nothing would ease my nervous condition but that."

At other times have you any desire for intercourse?
Yes. Very soon after period, [it is] more agreeable. Sometimes just before [period]. Much of time could have blotted [it] out and never missed it. Then another time wanted it. [She prefers intercourse] when not too tired, just before and just after [menses].

Is intercourse agreeable to you or not?
Yes, when not too tired & conditions are right.

Do you always have a venereal orgasm?
Always when she desires. Many times not.
   When you do, effect immediately afterwards?
   Sleepy, relaxed, less nervous, good.
   Effect next day?
   Feels well.
   When you do not, effect immediately afterwards?
   Nervous, strung up, not sleepy.
   Effect next day?
   No effect.

What do you believe to be the true purpose of intercourse?
   Necessity to man? to woman?
   [Yes] Because many [who are] unmarried are too nervous & do not recognize what the cause is.
   Pleasure?
   [Yes] for purpose of bringing about [reproduction].
   Reproduction?
   [Yes] highest purpose.
   What other reasons beside reproduction are sufficient to warrant intercourse?
   Individual health: a normal desire and a rational use of it tends to keep people healthier.

Have you ever used any means to prevent conception? If so, what?
Withdrawal sometimes.
   Effect on your health?
   None in either [husband or wife?]

What, to you, would be an ideal habit?
Once a week or [once every] ten days. When both want it.

Number 44

(Respondent Number 44 was forty-two when interviewed in 1913. She had had two children and two miscarriages. The length of time she had been married was not recorded.)

What knowledge of sexual physiology had you before marriage? (b) How did you obtain it?
No knowledge. Did not know what marriage meant.

1st intercourse how long after marriage?
2 or 3 days after marriage.

Did conception occur by choice or accident?
1st by choice. All others accidental.

Habit of intercourse, average number of times per week?
Formerly 2 [times] weekly. Now once in 2-3 wks. Depends on whether they have leisure.

Was intercourse held during pregnancy? If so, how often?
Rarely with 1st [child] during [entire pregnancy]. Not with 2nd [child].
   Had you any desire for it during this period?
   With 2nd one yes, not with 1st.

At other times have you any desire for intercourse?
Yes.
   At what time in relation to your menses?
   Following or preceding menstruation.

Is intercourse agreeable to you or not?
Yes.

Do you always have a venereal orgasm?
No. Conscious of suppression on part of woman. Time reaction slower.
   When you do, effect immediately afterwards?
   Rests better when she has orgasm. Temperamental uplift.
   When you do not, effect immediately afterwards?
   Very little difference.

What do you believe to be the true purpose of intercourse?
   Necessity to man?
   Yes.
   To woman?

Yes.
Pleasure?
Very strong. Psychological 2nd.
Reproduction?
Yes 1st.
What other reasons beside reproduction are sufficient to warrant intercourse?
If women enjoyed intercourse, the demands on them would be much less.
Males [have] less desire when [they are] more perfectly satisfied. Intellectual
work on part of husband—less leisure. [Intercourse produces] oneness [and is]
uplifting like music. [There is] very little that is animal about it. The comrade-
ship of it. [Remainder of response is unintelligible.]

Have you ever used any means to prevent conception? (a) If so, what?
After known miscarriage because husband did not wish her to conceive again until
she was strong. Douches of bichloride.
Effect on your health?
No effect.

What, to you, would be an ideal habit?
When desired by both.

2. Carlton C. Frederick, M.D., on the Manifestations of Nymphomania, 1907

The sexual instinct is not so common in woman as it is in man. With the latter it is,
under normal conditions of health and vigor, an ever-present, powerful impulse to
procreation. Sexual desire is entirely absent in a much larger number of women
than is generally supposed. If present it is ordinarily not so strong as it is in man. If
a woman has in her makeup the sexual instinct to the ordinary degree, that impulse
is only aroused by the man she loves, and for no other has she that feeling. There is
a small percentage of women in whom it is very strong, but relatively to the whole
number the percentage is small. . . . Fortunate it is for the morals of humanity that
woman generally is not so constituted sexually as is man, otherwise, as has been
aptly said, this world would be one vast brothel. Surely, to the influence of woman
we must look for the standard of moral tone, however high that may be. . . .

Nymphomania is an excessive development of sexual desire in the female, manifesting itself in various ways dependent upon the mental status, moral sense, environment, or social scale of the individual. . . . Masturbation is probably one of its
most prominent manifestations. . . . In general, women who have practised masturbation long are not satisfied by normal sexual indulgence, although the desire which
they have may lead them to such indulgence. . . . This is the rule with sexual perverts
of all kinds—the normal act is not one of gratification, or they would not be perverts.

Nymphomaniacs, especially among the insane and mildly insane, are liable to
resort to exposure of their persons or by lascivious movements in presence of men,

Carlton C. Frederick, "Nymphomania as a Cause of Excessive Venery," *American Journal of Obstetrics
and Diseases of Women and Children* 56 (1907): 807–812.

and thus invite coitus. But among those not insane such acts are seldom openly indulged in, but secretly they are often shameless. All sorts of degenerate practices
are followed by some. One of the most frequent is tribadism—the so-called "Lesbian Love," which consists in various degenerate acts between two women in order
to stimulate the sexual orgasm. Not an uncommon practice is the fondling of the
genitalia of small boys and babies and contact of the same. In fact, the numbers and
variations of practices are so various that it would take pages to mention them.

3. Letters to Margaret Sanger, Birth-Control Advocate, from American Wives and Husbands, 1920s

Number One

I had thought from my reading in magazines, etc., that after marriage the direct information necessary to prevent too large a family would become mine "on demand."
But to my amazement others older and supposedly wiser seem as ignorant as I. I was
nearly twenty-five when we married and had I realized this condition I should have
remained single a while longer. I was never very strong, and now as the mother of
three children I feel my little strength slowly going and know that the demands of
motherhood is the cause.

Already our doctor has warned me to take care of my health. Heart weak, liable
to lung trouble. Since we lost our second child I would not object to one other but I
would like better to be able to choose when.

After marriage I lived in the country on a farm and since I was from town
many neighbors thought I knew and appealed to me. It was almost with tears I had
to refuse to aid the poor creatures who seemed to think I knew because I was from
town. Oh, you indeed know their despair! I too have seen it. A woman, the mother
of nine children, appealed to me, but I was powerless to aid her. . . .

Number Two

I have a problem which to me and to those with whom I am concerned is very serious
and in the full meaning of the word, vital. I shall try to be candid and brief in stating
it knowing that with your great work you cannot afford to spend much time on any
individual. I am thirty-three years of age. Have been married for ten years. We have
an adopted child.

My wife has always been delicate and was some years ago severely injured in
an accident and a doctor told me she could never bear children. Knowing that it
probably meant her death if conception took place I have refrained from sexual intercourse, for my wife's welfare is more to me than anything else.

Now I am not under- or over-sexed but am a healthy strong normal man. Yet the
strain is very very hard not to live and have intercourse naturally. The intense desire
always balked has ill mental and physical effects and I fear may lead to estrange-
ment. But I need not dwell on this as you will understand it. I love my wife dearly

Margaret Sanger, *Motherhood in Bondage* (1928; reprint, Columbus: Ohio State University Press, 2000), 298–299, 341–343, 347. Reprinted by permission of Ohio State University Press.

and if she could only obey nature without the shadow of death as a penalty it would enable us to live normally and happily and do our work with mental faculties clear.

Number Three

I am thirty-four years old and am the mother of six children now and expect to become a mother again shortly. I dread the months to come very much as we haven't the means to hire help. I expect to do all my housework, take care of the children, do all the cooking and milk six cows, as I have done before, up to the day my baby is born. Being a mother, you know this is too much to expect of any woman. We live on a farm, but my husband is working at public work at the present time and don't have much time to work at home. I would not mind my work so much but about five years ago I had a very bad case of typhoid fever. I was bedfast for eight weeks. Had to have two trained nurses all the time. I was unconscious and had many hemorrhages the first few weeks of my sickness.

The worst thing of all is this: I love my husband as much as any woman could and it nearly breaks my heart when he is not affectionate to me or the children or when he says anything harsh. We get along good only for one thing. He says our family is already larger than it should be to take care of them right. I think too, that seven will be as many as I can care for properly.

He would rather stay away from me and not have intercourse at all rather than make the family larger. This don't please me for I know every time he doesn't come to me for a week or two he gets so contrary with me and children that there is no pleasure living in the house with him. I have never refused him his privilege once. He is very moderate in his passions. He has always been true to me and I to him and owing to my afflictions and desire to live happy with my husband.

I think Birth Control would be all right in our case. I love babies but I think we have had our share after we get the one we expect in a few months.

I am a Catholic and would not think of destroying a child after conception. Can you tell me of any sure way by which my husband and I can enjoy the privilege of married life without conception. It seems some people know how, but we don't. I know my life will be a torture if I cannot find a way of satisfying him without conceiving more children. He says this is our last and I know he means it and that he will keep away from me rather than conceive more. . . .

Number Four

In the first place, my husband and I started all wrong. We got married before we had enough money to keep house. We went to live with his folks where we still are and thought we could soon save enough to go by ourselves. Thirteen months after we were married our first baby was born, and in fifteen and a half months after our second baby came.

We love our baby girls dearly, but are so afraid of having more that we have had no intercourse since before the birth of the second child, three and one-half years ago tomorrow.

Although my husband says he is still faithful to me (and I have seen no indication that he isn't) naturally we are not very happy; we have a good many quarrels and he has told me a good many times that he could divorce me because of my refusing him. It is not that the sexual union is revolting to me, for it is not and has not been in a single instance, but I dread the expense of rearing more children and I am not very strong and everything worries me so. I cannot sleep nights through worrying about losing my husband and it makes me so cross and irritable and naturally I feel tired all the time. Can't you possibly help me?

4. Malcolm Bissell Reports on Birth Control Activism in Eastern Pennsylvania, 1925

In December 1921, the Pennsylvania Branch of the American Birth Control League was organised. Public meetings were held in Philadelphia in 1922 and 1923 under the auspices of this organisation, and a number of addresses on Birth Control were made in private homes. Subsequently the Pittsburgh group formed an independent organisation known as the Birth Control League of Allegheny County, not affiliated with any national organisation. The work in the eastern end of the state continued to be carried on under the original name and a public meeting was held at the College Club early in 1924. In the fall of 1924, however, it was decided to reorganize as the Eastern Pennsylvania Branch of the American Birth Control League. The present membership of the branch is 257.

Up to the present it cannot be said that the Birth Control movement has gained much headway in Pennsylvania. There are a number of reasons for this, but the principal one has undoubtedly been the lack of an effective campaign. Experience shows that spasmodic efforts and isolated meetings have relatively little effect in arousing sentiment and that a continuous and unremitting effort must be made to keep the subject of Birth Control agitated. The remarkable results obtained by Mr. Meves across the river in New Jersey are a most stimulating example of what can be accomplished by such work.

At the same time it must be admitted that the situation in Eastern Pennsylvania is peculiarly difficult. In the first place Philadelphia is a very conservative city and requires time to adjust itself to a new point of view. The community as a whole is not yet altogether sure that it is quite respectable to advocate Birth Control. In the second place, there is no satisfactory hall available for large public Birth Control discussions. The most centrally located hall is under the control of a particularly conservative group of a conservative religious denomination and its use has so far been denied us. We have therefore been obliged to hold all large public meetings in hotels, which has kept us from reaching as many people as we would in a hall. A third factor has been the difficulty of securing publicity. The Philadelphia newspapers are frankly afraid of giving too much space to Birth Control, and have even declined to accept paid advertisements of Birth Control meetings. The Quaker influence is still strong in the city and of course it must never be forgotten that Philadelphia is the seat of a Roman Catholic cardinal. . . .

Malcolm Bissell, "Report of the Eastern Pennsylvania Branch of the American Birth Control League, 1924–1925," in Margaret Sanger, ed., *International Aspects of Birth Control* (New York: American Birth Control League, 1925), 1: 167–171.

The final goal of all work in Pennsylvania must be a revision of the present state law, which is one of the most repressive in the union, forbidding doctors to give contraceptive information even to diseased women, and classing contraception in general with obscenity. We want to make it possible to establish clinics and permit doctors and nurses to give instruction to any married persons desirous of receiving it. A legislative campaign is therefore inevitable. At present, however, we do not believe the time is ripe for such a campaign. A vast amount of educational work must first be done, as much ignorance and misunderstanding of Birth Control still exists. This educational work must be our first concern. Our meeting on April 1st will be a big move in this direction, but it must be followed up by other meetings, large and small, and the subject must not be allowed to rest.

Present plans have two immediate objects in view: First, the establishment of local Birth Control organisations in every part of the state, and secondly, a systematic campaign of education which shall cover the whole state. We believe that small neighborhood meetings in private homes are one of the most effective means of reaching many people who would not attend a large public meeting. One such neighborhood meeting has already been held and much effort will be expended in this direction after our big Philadelphia meeting. This work can be carried on most effectively through local county, city or community Birth Control organisations, or such existing civic groups as are willing to undertake it. Hence the importance of establishing local organisations. In this work we shall co-operate as far as possible with the existing independent Birth Control League in Pittsburgh and with the branch in Reading, hoping that these groups will organize their respective territories. There should be Birth Control groups actively working in Harrisburg, Altoona, Erie, Williamsport, Scranton, Lancaster and other cities, and it is hoped that there will be soon. The first steps have been taken toward the organization of a Harrisburg branch.

With the establishment of such local groups throughout the state, addresses before chambers of commerce, Rotary clubs, women's clubs, labor organisations and church groups can be arranged and a powerful public sentiment built up. Then we will go to the legislature and *demand*, not ask, a revision of the law. Experience shows that the average legislator will not take a stand for Birth Control until a strong public opinion forces him to do so. Our strongest opposition is organised and we must organise to overcome it.

Special efforts need also to be made to get the active and open support of the medical profession. There seems to be a strongly conservative tendency among doctors in Philadelphia, but we are gradually compiling a list of physicians who are openly in favor of Birth Control. With this list as a nucleus, we hope to organise a meeting for doctors only in the near future. In this connection we cannot express too highly our appreciation of the co-operation of Dr. Kate W. Baldwin, our honorary president, who has been one of the chief sponsors of our organization, and of Dr. Howard K. Longshore, who is not only serving as a member of our executive committee, but has repeatedly and practically demonstrated his interest in a variety of ways.

We feel that nearly all of our task is before us, but that the prospects are encouraging. There are abundant signs that the public is ready to give its support to Birth Control. The Quaker element, although naturally conservative, is increasingly open-minded, and we find more and more people of influence who are willing to come out openly for Birth Control. We have already had several examples of what can be accomplished by a little effort and enthusiasm. One instance was the presentation of the subject of Birth Control at the annual meeting of the Old York Road Public Health Center in Jenkintown on January 26th, at which addresses were made by Mrs. Robertson Jones of the American Birth Control League, and Prof. Malcolm Bissell of Bryn Mawr College. Another is the arrangement of a Birth Control meeting of the Women's Club of Swarthmore this Friday, March 27th. In both these instances the discussion of Birth Control was the result of efforts of members of the Eastern Pennsylvania Branch. We hope and expect that this is only a beginning and that our next report will have a list of real achievements to chronicle.

5. Phyllis Blanchard and Carolyn Manasses Discuss the Ideals and Problems of Modern Marriage, 1930

Since marriage is looked upon as the good life by a majority of girls and young women, it becomes of utmost importance that they be prepared for making the best possible adjustments in this relationship. We have already stressed the inadequate sex education which most girls are given and indicated that this may interfere with the emotional responses in marriage. That girls are awakening to this danger, as well as to a realization of other marriage problems, is evident from the demands for courses on preparation for marriage which have been made by students in colleges and universities. That such courses were not offered until the young people themselves clamored for them is once again but a sign of academic and parental conservatism. The Y.W.C.A. has been more alert than many institutions of higher learning in sensing this need on the part of young women, and has sponsored study groups concerned with the subject of preparation for marriage in several communities. . . .

To be sure there is much more opportunity now than formerly to become intimately acquainted during the courtship period. Conversational freedom permits the young man and woman to discover each other's likes and dislikes, prejudices and ideals to a degree that was formerly impossible. Discussion of intimate subjects, such as the number of children wanted, the amount of previous sex experience, the attitude concerning the woman working after marriage, and the amount of liberty to be permitted in post-marital friendships with those of the opposite sex, provides at least a superficial basis of mutual understanding. There are those who think that such confidences pave the way to complete understanding and eliminate any cause for later dissensions; but there are others who believe that only by living together can two people really learn their true feelings and realize the problems of adjustment that have to be met. . . .

One thing which is necessary for a satisfying marriage experience is that husband and wife find each other sexually compatible. Yet sexual pleasure, especially for the woman, is not always easily and naturally attained. Too often a girl enters marriage with fears and inhibitions and conditioned responses toward sex which have been created as the result of unfortunate impressions received during childhood or adolescence. Innocent episodes of sex play in those early years may have been

Phyllis Blanchard and Carolyn Manasses, *New Girls for Old* (New York: Macaulay, 1930), 185–199.

met with attitudes of disgust or caused punishment to be bestowed by parents who thought such acts immoral. The girl may have forgotten long since the episodes that occurred and the things her parents said or did, but the feeling of shame may linger on, to prevent her wholehearted acceptance of sex relationships in marriage.

Again, emotional conflicts over masturbation may have entered into pre-marital experiences. The girl who once had such a habit, if told that it was a sign of abnormal and exaggerated sexual desires, may have felt guilty about it and struggled to control it. Then it may be difficult for her to give up this hard-won control of her sexual desires and the patterns of repression set up in connection with one aspect of sex behavior color her responses to the sex element in marriage. Because of a lurking fear that she may seem too passionate, and her husband may suspect what still seems to her a dreadful secret, she cannot give herself up to free enjoyment of his love.

Inadequate knowledge of contraceptive techniques, with a fear of the coming of children before they are really wanted, may prevent the wife from full and joyous participation in the sex relationship. Her anxiety as to consequences inhibits her complete surrender to passionate impulses.

These are only a few illustrations of the ways in which inadequate sex knowledge, or residuals of early experiences, may influence sex adjustments in marriage. Sexual compatibility may be only slightly attenuated as a result of such circumstances, or it may be more decidedly marred by the partial or complete frigidity of the wife. Moreover, leaving all these problems aside, there is still another part of her sex education which is likely to have been neglected; in all probability she will have only a hazy notion of the technique of intercourse. The supposedly passive rôle of the female has been too much taken for granted. Only in books on sex psychology, which are often restricted in circulation by the sales being confined to certain professional classes or are banned entirely as obscene literature, is there frank admission of woman's active participation. It is unfortunate that these volumes are not more readily accessible to the average person, for the young wife might gather valuable hints as to her part of the love life which might help her gain greater pleasure from it, and the young husband might be better prepared to make her introduction to the sex side of marriage a pleasant one. . . .

Marriage adjustments do not depend merely upon the attitudes toward sex, however. There are involved in every sexual partnership two personalities which act and react upon each other. Antagonisms arising in extra-sexual fields may cause anger and bitterness and the desire to hurt the opponent. These personality clashes interfere with the sense of harmony and unity which furnishes the perfect background for coming together in the sexual relationship. It is more than idealism which asks that friendliness, humor and mutual tolerance characterize the differences of opinion over financial policies or any other matter which must be settled between husband and wife; it is a very practical advantage to them in terms of prolongation of sexual compatibility. . . .

Just as the lessened emphasis upon the economic aspects of marriage has permitted a clearer perception of the elements of personality conflicts, so our modern sophistication with regard to sex matters has sharpened the focus of attention upon the physical relationship. When the sex side of marriage was regarded as pleasurable only for men, frigidity in a wife was no matter of grave concern. If the repression of her sex nature led to psychoneurotic traits, at least no one suspected that this was what was the matter, and therefore neither husband or wife worried about it. And perhaps it really was far less serious than the drainage of physical energy through many and frequent pregnancies in a pre-contraceptual age.

After hundreds of years of mild complaisance to wifely duties, modern women have awakened to the knowledge that they are sexual beings. And with this new insight the sex side of marriage has assumed sudden importance. The husband is no longer satisfied with good natured acquiescence; he must have a passionate response to his own desires. And the wife expects to find in him the perfect lover who will arouse ecstasies of sensual pleasure. With the introduction of contraceptives, and these new attitudes toward sex, it is no longer regarded as an outlet for merely masculine passions or as a means of procreation of the race, but rather as a way of adding to the fullness and joy of living. . . .

Again, even if the physical side of marriage is radiant during the first months and years, there is no guarantee that it will continue to be so. Situations change; illness, anxiety or age differences may destroy temporarily or permanently a relationship that was previously mutually satisfactory. There is even evidence from our researches in comparative psychology that sexual attraction tends normally to become attenuated after two partners have been continually together over a period of time, and can only be stimulated to any degree of intensity by a new individual. If this be so, we shall have to face the fact that the cult of sex for pleasure will inevitably lead us into certain dilemmas. We shall eventually have to choose between contentment with the memories of more poignant moments and remaining faithful to one person because of those tender associations and other bonds which have later come into existence, or contemplate the possibility of unfaithfulness or divorce. This facing of alternatives is but the logical outcome of the modern tendency to cast aside the concept of duty with respect to marriage except in relation to the welfare of children.

With the insight which we have recently been gaining into the personality and sex problems of marriage, there inevitably comes considerable skepticism toward all the formulas which have been proposed as universal panaceas which would enable men and women to obtain sexual happiness. So long as individuals remain handicapped by physical and emotional limitations, it is hardly possible for changes in the outer form of an institution to bring about the miracle of perfection. Modifications in the rigidity of institutional forms are desirable, in that this permits of more flexibility in working out personal adjustments, but it is unwise to expect more than that from them.

Our greatest hope for an increase of happiness in the relations between men and women depends upon the continuation of scientific research and further applications of science. Scientific methods of birth control, by contributing to the better health of women and reducing the economic burden through decreasing the number of children in the family, have certainly been an important factor in improving marital adjustment. It will become still more so as such information becomes available readily to a greater number of young people.

The scientific understanding and attitude toward sex offers another promise of happier adaptations in the future than there have been in the past. And the new psychology of human behavior, which helps us to self-understanding and to sympathetic comprehension of others, may do much to reduce personality conflicts between married people.

An especially promising movement is the modern interest in children and the rapid extension of the work which aims to help them make better personality adaptations. If we ever succeed in producing a race of individuals who are free from the emotional conflicts engendered by unwholesome childhood experiences, we may expect to see the responsibilities of marriage more easily accepted. In that day, adults will perhaps have achieved an emotional maturity which will permit them to refrain from making unreasonable demands upon others. Then, too, they will be more courageous in facing reality, so that they will not expect perfect and constant happiness in marriage; for they will understand that an imperfect balance of joy and grief exists in marriage because it is a part of life.

E S S A Y S

Bryn Mawr historian Sharon R. Ullman explores changes in heterosexual conduct in early-twentieth-century America, as well as the anxieties and backlash that such changes provoked. Her evidence of efforts to redefine female sexuality comes primarily from popular films of the era; for evidence of resistance to change, she examines court documents from statutory rape trials. Independent historian Margaret Gibson examines medical discussions of the late nineteenth and early twentieth centuries that acknowledged the presence of lesbians in American society but categorized these women as degenerate in mind as well as body. Nancy F. Cott of Harvard University shows that assumptions about the economic unity of men and women in marriage were reinforced by law in the twentieth century, even as women gained new levels of political and moral independence in marriage.

The Boundaries of Heterosexuality in Early-Twentieth-Century America

SHARON R. ULLMAN

Turn-of-the-century America witnessed a dramatic shift in gender relations. The Victorian world of homosocial relationships gradually gave way to one of heterosocial associations. American men and women have always socialized in some fashion; however, such connections—particularly among unmarried individuals—were closely regulated in the nineteenth century, an era of gender-segregated friendships and social networks. Though such networks survive to a degree in today's world, they retain but a shadow of their former substance. The complex, insular nature of those connections withered a century ago under pressure from a new sexual culture that reinforced the idea that men and women should be playmates together.

The sexual dangers of such new social alliances were readily apparent, and Progressive reform activity aimed at vice can be seen in this context. Yet the "obvious" problems over which the Progressives hyperventilated had less dramatic social consequences than did the infinitely more private renegotiations of sexual expectation that occurred between men and women as they came to depend upon each other for

Sharon R. Ullman, *Sex Seen: The Emergence of Modern Sexuality in America* (Berkeley and Los Angeles: University of California Press, 1997), 18–44. Copyright © 1998 The Regents of the University of California. Reprinted by permission.

social affirmation as well as sexual connection. Though playful sexuality provided the underpinnings for a form of parity between men and women, it introduced troubling anxiety as well. If women were no longer to act as Cerberus, guarding the gates to the sexual hell ever present in unleashed male lust, but instead were to be equal partners in the creation of a sexual understanding, how would the rules be made? How were the boundaries to be drawn? As female desire became incorporated into the popular and private visions of sexual morality at the turn of the century, both men and women confronted a world in flux.

Such questions frame many of the sexual representations found in court documents and early film. . . . Fears of unacceptable heterosexual practice and even deeper anxieties over what might be termed "anti-heterosexual" practice occupied an important place in the subtext of early film. Similarly, in responding to cases of statutory rape, communities attempted (with mixed success) to agree upon and articulate appropriate heterosexuality. Disagreement surfaced often, and a close reading of testimony uncovers sharp echoes of the cinematic discourses. Together, the films and the trials help illuminate the specific boundaries of and resistances to public heterosexuality. . . .

I

From the inception of film until the rise of serious censorship, a period encompassing the years 1896 to 1910, motion pictures demonstrated a surprising recognition of female desire and sexual availability. . . . No single moral vision predominated; sexuality remained an uncharted area open to exploration. . . . It is not simply that individual filmmakers and production companies created iconoclastic imagery to match their own sensibilities; rather, a full range of sexual imagery often appeared within the films of a single company or director. The cinema of this era was a world at play, and filmmakers very often played by depicting sexuality.

The first filmmakers explored a variety of questions that both reflected and ultimately helped shape heterosexual practice among unmarried people. Were women dominant or submissive? Holders of virtue or eager participants in sexual desire? Did male desire constitute inappropriate lechery or youthful pleasure? Could the public enjoy images of desire without transgressing earlier boundaries of moral traditions? Through these explorations—admittedly undertaken by a small number of men—a newly public heterosexual ethic emerged, subtly defining the limits of the possible and the expanse of the unacceptable.

One very popular and influential arena of sexual definition appeared in films that deployed a dominant female stereotype—the frustrated old maid. The image so sharply etched in traditional nineteenth-century wit reappeared in a series of movies that mocked unwed women. . . .

Gilbert Saroni, perhaps the most famous "old maid" in vaudeville, repeated his act for Edison Film in two separate shorts produced on March 1, 1901: "The Old Maid Having Her Picture Taken" and "The Old Maid in the Horsecar." "The Old Maid Having Her Picture Taken" offered a woman with haggard features and a sharp hook nose. She is notably more skinny and angular than women depicted in other films. The character has large puffy sleeves that look absurd when compared with the costumes worn by younger women in these films, and she carries the requisite fan, which can be used to indicate modesty or distress as needed.

The joke in "The Old Maid Having Her Picture Taken" revolves around the potency of her ugliness. Her countenance has remarkable destructive power. As she enters the room and surveys the wall hangings, they all drop to the floor; the mirror cracks as she primps before the photo session; and, naturally enough, the camera explodes when it is focused upon her. To modern eyes, it looks like an old joke, and no doubt it echoed with familiarity in 1901 as well. That familiarity is precisely the mechanism by which we are able to identify the woman as a sexual—or, in this case, asexual—icon. "The Old Maid in the Horsecar" had no discernible plot, but it reinforced the stereotype through dress and physical presentation. Saroni added a large mole to each cheek, exaggerated his character's long, unkempt ringlets of hair, and occasionally hid his face behind an open fan, seemingly giggling to exhibit a mock girlishness. The image alone provides a certain degree of humor, as does the juxtaposition of the old, broken-down figure and the new, modern conveyance. . . .

Similar old maid films of the period employ identical female imagery to convey a variety of physical and emotional jokes. All involve rejection of the old maid, whether by objects or by people. The dominating ridicule of this character indicates a socially agreed-upon repudiation of a certain form of older single woman. She stands as an icon of unacceptability—repelled and repellent. . . . The old maid represented a vision of female desire but also set limits on the type of woman who could appropriately exercise it.

One of the best examples in this genre, "The Disappointed Old Maid," tackled frustrated sexuality directly in 1903. As the film opens, a man dressed in black enters a bedroom through an unlatched window and crawls under the bed. An old maid in white nightclothes enters the room and begins to remove her shoes. As she leans over to do so, she sees the man under her bed. Clapping her hands together in delight, she smiles broadly and dances to the window in order to lock it and trap him inside. She reaches under the bed to pull him out but finds that he is only a large doll. As the film ends, she sits on the bed and cries, cradling the doll in her arms. Lacking in any subtlety whatsoever, "The Disappointed Old Maid" elevates the subtext of the old maid imagery to the surface and confronts it directly. These are women who wish to be sexual actors but are locked out of the world of desire. Men are incapable of feeling desire for them. In fact, in order to truly capture their lack of female sexual appeal, the old maid was best played by a man or made up to look like one.

. . . The old maid as specifically formulated in turn-of-the-century popular culture was a relatively recent construction, a response to an actual increase in the number of older single women and to the popular identification of such women with the women's rights movement. Both the demographic and the political aspects of the stereotype had some basis in truth. The 1890 and 1900 censuses did reflect significant increases in the number of women who never married, with a particularly high rate of nonmarriage among educated white women. Though not all college women supported suffrage and other feminist causes, many did—and all came to be tarred with the women's rights brush.

Women who did not marry incurred political and social scorn for another reason. The influx of eastern and southern European immigrants in the United States pushed the question into eugenic terms—the wrong people were reproducing. Educated women came primarily from white middle- and upper-class stock, the most desired element by dominant social norms. When these women refused to marry and reproduce, they forced a new concern into the public discourse. It is not a coincidence that the stereotypical asexual unmarried older woman emerged at this time as a source of popular humor. . . .

. . . The old maid warned women of the danger of thwarted desire and acted as an outer boundary to an emerging sexual sensibility; in a sense, she represented a photographic negative of appropriate female sexuality. In the emphatic dismissal of the old maid, we can also readily view an invitation to women to enter a public sexual dialogue previously reserved for males. This invitation may indeed have been a necessary response to a perceived increase in female resistance to heterosexual imperatives.

The proposition surfaces in early Edison and Biograph films that both reflected and provided models for a world of sexually engaged men *and* women. Many of the movies are remarkable in showing not only the sexual possibilities available to women but also the responsibility for initiation often placed upon them. Though some of this sexuality seems to be reserved for women characterized as wanton, much of it is not. Many "respectable" female characters find themselves happily ensconced in entanglements reflecting their own sexual desire. The images created an impression of active female sexuality and helped to establish women as agents of desire. . . .

. . . In one of the best-known early films, "What Demoralized the Barbershop" (made twice by Edison), the barbershop, a basement establishment of male privacy and prerogative, is thrown into an uproar at the sight of striped stockings worn by women walking past the street-level front door. Everyone in the shop reacts. The man getting his shoes shined won't sit still; the barber cranes his head to catch a glance and carelessly whips his huge razor across a squirming and screaming customer. Patrons knock things over trying to get a better look. The women are not unaware of the commotion they are causing; they stop at the doorway, lift their skirts, and show their legs through the open framed area over the men's heads.

Though such shenanigans seem tame by today's standards, these 1898 and 1901 productions lent early witness to the public dialogue on sexuality—particularly as it concerned male lust and female purity. In contradiction to the Progressive rhetoric about rapacious men, lust here is portrayed as a form of bumbling impotence that might wreak havoc inside the sanctuary of male isolation but otherwise poses little threat. The imagery of female instigation belonged to an ongoing counterdiscourse to reformer ideology which blamed male lechery on female wantonness.

There is little within the film to indicate anything about the character or class of the young ladies. Most films about disreputable young women made their low status quite plain. Here, status is not at issue; the humor comes from the recognition that these men are flustered by their sexual arousal at a "glimpse of stocking" and from the knowledge that the girls who wear those stockings are deliberately attempting to disrupt the male psyche. During this era the concept was sufficiently new to public discourse that the joke could emerge from the reversal of standard attitudes. Though this reversal humor would hold sway for several more years, the change in attitudes reflected in "What Demoralized the Barbershop" had now begun in earnest. . . .

Popular artists exploring sexual expression saw the female body as more than a skirt and a pair of legs. The body took on a specific physical reality, almost as a counter to the ethereal vision of the Victorian woman. Here, the movies clearly reflected a growing cultural trend that encouraged women to exercise and to see their bodies as a natural part of themselves instead of as an "animal" side to be shunned.

Doctors and educators in the late nineteenth century began to reject the prevailing medical view that physical activity was debilitating for middle- and upper-class women. Instead, physicians began to encourage women to engage in exercise and recreational activity. The debate over proper physical activity often centered on issues that were either openly or covertly sexual. Bicycle riding, for example, was a source of much controversy, as was swimming. Despite the argument, "physical culture," as it was called, became quite a rage among young women of the upper classes.

The connection between physical culture and a woman's capacity to take care of herself in the battle for sexual parity appeared often in films of the period. Numerous works satirized the craze and placed it in a sexual context. "The Physical Culture Lesson," made in 1906 by G. W. Bitzer (probably the most prolific early filmmaker), takes the otherwise unstated sexual potential and makes it explicit. A dark-suited man comes to give a young lady her calisthenics lesson. They seem to be in the dressing area of her home. As the instructor demonstrates each exercise, his pupil only replicates it partially, continually forcing him to reach over and guide her body with his hands. When she does a leg lift, he grabs her ankle and pulls it upward, exaggerating the movement. She primps at the dressing table in between exercises. At the end of the lesson, he sits down to rest, and she is pulled onto his lap. The film ends with them kissing as she sits on his lap. . . .

Images of female athleticism provided erotic representations because they placed women's bodies on display in a fashion that implied sexual access. Bitzer recognized and satirized that fact. His films on the subject simply showed the new phenomenon in all its startling irregularity. These first efforts seem to have served as some form of soft pornography; they are well in line with a number of films whose sole purpose was to show women engaging in some form of physical action in inappropriate, often suggestive clothing. By adding a specific sexual subtext through the plot, Bitzer reinforced an emerging public vision of a female body available to male desire. Moreover, women were eager participants in the creation and consumption of these images, skewed though they might be. The images were not intended exclusively for the rarefied world of private male lust but were instead aimed at the culture at large, becoming part of the free floating, unfettered social dialogue on relations between men and women. Women as well as men were to be in on the joke. The assumption that women would understand humor of such a sexual nature presupposes a fundamental recognition that women were engaged in the sexual dialogue. The films discussed here thus indicate shifts in both focus and audience. . . .

II

. . . The representations captured in these movies did not stand as the final statement of some "new" sexuality. Rather, they were attempts to reformulate existing public understandings governing heterosexuality. . . . In the world as on the screen, women came to be incorporated into a vision of desire and lust, both as objects and as participants. This transformation brought costs as well as pleasures, both for individuals unsure of the rules and for a society facing an uncertain future.

. . . Testimony and court documents from statutory rape trials in Sacramento, California, demonstrate that determining the rules for sexual activity was no easy matter at the turn of the century. In these proceedings we find a besieged traditional order trying with mixed success to shore up a waning moral and sexual ethic. Simultaneously, the records illustrate a readjustment of sexual values among those accused of misconduct as well as among their prosecutors and judges. The hard-working farmers and railroad employees who composed local juries did not decide cases of sexual transgression by applying a simple moral equation. Guilt and innocence in such matters became increasingly difficult to recognize. . . . As films soared in popularity during the first decade of the twentieth century, the private debate, as seen in the trials of young men accused of sexual crimes, roared fiercely. The gravity of those cases contrasted sharply with the lighthearted sexual humor presented by the films. Sexual negotiations may have seemed funny on screen, but to communities in transition the evidence of similar activity in their hometowns forced crises of moral order that often resulted in palpable rage.

Fourteen-year-old Almary Jones felt the full force of that rage after she began meeting John Salle secretly during the dog days of a Sacramento October in 1910. The rules for sexual behavior had become cloudy, and judgments about that behavior were difficult to make. Everyone testifying at the grand jury indictment for rape against Salle, a twenty-five-year-old Southern Pacific boiler-shop worker, had recognized that his involvement with Jones might cause trouble, and all claimed to have warned him. Salle acknowledged that although he thought Jones looked about sixteen, he suspected that she was younger. Salle pled guilty, and when he was finally sentenced to five years in prison it was agreed that a deservedly light punishment had been handed down.

Great sympathy was expressed for Salle, reflecting the confusion felt by the community. Even the judge, who seemed determined to assign blame away from the "little girl" in question, found Salle troublingly respectable: "This young man . . . is an earnest, hard worker. Everyone of his co-employees in the shops, where he works, speak well of him; many testified in the trial of those who were associated with him in the commission of this offense, and all spoke of the defendant as a hard working, good boy." His attorney pleaded with the court that "he is not a criminal. There is not anything criminal in him. From the first arrest of this young man up to the present moment, his conduct has been that of an exemplary, honest, straightforward young fellow." Reluctantly, the judge denied a defense request for probation and sentenced the defendant to prison, but those who bore witness agreed with Salle's attorney, who argued that "the circumstances surrounding his guilt should appeal to the manhood of every man here who hears his story."

Those circumstances reflected the private life of many such young men and women, including the dozens who testified in Salle's behalf. Salle and his friends played together in ways unfamiliar to a staid legal system that did not quite know what to do with them. Their play was energetic and engaged. It rested on a mutuality of interest between men and women and assumed at its base an understanding and acceptance of desire. The judge may have seen a "pretty little girl in short dresses to the knees . . . attending the primary school" when he looked at Almary Jones, but Salle and friends from both camps knew her as an independent young woman with more than a little sexual experience to guide her through relations with her new beau. All the differing impressions were true. John Salle was just as respectable as he seemed to be, and yet not so; Almary Jones was both innocent and "wild." In this they were much like their friends, and it is clear, as we read the text of this case, that neither Almary nor John was anybody special at all.

They met at a Saturday night dance, a regular weekly event that brought out people of a variety of ages and types. . . . The chaperoned dances at Turner Hall were considered a safe way for young people to meet each other. Almary, accompanied by her mother and friends, had every reason to know that this was proper behavior.

When she went to the dance for several weeks with one of her mother's female boarders, however, the stakes got a little higher. Almary and Mabel Springer found in each other the support they needed to explore their own sexual potential. Mabel and her husband, Morris, an independent roofer, lived in the Jones home in the summer and fall of 1910. She and Almary became friends and began to go to the Saturday night dances without Mrs. Jones. Almary met John Salle and his boiler-shop buddy Pete Kostena and then introduced them to Mabel Springer. Mabel paired off with Pete, and Almary joined up with John. Following the dance, the four went to the Eagle, a local restaurant catering to working-class patrons. They had some supper and a few beers (the grand jury was stunned to learn that the young Almary drank real lager, or, as she called it, "Bohemian Beer"), finally getting home at 1:30 A.M.

During the week Salle sent Jones a cryptic postcard urging the women to meet him and Pete at the corner of Seventh and K Streets at 8:00 P.M. on Thursday night. The four went to the theater, then to the Eagle, and then took a stroll through Capitol Park, the extensive and beautiful grounds surrounding the State Capitol. Almary and John lay in the grass, fondling and kissing, but when John said he wanted to "fuck," she put him off by telling him that she was "sick" with her "monthlies." They met again, by the same method, the next week. That evening, after going to the movies and making the requisite midnight visit to the Eagle, they decided to get a room. While still at the restaurant, Mabel spoke to Almary in the bathroom: "I told her that Kostena promised me ten dollars if I would stay with him, and she said she would stay also. I told her she hadn't better. She better go home. . . . She said she was going anyway. She said if Mr. Salle would give her some money, she would go; but she liked Pete [*sic*; corrected testimony to "John"], and she would go anyway." Mabel gave Almary advice on how to wash herself afterward, and the four took off in search of rooms. It was no small task. Three or four rooming houses turned them away. They finally found two basement rooms a few blocks from the Eagle.

An extremely reluctant witness, Almary testified about what happened next. Earlier, she apparently had given a comprehensive statement to the district attorney, but Almary now infuriated the grand jury by refusing to give detailed answers.

Q: Well, now just what did he do? What sort of objects did he put into you? What was the shape of it? Take your hand down from your mouth and the quicker you tell, the better. What was the shape of the object he put into you? Was it square?
A: No sir.
Q: Well, what was the shape? Do you know what it is called?
A: No sir.
Q: Well, if it was not square, what was the shape of it?
A: Round.
Q: Was it hard or soft?
A: Soft, I guess.
Q: Well, don't you know? Was it hard or soft? Well, whereabouts did he put it into you? What portion of you? Were you lying on your stomach or your back?
A: Back.

Q: What portion of your body did he put that into you? Did he put it into any opening on your body?

A: Yes sir.

Q: What do you use that opening for? Do you know what organ you use when you go to the toilet to pass water?

A: Yes sir.

Q: Was that the place he put the organ into you?

A: No sir.

Exasperated, the interrogator began to badger her even further, demanding to know why she was refusing to answer questions and whether anyone had spoken to her about the case or was cajoling her to marry Salle. She finally acknowledged that he had put the organ into the center of the opening between her legs. The jury then demanded to know the details of the penetration, . . . eventually getting her to spell out letter by letter ("f-u-c-k") the word Salle had used to describe their activity and finally to confess that she had told Salle that she was sixteen. . . .

The case troubled the community because innocence and guilt played little part. Though the case clearly fell within the legal definition of statutory rape, the jury had no stomach to convict. Within three or four years, almost all such cases of consensual activity would routinely result in probation for the man in question. The law, however, took time to catch up with society; in 1910, such flaunted sexual independence still remained within a context of criminality.

Yet assigning criminal responsibility was not the jury's only intent. The extensive questioning of Jones about the specifics of penetration was clearly meant to be a form of punishment. The law demanded that penetration be established for the case to be classified as statutory rape, so the questions may have been inevitable. But Salle, in his statement to the district attorney, had already confessed to having intercourse with Jones, making the questioning of Jones seem gratuitous. Further, the tone of the interrogation was stunningly assaultive. The grand jurors were enraged at Jones and used their power to humiliate her. They could see that her reluctance to testify did not reflect the shyness of a child, as they might have wished. Rather, the details of the case made readily apparent that Almary Jones knew the score. She also understood that these men were *her* prosecutors, not her protectors. Her refusal to respond seems to have been precisely what they thought it was, a willful rejection of their authority and a concern for her own "guilty" neck.

Almary Jones's decision to go on secret dates with John Salle reflected her own sexual sensibility. Though her court testimony was vague as to whether she had any earlier sexual experience, there was some indication that this was not her first encounter. Certainly, she understood the nature of her new relationship after the second date. . . . Her prior conversation with Mabel about getting money was explicit enough. What remained indisputable was the degree of autonomy exercised by Almary. She may not have understood everything she was getting into, but she certainly knew enough to lie to Salle about her age—and thus to guarantee that the enjoyable dangerous situation continued. . . .

It seems unlikely that either Almary Jones or Mabel Springer was coerced into an action against her moral code. To the contrary, both the married Mrs. Springer and the independent Miss Jones seem to have been fairly hell-bent on doing precisely what they wanted. Those wants included a few beers, some dancing, the picture show, and a little cash for a little sex with a couple of hard-working, respectable young fellows. Obtaining those rewards required the two women to do some negotiating with the young men, negotiations that had less to do with money than with the sex that might be available. Their agreements reflected both knowledge and a degree of accord between all parties as to what was appropriate and what could be had for what cost. None of the four challenged these fundamental understandings. It was not odd or "insulting," to use the language of the reformers, to the women that John and Pete had sexual designs on them. Almary and Mabel had their own scheme, and the men found this perfectly reasonable as well.

This mutuality of interest and purpose, a sensibility shared by all four parties and by their numerous friends, testifies to the altered sexual reality emerging at the beginning of the new century. Despite the judge's attempts to paint Almary Jones as an innocent victim, few of those involved agreed. Her eager participation in the relationship with Salle may have made her character dubious to many, but for others it must have reinforced the emergence of a new code of acceptable conduct. Just as the popular vision (as mediated on screen and stage) began to include female desire for the first time, private individuals—the first generation of young people impacted by and involved with the development of that vision—recognized women as active and equal players in sexual affairs. Women such as Almary and Mabel saw themselves as sexual actors in their own right; perhaps even more significant, the young men shared that sensibility with them. Negotiating a new sexual code did not necessarily entail an exchange of cash, although it certainly might. What that negotiation demanded was parity—a sense of, if not equal, at least equivalent desire by both men and women.

The testimony in the Salle case demonstrates well this symmetry. However, the consternation and confusion surrounding the case make it clear that this new public sexuality was as yet a language under construction. Its syntax and grammar remained undersigned, and its vocabulary still lay encoded in the conversations of the past. The grand jury inquisition of Almary Jones was but one particularly virulent reflection of the conflict between old and new. She received little sympathy, despite the assault upon her honor that would send John Salle to prison for five years. . . .

III

By World War I, the Victorian assumptions about sexuality which dominated Progressive rhetoric were in tatters. Public imagery of women no longer conveyed purity and chastity. The movies and popular stage had made clear that women were deeply interested in expressions of erotic desire. Women on the screen initiated sexual contact, took responsibility for its development, and often enjoyed its pleasures without ill consequence. Not surprisingly, reformers roared that such films utterly lacked moral content. But, of course, the films did have a moral ethos—it simply differed from that of late-nineteenth-century middle-class culture.

In reconstructing public heterosexuality, the films reflected and helped build consensus for a vision of women as sexual beings. This consensus crossed class lines in the white community; though films depicted some sexually active women as disreputable or working-class, the overwhelming majority were represented, both by dress and lifestyle, as middle-class or, at least, upwardly mobile. Although the burlesque girl may have been the symbol of sexual precociousness, the middle-class wife or girlfriend demonstrated an equal degree of pleasure in expressing her desire.

It is important to grasp the visual power of this moment. As the first films made their way through the country and enthralled a national audience, they presented images of women that rang true with many in the audience. At precisely the moment that the Progressive ideologies launched their assault on prostitution, vice, and male lust, the films offered a counterdiscourse that manipulated prostitution, redefined vice, and contextualized lust as a two-party action. The audiences listening to both ideologies rejected the Progressives, whose vision of the world bore so little resemblance to their own, and welcomed the films as affirmation and agreeable entertainment.

In towns like Sacramento, these discourses redefined public heterosexuality. Increasingly, judges who defended womanhood and the family as understood by the Progressives found themselves voices in the wilderness. They railed alone in communities that cared deeply about their members. These were small towns in which many people knew each other, had grown up together, and worked together as adults. If the people of Sacramento had no desire to prosecute and convict statutory rape cases by 1910, it was not because they had fallen prey to a nameless, alienating society that promoted immoral character. On the contrary, it was because everyone's name was known. The Progressive rhetoric made no sense to the people of Sacramento. They knew the people accused of sexual crimes and knew dozens of others who behaved similarly but were never charged. They could not see evil in these actions; they and their neighbors engaged in these same activities and considered them harmless. . . .

The inclusion of desire into female identity, a central focus of the heterosexual vision, was not a triumphant process. The women discussed here did not wake up one morning and march through the streets, ushering in a world of sexual "liberation." In their contravention of community authority, these women and men were punished. As time went on, men were punished less by the courts, but women began to be punished more. Moral "delinquency" and moral "imbecility" emerged as terms to explain female sexual expression. . . . The evidence from Sacramento and the early films testify to the conflicts faced by all participants as the emerging sensibility and the older codes wrestled for dominance in the arena of civic authority and the popular imagination.

American Doctors Define the Lesbian and Her Intellect, 1880–1949

MARGARET GIBSON

From the end of the nineteenth century through the first half of the twentieth, the female invert, homosexual, or lesbian made her debut in the writings and categories of American doctors. In this formative period, the lesbian body was a subject of increasingly lively discussion and vigorous scrutiny. Medical writers, including alienists, psychiatrists, neurologists, sexologists, and psychoanalysts, constructed

Margaret Gibson, "The Masculine Degenerate: American Doctors' Portrayals of the Lesbian Intellect, 1880–1949," *Journal of Women's History* 9, no. 4 (1998); 78–103. Reprinted by permission of Indiana University Press.

a variety of images of the new creature and of those body parts which they deemed relevant to her "perversion." While these investigators examined, directly or indirectly, a wide variety of organs and systems that might surprise a late-twentieth-century observer, two related topics that medical writers between 1880 and 1949 pinpointed as crucial subjects of study are still central to scientific studies of homosexuality: the lesbian intellect and brain. . . .

This article examines some of the multiple and frequently contradictory images of the lesbian intellect and the ways in which medical writers of the late nineteenth and early twentieth centuries attempted to reconcile them. In the first section, I discuss the general masculinity of the lesbian in medical writings of the time, the history of the brain in medial and biological writings, and the most prominent images of the lesbian brain and intellect that emerged. The latter sections of the article examine two discussions in the medical literature that expanded upon the significance of the lesbian intellect. The first of these debates is the flurry of concern that arose about women's education and its relationship to sexual deviance. . . . I argue that debates about women's education utilized the conflicting qualities of the lesbian intellect to discourage and regulate a trend toward women's higher education that doctors and others found disturbing. The final section of this article discusses medical writers' explicit consideration of the intellect in the determination of lesbians' (and male homosexuals') social value. A number of medical studies from the 1910s through the 1930s dealt with the defense and condemnation of the lesbian, and her brain and mental abilities were highlighted as indispensable pieces of evidence. In a somewhat bizarre sequence of articles in this time period, doctors also wrote in retaliation against outspoken homosexuals and their supporters, an episode that demonstrates the metaphorical importance of the discourse on the intellect as a way to manage perceived social threats. . . .

Embedded in my approach to the American medical establishment's relationship with lesbianism is the idea that homosexuality, or indeed any sexuality, is a historically variable entity I also assert that the creation of labels and categories of deviance serves a regulatory purpose, and doctors use medical forums as a way to quell perceived social threats. Medical studies of the human body are valuable social documents, and an analysis of the medical "construction" of the lesbian body reveals the concerns and assumptions of medical writers and their societies. A crucial theorist in this "constructivist" tradition is Michel Foucault, whose studies in the history of madness and sexuality have been seminal in the understanding of "deviance" as a regulatory category. . . . [T]he medicalization of lesbianism, frequently considered a form of "insanity" throughout this time period, and the lesbian body, which was the morphological representation of deviance, formed a crucial consolidation of medical and social responses to the various threats which the lesbian represented to her society.

To most medical commentators at the turn of the century, the lesbian's physical or psychological masculinity was her defining characteristic and was often essential to her categorization. . . . This identification of female homosexuality with masculinity was a historically stable phenomenon and was reflected to some degree in all of the major works on homosexuality throughout this time period. Masculinity was implied by the terms "sexual inversion," "sexual intermediacy," "third sex," and the medical illustrations of these diagnoses were often at least as concerned with gender transgression as sexual object choice. For example, in 1895, Havelock Ellis listed traits that might betray the invert's masculinity, including a "masculine type of larynx," an affinity for "masculine" activities like smoking, and a corresponding distaste for more "feminine" habits and duties. Similarly, in 1923, F. Stella Browne described "an invert of the most pronounced physical type . . . [whose physical traits] were so like those of a very young and very well-groomed youth, that all the staff of the school nicknamed her 'Boy.'" . . . Throughout this time period, lesbians could be considered "masculine" based on who found them attractive: if only "feminine" men were attracted to a woman, this was viewed as further evidence of her "masculine" charms.

Medical observers viewed the brain as a gendered organ, and as such its description and construction played a key role in the categorization of female homosexuality. While organs like ovaries or external genitalia might be more readily accepted as representative of gender or sex to a late-twentieth-century reader, the brain has a long history as an indicator of gender. The prominent historical association of the masculine with the rational and the feminine with the natural or bodily was central to the construction of a gendered brain. This split between the male mind and female body led to an image of the male or masculine brain as larger and more competent than the smaller, weaker female organ. . . .

The nineteenth century was an especially crucial time period in the creation and modification of the physically gendered brain. . . . Biological anthropologists in particular developed a fascination for the measurement of the human head and brain, which they then used to rank races, sexes, and other groups. The white man, especially the northern European and his (male) descendants, maintained his position as the possessor of the "largest" and most "advanced" brain. The white, male, upper-class brain was found not only to weigh more and occupy more cranial space than any competitors, but it also had a more developed forebrain (the traditional seat of the "higher functions") than that of black men, all women, or anybody else. Female brains were found to be significantly smaller, a finding which scientists argued could not be completely accounted for by any difference in stature. The replacement of cranial and cerebral measurements by intelligence testing in the early twentieth century, an American development, proved to be a smooth transition, as the racial, sexual, and socioeconomic hierarchies of the nineteenth century were strictly maintained. Intelligence, gender, race, and a variety of other traits directly corresponded to the qualities of the brain in scientific and medical accounts, all of which were crucial to the construction of the lesbian brain.

With the rapid proliferation of medical specialties at the turn of the century, a wide variety of medical professionals were studying the lesbian brain, including neurologists, alienists, psychiatrists, and eventually psychoanalysts and endocrinologists. At the same time, a number of common structures of the lesbian brain emerged, all of which were built on the assumption that the female homosexual was masculine. One of the earliest and most prominent images which doctors put forth of the gendered lesbian brain was that of "psychic hermaphroditism," or psychosexual hermaphroditism," in which a male brain resided in (or was trapped in) a female body, or, in the case of the male homosexual, a female brain resided in a male body. For example, James Kiernan described this phenomenon in an 1888 article on sexual perversions: "Without dealing with the question of the soul, which belongs to the domain of theology, it seems that a femininely functioning brain can occupy a male body, and vice versa." . . . The brain in this portrayal was a discrete entity, which could be removed from its "proper" sex and transplanted into the "improper" one as an effectual whole. . . .

. . . Endocrinology, which gained prominence in the 1920s through the 1940s, directly connected the brain with sexuality through hormonal vectors. This relationship was not new, since the phrenological theories of the early nineteenth century cast the brain as the seat of the sexual drive. In endocrinology, however, the presence of cerebral glands that controlled sex hormones sexualized the brain more directly by positioning it as a source of sexual feeling. . . .

As one might expect, . . . discussions of lesbian intelligence were intertwined with concerns about the organic brain. Thus, doctors frequently wrote about lesbians' superior intellectual abilities, although there was no clear consensus on whether a keen intellect caused lesbianism or reflected it. For example, in 1934, George Henry described a homosexual patient in this way: "During adolescence she preferred the company of girls who were of the intellectual type like herself and this preference caused boys to shun her." In this account, the social misstep of obvious female intelligence could make lesbianism a relative necessity; however, Henry's remark also implies that lesbianism created a homosocial grouping which relied on the shared (masculine) intellect of its members. . . . Sometimes doctors argued that the presence of a masculine or "advanced" intellect in a woman might lead to homosexuality, when combined with social pressures: "Our present social arrangements . . . artificially stimulate inversion and [we] have thus forfeited all right to condemn it. There is a huge, persistent, indirect pressure on women of strong passions and *fine brains* to find an emotional outlet with other women" (emphasis mine). Thus, whether "masculine" intelligence could be considered a cause or a side effect of female homosexuality, the connection between intellect and lesbianism relied on and reproduced sexual hierarchies in brain size and intelligence. This image of the lesbian brain would also be integral to debates about women's education.

Despite the potentially admirable traits that a masculine mind might bring to the lesbian body, degeneration and eugenic theories of the nineteenth and twentieth centuries, as well as contemporary social convictions, could not permit a consistent portrayal of lesbians as intellectually superior to other women. As Daniel Pick and others have noted, the rise of Darwinian evolutionary biology in the mid-nineteenth century created a legacy of degeneration concerns which lasted into the twentieth century in the social and eugenic theories of the Progressive Era. According to degeneration theory, humanity lived under the constant threat of evolutionary regression, a surfacing of animalistic or "uncivilized" traits. Medical writers believed that the boundaries of gender and sexuality were especially prone to and indicative of such degradation. . . . The theory that homosexuality was a hermaphroditic reversion, exemplified by Kiernan's work on inversion, implied that the lesbian occupied an inferior evolutionary rung, a status which both her masculinity and general "perversion" would confirm. These degenerative fears led doctors to scrutinize patients' heredity for such traits as insanity or alcoholism, the presence of which would support Krafft-Ebing's classification of sexual inversion as "a result of neuro-psychical degeneration." An article in the journal *Medicine* claimed that "aberrations of the sexual instinct are among the most striking stigmata of inherited nervous instability"—meaning that homosexuality indicated broader degeneration in an individual, and possibly in a society.

Insanity and feeblemindedness were especially direct vehicles for linking the lesbian intellect to "lower" rungs of the evolutionary and social ladder. Feeble-mindedness was a concern that entered the medical spotlight in the early twentieth century, in the height of Progressive Era eugenicist fervor, through the efforts of fig-ures like H. H. Goddard, who drew from and capitalized on popular anxieties about immigration. Feeblemindedness was seen as strongly congenital and hereditary, and was perceived as the prototypical barrier to a healthy and evolutionarily "strong" society, and the source of social evils such as crime. Thus, when Charles Ford's 1928–1929 discussion of lesbian relationships in institutions included the state-ment, "Many of the [lesbian] inmates are retarded in mental development and some are actually feebleminded," he was making a strong argument against the evolution-ary worth of the lesbian, as well as providing an image of the lesbian brain which directly contradicted the "masculine" lesbian intelligence of other accounts.

The other common image of the mentally degenerate lesbian was that of the insane homosexual. Lesbianism was regarded as a form of insanity, or otherwise associated with madness, from the earliest medical accounts of inversion through the 1940s and beyond. The doctors who treated female inversion or homosexuality of-ten depended on this association, since the professional expertise of these alienists, neurologists, psychiatrists, and psychologists lay in their understanding of insanity. In later accounts of homosexuality, this connection had especially strong signifi-cance for the lesbian intellect and its treatment. The 1930s and 1940s witnessed a rise in somatic explanations and treatments of mental disorder, which targeted the brain and nervous system as the cause of behavioral abnormality. . . .

. . . Another way in which doctors freely connected the lesbian's masculine brain with low evolutionary status was through the consideration of scientific and social hierarchies other than that of sex. Race, criminality, and socioeconomic status could serve as useful ways to undermine any connection between lesbianism and masculine superiority. Instead of simply constructing a lesbian brain that was similar to a male brain, doctors depicted a lesbian brain with characteristics similar to a nonwhite, or lower-class masculine brain. . . . By connecting female homosexuals' brains to other races, doctors could undermine any connotations of superiority that surrounded their intellectual masculinity. This strategy points to a multiplicity of masculinities that could be called upon in the construction of a lesbian intellect. The diversity of masculinities that were created by differences such as class and race was expanded upon through the creation of the lesbian herself. One of the most revealing examples of this role assigned to the lesbian intellect is found in debates about women's education. In these discussions, the lesbian intellect embodied a new form of degenerate masculinity that was to warn putatively "normal" women away from higher education.

Discussions of the lesbian intellect had implications for all women, especially women who challenged dominant ideas about male superiority. For example, in a turn-of-the-century account of degeneracy, Frank Lydston wrote a small section on "The Female Genius" in which he argued that female "geniuses" were essentially in-tersexed and degenerate, and gave the examples of Sappho, Cleopatra, George Sand,

and others to support the image of a sexually immoral female genius. Thus, the specter of an intelligent, sexually deviant woman became a threat to the status of any ambitious woman. As the following section will show, the taint of lesbianism that surrounded the New Woman and the female college student in the late nineteenth and early twentieth century created a legacy from which doctors and members of other social establishments could draw to suppress any threatening female intellectual or social ambition. In these discussions, the multiple images of the lesbian intellect provided a powerful and flexible way to delineate the proper roles of all women. Medical writers were able to sidestep the contradictions of the lesbian brain and intellect by using lesbianism itself as a connection between intelligence and degeneracy. Thus, instead of being split between two portrayals, the lesbian intellect became the manifestation of the hidden dangers of "masculine" achievement for women, revealing the degeneration that could follow the apparently innocuous goal of higher education. Medical writers became watchdogs for society, advocating prevention and early diagnosis. Education, they argued, was a process by which women might become masculine, and therefore lesbian, and ultimately degenerate.

The formative years of the medical classification of lesbianism were filled with conflicts about female education, which reached fever pitch at the turn of the century with the rise of women's colleges and the New Woman. New Women were usually college graduates who used their education as a stepping stone in creating careers, to the exclusion of marriage. New Women were often politically active, participating in many of the social reform movements that characterized the Progressive Era. In particular, many New Women joined suffrage movements and advocated more extensive rights for women. The anxieties surrounding the strong links between New Women and female political activity were reflected in their shared connections to lesbianism in medical accounts of the time period. . . .

One of the most influential nineteenth-century opponents of female higher education was Edward Clarke, a professor at the Harvard Medical School. His 1873 treatise, *Sex in Education: A Fair Chance for the Girls*, highlighted the multiple costs that education would impose on the female body, including illness and fatigue. The female brain, according to Clarke, could only be used at the expense of physical feminine qualities, since energy devoted to study would be diverted from the development of the healthy reproductive system that was so essential to society. While Clarke did not discuss female inversion or homosexuality, which the medical literature of the time had only begun to classify, he defined a relationship between women's education, masculinity, and both degeneration and arrested development that would remain critical associations into the next century. For example, Clarke wrote that "a woman . . . who has been defrauded by her education . . . is not so much of a woman, intellectually and morally, as well as physically." . . . Clarke then listed the possible "intellectual and psychical condition" of these overeducated women, which included "a dropping out of maternal instincts, and an appearance of Amazonian coarseness and force." Thus, Clarke's influential book represented an image of the pre-lesbian brain, which the earliest American accounts of female inversion would then incorporate into the constructions of a lesbian intellect. Furthermore, he had paved the way for others to use the lesbian intellect as a warning to college-bound women, by pointing to increased "masculinity" as the horror they should fear most in their consideration of higher education.

The later medical anxieties about the masculinizing or homosexualizing impact of education on women expanded on Clarke's themes and explicitly linked college or school life with an ominous lesbian presence. Turn-of-the-century doctors expressed growing concern about the seclusion of girls and women from male influence in single-sex schools and colleges. While girls who spent all their time with male friends were a source of anxiety, girls and women who showed no interest in interacting with boys and men were even more of a concern. Thus, the "school crush" between girls became a central figure in medical articles on lesbianism. . . .

The concern about lesbianism in colleges was so pervasive that even the desire of a woman to attend college could indicate her latent or active homosexuality, and such anxieties lasted far beyond the early twentieth century and the New Woman. For example, in a 1929 article, John Meagher wrote, "It has been observed that a woman who yearns only for higher education and neglects love, is usually the frigid type. Many homosexuals are intellectual and cultured, though sexually infantile." The publication of Katherine Bement Davis's 1929 book, *Factors in the Sex Life of Twenty-Two Hundred Women,* both created and underlined renewed concern about the connection between homosexuality and college. In a chapter entitled "Homosexuality: The Unmarried College Woman," Davis claimed: "My own observation in both educational and penological institutions leads me to believe that the phenomena described in this study [homosexual experiences] are much more widespread than is generally suspected, or than more administrators are willing to admit." One-half of the respondents to her surveys answered that they had "at any time experienced intense emotional relations with other women," and around half of this group answered that their relations were sexual in nature. The Davis study reinforced the connection between lesbianism and education, and implicitly contributed to the image of a masculine, lesbian brain that might be more educated or intelligent than the brain of a heterosexual woman. . . .

Doctors still had to deal with some contradictions between the images of the educated and the degenerate lesbian when it came to discussions of socioeconomic class. . . . If lesbianism were connected to the intelligent, wealthy, college-going elite, then this finding directly conflicted with the image of the lower-class (and therefore evolutionarily lower) lesbian who was found in so many other accounts. Some medical commentators attempted to incorporate both images of female homosexuality. Meagher wrote that "riches and poverty are more apt to favor homosexuality; the development of the average individual between these two classes is more apt to follow the normal course." Meagher's theory of sexuality and class reflected the case studies of most doctors in this time period: prostitutes, prisoners, and other representatives of the poor appeared opposite wealthy, hysterical, and overwrought girls in accounts of female homosexuality. . . .

While discussions of education could sometimes set aside the conflicts inherent in the construction of the lesbian brain, this task was more difficult to accomplish in studies that set out to determine the overall social status of the lesbian. . . . While most late-twentieth-century readers would expect all doctors in the early twentieth century to be ruthless in their evaluations of the homosexual (an assumption which is well-supported by most medical literature of the time), a number of doctors and other writers challenged these medical condemnations of homosexuality and homosexuals.

The resulting debates by no means overturned the overwhelming hostility of the medical profession toward women and homosexuals throughout this time period, but such discussion does indicate that medical opinions were not monolithic. More importantly for the consideration of the lesbian intellect, the debates that arose from these differences of opinion used the intellect and brain as valuable indicators of social worth.

. . . [O]pinions seem to be at their most diverse in the 1920s and 1930s. One possible reason for the multiplication of medical views of lesbianism in these later decades is a new awareness of female sexuality, springing from both the dissemination of Freudian thought into popular American culture and a widespread rebellion against "Victorianism"—which led doctors to consider asexuality or even "frigidity" as a problem in women, rather than natural to their sex. Furthermore, the publication of Radclyffe Hall's *The Well of Loneliness* in 1928 injected the image of the lesbian directly into the popular imagination of mid-twentieth-century America, while medical doctors became more likely to address homosexuality in a public forum. Finally, in the more urban areas of the country, there were increasingly visible homosexual communities.

Lesbians' "masculine" intelligence and large, advanced brains were frequently mentioned as a part of a defense of lesbianism, demonstrating the potential of this organ to contradict the image of the degenerate lesbian. . . . Florence Beery's "The Psyche of the Intermediate Sex" . . . described the homosexual (male or female) as "keen, quick, intuitive, sensitive, exceptionally tactful and [having] a great deal of understanding," and again emphasized intellectual qualities in her argument that homosexuals are "generally fine healthy specimens, well developed bodily, intellectual, and generally with a very high standard of conduct." Beery praised female homosexuals as "superwomen" and argued that the lesbian "is fitted for remarkable work in professional life or as managress of institutions, even as a ruler of a country." Jane MacKinnon's 1947 article in the *American Journal of Psychiatry* was a more restrained but heartfelt assertion of lesbians' worth. MacKinnon, a homosexual who was presumably writing under a pseudonym, wrote "The Homosexual Woman" as retaliation against mistaken images of lesbianism. While her article had a great deal in common with those of her contemporaries, instead of viewing insanity as a symbol of lesbians' degeneracy, MacKinnon blamed social stigma and consequent loneliness for lesbians' health problems, arguing, "You cannot keep a healthy state of mind if you are very lonely." MacKinnon did not explicitly claim lesbians' intelligence, but she underlined the social value of homosexual women's masculinity, writing "In many cases, she [the lesbian] is respected and admired for her manly qualities."

These assertions of the social worth of lesbians and homosexuals challenged the portrayal of the lesbian intellect as inferior and, to varying degrees, exploited the image of the unusually intelligent lesbian. In response to or in conjunction with such assertions of admirable lesbian qualities, some doctors reasserted their loathing or disapproval of homosexuality. Fears of the proud and defiant homosexual, or the medical writer who might create such a creature, became especially visible from the 1920s through the 1940s. As might be expected, these doctors used the abundant images of the degenerate homosexual, and especially the degenerate homosexual intellect, to contradict contemporaries like Beery and MacKinnon.

There was a surprisingly strong fear that homosexuals were becoming too power-ful, and that heterosexual superiority, or even equality, was under attack by social trends. . . . William J. Robinson's article, "My Views on Homosexuality," presented an especially strident objection to his colleagues who had "found that there were among them [homosexuals] people of high intellectual attainments. So far so good, and so far I am in full agreement. But some sexologists thought it necessary to 'go further' and even claimed that homosexuals were 'something superior to normal.'" Robinson asserted the abnormality and degeneracy of homosexuals, and stated "I have yet to see a great or even a capable thinker among them." . . . Such discussions of the correct social and medical attitude toward the homosexual indicate the im-portance of the intellect and brain as a determinant of the social hierarchy. Further-more, the arguments of these anxious individuals demonstrate the existence of a homosexual resistance to dominant medical beliefs that had even found some allies within the medical profession.

. . . A consideration of historical studies of the lesbian's intellect in light of her pre-sumed gender transgression has implications beyond the analysis of recent medical research. This discussion of the multiple images of the lesbian brain and intellect also offers a different perspective on how perceived gender qualities have affected the lesbian's place in her society. Other historians have struggled with the implica-tions of the "mythic mannish lesbian," to use Esther Newton's term. Newton, for ex-ample, argues that the visibly masculine lesbian represents a self-assertive adoption of medical stereotypes which allowed women like Radclyffe Hall and her famous protagonist from *The Well of Loneliness* to escape from the asexuality and invisibility of "romantic friendship." Others, like Carroll Smith-Rosenberg and Sherrie Inness, claim that the medical establishment's equation of homosexuality with masculinity was part of a successful strategy to limit the subversive power of the New Woman and lesbian. Inness argues that the visible, masculine lesbian was far less threatening to early twentieth-century American culture than the feminine lesbian who might slip by unnoticed. The medical writers cited in this article almost universally subscribed to the belief that the lesbian was somehow masculine, but they used this assumption very differently. The history of the lesbian intellect demonstrates that masculinity was not a unified quality in medical writings about homosexuality. Masculinity could be used to assert the intellectual prowess of the lesbian, it could be an indicator of the hermaphroditic evolutionary reversion of the invert, or it could be radically or socio-economically modified to produce the image of an ethnically-suspect, lower-class lesbian brain and intellect.

   The reconsideration of masculinity complicates the question: Is it more poten-tially subversive for a lesbian to be "masculine" or "feminine"? While it is true that the "mythic mannish lesbian" fulfilled the proscriptive formulas of the medical community, she also inserted herself into a morass of contradictory evaluations. The feminine lesbian was by no means a more comfortable subject for medical consider-ation. She was a contradiction in terms under Victorian considerations of female sexuality, since any overt sexuality in women was "hypersexuality" and essentially masculine. She might evade the notice not only of medical observers but also of the heterosexual men whose wives or lovers she coveted. But the feminine lesbian's invisibility placed her in the same category as other women in terms of her intellect, and so any claims of "superwoman" status would be denied her. Furthermore, she would only be considered "feminine" by medical writers for as long as she remained securely within the intellectual and social worlds seen as appropriate to her sex. Finally, being truly "feminine" in the contemporary meanings of the word was only open to those women who were in the middle and upper social classes, white, and native-born. In sum, the medical conceptions of degeneracy and gender provided neither a unified model that self-assertive lesbians might easily appropriate nor a straightforward monologue that simply pathologized and constrained them.

The Modern Architecture of Marriage

NANCY F. COTT

When Orville and Wilbur Wright sent a heavier-than-air machine into the sky over Kitty Hawk, North Carolina, to fly like a bird in December 1903, the flight was rightly seen as an augury of the new century. Many technologies that would make twentieth-century life distinctive, including telephones, electric power, the automobile, the movies, and the radio, came into being around the turn of the century. So did characteristics of the economy such as the consolidated national corporation, the moving assembly line, national brands, brand-name advertising, mass merchandising of consumer goods, and the white-collar and management occupations these created. Technological innovations such as electric lights and electrified urban transportation quickened the pace of life. Not only new immigrants but country folks were drawn toward towns and cities, so that the relative weight of the rural population diminished. New forms of civic life in local and national nonpartisan organizations grouped people together to pursue shared purposes; new forms of commercialized leisure such as vaudeville theaters, movies, window-shopping at department stores, public dance halls, and amusement parks beckoned wage-earners to entertainment and relaxation outside their homes.

Amidst wrenching changes in industry, technology, and the very composition of the American people—amidst what also seemed like sky-high openings to progress—public understandings of marriage were recreated. A twentieth-century shape for the institution began to come into focus. New possibilities for women outside wifehood and the home were perceived as the driving force, more than alterations in men's lives; but new patterns in women's lives were not simple or unidirectional and neither were signals about the institution of marriage. One shift was clear: government authorities eased up on political and moral strictures about marriage and concentrated more on enforcing its economic usefulness. In the twentieth century the public framework of marriage would be preeminently economic, preserving the husband's role as primary provider and the wife as his dependent—despite the growing presence of women in the labor force.

Public policy had always viewed the economic substructure of marriage as essential, but earlier, when the character of the American polity was still at risk, the relation of marriage to political citizenship and to the moral virtue of the citizenry

Nancy Cott, *Public Vows: A History of Marriage and the Nation* (Cambridge, Mass.: Harvard University Press, 2000), 156–179. Copyright © 2000 by Nancy F. Cott. Reprinted by permission of the publisher.

was more important to articulate. The nation originally had few technologies of governance to monitor and control a people strewn unevenly over a huge expanse of land. Monogamous marriages that distinguished citizen-heads of households had enormous instrumental value for governance, because orderly families, able to accumulate and transmit private property and to sustain an American people, descended from them. As the polity itself and national solidarity became firmly established between the Civil War and World War I, however, the serviceability of marriage as a form of direct political governance lessened. And as the post-Victorian generation enjoyed what they considered a sexual revolution, they gave up their parents' exaggerated public emphasis on linking monogamous morality to political virtue. The marital model in which the individuality and citizenship of the wife disappeared into her husband's legal persona had to go, logically, once women gained the vote in 1920.

Yet marital unity was rewritten economically in the provider/dependent model, a pairing in which the husband carried more weight. This public policy emphasis emerged, ironically, while the doctrine of coverture was being unseated in social thought and substantially defeated in the law. Blanche Crozier, an exceptional feminist legal commentator, wrote acerbically that "public policy" had taken the place of common law, becoming "the new explanation, the new basis of justification," for marital inequality. When she wrote in 1935, the economic bargain between a husband-provider and a wife-dependent had become the most important public stake in marriage. . . . This economic emphasis was less directly coercive than coverture had been. It operated more through incentives than through ultimatums. Yet because the economic figuration of marriage blurred lines between public policy, law, economy, and society, it was inescapable.

When the federal government was called upon during the Depression to include social entitlements in the definition of citizenship, this marital patterning became central. The New Deal announced a qualitative change in the powers of the nation-state. Following many nations in Europe, the federal government in the United States sought to support and reshape economic life more directly. Enacting its aims involved defining social categories—such as earner and dependent—and the social relations between them. In the process of broadening meanings of citizenship, New Deal policy innovations lent new support to the old economic underpinning of marital roles. . . . The federal government would offer social provision while bolstering the basic structure of male providership and affirming the male citizen's domestic rights. It would retain within the innovation of government-granted entitlements the norm of private provision by a male citizen/head of household for his wife and children—a norm central to the system of private business enterprise as well as to the conception of the male citizen.

This evolution in government's stake in marriage was far less visible or remarkable to Americans living in the early twentieth century than the revolutions going on in the world and around them. A single extraordinary decade of political and cultural rupture after 1910 produced World War I, the Bolshevik Revolution, Cubist and Futurist art, and Einstein's theory of special relativity. In American cities, standards of behavior were cleaving the generations, as work and leisure habits and sexual mores were being transformed. Women's behavior especially attracted commentary. Sex became political—that is, it was emblematic of changing power dynamics between women and men. In expressing some sexual initiatives, women were seizing a prerogative seen as men's, just as they were treading on "male" terrain in the labor force and reform politics. . . .

By the 1920s, femininity was associated more with sex appeal than with sexual modesty, as it had been earlier. . . . Sexual experimentation before marriage by couples in love moved out of the shadows; some exploratory premarital heterosexual activity was granted to be normal. . . . Nonetheless, sexual liberalization was very controversial. Its threat to strict monogamous morality caused contests in many arenas, including the Supreme Court and the state legislatures. The Supreme Court had to decide three cases, in 1904, 1908, and 1911, all of which dealt, conceptually, with wives' challenges to the sexual and intimate aspects of marital governance. In all of these cases the court proved a bastion of conservatism, even of reaction—trying to erect a seawall against the incoming tide of women's sexual self-assertions. The court did so by reaffirming the very core of marital unity, the husband's private control of his wife's body. The first case involved a wife's consenting adultery, and her husband's rights to gain damages from the lover. In deciding it, the court defined a husband's right to exclusive sexual intercourse as "a right of the highest kind, upon . . . which the whole social order rests" and called the wife's consent to the love affair irrelevant, because she was "in law incapable of giving any consent to affect the husband's rights." The second case justified use of Congress's ban on bringing women into the United States for prostitution or "other immoral purpose" to keep out a man who sought to enter with his mistress. The court here refused to distinguish among lovers, mistresses, prostitutes, and concubines, putting them all in the same "immoral" category. All these transgressive women were "hurtful to the cause of sound private and public morality," Justice John Harlan declared, because they displayed a common "hostility" to "the union for life of one man and one woman in the holy estate of matrimony," which was—he quoted from Francis Lieber—"the sure foundation of all that is stable and noble in our civilization." The court thus confirmed congressional power to legislate monogamous morality, and applied immigration law to reinstate the sexual double standard, when social behavior was defying both. Confident that Americans "almost universally held" its own view, the court ignored the expanding spectrum of sexual behavior.

The third case involved wife abuse. Congress had enacted a married woman's property and earnings statute for the District of Columbia. One of its provisions declared that wives had the capacity to sue "as fully and freely as if they were unmarried" for harms to themselves (torts, in legal language). On the basis of this law, an abused wife in the nation's capital sued her husband to recover damages for his tort of assault and battery on her. Had she been successful, her victory would have registered an enormous change in the institution of marriage. Suits *between* husband and wife (interspousal suits) were anathema to the doctrine of marital unity. Back in 1792, the jurist James Wilson had explained why: the "beautiful and striking" principle of marital unity presumed that "between husband and wife, there subsist or may subsist no difference of will or of interest." Wilson put "the matrimonial state" at a "far remove" from legal intervention except in "very pressing emergencies." This legal doctrine . . . implemented the husband's right to be the decision-maker in his household. The law trusted the husband's "honour" to exercise his marital governance justly. . . .

In the 1911 case *Thompson v. Thompson*, a majority of the justices on the U.S. Supreme Court . . . refused to believe that Congress intended the District of Columbia married women's statute "to revolutionize the law governing the relation of husband and wife as between themselves." They rejected the "radical and far-reaching" reading that a wife could sue her husband "for injuries to person or property as though they were strangers." Allowing interspousal tort suits would encourage wives and husbands to bring marital spats into the public spotlight, unnecessarily and inappropriately. Without even glancing at the way such public restraint perpetuated male dominance in the married couple, the court alluded to divorce as the remedy available to a battered wife suffering "atrocious wrongs." . . .

. . . Despite the court's intent to say otherwise, new behaviors in the early twentieth century had begun to blur the sharp lines of monogamous morality and had disrupted conventions of marital unity. In the always-contentious area of marriage across the color line, the 1910s and 1920s were explosive. In 1912, the marriage of the heavyweight boxer Jack Johnson, who was African American, to Lucille Cameron, a seventeen-year-old white prostitute, made sensational news. The marriage came on the heels of Johnson's defeat of the "great white hope," Jack Jeffries, in a championship match interpreted across the nation as a contest for racial supremacy. Cameron's parents attempted to charge Johnson with abduction, portraying their daughter as an innocent girl who came to the city, was snared into a life of sin, and succumbed to Johnson only because she was drunk. The federal government tried to show that Johnson and his friends ran an interstate prostitution ring. Because the couple had traveled across state lines, Johnson was successfully prosecuted under the Mann Act and had to spend a year in prison.

In the year after the couple married, fourteen state legislatures introduced bills to institute or strengthen bans on racial intermarriage, though none passed in northern states. . . . Some southern congressmen hoped to pass a constitutional amendment against racial intermarriage. The Johnson-Cameron marriage became such a flashpoint, touching off this renewed effort, because more and more frequent mixed marriages loomed on the horizon as the "Great Migration" of African Americans from the south proceeded. Mixed couples became more visible, especially in New York City's celebrated Harlem. . . . Black voters' pressure had much to do with the failure of new bans to pass in the north. Nonetheless, thirty states still nullified and/or punished marriage between whites and blacks in 1930—many of them, mainly in the west, treating marriage between whites and Asians the same way. Marriage was the most criminalized form of racially related conduct. Although these laws inhibited and stigmatized mixed couples, the behavior banned had leeway to advance elsewhere. Legislators knew they were making a prescriptive statement in passing or strengthening such laws; they could only contain, not eliminate the conduct they were stigmatizing.

If sexual norms, marital unity, and separation between black and white were all challenged by transformations taking place in the new century, the old relation between marriage and political citizenship was even more directly undercut. After three quarters of a century of suffragists' efforts, the U.S. Constitution was amended, in 1920, to prohibit sex discrimination in voting. . . . Wives, voting as individuals, could no longer be presumed to be represented by their husbands. In a clear insistence on this position, women activists moved quickly to eliminate the federal laws that bound a wife's nationality to her husband's and took away the citizenship of American women who married foreigners.

The result was the Cable Act, or Married Women's Independent Nationality Act, of 1922. Reflecting the reluctance of Congress to give up its long-term priority for the male citizen as family head and also the racial nationalism of immigration restriction, the act did not free a wife's citizenship entirely. An American woman who married a foreigner and stayed put in the United States would now remain the citizen she was. But she would lose her citizenship if she lived in her husband's country as much as two years, and she could not retain it at all if she married a man "ineligible for citizenship"—an Asian, a polygamist, or an anarchist. An American man suffered no such consequences for similar choices. . . . [T]he Cable Act contained inequalities that kept the principle of a wife's political individuality from being fully realized. These were eventually corrected with a series of legislative revisions, hard fought for by women's pressure groups, in 1930, 1931, and 1934.

Even stronger hesitations dogged women's accession to jury service. Jury service was a political right that had always been linked to voting capacity. Accordingly, a ripple of state statutes enabling women to be jurors followed ratification of the nineteenth amendment, as if this were obvious and right. But by 1923—in tandem with politicians' assessment that women were not going to vote as a bloc—this initial rush had stopped, and it became very, very difficult for advocates of equal jury service to make headway. . . .

. . . Opponents of women's jury service sometimes claimed that women were unsuitable because they were irrational and emotional. More often, they argued that jury service conflicted with women's more important responsibilities to be at home serving the needs of their husbands and children. Opponents thus took for granted that "women" were "wives," and gave more weight to marital and domestic obligations than to women's obligations as citizens. By 1938, twenty-six of the forty-eight states and the District of Columbia called women to jury service, but of those, only eleven required women to serve on equal terms with men. Men's service was mandatory (with very limited exceptions), while women could easily exempt themselves by claiming domestic responsibilities. Predictably, juries with very few women members resulted.

The nineteenth amendment might have been expected to transform the legal and political status of wives more thoroughly, given the prior importance of the husband's political representation of his wife, but continuity of the economic relation of husbands to wives minimized the transformation. . . . Alongside glamorous incarnations of the "working girl," unpaid housekeeping was still commonly regarded as women's inevitable vocation. This bisected vision was not entirely distorted, for relatively few women were regularly employed *after* they married. The proportion was increasing, but only 12 percent of wives with husbands present were in the labor force as of 1930. Marriage and motherhood were assumed to be every woman's hope, and despite some brave advocates' attempts to prove the contrary in the 1920s, marriage and motherhood were viewed as inconsistent with full-time employment for all but the economically pressed. . . .

Because of the increased employment of women workers, however, the vocation of wife-and-motherhood could now be seen as chosen rather than prescribed.

Women had alternatives. If a woman married, the consequences could be viewed simply as her individual choice. . . .

. . . Some voices countered this ideal view: in novels of social realism by intellectual women and those on the left, for example, in occasional complaining articles in women's magazines, and in the urban blues sung by African American women, more sardonic views of marriage could be seen and heard. "Marriage is too much of a compromise; it lops off a woman's life as an individual," wrote one politically active woman who remained unmarried. "Yet the renunciation too is a lopping off," she continued, genuflecting to expectations for "normality."

. . . Twentieth-century wives exercised far more legal and economic autonomy than their mothers and grandmothers had: by the mid-1930s virtually all the states had laws on their books enabling a wife to own her own property and to inherit an estate free of her husband's debts, to sue in court and make contracts (enabling her to conduct business on her own), to write a will, and if her husband deserted her, to act as a single woman economically. Judges ordinarily awarded mothers custody of children in cases of separation or divorce. Yet the modern wife's freedom from economic and other constraints was incomplete. The nineteenth amendment did not fully dismantle coverture. . . . Every state legally obliged the husband to support his wife, and his ownership of her labor corresponded to his support obligation. By the mid-1930s, twenty-eight states had explicitly granted the wife her wages when she worked for a third party, and only two states had explicitly denied the wife's right to her own earnings, while the rest hedged or complicated the question. But the sticking point, where the hand of the past showed itself most, was not her work in an office or shop or factory—it was her household labor, traditionally seen as her husband's domestic right. Even in states that had passed married women's earnings statutes, courts strongly tended to interpret a wife's household work as belonging to her husband, whether she was undertaking tasks for family members or keeping boarders or lodgers or washing laundry as a way to generate income.

. . . The laws requiring husbands' support—although by no means wholly effective inside marriage or out—had consequences in the labor market and in marital roles. Municipal officials and social workers saw new reason for enforcement of husbands' support obligations when millions of immigrants were being assimilated into American life in the early twentieth century. The frequency of men's desertion of their wives and families became a public issue, as charitable societies addressed themselves to the needs of poor mothers and children. These groups emphasized husbands' support obligations not only for the immediate purpose of reducing the need for public relief of female-headed households, but also for the longer-term purpose of making immigrant working-class men conform to American standards for marriage and the domestic environment.

. . . In response to public concern, most states made their laws harsher, setting higher fines or longer imprisonment for the husband who failed to support his wife and children. Many made nonsupport a felony rather than a misdemeanor. States allowed deserted wives to testify against their husbands in court, something previously impossible because coverture maintained that such testimony was self-incrimination, the two spouses being one person legally. . . . In implementing the support laws, courts looked to a man's public obligation (set by the state) more than to the wife's quality of life. When family courts ordered separation and support for abused wives, the husband had to make his payment to the court, rather than to the wife. The wife's own obligation of service did not go unnoticed. Harsh as they were on husbands, charity workers often blamed the deserted wives just as much, accusing them of failing to create the kinds of comfortable American homes in which husbands would want to stay put.

Laws making it a crime for the husband to shirk his obligations were strengthened further by many states during the Depression decade. Nonsupport cases, heard at family courts, served mainly to discipline wayward men among the working poor in an effort to keep public funds from being spent on their families. Implementation was always a problem. . . . Because courts were chary of intervening in an intact marriage, the husband's obligation to provide was rarely legally enforceable unless a marriage had effectively ended. If an unsupported wife obtained a court decree, there was no guarantee that her husband would deliver. If he was jailed for nonsupport, that hardly helped her (though he could be put on probation, on the condition that he work to support the family). When a middle-class wife went to court over nonsupport, the case was usually a prelude to divorce—and in some states a ground for it. As in *Thompson v. Thompson* at the Supreme Court earlier, the remedy for "atrocious wrongs" was still divorce, though it was not a remedy that could guarantee a vanished man's support of his ex-wife.

The innovation of "mothers' aid" or "mothers' pensions" in this era of commotion over marital desertion manifested a similar logic, emphasizing the economic substructure of marriage rather than offering alternatives to it. These state programs were meant to help "deserving" single mothers raise children in their own homes, to prevent children from being shunted to institutions, and to minimize child labor. Advocates thought that poor children without fathers would fare better at home with their mothers than in asylums or foster homes. They wanted the state (not private charities) to take the lead in providing the funds. Because of very widespread popular pressure, especially from middle-class women's clubs, mothers' aid programs spread like wildfire to almost every state in little more than a decade, beginning in 1911 The terminology of mothers' pensions expressed the most visionary advocates' wish to honor mothering as a labor on behalf of the public welfare. With the world's eyes focused on World War I, advocates argued that mothers performed as crucial a service to the state as soldiers did, so pensions were warranted.

Some radical women imagined state funding of motherhood as the way to eliminate women's economic reliance on men and inaugurate sexual freedom and childbearing unattached to marriage. That version was not the one put into practice. Mothers' pensions marked a significant breakthrough by taking up public responsibility for some level of economic welfare, but the programs left unfulfilled the promise to support single mothers and children with respect. The aid did not go to deserted wives, or unmarried mothers, but to widows. Advocates realized that political realities required compromise. Legislators would not accept programs that appeared to negate marriage or to lift the onus of support from a man's shoulders. . . . Aid to widows, on the other hand, brought in the state to supply the husband's place as provider after his death, sustaining his wife's appropriate economic dependency and childrearing role.

The "pensions" amounted more to a token than a sufficiency. The funds budgeted by states and counties were meager, never enough to cover all applicants. The grants were not enacted as a right of mother-citizens but rather as a response to need, and recipients were closely supervised to monitor continuing need and appropriate use. Local control in defining who was "deserving" made for highly variable coverage, enrolling high proportions of white immigrant mothers in the hope that the supervision accompanying the aid would serve as an Americanizing purpose, while discriminating against African American applicants in the south.

When the economic crisis of the Great Depression hit, new federal programs reinvoked the economic pattern of marital relationship in place at the state level. From the government's perspective, the huge problem of unemployment in the Depression called for bolstering men as providers, and women as their wives and dependents. President Franklin D. Roosevelt's administration reinforced that emphasis in responding to the Depression. The New Deal's mode of connecting social and economic welfare to political citizenship, necessary and promising as it was, did not bode equality between husbands and wives.

Millions lost their jobs in the 1930s and either remained jobless or took positions far inferior to their previous ones. Although women composed a quarter of the labor force, the focus of public concern about unemployment was working *men*, understood as providers for their families. Wives with paid jobs became the target of economic discrimination, on the widely accepted though fallacious thinking that the unemployment crisis would be solved if married women left the labor force. This outcry failed to recognize that the jobs men lost or sought were not the ones held by wives or by women at all, except in the case of some high-ranked professionals. Over 90 percent of women wage-earners were clustered in "women's work" in a very few occupations. Nonetheless, many private and public employers (public school systems, for instance) fired or refused to hire married women. Single women or widows, seen as having to support themselves, escaped most of this hostility, but those in desirable professional positions did not always escape being replaced by men.

When governments at any level removed married women from public sector jobs, it was an important signal to the nation about priorities in employment. The U.S. Congress fostered the exclusionary trend with Section 213 of the Economy Act of 1932, which prohibited two people of the same family from holding federal employment at the same time. Although it was gender-neutral in its language, in practice Section 213 meant dismissing from federal jobs those wives whose husbands also worked for the government, because the wife's job was almost always the lower-paid one and the one to be sacrificed. Nearly all of the fifteen hundred persons fired the first year that Section 213 went into effect were women. Women's organizations sprang into action opposing it, but five years of persistent lobbying were required before Section 213 was eliminated. Meanwhile a crop of state legislatures imitated its intent. As late as 1939, legislatures in twenty-six states were considering bills to bar married women from state jobs. Meanwhile, Depression poverty and male unemployment actually drove more married women to seek jobs. The negative climate meant that they got what others viewed as undesirable and ill-paid jobs—cleaning office buildings at night, for example. Amidst the condemnation, the proportion of wives in the labor force rose faster than ever before, going up from 12 percent to 17 percent during the 1930s.

Although putting the onus on married women workers may have diffused discontent, it had grave consequences for women workers. The diatribes against wives earning meant that the "working girl" was the only approved female wage-earner—someone passing through a phase of her life, for whom paid work was fleeting and not a continuing need and right, who could manage without equal work and did not merit the same say in government or in union policy as the "working man." This mind-set assumed that women with husbands belonged at home; a wife who persisted in working must be motivated either by dire need or callous personal self-ishness. Movies in the Depression decade played with this theme, starting with a glamorous, assertive "working girl" heroine who by the end of the film had usually opted for marriage and domesticity.

Working men's welfare was at the center of popular and social-scientific commentary and at the heart of New Deal domestic policies. . . . When President Roosevelt asserted that government had an "inescapable obligation" to "protect the citizen in his right to work and his right to live" no less than "in his right to vote," he sketched a prospect of social citizenship that began with the "right to life" and the "right to make a comfortable living" owed to every *man*. Attempts in federal agency after agency to shore up the nation's individuals and families during the economic crisis addressed the husband-father as the principal wage-earner and citizen. . . .

New Deal policy innovations revivified the fading connection between citizenship and marital role through economic avenues. These choices diluted the formal political equality of women and deeply imprinted marriage on citizenship entitlements, while refiguring what those entitlements were. Arguably the most important and lasting was the Social Security Act of 1935. This omnibus act had two major categories: social insurance and public assistance. In the social insurance category, which included unemployment compensation and the retirement benefits we still call "Social Security," recipients were envisioned as able-bodied (white, male) workers insuring themselves against untoward circumstances. In the public assistance category, which included aid to the blind and financial help for the indigent elderly not covered by Social Security, the recipient was imagined to be needy and dependent. Aid to Dependent Children (ADC), later . . . Aid for Families with Dependent Children (AFDC), or what [we] now call "welfare," was in the public assistance category.

From their inception, the social insurance programs were superior in payments and in reputation. They were known as programs that were not need-based but were financed by beneficiaries' contributions. Unemployment compensation and retirement benefits were premised on wages and on objective criteria for qualification. They were entitlements based on participation in paid employment. Public assistance, by contrast, was attuned to nonworkers or unpaid workers, was based on need rather than right, and was comparatively inferior in benefits and reputation. ADC, the assistance program reaching the most people, took mothers' aid as its model—continuing local administration and discretion over recipients, scrutinizing and supervising their lives to guarantee continuing deservingness. In return for a scanty stipend, a recipient had to be certified "a proper person, physically, mentally, and morally fit to bring up her children." This brought motherhood under surveillance, as had been true when the Union first instituted pensions for Civil War widows.

Both tracks of the Social Security Act confirmed marital roles, without being explicit about it. Retirement and unemployment insurance made no reference to gender or race, and employed wives could pay in and utilize both, and did. But the old-age insurance coverage in the 1935 act was partial, covering only about half of all workers by excluding part-time, seasonal, agricultural, domestic, philanthropic, and government employees (including teachers), and the self-employed. These were exactly the areas where women wage-earners, and African American and Latino men as well, were concentrated. More than 60 percent of women wage-earners were left uncovered, as though they were unearning wives. . . .The Social Security Act that passed, after the wheeling and dealing and bargain-trading of Congress, helped most those who needed help the least: white male employees with year-round work. These were the citizens whose "right to work" and "right to make a comfortable living" as well as "right to vote" the New Deal would try to guarantee. The priority given to the male citizen in the New Deal thus echoed the prominence of the (white) male immigrant in immigration policy of the early part of the century.

The shape and spirit of social policy in the United States were fatefully ordained by the Social Security Act's inherent differentiation between the male citizen-husband-provider and the female citizen-mother-dependent. . . . When amendments to Social Security were made later in the 1930s, the intent to reward the male citizen-worker became still clearer. Revising the system to pay out slightly more and improve the standard of living possible for some Americans, policy-makers did not extend coverage to excluded groups but rather gave more privileges to the citizen-worker-husbands who were already covered. Amendments passed in 1939 created "survivors' benefits" for the wives and minor children of men who died before the age [of] sixty-five (so long as the wife did not remarry). They also increased a man's retirement benefit by 50 percent if his wife lived with him, once she reached the age of sixty-five. A wife who had worked in covered employment could choose to collect the benefits accrued from her own contribution, or the benefits her husband would get on her behalf. Typically, an employed wife earned so little and her years of employment were so relatively few that 50 percent of her husband's benefit was more than her own whole benefit, and she chose the larger amount. (In 1996, men's and women's earning powers were still so disparate that nearly two thirds of women on Social Security collected as wives rather than earners.) . . .

Policy-makers' and congressmen's endorsement of these benefits for a male worker's family members was especially remarkable because the supplements contradicted the highly championed "equity" principle of the retirement benefit system. Being purposely tied to workers' contributions, retirement insurance was distinguished from a "dole," justified as harmonizing with the cherished American value of self-reliance. President Roosevelt said at the time it was "not charity"; the payroll taxes gave contributors "a legal, moral, and political right to collect their pensions and their unemployment benefits." Workers would receive benefits in proportion to what they paid in—this was called "equity." But the supplements added in 1939 meant that at sixty-five a married man who had worked right beside a single man for the same number of years, and paid the same amount in, got 50 percent more out of the system.

The policy-makers who crafted the amendments recognized that single men and all women contributors were being overtaxed, so to speak. They saw this as a useful incentive to men to marry and have families, and to women to be stay-at-home wives and mothers rather than entering the labor force. An "adequacy" function (what we would today call "welfare" function) was intended in the supplement, for the extra 50 percent would allow older couples a higher standard of living than the man's benefits alone could. Congress continued to insist on the equity of the contributory system in passing the amendments. Federal officialdom saw no violation of principle because their "common sense" allowed greater reward to the husband-citizen-workers than to others. The nation's political and economic reliance on male-headed monogamous families for well-being made this *ipso facto* equitable. . . .

Both men and women helped to draft New Deal public policy. The women involved, who formed a network around Eleanor Roosevelt, were themselves career-oriented and mostly self-supporting. Of an identifiable group of influential women policy-makers and reformers, two thirds had never been married, and even fewer had children. A quarter of them were involved with same-sex relationships. But they did not take themselves as the norm. Almost all these women thought that a full-time career could not be sustained successfully by a wife and mother. They assumed that most women wanted husbands and children, and would pursue only ill-paid or part-time employment at best. For the benefit of child nurture they preferred shoring up the husband-father's wages and security to increasing the mother's opportunities in the labor market. They did not push public policy to disrupt the pattern in which husbands remained principal earners and wives were homemakers and childrearers.

The New Deal's broader conception of citizenship, extending from the political into the economic and social realms, made the line between federal public authority and the private economy harder than ever to draw. Federal social provision renewed the economic substructure of marriage, and revivified social and economic features of marital unity just when legal writers were calling it legally archaic, "foreign to modern statutes." The early part of the new century had seen many opposing tides, the highest being the enfranchisement of women. Women's and men's arenas of possible accomplishment now overlapped far more. Marriage ideals had become less hierarchical amidst the language of true love and companionate partnership; more wives were in the labor force; in legal terms the wife's personal identity was freer of her husband's imprint; and a wider spectrum of sexual behavior had become acceptable. Yet the economic bedrock held fast below, and on it stood the public architecture of marriage.

FURTHER READING

Alexander, Ruth M. *The "Girl Problem": Female Sexual Delinquency in New York, 1900–1930* (1995).

Blee, Kathleen M. *Women of the Klan: Racism and Gender in the 1920s* (1991).

Brodie, Janet Farrell. *Contraception and Abortion in Nineteenth-Century America* (1994).

Cahn, Susan K. "From the 'Muscle Moll' to the 'Butch' Ballplayer: Mannishness, Lesbianism, and Homophobia in U.S. Women's Sport," *Feminist Studies* 19, no. 2 (summer 1993): 343–368.

Chauncey, George. *Gay New York: Gender, Urban Culture, and the Makings of the Gay Male World, 1890–1940* (1994).

Chen, Constance M. *"The Sex Side of Life": Mary Ware Dennett's Pioneering Battle for Birth Control and Sex Education* (1996).

Chesler, Phyllis. *Woman of Valor: Margaret Sanger and the Birth Control Movement in America* (1992).

D'Emilio, John, and Estelle Freedman. *Intimate Matters: A History of Sexuality in America* (1988).

Erickson, Julia A., with Sally A Steffen. *Kiss and Tell: Surveying Sex in the Twentieth Century* (2001).

Faderman, Lillian. *Odd Girls and Twilight Lovers: A History of Lesbian Life in Twentieth-Century America* (1991).

Fass, Paula. *The Damned and the Beautiful: American Youth in the 1920s* (1977).

Freedman, Estelle B. *Maternal Justice: Miriam Van Waters and the Female Reform Tradition* (1996).

Geppert, Alexander C. T. "Divine Sex, Happy Marriage, Regenerated Nation: Marie Stopes's Marital Manual *Married Love* and the Making of a Best Seller, 1918–1955," *Journal of the History of Sexuality* 8 (1998): 389–505.

Gordon, Linda. *Woman's Body, Woman's Right: A Social History of Birth Control in America* (1976).

Haag, Pamela. *Consent: Sexual Rights and the Transformation of American Liberalism* (1999).

Hine, Darlene Clark. "Rape and the Inner Lives of Black Women in the Middle West: Preliminary Thoughts on the Culture of Dissemblance," *Signs* 14 (1989): 912–920.

Hodes, Martha E., ed. *Sex, Love, Race: Crossing Boundaries in North American History* (1999).

Kunzel, Regina G. *Fallen Women, Problem Girls: Unmarried Mothers and the Professionalization of Social Work, 1890–1945* (1993).

Meyerowitz, Joanne. "Women, Cheesecake, and Borderline Material: Responses to Girlie Pictures in the Mid-Twentieth-Century U.S.," *Journal of Women's History* 8, no. 3 (winter 1996): 9–35.

Odem, Mary E. *Delinquent Daughters: Protecting and Policing Female Adolescent Sexuality in the Untied States, 1885–1920* (1995).

Pascoe, Peggy. "Miscegenation Law, Court Cases, and Ideologies of 'Race' in Twentieth-Century America," *Journal of American History* 83, no. 1 (June 1996): 44–69.

Peiss, Kathy. *Cheap Amusements: Working Women and Leisure in Turn-of-the-Century New York* (1986).

———. *Hope in a Jar: The Making of America's Beauty Culture* (1998).

Pivar, David. *Purity Crusade: Sexual Morality and Social Control, 1868–1900* (1973).

Reagan, Leslie J. *When Abortion Was a Crime: Women, Medicine, and the Law in the United States, 1867–1973* (1997).

Reed, James W. "The Birth Control Movement Before Roe v. Wade," *Journal of Policy History* 7 (1995): 22–52.

Rosen, Robyn L. "Federal Expansion, Fertility Control, and Physicians in the United States: The Politics of Maternal Welfare in the Interwar Years," *Journal of Women's History* 10, no. 3 (winter 1998): 53–73.

Rosen, Ruth. *The Lost Sisterhood: Prostitution in America, 1900–1918* (1982).

Sahli, Nancy. "Smashing: Women's Relationships Before the Fall," *Chrysalis,* no. 8 (summer 1979): 17–27.

Shade, William. "'A Mental Passion': Female Sexuality in Victorian America," *International Journal of Women's Studies* 1 (1978): 13–29.

Simmons, Christina. "African Americans and Sexual Victorianism in the Social Hygiene Movement," *Journal of the History of Sexuality* 4 (1993): 51–75.

Smith, Daniel Scott. "Family Limitation, Sexual Control, and Domestic Feminism in Victorian America," *Feminist Studies,* 1, no. 1 (spring 1973): 40–57.

Smith, Merril D. *Sex Without Consent: Rape and Sexual Coercion in America* (2002).

Snitow, Ann, et al., eds. *Powers of Desire: The Politics of Sexuality* (1983).

CHAPTER
12

Women in America
During the Great Depression
and New Deal

In 1929 the United States descended into the worst economic crisis of its history, a crisis that ruined thousands of businesses and left nearly one-quarter of the work force
unemployed by 1933. Hoping to restore the nation to prosperity, Franklin Delano
Roosevelt's administration intervened in unprecedented ways in society and the
economy: New Deal legislation created federal relief and jobs programs, boosted
unionization (and worker militancy), established Social Security and unemployment
funds, and mandated a federal minimum wage. Even though Roosevelt's New Deal
did not end the Great Depression, it did dramatically increase the regulatory powers
and social welfare obligations of the federal government, thereby altering the relationship between American citizens and the state.

Historians have long debated the significance of the Great Depression and New
Deal for women, questioning whether the economic crisis of the 1930s and the policy
innovations that it provoked caused Americans to affirm or forsake traditional gender roles and expectations. Some facts are well known and oft-repeated. For example,
Americans in great number expressed heightened anxiety about women's presence
in the work force during the Great Depression and seem to have supported, at least
tacitly, federal agencies, state governments, school districts, and various businesses
that fired or denied jobs to married women in an attempt to create work opportunities for married men. In addition, Eleanor Roosevelt and a network of liberal Democratic women became important figures in the New Deal bureaucracy, influencing
the development of policy and programs. Finally, the Great Depression was primarily
a crisis of consumption, not production, and policies of the 1930s sought to enhance
both the appeal of the marketplace and the purchasing power of American consumers,
most of whom were women.

But these simple facts raise more questions than they answer. How did women,
as individuals or in groups, try to define, protect, or advance their interests during
this decade of crisis and innovation? Did the Great Depression and New Deal alter
in significant ways women's identity or vulnerabilities in the labor force, the family,

the marketplace, or public life? How did the New Deal define women's interests, and to what extent did women of different class, race, and ethnic backgrounds profit from New Deal job programs, social welfare policies, or unionization efforts? The documents and essays in this chapter offer partial answers to these complex questions.

◈ D O C U M E N T S

Ann Marie Low, a single college-educated white woman, kept a diary during the 1930s while she and her North Dakota family struggled to withstand both the Great Depression and the Dust Bowl. Excerpted in Document 1, Low's diary records her feelings about lost job opportunities, family obligations, and marriage. In Document 2, Agnes Burns Wieck describes to the readers of *The Nation* in 1933 the militancy of miners' wives in Illinois who petitioned their governor to provide relief from intolerable poverty and bring an end to gross violations of miners' civil liberties. Writing for *Harper's Monthly Magazine,* Dorothy Dunbar Bromley examines in Document 3 women's great need for reliable contraception in the 1930s and the obstacles they confronted in trying to obtain it. In Document 4, P'ing Yu, a woman writer for the *Chinese Digest* in San Francisco in 1937, exposes the racism of white clubwomen in that city and thereby calls into question America's claim that it was one of the truly authentic democracies in a world beset by economic crisis and "race hatred." Writing for *The Daily Worker* in 1940, Louise Mitchell (Document 5) discloses the harsh conditions under which black women sought work in New York City during the Great Depression; as domestic servants they lacked job security and were ineligible for New Deal work benefits or entitlements.

1. Ann Marie Low Records Her Feelings About Life in the Dust Bowl, 1934

April 25, 1934, Wednesday

Last weekend was the worst dust storm we ever had. We've been having quite a bit of blowing dirt every year since the drouth started, not only here, but all over the Great Plains. Many days this spring the air is just full of dirt coming, literally, for hundreds of miles. It sifts into everything. After we wash the dishes and put them away, so much dust sifts into the cupboards we must wash them again before the next meal. Clothes in the closets are covered with dust.

Last weekend no one was taking an automobile out for fear of ruining the motor. I rode Roany to Frank's place to return a gear. To find my way I had to ride right beside the fence, scarcely able to see from one fence post to the next.

Newspapers say the deaths of many babies and old people are attributed to breathing in so much dirt.

May 7, 1934, Monday

The dirt is still blowing. Last weekend Bud and I helped with the cattle and had fun gathering weeds. Weeds give us greens for salad long before anything in the garden

Ann Marie Low, *Dust Bowl Diary* (Lincoln: University of Nebraska Press, 1984), 95–100. Copyright © 1984 by the University of Nebraska Press. Reprinted by permission of the publisher.

is ready. We use dandelions, lamb's quarter, and sheep sorrel. I like sheep sorrel best. Also, the leaves of sheep sorrel, pounded and boiled down to a paste, make a good salve.

Still no job. I'm trying to persuade Dad I should apply for rural school #3 out here where we went to school. I don't see a chance of getting a job in a high school when so many experienced teachers are out of work.

He argues that the pay is only $60.00 a month out here, while even in a grade school in town I might get $75.00. Extra expenses in town would probably eat up that extra $15.00. Miss Eston, the practice teaching supervisor, told me her salary has been cut to $75.00 after all the years she has been teaching in Jamestown. She wants to get married. School boards will not hire married women teachers in these hard times because they have husbands to support them. Her fiancé is the sole support of his widowed mother and can't support a wife, too. So she is just stuck in her job, hoping she won't get another salary cut because she can scarcely live on what she makes and dress the way she is expected to.

Dad argues the patrons always stir up so much trouble for a teacher at #3 some teachers have quit in mid-term. The teacher is also the janitor, so the hours are long.

I figure I can handle the work, kids, and patrons. My argument is that by teaching here I can work for my room and board at home, would not need new clothes, and so could send most of my pay to Ethel and Bud. . . .

May 21, 1934, Monday

Ethel has been having stomach trouble. Dad has been taking her to doctors though suspecting her trouble is the fact that she often goes on a diet that may affect her health. The local doctor said he thought it might be chronic appendicitis, so Mama took Ethel by train to Valley City last week to have a surgeon there remove her appendix.

Saturday Dad, Bud, and I planted an acre of potatoes. There was so much dirt in the air I couldn't see Bud only a few feet in front of me. Even the air in the house was just a haze. In the evening the wind died down, and Cap came to take me to the movie. We joked about how hard it is to get cleaned up enough to go anywhere. . . .

Sunday the dust wasn't so bad. Dad and I drove cattle to the Big Pasture. Then I churned butter and baked a ham, bread, and cookies for the men, as no telling when Mama will be back.

July 6, 1934, Friday

I am still herding cows, and it is awfully hot. Where they have eaten every weed and blade of grain. Bud is plowing so the ground will be softened to absorb rain (if it comes). He is very fed up and anxious to get away to school and fit himself for a job.

Poor Bud. He has worked so hard and saved so hard. He has done without nice clothes and never went to a dance or movie oftener than about once a year because he was saving every penny for college. He hoped his livestock would pay his way for four years. The price was so low he didn't sell any last year. This year they are worth less, and he absolutely must sell them because there is not enough feed for them and no money to buy feed. All the stock he has won't pay his way through one year of college. . . .

July 9, 1934, Monday

Saturday night Cap and I went to the movie, Claudette Colbert in *The Torch Singer.* Afterward he bought ice cream cones and we sat in the car in front of the store eating them. He brought up the subject of marriage. I reminded him that he promised, if I would go out with him occasionally, he would not mention marriage. I also pointed out the impossibility. He has to run the farm until Sonny is old enough and then will have nothing to start out on his own. I have to work until Ethel gets through college and can help Bud, at least two years. If she doesn't help Bud, we are looking at four years. Though I didn't mention it, in four years Cap will be thirty-six years old. Forget it.

He insisted he wants to get married now. Then I turned shrewish and said I'd seen him leave a dance last year with Joan. If he wants a wife, she would doubtless marry him.

He said he did take her home from a dance once, but there is absolutely nothing between him and Joan and I know it—I am all he wants and I know it.

"Let's not quarrel," I murmured. "Things will work out somehow."

He leaned back against the car seat, saying somberly, "Oh, how I wish it would rain."

The light from the store window was on his face. He is really a handsome man, with a John Barrymore profile and thick wavy auburn hair. Suddenly I seemed to see what his face will be someday—a tombstone on which is written the epitaph of dead dreams. I shivered.

"Oh, Sweetheart, you are cold and have no wrap. I'll take you home."

I didn't tell him I wasn't shivering from cold.

2. Agnes Burns Wieck Describes the March and Petition of Ten Thousand Miners' Wives, 1933

To the Editors of The Nation:

Ten thousand miners' wives marched to the State House in Springfield, Illinois, on January 26 and presented to Governor Horner a petition signed by the Illinois Women's Auxiliary of the Progressive Miners of America demanding the restoration of civil liberties in the coal fields of Christian and Franklin counties and immediate and adequate relief for the families of miners. The petition read, in part, as follows:

> We . . . have come to the seat of government in our State to seek redress from the oppressive and intolerable conditions in the coal fields of Illinois. Thousands of working-class housewives have marched to the State Capitol. This is an unusual event in the history of the State but these are unusual times. It is well for the State that we come while we still have faith in government, for that faith has been terrifically shaken during the past year.
>
> When it was no longer possible for our men to have a voice in determining the conditions under which they worked, because of the usurping of this right by the officials of the old union, they broke away from that organization, to which they had given long years of service and devotion, and established a new union that is responsive to the

Agnes Burns Wieck, Letter to the Editors, *The Nation,* March 1, 1933, 234–235. Reprinted with permission.

wishes of the rank and file. A reign of terror resulted . . . in which officials of the old union, the coal corporation, county and municipal authorities, and even the State joined—clubbing, tear-gassing, shooting, killing our people, bombing our homes, making it impossible for us to assemble or to enjoy any of the rights to which the Constitution of this nation entitled its citizens.

Not only are thousands of our people victims of terror but they are victims of hunger. . . . In ever-increasing numbers our people are losing their homes. . . . We women who live in rented homes are in constant dread of eviction. . . . We are forced to see our sick children go unattended by doctors. Savings have disappeared. . . . Moreover, our mining communities have been discriminated against in the matter of distribution of [State] aid.

Therefore, in the face of these intolerable conditions, we respectfully petition you, the Governor, and members of the Legislature of the State of Illinois: first, for the immediate and full restoration of civil liberties in the coal fields of Christian and Franklin counties; second, for increased and more equitable distribution of State aid . . . ; third, that you immediately pass legislation for unemployment insurance . . . ; and fourth, that you refuse to burden further the workers by the enactment of a sales tax to meet this unemployment emergency. . . .

Not only is our welfare at stake, but our faith in the ability and willingness of the government to protect and serve us is menaced. Dare you fail us now?

Governor Horner received us cordially—a big delegation of fifty local presidents and fourteen State officers. The day before, a Communist delegation trying to see him had been clubbed and forced out of his office when they would not accept his offer to receive a committee of five. Damage to the Governor's quarters resulted, and the next day when I arrived with 10,000 miners' wives the city was a bunch of nerves, with two companies of soldiers in readiness.

Our army was peaceful and well-disciplined, wanting mainly to demonstrate the solidarity of the new miners' union, which we certainly did. We women assembled in the armory, paraded through the streets with a motor-cycle police escort, and marched down Capitol Avenue to the State House grounds, where we massed about the statue of Lincoln and overflowed into the Capitol. We were in our uniforms—plain white smocks and head bands with our union's name. After I read the petition to the Governor, he replied point by point, with none of the politician's evasion but with statements far from satisfactory to us on unemployment insurance and increased State aid, to be financed not by a sales tax but by taxes on inheritances and high incomes.

The Governor declared he would see that the civil liberties of all citizens were maintained, by suasion if possible but if necessary by the use of any instrumentality in his power. However, he qualified his position on civil liberties by reminding us that an individual's rights do not transcend the community's rights. He did not make clear his stand in regard to the rights of minorities. He was very friendly and expressed his appreciation of our statement that we still have faith in government.

On the matter of settling the turmoil in the mine areas of Christian and Franklin counties, the Governor referred to the conferences he had been having with the two miners' organizations. He said the trouble could be settled if both sides would leave it entirely to him or to some other disinterested person, but that both sides refused to budge. We women demonstrated in the State capital that the Progressive Miners' Union is the dominant one—there are no women marching behind John Lewis to perpetuate the old union.

Since we presented our petition to the Governor, he has announced that he would select a committee of inquiry, which would not include a member of the Illinois National Guard, to investigate violations of civil liberties. I held a week of meetings in December, but when John Lewis returned from the Cincinnati convention, he ordered the sheriff to stop me, and as a result a thousand women were driven off the streets of West Frankfort and one woman slugged when we met to hold a public meeting. I am going back to Franklin County to see what the Governor's declaration means.

Belleville, Ill., January 28   AGNES BURNS WIECK
President, Illinois Women's Auxiliary,
Progressive Miners of America

February 16. Governor Horner's pledge that constitutional rights would be protected failed on February 5 when thugs and civil officers prevented a meeting in West Frankfort, Illinois, and clubbed women. We took the injured women to the Governor, who advised recourse to the courts, declaring that he could not intervene except at the sheriff's request.

A. B. W.

3. Dorothy Dunbar Bromley Comments on Birth Control and the Depression, 1934

"Nobody wanted Jimmy, but he was born anyhow." This caption appears, not on propaganda issued by the American Birth Control League, but on a flier recently distributed by the Cincinnati Committee on Maternal Health. The story told by Dr. Elizabeth Campbell, Chairman of the Medical Committee, is a graphic one. At the time Jimmy was born his father had been out of work for seventeen months, and the parents with five children were subsisting on a five dollars a week relief allowance. His mother, sick with worry before he came, did not want Jimmy. The community did not want him, as the city was already spending $350,000 on relief. Jimmy himself, had he had any say, could hardly have wanted to be born, for his short life meant only misery to him. His home was so cold that in four months time he died of pneumonia. His brief and painful life had cost the community a total of $130.02 for hospital, nursing, and medical care, for milk, for baby clothes, and for his burial. Was it fair to Jimmy to be born at this time? And was it fair to the community, which was already taking care of 21,380 families, that he should have been born?

Half of the women, Dr. Campbell says, who have applied during the past year to the Maternal Health Clinic of Cincinnati for contraceptive advice had unemployed husbands and all of them, for some good reason, feared the birth of another child. Dr. Campbell's arguments are frank and to the point. "Every child," she says, "has a right to be wanted. Hunger and fear cannot create a wholesome life for a baby. During this crisis the birth of those babies whose coming is a cause of dread, should be postponed until a better time, since the community cannot keep in health and decency the children that are here."

The situation in Cincinnati is no different from that in other cities. Proof is to be found in an economic health survey recently made by Milbank Memorial Foundation in co-operation with the United States Public Health Service, covering 8000 urban families in the lower-income groups living in ten different localities. Investigation showed that in 1932 there were 43 per cent more births in families without any employed workers than in families with one or more full-time workers. Families that were actually receiving relief had a birth rate 54 per cent higher than those not on relief. The study further showed that families who were poor in 1929 and continued in that condition in 1932 had the highest birth rate of all, while those who dropped below the $1200 a year level during the depression had a considerably higher birth rate than those with an income of from $1200 to $2000 a year. Summing up their conclusions, Messrs. Perrott and Sydenstricker, the authors of the study, say:

> Low social status, unemployment, and low income in 1932 went hand in hand with a high illness rate and increased malnutrition among children. It was in these same groups of families that a high birth rate prevailed. Whatever the broad implications of the findings may be, it is evident that a high birth rate during the depression prevailed in families which could least afford, from any point of view, to assume this added responsibility.

It might be supposed that there is a causal relation between men's idleness and their procreative activities, if the study did not show that the couples who were prolific in 1932 were prolific in 1929. The explanation of the differential birth rate in these 8000 families would seem to be that the man who shows no judgment about the number of children he sires is likely to be the man who loses his job in a crisis, perhaps because he lacks judgment all along the line. In this connection it is interesting to hear from Professor James H.S. Bossard of the Wharton School of Commerce and Finance, University of Pennsylvania, that in 1932, when the depression was perhaps at its crest, the highest marriage rates in Philadelphia prevailed in the areas of greatest unemployment.

The findings cited above are paralleled by another Milbank Fund study, recently made under the direction of the famous biologist, Dr. Raymond Pearl of Johns Hopkins University. This survey concerned contraceptive practices among 4945 hospitalized urban women of all classes, living in thirteen different States. The results showed, as was to be expected, that a much higher percentage of well-to-do and rich women were practicing birth control than poor white and colored women. But the study also showed, contrary to expectations, that the women of the well-to-do and rich classes who took no preventive measures were as fertile as the women of the poorer classes, colored women included. In other words, the failure on the part of the poorer classes to practice birth control appears alone to be responsible for their too rapid propagation.

Dr. Pearl had for many years questioned the social value of birth control. But his findings now lead him to the emphatic conclusion that "the national policy of prohibiting the free dissemination of accurate scientific information about birth control methods is adding definitely and measurably to the difficulty of the problems of poverty and unemployment with which our children and grandchildren will have to deal."

Dr. Pearl might have gone on to say that our national policy regarding birth control has added definitely and measurably to the enormous relief load which burdens the country to-day. It is as ironic as it is tragic that parents who cannot take care of the children they already have should have no choice but to bring more into the world. In one year's time—between October, 1932 and October, 1933 according to the Federal Unemployment Relief Census taken last October—there were as many as 233,822 children born to families who were receiving public relief. These families, 3,134,678 in number, also had 1,589,480 children from one to five years of age or, all told, 1,823,302 children under six years of age. Unfortunately we do not know exactly how many of the one-to-five-year-olds were born after 1929. But there can be no doubt that the majority of them were depression babies. Their entry into the world increased the strain on public health and hospital facilities as well as on the agencies that provide clothing. Their presence in over-large families has brought, as the Milbank study suggests, malnutrition and privation for existing children, since relief expenditures per child have been far from adequate.

The future will probably show that the children have borne the brunt of the depression. Of the 12,500,000 persons who were found in the October Census to be receiving relief, 42 per cent were under 16 years of age. This is a disproportionate number, since the 1930 Census showed that children of this age comprised only 26 per cent of the population. It is a tragic fact that over a third of the children subsisting on relief were under six years of age, or in their most formative period.

The ill health and hardships so often suffered by members of over-large families are argument enough for birth control. As Margaret Sanger has said, "There can be no justification for violating the right of every married woman to decide when and how often she shall undertake the physical and far-reaching responsibilities of motherhood." The argument that large families among the indigent are an additional burden on the taxpayer is hardly a generous one. Yet it may have its effect on legislators and their constituents who have so far been unmoved by humane considerations.

Unfortunately there is no way of estimating the cost of relief for the million or more babies born during the depression to families that were living on public funds in October, 1933. The sum total of relief expenditures, however, is sufficiently appalling. For the year 1933 all forms of public relief reached approximately $800,000,000. For the same year combined public and private expenditures are estimated by the Monthly Bulletin on Social Statistics, published by the Children's Bureau, to have been three times as great in 120 cities as they were in 1929. Professor James H.S. Bossard considers this a conservative estimate. In his forthcoming book *Social Change and Social Problems* he presents figures to prove that relief expenditures in the country at large have increased by a geometric ratio and that they were 16 times as great in 1933 as in 1929. The Children's Bureau figures also show that as the depression has progressed, the proportion of public, as against private, expenditures has increased from 74 per cent in 1929 to 94 per cent in 1934.

The moral of these figures is that the comfortable and well-to-do can no longer remain indifferent to the fate of the indigent. We have reached the point that England reached in 1919. Families and individuals in want are admitted to be a charge on government, and it is not likely that even a reactionary administration, should one come into power, would dare to discontinue public relief so long as there is unemployment on a large scale. Given present-day conditions in industry and increasing technological unemployment, there appears slight possibility that the relief problem will disappear. Mr. William Hodson, Commissioner of the Department of Public Welfare of New York City, predicts that "it will be many years before we pull ourselves out and have families now on relief, restored to independence and self-support."

The country has become birth-control-conscious. Economic conditions make family limitation in both the white-collar and the working class imperative. There can, therefore, be no turning back. It is only a question whether the setting up of clinics shall be left to lay organizations with limited facilities, and the wholesale distribution of doubtful products be further tolerated, or whether the medical profession will awaken to its clear duty. Mrs. Margaret Sanger and the American Birth Control League are ready and willing to turn over their self-imposed task to the profession, for they realize that only through wide medical practice and extensive research will better and simpler technics be evolved for the future.

The profession is at present in an anomalous position. Dr. J. Prentice Wilson, President of the Washington, D. C., Medical Association, points out, "At the 1933 meeting of the American Medical Association, Dr. Barton Cooke Hirst, chairman of the section on Obstetrics, Gynecology, and Abdominal Surgery, listed birth control as one of the four major problems in gynecology. At the same meeting a resolution asking that a committee be appointed to study the subject was defeated. Thus the A.M.A. placed itself on record as refusing to study one of the four major problems affecting the women of America."

A similar resolution was voted down in June of this year by the House of Delegates, despite the fact that it was favorably reported by the Committee on Public Health and Hygiene, as well as by the Council of the Section on Obstetrics and Gynecology. At the same convention a commercial exhibitor was allowed to feature a misleading film on the "safe period," which took no account of the doubts which scientists have expressed concerning it. Such action on the part of the A.M.A. is hardly calculated to inspire confidence in its devotion to scientific ideals

The women of the United States are waiting for the medical profession's help. All of the clinics in the country have in the past ten years taken care of probably not more than 160,000 women, while the number advised by private practitioners would hardly bring this figure up to half a million. It is quite possible that the majority of married people are using some more or less crude form of birth control. But only a small minority are instructed in reliable methods.

It is absurd that the legislators should wait for the doctors and the doctors should wait for the legislators to correct the situation. A movement is now on foot, started by Dr. Prentiss Willson, President of the District of Columbia Medical Society, to organize a National Medical Committee on State and Federal Contraceptive Legislation. It is to be hoped that the influential men on this committee will be able to break the deadlock that has so far been the fate of all contraceptive legislation.

There is no reason why the Roman Catholic Church should attempt to dictate either to the legislators or the A.M.A. Father Coughlin admitted, in testifying against the proposed Federal legislation before the House Judiciary Committee, that "63 per cent of the American population to-day profess no affiliated religion." "I recognize the fact," he went on, "that those people are favoring practical birth control. If that is their morals . . . I have no criticism to offer; that is their business."

But Father Coughlin had a criticism to offer or he would not have been testifying against the proposed bill. Amendment of the Federal law so as to admit contraceptive materials to the mails will hardly force "practical birth control" on the communicants of the Roman Catholic Church. Its priests will still be at liberty to lead their flocks as best they can. Because the Church is uncertain of its authority over its own members, it is attempting to dictate on a very vital subject to the majority of Americans, who *are not its communicants.* There could be no better proof that it is seeking to invade the domain that belongs to the State.

The only other opponents of a change in the laws are such Protestant fundamentalists as Canon William Sheafe Chase, who believe with Father Coughlin that birth control is synonymous with prostitution, and those population theorists who are alarmed by the falling birth rate. But these latter gentlemen have not proved that we should be any the worse off for having a stationary population. Over a century ago Malthus tried to alarm the world with his theory that human beings were increasing by a geometric ratio while the means of existence were increasing only by an arithmetic ratio. To-day Mgr. John A. Ryan and others argue that this country and the world at large need more and not fewer consumers. They ignore the fact that we also need fewer and not more workers.

Far more impressive—and alarming—are the Milbank Fund findings showing that the highest birth rate prevailed in 1932 (and doubtless still does) "in families which could least afford, from any point of view, to assume this added responsibility." It would be hard to deny that the drain on women's health, the broken marriages, the toll of abortions, the hardships suffered by over-large families subsisting on relief, are a medieval disgrace to a twentieth-century civilization.

4. P'ing Yu Publicizes a Shameful Demonstration of Racism Among White Clubwomen in California, 1937

Just when the world, the intelligent world, was getting nauseated with the patriotic purity purgings and the shameful spread of race hatred among the less democratic nations, and when we were vociferously praising the more enlightened ways of life and government in this country where we can still doff our hats to whomever we like, this had to happen to take the joy out of life. The "color line" once more became a point of issue and definitely caused a battle in the ranks of local American clubwomen when the constitution of the City and Country Federation of Women's Clubs was amended to bar non-Caucasian clubs from membership. Some of the much heated clubwomen, doing considerable chest-heaving, said that though they would be willing to work for "colored women," they wished—oh, so ardently—to reserve the right to choose their own club friends, and so on, ad nauseum.

It's just this high and mighty "holier than thou" attitude of "working for" and not "working with" people that makes this world so divided in spirit. I am sorry for the Federation. It had a wonderful chance, in this cosmopolitan San Francisco, to

P'ing Yu, "Color—Chafing to Clubwomen," *Chinese Digest* (March 1937): 10.

make world history for the cause of international peace and good will, but that's gone with the wind.

I don't like living alone, so I think I shall join the Commonwealth Club. Its members are talking of an Asia House where they can expand their inter-racial contacts—with no constitutional amendment to restrict them! I doff my bonnet to Mrs. Richard Simons, Mrs. W. F. C. Zimmerman, Mrs. Letitia Farber and Mrs. S. S. Abrams, leaders in the losing battle. Thank goodness, I can still do that.

5. Louise Mitchell Denounces the "Slave Markets" Where Domestics Are Hired in New York City, 1940

Every morning, rain or shine, groups of women with brown paper bags or cheap suitcases stand on street corners in the Bronx and Brooklyn waiting for a chance to get some work. Sometimes there are 15, sometimes 30, some are old, many are young and most of them are Negro women waiting for employers to come to the street corner auction blocks to bargain for their labor.

They come as early as 7 in the morning, wait as late as four in the afternoon with the hope that they will make enough to buy supper when they go home. Some have spent their last nickel to get to the corner and are in desperate need. When the hour grows late, they sit on boxes if any are around. In the afternoon their labor is worth only half as much as in the morning. If they are lucky, they get about 30 cents an hour scrubbing, cleaning, laundering, washing windows, waxing floors and wood-work all day long; in the afternoon, when most have already been employed, they are only worth the degrading sum of 20 cents an hour.

Once hired on the "slave market," the women often find after a day's back-breaking toil, that they worked longer than was arranged, got less than was promised, were forced to accept clothing instead of cash and were exploited beyond human endurance. Only the urgent need for money makes them submit to this routine daily.

Throughout the country, more than two million women are engaged in domestic work, the largest occupational group for women. About half are Negro women. . . .

Though many Negro women work for as little as two dollars a week and as long as 80 hours a week . . . they have no social security, no workmen's compensation, no old age security. . . .

The Women's Bureau in Washington points out that women take domestic work only as a last resort. Largely unprotected by law they find themselves at the mercy of an individual employer. Only two states, Wisconsin and Washington, have wage or hour legislation. But enforcement is very slack. . . .

The tradition of street corner markets is no new institution in this city. As far back as 1834, the statute books show, a place was set aside on city streets where those seeking work could meet with those who wanted workers. This exchange also functions for male workers. . . . At present markets flourish in the Bronx and

Louise Mitchell, "Slave Markets Typify Exploitation of Domestics," *The Daily Worker,* May 5, 1940. This document can also be found in Gerda Lerner, ed., *Black Women in White America: A Documentary History* (New York: Pantheon Books, 1972), 229–231.

Brooklyn where middle-class families live. However, this method of employment is also instituted in Greenwhich Village, Richmond and Queens. . .

The prosperity of the nation can only be judged by the living standards of its most oppressed group. State legislatures must pass laws to protect the health and work of the domestic. A world of education is still needed both for employees and employers.

Many civic and social organizations are now working toward improving conditions of domestics. Outstanding among these is the Bronx Citizens Committee for Improvement of Domestic Employees. The YWCA and many women's clubs are interested in the problem. Mayor LaGuardia . . . must be forced to end these horrible conditions of auction block hiring with the most equitable solution for the most oppressed section of the working class—Negro women.

✦ E S S A Y S

Annelise Orleck of Dartmouth College shows that working-class women, white and black, were not merely victims of poverty or misguided policy during the Great Depression and New Deal. Depression-era housewives became effective political activists, raising the consumer consciousness of Americans and forcing reductions in food, rent, and utility costs. Andrea Tone of the Georgia Institute of Technology likewise explores women's role as consumers. But unlike Orleck, Tone emphasizes women's inability to lessen their vulnerability in the marketplace. Desperate to achieve some degree of reproductive control, yet unable to obtain reliable contraceptives legally, female consumers in the 1930s purchased unregulated commercial products that had been proven neither safe nor efficacious.

Housewives Demand Economic Justice During the Great Depression

ANNELISE ORLECK

In her 1933 book, *It's Up to the Women,* Eleanor Roosevelt argued that mothers, through self-sacrifice and creativity, would save their families from the worst ravages of the Depression. There is abundant evidence to show that poor wives and mothers did approach their traditional responsibilities with heightened urgency during the Depression. They did not, however, suffer alone their inability to provide food or shelter for their families; nor did they sacrifice silently for the sake of their husbands and children. Quite the contrary. From the late 1920s through the 1940s, there was a remarkable surge of activism by working-class American housewives.

From New York City to Seattle; from Richmond, Virginia, to Los Angeles; and in hundreds of small towns and farm villages in between, poor wives and mothers staged food boycotts and antieviction demonstrations, created large-scale barter networks, and lobbied for food and rent price controls. Militant and angry, they

Annelise Orleck, "We Are That Mythical Thing Called the Public: Militant Housewives During the Great Depression," *Feminist Studies* 19, no. 1 (1993): 147–172. Reprinted by permission of the publisher, Feminist Studies, Inc.

demanded a better quality of life for themselves and their children. Echoing the language of trade unionism, they asserted that housing and food, like wages and hours, could be regulated by organizing and applying economic pressure. . . .

Housewives' activism, like that of every other group of Americans during the Depression era, was profoundly influenced by Franklin Roosevelt's New Deal. During the early years of the Depression, prior to the 1932 presidential election, housewives organized to stave off imminent disaster. Their focus was on self-help—setting up barter networks, gardening cooperatives, and neighborhood councils. After 1933, the tactics and arguments used by militant housewives reflected their acceptance of Roosevelt's corporatist vision. By the mid-1930s, poor and working-class housewives, like farmers and factory workers, had begun to see themselves as a group that could, by organizing and lobbying, force the New Deal state to respond to their needs. . . . Understanding their power as a voting bloc, house-wives lobbied in state capitals and in Washington, D.C. They also ran for electoral office in numerous locales across the country. . . . These were . . . women who accepted the traditional sexual division of labor but who found that the Depression had made it impossible for them to fulfill their responsibilities to the home without leaving it.

Housewife activists argued that the homes in which they worked were intimately linked to the fields and shops where their husbands, sons, and daughters labored; to the national economy; and to the fast-growing state and federal bureaucracies. . . . The housewives' rebellions that swept the country during the 1930s cannot be seen as only spontaneous outcries for a "just price." Like so many others during the Depression, working-class housewives were offering their own solutions to the failure of the U.S. economic system.

. . . [T]his essay focuses on three of the most active and successful urban housewives' groups: the New York-based United Council of Working-Class Women, the Seattle-based Women's Committee of the Washington Commonwealth Federation, and the Detroit-based Women's Committee against the High Cost of Living. . . . An examination of these three groups illustrates that although there were some important regional differences in housewives' political style and focus, there were also commonalities. Most significantly, each had a strong labor movement affiliation. Housewives' activism developed in union strongholds, flourishing in the Bronx and Brooklyn among the wives and mothers of unionized garment workers; in Detroit among the wives and mothers of United Auto Workers' (UAW) members; and in Seattle, among the wives of unionized workers who had begun to argue the importance of consumer organizing during the 1920s. . . . Union husbands' fights for higher wages during the 1910s had resulted in a fairly comfortable standard of living for many families by World War I. But spiraling inflation and the near-destruction of many trade unions during the 1920s eroded the working-class quality of life. By 1929 it had become increasingly difficult, even for families of employed union workers, to make ends meet.

The militance of the Depression-era housewives' movement was an outgrowth of this sudden and rapid decline in working-class families' standard of living. But it was also rooted in women organizers' own experiences in trade unions. . . . [T]he key organizers of the housewives' movement were all labor leaders before the Depression. In Seattle, Jean Stovel and Mary Farquharson were active in the American

Federation of Labor (AFL) before they became leaders of the Women's Committee of the Washington Commonwealth Federation. Detroit's Mary Zuk was the daughter of a United Mine Workers' member and was raised on the violent mine strikes of the 1920s. As a young woman she migrated to Detroit to work on an automobile assembly line and was fired for UAW organizing before founding the Detroit Women's Committee against the High Cost of Living. In New York, Rose Nelson was an organizer for the International Ladies' Garment Workers' Union (ILGWU) before she became co-director of the United Council of Working-Class Women (UCWCW). And the career of the best-known housewife organizer of the 1930s, Clara Lemlich Shavelson, illustrates the importance of both labor movement and Communist party links. (Only the New York organizers had explicit CP ties, although charges of CP involvement were leveled against nearly all the housewife leaders.)

Shavelson's career also roots the housewives' rebellions of the 1930s in a long tradition of Jewish immigrant women's agitation around subsistence issues. . . . Clara Lemlich came of age on Manhattan's Lower East Side where married women led frequent food boycotts and rent strikes during the first decade of the twentieth century. Long before she made the famous speech that set off the massive 1909 shirtwaist makers' strike—"I am tired of the talking; I move that we go on a general strike!"—Lemlich was aware that the principles of unionism could be applied to community activism.

Blacklisted by garment manufacturers after the 1909 strike, fired from her new career as a paid woman's suffrage advocate after conflicts with upper-class suffragists, Lemlich married printer Arthur Shavelson in 1913 and immediately began looking for ways to channel spontaneous outbursts of housewives' anger into an organizational structure. During World War I, the U.S. government made her task easier by mobilizing housewives in many city neighborhoods into Community Councils for National Defense. Now, when housewives decided to protest rapidly increasing food prices, they had an organizational structure to build on and halls in which to meet. In 1917 and 1919 Shavelson and other community organizers were able to spread meat boycotts and rent strikes throughout New York City by winning support from the community councils, as well as synagogue groups and women's trade union auxiliaries.

By 1926, when Shavelson established the United Council of Working-Class Housewives (UCWCH), she was working under the auspices of the Communist party. However, Shavelson's insistence on organizing women made her a maverick within the CP, as she had been in the labor and suffrage movements. The male leadership of the CP expressed little interest in efforts to win working-class wives to the party. And the women who ran the UCWCH put no pressure on women who joined the housewives' councils to also join the CP.

Around the same time that the united councils were founded, non-Communist organizers like Rose Schneiderman of the Women's Trade Union League (WTUL) and Pauline Newman and Fania Cohn of the ILGWU were also trying to bring housewives into the working-class movement. . . . As workers, women were segregated into the lowest-paid, least-skilled sectors of the labor force. . . . But as consumers, U.S. working class women spent billions of dollars annually. Organized as consumers, even poor women could wield real economic power. By the late 1920s, women organizers were ready to try to link the home to labor unions and government in a dynamic partnership—with wage-earning women and house-wives as full partners.

That goal brought women organizers into direct conflict with male leaders in the trade union movement and in the CP, who were unwilling to accept the home as a center of production or the housewife as a productive laborer. Nor did they see a relationship between production and consumption. Poor housewives, whatever their political stripe, understood that relationship implicitly. They responded to the neighborhood organizing strategy because they saw in it a chance to improve day-to-day living conditions for themselves and their families. Jean Stovel explained the surge of militance among Seattle housewives this way: "Women," she said, "have sold the idea of organization—their own vast power—to themselves, the result of bitter experience. We are that mythical thing called the public and so we shall demand a hearing." . . .

Between 1926 and 1933 housewives' self-help groups sprang up across the United States. . . . In Seattle, unemployed families organized quickly in the aftermath of the 1929 stock market crash; but then this was an unusually organized city, described by a local paper in 1937 as "the most unionized city in the country." . . . By 1931–32, 40,000 Seattle women and men had joined an exchange in which the men farmed, fished, and cut leftover timber from cleared land, while the women gathered food, fuel, and clothing. The women also ran commissaries where members could shop with scrip for household essentials. By 1934, an estimated 80,000 people statewide belonged to exchanges that allowed them to acquire food, clothing, and shelter without any money changing hands.

In larger cities like New York, Chicago, Philadelphia, and Detroit, self-help groups also sprang up during the early years of the Depression, but housewives there had little chance of making direct contact with farmers. Rather than establishing food exchanges, they created neighborhood councils that used boycotts and demonstrations to combat rising food prices. And, rather than rehabilitating abandoned buildings for occupation by the homeless, as the unemployed did in Seattle, housewives in larger cities battled with police to prevent evictions of families unable to pay their rents.

Tenant and consumer councils in those cities took hold in neighborhoods where housewives had orchestrated rent strikes and meat boycotts in 1902, 1904, 1907, 1908, and 1917. They organized in the same way as earlier housewife activists had done—primarily through door-to-door canvassing. Boycotts were sustained in the latter period, as in the earlier one, with picket lines and streetcorner meetings. Even their angry outbursts echoed the earlier housewives' uprisings: meat was destroyed with kerosene or taken off trucks and thrown to the ground. Flour was spilled in the streets, and milk ran in the gutters.

But although its links to earlier housewives' and labor union struggles are important, the 1930s' housewives' revolt was far more widespread and sustained, encompassing a far wider range of ethnic and racial groups than any tenant or consumer uprising before it. The earlier outbursts were limited to East Coast Jewish immigrant communities, but the housewives' uprising of the 1930s was nationwide and involved rural as well as urban women. It drew Polish and native-born housewives in Detroit, Finnish and Scandinavian women in Washington State, and Scandinavian farm wives in Minnesota. Jewish and Black housewives were particularly militant in New York, Cleveland, Chicago, Los Angeles, and San Francisco.

The 1930s' housewives' movement can also be distinguished from earlier housewives' actions by the sophistication and longevity of the organizations it generated. Depression-era housewives moved quickly from self-help to lobbying in state capitals and Washington, D.C. Leaders like the "diminutive but fiery" Mary Zuk of Detroit displayed considerable skill in their use of radio and print media. Their demands of government—regulation of staple food prices; establishment of publicly owned farmer-consumer cooperatives—reflected a complex understanding of the marketplace and the potential uses of the growing government bureaucracy.

Leaders of these groups also demonstrated considerable sophistication about forming alliances. Shortly after Roosevelt was elected president, hostilities between Communist and non-Communist women in the labor movement were temporarily set aside. AFL-affiliated women's auxiliaries and CP-affiliated women's neighborhood councils worked together to organize consumer protests and lobby for regulation of food and housing costs. This happened in 1933, well before the CP initiated its Popular Front policy urging members to join with "progressive" non-Communist groups and well before the Congress of Industrial Organizations extended its hand to Communists to rejoin the labor movement.

This rapprochement highlighted the desperation that gripped so many working-class communities during the Depression. Although anti-Communist charges were leveled against housewife organizers throughout the Depression, such accusations did not dampen the enthusiasm of rank-and-file council members. . . . Detroit housewife leader Catherine Mudra responded this way to charges of Communist involvement in the Detroit meat strike of 1935: "There may be some Communists among us. There are a lot of Republicans and Democrats too. We do not ask the politics of those who join. . . . All we want is to get prices down to where we can feed our families."

Despite this tolerance of Communist leadership, housewife organizers affiliated with the CP were careful not to push too hard. Party regulars like Clara Lemlich Shavelson were open about their political beliefs, but they did not push members of the housewives' councils to toe the party line. And they organized as mothers, not as Communists. . . .

In New York, ethnic bonding between women facilitated the growth of housewives' councils. Although many community organizers like Shavelson, Rose Nelson Raynes, Sonya Sanders, and Sophia Ocher were CP members, they were also genuine members of the communities they sought to organize, familiar with local customs, needs, and fears. They addressed crowds of housewives in Yiddish as well as English. And steering clear of Marxist doctrine, they emphasized ethnic and community ties in their speeches, likening housewives' councils to the women's charitable associations traditional in East European Jewish culture. . . .

This strength was also a weakness. As a result of New York's ethnic balkanization, the city's neighborhood councils were not ethnically diverse. Organizers tended to have most success organizing women of their own ethnic group. . . . As in New York, the Detroit and Seattle housewives' actions were initiated by immigrant women of a particular ethnic group—Polish Catholics in Detroit and Scandinavian Protestants in Seattle. Because those cities were less ghettoized than New York, organizers were more successful in creating coalitions that involved Black as well as white women; Protestants, Jews, and Catholics; immigrants and native born. However, ethnic differences were not unimportant, even outside New York. For example, American-born Protestants in the Detroit housewives' councils were far less confrontational in their tactics than their Polish, Jewish, or Black counterparts. They signed no-meat pledges rather than picketing butcher shops and handed in petitions rather than marching on city hall. . . .

Depression-era organizing against high food prices reached its peak during the summer of 1935. Working-class women activists from Communist and non-Communist organizations convened two regional conferences the previous winter, one for the East Coast, another for the Midwest, to coordinate protests against the sales tax and high cost of living. Representatives from AFL women's union auxiliaries, parents' associations, church groups, farm women's and Black women's groups attended. By that summer, they had laid plans for the most ambitious women's consumer protest to that time.

It began when the Chicago Committee against the High Cost of Living, headed by Dina Ginsberg, organized massive street meetings near the stockyards to let the meat packers know how unhappy they were with rising meat prices. New York housewives in the UCWCW quickly raised the ante by organizing a citywide strike against butcher shops. . . .

Housewives across the United States promptly joined in. Ten thousand Los Angeles housewives, members of the Joint Council of Women's Auxiliaries, declared a meat strike on June 8th that so completely shut down retail meat sales in the city that butchers cut prices by the next day. In Philadelphia, Chicago, Boston, Paterson, St. Louis, and Kansas City, newly formed housewives' councils echoed the cry of the New York strike: "Stop Buying Meat Until Prices Come Down!"

On June 15, a delegation of housewives from across the country descended on Washington, D.C., demanding that the Department of Agriculture enforce lower meat prices. Clara Lemlich Shavelson described the delegation's meeting with Secretary of Agriculture Henry Wallace. "The meat packers and the Department of Agriculture in Washington tried to make the strikers' delegation . . . believe that the farmer and the drought are to blame for the high price of food. But the delegation would not fall for this. They knew the truth."

The Polish housewives of Hamtramck, Michigan, a suburb of Detroit, did not believe Wallace's explanation either. A month after the end of the New York strike, thirty-two-year-old Mary Zuk addressed a mass demonstration of housewives gathered on the streets of Hamtramck to demand an immediate reduction in meat prices. When the reduction did not come by that evening, Zuk announced a meat boycott to begin the following day.

On July 27, 1935, Polish and Black housewives began to picket Hamtramck butcher shops, carrying signs demanding a 20 percent price cut throughout the city and an end to price gouging in Black neighborhoods. . . . Within a matter of days the meat boycott spread to other parts of Detroit, as housewives in several different ethnic communities hailed the onset of "a general strike against the high cost of living." Jewish women picketed kosher butcher shops in downtown Detroit neighborhoods. Protestant women in outlying regions such as Lincoln Park and River Rouge declined to picket or march but instead set up card tables on streetcorners to solicit no-meat pledges from passing housewives.

Housewives also sought government intervention. Detroit housewives stormed the city council demanding that it set a ceiling on meat prices in the metropolitan area. "What we can afford to buy isn't fit for a human to eat," Joanna Dinkfeld told the council. "And we can't afford very much of that." Warning the council and the state government that they had better act, Myrtle Hoaglund announced that she was forming a statewide housewives' organization. "We feel that we should have united action," she said. "We think the movement of protest against present meat prices can be spread throughout the state and . . . the nation." As evidence, she showed the city council bags of letters she had received from housewives around the country, asking her how to go about organizing consumer boycotts.

Throughout August the meat strikers made front-page news in Detroit and received close attention in major New York and Chicago dailies. The women staged mass marches through the streets of Detroit, stormed meat-packing plants, overturned and emptied meat trucks, and poured kerosene on thousands of pounds of meat stored in warehouses. . . . *Newsweek* reported housewives' demonstrations against the high price of meat in Indianapolis, Denver, and Miami. The *New York Times* reported violent housewives' attacks on meat warehouses in Chicago and in Shenandoah and Frackville, Pennsylvania. And Mary Zuk, the "strong-jawed 100 lb. mother of the meat strike," became a national figure. The Detroit post office announced that it was receiving letters from all over the country addressed only to "Mrs. Zuk—Detroit."

Although boycotts and strikes continued to be used as a tool in the housewives' struggle for lower prices, the movement became more focused on electoral politics as the decade wore on. Both Shavelson and Zuk used the prominence they'd gained through housewife activism to run for elected office. Shavelson ran for New York State Assembly in 1933 and 1938 as a "real . . . mother fighting to maintain an American standard of living for her own family as well as for other families. . . ." She did not win but she fared far better than the rest of the CP ticket.

Zuk ran a successful campaign for the Hamtramck City Council in April of 1936. Although the local Hearst-owned paper warned that her election would be a victory for those who advocate "the break-up of the family," Zuk was swept into office by her fellow housewives. She won on a platform calling for the city council to reduce rents, food prices, and utility costs in Hamtramck. After her election she told reporters that she was proof that "a mother can organize and still take care of her family."

In some ways what the Hearst papers sensed was really happening. Zuk's campaign represented an express politicization of motherhood and the family. On Mother's Day, 1936, seven hundred Zuk supporters rallied outside the city council to demand public funding for a women's healthcare clinic, childcare centers, playgrounds, and teen centers in Hamtramck. They also called for an end to evictions and construction of more public housing in their city. The government owed this to mothers, the demonstrators told reporters. . . .

Housewife activists also kept their sights on the federal government during this period. From 1935 to 1941, housewives' delegations from major cities made annual trips to Washington, D.C., to lobby for lower food prices. These trips stopped during World War II but resumed afterward with a concerted campaign to save the Office of Price Administration and to win federal funds for construction of public housing in poor neighborhoods.

The alliance of housewives' councils and women's union auxiliaries continued to grow through the late 1930s, laying the groundwork for two more nationwide meat strikes in 1948 and 1951. . . . But even as these actions made front-page news across the country, the housewives' alliance was breaking apart over the issue of Communist involvement. As early as 1933, the Washington State legislature had passed a bill requiring that Seattle take over the commissaries created by the unemployed two years earlier. Conservative politicians claimed that Communists had taken control of the relief machinery in the city and were seeking to indoctrinate the hungry. In 1939, Hearst newspapers charged that the housewives' movement nationwide was little more than a Communist plot to sow seeds of discord in the American home. The Dies Committee of the U.S. Congress took these charges seriously and began an investigation. U.S. entry into World War II temporarily ended the investigation but also quelled consumer protest, because the government instituted rationing and price controls.

Investigations of the consumer movement began again soon after the war ended. During the 1948 boycott, housewife leaders were charged by some with being too friendly to Progressive party presidential candidate Henry Wallace. In 1949, the House Committee on Un-American Activities began investigating the organizers of a 1947 housewives' march on Washington, and in 1950 they were ordered to register with the Justice Department as foreign agents. By the early 1950s national and local Communist-hunting committees had torn apart the movement, creating dissension and mistrust among the activists.

The unique alliance that created a nationwide housewives' uprising during the 1930s and 1940s would not reemerge, but it laid the groundwork for later consumer and tenant organizing. Housewives' militance politicized consumer issues nationwide. "Never has there been such a wave of enthusiasm to do something for the consumer," *The Nation* wrote in 1937. Americans have gained "a consumer consciousness," the magazine concluded, as a direct result of the housewives' strikes in New York, Detroit, and other cities. The uprising of working-class housewives also broadened the terms of the class struggle, forcing male union leaders to admit that "the roles of producer and consumer are intimately related."

Housewives' groups alleviated the worst effects of the Depression in many working-class communities by bringing down food prices; rent and utility costs; preventing evictions; and spurring the construction of more public housing, schools, and parks. By the end of World War II, housewives' activism had forced the government to play a regulatory role in food and housing costs. Militant direct action and sustained lobbying put pressure on local and federal politicians to investigate profiteering on staple goods. The meat strikers of 1935 and of 1948 through 1951 resulted in congressional hearings on the structure of the meat industry and in nationwide reductions in prices. The intense antieviction struggles led by urban housewives and their years of lobbying for public housing helped to convince New York City and other localities to pass rent-control laws. They also increased support in Congress for federally funded public housing.

Perhaps an equally important legacy of housewives' activism was its impact on the consciousness of the women who participated. "It was an education for the women," Brooklyn activist Dorothy Moser recalls, "that they could not have gotten any other way." Immigrant women, poor native white women, and Black women learned to write and speak effectively, to lobby in state capitals and in Washington, D.C., to challenge men in positions of power, and sometimes to question the power relations in their own homes. . . .

In defending their right to participate in a struggle that did not ideologically challenge the traditional sexual division of labor, many working-class housewives developed a new sense of pride in their abilities and a taste for political involvement. These women never came to think of themselves as feminists. They did, however, begin to see themselves as legitimate political and economic actors. During this period, poor wives and mothers left their homes in order to preserve them. In so doing, whether they intended to or not, they politicized the home, the family, and motherhood in important and unprecedented ways.

Women, Birth Control, and the Marketplace in the 1930s

ANDREA TONE

In 1933, readers of *McCall*'s probably noticed the following advertisement for Lysol feminine hygiene in the magazine's July issue:

> The most frequent eternal triangle:
> A HUSBAND . . . A WIFE . . . and her FEARS
> Fewer marriages would flounder around in a maze of misunderstanding and unhappiness if more wives knew and practiced regular marriage hygiene. Without it, some minor physical irregularity plants in a woman's mind the fear of a major crisis. Let so devastating a fear recur again and again, and the most gracious wife turns into a nerve-ridden, irritable travesty of herself.

Hope for the vexed woman was at hand, however. In fact, it was as close as the neighborhood store. Women who invested their faith and dollars in Lysol, the ad promised, would find in its use the perfect panacea for their marital woes. Feminine hygiene would contribute to "a woman's sense of fastidiousness" while freeing her from habitual fears of pregnancy. Used regularly, Lysol would ensure "health and harmony . . . throughout her married life."

The *McCall*'s ad, one of hundreds of birth control ads published in women's magazines in the 1930s, reflects the rapid growth of the contraceptive industry in the United States during the Depression. Birth control has always been a matter of practical interest to women and men. By the early 1930s, despite long-standing legal restrictions and an overall decline in consumer purchasing power, it had also become a profitable industry. Capitalizing on Americans' desire to limit family size in an era of economic hardship, pharmaceutical firms, rubber manufacturers, mail-order houses, and fly-by-night peddlers launched a successful campaign to persuade women and men to eschew natural methods for commercial devices whose efficacy could be "scientifically proven." In 1938, with the industry's annual sales exceeding $250 million, *Fortune* pronounced birth control one of the most prosperous new businesses of the decade. . . .

It was during the Depression that the structure of the modern contraceptive market emerged. Depression-era manufacturers were the first to create a mass market for contraceptives in the United States. Through successful advertising they heightened

Andrea Tone, "Contraceptive Consumers: Gender and the Political Economy of Birth Control in the 1930s," *Journal of Social History* 29, no. 3 (spring 1996): 485–506. Reprinted by permission.

demand for commercial birth control while building a permanent consumer base that facilitated the industry's subsequent expansion. Significantly, this consumer constituency was almost exclusively female. Condoms, the most popular commercial contraceptive before the Depression, generated record sales in the 1930s. But it was profits from female contraceptives—sales of which outnumbered those of condoms five to one by the late 1930s—that fuelled the industry's prodigious growth. Then, as now, women were the nation's leading contraceptive consumers.

An important feature distinguished the birth-control market of the 1930s from that of today, however: its illegality. Federal and state laws dating from the 1870s proscribed the inter-state distribution and sale of contraceptives. Although by the 1920s the scope of these restrictions had been modified by court interpretations permitting physicians to supply contraceptive information and devices in several states, the American Medical Association's ban on medically dispensed contraceptive advice remained intact. Neither legal restrictions nor medical disapproval thwarted the industry's ascent, however. Instead, they merely pushed the industry underground, beyond regulatory reach.

Contraceptive manufacturers in the 1930s exploited this vacuum to their advantage, retailing devices that were often useless and/or dangerous in a manner that kept the birth-control business on the right side of the law. The industry thrived within a grey market characterized by the sale of contraceptives under legal euphemisms. Manufacturers sold a wide array of items, including vaginal jellies, douche powders and liquids, suppositories, and foaming tablets as "feminine hygiene," an innocuous-sounding term coined by advertisers in the 1920s. Publicly, manufacturers claimed that feminine hygiene products were sold solely to enhance vaginal cleanliness. Consumers, literally deconstructing advertising text, knew better. Obliquely encoded in feminine hygiene ads and product packaging were indicators of the product's *real* purpose; references to "protection," "security," or "dependability" earmarked purported contraceptive properties.

Tragically, linguistic clues could not protect individuals from product adulteration or marketing fraud. Because neither the government nor the medical establishment condoned lay use of commercial contraceptives, consumers possessed no reliable information with which to evaluate the veracity of a product's claim. The bootleg status of the birth control racket left contraceptive consumers in a legal lurch. If an advertised product's implied claims to contraceptive attributes failed, they had no acceptable means of recourse. . . .

When Congress enacted the Comstock Act in 1873, a new nadir in reproductive rights had arrived. The anti-obscenity law, the result of the relentless campaigning of its namesake, purity crusader Anthony Comstock, proscribed, among other things, the private or public dissemination of any

> book, pamphlet, paper, writing, advertisement, circular, print, picture, drawing, or other representation, figure, or image on or of paper or other material, or any cast, instrument, or other article of an immoral nature, or any drug or medicine, or any article whatever for the prevention of conception.

Passed after minimal debate, the Comstock Act had long-term repercussions. Following Congress's lead, most states enacted so-called "mini" Comstock acts which criminalized the circulation of contraceptive devices and information within state lines.

Collectively, these restrictions demarcated the legal boundaries of permissible sexuality. Sexual intercourse rendered nonprocreative through the use of "unnatural"—that is, purchased—birth control was forbidden. Purity crusaders contended that if properly enforced, the Comstock and mini-Comstock acts would regulate birth control out of existence. Instead, they made birth control an increasingly dangerous, but no less popular, practice.

By the time state and federal legislatures had begun to abandon their laissez-faire attitude toward birth control, a fledgling contraceptive industry had already surfaced in the United States. Indeed, the two developments were integrally yoked: the initiative to regulate contraceptives arose out of the realization that there was a growing number to regulate. The nineteenth century witnessed the emergence of a contraceptive trade that sold for profit goods that had traditionally been prepared within the home. Douching powders and astringents, dissolving suppositories, and vaginal pessaries had supplemented male withdrawal and abstinence as mainstays of birth-control practice in pre-industrial America. . . . By the 1870s, condoms, douching syringes, douching solutions, vaginal sponges, and cervical caps could be purchased from mail-order houses, wholesale drug-supply houses, and pharmacies. Pessaries—traditionally used to support prolapsed uteruses but sold since the 1860s in closed-ring form as "womb veils"—could be obtained from sympathetic physicians. Thus when supporters of the Comstock Act decried the "nefarious and diabolical traffic" of "vile and immoral goods," they were identifying the inroads commercialized contraception had already made.

After the Comstock restrictions were passed, birth control continued to be sold, marketed for its therapeutic or cosmetic, rather than its contraceptive, value. Significantly, however, commercial contraceptive use became more closely associated with economic privilege. The clandestine nature of the market prompted many reputable firms—especially rubber manufacturers—to cease production altogether. Those that remained charged exorbitant prices for what was now illegal merchandise. For many wage-earning and immigrant families, the high price of contraceptives made them unaffordable. In addition, the suppression of birth-control information reduced the availability of published material on commercial and noncommercial techniques, as descriptions previously featured openly in pamphlets, books, journals, broadsides, and newspaper medical columns became harder to find. In effect, contraceptive information, like contraceptives themselves, became a privileged luxury.

Only in the 1930s were birth-control manufacturers able to create a mass market characterized by widespread access to commercial contraceptives. This market developed in response to a combination of important events. The birth-control movement of the 1910s and 1920s, spearheaded by Margaret Sanger, made birth control a household word (indeed, it was Sanger who introduced the term) and a topic of protracted debate and heated public discussion. Sanger insisted that women's sexual liberation and economic autonomy depended upon the availability of safe, inexpensive, and effective birth control. Sanger conducted speaking tours extolling the need for female contraception and published piercing indictments of "Comstockery" in her short-lived feminist newspaper *The Woman Rebel,* the *International Socialist Review,* and privately published pamphlets. In October 1916, she opened in Brooklyn the first birth-control clinic in the United States where she instructed neighborhood women on contraceptive techniques. The clinic's closure and Sanger's subsequent jail sentence only increased her notoriety. Sanger was not alone in her efforts to legit-imize contraception, of course. The birth control movement was a collective struggle waged by hundreds of individuals and organizations, including IWW locals, women's Socialist groups, independent birth control leagues, and the liberal-minded National Birth Control League. But Sanger's single-minded devotion to the birth-control cause and her casual and frequent defiance of the law captured the media spotlight. In the 1910s it was Sanger, more than anyone else, who pushed contraception into the public arena and who, quite unintentionally, set the stage for the commercial exploitation that followed.

. . . By the end of the 1920s, state and federal legal restrictions on birth control remained operative and unchanged. Doctors-only bills which, had they been suc-cessful, would have permitted physicians to prescribe birth control, were introduced and defeated in New York, Connecticut, Pennsylvania, Massachusetts, New Jersey, and California. . . .

Notwithstanding these legislative setbacks, significant advances were made. Capitalizing on a 1918 New York Court of Appeals ruling that exempted physicians from prosecution for prescribing contraception necessary to "cure or prevent dis-ease," Sanger opened the first permanent public birth-control clinic in the country in 1923. Within a year, the clinic had supplied contraceptive information to 1,208 women. By 1929, the number of medically supervised birth-control clinics across the country had increased to twenty-eight, almost all of which were affiliated with Sanger's parent organization, the American Birth Control League. Sanger was also responsible for facilitating the domestic manufacture of diaphragms and spermicidal jellies, clinics' contraception of choice. Frustrated by her inability to interest Ameri-can manufacturers in the manufacture of female contraceptives, Sanger persuaded her second husband, J. Noah H. Slee, president of the Three-In-One Oil Company, to smuggle German-made Mensinga diaphragms and contraceptive jellies in oil drums across the border near the firm's Montreal plant. The smuggling system worked, but not well: the method was unreliable and legally risky, the products acquired too few in number and vastly overpriced. In 1925, with Sanger's urging, Slee financed the Holland-Rantos Company which began manufacturing spring-type diaphragms and lactic acid jelly for Sanger's clinics.

The cumulative effect of these activities—the sensationalist tactics, the organiza-tional impetus, the failed legislative initiatives, and the expansion of public clinics — was to make Americans "birth control conscious." The popularization of the idea of birth control supplied the cultural backdrop to the economic birth-control boom of the 1930s. In the absence of government approval and regulation, the rising de-sire for contraceptives provided the perfect environment in which a bootleg trade could thrive. . . .

As the demand for birth control accelerated, the inability of existing institutions to satisfy it became apparent. By 1932, only 145 public clinics operated to service the contraceptive needs of the nation; twenty-seven states had no clinics at all. . . . Many women, spurred on by public attention to birth control but unable to secure the assistance needed to make informed contraception choices, took contraception—and their lives—into their own hands. . . .

That there was a commercial market to turn to was the result of liberalized legal restrictions that encouraged manufacturers to enter the birth-control trade.

The structure of the birth-control industry of the early 1930s was markedly different from that which preceded it only a few years earlier. From 1925 to 1928, Holland-Rantos had enjoyed a monopoly on the manufacture of diaphragms and contraceptive jellies in the United States; other manufacturers expressed little interest in producing articles that might invoke government prosecution and whose market was confined to a handful of non-profit clinics. A 1930 decision, *Youngs Rubber Corporation, Inc., v. C.I. Lee & Co., et al,* lifted legal impediments to market entry. The *Youngs* case, in which the makers of Trojan condoms successfully sued a rival company for trademark infringement, forced the court to decide whether the contraceptive business was legal, and thus legitimately entitled to trademark protection. The court ruled that in so far as birth control had "other lawful purposes" besides contraception, it could be legally advertised, distributed, and sold as a non-contraceptive device. The outcome of a dispute between rival condom manufacturers, the *Youngs* decision left its most critical mark on the female contraceptive market. Companies that had previously avoided the birth control business quickly grasped the commercial opportunities afforded by the court's ruling. Provided that no reference to a product's contraceptive features appeared in product advertising or on product packaging, female contraceptives could now be legally sold—not only to the small number of birth control clinics in states where physician-prescribed birth control was legal, but to the consuming public nation-wide. Manufacturers realized that the court's legal latitude would not affect the diaphragm market, monopolized, as it was, by the medical profession. Because diaphragms required a physician's fitting, the number of buyers, given financial and regional obstacles to this type of medical consultation, would remain proportionately small. Jellies, suppositories, and foaming tablets, on the other hand, possessed untapped mass-market potential. They could be used without prior medical screening. And because chemical compounds were cheaper to mass produce than rubber diaphragms, they could be sold at a price more women could afford.

By 1938, only twelve years after Holland-Randos had launched the female contraceptive industry in the United States, at least four hundred other firms were competing in the lucrative market. The $212 million industry acquired most of its profits from the sale of jellies, suppositories, tablets, and antiseptic douching solutions retailed over the counter as feminine hygiene and bought principally by women. . . . The contraceptive industry thrived in the 1930s precisely because, while capitalizing on public discussions of birth control to which the medical community contributed, it operated outside customary medical channels. Manufacturers supplied women with something that clinics and private physicians did not: birth control that was conveniently located, discreetly obtained, and, most importantly, affordably priced. While the going rate for a diaphragm and a companion tube of jelly ranged from four to six dollars, a dollar purchased a dozen suppositories, ten foaming tablets, or, most alluring of all, up to three douching units, depending on the brand. Contraceptive manufacturers pledged, furthermore, that customer satisfaction would not be sacrificed on the altar of frugality. They reassured buyers that bargain-priced contraceptives were just as reliable as other methods. Without lay guides to help them identify the disjunction between advertising hyperbole and reality, women could hardly be faulted for taking the cheaper path. By the late 1930s, purchases of diaphragms accounted for less than one percent of total contraceptive sales.

Manufacturers' grandiose claims aside, not all contraceptives were created alike. The dangers and deficiencies of birth control products were well known in the health and hygiene community. Concerned pharmacists, physicians, and birth-control advocates routinely reviewed and condemned commercial preparations. Experts agreed, for instance, that vaginal suppositories, among the most frequently used contraceptives, were also among the least reliable. Suppositories typically consisted of boric acid and/or quinine, ingredients not recognized as effective spermicides. Melting point variability posed an added problem. Suppositories, usually based in cocoa butter or gelatin, were supposed to dissolve at room temperature. In practice, weather extremes and corresponding fluctuations in vaginal temperature made suppositories' diffusion, homogeneity, and contraceptive attributes unpredictable. . . .

But critics reserved their hardest comments for the most popular, affordable, and least reliable contraceptive of the day, the antiseptic douche. Noting the method's alarming failure rate—reported at the time to be as high as seventy percent—they condemned the technique as mechanically unsound and pharmacologically ineffectual. . . . Scores of douching preparations, while advertised as modern medical miracles, contained nothing more than water, cosmetic plant extracts, and table salt. On the other hand, many others, including the most popular brand, Lysol disinfectant, contained cresol (a distillate of coal and wood) or mercury chloride, either of which, when used in too high a concentration, caused severe inflammation, burning, and even death. Advertising downplayed the importance of dilution by drawing attention to antiseptics' gentleness and versatility; single ads praising Lysol's safety on "delicate female tissues" also encouraged the money-wise consumer to use the antiseptic as a gargle, nasal spray, or household cleaner. . . .

Reports on douche-related deaths and injuries and the general ineffectiveness of popular commercial contraceptive were widely discussed among concerned constituents of the health community. Sadly, however, these findings failed to prod the medical establishment as a united profession to take a resolute stand against the contraceptive scandal. Nor, regrettably, did blistering indictments of manufacturing fraud trickle down to the lay press where they might have enabled women to make informed contraceptive choices. The numerous women's magazines that published feminine hygiene ads—from *McCall's* to *Screen Romances* to the *Ladies' Home Journal*—were conspicuously silent about the safety and efficacy of the products they tacitly endorsed. The paucity of information impeded the development of informed consumerism. In advertising text and in many women's minds, the euphemism "feminine hygiene" continued to signify reliable contraception. For unscrupulous manufacturers eager to profit from this identification, feminine hygiene continued to be a convenient term invoked to sell products devoid of contraceptive value.

Manufacturers absolved themselves of responsibility by reminding critics that by the letter of the law, their products were not being sold as contraceptives. If women incurred injuries or became pregnant while using feminine hygiene for birth control, that was their fault, not manufacturers'. . . . Added to the growing list of groups unwilling to expose the hucksterism of the birth-control bonanza was the federal government. Neither the Food and Drug Administration (FDA) nor the Federal Trade Commission (FTC) was in a strong position to rally to consumers' aid. The FDA, authorized to take action only against product mislabelling, was powerless to suppress birth-control manufacturers' rhetorically veiled claims. The FTC, in turn, regulated advertising, but only when one company's claims were so egregious as to constitute an unfair business practice. The subterfuge prevalent in all feminine hygiene marketing campaigns, as well as a unanimous desire on manufacturers' part to eschew protracted scrutiny, kept the FTC at bay. Sadly for the growing pool of female contraceptive consumers, without regulation and reliable standards for discriminating among products, the only way to discern a product's safety and efficacy was through trial and error.

Clamoring for a larger share of the hygiene market, manufacturers did their utmost to ensure that their product would be one women would want to try. . . . Ads conveyed the message that ineffective contraception led not only to unwanted pregnancies, but also to illness, despair, and marital discord. Married women who ignored modern contraceptive methods were courting life-long misery. "Almost before the honeymoon ends," one ad warned, "many a young bride is plagued by foreboding. She pictures the early departure of youth and charm . . . sacrificed on the altar of marriage responsibilities." . . . "Many marriage failures," one advertisement asserted authoritatively, "can be traced directly to disquieting wifely fears." "Recurring again and again," marriage anxieties were "capable of changing the most angelic nature, of making it nervous, suspicious, irritable." "I leave it to you," the ad concluded, "is it easy for even the kindliest husband to live with a wife like that?"

Having divulged the ugly and myriad hazards of unwanted pregnancy while saddling women with the burden of its prevention, advertisements emphasized that peace of mind and marital happiness were conditions only the market could bestow. . . . As advertisements reminded prospective customers, however, not all feminine-hygiene products were the same. The contraceptive consumer had to be discriminating. Hoping both to increase general demand for hygiene products and to inculcate brand loyalty, manufacturers presented their product as the one most frequently endorsed for its efficacy and safety by medical professionals. Dispelling consumer doubts by invoking the approval of the scientific community was not an advertising technique unique to contraceptive merchandising—the same strategy was used in the 1930s to sell women laxatives, breakfast cereal, and mouth wash. What was exceptional about contraceptive advertising, however, was that the experts endorsing feminine hygiene were not men. Rather, they were female physicians whose innate understanding of the female condition permitted them to share their birth-control expertise "woman to woman."

The Lehn and Fink corporation used this technique to make Lysol disinfectant douche the leading feminine-hygiene product in the country. In a series of full-page advertisements entitled "Frank Talks by Eminent Women Physicians," stern-looking European female gynecologists urged "smart-thinking" women to entrust their health only to doctor-recommended Lysol disinfectant douches. "It amazes me," wrote Dr. Madeleine Lion, "a widely recognized gynaecologist of Paris,"

> in these modern days, to hear women confess their carelessness, their lack of positive information, in the so vital matter of feminine hygiene. They take almost anybody's word . . . a neighbor's, an afternoon bridge partner's . . . for the correct technique. . . . Surely in this question of correct marriage hygiene, the modern woman should accept only the facts of scientific research and medical experience. The woman who does demand such facts uses 'Lysol' faithfully in her ritual of personal antisepsis.

Contraceptive manufacturers' creation of a mass market in the 1930s depended not only upon effective advertising, but also on the availability of advertised goods. Prospective customers needed quick, convenient, and multiple access to contraceptives. Manufacturers made sure that they had it. . . . The department store became the leading distributor of female contraceptives in the 1930s. By the mid 1930s women could purchase feminine hygiene products at a number of national chains, including Woolworth, Kresge, McLellan, and W. T. Grant. Already fashioned as a feminized space, department stores established sequestered "personal hygiene" departments where women could shop in a dignified and discreet manner for contraceptives and other products related to female reproduction such as sanitary napkins and tampons. Stores emphasized the exclusively female environment of the personal hygiene department as the department's finest feature. The self-contained department was not only separated from the rest of the store where "uncontrollable factors . . . might make for . . . embarrassment," but it was staffed solely by saleswomen trained in the "delicate matter of giving confidential and intimate personal advice to their clients." As one store assured female readers in the local newspaper: "Our Personal Hygiene Department [Has] Lady Attendants on Duty at all Times." Female clerks, furthermore, were instructed to respect the private nature of the department's transactions; sensitive, knowledgeable, and tactful, they were "understanding wom[en] with whom you may discuss your most personal and intimate problems." . . .

Manufacturers reasoned that many prospective female customers would not buy feminine hygiene in a store. Many did not live close enough to one, while others, notwithstanding the store's discretion, might remain uncomfortable with the public nature of the exchange. To eliminate regional and psychological obstacles to birth-control buying, companies sold feminine hygiene to women directly in their homes. Selling contraceptives by mail was one such method. Mail order catalogues, including those distributed by Sears, Roebuck and Montgomery Ward, offered a full line of female contraceptives; each catalogue contained legally-censored ads supplied by manufacturers. As a reward for bulk sales, mail-order houses received a discount from the companies whose products they sold. Other manufacturers bypassed jobbers and encouraged women to send their orders directly to the company. To eliminate the possibility of embarrassment, ads typically promised that the order would be delivered in "plain wrapper."

To create urban and working-class markets, dozens of firms hired door-to-door sales representatives to canvass urban districts. All representatives were women, a deliberate attempt on manufacturers' part to profit from the prudish marketing scheme that tried to convince women that, as one company put it, "There are some problems so intimate that it is embarrassing to talk them over with a doctor." At the Dilex Institute of Feminine Hygiene, for example, five separate female crews, each headed by a female crew manager, combed the streets of New York. The cornerstone of the company's marketing scheme was an aggressive sales pitch delivered by saleswomen dressed as nurses. As *Fortune* discovered in an undercover investigation, however, the Dilex canvassers had no medical background. In fact, the only qualification required for employment was previous door-to-door sales experience. Despite their lack of credentials, newly hired saleswomen were instructed to assume the role of the medical professional, a tactic the Institute reasoned would gain customers' trust, respect, and dollars. "You say you're a nurse, see?" one new recruit was told, "That always gets you in." . . . The saleswoman then attempted to peddle the company's top-of-the-line contraceptive kit. For seven dollars, a woman could purchase jelly, a douching outfit, an antiseptic douche capsule, and—most alarming of all—a universal "one-size-fits all" diaphragm. Poverty, women were told, was not an impediment to the personal happiness the company was selling: "luckily" for them, the Dilex kit was available on the installment plan.

Contraceptive companies' tactics paid off. By 1940, the size of the female contraceptive market was three times that of the 1935 market. The industry's unabated growth continued despite important changes in legal interpretation and medical attitudes in the late 1930s that might have reduced the industry's hold over American women. In 1936, the Supreme Court's *One Package* decision allowed physicians in every state to send and receive contraceptive devices and information. The following year, the American Medical Association reversed its long-standing ban on contraception, endorsing the right of a physician to prescribe birth control. The court's decision and the AMA's liberalized policy did not foster the immediate medicalization of birth control, a process that might have encouraged women to turn to the medical profession instead of the market for contraception. Indeed, in the short term, these sweeping changes proved remarkably inconsequential to the state of the industry. Many Americans could not afford the luxury of a personal physician, and only a minority lived close enough to the 357 public birth-control clinics operating in 1937 to avail themselves of clinic services. But of even more significance than medical barriers was manufacturers' enticing sales message. Companies' pledges to supply birth control that was affordable, immediate, and discreetly sold—either anonymously or in a completely feminized setting—continued to strike a responsive chord with American women. In addition, manufacturers promised what no lay guide could dispute: that what was bought from the market was as effective as doctor-prescribed methods. Out of pragmatic necessity and personal preference, most women worried about pregnancy prevention continued to obtain birth control from the contraceptive market. . . .

The commercialization of birth control in the 1930s illuminates the important but overlooked role of industry in shaping birth-control developments in the United States. Historians have typically framed birth-control history as a tale of doctors, lawmakers, and women's rights activists. The events of the 1930s suggest that we need to recast this story to include the agency of a new set of actors, birth-control manufacturers. The commercialization that manufacturers engendered at this time left an indelible imprint on the lives of ordinary women and men. It also revealed a world in which industry, gender, and reproduction were frequently and intimately intertwined.

◈ *F U R T H E R   R E A D I N G*

Blackwelder, Julia Kirk. *Women of the Depression: Caste and Culture in San Antonio, 1929–1939* (1984).
Boris, Eileen. *Home to Work: Motherhood and the Politics of Industrial Homework in the United States* (1994).
Clark, Claudia. *Radium Girls: Women and Industrial Health Reform, 1910–1935* (1997).
Cohen, Lizabeth. *Making a New Deal: Industrial Workers in Chicago, 1919–1939* (1990).

Cook, Blanche Weisen. *Eleanor Roosevelt: Volume One, 1884–1933* (1992).

Faue, Elizabeth. *Community of Suffering and Struggle: Women, Men, and the Labor Movement in Minneapolis, 1915–1945* (1991).

Gordon, Linda. *Pitied but Not Entitled: Single Mothers and the History of Welfare* (1994).

Kessler-Harris, Alice. *In Pursuit of Equity: Women, Men, and the Quest for Economic Citizenship in Twentieth-Century America* (2001).

Melosh, Barbara. *Engendering Culture: Manhood and Womanhood in New Deal Public Art and Theater* (1991).

Mettler, Suzanne B. *Dividing Citizens: Gender and Federalism in New Deal Public Policy* (1998).

Mink, Gwendolyn. *The Wages of Motherhood: Inequality in the Welfare State, 1917–1942* (1995).

Orleck, Annelise. *Common Sense and a Little Fire: Women and Working-Class Politics in the United States, 1900–1965* (1995).

Ross, B. Joyce. "Mary McLeod Bethune and the National Youth Administration: A Case Study of Power Relationships," *Journal of Negro History* 60 (1975): 1–28.

Roth, Darlene Rebecca. *Matronage: Patterns in Women's Organizations in Atlanta, Georgia, 1890–1940* (1994).

Ruiz, Vicki. *Cannery Women, Cannery Lives: Mexican Women, Unionization, and the California Food Processing Industry, 1930–1950* (1987).

———. *From Out of the Shadows: Mexican Women in Twentieth-Century America* (1998).

Salmond, John A. *Miss Lucy of the CIO: The Life and Times of Lucy Randolph Mason, 1882–1959* (1988).

Santillan, Richard. "Midwestern Mexican American Women and the Struggle for Gender Equality: A Historical Overview, 1920s–1960s," *Perspectives in Mexican American Studies* 5 (1995): 79–119.

Scharf, Lois. *To Work or to Wed: Female Employment, Feminism, and the Great Depression* (1980).

Sicherman, Barbara. *Alice Hamilton: A Life in Letters* (1984).

Storrs, Landon R.Y. *Civilizing Capitalism: The National Consumers' League, Women's Activism, and Labor Standards in the New Deal Era* (2000).

Sullivan, Patricia. *Days of Hope: Race and Democracy in the New Deal Era* (1996).

Swain, Martha H. *Ellen S. Woodward: New Deal Advocate for Women* (1995).

Wandersee, Winifred. *Women's Work and Family Values, 1920–1940* (1981).

Ware, Susan. *Beyond Suffrage: Women in the New Deal* (1981).

———. *Partner and I: Molly Dewson, Feminism, and New Deal Politics* (1987).

Wolcott, Victoria W. *Remaking Respectability: African-American Women in Interwar Detroit* (2001).

Women and the Disputed Meanings of Gender, Race, and Sexuality During World War II

Even as economic hardship continued in the United States and around the world, Americans confronted another crisis—the start of World War II in 1939. The war, rather than the New Deal, finally reinvigorated the industrial economy, prompted the creation of millions of new jobs, and brought an end to the Great Depression. However, the war also created new hardships and social instability for Americans, especially after the United States entered the war in response to Japan's attack on Pearl Harbor in December 1941.

Historians have long been interested in analyzing the significance of World War II for women, noting that it opened new doors for many women, yet also aroused great anxiety and resistance to racial, gender, and sexual equality. For example, the nation's involvement in World War II produced a temporary surge in new job opportunities for women in munitions work, related war industries, government service, and the armed forces. Women's entry into fields of work previously closed to them was aided by government propaganda, which tried to convince women that the new jobs were a form of patriotic service and required many of the same skills used by women in their own homes and kitchens. Nevertheless, even at the height of the war, government officials, family experts, and pundits in the mass media debated the merits of women's access to nontraditional jobs and looked forward to putting gender experimentation aside at the war's end. Often they expressed concern that women employed in positions or settings formerly reserved for men would abandon habits of nurture, modesty, and deference that were "natural" to their sex. What assumptions and fears were embedded in such concerns? What did women themselves think of wartime jobs? Did they work out of a sense of patriotism, out of a desire for the money, or for other reasons, and what did they want to do once the war ended? Were women treated fairly on the job, and did wartime employers try to comprehend or meet their needs? Did the expansion of job opportunities during the war benefit women of color as much as it did white women?

The war also provoked a dramatic upsurge in anti-Japanese prejudice, leading the Roosevelt administration to order the removal of nearly one hundred twenty thousand Japanese Americans then living on the West Coast to hastily constructed inland concentration camps. Japanese American women who were interned in these "relocation centers" suffered a sharp loss of civil liberties and dramatic reversals in their material circumstances. They were also denied any opportunity to take high-paying jobs in the war industry. How did they respond to the hardships and indignities of wartime internment? How did forced relocation alter their lives and sense of self as women and as Americans of Japanese heritage?

D O C U M E N T S

Norma Yerger Queen, a daycare worker in Utah, reported in 1944 on the difficulties faced by employed mothers in that state (Document 1). A prize-winning essay by black munitions worker Hortense Johnson appeared in *Opportunity* magazine in 1943 (Document 2). In June 1944, women from organizations such as the League of Women Voters and the Federation of Business and Professional Women's Clubs met at the White House to demand jobs for women in the U.S. State Department and claim a role for women in postwar foreign policy making. Document 3 contains a summary of that meeting. Document 4, drawn from an official history of the Women's Army Corps (WAC), describes women's impressive record of achievement in the Mediterranean and African theaters of war, as well as efforts to prevent or mitigate problems of health, discipline, and morale in the WAC.

1. Mrs. Norma Yerger Queen Reports on the Problems of Employed Mothers in Utah, 1944

My dear Mr. Hart [of the Office of War Information],

In reply to your questions about women working I should like to say that from March 1, 1943 to July 31, 1943 I was the Day Care Worker for our county and as such tried to learn the needs of day care for children of working mothers and to make possible the employment of women. Since then as child welfare worker for our county, I have continued to keep in touch with the need for women working, their problems & the attitudes of the community about it. We opened a day nursery for preschool children June 15th & closed Oct. 31st because it was never sufficiently used. It was more than well publicized but we finally decided that really not enough women with preschool children were employed to warrant keeping it open.

The people of this community all respect women who work regardless of the type of work. Women from the best families & many officers' wives work at our hospital. It is not at all uncommon to meet at evening parties in town women who work in the kitchens or offices of our hospital (Army–Bushnell–large general). The city mayor's wife too works there.

The church disapproves of women working who have small children. The church (L.D.S.) has a strong influence in our county.

Mrs. Norma Yerger Queen to Clyde Hart, March 26, 1944, files of Correspondence Panels Division, Office of War Information, General Archives, National Archives, Washington, D.C.

For the canning season in our county men's & women's clubs & the church all recruited vigorously for women for the canneries. It was "the thing to do" to work so many hrs. a week at the canneries.

I personally have encouraged officers' wives who have no children to get out and work. Those of us who have done so have been highly respected by the others and we have not lost social standing. In fact many of the social affairs are arranged at our convenience.

Some husbands do not approve of wives working & this has kept home some who do not have small children. Some of the women just do not wish to put forth the effort.

The financial incentive has been the strongest influence among most economic groups but especially among those families who were on relief for many years. Patriotic motivation is sometimes present but sometimes it really is a front for the financial one. A few women work to keep their minds from worrying about sons or husbands in the service.

In this county, the hospital is the chief employer of women. A few go to Ogden (20 miles away) to work in an arsenal, the depot, or the air field. When these Ogden plants first opened quite a few women started to work there, but the long commuting plus the labor at the plants plus their housework proved too much.

Many women thoroughly enjoy working & getting away from the home. They seem to get much more satisfaction out of it than out of housework or bringing up children. Those who quit have done so because of lack of good care for their children, or of inability to do the housework & the job.

We definitely found that having facilities for the care of children did not increase the number of women who worked. In 1942, the women kept saying they couldn't go to the canneries because they had no place to leave their children. In 1943 everyone knew we had the day nursery & private homes available & still there was difficulty in recruiting. One of the big reasons we got the nursery was to help in our canning & poultry seasons.

Most all jobs are secured thro our U.S.E.S. so I assume people know about it. It runs frequent stories in our local paper.

I am convinced that if women could work 4 days a week instead of 5½ or 6 that more could take jobs. I found it impossible to work 5½ days & do my housework but when I arranged for 4 days I could manage both. These days one has to do everything—one cannot buy services as formerly. For instance—laundry. I'm lucky. I can send out much of our laundry to the hospital but even so there is a goodly amount that must be done at home—all the ironing of summer dresses is very tiring. I even have to press my husband's trousers—a thing I never did in all my married life. The weekly housecleaning—shoe shining—all things we formerly had done by others. Now we also do home canning. I never in the 14 yrs. of my married life canned one 1 jar. Last summer I put up dozens of quarts per instructions of Uncle Sam. I'm only one among many who is now doing a lot of manual labor foreign to our usual custom. I just could not take on all that & an outside job too. It is no fun to eat out—you wait so long for service & the restaurants cannot be immaculately kept—therefore it is more pleasant & quicker to cook & eat at home even after a long day's work. I've talked with the personnel manager at the hospital & he agrees that fewer days a week would be better. The canneries finally took women for as little as 3 hrs. a day.

This is a farming area & many farm wives could not under any arrangements take a war job. They have too much to do at their farm jobs & many now have to go into the fields, run tractors & do other jobs formerly done by men. I marvel at all these women are able to do & feel very inadequate next to them. Some do work in Ogden or Brigham during the winter months.

Here is the difference between a man working & a woman as seen in our home—while I prepare the evening meal, my husband reads the evening paper. We then do the dishes together after which he reads his medical journal or cogitates over some lecture he is to give or some problem at his lab. I have to make up grocery lists, mend, straighten up a drawer, clean out the ice box, press clothes, put away anything strewn about the house, wash bric a brac, or do several of hundreds of small "woman's work is never done stuff." This consumes from 1 to 2 hrs. each evening after which I'm too weary to read any professional social work literature & think I'm lucky if I can keep up with the daily paper, Time Life or Reader's Digest. All this while my husband is relaxing & resting. When I worked full time, we tried doing the housecleaning together but it just didn't click. He is responsible for introducing penicillin into Bushnell & thus into the army & there were so many visiting brass hats & night conferences he couldn't give even one night a week to the house. Then came a mess of lectures at all kinds of medical meetings—he had to prepare those at home. I got so worn out it was either quit work or do it part time.

This has been a lot of personal experience but I'm sure we are no exception. I thought I was thro working in 1938. My husband urged me to help out for the war effort—he's all out for getting the war work done & he agreed to do his share of the housework. He is not lazy but he found we could not do it. I hope this personal experience will help to give you an idea of some of the problems.

2. Hortense Johnson Describes Black Women and the War Effort, 1943

Of course I'm vital to victory, just as millions of men and women who are fighting to save America's chances for Democracy, even if they never shoulder a gun nor bind a wound. It's true that my job isn't so exciting or complicated. Perhaps there are millions of girls who could do my job as well as I—certainly there are thousands. I am an inspector in a war plant. For eight hours a day, six days a week, I stand in line with five other girls, performing a routine operation that is part of our production schedule. We inspect wooden boxes that are to hold various kinds of munitions, and that range in size from eight inches to six feet. When we approve them they are ready to be packed with shells, bombs, fuses, parachutes—and other headaches for Hitler and Hirohito.

Not much to that, you say. Well, that all depends on the way you look at it. A missing or projecting nail, a loose board or hinge—these are some of the imperfections that we watch for. If we miss them, they may be checked later on, or they may not. If they are not, they may mean injury for a fellow worker on a later operation

Hortense Johnson, "First Essay," *Opportunity* 21 (April 1943); 50–51.

or an explosion in another part of the plant with dozens of lives lost—or they might even spell disaster for American soldiers in a tight spot in North Africa.

Did I say my job isn't exciting or complicated? I take that back. It may be a simple matter to inspect one box or a dozen, but it's different when you are handling them by the hundreds. The six of us in my crew sometimes inspect as many as fourteen or fifteen hundred boxes during one shift. That means two hundred and fifty apiece—an average of one every two minutes, regardless of size and not counting any rest periods. Try that sometime and see if it's a simple job! You stand at your bench all day long, with rest periods sometimes seeming years apart. You fight against the eye fatigue that might mean oversight. You probe with your fingers and tap here and there. Your back aches, your legs get weary, your muscles scream at you sometimes—groan at you all the time. But the dozen and one little operations must be carried on smoothly and efficiently if your work output is to keep up. It's exciting all right, and it's plenty complicated—in the same way that jungle warfare must be, hard and painstaking and monotonous—until something goes off with a bang!

And then when your shift is finished, you stalk off stiffly to the washroom and hurry to get ready for the bus that brings you forty-five miles back from the plant to your home in the city. You slip on an extra sweater and heavy woolen socks, because the unheated bus is apt to be cold and damp. Even when you get into the bus your day's jog isn't over, for you work almost as hard as the driver. You strain with him to see through the heavy winter fog that blankets the highway. You watch with him for the tricky ice that waits at curves to throw you into dangerous skids. When sleet has covered the road and made all travel seem suicidal, you sit ready to get out at the worst spots and walk with the rest of your crowd until the bus pulls across to safety.

So when you get back home, you're glad to jump into bed and die until morning—or until your alarm-clock tells you it's morning, no matter how black it is. Then your two-hour experience of traveling back to the job begins all over again, because in spite of rain, snow, cold or illness, the job is there to be done, and you're expected to do your share. It never occurs to you to figure out how much money you're making, because it isn't much anyhow—after you've had your victory tax deducted, paid for your war bond, set aside money for your bus commutation ticket. By the time you've given grandmother the food and rent money, and paid the doctor for helping you to fight off your frequent colds, and bought the extra-heavy clothes the job calls for, you're just about where the boys in New Guinea are. Don't let Senator Wheeler fool you with his talk about "high wages for war workers!"

So if it's as tough as all that—and it is!—why do you stick on the job? Why did you leave the comfortable job you held with a city business house? Why don't you go back to it and make as much money as you're making now? Why? Because it's not that easy to leave, and it's not that tough to stay! Of course the work is hard and sometimes dangerous, but victory in this war isn't going to come the easy way, without danger. And we brown women of America need victory so much, so desperately. America is a long way from perfect. We resent the racial injustices that we meet every day of our lives. But it's one thing to resent and fight against racial injustices; it's another thing to let them break your spirit, so that you quit this struggle and turn the country over to Hitler and the Talmadges and Dies' who will run this country if Hitler wins. America can't win this war without all of us, and we know it. We must prove it to white Americans as well—that our country can't get along without the labor and sacrifice of her brown daughters, can't win unless we *all* fight and work and save.

So the hardships of war work become willing sacrifices to victory, not to victory for Democracy, but to victory by a country that some day, please God, will win Democracy. In such a spirit, even some of the hardships are forgotten in the daily rewards of the job. After all, we *are* working today and drawing regular pay checks. . . . Frayed nerves and short tempers show themselves sometimes, and that's understandable, but a real quarrel seldom develops. Ill-tempered remarks are usually understood, and passed over without comeback.

I imagine that our boys at the front develop the same kind of tolerance, the same kind of partnership, for the same reason. Wouldn't it be great if the white workers who are fellow-fighters with us in war production, would develop more of the same spirit of partnership? What can we do to make them realize that colored people must be given equal opportunity in every walk of life to make that partnership real—to build an impregnable, free, and democratic America. . . .

I'm not fooling myself about this war. Victory won't mean victory for Democracy —yet. But that will come later, because most of us who are fighting for victory today will keep on fighting to win the peace—maybe a long time after the war is over, maybe a hundred years after. By doing my share today, I'm keeping a place for some brown woman tomorrow, and for the brown son of that woman the day after tomorrow. Sterling Brown once wrote, "The strong men keep a-comin' on," and millions of those men have dark skins. There will be dark women marching by their side, and I like to think that I'm one of them.

3. Women Meet at the White House to Claim a Role in Postwar Foreign Policy Making, 1944

The tasks of war, of peace, of nation-planning must be shared by men and women alike. No part of the citizenry holds a greater state in the democratic way of life, in plans for the reconstruction of an ordered world, than the women of the nation. Women have been called upon to share the burdens of war, to stand side by side with men on the production line and to complement men in the fighting services. So women must share in the building of a post-war world fit for all citizens—men and women—to live and work in freely side by side.

Eloquent appeals to women to prepare themselves to render the greatest possible service to society in national and international councils have recently been uttered by women leaders here and abroad. They have urged that women should participate in any decisions for the future, now or later.

So far, very few women have shared in the councils of national and international policy-making bodies. Yet, there are women in every country who are qualified and ready to contribute. We note with encouragement the recent appointments of women as United States delegates to the Food Conference, the United Nations Relief and

From "Women and Post-War Policy-Making," A Summary Statement Adopted by the White House Conference, June 14, 1944, on How Women May Share in Post War Policy Making. Reprinted in the *Journal of the American Association of University Women* 37, no. 4 (summer 1944): 198.

Rehabilitation Conference, the Conference of Allied Ministers of Education in London, and the International Labor Organization Conference.

Current developments make this the crucial moment for women and women's organizations to press for the inclusion of qualified women as United States delegates and advisers to international conferences and as members of national policy-making bodies. Therefore, we, a group of 200 representative women, meeting in Washington at the White House on June 14, 1944, express our conviction that women should take definite action now in order to implement the significant statements of women leaders the world around, to see that women have a share in national and international planning, to see that women's proper contributions are made "in giving all the world a chance to envision something a little better than has been known before."

We therefore resolve that we will take every step within our power to further the active participation of qualified women in positions of responsibility pertaining to the conduct of public affairs, national and international.

4. The Challenges of Maintaining the Health, Discipline, and Morale of the Women's Army Corps in North Africa and the Mediterranean During World War II

Fifth Army Wacs

The [Mediterranean] theater's most unusual experiment in WAC employment was that of the Fifth Army Wacs, who claimed the honor of being the first Wacs to set foot in Italy, and in fact on the continent of Europe. Although never more than sixty women were involved, the experiment was considered to be potentially more important than its size would indicate, since it might determine the degree to which women could in future emergencies make up part of tactical units.

When the Fifth Army jumped off for Italy, the Wacs were not too far behind it, arriving in Caserta, via Naples, on 17 November 1943 under the command of 1st Lt. Cora M. Foster. The T/O called for 10 telephone operators, 7 clerks, 16 typists, 10 stenographers, 1 administrative clerk, and cooks and other cadre. In late January the unit split into forward and rear echelons, and the forward echelon, including all telephone operators and some stenographers, moved into the bivouac area near Presenzano. Here the women lived in pyramidal tents and worked chiefly in the Fifth Army's mobile switchboard trailer. By March the rear echelon was also in tents near Sparanise. Unit records noted that the women "thrived on it; the sick call rate dropped way down."

For the rest of the Italian campaign, the units followed the Fifth Army up the peninsula, usually being located from twelve to thirty-five miles behind the front lines. From June to September the forward echelon's longest stay in any one place was five weeks, the average being two. The women lived in whatever billets were available—schools, factories, apartments, and chiefly tents. The forward section spent most of the winter of 1944–45 living in tents in the mountains above Florence.

Mattie E. Treadwell, *The Women's Army Corps,* Office of the Chief of Military History, Department of the Army (Washington, D.C.: GPO, 1953), 371–374.

The women usually wore enlisted men's wool shirts, trousers, and combat boots, and carried only the few necessities that could be moved forward with them.

The unit proved unusually successful. It received Lt. Gen. Mark W. Clark's praise as well as being one of the few to receive both the Fifth Army Plaque with clasp, in 1944, and the Meritorious Service Unit Plaque in 1945. There were twenty-seven awards of the Bronze Star. The forward echelon included some of the most skilled telephone operators on the Continent, able in a matter of minutes to get through the complicated communications networks to the commanding officer of any unit sought by General Clark. The unit's morale and *esprit de corps* were perhaps the highest in the theater's WAC units. Its members wore the Fifth Army's green scarf. "They were," said Colonel Coleman, "Fifth Army first and Wacs second—perhaps the best-integrated unit in the theater."

The dangers of a combat area did not present any great problem in this case. During the last days in Anzio, air raids offered the nuisance of noise and falling shell fragments, but fortunately the area had just been vacated by a combat unit that had left adequate foxholes and dugouts. The Wacs were lucky in having no injuries, in spite of some close calls. During the advance up the peninsula, they were frequently within sound of long-range artillery, and almost always in an area of complete blackout, but required no guard except the usual one that patrolled the entire camp. Italian service troops ordinarily set up the WAC and Nurse Corps tents, and the Wacs took them down themselves, with the aid of two Italian laborers to load them on trucks.

In spite of the fatigue that developed from repeated moves, officers noted that the women "griped and complained less than soldiers in rear areas." Signal Corps units in rear areas were surprised, upon offering Wacs rotation to less exhausting conditions, to find that not one telephone operator would agree to quit the Fifth Army unit. . . .

. . . The longer hours, the lack of privacy, the necessity for wearing clothing designed for men, all seemed to have little effect. Telephone operators seemed to be immune from the illness and tension experienced by women on identical shift work in more permanent companies a few score miles to the rear. Rude remarks from occasional unfriendly males, which caused a morale problem among Wacs elsewhere, were more or less brushed aside by women too busy to notice them and too assured of their own usefulness to doubt it. Under the circumstances, the staff director considered it a pity that all Wacs could not be employed in such units.

WAC advisers recommended that any such groups, for best success, be carefully selected. The best-suited type of woman was believed to be one whose physical stamina was average or better, who liked outdoor life, and who was well balanced mentally and emotionally. In a small isolated group, it was found fatal to include those with irritating habits and mannerisms—overtalkative, grouchy, or erratic. The ambitious or the highly qualified woman was also not a good choice, since top supervisory jobs in a tactical headquarters did not go to women, nor did they receive the high grades that those in rear areas did, many still being privates after two years. Emotional self-control was also vital, since the women were constantly surrounded by men, especially by combat troops coming back for a rest. Besides fending off advances, said the staff director, "The Wacs had to listen to the men and let them blow off steam, and this put an additional strain on the women's nerves." A mature woman was found preferable, especially one whose only interest was not the opposite sex. The lone company officer who accompanied each section had to be especially self-reliant and self-sufficient; her conduct necessarily had to be above reproach.

✦ E S S A Y S

University of Arizona professor Karen Tucker Anderson examines the discrimination faced by black women during World War II. Black women were able to move out of the rural South into urban industrial centers, but they were denied access to many well-paying jobs, despite a chronic labor shortage. Valerie Matsumoto of UCLA looks at the lives of Japanese American women during World War II. While the relocation camps tended to undermine family harmony, internment presented young women with new opportunities for work, travel, and education. Leisa D. Meyer of William and Mary investigates the challenges faced by Americans who supported women's inclusion in the military during World War II yet believed that female "soldiers" had to uphold conventional notions of femininity and female sexual respectability.

Persistent Discrimination Against Black Women During World War II

KAREN TUCKER ANDERSON

As a result of the increasing demand for workers in all categories of employment, and especially in the high-paying manufacturing sector, the full employment economy of World War II posed the most serious challenge in American history to the traditional management preference for white male labor in primary-sector jobs. The war years were especially important for blacks, who benefited from an expanding labor force, changing racial values, a revitalized migration out of the rural South, and the attempted enforcement of equal employment opportunity under a presidential executive order. Although scholars have given some attention to the labor-force fortunes of blacks in the war economy, few have considered the impact of the wartime expansion on black women, who constituted 600,000 of the 1,000,000 blacks who entered paid employment during the war years. Those who have focused on black women have stressed the degree to which the war opened new job categories and fostered mobility. William Chafe, for example, contends that the opportunities generated by the wartime economy and the long-term changes they fostered constituted a "second emancipation" for black women. According to Dale L. Hiestand, occupational shifts by black women workers during the 1940s promoted substantial income improvement.

A careful examination of the labor-force status of black women during the 1940s brings into question such sanguine pronouncements. Focusing on the wartime experiences of black women provides insight into the nature of prejudice as manifested and experienced by women and into the sources and mechanisms of labor-force discrimination in a particular historical context. It also facilitates an examination

Karen Tucker Anderson, "Last Hired, First Fired: Black Women Workers During World War II," *Journal of American History* 69 (June 1982): 82–97. Reprinted by permission of the Organization of American Historians.

of the relative importance of managerial intransigence and coworker prejudice in perpetuating discriminatory employment practices. In addition, it gives an indication of the importance of tight labor markets in fostering economic mobility for minority group women.

Labor force statistics support the contention that the war marked an important break with the historic allocation of work by race and sex. Between 1940 and 1944 the proportion of employed black women engaged in domestic service declined from 59.9 percent to 44.6 percent, although their share of jobs in this field increased because white women exited from private household work in even greater proportions. In addition, the percentage of the black female labor force in farm work was cut in half, as many from the rural South migrated to urban areas in response to the demand for war workers. The shift of large numbers of black women from work in farms and homes to work in factories resulted in the proportion of black females employed in industrial occupations rising from 6.5 percent to 18 percent during the war. A comparable expansion also occurred in personal service work outside of the private household, which claimed 17.9 percent of black women workers in 1944.

To stress only the improvement wrought during the war, however, is to understate the extent to which discrimination persisted and to ignore the fact that the assumptions of a historically balkanized labor force continued to determine the distribution of the benefits of a full employment economy. When faced with a shortage of white male workers, employers had various options. They could seek workers from other areas of the country, hoping that this would enable them to minimize the changes produced by the wartime expansion, or they could rely on underutilized elements of the local labor supply—workers in nonessential employment, women, blacks, and older and younger workers. If unable to secure large numbers of white male in-migrants and unwilling to modify hiring patterns too drastically, they could limit production, sacrificing output to prejudice.

Those who decided to employ substantially increased numbers of women and/or minorities established a complex hierarchy of hiring preferences based on the composition of the local labor force and the nature of the work to be done. In light industries, women workers became the first recourse of employers unable to recruit large numbers of white males. In the airframe industry, for example, women constituted 40.6 percent of the employees by November 1943, while blacks claimed only 3.5 percent of airframe jobs. Employers in heavy industries, by contrast, sought minority males as a preferred source of labor, with the result that the level of utilization of women depended on the minority population of an area. In Baltimore, for example, blacks comprised up to 20 percent of the shipbuilding workers while women represented only 4 percent. Seattle, which had only a small black population, relied on women for 16 percent of its shipyard employees.

Whatever the hierarchy of preference, however, black women could always be found at the bottom. The dramatic expansion of jobs for women did not necessarily mean the opening up of new categories of employment for minority group women. A survey conducted by the United Auto Workers (UAW) in April 1943 found that only 74 out of 280 establishments that employed women in production work were willing to hire black women. Similarly, a 1943 study by the National Metal Trades Association revealed that only twenty-nine out of sixty-two plants that used women workers had black women in their employ. Moreover, most of them used black women only in janitorial positions. Even some employers willing to hire white women and black men in large numbers balked at including black women in their work forces. At the Wagner Electric Corporation in Saint Louis, for example, 64 percent of the employees were white women, 24 percent were black males, and 12 percent were white males. The company refused to hire black women throughout the war, even in the face of a January 1945 order from the President's Committee on Fair Employment Practice (FEPC) to cease all discrimination.

Because of the mobilization of large numbers of young men by the military, the availability of white women for aircraft and munitions work, the nature of the jobs being created during the war, and the depth of the prejudice against black women, the male labor force proved to be more racially flexible than the female labor force. While the number of all blacks employed in manufacturing increased 135 percent between April 1940 and January 1946, the number of black women in such work rose only 59 percent. Blacks made their greatest wartime gains in heavily male-employing industrial fields; by January 1945 they constituted 25 percent of the labor force in foundries, 11.7 percent in shipbuilding, and 11.8 percent in blast furnaces and steel mills. By contrast, nonwhites accounted for only 5.8 percent of employees in aircraft and 2.7 percent of those in electrical equipment production. In the traditional female fields of clerical and sales, the gains of black women were negligible— their share of female clerical jobs rose from 0.7 percent to 1.6 percent while their proportion in the female sales force declined from 1.2 percent to 1.1 percent.

One of the most important and obdurate of the industries that fought the employment of black women during the war was the auto industry. Led by the negative example of the Ford Motor Company, which refused to hire nonwhite women in any but token numbers, the auto companies persisted in rejecting trained black female applicants or in limiting their employment to a few work categories until very late in the war. When referred to the automakers by the United States Employment Service (USES) in response to calls for women workers, black women found that the white women accompanying them would be hired immediately while they would be told to await a later call, a call that would never come. When Samella Banks, along with five white women, applied to Cadillac Motor Company in November 1942, she was told that there might be a janitress opening in a day or two while they were hired as welder trainees. As a result, much of the expansion of the female labor force in industrial work occurred before economic or political pressures necessitated the hiring of black women. By February 1943 nonwhite women had claimed only 1,000 of the 96,000 jobs held by women in major war industries in Detroit. Consequently, most nonwhite females were confined to work in low-paying service and other unskilled categories, and those who landed industrial jobs had so little seniority that their postwar fate was guaranteed.

As was generally the case with wartime racial discrimination in employment, the most frequent employer rationale for excluding nonwhite women was the fear that white opposition to the change might cause work slowdowns or strikes. An examination of the nature and goals of coworker prejudice during the war years provides some possible answers to the question of whether such prejudice is rooted in an aversion to social contact in a context of equality or is primarily a calculated attempt on the part of whites to maintain an exploitative economic advantage. When the former issue is the basic concern, it is manifested in a desire to exclude blacks altogether or to segregate them on the job. When the latter is the wellspring of white workplace prejudice, it is evidenced, not in a wish to segregate black workers, but in an attempt to prevent the hiring of blacks or to limit them to particular low-paying job categories.

During the war years, white male hostility to expanded job opportunities for black men focused primarily on the issue of promotion rather than on hiring or segregation. Although some strikes occurred when black men were admitted to entry-level jobs or over the issue of integrating the workplace, most white-male hate strikes took place when black male workers were promoted into jobs at higher skill and pay levels. This was a product of the fact that black men had been employed as janitors and unskilled laborers in many defense industries prior to the war and sought promotions as opportunities expanded. White males thus seemed to be concerned primarily with maintaining their advantaged economic position. Moreover, their resistance to the elimination of discrimination was more tenacious and more effective than was the opposition of white women to the opening of opportunities for black women. Control over labor unions, whose opposition to black entry into previously white jobs proved an effective barrier to change in many cases, gave white males more power to translate prejudice into employer discrimination.

For women workers, on the other hand, the desire to maintain social distance, rather than a wish to safeguard economic prerogatives, seemed to be the dominant motivation in many cases. White female workers frequently objected to working closely with black women or sharing facilities with them because they feared that blacks were dirty or diseased. Work stoppages occurred in several places after the introduction of black women into the female work force. More than 2,000 white women employed at the U.S. Rubber plant in Detroit walked off the job in March 1943, demanding separate bathroom facilities. A similar walkout occurred at the Western Electric plant in Baltimore in summer 1943. In both cases management refused to segregate the facilities and appealed to patriotic and egalitarian values to persuade the striking workers to return to their jobs. Significantly, the one hate strike by white women workers that focused on upgrading as well as integration, the Dan River strike in 1944, was in a traditional female-employing industry. . . .

As a result of the idiosyncratic nature of employer practices during the war, some areas and some employers offered greater employment opportunities for black women than others. Aircraft plants in the Los Angeles area, for example, began hiring black women for production work relatively early by comparison with similar operations in other areas of the country. As a result, by 1945 black women could be found doing industrial work in all Los Angeles aircraft plants; 2,000 were employed by North American Aviation alone. Among the automakers, the Briggs plant in Detroit deviated from industry patterns and hired substantial numbers of black women. In Saint Louis, where defense industry discrimination against black women was the general rule, the Curtiss-Wright Company and the U.S. Cartridge Company eased the situation somewhat by providing industrial jobs for hundreds of nonwhite women. These examples, however, were not typical of employer response; restrictive hiring and segregation remained the rule, even in industries faced with severe labor shortages. Nowhere was this truer than in the South, where traditional practices remained virtually unchanged.

Even when defense employers broke with tradition and hired nonwhite women, they generally segregated them from other women workers and employed them only for certain kinds of work, usually that which was arduous, dirty, hot, or otherwise disagreeable. A cursory study of black women workers done by the Women's Bureau of the United States Department of Labor in 1945 revealed that in many cases non-white women were disproportionately represented among women employed in out-side labor gangs, in foundries, and in industrial service work. On the ore docks of the Great Lakes, for example, the survey found women, predominantly black, shoveling the leavings of ore from the bottoms of ships onto hoists. According to the USES, the meat-packing industry in Detroit resorted to black women in large numbers during the war years to take jobs others had spurned. On the railroads minority group women found employment in substantial numbers as laborers, loaders, car cleaners, and waitresses. The city of Baltimore first broke with its policy of hiring only whites for street-cleaning work in the immediate prewar period when it began hiring black males; by 1943, when the black male labor force was completely exhausted, the city turned to the only labor reserve left—the large numbers of unemployed and under-employed black females.

The insistence by some employers on segregated work arrangements and facil-ities served as a rationale for excluding black women altogether or limiting their numbers to conform to physical plant requirements. The Glenn Martin Aircraft Company, for example, hired the same proportion of nonwhite women for its inte-grated plant in Omaha, where the black population was quite small, as it did for its Baltimore operations, where black women constituted a substantial proportion of the local labor supply. In Baltimore, however, their numbers were limited because they had to be assigned only to a small separate subassembly plant. A small aircraft parts firm in Los Angeles asserted that it could not hire black women because it separated workers by sex as well as by race and could not further complicate its managerial and supervisory difficulties. At the Norfolk Navy Yard, management excluded black women from most production jobs on the grounds that women workers had to be segregated by race, although the racial integration of male workers was an accomplished fact. As a result, black men worked in a wide variety of jobs at all skill levels in the yard while the jobs assigned to women were virtually monopo-lized by whites. . . .

The major agency charged with enforcing equal opportunity in employment regardless of race, religion, or national origin was the FEPC, an agency created in 1941 by executive order of President Franklin D. Roosevelt in response to a threat-ened march on Washington by civil rights groups protesting discriminatory policies by war contractors. Although the FEPC could theoretically recommend the removal of war contracts from those who continued to discriminate and the WMC [War Manpower Commission] could restrict work permits to enforce federal hiring poli-cies, the federal government was not inclined to hamper the production of essential war materials in order to foster racial equity. As a result, the agency had to rely on behind-the-scenes negotiations and the possibility of adverse publicity generated by public hearings. Although effective in some cases, such tools proved ineffectual against recalcitrant violators, whose ranks included some major war industries. The large volume of complaints and the bureaucratic delays inherent in the situation facilitated evasion, even on the part of blatant violators officially ordered to cease restrictive hiring practices. Moreover, the reliance on individual, documented com-plaints rather than on employer hiring patterns as the basis for action hampered effective enforcement.

The decision by Roosevelt to place the FEPC under the jurisdiction of the WMC in July 1942 also handicapped the agency in its efforts to end employment discrimination. WMC head Paul McNutt, never enthusiastic regarding the FEPC's goals and afraid that they were incompatible with his agency's responsibility for allocating scarce manpower within war industries, canceled scheduled FEPC hearings on discrimination by the railroads and generally made racial equity a low priority within WMC. Even after the FEPC was removed from the WMC in May 1943, it was hampered in its efforts to enforce the law by the unwillingness of southern representatives of the WMC and the USES to cooperate in reporting and seeking to change discriminatory practices. Although the USES had agreed in September 1943 to refuse to fill employer requests for workers when they included racial restrictions, its agents in the South frequently disregarded this directive. Thus, when blacks with defense training applied for appropriate work, they were often referred to jobs outside the area. The persistence of discrimination, despite a federal commitment to eliminate it, hampered the ability of all blacks, male and female, to find industrial employment in the region that still claimed a majority of the black population.

In its official policies the FEPC treated discrimination against black women as seriously as discrimination against black males, although its rate of success enforcing compliance in women's cases lagged somewhat behind the rate for men. After its 1944 hearings in Saint Louis, the FEPC ruled that a company that hired black males while discriminating against black women was still in violation of the executive order, noting that "partial compliance is partial violation." Despite pressure from civil rights groups on behalf of black women workers and occasional threats of strikes by black male workers, the equal opportunity machinery of the government proved unable to aid minority women in any substantial way. By the time the agency had investigated, negotiated, or held hearings, much valuable time had been lost. For women, this could be especially damaging because it meant that anything beyond token conformity could be jeopardized by employer unwillingness to expand the female work force late in the war.

The Carter Carburetor Company in Saint Louis, for example, managed a minimal compliance with an FEPC order to cease discriminating when it came to black men, but refused in April 1944 to hire any black women on the grounds that it had no intention of hiring any more women. Although the government continued to pressure the company, it stood by its policies. The Allied Tent Manufacturing Company in New Orleans claimed to have instituted a nondiscriminatory policy regarding women workers when it announced its intention in June 1945 to replace all its women machine operators with men (white and black), having decided that women workers had proved themselves "unsatisfactory." Federal enforcement officials thus found that labor-market forces late in the war provided a rationale and a means for continued resistance by those employers intent on circumventing federal hiring policies regarding black women.

The organization that was most cognizant of persisting discrimination against black women and most active in fighting against it was the National Association for the Advancement of Colored People (NAACP). As early as August 1942, Detroit NAACP officer Gloster Current wrote to McNutt of the WMC, complaining that the Ford Motor Company was discriminating against black females as it hired thousands of whites for work at the Willow Run Bomber Plant. In March 1943 the Detroit NAACP cooperated with the United Auto Workers Inter-Racial Committee in staging a large rally to protest continued discrimination against black women in hiring and black men in promotion on the part of Detroit's war industries. Thereafter both groups continued to pressure employers and government officials at all levels on the issue. In a statement prepared for presentation to the House manpower committee, the NAACP evinced its awareness that the situation was not unique to Detroit but was a national problem resulting in the serious underutilization of black womanpower. . . .

Job retention was a serious issue for those women who landed industrial work during the war. The persistence of discrimination and the late entry of black women into production work, rather than their on-the-job conduct, meant that nonwhite females were more likely than others to experience layoffs resulting from contract completions or seasonal cutbacks. Once fired, they faced great difficulties in finding comparable work. According to an official of the Baltimore Urban League, white women there with industrial experience were easily reabsorbed by war industries while black women were being referred by the USES to work as maids, counter girls, and laundry pressers. As would be the case for all unemployed women after the war, those who turned down such jobs faced the possibility of losing their unemployment benefits for refusing suitable work. Black women thus experienced a much greater degree of job discontinuity than others during the war, hampering their ability to accumulate seniority.

Once the war was over and American industry began its postwar contraction, those black women who had held industrial jobs during the war found that their concentration in contracting industries, their low seniority, and their sex contributed to employment difficulties in the postwar period. American women, black and white, were overrepresented among those experiencing layoffs in durable good industries. When management began rehiring workers in the reconversion period, it reinstituted most prewar discriminatory policies regarding working women, even to the point of disregarding their seniority rights, a practice facilitated by union acquiescence. USES officials reinforced employer policies by denying unemployment benefits to those women who refused referrals to jobs in traditional female-employing fields. To a greater extent than white women, black women were victimized by the postwar eviction of women from jobs in durable goods industries. . . .

In other work categories black women fared somewhat better in the postwar years. Although some apparently lost employment in service, sales, and clerical work as a result of competition from displaced white women, most managed to maintain their hold on lower-level jobs in the female work force. Despite attempts by USES officials in some local offices to force black women to return to domestic service work by threatening to withhold unemployment compensation benefits, enough job opportunities in other categories remained available to prevent a massive return to household work. Even so, domestic service remained the primary occupation of black women, providing employment to 782,520 in 1950, 40 percent of the black female work force.

As a result of the wartime experience, black women made substantial progress in the operatives occupational category, although their position in this area deteriorated somewhat in the late 1940s. One of the most important areas of expansion for nonwhite women was the apparel industry, which witnessed a 350 percent increase in black female employment during the 1940s. By 1950, it offered employment to

56,910 black women and ranked second in the operatives category behind laundry and dry cleaning establishments, where 105,000 black females were employed. Other major sources of industrial work for women, including textiles, remained virtually closed to blacks during the 1940s. In the durable goods industries, which had experienced the greatest wartime expansion, black women were a rarity in the postwar period. In 1950, only 60 black women held jobs as operatives in aircraft plants, while 2,730 claimed similar positions in the auto industry.

In the long run, the greatest benefit of the wartime experience for black women workers derived from their movement in large numbers out of the poverty of the rural South to the possibilities provided by an urban, industrialized economy. The extent to which those possibilities were realized in the decade of the 1940s can be overstated, however. Both during and after the war, black women entered the urban female labor force in large numbers only to occupy its lowest rungs. Largely excluded from clerical and sales work, the growth sectors of the female work force, black women found work primarily in service jobs outside the household and in unskilled blue-collar categories. Although many experienced some upward mobility during the war, their relative position within the American economy remained the same.

Wartime circumstances illustrate the extent to which an economic system that had historically allocated work according to race and sex could tolerate a high level of unemployment and underemployment even in a time of labor shortage in order to minimize the amount of change generated by temporary and aberrant conditions. By stressing the modification of traditional patterns fostered by rapid economic growth, scholars ignore the degree to which prejudices inhibited change and constrained the rate of economic expansion even in the face of strong patriotic, political, and economic incentives favoring expanded output at all costs. For black women, especially, what is significant about the war experience is the extent to which barriers remained intact.

Japanese American Women During World War II

VALERIE MATSUMOTO

The life here cannot be expressed. Sometimes, we are resigned to it, but when we see the barbed wire fences and the sentry tower with floodlights, it gives us a feeling of being prisoners in a "concentration camp." We try to be happy and yet oftentimes a gloominess does creep in. When I see the "I'm an American" editorial and write-ups, the "equality of race etc."—it seems to be mocking us in our faces. I just wonder if all the sacrifices and hard labor on [the] part of our parents has gone up to leave nothing to show for it?

—LETTER FROM SHIZUKO HORIUCHI,
POMONA ASSEMBLY CENTER, MAY 24, 1942

Thirty years after her relocation camp internment, another Nisei woman, the artist Miné Okubo, observed, "The impact of the evacuation is not on the material and the physical. It is something far deeper. It is the effect on the spirit." Describing the

Valerie Matsumoto, "Japanese American Women During World War II," *Frontiers* 8 (1984): 6–14—with abridgements as approved by Valerie Matsumoto.

lives of Japanese American women during World War II and assessing the effects of the camp experience on the spirit are complex tasks: factors such as age, generation, personality, and family background interweave and preclude simple generalizations. In these relocation camps Japanese American women faced severe racism and traumatic family strain, but the experience also fostered changes in their lives: more leisure for older women, equal pay with men for working women, disintegration of traditional patterns of arranged marriages, and, ultimately, new opportunities for travel, work, and education for the younger women.

I will examine the lives of Japanese American women during the trying war years, focusing on the second generation—the Nisei—whose work and education were most affected. The Nisei women entered college and ventured into new areas of work in unfamiliar regions of the country, sustained by fortitude, family ties, discipline, and humor. My understanding of their history derives from several collections of internees' letters, assembly center and relocation camp newspapers, census records, and taped oral history interviews that I conducted with eighty-four Nisei (second generation) and eleven Issei (first generation). Two-thirds of these interviews were with women. . . .

A century ago, male Japanese workers began to arrive on American shores, dreaming of making fortunes that would enable them to return to their homeland in triumph. For many, the fortune did not materialize and the shape of the dream changed: they developed stakes in small farms and businesses and, together with wives brought from Japan, established families and communities.

The majority of Japanese women—over 33,000 immigrants—entered the United States between 1908 and 1924. The "Gentlemen's Agreement" of 1908 restricted the entry of male Japanese laborers into the country but sanctioned the immigration of parents, wives, and children of laborers already residing in the United States. The Immigration Act of 1924 excluded Japanese immigration altogether.

Some Japanese women traveled to reunite with husbands; others journeyed to America as newlyweds with men who had returned to Japan to find wives. Still others came alone as picture brides to join Issei men who sought to avoid army conscription or excessive travel expenses; their family-arranged marriages deviated from social convention only by the absence of the groom from the *miai* (preliminary meeting of prospective spouses) and wedding ceremony. Once settled, these women confronted unfamiliar clothing, food, language, and customs as well as life with husbands who were, in many cases, strangers and often ten to fifteen years their seniors.

Most Issei women migrated to rural areas of the West. Some lived with their husbands in labor camps, which provided workers for the railroad industry, the lumber mills of the Pacific Northwest, and the Alaskan salmon canneries. They also farmed with their husbands as cash or share tenants, particularly in California where Japanese immigrant agriculture began to flourish. In urban areas, women worked as domestics or helped their husbands run small businesses such as laundries, bath houses, restaurants, pool halls, boarding houses, grocery stores, curio shops, bakeries, and plant nurseries. Except for the few who married well-to-do professionals or merchants, the majority of Issei women unceasingly toiled both inside and outside the home. They were always the first to rise in the morning and the last to go to bed at night.

The majority of the Issei's children, the Nisei, were born between 1910 and 1940. Both girls and boys were incorporated into the family economy early, especially those living on farms. They took care of their younger siblings, fed the farm animals, heated water for the *furo* (Japanese bath), and worked in the fields before and after school—hoeing weeds, irrigating, and driving tractors. Daughters helped with cooking and cleaning. In addition, all were expected to devote time to their studies: the Issei instilled in their children a deep respect for education and authority. They repeatedly admonished the Nisei not to bring disgrace upon the family or community and exhorted them to do their best in everything.

The Nisei grew up integrating both the Japanese ways of their parents and the mainstream customs of their non-Japanese friends and classmates—not always an easy process given the deeply rooted prejudice and discrimination they faced as a tiny, easily identified minority. Because of the wide age range among them and the diversity of their early experiences in various urban and rural areas, it is difficult to generalize about the Nisei. Most grew up speaking Japanese with their parents and English with their siblings, friends, and teachers. Regardless of whether they were Buddhist or Christian, they celebrated the New Year with traditional foods and visiting, as well as Christmas and Thanksgiving. Girls learned to knit, sew, and embroider, and some took lessons in *odori* (folk dancing). The Nisei, many of whom were adolescents during the 1940's, also listened to the *Hit Parade*, Jack Benny, and *Gangbusters* on the radio, learned the jitterbug, played kick-the-can and baseball, and read the same popular books and magazines as their non-Japanese peers.

The Issei were strict and not inclined to open displays of affection towards their children, but the Nisei were conscious of their parents' concern for them and for the family. This sense of family strength and responsibility helped to sustain the Issei and Nisei through years of economic hardship and discrimination: the West Coast anti-Japanese movement of the early 1920's, the Depression of the 1930's, and the most drastic ordeal—the chaotic uprooting of the World War II evacuation, internment, and resettlement. . . .

The bombing of Pearl Harbor on December 7, 1941, unleashed war between the United States and Japan and triggered a wave of hostility against Japanese Americans. On December 8, the financial resources of the Issei were frozen, and the Federal Bureau of Investigation began to seize Issei community leaders thought to be strongly pro-Japanese. Rumors spread that the Japanese in Hawaii had aided the attack on Pearl Harbor, fueling fears of "fifth column" activity on the West Coast. Politicians and the press clamored for restrictions against the Japanese Americans, and their economic competitors saw the chance to gain control of Japanese American farms and businesses.

Despite some official doubts and some differences of opinion among military heads regarding the necessity of removing Japanese Americans from the West Coast, in the end the opinions of civilian leaders and Lieutenant General John L. DeWitt—head of the Western Defense Command—of Assistant Secretary of War John McCloy and Secretary of War Henry Stimson prevailed. On February 19, 1942, President Franklin Delano Roosevelt signed Executive Order 9066, arbitrarily suspending the civil rights of American citizens by authorizing the removal of 110,000 Japanese and their American-born children from the western half of the Pacific Coastal States and the southern third of Arizona.

During the bewildering months before evacuation, the Japanese Americans were subject to curfews and to unannounced searches at all hours for "contraband" weapons, radios, and cameras; in desperation and fear, many people destroyed their belongings from Japan, including treasured heirlooms, books, and photographs. Some families moved voluntarily from the Western Defense zone, but many stayed, believing that all areas would eventually be restricted or fearing hostility in neighboring states.

Involuntary evacuation began in the spring of 1942. Families received a scant week's notice in which to "wind up their affairs, store or sell their possessions, close up their businesses and homes, and show up at an assembly point for transportation to an assembly center." Each person was allowed to bring only as many clothes and personal items as he or she could carry to the temporary assembly centers that had been hastily constructed at fairgrounds, race tracks, and Civilian Conservation Corps camps: twelve in California, one in Oregon, and one in Washington.

The rapidity of evacuation left many Japanese Americans numb; one Nisei noted that "a queer lump came to my throat. Nothing else came to my mind, it was just blank. Everything happened too soon, I guess." As the realization of leaving home, friends, and neighborhood sank in, the numbness gave way to bewilderment. A teenager at the Santa Anita Assembly Center wrote, "I felt lost after I left Mountain View [California]. I thought that we could go back but instead look where we are." . . .

Overlying the mixed feelings of anxiety, anger, shame, and confusion was resignation. As a relatively small minority caught in a storm of turbulent events that destroyed their individual and community security, there was little the Japanese Americans could do but shrug and say, *"Shikata ga nai,"* or, "It can't be helped," the implication being that the situation must be endured. The phrase lingered on many lips when the Issei, Nisei, and the young Sansei (third generation) children prepared for the move—which was completed by November 1942—to the ten permanent relocation camps organized by the War Relocation Authority: Topaz, Utah; Poston and Gila River, Arizona; Amache, Colorado; Manzanar and Tule Lake, California; Heart Mountain, Wyoming; Minidoka, Idaho; Denson and Rohwer, Arkansas. Denson and Rohwer were located in the swampy lowlands of Arkansas; the other camps were in desolate desert or semi-desert areas subject to dust storms and extreme temperatures reflected in the nicknames given to the three sections of the Poston Camp: Toaston, Roaston, and Duston.

The conditions of camp life profoundly altered family relations and affected women of all ages and backgrounds. Family unity deteriorated in the crude communal facilities and cramped barracks. The unceasing battle with the elements, the poor food, the shortages of toilet tissue and milk, coupled with wartime profiteering and mismanagement, and the sense of injustice and frustration took their toll on a people uprooted, far from home.

The standard housing in the camps was a spartan barracks, about twenty feet by one hundred feet, divided into four to six rooms furnished with steel army cots. Initially each single room or "apartment" housed an average of eight persons; individuals without kin nearby were often moved in with smaller families. Because the partitions between apartments did not reach the ceiling, even the smallest noises traveled freely from one end of the building to the other. There were usually fourteen barracks in each block, and each block had its own mess hall, laundry, latrine, shower facilities, and recreation room.

Because of the discomfort, noise, and lack of privacy, which "made a single symphony of yours and your neighbors' loves, hates, and joys," the barracks often became merely a place to "hang your hat" and sleep. As Jeanne Wakatsuki Houston records in her autobiography, *Farewell to Manzanar,* many family members began to spend less time together in the crowded barracks. The even greater lack of privacy in the latrine and shower facilities necessitated adjustments in former notions of modesty. There were no partitions in the shower room, and the latrine consisted of two rows of partitioned toilets "with nothing in front of you, just on the sides. Lots of people were not used to those kind of facilities, so [they'd] either go early in the morning when people were not around, or go real late at night. . . . It was really something until you got used to it."

The large communal mess halls also encouraged family disunity as family members gradually began to eat separately: mothers with small children, fathers with other men, and older children with their peers. "Table manners were forgotten," observed Miné Okubo. "Guzzle, guzzle, guzzle; hurry, hurry, hurry. Family life was lacking. Everyone ate wherever he or she pleased." Some strategies were developed for preserving family unity. The Amache Camp responded in part by assigning each family a particular table in the mess hall. Some families took the food back to their barracks so that they might eat together. But these measures were not always feasible in the face of varying work schedules; the odd hours of those assigned to shifts in the mess halls and infirmaries often made it impossible for the family to sit down together for meals.

Newspaper reports that Japanese Americans were living in luxurious conditions angered evacuees struggling to adjust to cramped quarters and crude communal facilities. A married woman with a family wrote from Heart Mountain:

> Last weekend, we had an awful cold wave and it was about 20° to 30° below zero. In such a weather, it's terrible to try going even to the bath and latrine house. . . . It really aggravates me to hear some politicians say we Japanese are being coddled, for *it isn't so*!! We're on ration as much as outsiders are. I'd say welcome to anyone to try living behind barbed wire and be cooped in a 20 ft. by 20 ft. room. . . . We do our sleeping, dressing, ironing, hanging up our clothes in this one room.

After the first numbness of disorientation, the evacuees set about making their situation bearable, creating as much order in their lives as possible. With blankets they partitioned their apartments into tiny rooms and created benches, tables, and shelves as piles of scrap lumber left over from barracks construction vanished; victory gardens and flower patches appeared. Evacuees also took advantage of the opportunity to taste freedom when they received temporary permits to go shopping in nearby towns. These were memorable occasions. A Heart Mountain Nisei described what such a trip meant to her in 1944:

> [F]or the first time since being behind the fences, I managed to go out shopping to Billings, Montana—a trip about 4 hours ride on train and bus. . . . It was quite a mental relief to breathe the air on the outside. . . . And was it an undescribable sensation to be able to be dressed up and walk the pavements with my high heel shoes!! You just can't imagine how full we are of pent-up emotions until we leave the camp behind us and see

the highway ahead of us. A trip like that will keep us from becoming mentally narrow. And without much privacy, you can imagine how much people will become dull.

Despite the best efforts of the evacuees to restore order to their disrupted world, camp conditions prevented replication of their prewar lives. Women's work experiences, for example, changed in complex ways during the years of internment. Each camp offered a wide range of jobs, resulting from the organization of the camps as model cities administered through a series of departments headed by Caucasian administrators. The departments handled everything from accounting, agriculture, education, and medical care to mess hall service and the weekly newspaper. The scramble for jobs began early in the assembly centers and camps, and all able-bodied persons were expected to work.

Even before the war many family members had worked, but now children and parents, men and women all received the same low wages. In the relocation camps, doctors, teachers, and other professionals were at the top of the pay scale, earning $19 per month. The majority of workers received $16, and apprentices earned $12. The new equity in pay and the variety of available jobs gave many women unprecedented opportunities for experimentation, as illustrated by one woman's account of her family's work in Poston:

> First I wanted to find art work, but I didn't last too long because it wasn't very interesting . . . so I worked in the mess hall, but that wasn't for me, so I went to the accounting department—time-keeping—and I enjoyed that, so I stayed there. . . . My dad . . . went to a shoe shop . . . and then he was block gardener. . . . He got $16. . . . [My sister] was secretary for the block manager; then she went to the optometry department. She was assistant optometrist; she fixed all the glasses and fitted them. . . . That was $16.

As early as 1942, the War Relocation Authority began to release evacuees temporarily from the centers and camps to do voluntary seasonal farm work in neighboring areas hard hit by the wartime labor shortage. The work was arduous, as one young woman discovered when she left Topaz to take a job plucking turkeys:

> The smell is terrific until you get used to it. . . . We all wore gunny sacks around our waist, had a small knife and plucked off the fine feathers.
>
> This is about the hardest work that many of us have done—but without a murmur of complaint we worked 8 hours through the first day without a pause.
>
> We were all so tired that we didn't even feel like eating. . . . Our fingers and wrists were just aching, and I just dreamt of turkeys and more turkeys.

Work conditions varied from situation to situation, and some exploitative farmers refused to pay the Japanese Americans after they had finished beet topping or fruit picking. One worker noted that the degree of friendliness on the employer's part decreased as the harvest neared completion. Nonetheless, many workers, like the turkey plucker, concluded that "even if the work is hard, it is worth the freedom we are allowed."

Camp life increased the leisure of many evacuees. A good number of Issei women, accustomed to long days of work inside and outside the home, found that the communally prepared meals and limited living quarters provided them with spare time. Many availed themselves of the opportunity to attend adult classes taught by both evacuees and non-Japanese. Courses involving handcrafts and traditional Japanese arts such as flower arrangement, sewing, painting, calligraphy, and wood carving became immensely popular as an overwhelming number of people turned to art for recreation and self-expression. Some of these subjects were viewed as hobbies and leisure activities by those who taught them, but to the Issei women they represented access to new skills and a means to contribute to the material comfort of the family.

The evacuees also filled their time with Buddhist and Christian church meetings, theatrical productions, cultural programs, athletic events, and visits with friends. All family members spent more time than ever before in the company of their peers. Nisei from isolated rural areas were exposed to the ideas, styles, and pastimes of the more sophisticated urban youth; in camp they had the time and opportunity to socialize—at work, school, dances, sports events, and parties—in an almost entirely Japanese American environment. Gone were the restrictions of distance, lack of transportation, interracial uneasiness, and the dawn-to-dusk exigencies of field work.

Like their noninterned contemporaries, most young Nisei women envisioned a future of marriage and children. They—and their parents—anticipated that they would marry other Japanese Americans, but these young women also expected to choose their own husbands and to marry "for love." This mainstream American ideal of marriage differed greatly from the Issei's view of love as a bond that might evolve over the course of an arranged marriage that was firmly rooted in less romantic notions of compatibility and responsibility. The discrepancy between Issei and Nisei conceptions of love and marriage had sturdy prewar roots; internment fostered further divergence from the old customs of arranged marriage.

In the artificial hothouse of camp, Nisei romances often bloomed quickly. As Nisei men left to prove their loyalty to the United States in the 442nd Combat Team and the 100th Battalion, young Japanese Americans strove to grasp what happiness and security they could, given the uncertainties of the future. Lily Shoji, in her "Fem-a-lites" newspaper column, commented upon the "changing world" and advised Nisei women:

> This is the day of sudden dates, of blind dates on the up-and-up, so let the flash of a uniform be a signal to you to be ready for any emergency. . . . Romance is blossoming with the emotion and urgency of war.

In keeping with this atmosphere, camp newspaper columns like Shoji's in *The Mercedian, The Daily Tulean Dispatch*'s "Strictly Feminine," and the *Poston Chronicle*'s "Fashionotes" gave their Nisei readers countless suggestions on how to impress boys, care for their complexions, and choose the latest fashions. These evacuee-authored columns thus mirrored the mainstream girls' periodicals of the time. Such fashion news may seem incongruous in the context of an internment camp whose inmates had little choice in clothing beyond what they could find in the Montgomery Ward or Sears and Roebuck mail-order catalogues. These columns, however, reflect women's efforts to remain in touch with the world outside the barbed wire fence; they reflect as well women's attempt to maintain morale in a drab, depressing environment. . . .

Relocation began slowly in 1942. Among the first to venture out of the camps were college students, assisted by the National Japanese American Student Relocation Council, a nongovernmental agency that provided invaluable placement aid to 4,084 Nisei in the years 1942–46. Founded in 1942 by concerned educators, this organization persuaded institutions outside the restricted Western Defense zone to accept Nisei students and facilitated their admissions and leave clearances. A study of the first 400 students to leave camp showed that a third of them were women.

Because of the cumbersome screening process, few other evacuees departed on indefinite leave before 1943. In that year, the War Relocation Authority tried to expedite the clearance procedure by broadening an army registration program aimed at Nisei males to include all adults. With this policy change, the migration from the camps steadily increased.

Many Nisei, among them a large number of women, were anxious to leave the limbo of camp and return "to normal life again." With all its work, social events, and cultural activities, camp was still an artificial, limited environment. It was stifling "to see nothing but the same barracks, mess halls, and other houses, row after row, day in and day out, it gives us the feeling that we're missing all the freedom and liberty." An aspiring teacher wrote: "Mother and father do not want me to go out. However, I want to go so very much that sometimes I feel that I'd go even if they disowned me. What shall I do? I realize the hard living conditions outside but I think I can take it." Women's developing sense of independence in the camp environment and their growing awareness of their abilities as workers contributed to their self-confidence and hence their desire to leave. Significantly, Issei parents, despite initial reluctance, were gradually beginning to sanction their daughters' departures for education and employment in the Midwest and East. One Nisei noted:

> [Father] became more broad-minded in the relocation center. He was more mellow in his ways. . . . At first he didn't want me to relocate, but he gave in. . . . I said I wanted to go [to Chicago] with my friend, so he helped me pack. He didn't say I could go . . . but he helped me pack, so I thought, "Well, he didn't say no."

The decision to relocate was a difficult one. It was compounded for some women because they felt obligated to stay and care for elderly or infirm parents, like the Heart Mountain Nisei who observed wistfully. "It's getting so more and more of the girls and boys are leaving camp, and I sure wish I could but mother's getting on and I just can't leave her." Many internees worried about their acceptance in the outside world. The Nisei considered themselves American citizens, and they had an allegiance to the land of their birth: "The teaching and love of one's own birth place, one's own country was . . . strongly impressed upon my mind as a child. So even though California may deny our rights of birth, I shall ever love her soil." But evacuation had taught the Japanese Americans that in the eyes of many of their fellow Americans, theirs was the face of the enemy. Many Nisei were torn by mixed feelings of shame, frustration, and bitterness at the denial of their civil rights. These factors created an atmosphere of anxiety that surrounded those who contemplated resettlement: "A feeling of uncertainty hung over the camp; we were worried about the future. Plans were made and remade, as we tried to decide what to do. Some were ready to risk anything to get away. Others feared to leave the protection of the camp."

Thus, those first college students were the scouts whose letters back to camp marked pathways for others to follow. May Yoshino sent a favorable report to her family in Topaz from the nearby University of Utah, indicating that there were "plenty of schoolgirl jobs for those who want to study at the University." Correspondence from other Nisei students shows that although they succeeded at making the dual transition from high school to college and from camp to the outside world, they were not without anxieties as to whether they could handle the study load and the reactions of the Caucasians around them. . . .

Several incidents of hostility did occur, but the reception of the Nisei students at colleges and universities was generally warm. Topaz readers of *Trek* magazine could draw encouragement from Lillian Ota's "Campus Report." Ota, a Wellesley student, reassured them: "During the first few days you'll be invited by the college to teas and receptions. Before long you'll lose the awkwardness you might feel at such doings after the months of abnormal life at evacuation centers." Although Ota had not noticed "that my being a 'Jap' has made much difference on the campus itself," she offered cautionary and pragmatic advice to the Nisei, suggesting the burden of responsibility these relocated students felt, as well as the problem of communicating their experiences and emotions to Caucasians.

> It is scarcely necessary to point out that those who have probably never seen a nisei before will get their impression of the nisei as a whole from the relocated students. It won't do you or your family and friends much good to dwell on what you consider injustices when you are questioned about evacuation. Rather, stress the contributions of [our] people to the nation's war effort.

Given the tenor of the times and the situation of their families, the pioneers in resettlement had little choice but to repress their anger and minimize the amount of racist hostility they encountered.

In her article "a la mode," Marii Kyogoku also offered survival tips to the departing Nisei, ever conscious that they were on trial not only as individuals but as representatives of their families and their generation. She suggested criteria for choosing clothes and provided hints on adjustment to food rationing. Kyogoku especially urged the evacuees to improve their table manners, which had been adversely affected by the "unnatural food and atmosphere" of mess hall dining:

> You should start rehearsing for the great outside by bringing your own utensils to the dining hall. It's an aid to normality to be able to eat your jello with a spoon and well worth the dishwashing which it involves. All of us eat much too fast. Eat more slowly. All this practicing should be done so that proper manners will seem natural to you. If you do this, you won't get stagefright and spill your water glass, or make bread pills and hardly dare to eat when you have your first meal away from the centers and in the midst of scrutinizing caucasian eyes.

Armed with advice and drawn by encouraging reports, increasing numbers of women students left camp. A postwar study of a group of 1,000 relocated students showed that 40 percent were women. The field of nursing was particularly attractive to Nisei women; after the first few students disproved the hospital administration's fears of their patients' hostility, acceptance of Nisei into nursing schools grew. By July 1944, there were more than 300 Nisei women in over 100 nursing programs in twenty-four states. One such student wrote from the Asbury Hospital in Minneapolis: "Work here isn't too hard and I enjoy it very much. The patients are very nice people and I haven't had any trouble as yet. They do give us a funny stare at the beginning but after a day or so we receive the best compliments." ·

The trickle of migration from the camps grew into a steady stream by 1943, as the War Relocation Authority developed its resettlement program to aid evacuees in finding housing and employment in the East and Midwest. A resettlement bulletin published by the Advisory Committee for Evacuees described "who is relocating":

Mostly younger men and women, in their 20s or 30s; mostly single persons or couples with one or two children, or men with larger families who come out alone first to scout opportunities and to secure a foothold, planning to call wife and children later. Most relocated evacuees have parents or relatives whom they hope and plan to bring out "when we get re-established."

In early 1945, the War Department ended the exclusion of the Japanese Americans from the West Coast, and the War Relocation Authority announced that the camps would be closed within the year. By this time, 37 percent of the evacuees of sixteen years or older had already relocated, including 63 percent of the Nisei women in that age group.

For Nisei women, like their non-Japanese sisters, the wartime labor shortage opened the door into industrial, clerical, and managerial occupations. Prior to the war, racism had excluded the Japanese Americans from most white-collar clerical and sales positions, and, according to sociologist Evelyn Nakano Glenn, "the most common form of nonagricultural employment for the immigrant women (issei) and their American-born daughters (nisei) was domestic service." The highest percentage of job offers for both men and women continued to be requests for domestic workers. . . . However, Nisei women also found jobs as secretaries, typists, file clerks, beauticians, and factory workers. By 1950, 47 percent of employed Japanese American women were clerical and sales workers and operatives; only 10 percent were in domestic service. The World War II decade, then, marked a turning point for Japanese American women in the labor force.

Whether they were students or workers, and regardless of where they went or how prepared they were to meet the outside world, Nisei women found that leaving camp meant enormous change in their lives. Even someone as confident as Marii Kyogoku, the author of much relocation advice, found that reentry into the Caucasian-dominated world beyond the barbed wire fence was not a simple matter of stepping back into old shoes. Leaving the camps—like entering them—meant major changes in psychological perspective and self-image.

> I had thought that because before evacuation I had adjusted myself rather well in a Caucasian society, I would go right back into my former frame of mind. I have found, however, that though the center became unreal and was as if it had never existed as soon as I got on the train at Delta, I was never so self-conscious in all my life.

Kyogoku was amazed to see so many men and women in uniform and, despite her "proper" dining preparation, felt strange sitting at a table set with clean linen and a full set of silverware.

> I felt a diffidence at facing all these people and things, which was most unusual. Slowly things have come to seem natural, though I am still excited by the sounds of the busy city and thrilled every time I see a street lined with trees. I no longer feel that I am the cynosure of all eyes.

Like Kyogoku, many Nisei women discovered that relocation meant adjustment to "a life different from our former as well as present way of living" and, as such, posed a challenge. Their experiences in meeting this challenge were as diverse as their jobs and living situations.

"I live at the Eleanor Club No. 5 which is located on the west side," wrote Mary Sonoda, working with the American Friends Service Committee in Chicago:

I pay $1 per day for room and two meals a day. I also have maid service. I do not think that one can manage all this for $1 unless one lives in a place like this which houses thousands of working girls in the city. . . . I am the only Japanese here at present. . . . The residents and the staff are wonderful to me. . . . I am constantly being entertained by one person or another.

The people in Chicago are extremely friendly. Even with the Tribune screaming awful headlines concerning the recent execution of American soldiers in Japan, people kept their heads. On street cars, at stores, everywhere, one finds innumerable evidence of good will.

Chicago, the location of the first War Relocation Authority field office for supervision of resettlement in the Midwest, attracted the largest number of evacuees. Not all found their working environment as congenial as Mary Sonoda did. Smoot Katow, a Nisei man in Chicago, painted "another side of the picture":

I met one of the Edgewater Beach girls. . . . From what she said it was my impression that the girls are not very happy. The hotel work is too hard, according to this girl. In fact, they are losing weight and one girl became sick with overwork. They have to clean about fifteen suites a day, scrubbing the floors on their hands and knees. . . . It seems the management is out to use labor as labor only. . . . The outside world is just as tough as it ever was.

These variations in living and work conditions and wages encouraged and sometimes necessitated a certain amount of job experimentation among the Nisei.

Many relocating Japanese Americans received moral and material assistance from a number of service organizations and religious groups, particularly the Presbyterians, the Methodists, the Society of Friends, and the Young Women's Christian Association. . . .

The Nisei also derived support and strength from networks—formed before and during the internment—of friends and relatives. The homes of those who relocated first became way stations for others as they made the transition into new communities and jobs. In 1944, soon after she obtained a place to stay in New York City, Miné Okubo found that "many of the other evacuees relocating in New York came ringing my doorbell. They were sleeping all over the floor!" Single women often accompanied or joined sisters, brothers, and friends as many interconnecting grapevines carried news of likely jobs, housing, and friendly communities. Ayako Kanemura, for instance, found a job painting Hummel figurines in Chicago; a letter of recommendation from a friend enabled her "to get my foot into the door and then all my friends followed and joined me." Although they were farther from their families than ever before, Nisei women maintained warm ties of affection and concern, and those who had the means to do so continued to play a role in the family economy, remitting a portion of their earnings to their families in or out of camp, and to siblings in school.

Elizabeth Ogata's family exemplifies several patterns of resettlement and the maintenance of family ties within them. In October 1944, her parents were living with her brother Harry who had begun to farm in Springville, Utah; another brother and sister were attending Union College in Lincoln, Nebraska. Elizabeth herself had moved to Minneapolis to join a brother in the army, and she was working as an operative making pajamas. "Minn. is a beautiful place," she wrote, "and the people are so nice. . . . I thought I'd never find anywhere I would feel at home as I did in Mt. View [California], but I have changed my mind." Like Elizabeth, a good number of the 35,000 relocated Japanese Americans were favorably impressed by their new homes and decided to stay.

The war years had complex and profound effects upon Japanese Americans, uprooting their communities and causing severe psychological and emotional damage. The vast majority returned to the West Coast at the end of the war in 1945—a move that, like the initial evacuation, was a grueling test of flexibility and fortitude. Even with the assistance of old friends and service organizations, the transition was taxing and painful, the end of the war meant not only long-awaited freedom but more battles to be fought in social, academic, and economic arenas. The Japanese Americans faced hostility, crude living conditions, and a struggle for jobs. Few evacuees received any compensation for their financial losses, estimated conservatively at $400 million, because Congress decided to appropriate only $38 million for the settlement of claims. It is even harder to place a figure on the toll taken in emotional shock, self-blame, broken dreams, and insecurity. One Japanese American woman still sees in her nightmares the watchtower searchlights that troubled her sleep forty years ago

The war altered Japanese American women's lives in complicated ways. In general, evacuation and relocation accelerated earlier trends that differentiated the Nisei from their parents. Although most young women, like their mothers and non-Japanese peers, anticipated a future centered around a husband and children, they had already felt the influence of mainstream middle-class values of love and marriage and quickly moved away from the pattern of arranged marriage in the camps There, increased peer group activities and the relaxation of parental authority gave them more independence. The Nisei women's expectations of marriage became more akin to the companionate ideals of their peers than to those of the Issei.

As before the war, many Nisei women worked in camp, but the new parity in wages they received altered family dynamics. And though they expected to contribute to the family economy, a large number did so in settings far from the family, availing themselves of opportunities provided by the student and worker relocation programs. In meeting the challenges facing them, Nisei women drew not only upon the disciplined strength inculcated by their Issei parents but also upon firmly rooted support networks and the greater measure of self-reliance and independence that they developed during the crucible of the war years.

The Regulation of Sexuality and Sexual Behavior in the Women's Army Corps During World War II

LEISA D. MEYER

Several years after World War II ended, a journalist summed up the difficulties the Women's Army Corps encountered in recruiting women by observing:

> Of the problems that the WAC has, the greatest one is the problem of morals . . . of convincing mothers, fathers, brothers, Congressmen, servicemen and junior officers that women really can be military without being camp followers or without being converted into rough, tough gals who can cuss out the chow as well as any dogface. . . .

Leisa D. Meyer, "Creating G.I. Jane: The Regulation of Sexuality and Sexual Behavior in the Women's Army Corps during World War II," *Feminist Studies* 18, no. 3 (fall 1992): 581–601. Reprinted by permission of the publisher, Feminist Studies, Inc.

The sexual stereotypes of servicewomen as "camp followers" or "mannish women," prostitutes or lesbians, had a long history both in the construction of notions of femaleness in general and in the relationship of "woman" and "soldier" in particular. Historically, women had been most visibly associated with the military as prostitutes and crossdressers. The challenge before women and men who wanted to promote "women" as "soldiers" during World War II was how to create a new category which proclaimed female soldiers as both sexually respectable and feminine. The response of Oveta Culp Hobby, the Women's Army Corps director, to this challenge was to characterize female soldiers as chaste and asexual; such a presentation would not threaten conventional sexual norms. Clashing public perceptions of servicewomen and internal struggles within the U.S. Army over the proper portrayal and treatment of military women were the crucibles in which this new category was created. Such struggles profoundly shaped the daily lives of women in the Women's Army Auxiliary Corps (WAAC) and the Women's Army Corps (WAC) and framed the notorious lesbian witchhunts of the mid- to late-forties.

This article focuses on the regulation and expression of women's sexuality within the army during World War II. I will examine the debates between female and male military leaders over the most appropriate methods of controlling female soldiers' sexual behavior and the actions and responses of army women themselves to the varied and often conflicting rulings emanating from WAAC/WAC Headquarters and the War Department. Framed by public concern with the possibilities of both the sexual independence and sexual victimization of servicewomen, the interactions between and among these groups illuminate the ongoing tension between the mutually exclusive, gendered categories "woman" and "soldier."

The entrance of some women into the army paralleled the movement of other women into nontraditional jobs in the civilian labor force as the need for full utilization of all resources during World War II brought large numbers of white, married women into the labor force for the first time and created opportunities for many women and people of color in jobs historically denied them. Women's service in the armed forces was especially threatening, however, because of the military's function as the ultimate test of "masculinity."

The definition of the military as a masculine institution and the definition of a soldier as a "man with a gun who engages in combat" both excluded women. Moreover, military service had historically been the obligation of men during wartime, and the presence of female soldiers in the army suggested that women were abdicating their responsibilities within the home to usurp men's duty of protecting and defending their homes and country. Thus, the establishment of the WAAC in May 1942, marking women's formal entrance into this preeminently masculine domain, generated heated public debate. It heightened the fears already generated by the entry of massive numbers of women in the civilian labor force and by the less restrictive sexual mores of a wartime environment. . . .

In a culture increasingly anxious about women's sexuality in general, and homosexuality in particular, the formation of the WAAC, a women-only environment within an otherwise wholly male institution, sparked a storm of public speculation as to the potential breakdown of heterosexual norms and sexual morality which might result. Not surprisingly, these concerns focused on the potentially "masculinizing" effect the army might have on women and especially on the disruptive influence the

WAAC would have on sexual standards. Public fears were articulated in numerous editorials and stories in newspapers and journals, as well as in thousands of letters to the War Department and the newly formed WAAC Headquarters in Washington, D.C. These anxieties were expressed in accusations of heterosexual promiscuity and lesbianism and concerns over women's lack of protection within the military. Among other allegations, the public expressed fear that, in forming the WAAC, the military was trying to create an organized cadre of prostitutes to service male GI's. . . .

The sexual stereotypes of the female soldier as "loose" or "mannish" were seen both as inherent in women's military service *and* as a product of the particular kinds of women believed to be most likely to enter the WAAC. In other words, the army either attracted women who were already "sexually deviant," or the experience of military life would make them that way. In addition, the corollary to concerns with women's sexual agency [was] discussions of army women as potential sexual victims. Integral to this contention were questions of who would protect women inside the military. Removed from the control of their families, what would the state's control of servicewomen mean?

The army's response to this negative publicity was orchestrated by Col. Hobby. She organized this response around the need to assure an anxious public that service-women had not lost their "femininity." Hobby's definition of "femininity" was rooted in the Victorian linkage between sexual respectability and female passionlessness. As a result she characterized the woman soldier as chaste, asexual, and essentially middle-class. For example, in cooperation with the War Department she arranged public statements by a number of religious leaders who assured all concerned that the army was a safe and moral environment for young women, and further, that women who joined the WAAC/WAC were of the highest moral character and from "good family backgrounds." She characterized the WAAC/WAC as acting *in loco parentis*, as a guardian of young women's welfare and morals. And to demonstrate that the WAAC/WAC attracted "better-quality" women, Hobby emphasized the greater educational requirements mandated for women compared with their male counterparts, illustrated by the high ratio of women with college degrees. Thus, in countering allegations that to join the WAAC/WAC meant to "lower one's self," army propaganda reflected and supported contemporary definitions of respectability which explicitly connected class status and sexual morality.

These pronouncements on sexual respectability coincided with other army public relations campaigns aimed at defusing public concerns with homosexuality. In these efforts, attempts to limit the visibility of lesbians in the women's corps were linked with the implicit encouragement of heterosexuality. In responding to fears that the military would make women "mannish" or would provide a haven for women who were "naturally" that way, for instance, some army propaganda highlighted the femininity of WAAC/WAC recruits and stressed their sexual attractiveness to men. These articles assured an anxious public that "soldiering hasn't transformed these Wacs into Amazons—far from it. They have retained their femininity." Presenting women in civilian life in the period as sexually attractive to men did not necessarily imply that they were sexually available. However, public hostility toward women's entrance into the military and conjecture over the army's "real need" for Waacs/Wacs frequently focused on the potential for women's sexual exploitation and/or agency within the army. The army's policy of portraying servicewomen as feminine and sexually attractive to men worked to both contest the image of the female soldier as a "mannish" woman, or lesbian, *and* to reinforce the public characterizations of Waacs/Wacs as heterosexually available. Hobby's efforts to control the effects of these campaigns was to emphasize that Waacs/Wacs remained passionless and chaste while in the military and that their sexual behavior in the military was, and should be, profoundly different from that of men in the same institution.

The framework created by Hobby and disseminated in military propaganda efforts was occasionally undercut by the conflicting responses to the question of whether Waacs/Wacs should be treated and utilized as "soldiers" or as "women." On several occasions the male army hierarchy, much to Hobby's dismay, attempted to treat the regulation and control of women's sexuality and sexual behavior in the same manner as that of male soldiers. The army's approach to the issue of sexual regulation and control for men stressed health and combat readiness among troops, not morality. In fact, the army expected and encouraged heterosexual activity among male soldiers and controlled male sexuality with regulations prohibiting sodomy and addressing the prevention and treatment of venereal disease, as well as more informal mechanisms upholding prohibitions on interracial relationships. The male military hierarchy's desire for uniformity collided with the female WAAC director's firm belief in different moral standards for women and her insistence that this difference be reflected in army regulations. This struggle was clearly represented in the army's battle to fight the spread of venereal disease within its ranks.

Hobby believed the army's venereal disease program for men, premised on the assumption of heterosexual activity, would seriously damage the reputation of the corps if applied to women and would undermine her efforts to present Waacs as sexless, not sexual. Her strategy of moral suasion clashed with the U.S. surgeon general's efforts to institute a system of chemical prophylaxis in the women's corps. The surgeon general's plan for control of venereal disease in the WAAC included a full course of instruction in sex education and the distribution of condoms in slot machines placed in latrines so that even "modest" servicewomen might have access to them. This program was completely rejected by Hobby. She argued that even proposing such measures placed civilian and military acceptance of the WAAC in jeopardy. She pointed to public fears of women's military service and accusations of immorality already present as evidence that the course proposed by the surgeon general would result in catastrophic damage to the reputation of the WAAC and seriously hamper her efforts to recruit women to the corps.

Her concern was not with venereal disease per se, but rather with creating an aura of respectability around the WAAC. Her victory in this struggle resulted in the development of a social hygiene pamphlet and course which stressed the "high standards" of moral conduct (i.e., chastity) necessary for members of the corps and the potential damage one woman could do through her misbehavior or immoral conduct. The pamphlet, distributed to all WAAC officers, discussed venereal disease only in reference to the "frightful effects" of the disease on women and children, the difficulties in detection and treatment, and the ineffectiveness of all prophylactic methods for women. Hobby supported combining this policy with the maintenance of strict enlistment standards. She believed that if the corps accepted only "high types of women," no control measures would be necessary. . . .

Hobby's fears of the adverse public reaction that might result from the distribution of prophylactics information and equipment to Waacs were confirmed by the slander campaign against the WAAC/WAC which started in mid-1943 and continued through early 1944. This "whispering campaign" began with the publication of a nationally syndicated article which reported that in a secret agreement between the War Department and the WAAC, contraceptives would be issued to all women in the army. This piece provoked a storm of public outcry and marked the resurgence of accusations of widespread sexual immorality in the women's corps. . . .

Public fears that the only "real uses" the army had for women were sexual were exacerbated by male officers who claimed that the most important function of the WAAC/WAC was not the soldierly duties it performed but the positive impact the women had on the "morale" of male soldiers. Although "morale boosting" did not necessarily imply prostitution or sexual service, the two were often linked in the public consciousness. For example, one army investigator reported that in Kansas City, Kansas, it was believed that "Waacs were issued condoms and enrolled solely for the soldier's entertainment, serving as 'morale builders' for the men and nothing more." Hobby worked to eliminate all references to Waacs/Wacs being used for "morale purposes," believing that these bolstered public concerns with heterosexual immorality in the corps.

In addition, the occasional use of WAAC/WAC units to control male sexuality seemed to confirm suspicions that the role the army envisioned for women was sexual. For example, African American WAAC/WAC units were in general stationed only at posts where there were Black male soldiers present. In part this was a product of the army's policy of segregating its troops by race. However, white officers, particularly at southern posts, also explicitly referred to the "beneficial" presence of African American WAAC/WAC units as a way to insure that Black male troops would not form liaisons with white women in the surrounding communities. Thus, in this instance, African American WAAC/WAC units were used by the army as a means of upholding and supporting prohibitions on interracial relationships. Similarly, in December 1944, Field Marshall Sir Bernard L. Montgomery proposed using white American WAC and British Auxiliary Territorial Service units in the Allied occupation of Germany to curb the fraternization of male GI's in the U.S. and British armies with enemy (German) women, especially prostitutes. Field Marshall Montgomery's proposal was made public in a number of articles and editorials and harshly criticized by WAC Headquarters, as well as by Wacs stationed overseas in the European theater of operations. It is clear from these examples that military policy and practice were sometimes contradictory.

This situation was made more complicated by the fact that Waacs/Wacs and male soldiers regularly dated and socialized. This was particularly true in overseas theaters of war where military women were often the only U.S. women in the area. The only army regulations dealing with the social interaction of female and male military personnel were long-standing rules against fraternization between officers and enlisted personnel. Again the question arose of whether Waacs/Wacs should be treated like all other soldiers or if allowances should be made for female/male interactions across the caste lines established by the military. No clear answer to this query developed during World War II. In practice, the regulations concerning the socializing of male officers and female enlisted personnel and vice-versa varied from post to post and over different theaters. Many Waacs/Wacs were extremely vocal in their resentment of what they perceived as army policies dictating whom they should not date. When fraternization policies were enforced between women and men, it was usually the Waac/Wac who was punished, not the male soldier or officer, if discovered in violation of these regulations. This practice made it clear that it was women's responsibility to say "no" to these encounters and reinforced the sexual double standard which excused men's heterosexual activity and punished that of women. . . .

The army's negotiation between anxieties about assertive female sexuality, whether heterosexual or homosexual, and the realities of servicewomen's sexual vulnerability to abuse by male GI's and officers can be seen by examining the army's efforts to control the sexuality of servicewomen in the Southwest Pacific Area. Upon arrival in Port Moresby, New Guinea, in May 1944, Wacs found their lives unexpectedly restricted. The theater headquarters directed that in view of the great number of white male troops in the area, "some of whom allegedly had not seen a nurse or other white woman in 18 months," Wacs should be locked within their barbed wire compound at all times except when escorted by armed guards to work or to approved group recreation. No leaves, passes, or one-couple dates were allowed at any time. Many Wacs found these restrictions unbearable and patronizing and complained that they were being treated as criminals and children. The mounting complaints from women at WAC Headquarters and rumors of plummeting morale moved Hobby to protest to the War Department and ask for a discontinuation of what many Wacs referred to as the "concentration camp system." The War Department responded that it was in no position to protest command policies, especially because the theater authorities insisted that the system was required "to prevent rape of Wacs by Negro troops in New Guinea." Societal stereotypes of African American men, in particular, as rapists, and of male sexuality, in general, as dangerous for women, were used to defend the extremely restrictive policies of the military toward Wacs in the Southwest Pacific Area. In this situation the army stepped in as the surrogate male protector defending white military women's honor and virtue by creating a repressive environment designed to insure a maximum of "protection" and supervision.

One consequence of the controls placed on women's heterosexual activities in the Southwest Pacific Area was a series of rumors in late 1944 claiming widespread homosexuality among Wacs in New Guinea. The concerns originated in letters of complaint from several Wacs stationed there who asserted that restrictive theater policies created an ideal habitat for some women to express and explore their "abnormal sexual tendencies." The War Department and Hobby sent a WAC officer to the theater to investigate the rumors. The report issued by Lt. Col. Mary Agnes Brown, the WAC staff director, noted that although homosexuality was certainly not widespread, several incidences of such behavior had occurred. Lieutenant Colonel Brown felt that the situation was accentuated by the rigid camp security system to which Wacs were subjected. She suggested increasing Wacs' opportunities for recreation "with a view of maintaining the normal relationships between men and women that exist at home and avoid the creation of abnormal conditions which otherwise are bound to arise." When faced with a choice of protecting women from men or "protecting" them from lesbian relationships which might occur in a sex-segregated and restricted compound, Lieutenant Colonel Brown's recommendation was to protect servicewomen from the possibility of homosexuality.

The more repressive framework created by Hobby to control women's sexuality in the face of public antagonism was also challenged by women, both heterosexual and lesbian, who asserted their autonomy and right to find their own means of sexual expression within the authoritarian structure of the army. Indeed, heterosexual women sometimes manipulated fears of homosexuality in the women's corps to expand their own opportunities for heterosexual activity. They accused female officers who enforced army regulations against fraternization of male and female officers and enlisted personnel of being "antimale" and discouraging "normal" heterosexual interactions. For example, in February 1944, Capt. Delores Smith was ordered to report for duty as the commanding officer of the Army–Air Forces WAC Detachment at Fort Worth, Texas. As a new commanding officer, Captain Smith sought the help and advice of her officer staff in familiarizing herself with the company and environment. Receiving little support from her officers, she turned for advice to the ranking enlisted woman, Sgt. Norma Crandall. Shortly after her arrival, Smith reprimanded several of her company officers for allowing enlisted men to frequent the WAC barracks and mess hall. In addition, she cautioned these officers on their fraternization with male enlisted personnel. Two weeks later these officers brought charges of homosexuality against Captain Smith. They cited her restrictions on female/male interactions on post, her "dislike" of socializing with servicemen, and her "close association" with the enlisted woman, Sergeant Crandall, as evidence of her "abnormal tendencies." Despite the lack of concrete documentation to support these accusations, Hobby and the Board of Inquiry felt that to allow Captain Smith to continue as a WAC officer would only damage the reputation of the corps, and she was forced to resign from service.

The WAC officers at Fort Worth were angered by what they perceived as the imposition of unfair restrictions on their social lives by Captain Smith. They responded by invoking homophobic anxieties. In doing so they simultaneously defended their right to choose how and with whom they would socialize and reinforced social taboos and army proscriptions against lesbianism. The "lesbian threat" thus became a language of protest to force authorities to broaden their heterosexual privilege.

Lesbian servicewomen, like their heterosexual counterparts, also tried to create their own space within the WAC. In these efforts army lesbians were affected by the contradiction between official proscriptions of homosexuality and the WAC's informal policies on female homosexuality, which were quite lenient. . . . Army regulations providing for the undesirable discharge of homosexuals were rarely used against lesbians in the WAC, and WAC officers were warned to consider this action only in the most extreme of situations. Hobby felt that such proceedings would only result in more intensive public scrutiny and disapproval of the women's corps. Instead, it was suggested that WAC officers use more informal methods of control. These including shifting personnel and room assignments, transferring individuals to different posts, and as was exemplified in New Guinea, insuring that corps members were provided with "opportunities for wholesome and natural companionship with men." . . . In addition, on several posts informal WAC policy prohibited women from dancing in couples in public and cautioned against the adoption of "mannish" hairstyles. WAC leaders were concerned primarily with the image of the corps, and Hobby felt that the adverse publicity generated by intense screening procedures, investigations, and court-martials of lesbians within the WAC could only hurt the corps. Thus, as historian Allan Bérubé has noted in his work on gay GI's during World War II, the expanding antihomosexual apparatus of the military was focused much more closely on regulating and screening for male homosexuals than for their female counterparts.

Within these parameters, lesbians within the WAC developed their own culture and methods of identifying one another, although the risks of discovery and exposure remained. The court-martial of T. Sgt. Julie Farrell, stationed at an army school in Richmond, Kentucky, provides an interesting example of this developing culture and its limits. Although she was given an undesirable discharge because of "unsuitability for military service," Technical Sergeant Farrell's court-martial focused on her alleged homosexuality. According to the testimony of Lt. Rosemary O'Riley, Farrell approached her one evening, depressed at what she felt were the army's efforts to make her "suppress her individuality," including criticisms and reprimands for her "mannish hairstyle" and "masculine behavior." Receiving a sympathetic response, Farrell went on to ask the lieutenant if she understood "double talk" and if she had ever been to San Francisco. It is clear that these questions were used by Farrell to determine if it was safe to discuss issues of homosexuality with O'Riley. When the lieutenant answered in the affirmative to her queries, Farrell went on to speak more explicitly of the "natural desires" of women which the military attempted to suppress. She ended with what Lieutenant O'Riley later termed as a "humiliating suggestion." Farrell was surprised by O'Riley's insistence that she had "no interest in such things" and remarked, "Well, when you first came on this campus we thought that maybe you were one of us in the way you walked." . . .

Lieutenant O'Riley's reports of Farrell's comments and behavior resulted in a court-martial proceeding against Technical Sergeant Farrell. In the course of this proceeding it was argued that in addition to this latest breach of military regulations, Farrell had already been the subject of "malicious gossip and rumor." Most damaging, however, were love letters between Farrell and a WAAC officer, Lieutenant Pines, that were entered as evidence. The tender and explicit discussions of the women's relationship contained within these letters were crucial to the decision of the board to dismiss Farrell from service. Lieutenant Pines avoided prosecution by claiming that the interactions described in the letters occurred only in the imagination of Farrell. Pines covered herself by asserting that she had kept the letters because of her own suspicions of Farrell. Thus, in saving herself, Pines sealed the fate of her lover.

Despite the opportunities for creating and sustaining a lesbian identity or relationship within the WAAC/WAC, the process was also fraught with danger and uncertainty. Army policies provided a space in which female homosexuals could exist, recognize one another, and develop their own culture. Yet this existence was an extremely precarious one, framed by army regulations which also provided for the undesirable discharge of homosexuals, female and male. These regulations could be invoked at any time and were widely used in purges of lesbians from the military in the immediate postwar years, purges that were in part the result of the army's decreasing need for women's labor. In these efforts the army utilized the techniques illustrated in Julie Farrell's court-martial, enabling some women to protect themselves by accusing others of lesbianism. In addition, some lesbians used heterosexual privilege and respectability to obscure their sexual identity by getting married or becoming pregnant in order to leave the army and protect themselves and their lovers. Pat Bond, a lesbian ex-Wac who married a gay GI to avoid prosecution, described one of these purges at a base in Japan: "Every day you came up for a court-martial against one of your friends. They turned us against each other. . . . The only way I could figure out to save my lover was to get out. If I had been there, they could have gotten us both because other women would have testified against us."

The tensions between agency and victimization illustrated here are character- istic of women's participation within the U.S. Army during World War II. Hobby's attempts to portray Wacs as sexless and protected in response to accusations of het- erosexual promiscuity were undercut by the need also to present Wacs as feminine and sexually attractive to men to ease fears that the military would attract or produce "mannish women" and lesbians. In addition, the army's occasional utilization of WAC units to control male sexuality seemed to confirm the belief that women's role within the military was sexual. Within this confusing and fluctuating environment and in negotiation with army regulations and public opinion, Wacs tried to define their own sexuality and make their own sexual choices. Their actions sometimes challenged and other times reinforced entrenched gender and sexual ideologies and were crucial to the development of a role for women within the military. The process of creating a category of "female soldier" was defined by these interactions between Wacs, the army hierarchy (which was often divided along gender lines), and public opinion. The reformulation and reconstruction of gender and sexual norms involved in this process did not end with the war but is still going on today. Women's service continues to be circumscribed by debates over the contradictory concepts of "woman" and "soldier," and servicewomen continue to grapple with the sexual images of dyke and whore framing their participation.

F U R T H E R   R E A D I N G

Anderson, Karen Tucker. *Wartime Women: Sex Roles, Family Relations, and the Status of Women During World War II* (1981).

Baker, M. Joyce. *Images of Women in Film: The War Years, 1941–1945* (1981).

Bentley, Amy. *Eating for Victory: Food Rationing and the Politics of Domesticity* (1998).

Bérubé, Allan. *Coming Out Under Fire: The History of Gay Men and Women in World War II* (1990).

Campbell, D'Ann. *Women at War with America* (1984).

Chafe, William. *The American Woman: Her Changing Social, Economic, and Political Roles, 1920–1970* (1972).

Costello, John. *Virtue Under Fire: How World War II Changed Our Social and Sexual Attitudes* (1985).

Glenn, Evelyn Nakanno. *Issei, Nisei, War Bride: Three Generations of Japanese American Women in Domestic Service* (1986).

Gluck, Sherna Berger, ed. *Rosie the Riveter Revisited: Women, the War, and Social Change* (1987).

Goossen, Rachel Walker. *Women Against the Good War: Conscientious Objection and Gender in the American Home Front, 1941–1947* (1997).

Hartmann, Susan. *The Home Front and Beyond* (1982).

Hoff-Wilson, Joan, and Marjorie Lightman, eds. *Without Precedent: The Life and Career of Eleanor Roosevelt* (1984).

Honey, Maureen. *Creating Rosie the Riveter: Class, Gender, and Propaganda During World War II* (1984).

———, ed. *Bitter Fruit: African American Women in World War II* (1999).

Kesselman, Amy. *Fleeting Opportunities: Women Shipyard Workers in Portland and Vancouver During World War II and Reconversion* (1990).

Light, Jennifer S. "When Computers Were Women," *Technology and Culture* 40 (1999): 455–483.

Matsumoto, Valerie J. *Farming the Home Place: A Japanese American Community in California, 1919–1982* (1993).

Meyer, Leisa D. *Creating G.I. Jane: Sexuality and Power in the Women's Army Corps During World War II* (1996).

Milkman, Ruth. *Gender at Work: The Dynamics of Job Segregation by Sex During World War II* (1988).

Quick, Paddy. "Rosie the Riveter: Myths and Realities," *Radical America* 9 (1975): 115–132.

Rupp, Leila. *Mobilizing Women for War* (1978).

Schweitzer, Mary. "World War II and Female Labor Force Participation Rates," *Journal of Economic History* 40 (1980): 89–95.

Sherman, Janann. *No Place for a Woman: A Life of Senator Margaret Chase Smith* (2000).

Skold, Karen Beck. "The Job He Left Behind: American Women in the Shipyards During World War II," in Carol Berkin and Clara Lovett, eds., *Women, War, and Revolution* (New York: Holmes & Meier, 1980), 55–75.

Tucker, Sherrie. "Working the Swing Shift: Women Musicians During World War II," *Labor's Heritage* 8 (1996): 46–66.

CHAPTER
14

Women and the Feminine
Ideal in Postwar America

*Throughout the 1940s and 1950s, American men and women married earlier and
had larger families than their own parents had had, reversing a long-standing
downward trend in the nation's birth rate. The parents of the baby-boom generation
moved by the thousands to suburban neighborhoods, where child rearing became the
focal point of private and public life. Meanwhile, movies and popular magazines
gave generous coverage to family matters and seemed to revive, though with a modern twist, a feminine ideal based in domesticity. Writing for the lay public, many
educators and mental health professionals stressed the "naturalness" of women's
identification with marriage and motherhood and the critical importance to society's
well-being of women's investment in domesticity.*

*Historians have vigorously debated the meaning of womanhood in the postwar
era. What are we to make of the nation's popular celebration of a domestic feminine
ideal? Was this ideal in some way shaped by the political context, by the nation's
Cold War policies and concerns? Did the popular media offer Americans alternative
images of womanhood? Can we know how women responded to representations in
the popular media? Just as importantly, did definitions of womanhood differ for
women of distinct social, sexual, or racial groups? Finally, how and under what
circumstances did women ignore, subvert, or manipulate normative standards of
postwar womanhood? With what gains and at what cost?*

◆ D O C U M E N T S

In 1946 Louisa Church Randall wrote an article for *American Home* magazine (excerpted in Document 1) that explored the vital duties of parents who lived in a nation
worried about Soviet expansionism and atomic warfare. Randall urged men and women
to regard parenting as a noble duty; interestingly, she also urged them to embrace gender
equity. Psychiatrist Marynia F. Farnham and her colleague sociologist Ferdinand Lundberg, coauthors of *Modern Woman: The Lost Sex* (1947), had no use for gender equity;
instead, as staunch antifeminists they offered strong praise for women who devoted
themselves to domesticity and called women who tried to compete with men "neurotic"

and "unfeminine." An excerpt from *Modern Woman* appears as Document 2. Also writing in 1947, but from a decidedly feminist perspective, Pauli Murray, an African American deputy attorney general for California, described the rebellion of educated and professional black women against racial and sexual subordination. In an article published in the *Negro Digest* (Document 3), Murray particularly lamented the tendency of black men to vent against black women frustrations borne of racism. In Document 4, Joyce Johnson, a young woman who was part of the nonconformist "Beat" generation, describes what it was like to obtain an illegal abortion in New York City in 1955. Document 5 is a letter from a black reader to *The Ladder,* America's first lesbian magazine, which began publication in 1956. Together, these documents point both to the varied social identities that women endorsed in the postwar decades and to the obstacles they encountered in realizing their goals.

1. Louisa Randall Church Explores the Duties of Parents as Architects of Peace, 1946

On that day in August 1945, when the first atomic bomb fell on Hiroshima, new concepts of civilized living, based on the obligations of world citizenship and unselfish service to mankind, were born. Out of the smoke and smoldering ruins arose a great cry for leadership equipped to guide the stricken people of the world along the hazardous course toward peace. On that day parenthood took on added responsibilities of deep and profound significance.

Today, months later, lacking sufficient and adequate leadership the nations of the earth flounder in a perilous state of distrust, suspicion, confusion and impotency. As one historian has said, "We stand at the very door of a golden age fumbling at the lock." How right he is.

Frightened scientists warn us of dire disaster—unspeakable catastrophe—the possible atomic murder of millions of peace-loving human beings. They tell us that bombs never again will come in ones and twos; they will come in hundreds, even thousands. More frightening still, they say there is no defense. Surely, in all history, the parents of the world were never so challenged.

However, there is a defense—an impregnable bulwark—which lies in meeting the world's desperate cry for leadership. Upon the shoulders of parents, everywhere, rests the tremendous responsibility of sending forth into the next generation men and women imbued with a high resolve to work together for everlasting peace.

There is no time to lose. We must gear our thoughts and actions for this new task as we did for winning the war. The noble instincts—sacrifice, heroism, generosity, unselfishness—which stirred us to action then must stir us now.

In every American home parents ought to be thinking and talking about these questions. What has caused the scarcity of qualified leaders? What are the requirements of worthy citizenship from which leaders can be expected to emerge? What changes must be made in our concepts of family living and parenthood if our children are to become wise, co-operative, courageous world citizens? How can parents

Louisa Randall Church, "Parents, Architects of Peace," *American* Home 36, no. 6 (November 1946): 18–19.

help to eradicate the underlying causes of war: poverty and despair, inequality of opportunity, hatred and greed? . . .

In order to develop the qualities of leadership necessary to insure peace—vision to see the needs of all humanity, willingness to work, sacrifice and co-operate for a common goal—parents must give their children not social security but personal security.

Personal security is attained only when the individual has achieved an inner harmony of spirit, self-confidence and a sense of mastery—in short—when he has achieved complete triumph over himself and his environment. Only then can he meet the exigencies of worthy citizenship in the world of tomorrow. Personal security cannot be bought for or taught to a child. It is a by-product of harmonious family living which is based on: **(1) Love and Affection.** Psychologists tell us our first duty is to surround a child, from the moment of birth, with a never-failing love, affection and the assurance of being wanted. . . . When we push a child aside as a nuisance, ignore his needs, allow ourselves to become bored with his care, or fail to accept him as a real person, is it strange that he becomes confused and troublesome? . . .

(2) Equal Rights. Parenthood is a partnership for the mutual welfare of the father and the mother, the children and the whole society and should be governed by the rules which apply to all professional partnerships. In the discipline of their children, in policies of home management or control of family finances neither father nor mother should reign supreme. There can be no harmony in a home where favoritism is shown, where the spirit of rivalry and competitive striving is encouraged or where equality of opportunity is denied. Since, more and more, women will be taking their rightful places in world affairs, girls should be provided with the same opportunities, intellectually, professionally, socially and economically as boys.

(3) Discipline. It is in the home that a child should develop his first sense of responsibility to himself and to others. From intelligent guidance in habit formation he gains self-reliance, self-control and self-direction. Such self-discipline cannot be achieved by parental tyranny which molds a child according to selfish ambitions and foolish pride. It cannot be achieved by pampering. . . .

(4) Freedom. Unless a child senses a growing inner freedom to think, act, and achieve according to his interests, his talents, his abilities and his ambitions, he cannot gain the sense of security which is his right. Parents who go through life, pruning shears in hand—clipping here, clipping there every spontaneous outburst of enthusiasm which fails to conform to their plans and desires for their children are building future robots.

(5) Enrichment. . . . A child's desire for self-expression and recognition is a basic personality need. Parents have no greater responsibility than to provide him with opportunities to develop hobbies which will open to him the world of arts, crafts and mechanical skills. Essential to his personal security, his ability to co-operate with others and to a high standard of social behavior are friendships and contacts with people from all walks of life. . . .

(6) Co-operation. Good behavior of the individual is basic to harmony in the group. Obedient, thoughtful, helpful, unselfish children are a reflection of the parent's ability to co-operate with them, and to win co-operation from them. . . . Nothing in parenthood is more important than . . . willingness to share in the dreams, ambitions and problems of their children—to share those rare, golden moments when a child bares his mind, heart and soul. At such moments parental guidance can go into action and do its best work in wise, constructive counselling. At such moments, listening with honest sincerity and understanding breeds in a child confidence, a sense of inner security and power. When he feels security in the home he will feel at home in his community, his nation and the world. . . . There is no place in today's world for the "getters"—those who seem, always, to be in trouble, who create tensions, who cause most of the problems of society. Leaders of a new stamp—the "givers" will be needed, not alone at the peace table, but in community activities, church life, education, public welfare services and youth groups.

(7) **Education.** . . . The time has come when potential parents should be trained for the serious business of marriage, family living, and parenthood. . . . One thing is certain: parents cannot create harmony in the home and personal security in their children if they, themselves, lack the assurance and confidence which comes from knowledge gained in advance of need. School officials, everywhere, and citizens, too, should give active support to the idea of training for parenthood. . . .

Success as a parent involves the expenditure not of money and material advantages, but of one's self; one's time, imagination, skill and effort; one's companionship and counsel; one's faith, patience and love. It involves a knowledge and an acceptance of the obligations of marriage; an understanding of the needs of children, and a willingness to co-operate with schools, churches and civic agencies for their welfare. When we build personal security not alone for our own child but for all children, everywhere, then we shall, indeed, be architects of peace!

2. Psychiatrist Marynia F. Farnham and Sociologist Ferdinand Lundberg Denounce Modern Woman as the "Lost Sex," 1947

The woman arriving at maturity today does so with certain fixed attitudes derived from her background and training. Her home life, very often, has been distorted. She has enjoyed an education identical with that of her brother. She expects to be allowed to select any kind of work for which she has inclination and training. She also, generally, expects to marry. At any rate, she usually intends to have "a go" at it. Some women expect to stop working when they marry; many others do not. She expects to find sexual gratification and believes in her inalienable right so to do. She is legally free to live and move as she chooses. She may seek divorce if her marriage fails to gratify her. She has access to contraceptive information so that, theoretically, she may control the size and spacing of her family. In very many instances, she owns and disposes of her own property. She has, it appears, her destiny entirely in her own hands.

All of this serves less to clarify and simplify her life than to complicate it with conflict piled on conflict. These conflicts are between her basic needs as a woman

Selected excerpts from *Modern Woman: The Lost Sex* by Ferdinand Lundberg and Marynia F. Farnham (New York: Harper and Brothers Publishers, 1947), 232–241. Copyright 1947 by Ferdinand Lundberg and Marynia F. Farnham. Copyright renewed. Reprinted by permission of HarperCollins Publishers, Inc.

and the destiny she has carved out for herself—conflicts between the head and the heart, if you will. . . .

Thus she finds herself squarely in the middle of the most serious kind of divided purpose. If she is to undertake occupation outside her home with any kind of success, it is almost certain in the present day to be time-consuming and energy-demanding. So it is also with the problems she faces in her home. Certainly the tasks of a woman in bearing and educating children as well as maintaining, as best she may, the inner integrity of her home are capable of demanding all her time and best attention. However, she cannot obtain from them, so attenuated are these tasks now, the same sort of community approval and ego-satisfaction that she can from seemingly more challenging occupations which take her outside the home. Inevitably the dilemma has led to one compromise after another which we see exemplified on every hand in the modern woman's adaptation—an uneasy patchwork. . . .

It is becoming unquestionably more and more common for the woman to attempt to combine both home and child care and an outside activity, which is either work or career. Increasing numbers train for professional careers. When these two spheres are combined it is inevitable that one or the other will become of secondary concern and, this being the case, it is certain that the home will take that position. This is true, if only for the practical reason that no one can find and hold remunerative employment where the job itself doesn't take precedence over all other concerns. All sorts of agencies and instrumentalities have therefore been established to make possible the playing of this dual role. These are all in the direction of substitutes for the attention of the mother in the home and they vary from ordinary, untrained domestic service through the more highly trained grades of such service, to the public and private agencies now designed for the care, supervision and emotional untanglement of the children. The day nursery and its more elegant counterpart, the nursery school, are outstanding as the major agencies which make it possible for women to relinquish the care of children still in their infancy.

All these services and facilities produce what appears on the surface to be a smoothly functioning arrangement and one that provides children with obviously highly trained, expert and efficient care as well as with superior training in early skills and techniques and in adaptation to social relations. This surface, however, covers a situation that is by no means so smoothly functioning nor so satisfying either to the child or the woman. She must of necessity be deeply in conflict and only partially satisfied in either direction. Her work develops aggressiveness, which is essentially a denial of her femininity. . . .

Work that entices women out of their homes and provides them with prestige only at the price of feminine relinquishment, involves a response to masculine strivings. The more importance outside work assumes, the more are the masculine components of the woman's nature enhanced and encouraged. In her home and in her relationship to her children, it is imperative that these strivings be at a minimum and that her femininity be available both for her own satisfaction and for the satisfaction of her children and husband. She is, therefore, in the dangerous position of having to live one part of her life on the masculine level, another on the feminine. It is hardly astonishing that few can do so with success. One of these tendencies must of necessity achieve dominance over the other. The plain fact is that increasingly we are observing the masculinization of women and with it enormously dangerous consequences to the home, the children (if any) dependent on it, and to the ability of the woman, as well as her husband, to obtain sexual gratification. . . .

The dominant direction of feminine training and development today . . . discourages just those traits necessary to the attainment of sexual pleasure: receptivity and passiveness, a willingness to accept dependence without fear or resentment, with a deep inwardness and readiness for the final goal of sexual life—impregnation. It doesn't admit of wishes to control or master, to rival or dominate. The woman who is to find true gratification must love and accept her own womanhood as she loves and accepts her husband's manhood. Women's rivalry with men today, and the need to "equal" their accomplishments, engenders all too often anger and resentfulness toward men. Men, challenged, frequently respond in kind. So it is that women envy and feel hostile to men for just the attributes which women themselves require for "success" in the world. The woman's unconscious wish herself to possess the organ upon which she must thus depend militates greatly against her ability to accept its vast power to satisfy her when proffered to her in love.

Many women can find no solution to their dilemma and are defeated in attempts at adaptation. These constitute the array of the sick, unhappy, neurotic, wholly or partly incapable of dealing with life. . . .

It is not only the masculine woman who has met with an unhappy fate in the present situation. There are still many women who succeed in achieving adult life with largely unimpaired feminine strivings, for which home, a husband's love and children are to them the entirely adequate answers. It is their misfortune that they must enter a society in which such attitudes are little appreciated and are attended by many concrete, external penalties. Such women cannot fail to be affected by finding that their traditional activities are held in low esteem and that the woman who voluntarily undertakes them is often deprecated by her more aggressive contemporaries. She may come to believe that her situation is difficult, entailing serious deprivations, as against the more glamorous and exciting life other women seemingly enjoy. She may be set away from the main stream of life, very much in a backwater and fearful lest she lose her ability and talents through disuse and lack of stimulation. She may become sorry for herself and somewhat angered by her situation, gradually developing feelings of discontent and pressure. As her children grow older and require less of her immediate attention, the feelings of loss increase.

. . . In this way she may easily and quickly develop attitudes of discontent and anger injurious to her life adjustment. She may begin to malfunction sexually, her libidinal depths shaken by her ego frustrations.

So it is that society today makes it difficult for a woman to avoid the path leading to discontent and frustration and resultant hostility and destructiveness. Such destructiveness is, unfortunately, not confined in its effects to the woman alone. It reaches into all her relationships and all her functions. As a wife she is not only often ungratified but ungratifying and has, as we have noted, a profoundly disturbing effect upon her husband. Not only does he find himself without the satisfactions of a home directed and cared for by a woman happy in providing affection and devotion, but he is often confronted by circumstances of even more serious import for his own emotional integrity. His wife may be his covert rival, striving to match him in every aspect of their joint undertaking. Instead of supporting and encouraging his manliness and wishes for domination and power, she may thus impose upon him feelings of insufficiency and weakness. Still worse is the effect upon his sexual satisfactions. Where the woman is unable to admit and accept dependence upon her husband as the source of gratification and must carry her rivalry even into the act of love, she will seriously damage his sexual capacity. To be unable to gratify in the sexual act is for a man an intensely humiliating experience; here it is that mastery and domination, the central capacity of the man's sexual nature, must meet acceptance or fail. So it is that by their own character disturbances these women succeed ultimately in depriving themselves of the devotion and power of their husbands and become the instruments of bringing about their own psychic catastrophe.

But no matter how great a woman's masculine strivings, her basic needs make themselves felt and she finds herself facing her fundamental role as wife and mother with a divided mind. Deprived of a rich and creative home in which to find self-expression, she tries desperately to find a compromise. On the one hand she must retain her sources of real instinctual gratification and on the other, find ways of satisfying her need for prestige and esteem. Thus she stands, Janus-faced, drawn in two directions at once, often incapable of ultimate choice and inevitably penalized whatever direction she chooses.

3. African American Pauli Murray Explains Why Negro Girls Stay Single, 1947

There exists in the United States a system of discrimination based upon sex which I call "Jane Crow" because it is so strikingly similar to "Jim Crow," or prejudice based upon race.

Women still occupy a subordinate position as citizens of the American community, even though they may represent a majority of the potential voting population. The rationalizations upon which this sex prejudice rests are often different from those supporting racial discrimination in label only.

I should like to cite two examples of this prejudice. Harvard University, for three centuries the "prestige" school of presidents, supreme court justices, ambassadors and financiers, still does not permit a woman student to darken the doors of its law school, although I am unaware of any special relation between legal acumen and sex identity. Recently, however, Harvard Law School did weaken to the degree that a Hunter College graduate, Soia Memchikoff, was appointed as a member of the law school faculty.

Secondly, I winced considerably the other day when, upon picking up a copy of Ebony Magazine, a Negro pictorial publication, and seeing a current "spread" on Negro lawyers, I saw the pictures of many personal friends and associates of mine but observed that Negro women lawyers were conspicuous by their absence. . . . I wondered what quirk of the editor's attitude had permitted him or her to ignore the contributions of women attorneys like Edith Alexander and Judge Jane Bolin, just to mention two of our outstanding lawyers who have won their spots unquestionably in the legal profession.

These two "case studies" suggest that despite their numerical size, women in the United States and perhaps throughout the world, with rare exceptions, are a minority

Pauli Murray, "Why Negro Girls Stay Single," *Negro Digest* (July 1947): 4–8.

group and suffer minority status. This minority status operates independently of race, religion or politics.

Every time I begin to bemoan the submerged status of the Negro woman among my white women friends, they hastily assure me that my problems are not unique and that they suffer just as much from "Jane Crow" as I do, particularly when it comes to advancement in their professional endeavors.

Within this framework of "male supremacy" as well as "white supremacy" the Negro woman finds herself at the bottom of the economic and social scale.

She is obviously in a state of revolt. This revolt proceeds in part from the consciousness on the part of the Negro woman that she has been compelled to act as breadwinner and cementer of family relationships in the Negro community since its inception. Historically, few Negro women have belonged to the leisure class, and what few social privileges they now enjoy have very often come "the hard way."

The rebellion against racial and sexual status is felt most keenly among Negro college-trained and professional women. With reference to my own generation, people now in their thirties, it is a matter of history that more Negro women proportionately have availed themselves of higher education than Negro men.

The complete hopelessness and dejection which led Negro boys of my age group to abandon their studies in droves before they completed a high school education or a trade, and to flounder about for years without vocational direction, is one of the tragic sources of frustration to the Negro woman of marriageable age. If professionally trained, she finds a shortage of her educational peers among men in Negro circles. She very often cannot find a mate with whom she can share all the richness of her life in addition to its functional aspects.

Having stayed in school far beyond the period of the average Negro boy, she now emerges with certain educational skills and often has a potential earning power far beyond the range of the majority of available single males—a social handicap if she wants marriage. Men usually shy away from women more highly trained than they are when the question of marriage is involved. It is too great a threat to their security.

Since the chances of the Negro trained woman for economic security are necessarily precarious because of the general underprivileged economic status of the Negro minority, in her relationship to the Negro male she can hope for little beyond emotional security.

But here again she is defeated. Emotional security arises from mature relationships among free and uninhibited individuals. The American Negro male is not prepared to offer emotional security because he has rarely, if ever, known it himself. His own emotional balance is that of a blindfolded tightrope walker before a jeering crowd. His submerged status in American life places unnatural stresses and strains upon his already inadequate equipment inherited from an immature democracy.

Our general mis-education of the sexes and our outmoded social tabus have helped to form rigid moulds into which the sexes are poured and which determine in advance the role men and women are to play in community life. Men are expected to act as if they are the lords of creation, the breadwinners and the warriors of our time and of all time. They play the role with varying degrees of ham-acting and success. . . .

The discerning eye soon discovers that many Negro men are well marked products of this sex mis-education. Charming individual exceptions appear here and there, but they are few. The Negro man who attempts to play the role of the dominant sex in a setting where the Negro woman has partially emancipated herself by dint of hard labor is face to face with emotional disaster. Particularly is this true in the case of the trained Negro woman who has become perhaps the most aggressive of the human species.

This impending emotional disaster is born of the contradictions in the life of the Negro male. He is the victim of constant frustration in his role as a male because socially he is subordinate to the white woman although he is trained to act as a member of the dominant sex. He is required to fit his human emotions into a racially determined pattern which may have nothing to do with his desires.

There is no earthly reason why a Negro man should not admire in a clean and healthy sort of way physical beauty, whether the bearer of the beauty be a Nordic Blonde or a West Indian Bronze. There is no reason why the Negro man today should find the white woman less attractive than did his white slave-owning ancestor find the African slavewoman desirable. Yet what sister of a Negro boy or man today does not know the family terror at the thought that some unguarded and unconscious look or gesture, though completely spontaneous and meaningless, may lead straight to ostracism, the faggot or the lynchman's noose!

The frustrations implicit in being a Negro are not only catastrophic to the Negro male's emotions, but lead him often to vent his resentments upon the Negro woman who may become his sex partner. The situation may be described in the homely saying, "Pa beats Ma, Ma beats me, and I beat hell out of the cat." Here, the Negro woman is without doubt "the cat."

On top of these difficulties, census figures suggest an unbalance between the sexes within racial groupings. Negro females far outnumber Negro males.

If the emotional security of the Negro woman depends upon proper mating and marriage, she is confronted with the inexorable logic of numbers which demands that she find a mate elsewhere than among Negro males, unless the American society which enforces bi-racialism also permits legal racial polygamy. From a biological and functional point of view, the logical solution to a shortage of available Negro males would be that Negro women find their mates in other ethnic groups.

This alternative faces the practical difficulty that there is a shortage of available males of marriageable age today in all groups. Secondly, to consciously seek interracial marriage would be denounced as sheer "treason" in the eyes of the "no social equality" advocates throughout the country. Yet, what other alternatives are open?

On the other hand, our racial stockades being what they are, Negro men who are in the market for Negro wives are not required to face honest and above-board competition from white members of their sex. Few white men are either mature or courageous enough to lift their emotional attractions for Negro women outside of the red light districts within the ghetto or the sub-rosa arrangements outside the ghetto into the clean light of healthy sex relationships looking toward legal marriage.

The Negro male, therefore, not only has no outside stimulus which operates to force him to improve his relationships with the Negro woman, but more damning, he stores up huge resentments against his rival, the white male who "slinks across the line" after dark, and very often turns this resentment upon himself and the Negro woman.

All of this contributes to a Jungle of human relationships, aggravates among Negroes the alienation of the sexes, intensifies homosexuality and often results in a rising incidence of crimes of passion, broken homes and divorces.

The problem of the Negro male cannot be solved within the Negro group unless it is being resolved simultaneously in the larger society. Readers of Negro periodicals will recall that Miss Almena Davis, editor of the Los Angeles Tribune, attempted more than a year ago to articulate the resentment of the Negro woman against the exposed position in which she finds herself by directing a critical editorial toward the sex habits of the Negro male. She won the Willkie Award in Journalism for her pains but incurred the wrath of almost every Negro male journalist in the country. Ann Petry added another fragment to the growing literature of revolt "from way down under," with her recent article, "What's Wrong With Negro Men," in NEGRO DIGEST. I have now jumped into the arena with both feet. What I think Almena Davis, Ann Petry and Pauli Murray are trying to say from their varied approaches is this:

We desire that the Negro male accept the Negro female as his equal and treat her accordingly and that he cease his ruthless aggression upon her and his emotional exploitation of her made possible by her admittedly inferior position as a social human being in the United States. That he strive for emotional maturity himself and see the Negro woman as a personality, an individual with infinite potentialities, and that in turn he require from the Negro woman an equal maturity and acceptance of responsibility in human relationships. That he maintain the dignity and respect for human personality with relation to the Negro woman in the sanctity of the marital chamber which he is expected to show in the law office or other professional set-up.

Despite the numerous limitations forced upon Negro men and women by our society, nevertheless certain improvements between the sexes are desirable and can be achieved.

4. Nonconformist Joyce Johnson Recounts Her Experience in Obtaining an Illegal Abortion in New York City, 1955

In June I didn't get my period. First it was a little late, and then a lot, but I still thought it would come anyway, and I waited, thinking I felt it sometimes. But finally it didn't come. A tangible, unbelievable fact, like sealed doom.

I was going to have a baby. But it was impossible for me to have a baby. . . .

The father was a child of my own age—a wrecked boy I'd known from Columbia who already had a drinking problem and lived, doing nothing, with his parents in Connecticut. I didn't love this boy. Sometimes you went to bed with people almost by mistake, at the end of late, shapeless nights when you'd stayed up so long it almost didn't matter—the thing was, not to go home. Such nights lacked premeditation, so you couldn't be very careful; you counted on a stranger's carefulness. The boy promised to pull out before the danger—but he didn't. And although I could have reminded him of his promise in time, I didn't do that either, remembering too late it was the middle of the month in a bedroom on East Ninety-sixth Street that smelled of smoke and soiled clothing, with leftover voices from that night's party outside the closed door.

I'd gotten a therapist by then—a $7.50 man, a rejected boyfriend of the woman whose apartment I was living in. I told him my problem. "I see," he said, rubbing his large chin, staring out over Central Park West.

There was a box of Kleenex on the small Danish-modern table near my head. He had pointedly placed boxes of tissues in several locations in his office. But I never cried.

I explained to this therapist why I didn't see how I could become a mother. Aside from being twenty years old, I lived on fifty dollars a week and had cut myself off from my family. I said I would rather die. And then I asked him what Elise had told me to: "Could you get me a therapeutic abortion?" (I'd never heard the term before she explained what it meant.)

"Oh, I wouldn't even try," he said.

I hadn't thought he wouldn't try.

Life was considered sacred. But independence could be punishable by death. The punishment for sex was, appropriately, sexual.

There were women in those days who kept slips of paper, like talismans to ward off disaster, on which were written the names of doctors who would perform illegal abortions. Neither Elise nor I knew any of these women. You had to ask around. You asked friends and they asked friends, and the ripples of asking people widened until some person whose face you might never see gave over the secret information that could save you. This could take time, and you only had two months, they said, and you'd lost one month anyway, through not being sure.

The therapist called my roommate, got from her the name of the boy who had made me pregnant. He called the boy and threatened to disclose the whole matter to his parents unless the boy came up with the money for an illegal abortion. The boy called me, drunk and wild with fear. I hadn't expected anything of this boy except one thing—that when I had an abortion he'd go there with me; there had to be someone with you, I felt, that you knew. But as for blaming this boy—I didn't. I knew I had somehow let this happen to me. There had been a moment in that bedroom on Ninety-sixth Street, a moment of blank suspension, of not caring whether I lived or died. It seemed important to continue to see this moment very clearly. I knew the boy wouldn't come with me now.

I went to see the therapist one last time to tell him he had done something terribly wrong.

"Yes," he admitted, looking sheepish. "I've probably made a mistake."

I said, "I'm never coming back. I owe you thirty-seven fifty. Try and get it."

Someone finally came up with a person who knew a certain doctor in Canarsie. If you called this person at the advertising agency where he worked, he wouldn't give you the doctor's name—he'd ask you if you wanted to have a drink with him in the Rainbow Room, and over martinis he might agree to escort you out to see the doctor. This person wasn't a great humanitarian; he was a young man who had a weird hobby—taking girls to get abortions. He'd ask you if you wanted to recuperate afterward at his house on Fire Island. You were advised to say no.

Blind dates were a popular social form of the fifties. As I sat in the cocktail lounge of the Rainbow Room, staring through the glass doors at crew-cutted young men in seersucker suits who came off the elevator lacking the red bow tie I'd been told to watch out for, I realized that despite the moment in the bedroom, I probably didn't want to die, since I seemed to be going to an enormous amount of effort to remain living. If it happened that I died after all, it would be an accident.

He turned up a half-hour late in his blue and white stripes. "Why, you're pretty," he said, pleased. He told me he liked blondes. He made a phone call after we had our drinks, and came back to the table to say the doctor would see us that night. "I hope you don't have anything lined up," he said.

He offered me sticks of Wrigley spearmint chewing gum on the BMT to Canarsie. People in jokes sometimes came from there, but I'd never been to that part of Brooklyn in my life.

Canarsie was rows of small brick houses with cement stoops and yards filled with wash and plaster saints. Boys were playing stickball in the dusk. You could disappear into Canarsie.

The doctor seemed angry that we had come, but he led us into his house after we rang the bell, and switched on a light in his waiting room. He was fat, with a lot of wiry grey hair on his forearms; a white shirt wet and rumpled with perspiration stretched over his belly. The room looked like a room in which only the very poor would ever wait. There were diplomas on the walls, framed behind dusty glass; I tried to read the Latin. He glared at me and said he wanted me to know he did tonsillectomies. To do "the other"—he didn't say *abortions*—disgusted him. I made efforts to nod politely.

My escort spoke up and said, "How about next week?"

"All right. Wednesday."

I felt panic at the thought of Wednesday. What if my mother called the office and found out I was sick, and came running over to the apartment? "No," I said, "Friday. It has to be Friday."

"Friday will cost you extra," the doctor said. . . .

I'd managed to borrow the five hundred dollars from a friend in her late twenties, who'd borrowed it from a wealthy married man who was her lover. With the cash in a sealed envelope in my purse. I stood for an hour that Friday morning in front of a cigar store on Fourteenth Street, waiting for the young advertising executive. I got awfully scared that he wouldn't come. Could I find the doctor's house myself in those rows of nearly identical houses?

There was a haze over Fourteenth Street that made even the heat seem grey. I stared across the street at Klein's Department Store, where my mother had taken me shopping for bargains, and imagined myself dying a few hours later with the sign KLEIN'S the last thing that flashed through my consciousness.

But finally the young man did materialize out of a cab. "Sorry to have kept you waiting." He'd brought some back issues of *The New Yorker,* and planned to catch up on his reading during the operation.

Upstairs in Canarsie, the doctor who did tonsillectomies had a room where he only did abortions. A freshly painted room where every surface was covered with white towels. He himself put on a mask and a white surgeon's gown. It was as if all that white was the color of his fear.

"Leave on the shoes!" he barked as I climbed up on his table almost fully clothed. Was I expected to make a run for it if the police rang his doorbell in the middle of the operation? He yelled at me to do this and do that, and it sent him into a rage that my legs were shaking, so how could he do what he had to do? But if I didn't want him to do it, that was all right with him. I said I wanted him to do it. I was crying. But he wouldn't take the money until after he'd given me the local anesthetic. He gave me one minute to change my mind before he handed me my purse.

The whole thing took two hours, but it seemed much longer through the pain. I had the impression that this doctor in all his fear was being extremely careful, that I was even lucky to have found him. He gave me pills when it was over, and told me I could call him only if anything went wrong. "But don't ever let me catch you back here again, young lady!"

I staggered down the cement steps of his house with my life. It was noon in Canarsie, an ordinary day in July. My escort was saying he thought it would be hard to find a cab, we should walk in the direction of the subway. On a street full of shops, I leaned against the window of a supermarket until he flagged one down. Color seemed to have come back into the world. Housewives passed in floral nylon dresses; diamonds of sunlight glinted off the windshields of cars.

On the cab ride across the Manhattan Bridge, the young man from the ad agency placed his hand on my shoulder. "I have this house out on Fire Island," he began. "I thought that this weekend—"

"No thanks," I said. "I'll be okay in the city."

He removed his hand, and asked if I'd drop him off at his office—"unless you mind going home alone."

I said I'd get there by myself.

5. A Letter to the Editor of *The Ladder* from an African American Lesbian, 1957

Please find enclosed a money order for $2.00. I should like to receive as many of your back issues as that amount will cover. In the event $2.00 is in excess of the cost of six issues—well, fine. Those few cents may stand as a mere downpayment toward sizeable (for me, that is) donations I know already that I shall be sending to you.

I hope you are somewhat interested in off-the-top-of-the-head reactions from across the country because I would like to offer a few by way of the following:

(1) I'm glad as heck that you exist. You are obviously serious people and I feel that women, without wishing to foster any strict *separatist* notions, homo or hetero, indeed have a need for their own publications and organizations. Our problems, our experiences as women are profoundly unique as compared to the other half of the human race. Women, like other oppressed groups of one kind or another, have particularly had to pay a price for the intellectual impoverishment that the second class status imposed on us for centuries created and sustained. Thus, I feel that THE LADDER is a fine, elementary step in a rewarding direction.

L. H. N., *The Ladder* 1, no. 8 (May 1957): 26.

(2) Rightly or wrongly (in view of some of the thought provoking discussions I have seen elsewhere in a homosexual publication) I could not help but be encouraged and relieved by one of the almost subsidiary points under Point I of your declaration of purpose, "(to advocate) a mode of behaviour and dress acceptable to society." As one raised in a cultural experience (I am a Negro) where those within were and are forever lecturing to their fellows about how to appear acceptable to the dominant social group, I know something about the shallowness of such a view as an end in itself.

The most splendid argument is simple and to the point, Ralph Bunche, with all his clean fingernails, degrees, and, of course, undeniable service to the human race, could still be insulted, denied a hotel room or meal in many parts of our country. (Not to mention the possibility of being lynched on a lonely Georgia road for perhaps having demanded a glass of water in the wrong place.)

What ought to be clear is that one is oppressed or discriminated against because one is different, not "wrong" or "bad" somehow. This is perhaps the bitterest of the entire pill. HOWEVER, as a matter of facility, of expediency, one has to take a critical view of revolutionary attitudes which in spite of the BASIC truth I have mentioned above, may tend to aggravate the problems of a group.

I have long since passed that period when I felt personal discomfort at the sight of an ill-dressed or illiterate Negro. Social awareness has taught me where to lay the blame. Someday, I expect, the "discreet" Lesbian will not turn her head on the streets at the sight of the "butch" strolling hand in hand with her friend in their trousers and definitive haircuts. But for the moment, it still disturbs. It creates an impossible area for discussion with one's most enlightened (to use a hopeful term) heterosexual friends. Thus, I agree with the inclusion of that point in your declaration to the degree of wanting to comment on it.

(3) I am impressed by the general tone of your articles. The most serious fault being at this juncture that there simply is too little.

(4) Would it be presumptuous or far-fetched to suggest that you try for some overseas communications? One hears so much of publications and organizations devoted to homosexuality and homosexuals in Europe; but as far as I can gather these seem to lean heavily toward male questions and interests.

Just a little afterthought: considering Mattachine; Bilitis, ONE; all seem to be cropping up on the West Coast rather than here where a vigorous and active gay set almost bump one another off the streets—what is it in the air out there? Pioneers still? Or a tougher circumstance which inspires battle? Would like to hear speculation, light-hearted or otherwise.

L. H. N.
New York, N.Y.

◈ *E S S A Y S*

Joanne Meyerowitz of Indiana University contends that America's postwar popular media "delivered multiple messages" to women, simultaneously glorifying and subverting domesticity. Scholar Rickie Solinger, in an examination of the politics of abortion in America from 1950 to 1970, argues that postwar turmoil among medical doctors over the issue of abortion produced hospital policies that curtailed women's already limited ability to end unwanted pregnancies safely and legally. These essays offer a number of ways of looking at the construction of female identity in the postwar era.

Competing Images of Women in Postwar Mass Culture

JOANNE MEYEROWITZ

In 1963 Betty Friedan published *The Feminine Mystique,* an instant best seller. Friedan argued, often brilliantly, that American women, especially suburban women, suffered from deep discontent. In the postwar era, she wrote, journalists, educators, advertisers, and social scientists had pulled women into the home with an ideological stranglehold, the "feminine mystique." This repressive "image" held that women could "find fulfillment only in sexual passivity, male domination, and nurturing maternal love." It denied "women careers or any commitment outside the home" and "narrowed woman's world down to the home, cut her role back to housewife." In Friedan's formulation, the writers and editors of mass-circulation magazines, especially women's magazines, were the "Frankensteins" who had created this "feminine monster." In her defense of women, Friedan did not choose a typical liberal feminist language of rights, equality, or even justice. Influenced by the new human potential psychology, she argued instead that full-time domesticity stunted women and denied their "basic human need to grow." For Friedan, women and men found personal identity and fulfillment through individual achievement, most notably through careers. Without such growth, she claimed, women would remain unfulfilled and unhappy, and children would suffer at the hands of neurotic mothers.

The Feminine Mystique had an indisputable impact. Hundreds of women have testified that the book changed their lives, and historical accounts often credit it with launching the recent feminist movement. But the book has also had other kinds of historical impact. For a journalistic exposé, Friedan's work has had a surprisingly strong influence on historiography. In fact, since Friedan published *The Feminine Mystique,* historians of American women have adopted wholesale her version of the postwar ideology. While many historians question Friedan's homogenized account of women's actual experience, virtually all accept her version of the dominant ideology, the conservative promotion of domesticity.

According to this now-standard historical account, postwar authors urged women to return to the home while only a handful of social scientists, trade unionists, and feminists protested. As one recent rendition states: "In the wake of World War II . . . the short-lived affirmation of women's independence gave way to a pervasive endorsement of female subordination and domesticity." Much of this secondary literature relies on a handful of conservative postwar writings, the same writings cited liberally by Friedan. In particular, the work of Dr. Marynia F. Farnham, a viciously antifeminist psychiatrist, and her sidekick, sociologist Ferdinand Lundberg, is invoked repeatedly as typical of the postwar era. In this standard account, the domestic ideology prevailed until such feminists as Friedan triumphed in the 1960s.

When I first began research on the postwar era, I accepted this version of history. But as I investigated the public culture, I encountered what I then considered exceptional evidence—books, articles, and films that contradicted the domestic

Joanne Meyerowitz, "Beyond the Feminine Mystique: A Reassessment of Postwar Mass Culture, 1946–1958," *Journal of American History* 79, no. 4 (March 1993): 1455–1482. Reprinted by permission of the Organization of American Historians.

ideology. I decided to conduct a more systematic investigation. This essay reexamines the middle-class popular discourse on women by surveying mass-circulation monthly magazines of the postwar era (1946–1958). The systematic sample includes nonfiction articles on women in "middlebrow" magazines (*Reader's Digest* and *Coronet*), "highbrow" magazines (*Harper's* and *Atlantic Monthly*), magazines aimed at African Americans (*Ebony* and *Negro Digest*), and those aimed at women (*Ladies' Home Journal* and *Woman's Home Companion*). The sample includes 489 nonfiction articles, ranging from Hollywood gossip to serious considerations of gender. In 1955 these magazines had a combined circulation of over 22 million. Taken together, the magazines reached readers from all classes, races, and genders, but the articles seem to represent the work of middle-class journalists, and articles written by women seem to outnumber ones by men.

My goal in constructing this sample was not to replicate Friedan's magazine research, which focused primarily on short story fiction in four women's magazines. Rather my goal was to test generalizations about postwar mass culture (that is, commodified forms of popular culture) by surveying another side of it. To this end, I chose nonfiction articles in a larger sample of popular magazines. Some of the magazines of smaller circulation, such as *Harper's* and *Negro Digest,* were perhaps outside the "mainstream." But including them in the sample enabled me to incorporate more of the diversity in American society, to investigate the contours of a broader bourgeois culture and some variations within it. Since my conclusions rest on a sample of nonfiction articles in eight popular magazines, they can provide only a tentative portrait of postwar culture. Future studies based on different magazines or on fiction, advertisements, films, television, or radio will no doubt suggest additional layers of complexity in mass culture and different readings of it.

. . . For Betty Friedan and for some historians, popular magazines represented a repressive force, imposing damaging images on vulnerable American women. Many historians today adopt a different approach in which mass culture is neither monolithic nor unrelentingly repressive. In this view, mass culture is rife with contradictions, ambivalence, and competing voices. We no longer assume that any text has a single, fixed meaning for all readers, and we sometimes find within the mass media subversive, as well as repressive, potential.

With a somewhat different sample and a somewhat different interpretive approach, I come to different conclusions about postwar mass culture than did Friedan and her followers. Friedan's widely accepted version of the "feminine mystique," I suggest, is only one piece of the postwar cultural puzzle. The popular literature I sampled did not simply glorify domesticity or demand that women return to or stay at home. All of the magazines sampled advocated both the domestic and the nondomestic, sometimes in the same sentence. In this literature, domestic ideals coexisted in ongoing tension with an ethos of individual achievement that celebrated nondomestic activity, individual striving, public service, and public success. . . .

In popular magazines, the theme of individual achievement rang most clearly in the numerous articles on individual women. These articles appeared with frequency throughout the postwar era: they comprised over 60 percent, or 300, of the 489 nonfiction articles sampled. These articles usually recounted a story of a woman's life or a particularly telling episode in her life. In formulaic accounts, they often constructed what one such article labeled "this Horatio Alger success story—feminine version." Of these articles, 33 percent spotlighted women with unusual talents, jobs, or careers, and another 29 percent focused on prominent entertainers. Typically they related a rise to public success punctuated by a lucky break, a dramatic come back, a selfless sacrifice, or a persistent struggle to overcome adversity. Such stories appeared in all of the magazines sampled, but they appeared most frequently in the African-American magazines, *Ebony* and *Negro Digest,* and the white "middlebrow" magazines, *Coronet* and *Reader's Digest.* Journalists reworked the formula for different readers: In *Negro Digest,* for example, articles returned repeatedly to black performers who defied racism; in *Reader's Digest* they more often addressed white leaders in community service. In general, though, the articles suggested that the noteworthy woman rose above and beyond ordinary domesticity. Or, as one story stated, "This is the real-life fairy tale of a girl who hurtled from drab obscurity to sudden, startling fame."

At the heart of many such articles lay a bifocal vision of women both as feminine and domestic and as public achievers. In one article, "The Lady Who Licked Crime in Portland," the author, Richard L. Neuberger, juxtaposed domestic stereotypes and newsworthy nondomestic achievement. The woman in question, Dorothy McCullough Lee, was, the article stated, an "ethereally pale housewife" who tipped "the scales at 110 pounds." But more to the point, she was also the mayor of Portland, Oregon, who had defeated, single-handedly it seems, the heavyweights of organized crime. Before winning the mayoral election in 1948, this housewife had opened a law firm and served in the state legislature, both House and Senate, and as Portland's commissioner of public utilities. Despite her "frail, willowy" appearance, the fearless mayor had withstood ridicule, recall petitions, and threatening mail in her "relentless drive" against gambling and prostitution. She was, the article related without further critique, a "violent feminist" who had "intense concern with the status of women." And, according to all, she was "headed for national distinction." The article concluded with an admiring quotation describing Mayor Lee's fancy hats as the plumes of a crusading knight in armor. Here the feminine imagery blended with a metaphor of masculine public service. . . .

While feminine stereotypes sometimes provided convenient foils that enhanced by contrast a woman's atypical public accomplishment, they also served as conservative reminders that all women, even publicly successful women, were to maintain traditional gender distinctions. In their opening paragraphs, numerous authors described their successful subjects as pretty, motherly, shapely, happily married, petite, charming, or soft voiced. This emphasis on femininity and domesticity (and the two were often conflated) seems to have cloaked a submerged fear of lesbian, mannish, or man-hating women. This fear surfaced in an unusual article on athlete Babe Didrikson Zaharias. In her early years, the article stated, the Babe's "boyish bob and freakish clothes . . . [her] dislike of femininity" had led observers to dismiss her as an "Amazon." But after her marriage, she "became a woman," a transformation signaled, according to the approving author, by lipstick, polished nails, and "loose, flowing" hair as well as by an interest in the domestic arts of cooking, sewing, and entertaining. In this article, as in others, allusions to femininity and domesticity probably helped legitimate women's public achievements. Authors attempted to reassure readers that conventional gender distinctions and heterosexuality remained intact even as women competed successfully in work, politics, or sports. . . .

Nonetheless, the emphasis on the domestic and feminine should not be over-stated; these articles on women's achievement did not serve solely or even primarily as lessons in traditional gender roles. The theme of nondomestic success was no hidden subtext in these stories. In most articles, the rise to public achievement was the first, and sometimes the only, narrative concern. When addressing both the domestic and the nondomestic, these articles placed public success at center stage: they tended to glorify frenetic activity, with domesticity at best a sideshow in a woman's three-ring circus. . . .

Marriage and domesticity were not prerequisites for star status in magazine stories. Over one-third of the articles on individual women featured unmarried women, divorced women, or women of unmentioned marital status. The African-American magazines seemed least concerned with marital status, but all of the maga-zines included articles that did not conjoin public success with connubial harmony. While a few such articles advocated marriage, others discounted it directly. Still other articles related the public achievements of divorced women, with consistent sympathy for the women involved. . . .

Magazines articles, of course, do not reveal the responses of readers. Formulaic stories of success do not seem to have provoked controversy: those magazines that published readers' responses rarely included letters regarding these stories. Some supplementary evidence, however, suggests that the language used in success stories also appeared in the language of at least some readers. The *Woman's Home Compan-ion* conducted opinion polls in 1947 and 1949 in which readers named the women they most admired. In both years the top four women were Eleanor Roosevelt, Helen Keller, Sister Elizabeth Kenny (who worked with polio victims), and Clare Boothe Luce (author and congresswoman), all distinctly nondomestic women. Why did readers select these particular women? They seemed to offer the same answers as the success stories: "courage, spirit, and conviction," "devotion to the public good," and "success in overcoming obstacles." While a feminine version of selfless sacrifice seems to have won kudos, individual striving and public service superseded devotion to home and family.

On the one hand, one might see these success stories as pernicious. They applied to women a traditionally male, middle-class discourse of individual achievement that glorified a version of success, honor, and fulfillment that was difficult enough for middle-class white men, highly unlikely for able-bodied women of any class and race, and nearly impossible for the ill, disabled, and disfigured. As fantasies of unlikely success, they offered false promises that hard work brought women public reward. They probably gave women readers vicarious pleasure or compensatory esteem, but they provided no real alternatives to most women's workaday lives. They usually downplayed the obstacles that women faced in the public arena, and they implicitly dismissed the need for collective protest. Further, they did not overtly challenge traditional gender roles. With frequent references to domesticity and femi-ninity, narrowly defined, they reinforced rigid definitions of appropriate female be-havior and sexual expression, and they neglected the conflicts between domestic and nondomestic demands that many women undoubtedly encountered.

On the other hand, these articles subverted the notion that women belonged at home. They presented a wide variety of options open to women and praised the women who had chosen to assert themselves as public figures. They helped readers, male and female, envision women in positions of public achievement. They tried openly to inspire women to pursue unusual goals, domestic or not, and they sometimes suggested that public service brought more obvious rewards than devotion to family. By applauding the public possibilities open to women, including married women, they may have validated some readers' nondomestic behavior and sharpened some readers' discontent with the constraints they experienced in their domestic lives. At least one contemporary observer noticed this subversive side to stories of individual success. Dr. Marynia Farnham, the antifeminist, railed not only against the "propaganda of the feminists'" but also against "stories about famous career women," which, she claimed, undermined the prestige of motherhood. . . .

The postwar popular discourse on women, then, did not simply exhort women to stay at home. Its complexity is also seen in . . . articles that addressed questions of gender directly. The topics of those articles ranged from women in India to premenstrual tension, but most fell into four broad categories: women's paid work, women's political activism, marriage and domesticity, and glamour and sexuality. . . .

On the issue of paid employment, there was rough consensus. Despite concerns for the postwar economy, journalists in this sample consistently defended wage work for women. Articles insisted that women, including married women, worked for wages because they needed money. . . . Articles praised women workers in specific occupations, from secretaries to doctors. These articles related exciting, stimulating, or rewarding job possibilities or the "practically unlimited" opportunities allegedly available to women. Like the success stories, these articles sometimes encouraged individual striving. "Advancement," one such article claimed, "will be limited only by [a woman's] intelligence, application, and education." The African-American magazines, *Ebony* and *Negro Digest,* alert to racism, showed more explicit awareness of institutional barriers to individual effort and sometimes noted discrimination based not only on race but also on gender. One article, for example, not only praised black women doctors but also denounced the "stubborn male prejudice" faced by "petticoat medics." In general, though, the articles on specific occupations did not attack sexism or the sexual division of labor directly; they simply encouraged women to pursue white-collar jobs in business and the professions.

Beneath the consensus, though, a quiet debate exposed the tensions between the ideals of nondomestic achievement and of domestic duty. Echoing earlier debates of the 1920s, some authors advised women to subordinate careers to home and motherhood while others invited women to pursue public success. The question of careers was rarely discussed at any length, and the relative silence itself underscores how postwar popular magazines often avoided contended issues. But throwaway lines in various articles sometimes landed on one side of the debate or the other. In a single article in *Ebony,* for example, one unmarried career woman warned readers, "Don't sacrifice marriage for career," while another stated, "I like my life just as it is." . . .

The postwar popular magazines were more unequivocally positive on increased participation of women in politics. The *Ladies' Home Journal,* not known for its feminist sympathies, led the way with numerous articles that supported women as political and community leaders. In 1947, lawyer and longtime activist Margaret Hickey, former president of the National Federation of Business and Professional Women's Clubs, launched the *Journal*'s monthly "Public Affairs Department," which encouraged women's participation in mainstream politics and reform. In one article, Hickey stated bluntly, "Make politics your business. Voting, office holding, raising your voice for new and better laws are just as important to your home and your family as the evening meal or spring house cleaning." Like earlier Progressive reformers, Hickey sometimes justified nondomestic political action by its benefits to home and family, but her overall message was clear: women should participate outside the home, and not just by voting. . . .

Reports on women politicians stressed the series' recurring motif, "They Do It . . . You Can Too." This article presented women politicians as exemplars. With direct appeals to housewives, it praised women who ran for office, even mothers of "babies or small children" who could "find time and ways to campaign and to win elections." It presented political activism not only as a public service but also as a source of personal fulfillment. For women who held political office, it claimed, "there is great pride of accomplishment and the satisfaction of 'doing a job.'" . . .

Historians sometimes contend that the Cold War mentality encouraged domesticity, that it envisioned family life and especially mothers as buffers against the alleged Communist threat. But Cold War rhetoric had other possible meanings for women. In the *Ladies' Home Journal,* authors often used the Cold War to promote women's political participation. One such approach contrasted "free society" of the United States with Soviet oppression, including oppression of women. . . . Other articles stressed that Soviet citizens, male and female, did not participate in a democratic process. American women could prove the strength of democracy by avoiding "citizen apathy," by "giving the world a lively demonstration of how a free society can serve its citizens," by making "free government work well as an example for the undecided and unsatisfied millions elsewhere in the world." . . .

The role of the housewife and mother was problematic in the postwar popular discourse. On the one hand, all of the magazines assumed that women wanted to marry, that women found being wives and mothers rewarding, and that women would and should be the primary parents and housekeepers. In the midst of the baby boom, some articles glorified the housewife, sometimes in conscious attempts to bolster her self-esteem. On the other hand, throughout the postwar era, numerous articles portrayed domesticity itself as exhausting and isolating, and frustrated mothers as overdoing and smothering. Such articles hardly glorified domesticity. They provided their postwar readers with ample references to housewife's discontent. . . .

In the postwar magazines, marriage also presented problems. . . . An article in *Ebony* stated, "Most women would rather be married than single but there are many who would rather remain single than be tied to the wrong man." The magazines gave readers contrasting advice on how to find a good husband. One article told women, "Don't fear being aggressive!," while another considered "aggressive traits" as "handicaps . . . in attracting a husband." Within marriage as well, journalists seemed to anticipate constant problems, including immaturity, incompatibility, and infidelity. They saw divorce as a difficult last resort and often advised both husbands and wives to communicate and adjust.

. . . Postwar authors did not, as Friedan's *Feminine Mystique* would have it, side automatically with "sexual passivity, male domination, and nurturing maternal love." They portrayed the ideal marriage as an equal partnership, with each partner intermingling traditional masculine and feminine roles. One article insisted: "The healthy, emotionally well-balanced male . . . isn't alarmed by the fact that women are human, too, and have an aggressive as well as a passive side. . . . He takes women seriously as individuals." This article and others condemned men who assumed an attitude of superiority. . . . Yet, to many it seemed that "individualism" could go too far and upset modern marriage. While husbands might do more housework and wives might pursue nondomestic activities, men remained the primary breadwinners and women the keepers of the home. . . .

The postwar magazines seemed least willing to entertain alternatives in the area of sexuality. As Friedan argued, popular magazines emphasized glamour and allure, at least for young women, and as Elaine Tyler May has elaborated, they tried to domesticate sexual intercourse by containing it within marriage. Magazines presented carefully framed articles with explicit directives about appropriate behavior. Young women were to make themselves attractive to men, and married women were to engage in mutually pleasing sexual intercourse with their mates. Articles presented "normal" sex through voyeuristic discussion of sexual problems, such as pregnancy before marriage and frigidity after. Other forms of sexual expression were rarely broached, although one article in *Ebony* did condemn "lesbians and nymphomaniacs" in the Women's Army Corps.

While all of the magazines endorsed a manicured version of heterosexual appeal, the African-American magazines displayed it most heartily. This may have reflected African-American vernacular traditions, such as the blues, that rejected white middle-class injunctions against public sexual expression. But it also reflected an editorial decision to construct glamour and beauty as political issues in the fight against racism. Articles admired black women's sex appeal in a self-conscious defiance of racist white standards of beauty. In this context what some feminists today might read as sexual "objectification" presented itself as racial advancement, according black womanhood equal treatment with white. Thus, *Ebony,* which in most respects resembled a white family magazine like *Life,* also included some of the mildly risqué cheesecake seen in white men's magazines like *Esquire.* One editorial explained: "Because we live in a society in which standards of physical beauty are most often circumscribed by a static concept of whiteness of skin and blondeness of hair, there is an aching need for someone to shout from the housetops that black women are beautiful." . . .

Still, despite the magazines' endorsement of feminine beauty and heterosexual allure, Friedan's polemical claim that "American women have been successfully reduced to sex creatures" seems unabashedly hyperbolic. Try as they might, popular magazines could not entirely dictate the responses of readers. In most cases, we have little way of knowing how readers responded to magazine articles, but in the case of sex appeal we have explicit letters of dissent. In the African-American magazines, some readers, women and men both, objected to the photos of semiclad women. One woman complained that the "so-called beauties" were "really a disgrace to all women." And another protested "those girl covers and the . . . so-called realism (just a cover up name for cheapness, coarseness, lewdness, profanity and irreverence)." . . .

In his ground-breaking 1972 book, *The American Woman,* William Henry Chafe offers what still stands as the best summary of the debates on womanhood in the postwar era. In Chafe's reconstruction, a popular "antifeminist" position, promoted by such authors as Farnham and Lundberg, stood opposed to a more feminist "sociological" perspective, promoted primarily by social scientists such as Mirra Komarovsky and Margaret Mead. While the antifeminists insisted on marriage and domesticity, the social scientists called for new gender roles to match modern conditions. In the popular magazines sampled for this essay, this debate rarely surfaced. Articles sometimes drew on one position or even both, but the vast majority did not fall clearly into either camp. Still, the antifeminist position did appear occasionally as did an opposing "women's rights" stance. These positions emerged in various magazines, but they both appeared most unequivocally in the highbrow magazines, the *Atlantic Monthly* and *Harper's,* which did not avoid controversy as assiduously as did others.

The antifeminist authors promoted domesticity as a woman's only road to fulfillment. Women should not compete with men, they argued; instead, they should defer to, depend on, and even wait on men, especially their husbands. According to these conservatives, women and men differed fundamentally, and attempts to diminish sexual difference would lead only to unhappiness. Often invoking a version of Freudian thought, these authors sometimes engaged in psychological name-calling in which they labeled modern woman neurotic, narcissistic, unfeminine, domineering, nagging, lazy, materialistic, and spoiled. These conservative arguments and the attendant name-calling were by no means typical of popular discourse. Of the 489 articles sampled, only 9, or less than 2 percent, even approached such starkly conservative claims.

This is where the oft-cited Dr. Marynia Farnham stood in the postwar discourse, at the conservative margin rather than at the center. For Farnham, modern women who attempted to compete with men or expressed discontent with their natural career as mothers suffered from mental instability, bitterness, and worse. Industrialization, Farnham claimed, had undermined women's productive functions in the home. Women, "frustrated at the inmost core of their beings," attempted tragically to emulate men in the world of work, led "aimlessly idle," "parasitic" lives as frigid housewives, or indulged in "overdoting, overstrict or rejecting" mothering, with a cumulative outcome of neurotic children, including future Adolph Hitlers. Farnham called for a renewed commitment to motherhood, dependence on men, and "natural" sexual passivity. She spelled out these arguments in ceaseless detail in her 1947 book, *Modern Woman: The Lost Sex,* coauthored with Ferdinand Lundberg.

Although Farnham's position had some influence, especially among psychologists, it did not represent the mainstream in the mass culture; rather, it generated "a storm of controversy." Book reviews, some of them scathing, called *Modern Woman* "neither socially nor medically credible," "dogmatic and sensational," "intensely disturbing," "unfair," and "fundamentally untrue." And Farnham's articles in *Coronet* provoked enough letters that the editors promised to include opposing viewpoints in future issues, this in a magazine that generally avoided any inkling of debate. While bits and pieces of Farnham's arguments appeared in other popular magazines, the antifeminist position was rejected more often than embraced. In the era of positive thinking, magazines tended toward more upbeat and celebratory representations of women.

Also at the boundaries of the discourse, a few "women's rights" articles counterbalanced the conservative extreme. . . . While conservatives insisted on domestic ideals, women's rights advocates insisted on women's right to nondomestic pursuits. Like the antifeminists, the authors of these articles often argued that women's functions in the home had declined, and they, too, often found the modern house-wife restless and discontented. These authors, however, condemned isolation in the home and subordination to men. They admired women who pursued positions of public responsibility and leadership, and they identified and opposed discrimination in the workplace and in politics. They insisted that women were individuals of infinite variety. In *Harper's,* Agnes Rogers wrote, "[T]here would be a healthier distribution of civic energy if more attention were paid to individuals as such and if it were not assumed that men hold the executive jobs and women do what they are told." In contrast with antifeminist writings, these articles either downplayed sex differences or derogated men for their militaristic aggression of "masculine self-inflation." The women's rights articles were only slightly less common than the antifeminist attacks. (With a conservative count, there were five, about 1 percent of the sample.) Like the antifeminist articles, they sometimes generated controversy, especially when readers read them as frontal attacks on the full-time housewife.

The antifeminists and the women's rights advocates competed for mainstream attention. Both tempered their arguments in seeming attempts to broaden appeal: antifeminists sometimes disavowed reactionary intention and denied that married women had to stay in the home, and women's rights advocates sometimes disavowed feminist militance and denied that married women had to have careers. Through the 1950s, though, neither position in any way controlled or dominated the public discourse, at least as seen in nonfiction articles in popular magazines. Both antifeminists and women's rights advocates clearly represented controversial minority positions. . . .

Why does my version of history differ from Betty Friedan's? The most obvious, and the most gracious, explanation is that we used different, though overlapping, sources. The nonfiction articles I read may well have included more contradictions and more ambivalence than the fiction on which Friedan focused. But there are, I think, additional differences in approach. Friedan did not read the popular magazines incorrectly, but she did, it seems, cite them reductively. . . . For the postwar era, she cited both fiction and nonfiction stories on domesticity. But she downplayed the articles on domestic problems (belittling one by saying "the bored editors . . . ran a little article"), ignored the articles on individual achievement, and dismissed the articles on political participation with a one-sentence caricature. Her forceful protest against a restrictive domestic ideal neglected the extent to which that ideal was already undermined.

My reassessment of the "feminine mystique" is part of a larger revisionist project. For the past few years, historians have questioned the stereotype of postwar women as quiescent, docile, and domestic. Despite the baby boom and despite discrimination in employment, education, and public office, married women, black and white, joined the labor force in increasing numbers, and both married and unmarried women participated actively in politics and reform. Just as women's activities were more varied and more complex than is often acknowledged, so, I argue, was the postwar popular ideology. Postwar magazines, like their prewar and wartime predecessors, rarely presented direct challenges to the conventions of marriage or motherhood, but they only rarely told women to return to or stay at home. They included stories that glorified domesticity, but they also expressed ambivalence about domesticity, endorsed women's nondomestic activity, and celebrated women's public success. They delivered multiple messages, which women could read as sometimes supporting and sometimes subverting the "feminine mystique." . . .

Women and the Politics of Hospital Abortion Committees, 1950–1970

RICKIE SOLINGER

This essay reviews discussion within the medical community in the postwar years concerning contraindications to pregnancy and the circumstances, if any, justifying therapeutic abortion. Such discussions reflect broader cultural attitudes toward women, mothers, babies, and pregnancy in the postwar era. They also illuminate the turmoil within the profession over these issues and the uneasy, insecure, but sometimes enduring, resolutions physicians devised to quell internal dissension and reinforce medical authority in the two decades immediately preceding *Roe v. Wade.* . . .

Dissension over abortion within the medical community was not a long-standing . . . problem. The post–Civil War state laws against abortion, which turned back the traditional right of girls and women to abort in the first trimester of pregnancy, stipulated that abortions were permissible only in cases where, due to a medical condition, the pregnant woman's life was in danger. These new, late-nineteenth-century laws granted the determination to licensed physicians only. Through the late 1940s, legal abortions were performed often and routinely in most hospitals across the country. Medically approved contraindications to pregnancy included cardiovascular conditions . . . ; kidney dysfunction . . . ; neurologic diseases . . . ; toxemia; respiratory disease . . .; uterine disease . . . ; orthopedic problems; and blood diseases such as leukemia, ulcerative colitis, diabetes, premature separation of the placenta, otosclerosis, bowel obstruction, lupus, and thyrotoxicosis. Physicians occasionally performed abortions on women suffering from severe psychiatric disorders.

With such an extensive list of contraindications to pregnancy, abortion ratios at some hospitals were high in various decades before 1950, especially in comparison to what they would soon be, for example: 1 abortion to every 76 live births at Bellevue Hospital in New York; 1 to every 167 at New York Lying-In; and 1 to every 169 deliveries at Iowa University Hospital. Given the state of medical knowledge and the range of medical options, as well as prevailing ideas about the physical toll pregnancy took on women, non-Catholic physicians were often willing to sacrifice the pregnancy in favor of the well-being of the woman. Medical decisions concerning these matters were often predicated upon an assumption that pregnancy itself was a physical event or a medical condition which happened to girls and women, sometimes under conditions that were not physically or medically favorable. In these cases, it could be assumed that pregnancy could interact with and worsen a

Rickie Solinger, "'A Complete Disaster': Abortion and the Politics of Hospital Abortion Committees, 1950–1970," *Feminist Studies* 19, no. 2 (summer 1993): 241–268. Reprinted by permission of the publisher, Feminist Studies, Inc.

preexisting condition. . . . This perspective assumed that the woman's body was an integrated system which the pregnancy *could* undermine or disintegrate. The pregnancy itself might well take precedence over disease as the more destructive agent. Where contraindications existed, pregnancy—or the "unborn child" was not granted precedence, or healing power, or constructed as a special condition virtually separate from the biological body or psychological mind of the impregnated female. The pregnancy was an additive, not an autonomous factor. . . . In short, abortion served a function when pregnancy invaded and threatened a woman's body.

By the early postwar years, the medical consensus about the indications for abortion had fractured, and therapeutic abortion rates were plummeting in hospitals across the country. One authoritative study reported that the therapeutic abortion rate per 1,000 live births in the United States declined from 5.1 in 1943 to 2.9 in 1953, a 43 percent decline. . . .

The sharp decline in legal, therapeutic abortions performed in hospitals reflected the fact that by mid-century, mainstream medical opinion held that medical-technological and obstetrical advances obviated the need to interrupt pregnancy for most of the medical conditions previously considered incompatible with pregnancy. . . . Shared access to new technologies and treatments, however, did not mean that physicians shared a professional opinion about when and how these innovations should be applied. In fact, the new medical developments gave rise to a very complicated situation for physicians; the situation could be called a *crisis* which extended over a twenty-year period, at least.

The crisis derived, in part, from a profoundly paradoxical relationship between medical progress, the law, and politics. On the one hand, physicians were scientific and humanitarian heroes for subduing the role of pregnancy as an "added burden" and for devising methodologies to conquer diseases threatening to pregnancy and the pregnant female. On the other hand, state laws still required that the life of the pregnant women must be medically endangered to permit abortion. The legal system persisted in requiring a condition that the medical system said rarely existed. Consequently, legal demands were at odds with medical advances which claimed to have virtually removed the basis for medical judgments concerning indications for abortions.

Given their continuing legal relationship to abortion, however, and their interest in sustaining medical authority over pregnant women, physicians struggled to establish new bases for medical decision making. By the early 1950s, a number of physicians were airing these struggles before the medical community in the pages of the most prestigious medical journals in the United States. They described a bitterly contentious intraprofessional situation. The reports indicated that any sense of common purpose among physicians considering abortion had been severely underminded in the aftermath of medical advances. . . . Two Chicago physicians asserted that no agreement among medical doctors can "be achieved regarding either individual indications [for abortions] or general principles." Another physician called his attempt to study the therapeutic abortion situation "a complete disaster" because "the categories of opinion were almost equal in number to the men concerned."

. . . [M]any felt that the new disunity over the abortion issue hurt the standing of physicians as expert, objective practitioners of medical science. Dissension also raised questions about the source and scope of medical authority. One physician observed, unhappily, that "if interruption of a pre-viable pregnancy is requested, the law at present dictates what medical opinion should be." . . . Others expressed deep uneasiness that they were facing pressures to look beyond their traditional subject—the physical condition of the individual pregnant woman. They were being urged, inappropriately, to include social factors in their medical diagnoses.

The rise of psychiatric indications as grounds for abortion solved the issue of medical authority for many practitioners but deepened the uneasiness of many others not convinced in the 1950s that psychiatry belonged within the ranks of medical science. A Cleveland obstetrician identified his hospital's biggest abortion problem as "those cases done for psychiatric indications, many times questionable psychiatric reasons." Another obstetrician wrote that "medical men . . . have been able to markedly reduce the therapeutic abortion rate throughout the country only to find that this least justifiable of all indications, psychiatric reasons, has been allowed to run rampant." . . . Psychiatrists were portrayed in this way as pawns of importuning women, unlike real medical doctors who initiated any abortion decision in the interest of their passive, pregnant patients. . . .

By the mid-1950s, most non-Catholic hospitals had begun to address their vulnerability in relation to abortion by finding ways to reassert medical authority over the issue and to sustain physicians' control over pregnant girls and women. Two strategies governed this process in a great many hospitals across the country. First, physicians recognized that they had to reassemble themselves as a collectivity from which professional expert diagnoses and decisions regarding individual women could be issued in one voice. In this setting, psychiatrists could be team players. They could bring their special perspective on the individual into the arena of experts and thus come to the aid of the profession while validating their own standing. Second, physicians redefined pregnancy in relation to women's bodies in such a way as to efface the woman herself while giving precedence to the law and the fetus. Again, psychiatrists played a pivotal role in accomplishing the redefinition.

By the mid-1950s, in many hospitals, physicians assembled themselves collectively into abortion boards or committees. As a group, obstetricians, cardiologists, psychiatrists, and others considered abortion recommendations and requests and issued definitive decisions on each case. The chief of a department of obstetrics and gynecology in a large northeastern hospital described the way decisionmaking processes changed in many hospitals in the early 1950s.

> At Mount Sinai Hospital [in New York], before [Alan Guttmacher's innovations], a request for therapeutic abortion merely had to be signed by two senior staff members. Guttmacher established the abortion committee of five members: the chief in medicine, representatives of pediatrics and of surgery, the chief of psychiatry, and the chief of obstetrics and gynecology who acts as chairman. Requests to the committee must be supported by two consultants recommending the procedure and outlining the indications for it. One of the consultants must appear before the committee to answer additional questions. The committee must be unanimous in its approval of any request.

These committees protected physicians, individually and as a profession, in a number of ways. Of paramount importance to many was the legal protection the boards provided. . . . Rudolph W. Holmes insisted that because the law drew such a "tenuous" line of demarcation between legal and illegal abortions, "it behooves medical staffs of all reputable hospitals to institute [abortion boards]. It would be a great protection to the operator as well as a deterrent to dangerous aspersions by outsiders." For many concerned physicians, insiders could be as dangerous as outsiders. These medical doctors felt that committees functioned best to mute, neutralize, or "curb liberal obstetricians" favoring too many abortions or abortions on questionable grounds. . . .

These interests in reputation and control were undoubtedly central concerns of many physicians in part because so many of them spoke and behaved one way publicly and another way privately. For example, a number of professional, illegal abortionists who conducted thriving businesses in this era have reported that hundreds of medical doctors—surely among them, those who publicly claimed medical, hospital control over abortion decisions—routinely referred clients for illegal abortions. By insisting on the righteousness of the mechanisms of hospital abortion committees, physicians could disassociate themselves from professional and public concerns about widespread illegal abortions, thus diminishing personal vulnerability and, perhaps, individual crises of conscience. . . .

Many contemporary commentators referred to the actual legal vulnerability of physicians who performed abortions as a "phantom," and many pointed out that "no reputable physician has ever been convicted for performing an abortion in a reputable hospital." This was the case both before and after abortion committees began to operate. It seems probable, then, that the most valuable service the boards actually performed was to bolster the image of physicians as members of a highly functioning professional body guided by scientific expertise and collective wisdom. The committee could transform public dissension within the medical community into public harmony, and at the same time, reduce the incidence of abortion. . . .

Moreover, physicians could more confidently assert their right and duty to retain medical control over the abortion decision once they established the committee as a respectable forum dedicated to processing individual women in an orderly fashion. In short order, the committee became a vehicle for bringing professional wisdom to bear on the issue, in part as a way to forestall the situation "where the decision for abortion may be made by legal, social or welfare groups outside of the profession." . . .

As physicians assumed a judicial role regarding individual requests for abortion—whether the requests originated with the obstetrician, another medical specialist, or the pregnant woman herself—inevitably, committee physicians, donning their robes in earnest, perceived the individual woman as "on trial." Unfortunately, however, in many cases, the cardinal principle of the U.S. legal system seems to have been inoperative. Physicians warned each other not to assume the woman's innocence. A New York medical doctor put it this way: "The physician must have a high index of suspicion for the patient who tries to pull a fast one." The source of danger was the "individual [woman] seeking to satisfy selfish needs." . . . One physician spoke for many of his colleagues when he warned of the "clever, scheming women, simply trying to hoodwink the psychiatrist and obstetrician," when they asked permission to abort. Another identified "woman's main role here on earth as conceiving, delivering and raising children." Thus, he concluded, any woman who claims not to want a certain pregnancy, must not be believed. In this environment, it is not surprising that, as one physician put it, "we have had a great many less requests for abortion [in his California hospital] since the patient and the doctor know that the patient must . . . have her case become an open trial so to speak to be decided on its merits." . . .

. . .[A]lthough the psychiatric perspective had been initially problematic for many medical doctors involved in abortion determinations, by the late 1950s, the situation had changed. By this time, the abortion committees had provided psychiatrists with a rich proving ground for their specialty. According to a number of essayists, psychiatrists did rise to the aid of their colleagues by providing the expert basis for medical decisionmaking and medical control that would have otherwise been lacking. As the biology of both disease pathology and pregnancy became less mystified and less remote because of medical-technological advances, psychiatrists stepped in, forestalling the possible empowerment of the pregnant patient. Psychiatrists constructed and drew on the unconscious as an entity which was only accessible to, and could only be decoded by, the expert. One physician observed, "If we have learned anything in psychiatry, we have learned to respect the unconscious far more than the conscious and we have learned not to take [abortion requests] at face value." Another demonstrated how this observation worked in practice. "An example is a woman who comes in seemingly with an unambivalent wish to be aborted which, upon interview, turns out to be an unconscious attempt on her part to punish her husband." Such a discovery, as the basis of diagnosis, could only be available to the physician.

This physician and many of his colleagues were, in part, responding to the new pressure from many women in their offices initiating requests for legal, therapeutic abortions. They were also responding from a new definition of pregnancy itself which emerged following the decline of medical indications for the interruption of pregnancy and alongside the validation of the psychiatric perspective.

Pregnancy became, at this time, a state inhering to the woman-as-custodian, but the pregnant woman and fetus no longer presented an integrated system. . . . After medical doctors determined that there were no longer any medical contraindications to pregnancy, pregnancy ceased to be a physical issue. Physicians now argued that "for most conditions, the natural history of the disease is not influenced deleteriously by an intercurrent pregnancy. Convertly, neither is the course of pregnancy seriously affected by a complicating medical condition."

Neither did physicians consider pregnancy a psychological issue. One argued: "Statistical analysis shows that childbearing has only a small influence on the mental disorders of women and that the majority of individuals predisposed to mental disorder go through childbirth unscathed." . . . In essence, pregnancy was most centrally a *moral* issue, but the moral ground had shifted. As the fetus was constructed as a little person, medical doctors constructed the pregnant woman's body as a safe reproductive container. The woman, along with her physician, had the moral duty, to sustain the container as fit. One obstetrician explained the suitability of women for this role. "Woman is a uterus surrounded by a supporting organism and a directing personality." Completely effaced, the woman-as-uterus simply housed the child. . . .

Drawing on the innovative notions of pregnancy and pregnant women, psychiatrists were prepared to explain the behavior of the growing number of women asking medical doctors for abortions in the postwar years. Their explanations created a broad category of women who were, by definition, in the absence of traditional medical problems, *morally* and psychologically unsuited for childbearing and certainly for motherhood because they were unwilling to serve as pregnancy vessels. Where there was an unhappily pregnant woman, there was a defective vessel. Many medical doctors agreed that an abortion *could* be performed on such a woman, but the procedure would not help as the problem was not the pregnancy. The problem was called a "psychiatric disorder" involving the woman's denial of her destiny and "amendable to treatment" as such. But the tone of the diagnosis, like the tone so often used to judge women on one grounds or another in these years, dripped with moral rectitude and condemnation. One psychiatrist identified the request for abortion "as proof [of the petitioner's] inability and failure to live through the destiny of being a woman." . . .

A physician who responded to such a woman's expressed desire to violate her destiny was, according to many, in serious error. One highly experienced author-psychiatrist placed women who chose abortion on a sullied moral plane when he asserted that he had "never seen a patient who has not had guilt feelings about a previous . . . abortion." Others felt that because the pregnancy itself was not the source of difficulty, an abortion did not solve a woman's problems but could create serious problems for her. For example,

> [Abortion] coupled with ideas of guilt, self-deprecation, some recurrent preoccupation centering around the abortion and the general theme of "I let them kill my baby" might well disturb a poorly integrated personality even to psychotic proportions. Feelings of love, admiration and respect for the male partner . . . may well be distorted in the aborted woman to ideas of disgust, hate, and disrespect; "He gave me a baby then took it away." The unconscious motivation and even the flow of emotions during the readjustments to a normal sexual nonpregnancy cycle may result in deeply engrained feelings of hostility toward the husband. Abortions we may say can produce psychotic cicatrix.

Well-known to unhappily pregnant women in the postwar era, however, was one method of resistance that sometimes cut through the language of morality; the threat of suicide. This condition alone raised the specter for medical doctors of a reintegrated mind, body, and pregnancy. A pregnant woman's threat of suicide suggested that the woman might destroy the reproductive container which gave definition to her very existence. Women recognized early that they could get their medical doctors' attention by making such a threat, but many physicians found it easier to believe that a woman was using her pregnancy rather than throwing away her destiny. Thus, physicians proceeded very cautiously in this area. One wrote that "a mere threat of suicide or even an abortive attempt at suicide is not in itself regarded as a medical indication for therapeutic abortion; it may be nothing more than an effort to blackmail the surgeon into performing the operation." . . .

[A] survey reported in the *Stanford Law Review* provides an excellent example of a suicidal pregnant woman who physicians were willing to believe deserved an abortion. An unprecedented 80 percent of reporting hospitals agreed to sanction abortion in this hypothetical case.

> Mrs. C. is 32 years old and is the mother of children, aged 7, 4, and 3. Following the birth of her last child, she had what was diagnosed as a postpartum depression in which she became completely withdrawn. She was hospitalized in a state hospital for 6 months during which time she had electroshock therapy with some improvement. She has remained under psychiatric care since then but she still becomes depressed very easily and talks freely about committing suicide, saying that her family will be better off without the burden of her care.

Four weeks ago it was diagnosed that she was approximately 4 weeks' pregnant. The news of this precipitated a severe emotional crisis. This has been manifested by vomiting, spells of uncontrollable crying lasting for hours at a time, at which time the patient locked herself in her room. She threatened suicide several times in the last four weeks, saying that she could never be a "good mother" and that she was a "useless member of society."

Last night Mrs. C. was found unconscious on the floor of her living room. There was an empty bottle, which should have contained approximately eighteen sleeping pills, in her bedroom. She was taken to the hospital and has apparently responded to vigorous therapy for her barbiturate overdose.

Mrs. C.'s case evoked near-consensus because this woman demonstrated her commitment to destroy the reproductive container she had become. Only in the case of such a demonstration could the moral dimension be eclipsed and the condition of pregnancy assume its previous status as an "added burden" or a destructive agent.

The other way that physicians frequently revealed their commitment to the new construction of women's bodies as reproductive containers was in their association of therapeutic abortion with simultaneous sterilization. . . . The prevalence of sterilization was widely featured in the obstetrical and psychiatric literature of the day, specifically in cases involving what one prominent expert called the "tainted individual." One group of obstetricians found that "some women desiring an abortion were required to have a simultaneous sterilization operation as a condition of approval of the abortion in from one-third to two-thirds of [those] teaching hospitals [studied] in different regions of the country. In all, 53.6 percent of teaching hospitals made this a requirement for some of their patients." Another physician reported his finding of a 40 percent concomitant sterilization rate in all U.S. hospitals in the 1940s and 1950s. . . .

Some physicians justified simultaneous sterilization on the grounds that any woman ill enough to warrant abortion should never again be pregnant. Others shared this position but shifted the emphasis on to the medical doctor's dilemma: "A serious effort is made to control [by sterilization] the need for dealing with the same problem in the same patient twice." A California psychiatrist described what he felt was a strong trend among medical doctors, "penalizing" by sterilization the patient who "needs" a therapeutic abortion. He explained the practice this way: "Often, the surgeon's stipulation for sterilization may reflect his reluctance to perform the abortion, his misunderstanding of its necessity, and his resentment of the psychiatric indications." Another commentator felt that some physicians in this era resented sexual women more than they resented psychiatry: "The abortion committee [at one hospital] evaluated all patients in terms of recommendations for sterilization. Medical grounds for this 'final solution' to 'promiscuous' abortions were forcefully debated by individual members and typically included the physician's evaluation of the woman's condition and moral character." The widespread use of sterilization, whatever the expressed justification, seems to suggest that many physicians in the postwar era were willing to use the sterilization option to cap the defective reproductive container. . . .

One physician, unhappy about the coupling of sterilization and therapeutic abortion in U.S. hospitals, observed that this practice actually drove women to illegal abortionists to escape the likelihood that a legal abortion would entail the permanent loss of their fertility. He added, "I would like to point that out, because the package [therapeutic abortion–sterilization] is so frequent I therefore consider them fortunate to have been illegally rather than therapeutically aborted, and thus spared sterilization." This aspect of the discussion foreshadowed, of course, the legal institutionalization, in our time, of the link between abortion and sterilization, via the Hyde Amendment.

The literature reviewed in this essay makes it clear that some influential medical doctors in the postwar era derived professional strength and ideological coherence from abortion committees and from a new, disembodied definition of pregnancy. But by the middle of the 1960s, it was also clear that the same factors which had pushed physicians into a defensive posture in the early postwar years continued to exert considerable pressures on the profession. These and additional factors combined to facilitate the eclipse of medical authority over the abortion decision much sooner than many practitioners had predicted.

Over time, the committees themselves could not sustain the image of professional unity and scientific purpose, even if an individual hospital could issue abortion decisions with one voice. Harold Rosen, a prominent medical doctor interested in abortion reform, noted widespread inconsistencies between hospital abortion committees in the mid-1960s which hurt the credibility of the profession.

> Not infrequently, for instance, the abortion board of one hospital, but not another, may refuse to accept a recommendation for interruption; on nine separate occasions during the past seven years, patients who have been seen in consultation in one hospital have afterwards been therapeutically aborted at adjacent hospitals with, at times, almost the same visiting staff.

At the heart of this apparent capriciousness was a continuing inability among physicians to agree on indications, even medical indications.

> If physicians do not wish to force a specific woman to carry a specific pregnancy to term, and if that woman is actually suffering from some severe physical disease then, but only then, the pathological process, provided it falls within certain categories, is in certain hospitals and by certain physicians and hospital boards considered sufficient indication for interruption. In others, it is not. . . .

. . . Other factors which exerted increasing pressure in the abortion arena include first, of course, women's growing insistence on breaking the link between law and medicine, so that women themselves could take the power to decide who was a mother and to decide when a woman was a mother. After the rubella epidemic and the thalidomide episode of the early 1960s, women also began to insist on a legal, publicly sanctioned right to decide who was a child. The sensationally and intrusively reported plight of Sherri Finkbine in 1962 raised, above all, the specter of the pregnant woman's right to reject a fetus deeply damaged by thalidomide.

Additional pressures which struck at medical authority came from the flowering of the quality of life (or "life-style") ethic among the middle-class in the United States which undermined the acceptability of the simple life/death dichotomy that the law mandated must govern abortion decisions. Also, in the 1960s as social criticism seeped back into mainstream public discourse, some physicians began to accept and use a definition of the purpose of medicine—in this case, of indications for abortion, which placed unhappily pregnant women in desperate social and economic contexts. . . .

Of equal or greater importance to all these pressures undermining medical authority in the abortion arena by the mid-1960s was widespread concern and fear among whites in the United States about the "population explosion," rising welfare costs, the civil rights movement, and the "sexual revolution." Critics of these social, political, and cultural phenomena tended to target women's bodies and their reproductive capacity as a source of danger to the fabric of U.S. society. Demedicalizing and decriminalizing the abortion decision became one way to diminish the damage women's bodies could do.

This essay leaves unexplored many issues that would shed additional light on the concerns and strategies of medical doctors sitting on hospital abortion committees in the postwar era. These include physicians' attitudes toward abortion and women of various races, ethnicities, and classes. Much research is needed in this area. The essay does not explore medical doctors' attitudes toward and relationships with illegal abortionists, a subject well worth pursuing. Also left unexplored are the sources and complex nature of physicians' changing attitudes toward abortion in the 1960s and 1970s. Pregnant women themselves have not been given voice in this essay.

But the subjects of this study, a highly visible segment of the medical community, have been given voice here in order to allow us to consider what was at issue for many physicians in the immediate pre–*Roe v. Wade* decades. What is most striking in the literature reviewed for this essay is that, with the exception of the few articles prepared by Catholic medical doctors, the physicians who wrote on the abortion issue were not primarily concerned with the issue of when life begins. They were, however, very concerned with what they took to be their role in the postwar cultural mandate to protect and preserve the links between sexuality, femininity, marriage, and maternity. They were also deeply concerned about their professional dignity and about devising strategies to protect and preserve the power, the prerogatives, and the legal standing of the medical profession.

An important strategy of many physicians in this era was to draw on the vulnerability of pregnant women to construct a definition of pregnancy that effaced the personhood of the individual pregnant woman. This definition created a safe place for the fetus and also for the physician forced by law to adjudicate the extremely personal decisions of women, many of whom were resisting effacement. The subordination of the pregnant woman to the fetus revitalized medical participation in the abortion decision because the medical doctor was now required to make sure that the woman stayed moral, that is, served her fetus correctly. These postwar ideas demonstrate the relationship between scientific advances and ideological positions regarding women, pregnant women, pregnancy, and fetuses.

◈ *F U R T H E R   R E A D I N G*

Black, Allida M. *Casting Her Own Shadow: Eleanor Roosevelt and the Shaping of Postwar Liberalism* (1996).

Chafe, William. *The Paradox of Change: American Women in the Twentieth Century* (1991).

Coontz, Stephanie. *The Way We Never Were: American Families and the Nostalgia Trap* (1992).

Faderman, Lillian. *Odd Girls and Twilight Lovers: A History of Lesbian Life in Twentieth-Century America* (1991).

Feldstein, Ruth. *Motherhood in Black and White: Race and Sex in American Liberalism, 1930–1965* (2000).

Gans, Herbert. *The Levittowners: Ways of Life and Politics in a New Suburban Community* (1967).

Glendon, Mary Ann. *A World Made New: Eleanor Roosevelt and the Universal Declaration of Human Rights* (2001).

Harrison, Cynthia. *On Account of Sex: The Politics of Women's Issues, 1945–1968* (1988).

Horowitz, Daniel. *Betty Friedan and the Making of the Feminine Mystique: The American Left, the Cold War, and American Feminism* (1998).

Jackson, Kenneth T. *Crabgrass Frontier: The Suburbanization of the United States* (1985).

Jones, Jacqueline. *Labor of Love, Labor of Sorrow: Black Women, Work, and the Family from Slavery to the Present* (1985).

Kaledin, Eugenia. *Mothers and More: American Women in the 1950s* (1984).

Kennedy, Elizabeth Lapovsky, and Madeline D. Davis. *Boots of Leather, Slippers of Gold: The History of a Lesbian Community* (1993).

Komarovsky, Mirra. *Blue Collar Marriage* (1964).

Laughlin, Kathleen A. *Women's Work and Public Policy: A History of the U.S. Department of Labor, 1945–1970* (2000).

Luibheid, Eithne. "'Looking Like a Lesbian': The Organization of Sexual Monitoring at the United States–Mexican Border," *Journal of the History of Sexuality* 8 (1998): 477–505.

Lynn, Susan. *Progressive Women in Conservative Times: Racial Justice, Peace, and Feminism, 1945 to the 1960s* (1992).

Marsh, Margaret. *Suburban Lives* (1990).

McEnaney, Laura. *Civil Defense Begins at Home: Militarization Meets Everyday Life in the Fifties* (2000).

Meyerowitz, Joanne, ed. *Not June Cleaver: Women and Gender in Postwar America, 1945–1960* (1994).

Richards, Yevette. *Maida Springer, Pan-Africanist and International Labor Leader* (2000).

Rossiter, Margaret W. *Women Scientists in America: Before Affirmative Action, 1940–1972* (1995).

Rupp, Leila J., and Verta Taylor. *Surviving the Doldrums: The American Women's Rights Movement, 1945 to the 1960s* (1987).

Sherman, Janann. *No Place for a Woman: A Life of Senator Margaret Chase Smith* (2000).

Solinger, Rickie. *Wake Up Little Susie: Single Pregnancy and Race Before Roe v. Wade* (1992).

Weiss, Jessica. *To Have and to Hold: Marriage, the Baby Boom, and Social Change* (2000).

Weiss, Nancy Pottishman. "The Invention of Necessity: Dr. Benjamin Spock's 'Baby and Child Care'" *American Quarterly* 29 (winter 1977): 519–546.

CHAPTER
15

Women Confront Oppression
and Demand Change,
the 1960s and 1970s

The 1960s and 1970s were years of extraordinary political and cultural unrest in the United States. Young adults, members of the baby-boom generation, participated in a frontal attack on American society and its institutions, condemning the nation's misuse of military power around the globe, especially in Vietnam, and its indifference to oppression and inequality at home. Women of varied class, race, and ethnic backgrounds devoted tremendous energy to the political movements of the era, including the civil rights and Black Power struggles and the antiwar, antipoverty, and labor movements. In the late 1960s, some women—many of them former members of the Student Non-Violent Coordinating Committee and Students for a Democratic Society and nearly all of them white and middle class launched a new radical feminist movement. Radical feminists organized small consciousness-raising groups that combined investigations of gender discrimination in employment, education, and politics with analyses of gender oppression in private, familial, and sexual contexts. Like Black Power activists, they were often frankly separatist, doubting the dominant society's willingness to grant women (or blacks) true equality. Meanwhile, older and more moderate women (mostly white and middle class) formed the National Organization for Women (NOW) in 1966, adopting integrationist goals that paralleled those of the National Association for the Advancement of Colored People and the Southern Christian Leadership Conference. The two branches of feminism often argued over goals and tactics, but together they helped to bring about massive changes in attitudes toward the role of women in American society.

By the early 1970s, African American women and Chicanas had also begun to form organizations that addressed explicitly the intersections of racial, ethnic, and sexual oppression, and they challenged white feminists to broaden the agenda of the women's movement. Simultaneously, working-class and professional women began to organize across racial and ethnic lines to demand access to fields of employment still closed to women. Women of varied racial and ethnic backgrounds also participated in the sexual revolution of the era, often trying to bring a feminist consciousness

to a quest for "free love." Lesbian feminists claimed the right to free themselves from
the bonds of heterosexuality. Straight and lesbian women demanded that Americans
acknowledge rape as a crime of violence against women; so, too, women of varied
backgrounds demanded an end to the criminalization of abortion, arguing that prohibitions against abortion unjustly limited women's reproductive and sexual freedom
and forced them to seek abortions from illegal and unsafe practitioners. Responding
to feminists, liberal doctors, and reform-minded lawyers, the Supreme Court struck
down existing laws against abortion in Roe v. Wade *(1973) and ruled in favor of
women's unrestricted right to abortion in the first trimester of pregnancy.*

*The documents and essays in this chapter explore the circumstances that pro-
voked feminist activism during these two decades, the critical importance of race
and ethnicity in the women's movement, and the varied meanings of the sexual
revolution for women. Women uncovered and challenged the linked politics of
gender, class, race, and sexuality with extraordinary urgency during these times.
They produced meaningful change but would also encounter powerful forces of
resistance and reaction.*

D O C U M E N T S

In 1963 Betty Friedan described "the problem that has no name" (Document 1) in her
book *The Feminine Mystique,* trying to give voice to (white middle-class) women confined to lives of domesticity. In 1966, the founding statement of NOW (extracted in
Document 2) laid out the organization's central premises. Mirta Vidal wrote an essay
in 1971 (Document 3) on the critical importance of feminism for Chicanas. That same
year, Susan Griffin brought rape to the attention of Americans (Document 4), calling
the profoundly misunderstood act the "all-American crime." The Supreme Court's 1973
ruling in *Roe* v. *Wade* is excerpted in Document 5. Writing in 1978, Lindsy Van Gelder
reports on an unusually important sex-discrimination lawsuit against the *New York Times*
(Document 6).

1. Betty Friedan Reveals the "Problem That Has No Name," 1963

The problem lay buried, unspoken, for many years in the minds of American
women. It was a strange stirring, a sense of dissatisfaction, a yearning that women
suffered in the middle of the twentieth century in the United States. Each suburban
wife struggled with it alone. As she made the beds, shopped for groceries, matched
slipcover material, ate peanut butter sandwiches with her children, chauffeured Cub
Scouts and Brownies, lay beside her husband at night—she was afraid to ask even
of herself the silent question—"Is this all?"

For over fifteen years there was no word of this yearning in the millions of
words written about women, for women, in all the columns, books and articles by
experts telling women their role was to seek fulfillment as wives and mothers.
Over and over women heard in voices of tradition and of Freudian sophistication

Betty Friedan, *The Feminine Mystique* (New York: Dell, 1963), 11–16, 21–22, 27. Copyright © 1983,
1974, 1973, 1963 by Betty Friedan. Used by permission of W. W. Norton & Company, Inc.

that they could desire no greater destiny than to glory in their own femininity. Experts told them how to catch a man and keep him, how to breastfeed children and handle their toilet training, how to cope with sibling rivalry and adolescent rebellion; how to buy a dishwasher, bake bread, cook gourmet snails, and build a swimming pool with their own hands; how to dress, look, and act more feminine and make marriage more exciting; how to keep their husbands from dying young and their sons from growing into delinquents. They were taught to pity the neurotic, unfeminine, unhappy women who wanted to be poets or physicists or presidents. They learned that truly feminine women do not want careers, higher education, political rights— the independence and the opportunities that the old-fashioned feminists fought for. Some women, in their forties and fifties, still remembered painfully giving up those dreams, but most of the younger women no longer even thought about them. A thousand expert voices applauded their femininity, their adjustment, their new maturity. All they had to do was devote their lives from earliest girlhood to finding a husband and bearing children. . . .

The suburban housewife—she was the dream image of the young American women and the envy, it was said, of women all over the world. The American housewife—freed by science and labor-saving appliances from the drudgery, the dangers of childbirth and the illnesses of her grandmother. She was healthy, beautiful, educated, concerned only about her husband, her children, her home. She had found true feminine fulfillment. As a housewife and mother, she was respected as a full and equal partner to man in his world. She was free to choose automobiles, clothes, appliances, supermarkets; she had everything that women ever dreamed of.

In the fifteen years after World War II, this mystique of feminine fulfillment became the cherished and self-perpetuating core of contemporary American culture. Millions of women lived their lives in the image of those pretty pictures of the American suburban housewife, kissing their husbands goodbye in front of the picture window, depositing their stationwagonsful of children at school, and smiling as they ran the new electric waxer over the spotless kitchen floor. They baked their own bread, sewed their own and their children's clothes, kept their new washing machines and dryers running all day. They changed the sheets on the beds twice a week instead of once, took the rug-hooking class in adult education, and pitied their poor frustrated mothers, who had dreamed of having a career. Their only dream was to be perfect wives and mothers; their highest ambition to have five children and a beautiful house, their only fight to get and keep their husbands. They had no thought for the unfeminine problems of the world outside the home; they wanted the men to make the major decisions. They gloried in their role as women, and wrote proudly on the census blank: "Occupation: housewife."

For over fifteen years, the words written for women, and the words women used when they talked to each other, while their husbands sat on the other side of the room and talked shop or politics or septic tanks, were about problems with their children, or how to keep their husbands happy, or improve their children's school, or cook chicken or make slipcovers. Nobody argued whether women were inferior or superior to men; they were simply different. Words like "emancipation" and "career" sounded strange and embarrassing; no one had used them for years. When a Frenchwoman named Simone de Beauvoir wrote a book called *The Second Sex,* an American critic commented that she obviously "didn't know what life was all about," and besides, she was talking about French women. The "woman problem" in America no longer existed.

If a woman had a problem in the 1950's and 1960's, she knew that something must be wrong with her marriage, or with herself. Other women were satisfied with their lives, she thought. What kind of a woman was she if she did not feel this mysterious fulfillment waxing the kitchen floor? She was so ashamed to admit her dissatisfaction that she never knew how many other women shared it. If she tried to tell her husband, he didn't understand what she was talking about. She did not really understand it herself. For over fifteen years women in America found it harder to talk about this problem than about sex. Even the psychoanalysts had no name for it. When a woman went to a psychiatrist for help, as many women did, she would say, "I'm so ashamed," or "I must be hopelessly neurotic." "I don't know what's wrong with women today," a suburban psychiatrist said uneasily. "I only know something is wrong because most of my patients happen to be women. And their problem isn't sexual." Most women with this problem did not go to see a psychoanalyst, however. "There's nothing wrong really," they kept telling themselves. "There isn't any problem."

But on an April morning in 1959, I heard a mother of four, having coffee with four other mothers in a suburban development fifteen miles from New York, say in a tone of quiet desperation, "the problem." And the others knew, without words, that she was not talking about a problem with her husband, or her children, or her home. Suddenly they realized they all shared the same problem, the problem that has no name. They began, hesitantly, to talk about it. Later, after they had picked up their children at nursery school and taken them home to nap, two of the women cried, in sheer relief, just to know they were not alone.

Gradually I came to realize that the problem that has no name was shared by countless women in America. As a magazine writer I often interviewed women about problems with their children, or their marriages, or their houses, or their communities. But after a while I began to recognize the telltale signs of this other problem. I saw the same signs in suburban ranch houses and split-levels on Long Island and in New Jersey and Westchester County; in colonial houses in a small Massachusetts town; on patios in Memphis; in suburban and city apartments; in living rooms in the Midwest. Sometimes I sensed the problem, not as a reporter, but as a suburban housewife, for during this time I was also bringing up my own three children in Rockland County, New York. I heard echoes of the problem in college dormitories and semi-private maternity wards, at PTA meetings and luncheons of the League of Women Voters, at suburban cocktail parties, in station wagons waiting for trains, and in snatches of conversation overheard at Schrafft's. The groping words I heard from other women, on quiet afternoons when children were at school or on quiet evenings when husbands worked late, I think I understood first as a woman long before I understood their larger social and psychological implications.

Just what was this problem that has no name? What were the words women used when they tried to express it? Sometimes a woman would say "I feel empty somehow . . . incomplete." Or she would say, "I feel as if I don't exist." Sometimes she blotted out the feeling with a tranquilizer. Sometimes she thought the problem was with her husband, or her children, or that what she really needed was to redecorate her house, or move to a better neighborhood, or have an affair, or another baby. Sometimes, she went to a doctor with symptoms she could hardly describe: "A tired feeling . . . I get so angry with the children it scares me . . . I feel like crying without any reason." (A Cleveland doctor called it "the housewife's syndrome.") . . .

Most men, and some women, still did not know that this problem was real. But those who had faced it honestly knew that all the superficial remedies, the sympathetic advice, the scolding words and the cheering words were somehow drowning the problem in unreality. A bitter laugh was beginning to be heard from American women. They were admired, envied, pitied, theorized over until they were sick of it, offered drastic solutions or silly choices that no one could take seriously. They got all kinds of advice from the growing armies of marriage and child-guidance counselors, psychotherapists, and armchair psychologists, on how to adjust to their role as housewives. No other road to fulfillment was offered to American women in the middle of the twentieth century. Most adjusted to their role and suffered or ignored the problem that has no name. It can be less painful for a woman, not to hear the strange, dissatisfied voice stirring within her.

It is no longer possible to ignore that voice, to dismiss the desperation of so many American women. This is not what being a woman means, no matter what the experts say. For human suffering there is a reason; perhaps the reason has not been found because the right questions have not been asked, or pressed far enough. I do not accept the answer that there is no problem because American women have luxuries that women in other times and lands never dreamed of; part of the strange newness of the problem is that it cannot be understood in terms of the age-old material problems of man: poverty, sickness, hunger, cold. The women who suffer this problem have a hunger that food cannot fill. It persists in women whose husbands are struggling internes and law clerks, or prosperous doctors and lawyers; in wives of workers and executives who make $5,000 a year or $50,000. It is not caused by lack of material advantages; it may not even be felt by women preoccupied with desperate problems of hunger, poverty or illness. And women who think it will be solved by more money, a bigger house, a second car, moving to a better suburb, often discover it gets worse.

It is no longer possible today to blame the problem on loss of femininity: to say that education and independence and equality with men have made American women unfeminine. I have heard so many women try to deny this dissatisfied voice within themselves because it does not fit the pretty picture of femininity the experts have given them. I think, in fact, that this is the first clue to the mystery: the problem cannot be understood in the generally accepted terms by which scientists have studied women, doctors have treated them, counselors have advised them, and writers have written about them. Women who suffer this problem, in whom this voice is stirring, have lived their whole lives in the pursuit of feminine fulfillment. They are not career women (although career women may have other problems); they are women whose greatest ambition has been marriage and children. For the oldest of these women, these daughters of the American middle class, no other dream was possible. The ones in their forties and fifties who once had other dreams gave them up and threw themselves joyously into life as housewives. For the youngest, the new wives and mothers, this was the only dream. They are the ones who quit high school and college to marry, or marked time in some job in which they had no real interest until they married. These women are very "feminine" in the usual sense, and yet they still suffer the problem. . . .

If I am right, the problem that has no name stirring in the minds of so many American women today is not a matter of loss of femininity or too much education, or the demands of domesticity. It is far more important than anyone recognizes. It is the key to these other new and old problems which have been torturing women and their husbands and children, and puzzling their doctors and educators for years. It may well be the key to our future as a nation and a culture. We can no longer ignore that voice within women that says: "I want something more than my husband and my children and my home."

2. NOW Issues Its Statement of Purpose, 1966

We, men and women who hereby constitute ourselves as the National Organization for Women, believe that the time has come for a new movement toward true equality for all women in America, and toward a fully equal partnership of the sexes, as part of the world-wide revolution of human rights now taking place within and beyond our national borders.

The purpose of NOW is to take action to bring women into full participation in the mainstream of American society now, exercising all the privileges and responsibilities thereof in truly equal partnership with men.

We believe the time has come to move beyond the abstract argument, discussion and symposia over the status and special nature of women which has raged in America in recent years; the time has come to confront, with concrete action, the conditions that now prevent women from enjoying the equality of opportunity and freedom of choice which is their right as individual Americans, and as human beings.

NOW is dedicated to the proposition that women first and foremost are human beings, who, like all other people in our society, must have the chance to develop their fullest human potential. We believe that women can achieve such equality only by accepting to the full the challenges and responsibilities they share with all other people in our society, as part of the decision-making mainstream of American political, economic and social life.

We organize to initiate or support action, nationally or in any part of this nation, by individuals or organizations, to break through the silken curtain of prejudice and discrimination against women in government, industry, the professions, the churches, the political parties, the judiciary, the labor unions, in education, science, medicine, law, religion and every other field of importance in American society. . . .

There is no civil rights movement to speak for women, as there has been for Negroes and other victims of discrimination. The National Organization for Women must therefore begin to speak.

National Organization for Women, Statement of Purpose, 1966.

WE BELIEVE that the power of American law, and the protection guaranteed by the U.S. Constitution to the civil rights of all individuals, must be effectively applied and enforced to isolate and remove patterns of sex discrimination, to ensure equality of opportunity in employment and education, and equality of civil and political rights and responsibilities on behalf of women, as well as for Negroes and other deprived groups.

We realize that women's problems are linked to many broader questions of social justice; their solution will require concerted action by many groups. Therefore, convinced that human rights for all are indivisible, we expect to give active support to the common cause of equal rights for all those who suffer discrimination and deprivation, and we call upon other organizations committed to such goals to support our efforts toward equality for women.

WE DO NOT ACCEPT the token appointment of a few women to high-level positions in government and industry as a substitute for a serious continuing effort to recruit and advance women according to their individual abilities. To this end, we urge American government and industry to mobilize the same resources of ingenuity and command with which they have solved problems of far greater difficulty than those now impeding the progress of women.

WE BELIEVE that this nation has a capacity at least as great as other nations, to innovate new social institutions which will enable women to enjoy true equality of opportunity and responsibility in society, without conflict with their responsibilities as mothers and homemakers. In such innovations, America does not lead the Western world, but lags by decades behind many European countries. We do not accept the traditional assumption that a woman has to choose between marriage and motherhood, on the one hand, and serious participation in industry or the professions on the other. We question the present expectation that all normal women will retire from job or profession for ten or fifteen years, to devote their full time to raising children, only to reenter the job market at a relatively minor level. This in itself is a deterrent to the aspirations of women, to their acceptance into management or professional training courses, and to the very possibility of equality of opportunity or real choice, for all but a few women. Above all, we reject the assumption that these problems are the unique responsibility of each individual woman, rather than a basic social dilemma which society must solve. True equality of opportunity and freedom of choice for women requires such practical and possible innovations as a nationwide network of child-care centers, which will make it unnecessary for women to retire completely from society until their children are grown, and national programs to provide retraining for women who have chosen to care for their own children full time.

WE BELIEVE that it is as essential for every girl to be educated to her full potential of human ability as it is for every boy—with the knowledge that such education is the key to effective participation in today's economy and that, for a girl as for a boy, education can only be serious where there is expectation that it will be used in society. We believe that American educators are capable of devising means of imparting such expectations to girl students. Moreover, we consider the decline in the proportion of women receiving higher and professional education to be evidence of discrimination. This discrimination may take the form of quotas against the admission of women to colleges and professional schools; lack of encouragement by parents, counselors and educators; denial of loans or fellowships; or the traditional or arbitrary procedures in graduate and professional training geared in terms of men, which inadvertently discriminate against women. We believe that the same serious attention must be given to high school dropouts who are girls as to boys.

WE REJECT the current assumptions that a man must carry the sole burden of supporting himself, his wife, and family, and that a woman is automatically entitled to lifelong support by a man upon her marriage, or that marriage, home and family are primarily woman's world and responsibility—hers, to dominate, his to support. We believe that a true partnership between the sexes demands a different concept of marriage, an equitable sharing of the responsibilities of home and children and of the economic burdens of their support. We believe that proper recognition should be given to the economic and social value of homemaking and child care. To these ends, we will seek to open a reexamination of laws and mores governing marriage and divorce, for we believe that the current state of "half-equality" between the sexes discriminates against both men and women, and is the cause of much unnecessary hostility between the sexes.

WE BELIEVE that women must now exercise their political rights and responsibilities as American citizens. They must refuse to be segregated on the basis of sex into separate-and-not-equal ladies' auxiliaries in the political parties, and they must demand representation according to their numbers in the regularly constituted party committees—at local, state, and national levels—and in the informal power structure, participating fully in the selection of candidates and political decision-making, and running for office themselves.

IN THE INTERESTS OF THE HUMAN DIGNITY OF WOMEN, we will protest and endeavor to change the false image of women now prevalent in the mass media, and in the texts, ceremonies, laws, and practices of our major social institutions. Such images perpetuate contempt for women by society and by women for themselves. We are similarly opposed to all policies and practices—in church, state, college, factory, or office—which, in the guise of protectiveness, not only deny opportunities but also foster in women self-denigration, dependence, and evasion of responsibility, undermine their confidence in their own abilities and foster contempt for women.

NOW WILL HOLD ITSELF INDEPENDENT OF ANY POLITICAL PARTY in order to mobilize the political power of all women and men intent on our goals. We will strive to ensure that no party, candidate, President, senator, governor, congressman, or any public official who betrays or ignores the principle of full equality between the sexes is elected or appointed to office. If it is necessary to mobilize the votes of men and women who believe in our cause, in order to win for women the final right to be fully free and equal human beings, we so commit ourselves.

WE BELIEVE THAT women will do most to create a new image of women by *acting* now, and by speaking out in behalf of their own equality, freedom, and human dignity—not in pleas for special privilege, nor in enmity toward men, who are also victims of the current half-equality between the sexes—but in an active, self-respecting partnership with men. By so doing, women will develop confidence in their own ability to determine actively, in partnership with men, the conditions of their life, their choices, their future and their society.

3. Mirta Vidal Reports on the Rising Consciousness of the Chicana About Her Special Oppression, 1971

At the end of May 1971, more than 600 Chicanas met in Houston, Texas, to hold the first national conference of Raza women. For those of us who were there it was clear that this conference was not just another national gathering of the Chicano movement.

Chicanas came from all parts of the country inspired by the prospect of discussing issues that have long been on their minds and which they now see not as individual problems but as an important and integral part of a movement for liberation.

The resolutions coming out of the two largest workshops, "Sex and the Chicana" and "Marriage—Chicana Style," called for "free, legal abortions and birth control for the Chicano community, controlled by *Chicanas.*" As Chicanas, the resolution stated, "we have a right to control our own bodies." The resolutions also called for "24-hour child-care centers in Chicano communities" and explained that there is a critical need for these since "Chicana motherhood should not preclude educational, political, social and economic advancement."

While these resolutions articulated the most pressing needs of Chicanas today, the conference as a whole reflected a rising consciousness of the Chicana about her special oppression in this society.

With their growing involvement in the struggle for Chicano liberation and the emergence of the feminist movement, Chicanas are beginning to challenge every social institution which contributes to and is responsible for their oppression, from inequality on the job to their role in the home. They are questioning "machismo," discrimination in education, the double standard, the role of the Catholic Church, and all the backward ideology designed to keep women subjugated. . . .

The oppression suffered by Chicanas is different from that suffered by most women in this country. Because Chicanas are part of an oppressed nationality, they are subjected to the racism practiced against La Raza. Since the overwhelming majority of Chicanos are workers, Chicanas are also victims of the exploitation of the working class. But in addition, Chicanas, along with the rest of women, are relegated to an inferior position because of their sex. Thus, Raza women suffer a triple form of oppression: as members of an oppressed nationality, as workers, *and* as women. Chicanas have no trouble understanding this. At the Houston conference 84 percent of the women surveyed felt that "there is a distinction between the problems of the Chicana and those of other women."

On the other hand, they also understand that the struggle now unfolding against the oppression of women is not only relevant to them, but *is* their struggle.

Because sexism and male chauvinism are so deeply rooted in this society, there is a strong tendency, even within the Chicano movement, to deny the basic right of Chicanas to organize around their own concrete issues. Instead they are told to stay away from the women's liberation movement because it is an "Anglo thing."

We need only analyze the origin of male supremacy to expose this false position. The inferior role of women in society does not date back to the beginning of time. In fact, before the Europeans came to this part of the world women enjoyed a position of equality with men. The submission of women, along with institutions such as the church and the patriarchy, was imported by the European colonizers, and remains to this day part of Anglo society. Machismo—in English, "male chauvinism"—is the one thing, if any, that should be labeled an "Anglo thing."

When Chicano men oppose the efforts of women to move against their oppression, they are actually opposing the struggle of every woman in this country aimed at changing a society in which Chicanos themselves are oppressed. They are saying to 51 percent of this country's population that they have no right to fight for their liberation.

Moreover, they are denying one half of La Raza this basic right. They are denying Raza women, who are triply oppressed, the right to struggle around their specific, real, and immediate needs.

In essence, they are doing just what the white male rulers of this country have done. The white male rulers want Chicanas to accept their oppression because they understand that when Chicanas begin a movement demanding legal abortions, child care, and equal pay for equal work, this movement will pose a real threat to their ability to rule.

Opposition to the struggles of women to break the chains of their oppression is not in the interest of the oppressed but only in the interest of the oppressor. And that is the logic of the arguments of those who say that Chicanas do not want to or need to be liberated. . . .

Stripped of all rationalizations, when Chicanos deny support to the independent organization of Chicanas, what they are saying is simply that Chicanas are not oppressed. And that is the central question we must ask: are Chicanas oppressed?

All other arguments aside, the fact is that Chicanas *are* oppressed and that the battles they are now waging and will wage in the future, are for things they need: the right to legal abortions, the right to adequate child care, the right to contraceptive information and devices, the right to decide how many children they do or do not want to have. In short, the right to control their own bodies. . . .

Coupled with this campaign to repeal all abortion laws, women are fighting to end all forced sterilizations, a campaign in which Chicanas will play a central role. This demand is of key importance to Chicanas who are the victims of forced sterilizations justified by the viciously racist ideology that the problems of La Raza are caused by Raza women having too many babies.

In line with other brutal abuses of women, Chicanas have been used as guinea pigs for experimentation with contraception. This was done recently in San Antonio by a doctor who wanted to test the reaction of women to birth control pills. Without informing them or asking their opinion, he gave some of the women dummy pills (placebos) that would not prevent conception, and as a result some of the women became pregnant. When questioned about his action, his reply was: "If you think you can explain a placebo test to women like these you never met Mrs. Gomez from the West Side."

The feminist movement today provides a vehicle for organizing against and putting an end to such racist, sexist practices. And that is what women are talking about when they talk about women's liberation.

Another essential fight that Chicanas have begun is around the need for adequate child care. While billions of dollars are spent yearly by this government on war, no money can be found to alleviate the plight of millions of women who, in addition to being forced to work, have families to care for. . . .

Demands such as twenty-four hour child-care centers financed by the government and controlled by the community, are the kinds of concrete issues that Chicanas are fighting for. As Chicanas explain in "A Proposal for Childcare," published in *Regeneración,* "Child care must be provided as a public service, like public schools, unemployment insurance, social security, and so forth. The potential for a mass movement around this initiative is clear."

An important aspect of the struggles of Chicanas is the demand that the gains made through their campaigns be *controlled by Chicanas.* The demand for community control is a central axis of the Chicana liberation struggle as a whole. Thus, when Chicanas, as Chicanas, raise demands for child-care facilities, abortion clinics, etc., controlled by Chicanas, their fight is an integral part of the Chicana liberation struggle.

When Chicanas choose to organize into their own separate organizations, they are not turning away from La Causa or waging a campaign against men. They are saying to Chicanos: "We are oppressed as Chicanas and we are moving against our oppression. Support our struggles." The sooner that Chicanos understand the need for women to struggle around their own special demands, through their own organizations, the further La Raza as a whole will be on the road toward liberation.

It is important to keep in mind that many of the misunderstandings that have arisen so far in the Chicano movement regarding Chicanas are due primarily to the newness of this development, and many will be resolved through the course of events. One thing, however, is clear—Chicanas are determined to fight. . . .

The struggle for women's liberation is the Chicana's struggle, and only a strong independent Chicana movement, as part of the general women's liberation movement and as part of the movement of La Raza, can ensure its success.

4. Susan Griffin Calls Rape the "All-American Crime," 1971

I have never been free of the fear of rape. From a very early age I, like most women, have thought of rape as part of my natural environment—something to be feared and prayed against like fire or lightning. I never asked why men raped; I simply thought it one of the many mysteries of human nature.

I was, however, curious enough about the violent side of humanity to read every crime magazine I was able to ferret away from my grandfather. Each issue featured at least one "sex crime," with pictures of a victim, usually in a pearl necklace, and of the ditch or the orchard where her body was found. I was never certain why the victims were always women, nor what the motives of the murderer were, but I did guess that the world was not a safe place for women. I observed that my

Susan Griffin, "Rape: The All-American Crime," *Ramparts* 10, no. 3 (1971): 26–35. Reprinted by permission of the author.

grandmother was meticulous about locks, and quick to draw the shades before any-one removed so much as a shoe. I sensed that danger lurked outside.

At the age of eight, my suspicions were confirmed. My grandmother took me to the back of the house where the men wouldn't hear, and told me that strange men wanted to do harm to little girls. I learned not to walk on dark streets, not to talk to strangers, or get into strange cars, to lock doors, and to be modest. She never ex-plained why a man would want to harm a little girl, and I never asked.

If I thought for a while that my grandmother's fears were imaginary, the illu-sion was brief. That year, on the way home from school, a schoolmate a few years older than I tried to rape me. Later, in an obscure aisle of the local library (while I was reading *Freddy the Pig*) I turned to discover a man exposing himself. Then, the friendly man around the corner was arrested for child molesting.

My initiation to sexuality was typical. Every woman has similar stories to tell—the first man who attacked her may have been a neighbor, a family friend, an uncle, her doctor, or perhaps her own father. And women who grow up in New York City always have tales about the subway.

But though rape and the fear of rape are a daily part of every woman's con-sciousness, the subject is so rarely discussed by that unofficial staff of male intel-lectuals (who write the books which study seemingly every other form of male activity) that one begins to suspect a conspiracy of silence. And indeed, the obscurity of rape in print exists in marked contrast to the frequency of rape in reality, for *forcible rape is the most frequently committed violent crime in America today*. The Federal Bureau of Investigation classes three crimes as violent: murder, aggravated assault and forcible rape. In 1968, 31,060 rapes were *reported*. According to the FBI and independent criminologists, however, to approach accuracy this figure must be multiplied by at least a factor of ten to compensate for the fact that most rapes are not reported; when these compensatory mathematics are used, there are more rapes committed than aggravated assaults and homicides.

When I asked Berkeley, California's Police Inspector in charge of rape investi-gation if he knew why men rape women, he replied that he had not spoken with "these people and delved into what really makes them tick, because that really isn't my job. . . ." However, when I asked him how a woman might prevent being raped, he was not so reticent, "I wouldn't advise any female to go walking around alone at night . . . and she should lock her car at all times." The Inspector illustrated his warning with a grisly story about a man who lay in wait for women in the back seats of their cars, while they were shopping in a local supermarket. This man eventually murdered one of his rape victims. "Always lock your car," the Inspector repeated, and then added, without a hint of irony, "Of course, you don't have to be paranoid about this type of thing." . . .

If a male society rewards aggressive, domineering sexual behavior, it contains within itself a sexual schizophrenia. For the masculine man is also expected to prove his mettle as a protector of women. To the naive eye, this dichotomy implies that men fall into one of two categories: those who rape and those who protect. In fact, life does not prove so simple. In a study euphemistically entitled "Sex Aggression by College Men," it was discovered that men who believe in a double standard of morality for men and women, who in fact believe most fervently in the ultimate value of virginity, are more liable to commit "this aggressive variety of sexual exploitation." . . .

In the system of chivalry, men protect women against men. This is not unlike the protection relationship which the mafia established with small businesses in the early part of this century. Indeed, chivalry is an age-old protection racket which depends for its existence on rape.

According to the male mythology which defines and perpetuates rape, it is an animal instinct inherent in the male. The story goes that sometime in our prehistorical past, the male, more hirsute and burly than today's counterparts, roamed about an uncivilized landscape until he found a desirable female. (Oddly enough, this female is *not* pictured as more muscular than the modern woman.) Her mate does not bother with courtship. He simply grabs her by the hair and drags her to the closest cave. Presumably, one of the major advantages of modern civilization for the female has been the civilizing of the male. We call it chivalry.

But women do not get chivalry for free. According to the logic of sexual politics, we too have to civilize our behavior. (Enter chastity. Enter virginity. Enter monogamy.) For the female, civilized behavior means chastity before marriage and faithfulness within it. Chivalrous behavior in the male is supposed to protect that chastity from involuntary defilement. The fly in the ointment of this otherwise peaceful system is the fallen woman. She does not behave. And therefore she does not deserve protection. Or, to use another argument, a major tenet of the same value system: what has once been defiled cannot again be violated. One begins to suspect that it is the behavior of the fallen woman, and not that of the male, that civilization aims to control.

The assumption that a woman who does not respect the double standard deserves whatever she gets (or at the very least "asks for it") operates in the courts today. While in some states a man's previous rape convictions are not considered admissible evidence, the sexual reputation of the rape victim is considered a crucial element of the facts upon which the court must decide innocence or guilt.

The court's respect for the double standard manifested itself particularly clearly in the case of the People v. Jerry Plotkin. Mr. Plotkin, a 36-year-old jeweler, was tried for rape last spring in a San Francisco Superior Court. According to the woman who brought the charges, Plotkin, along with three other men, forced her at gunpoint to enter a car one night in October 1970. She was taken to Mr. Plotkin's fashionable apartment where he and the three other men first raped her and then, in the delicate language of the *S.F. Chronicle,* "subjected her to perverted sex acts." She was, she said, set free in the morning with the warning that she would be killed if she spoke to anyone about the event. She did report the incident to the police who then searched Plotkin's apartment and discovered a long list of names of women. Her name was on the list and had been crossed out.

In addition to the woman's account of her abduction and rape, the prosecution submitted four of Plotkin's address books containing the names of hundreds of women. Plotkin claimed he did not know all of the women since some of the names had been given to him by friends and he had not yet called on them. Several women, however, did testify in court that Plotkin had, to cite the *Chronicle,* "lured them up to his apartment under one pretext or another, and forced his sexual attentions on them."

Plotkin's defense rested on two premises. First, through his own testimony Plotkin established a reputation for himself as a sexual libertine who frequently picked up girls in bars and took them to his house where sexual relations often took place. He was the Playboy. He claimed that the accusation of rape, therefore, was false—this incident had simply been one of many casual sexual relationships, the victim one of many playmates. The second premise of the defense was that his accuser was also a sexual libertine. However, the picture created of the young woman (fully 13 years younger than Plotkin) was not akin to the light-hearted, gay-bachelor image projected by the defendant. On the contrary, the day after the defense cross-examined the woman, the *Chronicle* printed a story headlined, "Grueling Day For Rape Case Victim." (A leaflet passed out by women in front of the courtroom was more succinct, "rape was committed by four men in a private apartment in October; on Thursday, it was done by a judge and a lawyer in a public courtroom.")

Through skillful questioning fraught with innuendo, Plotkin's defense attorney James Martin MacInnis portrayed the young woman as a licentious opportunist and unfit mother. MacInnis began by asking the young woman (then employed as a secretary) whether or not it was true that she was "familiar with liquor" and had worked as a "cocktail waitress." The young woman replied (the *Chronicle* wrote "admitted") that she had worked once or twice as a cocktail waitress. The attorney then asked if she had worked as a secretary in the financial district but had "left that employment after it was discovered that you had sexual intercourse on a couch in the office." The woman replied, "That is a lie. I left because I didn't like working in a one-girl office. It was too lonely." Then the defense asked if, while working as an attendant at a health club, "you were accused of having a sexual affair with a man?" Again the woman denied the story, "I was never accused of that."

Plotkin's attorney then sought to establish that his client's accuser was living with a married man. She responded that the man was separated from his wife. Finally he told the court that she had "spent the night" with another man who lived in the same building.

At this point in the testimony the woman asked Plotkin's defense attorney. "Am I on trial? . . . It is embarrassing and personal to admit these things to all these people. . . . I did not commit a crime. I am a human being." The lawyer, true to the chivalry of his class, apologized and immediately resumed questioning her, turning his attention to her children. (She is divorced, and the children at the time of the trial were in a foster home.) "Isn't it true that your two children have a sex game in which one gets on top of another and they—" "That is a lie!" the young woman interrupted him. She ended her testimony by explaining "They are wonderful children. They are not perverted."

The jury, divided in favor of acquittal ten to two, asked the court stenographer to read the woman's testimony back to them. After this reading, the Superior Court acquitted the defendant of both the charges of rape and kidnapping. . . .

Rape is an act of aggression in which the victim is denied her self-determination. It is an act of violence which, if not actually followed by beatings or murder, nevertheless always carried with it the threat of death. And finally, rape is a form of mass terrorism, for the victims of rape are chosen indiscriminately, but the propagandists for male supremacy broadcast that it is women who cause rape by being unchaste or in the wrong place at the wrong time—in essence, by behaving as though they were free.

5. The Supreme Court Legalizes Abortion in *Roe* v. *Wade*, 1973

Mr. Justice Blackmun delivered the opinion of the Court.

This Texas federal appeal and its Georgia companion. *Doe* v. *Bolton,* present constitutional challenges to state criminal abortion legislation. The Texas statutes under attack here are typical of those that have been in effect in many States for approximately a century. The Georgia statutes, in contrast, have a modern cast and are a legislative product that, to an extent at least, obviously reflects the influences of recent attitudinal change, of advancing medical knowledge and techniques, and of new thinking about an old issue.

We forthwith acknowledge our awareness of the sensitive and emotional nature of the abortion controversy, of the vigorous opposing views, even among physicians, and of the deep and seemingly absolute convictions that the subject inspires. One's philosophy, one's experiences, one's exposure to the raw edges of human existence, one's religious training, one's attitudes toward life and family and their values, and the moral standards one establishes and seeks to observe, are all likely to influence and to color one's thinking and conclusions about abortion.

In addition, population growth, pollution, poverty, and racial overtones tend to complicate and not to simplify the problem.

Our task, of course, is to resolve the issue by constitutional measurement, free of emotion and of predilection. We seek earnestly to do this, and, because we do, we have inquired into, and in this opinion place some emphasis upon, medical and medical-legal history and what that history reveals about man's attitudes toward the abortion procedure over the centuries. . . .

It perhaps is not generally appreciated that the restrictive criminal abortion laws in effect in a majority of States today are of relatively recent vintage. Those laws, generally proscribing abortion or its attempt at any time during pregnancy except when necessary to preserve the pregnant woman's life, are not of ancient or even of common-law origin. Instead, they derive from statutory changes effected, for the most part, in the latter half of the 19th century. . . .

Three reasons have been advanced to explain historically the enactment of criminal abortion laws in the 19th century and to justify their continued existence.

It has been argued occasionally that these laws were the product of a Victorian social concern to discourage illicit sexual conduct. Texas, however, does not advance this justification in the present case, and it appears that no court or commentator has taken the argument seriously. . . .

Roe v. *Wade*, 410 U.S. 113 (1973).

A second reason is concerned with abortion as a medical procedure. When most criminal abortion laws were first enacted, the procedure was a hazardous one for the woman. . . . Thus, it has been argued that a State's real concern in enacting a criminal abortion law was to protect the pregnant woman, that is, to restrain her from submitting to a procedure that placed her life in serious jeopardy.

Modern medical techniques have altered this situation. Appellants and various amici refer to medical data indicating that abortion in early pregnancy, this is, prior to the end of the first trimester, although not without its risk, is now relatively safe. Mortality rates for women undergoing early abortions, where the procedure is legal, appear to be as low as or lower than the rates for normal childbirth. Consequently, any interest of the State in protecting the woman from an inherently hazardous procedure, except when it would be equally dangerous for her to forgo it, has largely disappeared. Of course, important state interests in the area of health and medical standards do remain. . . .

The third reason is the State's interest—some phrase it in terms of duty—in protecting prenatal life. Some of the argument for this justification rests on the theory that a new human life is present from the moment of conception. The State's interest and general obligation to protect life then extends, it is argued, to prenatal life. Only when the life of the pregnant mother herself is at stake, balanced against the life she carries within her, should the interest of the embryo or fetus not prevail. Logically, of course, a legitimate state interest in this area need not stand or fall on acceptance of the belief that life begins at conception or at some other point prior to live birth. In assessing the State's interest, recognition may be given to the less rigid claim that as long as at least *potential* life is involved, the State may assert interests beyond the protection of the pregnant woman alone. . . .

The Constitution does not explicitly mention any right of privacy. In a line of decisions, however, the Court has recognized that a right of personal privacy, or a guarantee of certain areas or zones of privacy, does exist under the Constitution. . . .

This right of privacy, whether it be founded in the Fourteenth Amendment's concept of personal liberty and restrictions upon state action, as we feel it is, or, as the District Court determined, in the Ninth Amendment's reservation of rights to the people, is broad enough to encompass a woman's decision whether or not to terminate her pregnancy. The detriment that the State would impose upon the pregnant woman by denying this choice altogether is apparent. Specific and direct harm medically diagnosable even in early pregnancy may be involved. Maternity, or additional offspring, may force upon the woman a distressful life and future. Psychological harm may be imminent. Mental and physical health may be taxed by child care. There is also the distress, for all concerned, associated with the unwanted child, and there is the problem of bringing a child into a family already unable, psychologically and otherwise, to care for it. In other cases, as in this one, the additional difficulties and continuing stigma of unwed motherhood may be involved. All these are factors the woman and her responsible physician necessarily will consider in consultation.

On the basis of elements such as these, appellant and some amici argue that the woman's right is absolute and that she is entitled to terminate her pregnancy at whatever time, in whatever way, and for whatever reason she alone chooses. With this we do not agree. Appellant's arguments that Texas either has no valid interest at all in regulating the abortion decision, or no interest strong enough to support any limitation upon the woman's sole determination, is unpersuasive. The Court's decisions recognizing a right of privacy also acknowledge that some state regulation in areas protected by that right is appropriate. As noted above, a State may properly assert important interests in safeguarding health, in maintaining medical standards, and in protecting potential life. At some point in pregnancy, these respective interests become sufficiently compelling to sustain regulation of the factors that govern the abortion decision. The privacy right involved, therefore, cannot be said to be absolute. . . .

We, therefore, conclude that the right of personal privacy includes the abortion decision, but that this right is not unqualified and must be considered against important state interests in regulation. . . .

The appellee and certain amici argue that the fetus is a "person" within the language and meaning of the Fourteenth Amendment. In support of this, they outline at length and in detail the well-known facts of fetal development. If this suggestion of personhood is established, the appellant's case, of course, collapses, for the fetus' right to life is then guaranteed specifically by the Amendment. The appellant conceded as much on reargument. On the other hand, the appellee conceded on reargument that no case could be cited that holds that a fetus is a person within the meaning of the Fourteenth Amendment.

The Constitution does not define "person" in so many words. Section 1 of the Fourteenth Amendment contains three references to "person." The first, in defining "citizens," speaks of "persons born or naturalized in the United States." The word also appears both in the Due Process Clause and in the Equal Protection Clause. "Person" is used in other places in the Constitution. . . . But in nearly all these instances, the use of the word is such that it has application only postnatally. None indicates, with any assurance, that it has any possible prenatal application.

All this, together with our observation, supra, that throughout the major portion of the 19th century prevailing legal abortion practices were far freer than they are today, persuades us that the word "person" as used in the Fourteenth Amendment, does not include the unborn. . . .

Texas urges that, apart from the Fourteenth Amendment, life begins at conception and is present throughout pregnancy, and that, therefore, the State has a compelling interest in protecting that life from and after conception. We need not resolve the difficult question of when life begins. When those trained in the respective disciplines of medicine, philosophy, and theology are unable to arrive at any consensus, the judiciary, at this point in the development of man's knowledge, is not in a position to speculate as to the answer. . . .

With respect to the State's important and legitimate interest in the health of the mother, the "compelling" point, in the light of present medical knowledge, is at approximately the end of the first trimester. This is so because of the now-established medical fact that until the end of the first trimester mortality in abortion may be less than mortality in normal childbirth. It follows that, from and after this point, a State may regulate the abortion procedure to the extent that the regulation reasonably relates to the preservation and protection of maternal health. . . .

With respect to the State's important and legitimate interest in potential life, the "compelling" point is at viability. This is so because the fetus then presumably has the capability of meaningful life outside the mother's womb. State regulation protective of fetal life after viability thus has both logical and biological justifications. If the State is interested in protecting fetal life after viability, it may go so far as to pro-scribe abortion during that period, except when it is necessary to preserve the life or health of the mother. . . .

To summarize and to repeat:

1. A state criminal abortion statute of the current Texas type, that excepts from criminality only a *life-saving* procedure on behalf of the mother, without regard to pregnancy stage and without recognition of the other interests involved, is violative of the Due Process Clause of the Fourteenth Amendment.
   a. For the stage prior to approximately the end of the first trimester, the abor-tion decision and its effectuation must be left to the medical judgment of the pregnant woman's attending physician.
   b. For the stage subsequent to approximately the end of the first trimester, the State, in promoting its interest in the health of the mother, may, if it chooses, regulate the abortion procedure in ways that are reasonably related to mater-nal health.
   c. For the stage subsequent to viability, the State in promoting its interest in the potentiality of human life may, if it chooses, regulate, and even proscribe, abortion except where it is necessary, in appropriate medical judgment, for the preservation of the life or health of the mother. . . .

Mr. Justice White, with whom Mr. Justice Rehnquist joins, dissenting.

At the heart of the controversy in these cases are those recurring pregnancies that pose no danger whatsoever to the life or health of the mother but are, neverthe-less, unwanted for any one or more of a variety of reasons—convenience, family planning, economics, dislike of children, the embarrassment of illegitimacy, etc. The common claim before us is that for any one of such reasons, or for no reason at all, and without asserting or claiming any threat to life or health, any woman is en-titled to an abortion at her request if she is able to find a medical advisor willing to undertake the procedure.

The Court for the most part sustains this position: During the period prior to the time the fetus becomes viable, the Constitution of the United States values the convenience, whim, or caprice of the putative mother more than the life or poten-tial life of the fetus; the Constitution, therefore, guarantees the right to an abortion as against any state law or policy seeking to protect the fetus from an abortion not prompted by more compelling reasons of the mother.

With all due respect, I dissent. I find nothing in the language or history of the Constitution to support the Court's judgment. The Court simply fashions and an-nounces a new constitutional right for pregnant mothers and, with scarcely any rea-son or authority for its action, invests that right with sufficient substance to override most existing state abortion statutes. The upshot is that the people and the legisla-tures of the 50 States are constitutionally disentitled to weigh the relative importance of the continued existence and development of the fetus, on the one hand, against a spectrum of possible impacts on the mother, on the other hand. As an exercise of raw judicial power, the Court perhaps has authority to do what it does today; but in my view its judgment is an improvident and extravagant exercise of the power of judicial review that the Constitution extends to this Court.

6. Lindsy Van Gelder Reports on the "World Series of Sex-Discrimination Suits," 1978

The New York *Times* has long been known to the press corps and media buffs as "the Good Gray Lady." The term is not without endearment, but it refers only to the *Time*'s somber (some would say stuffy) sense of itself as both the Number One newspaper of record and the influential editorialist of liberal Establishment values. The far livelier tabloid *Daily News* is read by many more New Yorkers, but the *Times* is the Bible of the upwardly mobile and professional classes—and its editors fancy the Good Gray Lady the collective information font . . . for the cultural, financial, educational, and political elite.

"Ladies" and other females, however, are in comparatively scant supply at the *Times,* and the prevailing pigmentation is white.

The *Times* itself conceded this point last November in an editorial entitled "The Complaints of White Men," its response to charges that affirmative action programs for women and minorities constitute "reverse discrimination" against white males. "As the list of our company officers testify each day on this page," the editorial began, "we are an institution run mostly by white men. As in most other institutions, women and non-whites came later than white men into the hierarchies from which our managers have been chosen. Recognizing the inadequacy of the result, and faced with social and legal pressures that we ourselves helped to generate, we have undertaken corrective measures, affirmative action, to expand opportunity in our company." . . .

It is thus somewhat of a blow to the Gray Lady's image of fairness and rectitude that the newspaper is currently the target of employment discrimination suits brought under Title VII of the Civil Rights Act by both female and minority personnel. . . . Although most sex-discrimination cases that go as far through the federal machinery as the *Times* suit has are settled out of court, the paper's management, insisting they have not discriminated, is determined to see this one through the courts, and the case is scheduled to go to trial this fall. (The separate minority suit is at an earlier legal stage.) Given the cast of characters and the issues being raised, the women's day in court already promises to be the Title VII World Series.

It all began five years ago when a group of *Times* women—including reporters, clerks, telephone solicitors, and other non-newsroom personnel—began meeting among themselves and later with publisher Arthur O. (Punch) Sulzberger to discuss their grievances. It was only after they became convinced that they would find no redress through informal "gentlemanly" channels that they contacted attorneys Harriet Rabb and Howard Rubin, co-directors of Columbia Law School's Employment Rights Project. A by-now almost legendary Title VII specialist, Rabb is an outspoken feminist who has chalked up victories for women employees at *Reader's Digest, Newsweek,* New York Telephone, and a dozen Wall Street law firms.

Several women formally filed charges with the Equal Employment Opportunity Commission in the spring of 1973. It was difficult for the *Times* to dismiss the original group as a band of no-talent radical malcontents since they included several of

Lindsy Van Gelder, "Women vs. The New York 'Times': The World Series of Sex-Discrimination Suits," *Ms. Magazine* 7, no. 3 (September 1978): 66–68, 104. Reprinted by permission of the author.

the paper's most respected female staff members. One was star political reporter Eileen Shanahan (now with the Department of Health, Education, and Welfare), whose annual salary was $2,500 less than that of the average male in the *Time's* Washington bureau. Another was Elizabeth Boylan, known professionally as Betsy Wade, then chief of the paper's foreign copydesk, and once glowingly described in an in-house *Times* publication as being able to do "a man's work with a woman's delicacy." Wade, who earns more than her average male colleague, charged that for 10 years she had coveted the post of assistant news editor and had been passed over in favor of at least nine men.

The women won a significant point when the federal court ruled that theirs was a class action suit, which meant that they could act on behalf of all female *Times* employees. A cohesive women's caucus now exists at the paper.

"There's a real feeling of camaraderie among us," according to one member— perhaps all the more surprising since journalists tend traditionally to be apolitical loners, and the *Times* in particular is known for its Byzantine newsroom competitiveness. . . .

According to one male former *Times* executive, sexism does indeed exist there, but in a genteel form in keeping with the overall tone of the paper: "The editors look around furtively before they make their tits-and-ass cracks." . . .

The ex-*Times*man recalled being introduced to Betsy Wade by managing editor Seymour Topping in 1969 and later being told by Topping that Wade was "a really fine newspaperwoman. If she weren't a woman, she'd be in the bullpen [the main news desk] right now!" Since the initiation of the women's suit, he added, *Times* executives have given a great deal of lip service to hiring and promoting women. But he's skeptical: "Abe Rosenthal [executive editor] would get up at meetings, roll his eyes heavenward, and moan about 'our problem' and how he wanted to see some blacks and women around the place. Then last year he personally hired three people—all white, middle-class men."

The rumor in the city room is that Rosenthal and publisher Sulzberger made the decision not to settle out of court with the women's caucus, although it is also said that some other top executives were dismayed by this decision. By many accounts, however, women have no special monopoly on generally rough treatment at the hands of management. "Listen," said one reporter. "Blacks are oppressed at the *Times*. Gays are oppressed. But even white Jewish males feel oppressed. They're an equal opportunity oppressor." Since a great many journalists feel that the *Times* is the pinnacle of the profession, they are apparently willing to endure a fair amount of psychic scarring in exchange for a *Times* byline.

The upcoming trial will at least in part be a war of numbers. Harriet Rabb and her colleagues have amassed a staggering array of statistics purporting to show that the *Times* discriminates against women at all levels, from editors to cleaning women, in hiring, promotions, pay, assignments, among other areas. For example:

- Scores of positions at the *Times* have never been held by women.
- A 1977 government report based on personnel information supplied by the *Times* concluded that women were "underutilized" in 27 out of 37 divisions.
- According to Rabb's proposed pretrial order, the number of men employed by the *Times* in "craft union" jobs (*i.e.*, printers, newspaper deliverers, press workers, et cetera) in 1976 was 5,760. The number of women in such jobs was 19. Among

white-collar workers and professionals, as of January, 1976, 26.2 percent were women—at a time when fully 40 percent of the U.S. and New York labor force as a whole was female.

• As of January, 1976, males averaged higher salaries in 73.4 percent of all jobs than women. The difference between the average male and female salary was $5,159 a year. Even when length of service, total work experience, and education are factored in, the *Times* pays men an average $3,735 more a year than women are paid.

• In 1976, when the *Times* conducted a performance evaluation of its reporters, 18 men who were ranked "OK But Needs Improvement To Meet Normal Requirements" or "Satisfactory," earned more than women receiving the highest rating of "Better than Most."

Rabb's research also turned up a number of less-than-enlightened interoffice memos. One evaluated the "work" of a woman in the circulation and promotion department this way: "Very pleasant. Good at shorthand and typing. Her chief ambition is probably to get married. Has a good figure and is not restrained about dressing it to advantage." Another was a response from the Sunday editor to a *Times* employee who had recommended a female job applicant: "What does she look like? Twiggy? Lynn Redgrave? Perhaps you ought to send over her vital statistics, or a picture in a bikini." A third memo praised a female mail clerk, adding "I would make her my first assistant if she were a man." Another goodie brought forth in a proposed pretrial order was the fact that a female foreign correspondent—one of the few ever for the *Times*—was once ordered out of Vietnam to cover the Paris fashion collections, something no male war correspondent was ever assigned to do.

For its part, the *Times* has marshaled its own statistical analysis prepared by Dean Seymour Wolfbein of the Temple University School of Business Administration. Wolfbein's conclusions, set forth in a pretrial affidavit, fail to address the question of pay differentials, but maintain "that there is no systematic pattern of underutilization of women at the *Times*." While the proportion of women at the *Times* rose by only 9/10 of a percentage point between 1970 and 1976, according to the affidavit, the number of women in upper-echelon jobs almost quadrupled which was offered as proof of "a redeployment of women workers from the office and clerical category up the occupational ladder."

The *Times* also answers charges of discrimination in promotion, salary, and assignment, at least in the newsroom, by noting that the deployment of reporters and editors is a fairly subjective process, in which people are judged by intangibles such as "news judgment" rather than by what graduate degrees they have or how long they've been on the job. Executive vice-president James Goodale added that "women, for reasons I don't think are our fault, don't constitute a large talent pool in the thirty to forty-five age group, where you would find people for middle-management jobs." . . .

According to Goodale, the *Times* views itself as being "at the top of the list" in progressive hiring policies, and claims that "our institutional credibility is being attacked" by the suit. Goodale was asked if the *Times* wasn't in any case saddled with a credibility problem by the fact that the majority of its female reporters—women paid to exercise their news judgment—believe that they are discriminated against. How could so many intelligent women be so misled? "I don't know. You'll have to ask them that," Goodale replied.

The women in turn have mixed feelings about the upcoming trial. "The suit has definitely raised the editors' consciousnesses," said one. "You can see it in the news coverage. I'm not sure, for instance, if we would have had a Page One continuing series on the Equal Rights Amendment without the pressure of the suit. [Though their editorial page came out against extension.] And they do seem to have more women in top jobs in the last few months—although all of them are women from the outside, not people involved with the suit." . . .

While Harriet Rabb will attempt to prove a pattern of discrimination at the *Times,* the paper's attorneys will in many cases be countering that a specific woman didn't get a specific job, raise, or assignment because she just plain wasn't good enough—a prospect that both sides view as regrettable, but unavoidable. "The idea of going to trial doesn't fill me with radical fervor," admitted one *Times* woman. "Everybody's going to be spattered with mud, and it won't do any of our careers any good. But at this point our basic contention is so clear-cut that there's just no question of turning back."

◆ *E S S A Y S*

Independent historian Anne Standley examines the role and consciousness of black women in the civil rights movement. She argues that black women activists were reluctant to acknowledge or challenge sexism in the movement, fearing that to do so would undercut black men or divert attention from the issue of racism. Nancy MacLean of Northwestern University explores the history of affirmative action in the 1970s, arguing that through the use of affirmative–action laws, working-class women made long-lasting contributions to modern feminism. Jane Gerhard of Harvard University analyzes the impact of second wave feminists on sexual values. In demanding female sexual freedom, feminists challenged the widely-held view that "normal" women were heterosexual and passive in their erotic relations.

The Role of Black Women in the Civil Rights Movement

ANNE STANDLEY

The role of black women in the civil rights movement has received scant attention from historians. Most studies of the movement have examined such organizations as the Southern Christian Leadership Conference, the Student Nonviolent Coordinating Committee, the Congress of Racial Equality, and the National Association for the Advancement of Colored People, and accordingly have focused on the black ministers who served as officers in those organizations, all of whom were men. Harvard Sitkoff's list of the leaders of the movement, for example, consisted exclusively of men—Martin Luther King, Jr., of SCLC, James Forman and John Lewis of SNCC, James Farmer of CORE, Roy Wilkins of the NAACP, and Whitney Young of the National Urban League. The accounts of other historians, such as Aldon Morris, Clayborne Carson, and August Meier, also showed male preachers spearheading

---

Anne Standley, "The Role of Black Women in the Civil Rights Movement," in Darlene Clark Hine, ed. *Black Women's History: Theory and Practice* 10 (Brooklyn, N.Y.: Carlson Pub., 1990), 183–201.

the various protests—boycotts of bus companies and white-owned businesses, voter registration drives, and marches—that constituted the movement. Likewise, the vast majority of students leading the sit-ins and freedom rides named by Sitkoff were men. He cited only two of the many women who held positions of leadership in the movement—Fannie Lou Hamer, who was elected delegate to the Democratic National Convention by the Mississippi Freedom Democratic Party in 1964, and Ella Baker, executive secretary of SCLC—and understated their influence. . . .

The argument that men were the principal leaders of the civil rights movement is not wholly inaccurate. According to women who achieved prominence within the movement, such as Septima Clark, who trained teachers of citizenship schools for SCLC, or Ella Baker, and historians Jacqueline Jones and Paula Giddings, the ministers' sexism and authoritarian views of leadership prevented women from assuming command of any of the movement organizations. Indeed, in light of the advantages men possessed in establishing themselves as leaders of the movement—the preachers' virtual monopoly on political power within the black community and the exclusion of women from the ministry in many black churches—it is remarkable that any women achieved positions of authority.

Yet, in fact, women exerted an enormous influence, both formally, as members of the upper echelon of SNCC, SCLC, and the Mississippi Freedom Democratic Party, and informally, as spontaneous leaders and dedicated participants. Many of the protests that historians describe as led by ministers were initiated by women. For example, Martin Luther King, Jr., is usually cited as the leader of the Montgomery Bus Boycott, since it was King who was appointed director of the organization that coordinated the boycott, the Montgomery Improvement Association. Yet the boycott was started by a woman, Jo Ann Robinson, and by the women's group that she headed, the Women's Political Council. Black women directed voter registration drives, taught in freedom schools, and provided food and housing for movement volunteers. As members of the MFDP, women won positions as delegates to the national Democratic convention in 1964 and as representatives to Congress. They demonstrated a heroism no less than that of men. They suffered the same physical abuse, loss of employment, destruction of property, and risk to their lives.

Black women also deserve credit for the refusal within the movement to accept halfway measures towards eradicating Jim Crow practices. Fannie Lou Hamer's rejection of the compromise offered the MFDP delegation at the Democratic National Convention in 1964 typified the courage of black women, who formed the majority of the preachers' congregations and whose pressure forced the ministers in SCLC, CORE, and other movement associations to persist in the face of white opposition to their demands. Paula Giddings reported that when the ministers of Montgomery met after the first day of the bus boycott to discuss whether to continue the boycott, they agreed on the condition that their names not be publicized as the boycott leaders. E. D. Nixon, former head of the Montgomery NAACP, shamed them into giving their public endorsement by reminding them of the women to whom they were accountable: "How you gonna have a mass meeting, gonna boycott a city bus line without the white folks knowing about it? You guys have went around here and lived off these poor washerwomen all your lives and ain't never done nothing for 'em. Now you got a chance to do something for 'em, you talking about you don't want the White folks to know about it."

As well, black women were responsible for the movement's success in generating popular support for the movement among rural blacks. Ella Baker convinced SCLC to jettison plans to take control of SNCC, allowing the student-run group to remain independent of the other movement organizations and to adopt, with Baker's encouragement, an egalitarian approach to decisionmaking. Because SNCC workers formulated the organization's objectives by soliciting the views of members of black communities in which the volunteers worked, they were able to build considerable grass-roots support for the movement.

Despite the exclusion of black women from top positions in movement organizations and the little recognition they received from either blacks or whites for their contributions, the published accounts of black women activists suggest that the movement gave women as well as men a sense of empowerment. . . . Yet these women differed in their analyses of the cause of the racial oppression that they combatted. Two of the older women leaders—Daisy Bates, who was president of the NAACP State Conference of Branches, and who led the integration of Central High School in Little Rock, Arkansas, and Jo Ann Robinson—and a younger leader, Diane Nash, who organized sit-ins and freedom rides for SNCC, viewed racism as politically motivated. They believed that if blacks could obtain the vote, white politicians would be forced to act against racial discrimination at the polls, segregated schools, and the varied forms of extralegal violence carried out against blacks. Blacks could use their political influence to improve their economic status, which in turn would enhance their image among whites.

Because they saw themselves as having to convince whites to support the movement, and because they identified so completely with the struggle for civil rights, Bates, Robinson, and Nash refrained from making critical judgments about the movement or their roles within it. . . . Consequently their behavior showed contradictions—on the one hand a boldness in initiating protests and applying pressure on whites in power, while at the same time a submissiveness in their acceptance of the authority of the black male clergy.

Jo Anne Robinson was born in 1916 in Colloden, Georgia, twenty-five miles from Macon. She was the youngest of twelve children. Her family subsequently moved to Macon, where she graduated first in her class from an all black high school. Robinson received a bachelor's degree from Georgia State College in Fort Valley, taught for five years at a public school in Macon, and earned a master's degree in English literature from Atlanta University. In 1949, after teaching for a year at Mary Allen College in Crockett, Texas, she moved to Montgomery to join the faculty at Alabama State University. Robinson chaired the Women's Political Council in Montgomery, an organization of professional women that sought to raise the status of blacks by working with juvenile and adult delinquents and organizing voter registration. She also served on the Executive Board of the Montgomery Improvement Association and edited the MIA newsletter.

Robinson declared that in publishing her memoir, she hoped to improve whites' image of blacks by demonstrating blacks' courage, dedication, and self-discipline in their fight for their rights. Robinson saw the movement as blacks' attempt to overcome the circumstances that degraded them—to secure the same living conditions and opportunities as whites—so as to live decently and thereby prove their equality with whites. . . .

Robinson's view of the movement as the first step towards blacks' redemption in the eyes of whites, and the role she assumed as the movement's publicist, left little room for a candid evaluation of the male leadership or for challenging its authority. She briefly criticized the ministers in Montgomery for their timidity, stating that only when they read a circular advertising the bus boycott and realized that "all the city's black congregations were quite intelligent on the matter and were planning to support the one-day boycott with or without the ministers' leadership" did they endorse it. She offset this reproach, however, with praise for the preachers' work, and attributed the boycott's success to the clergymen.

> Had it not been for the ministers and the support they received from their wonderful congregations, the outcome of the boycott might have been different. The ministers gave themselves, their time . . . and their leadership . . . which set examples for the laymen to follow. They gave us confidence, faith in ourselves, faith in them and their leadership, that helped the congregations to support the movement every foot of the way.

In her memoir, *The Long Shadow of Little Rock,* Daisy Bates displayed similar contradictions between her readiness to confront her white oppressors, which she demonstrated both as a child and as an adult, and her acceptance of what she regarded as a flawed black leadership. Bates grew up in southern Arkansas, in a town controlled by a sawmill company. She first experienced discrimination at the age of eight, when a white grocer refused to serve her until he had waited on all of the white customers. . . .

Bates not only challenged whites while growing up; she also defied the authority of her parents and members of the black community. . . . Bates's narrative showed that as an adult, she continued to challenge those in power. She met with the governor of Arkansas and the U.S. Attorney to urge them, unsuccessfully, to respond to the whites' violence. In contrast, however, she appears to have deferred to the male leadership in the black community. She made only a passing reference to her irritation at the black ministers' silence in the face of the whites' terrorism carried out against the black students, suggesting that she suppressed her frustration. In her conclusion, she assailed Congress and the Eisenhower administration for their lackluster support of desegregation, but like Robinson, refrained from placing any blame for the movement's slow progress on its leadership.

One can see similar inconsistencies in the actions of Diane Nash, a SNCC volunteer. Nash grew up in Chicago and came to Nashville to attend Fisk University. Nash's shock at the segregation of restaurants, water fountains, and other public facilities in the south prompted her to join SNCC. In 1965, Nash wrote an article for *Ebony* that implied that she accepted the prevailing view that the civil rights movement, and specifically SCLC, should be led primarily by men. Nash's article, "The Men Behind Martin Luther King" profiled the male staff members of SCLC. She depicted the women on the staff, who numbered three out of a total of twelve, as important but peripheral figures. . . . At no point did Nash question the women's secondary status with SCLC.

Nash's prominence in protest efforts, however, seemed to contradict the unspoken assumption of her article that men should lead the movement. Nash chaired the central committee of the sit-in movement in Nashville. She also assembled a second group of freedom riders to continue the journey when harassment forced the first group to disperse in Birmingham before they reached their destination of New Orleans. . . .

While Bates, Robinson, and Nash attributed racism to blacks' lack of representation in the political process, the majority of black women leaders who left accounts of their experiences regarded racial oppression as symptomatic of a structurally flawed society. Disheartened by the movement's fragmentation in the late sixties and by what they regarded as its limited success, they concluded that racial oppression formed part of a larger system of inequities that characterized American society and that could not be eradicated without addressing the other injustices to which it was connected. One activist who became disillusioned was Jean Smith, a student at Howard University who registered voters for SNCC in 1963 and who organized the MFDP meetings that elected an integrated delegation to the Democratic National Convention in 1964. Smith maintained that the right to vote, while unifying the black community and giving blacks the confidence to assert themselves and challenge racist laws or customs, had proved ineffectual in diminishing white hegemony and improving the living conditions of blacks.

> The best way to understand is to look at what the Negro people who cast their lot with the Movement believed. They believed, I think, that their participation in the drive for voting rights would ultimately result in the relief of their poverty and hopelessness. They thought that with the right to vote they could end the exploitation of their labor by the plantation owners. They thought they could get better schools for their children; they could get sewers dug and sidewalks paved. They thought they could get adequate public-health facilities for their communities. And of course they got none of these. . . . They believed there was a link between representation in government and making that government work for you. What they—and I—discovered was that for some people, this link does not exist. . . .

This disenchantment with the civil rights movement led some activists to temporarily embrace separatism. Smith, for example, in 1968 argued for a self-sufficient black community as the solution to blacks' political impotence. . . . Two years earlier, in 1966, [Joyce] Ladner [a SNCC volunteer] had also abandoned integration as a goal, convinced by the unrelenting brutality of whites that black power offered the most effective means of improving the status of blacks.

> When Vernon Dahmier [Ladner's mentor] was killed, my faith in integration was shaken. I found myself trying to justify my belief that "Black and white together" was still the solution to the race problem. . . . What Blacks needed to do, I thought, was to unite as a group and develop their own institutions and communities. What they needed was Black power! . . .

In addition to embracing separatism, Ladner turned to marxism for a diagnosis and a solution to racial oppression, along with Frances Beale, a former SNCC activist. Ladner asserted that in aspiring to middle-class goals of upward mobility and wealth, blacks condoned a structure of economic inequality. For Ladner, it was not blacks' lowly position in the hierarchy, but their acceptance of a capitalist economy which required a hierarchy, in which the fortunes of a few came from the exploitation of many, that oppressed them. Similarly, Frances Beale claimed that the feminists who sought only to improve their own position, demanding, for example, equal pay for equal work, failed to attack capitalism as the root of inequality and thus perpetuated an unjust system. . . .

Robinson, Bates and Nash sought to present a united front to white authorities. Consequently, they suppressed their differences with the male leadership. In contrast, the other activists aired their disagreements with the men managing the movement organizations, although most did so only in hindsight.

Only two of the women, Ella Baker and Septima Clark, confronted the male leaders of the movement while working with them to challenge their policies. Baker, like Robinson and Bates, belonged to the older generation of women civil rights leaders. She was 57 when SCLC appointed her as executive secretary in 1960. Baker was born in 1903 in Norfolk, Virginia. . . . Baker's father waited on tables for the Norfolk-Washington ferry; her mother tended to the sick in the community. After graduating from Shaw University in Raleigh, Baker began a long career of activism. She worked for a WPA [Works Progress Administration] consumer education project in New York City during the depression. The NAACP hired her in 1938 to recruit members and raise money in the south, and five years later named her national director of branches. Baker helped found SNCC in 1960. In 1964 she gave the keynote address at the MFDP convention in Jackson and established the MFDP Washington office.

Baker's readiness to confront the male officers in SCLC may have come in part from her commitment to participatory decisionmaking. . . . Baker's account of the debate within SCLC on a strategy to bring SNCC under SCLC's control showed her opposing SCLC's hierarchical style of management—her efforts to democratize the leadership of the movement by lobbying for an autonomous SNCC, and her refusal to defer to King.

> The Southern Christian Leadership Conference felt that they could influence how things went. They were interested in having the students become an arm of SCLC. They were most confident that this would be their baby, because I was their functionary and I had called the meeting. At a discussion called by the Reverend Dr. King, the SCLC leadership made decisions [about] who would speak to whom to influence the students to become part of SCLC. Well, I disagreed. There was no student at Dr. King's meeting. I was the nearest thing to a student, being the advocate, you see. I also knew from the beginning that having a woman be an executive of SCLC was not something that would go over with the male-dominated leadership. And then, of course, my personality wasn't right, in the sense I was not afraid to disagree with the higher authorities. I wasn't one to say, yes, because it came from the Reverend King. So when it was proposed that the leadership could influence the direction by speaking to, let's say, the man from Virginia, he could speak to the leadership of the Virginia student group, and the assumption was that having spoken to so-and-so, so-and-so would do what they wanted done, I was outraged. I walked out.

Septima Clark, the other activist who challenged the male staff of SCLC, was also a member of the older generation of women civil rights leaders. Clark was born in 1898 in Charleston, North Carolina. She taught in the Charleston public schools until she lost her job in 1956 when the legislature passed a law prohibiting state employees from belonging to the NAACP. The Highlander Folk School, which brought blacks and whites together to discuss social issues at a farm in Tennessee, hired Clark to lead workshops training members of rural communities to teach their neighbors to read and to register to vote. In 1961, when the Tennessee legislature moved to close Highlander, SCLC and the United Church of Christ provided the funds to enable Clark to continue organizing citizenship schools, which in 1964 numbered 195.

Clark talked freely about what she saw as the sexism of the SCLC staff.

I was on the executive staff of the SCLC, but the men on it didn't listen to me too well. They like to send me into many places, because I could always make a path in to get people to listen to what I have to say. But those men didn't have any faith in women, none whatsoever. They just thought that women were sex symbols and had no contributions to make. That's why Reverend Abernathy would say continuously, "Why is Mrs. Clark on this staff?" Dr. King would say, "Well she has expanded our program. She has taken it into eleven deep south states." Rev. Abernathy'd [*sic*] come right back the next time and ask again.

I had a great feeling that Dr. King didn't think much of women either. . . . [W]hen I was in Europe with him, when he received the Nobel Peace Prize in 1964, the American Field Service Committee people wanted me to speak. In a sort of casual way he would say "Anything I can't answer, ask Mrs. Clark." But he didn't mean it, because I never did get the chance to do any speaking to the AFS committee in London or to any of the other groups.

Like Baker, Clark communicated to King her differences with his style of leadership, urging him in a letter to run SCLC more democratically by delegating authority. She also attacked other ministers for their dependence on King, in which they assumed that only King could lead the movement, and for their belief that to suggest expanding the leadership of the movement cast doubt on King's own capabilities. . . .

Kathleen Cleaver . . . reported in 1971 that she joined the women's movement because she observed while working for SNCC, beginning in 1966, that women did most of the work but that few women held positions of authority. Those women who obtained administrative posts, Cleaver noticed, carried the double burden of their jobs and their duties as wives and mothers, and also had to contend with the male staff members' refusal to accept them as their equals. Cleaver attributed the death of Ruby Doris Smith, Executive Secretary of SNCC, to sheer exhaustion from the many demands and from having to fight racism and sexism simultaneously. "What killed Ruby Doris was the constant outpouring of work, work, work, with being married, having a child, the constant conflicts, the constant struggles that she was subjected to because she was a woman."

A letter written in 1977 by Cynthia Washington, who directed a freedom project for SNCC in Mississippi in 1963, suggested that the position of black women in the movement was more ambiguous than the deference of Robinson, Bates, or Nash to the male leadership, or the anger of Baker, Clark, or Cleaver at women's subordinate status indicated. . . .

During the fall of 1964, I had a conversation with Casey Hayden about the role of women in SNCC. She complained that all the women got to do was type, that their role was limited to office work no matter where they were. What she said didn't make any particular sense to me because, at the time, I had my own project in Bolivar County, Mississippi. A number of other black women also directed their own projects. What Casey and other white women seemed to want was an opportunity to prove they could do something other than office work. I assumed that if they could do something else, they'd probably be doing that.

Washington said that while some black men viewed the women as inferior— she quoted Stokely Carmichael's jeer that the only position for women in SNCC was prone—she believed that the authority she enjoyed as project director demonstrated that few shared his view. "Our relative autonomy as projects directors seemed to deny or override his statement. We were proof that what he said wasn't true—or so we thought." . . . Yet Washington . . . later concluded that sexism did exist, despite her lack of awareness of it at the time. "In fact, I'm certain that our single-minded focus on the issues of racial discrimination and the black struggle for equality blinded us to other issues."

The ambiguity in the status of women in the movement brought out by Washington's letter paralleled the activists' ambivalence towards the male leaders, in which even those women who criticized the male activists for their condescending attitudes towards women did not hold the men responsible for their sexism. Some, such as Clark, saw the men's treatment of women as reflecting their hostility towards a racially oppressive society that put down black men even more than black women. Clark thought that black men's sexism was a reaction against their overprotective mothers, who tried to shield their sons from the violence of whites to which black men were particularly susceptible. . . .

Other movement workers, such as Beale and Cleaver, blamed capitalism as well as racism for black men's discrimination against women. Sexism, like racism, they argued, was a device by which whites reinforced the exploitation of the masses. Just as racism perpetuated lower-class whites' poverty by preventing them from joining forces with blacks to overthrow their oppressors, so too, by internalizing the sexism of whites, black men contributed to the marginal economic status of blacks. Their complicity in the segregation of jobs by sex, which limited black women's access to all but the lowest paid jobs, and which treated women as a source of surplus labor and as strikebreakers, impoverished blacks as a group.

Cleaver agreed with Clark that black men developed sexist attitudes because they were oppressed, although Cleaver saw their oppression as economic. The black men, according to Cleaver, resented the "strong" role black women had had to assume as breadwinners as well as mothers. They vented their frustration by asserting their power over women—treating them as inferior, abusing them—or by abandoning their families to escape their guilt at their inability to find employment. . . .

All of the women leaders agreed that discrimination against women was of secondary importance to the subjection of all blacks and the inequitable distribution of power in society. Cleaver, for example, insisted that to focus on sexism diverted blacks from attacking the root of all injustice, "colonization," or economic exploitation of white women and minority men and women. . . .

Moreover, these activists held differing views of the relationship between the status of black women and that of blacks as a whole. Cleaver thought that women's equality was a necessary precondition to achieve the equality of all blacks—a means of ensuring the full utilization of blacks' resources. . . . Ladner, on the other hand, feared that the assertiveness of women made black men look relatively weak, . . . and hindered the men from proving their equality to whites. . . .

The inconsistencies in the behavior of these women leaders, in which they challenged white authorities but deferred to black ministers, or criticized the male activists, but only in hindsight, or directly challenged the male officers of movement organizations, yet nevertheless accepted their leadership, cannot entirely be explained by their various theories on the source of racism. Indeed, only in the case of three of the activists, Robinson, Bates, and Nash, do their ideologies seem consistent with their actions. A more plausible explanation for their contradictory behavior is that these women, for the reasons given by Washington, did not consider themselves oppressed by black men, either in or out of the movement, and in some respects believed that black men were worse off than black women. Consequently they did not seek to change their roles in the movement. In addition, the women had conflicting feelings about whom to hold responsible for sexism, if they thought that it did exist, and were uncertain as to how the assertion of their rights as women would affect the status of blacks as a group. These women leaders' reflections suggest that the role of black women in the civil rights movement, largely ignored by historians, was complicated by their ambivalence about what it ought to be and defies a definitive answer.

Uncovering the History of Working Women and Affirmative Action in the 1970s

NANCY MACLEAN

In 1993, the New York City Fire Department issued a curious order: no pictures could be taken of Brenda Berkman, on or off duty, inside or outside of a firehouse. Berkman was a firefighter, a fifteen-year veteran of the force. The order was the latest shot in a protracted battle against Berkman and others like her: women claiming the ability to do a job that had been a men's preserve for all the New York City Fire Department's 117-year, tradition-conscious history. The struggle began in 1977, when the city first allowed women to take the Firefighter Exam—and then promptly changed the rules on the physical agility section when 400 women passed the written portion of the test. Five years and a victorious class-action suit for sex discrimination later, forty-two women passed the new, court-supervised tests and training and went on to become the first female firefighters in New York's history. Among them was Berkman, founding president of the United Women Firefighters, and the most visible and outspoken of the group.

Their struggle dramatizes many elements in the larger story of women and affirmative action, which involved remaking "women's jobs" as well as braving male bastions. What Berkman and her colleagues encountered when they crossed those once-undisputed gender boundaries was not simply reasoned, judicious skepticism from people who doubted the capacity of newcomers to do the job. Repeatedly, what they met was elemental anger that they would even dare to try. Hostile male coworkers used many tactics to try to drive the women out, including hate mail, telephoned death threats, sexual harassment, refusing to speak to them for months on end, scrawling obscene antifemale graffiti in firehouses, and organizing public demonstrations against them. Male firefighters also slashed the tires of women's cars, urinated in their boots, and, in one instance, tried to lock a woman in a kitchen that they had filled with tear gas. Sometimes, the men resorted to violence: one woman was raped, and a few others endured less grave sexual assaults. Some men even carried out potentially deadly sabotage—as when one newcomer found herself deserted by her company in a burning building and left to put out a four-room fire on her own.

Nancy MacLean, "The Hidden History of Affirmative Action: Working Women's Struggles in the 1970s and the Gender of Class," *Feminist Studies* 25, no. 1 (spring 1999): 43–78. Reprinted by permission of the publisher, Feminist Studies, Inc.

Frozen out by white male coworkers and betrayed by the firefighters union, the women found their only dependable internal allies in the Vulcan Society, the organization of Black male firefighters, who had themselves fought a long battle against discrimination in the department. They now stood by the women, even to the point of testifying in support of their class-action suit, despite "enormous pressure to remain silent." The tensions surrounding the entrance of women into the fire department were explosive although women constituted a mere 0.3 percent of the city's 13,000-member uniformed fire force. The no-photographs order from the top, the uncoordinated acts of hostility from would-be peers, as well as the support of the Vulcan Society, signal us that a great deal was at stake. Even in cases less egregious than the New York firefighters, boundary crossing backed by affirmative action affected something that mattered deeply to many men, especially many white men, in a way that often transcended logic.

Yet, historians of the modern United States have only begun to examine workplace-based sex discrimination and affirmative action struggles such as those of the United Women Firefighters. More attention is in order. On the one hand, disgust with discrimination and low-paying, dead-end jobs moved large numbers of working women to collective action in the last quarter-century. On the other hand, these struggles produced an unprecedented assault not just on previously unyielding patterns of occupational sex and race segregation and the economic inequality stemming from them but also on the gender system that sustained men's power and women's disadvantage and marked some women as more appropriate for certain types of work than others. *"Work* is," after all, *"a gendering process,"* as the scholar of technology Cynthia Cockburn has observed—and, one might add, a race-making process as well. "While people are working, they are not just producing goods and services," Cockburn argues, "they are also producing *culture."* . . .

In challenging discrimination and demanding affirmative action, . . . the struggles described here redefined gender, race, and class by undermining associations built up over more than a century. . . . These associations led women and men to have some sharply different experiences of what it meant to be working class. And although my focus here is on the transformation in class and gender specifically, race is deeply embedded in both of these categories and in the associations they carry, if not always accessible in the extant sources. Wage-earning women in 1965, for example, could not expect that the jobs available to them would pay enough to live in modest comfort, certainly not with children; they *could* expect to have to provide personal services to the men in their work places, to clean up after them, and to endure demeaning familiarities from them as a condition of employment. Working-class white men, by contrast, had their own indignities to endure. But they might at least hope for a job that would provide a "family wage," and they could expect that no boss or co-worker would ask them to do domestic chores or grope them on the job.

Anti-discrimination and affirmative action struggles challenged this system of expectations and the patterns of inequality it perpetuated. Time and again, the system-recasting properties of affirmative action proved necessary to ensure equal treatment. Breaking down job ghettos and the habits that kept them in place required new practices such as wider advertising of job openings, recruitment from new sources, the analysis of jobs to determine skill requirements, the setting up of training programs to teach those skills, and in some cases the setting of specific numerical goals and timetables for recruiting and promoting women (impugned misleadingly by critics as "quotas"). By performing old work in new ways and by breaking into jobs formerly closed to them, the women involved in these efforts began, in effect, to reconstitute gender, and with it class, permanently destabilizing the once-hegemonic distinction between "women's work" and "men's work." To reconstitute is not to root out, of course: class inequality is if anything more shamelessly robust today than it was a quarter-century ago. Yet the *meaning* of particular class positions and experiences has shifted with the entrance of minority men and women of all groups in ways that demand attention. That we have forgotten how dramatic and radical a departure this was is a tribute to the success of their efforts.

Concentrating so heavily on gender and class in a discussion of affirmative action will strike many readers as odd and with good reason. Black civil rights organizations struggled for generations against employment discrimination, and it was their organizing that secured the most significant reforms to combat it. African Americans have also borne the brunt of recent attacks on affirmative action and the larger project of white racial revanchism that drives them. Indeed, so single-mindedly do contemporary critics of affirmative action focus on Blacks that one would never know from their arguments that the policy has served other groups. This sleight of hand has left both affirmative action and African Americans more vulnerable than they would be if the policy's other beneficiaries were acknowledged. Rather than accept the terms of debate used by affirmative action critics, then, this work seeks to bring into discussion another key group involved in the modern struggle against employment discrimination and the responses its members encountered. Recovering women's relationship to affirmative action also seems important in its own right, because women—especially white women—are so often cast as "free riders" in the discourse, as passive beneficiaries living off the labors of others. This article aims to combat the historical amnesia which makes that image possible and to recognize in the process the cross-racial coalitions built among working-class women at a time when few of their more affluent counterparts yet saw this as a priority. . . .

In what follows, I will sketch out a preliminary reading of the story of women and affirmative action, focusing on three types of collective action that became widespread in the 1970s. In the first type, a decentralized mass movement arose as working women across the country took hold of the new ideas in circulation about gender, applied them to their own situations, and agitated for change, typically through the vehicle of ad hoc women's caucuses that involved women in a range of job categories. In the second type, full-time organizers sought to expand these caucus efforts into citywide organizations for working women in clerical jobs. And in the third variant, individual low-income women and advocates for them turned to affirmative action as an antipoverty strategy for women, particularly female household heads, and began a concerted push for access to "nontraditional" blue-collar jobs for women. Those involved in all three efforts worked to mobilize working women across racial and ethnic lines. Although smaller numbers of women of color became involved in the first two forms of collection action, they became especially visible in campaigns for "nontraditional" employment. . . .

. . . [T]he first big challenges to sex discrimination in the 1960s . . . came from wage-earning women in factory jobs, who discovered a new resource in legislation won by the civil rights movement in 1964. "Although rarely discussed in class terms," the Civil Rights Act's prohibition on race and sex discrimination in employment (Title VII), as the legal scholar Cynthia Deitch has pointed out, "had an unprecedented impact on class relations." . . . When the Equal Employment Opportunities Commission (EEOC) opened for business in the summer of 1965, all observers were stunned at the number of women's complaints, which made up more than one-fourth of the total. Some 2,500 women in the initial year alone, overwhelmingly working-class and often trade union members, challenged unequal wages, sex-segregated seniority lists, unequal health and pension coverage, and male-biased job recruitment and promotion policies—among other things. Alice Peurala, for example, who had been stymied each time she tried for promotion since she was first hired at U.S. Steel Corporation in 1953, said that when the Civil Rights Act came along "I thought, here's my chance." The protests of women such as Peurala, we can see now, prompted the development of an organized feminist movement. It was, after all, the EEOC's negligence in handling these charges of sex discrimination that led to the formation of NOW, whose founders included labor organizers and women of color as well as their better-known, affluent, white counterparts. . . .

Such efforts were brought to the attention of a broad audience by the mass media. By the early 1970s, television news, magazines, and newspapers all carried stories about sex discrimination in employment and women's struggles against it, as well as reports of the wider women's movement. Whether the reporters were sympathetic, hostile, or patronizing, their coverage . . . stimulated women to look at their jobs afresh and to imagine class itself in new ways. By 1970, large numbers of American women began to act on this new thinking at work. Borrowing a tactic from mostly male, blue-collar African Americans, and taking strength from the general ferment among rank-and-file workers in the early 1970s symbolized by the famed Lordstown wildcat strike, these women joined together with like-minded coworkers to organize women's caucuses as their characteristic vehicle of struggle. The caucuses embodied, in effect, a new social theory: Blacks of both sexes and women of all races who joined together implicitly announced that traditional class tools—such as unions—were ill suited to the issues that concerned them. In form, the caucuses crossed divisions of occupation in order to overcome the isolation and competition that allowed their members to be pitted against one another. Using separate structures, they fought not simply to achieve racial and gender integration at work but also to redefine it.

Having first appeared about 1970, the caucuses spread rapidly within a few years, one sparking the next like firecrackers on a string. . . . Women were organizing in steel plants and auto factories, in banks and large corporations, in federal and university employment, in trade unions and professional associations, and in newspaper offices and television networks. Few sites remained undisturbed. . . . Caucuses not only developed a critical consciousness among working women but they also won tangible improvements. Without their efforts, Title VII would have been a dead letter for women.

These early women's caucuses nearly always came about because a few women suddenly rejected some expectation arising from contemporary constructions of gender and class. . . . Time after time, the fresh recognition of some longstanding practice as sexist—a practice usually first identified as such in the course of casual lunchtime conversation among female coworkers—impelled women to organize.

Often a small slight triggered a sense that a broader pattern of discrimination had just been revealed. For example, . . . the refusal of editors at the *New York Times* to allow the title "Ms." in the paper led several women on staff to wonder whether "this style rigidity was symptomatic of more basic problems."

. . . [T]he resulting *New York Times* Women's Caucus . . . challenged the newspaper to practice the fairness it preached to its readers. Prompted by the editors' curious resistance to nonsexist language, nine female employees in the news department began to compare experiences in 1972. Ironically, the *New York Times* had once boasted in an advertisement that one of the leaders, then a copy editor, had a "passion for facts." Now, however, the facts so carefully assembled by Betsy Wade, the self-proclaimed "Mother Bloor" of this particular struggle, brought less pride to management. The investigation and organizing continued until eighty women drew up a petition that complained of sex-based salary inequities; the confinement of women to poorer-paying jobs; the failure to promote female employees even after years of exemplary service; and their total exclusion from nonclassified advertising sales, management, and policy-making positions. The more women came to understand and label discrimination, the more of it they discovered. When "nothing happened" to address their complaints, the women secured a lawyer and filed charges with the EEOC. In turning to the state, they found they had to broaden their ranks beyond the original group to include secretarial staff and classified ad workers. . . . Ultimately, in 1974, the enlarged group filed a class-action suit for sex discrimination on behalf of more than 550 women in all job categories at the *New York Times,* including reporters, clerks, researchers, classified salespeople, and data processors. For the next four years, as the suit wound its way through the courts, the caucus held meetings, put out newsletters, and continued to agitate. By 1978, management was willing to concede. Settling out of court, the *New York Times* compensated female employees for past discrimination and agreed to a precedent-setting affirmative action plan. "Considering where we were in 1972," said one of the original plaintiffs, the settlement was "the sun and the moon and the stars."

That settlement highlights a more common pattern: in virtually every case where women's caucuses came together, demands for affirmative action emerged logically out of the struggle against discrimination. So striking is this pattern that I have yet to come across a case in which participants did *not* see affirmative action as critical to the solution. Examples are legion: they range from the *New York Times* group, to steel workers, telephone operators, and NBC female employees, of whom two-thirds (600 of 900) were secretaries when they began organizing in 1971. Even the Coalition of Labor Union Women (CLUW), loyal to a trade union officialdom skeptical about affirmative action, came out strongly in its favor. Prioritizing seniority over diversity where the two came in conflict, CLUW nonetheless fought to establish affirmative action for women—and to keep it in place. The logic appeared inescapable: if male managers had for so many years proven oblivious to women's abilities and accomplishments and unwilling to stop preferring men when they hired and promoted, and if women themselves could have been unaware of or resigned to the discrimination taking place, then something was needed to counterbalance that inertia. Successful efforts by African American men to wield affirmative action as a battering ram against discrimination only reinforced women's resolve. Time and again, it was affirmative action that women embraced to open advertising of jobs, broaden outreach for recruitment, introduce job analysis and training, set specific numerical goals for recruiting and promoting women, and mandate timetables for achieving these changes, all commitments for which management would be held accountable. . . .

Yet, the largest single number of wage-earning women—one in three—remained in clerical jobs, and they became the target of the second kind of organizing initiative. These jobs were among the most sex segregated: in 1976, for example, women made up 91.1 percent of bank tellers and 98.5 percent of secretaries and typists. The income of clerical workers fell below that of male wage earners in every category except farming. Seeking to make the women's movement more relevant to working-class women, some feminists set out in 1973 to develop an organizing strategy geared to women office workers and to build a network that could spread the new consciousness. "The women's movement was not speaking to large numbers of working women," remembered Karen Nussbaum, one of the national leaders of the effort, "we narrowed the focus of our concerns, in order to broaden our base." Among the groups thus created were 9 to 5 (Boston), Women Employed (Chicago), Women Office Workers (New York), Cleveland Women Working, Women Organized for Employment (San Francisco), and Baltimore Working Women. By the end of the 1970s, a dozen such groups existed and had affiliated with an umbrella network called Working Women; together, they claimed a membership of eight thousand. The racial composition of the groups varied by locality, but Black women appeared to participate in larger numbers in these than in the women's caucuses, sometimes making up as much as one-third of the membership.

What linked all the members together was a categorical rejection of the peculiar gender burdens of their work: above all, the low pay and demands for personal service. Of these expectations, making and fetching coffee for men quickly emerged as the most resented emblem of women's status. Of the low pay, one contemporary said: "As long as women accepted the division of work into men's and women's jobs—as long as they *expected* to earn less because women *deserved* less—the employers of clerical workers had it easy." Now, however, the women active in these groups insisted on their standing as full-fledged workers who deserved, in what came to be the mantra of the movement, both "rights and respect." Appropriating National Secretaries' Day for their own purposes, the groups demonstrated for "Raises, Not Roses!" and a "Bill of Rights" for office workers. "What we're saying," as one 9 to 5 speaker explained in 1974, "is that an office worker is not a personal servant, and she deserves to be treated with respect and to be compensated adequately for her work." . . .

Neither professional associations nor unions, office worker organizations constituted a new model, one that used research, creative publicity, and media-savvy direct action to develop a mass membership and power base. Increasing wages and respect for office workers were their top concerns, but not far behind was securing and monitoring affirmative action programs. From the beginning, organizers understood the problems of women office workers in terms of discrimination: poor pay, blocked mobility, and gender-specific personal affronts—or, one might say, economics, social structure, and culture. They therefore turned to the legal tools provided by Title VII of the Civil Rights Act and Revised Order No. 4 (the federal regulation stipulating that federal contractors must practice affirmative action for women). In the late 1970s, for example, sometimes working with local NOW chapters, all the Working Women affiliates took up a campaign targeting sex discrimination in banks.

After distributing job surveys to female bank employees, the chapters held public hearings and demonstrations to publicize the results and prodded government anti-discrimination agencies to take action. Ultimately, these investigations resulted in several major settlements featuring novel affirmative action plans. . . .

As women's caucuses and office worker groups continued into the late 1970s, a new form of organizing for affirmative action spread: training and placement of women in "nontraditional" blue-collar jobs, particularly in construction. Here, advocates of gender equity came up more directly against sex-typed class consciousness among craftsmen who by long tradition equated working-class pride and "defiant egalitarianism" vis-à-vis bosses with, as the labor historian David Montgomery once observed, "patriarchal male supremacy." Feminists turned to the nontraditional work strategy in the belief that as women got access to these jobs and the higher wages they offered, their movement out of the female job ghetto would also relieve the overcrowding that pulled down women's wages. Men without college educations had long found in these jobs both good wages and personal pride; that women were steered away from even considering them was itself a mark of gender discrimination. Building on the reforms wrested by civil rights workers and women's caucuses, the new initiatives marked both a more self-conscious attempt to relieve female poverty and a more frontal challenge to the sexual division of labor in working-class jobs. . . .

One of the pioneer organizations was Advocates for Women, founded in San Francisco in 1972. Its founders self-consciously broke ranks with women's movement organizations such as NOW that seemed ever more single-mindedly focused on the Equal Rights Amendment and the concerns of better-off women. Taking advantage of newly available federal funds, Advocates for Women began recruiting and training women for nontraditional jobs. Directed by a Latina, Dorothea Hernandez, the organization aimed to reach "women of all races and cultures with emphasis on low-income women who must support themselves and their families." The rationale for the effort was to the point: "Poverty is a woman's problem"; hence, "women need money." The best way to ensure their access to it was through their own earnings. This strategy seemed more reliable than indirect claims on men's paychecks and more generous and empowering than Aid to Families with Dependent Children (AFDC). But the low-paying occupations into which most women were shunted wouldn't provide enough money to escape poverty, particularly to those with limited educations and work experiences. Advocates for Women reasoned that government-mandated affirmative action could be made to work for women in the construction industry. Because the skilled trades had long enabled men with only high school educations to secure good incomes, these jobs ought to be able to do the same for women—if they had the needed advocacy, training, and support services. . . .

Over the next few years, variations on the basic nontraditional jobs model sprang up in locations across the country. By mid-decade, 140 women's employment programs were in operation, from San Francisco, New York, Chicago, and Washington, D.C., to Atlanta, Dayton, Louisville, Raleigh, San Antonio, and Wichita. In an initiative launched in 1979, over ninety of them, from twenty-seven states, joined together to form the Women's Work Force Network, which soon created a Construction Compliance Task Force to facilitate women's entrance into the building trades. Women of color tended to be prominently involved, both as workers and as leaders. . . .

Even in the Appalachian South, often thought of as a bulwark of tradition, women began to organize for access to the better-paying work long monopolized by men. In 1977, several women who had grown up in the region's coal fields set up the Coal Employment Project "to help women get and keep mining jobs." Within a year, working with regional NOW chapters, they had filed complaints against 153 leading coal companies for practicing blatant sex discrimination in all areas: men comprised 99.8 percent of all coal miners and 98.6 percent of all persons employed in *any* capacity in the coal industry. Women's interest in this work expanded in tandem with their access. The number of female underground coal miners grew from zero in 1973, to over 3,500 by the end of 1981, when they comprised 2 percent of the work force. Often widowed or divorced and raising children on their own, coal-mining women took these jobs for the same reasons that led other women to construction sites: the work paid more than three times as much as they could get elsewhere. To the extent that working-class women could get jobs in Appalachia, after all, it was nearly always as waitresses, store clerks, or unskilled operatives in factories that came to the region for its low wages. More challenging than these "women's jobs," mining also held more interest and prestige. To women who had grown up in the area, coal was, as one put it, "part of our heritage," it was "part of who we are." "Women go into mining for the money," summed up one reporter: "They stay, they say, because they like it."

These endeavors marked an explicit feminist challenge not only to prevailing ideas of employment as something that fitted men for self-reliance and women for dependence on and service to men but also to the public policy model enshrined in the War on Poverty. Constructed on the premises set forth in the Moynihan Report, which explicitly argued that the problem for poor Black families was that so many were female-headed, this approach assumed that the key task was to generate jobs for poor men, particularly Black men, that would enable them to support families. Women's employment at best signaled family pathology; at worst, it created it, by depriving men of rightful dominance. Disparaged today, this thinking exerted a powerful influence through the 1970s, not just in government but in civil rights and Black nationalist circles as well. Participants in women's nontraditional employment programs, Black and white, argued a very different case. Not only were large numbers of women likely to continue heading families: they had a right to do so in comfort and dignity. Poor men needed good jobs, to be sure, but so did poor women. Society should not expect gains for one to come at the expense of the other. This position had far-reaching ramifications. Saying good riddance to both the old family-wage system and the privations and humiliations of AFDC, it aimed at a new model, a model in which women could build families from positions of autonomy and power, heading or coheading households while being recognized as full citizens at the same time. "Money meant independence," a divorced electrician explained, "a trade meant . . . being able to support my family without having a man around, if I couldn't find a decent man to relate to the family."

If we look at these initiatives in light of theories that gender is constituted through performance and see these women as engaged in performances that revised existing notions of womanhood and manhood alike, richer, subtler meanings emerge. Performing nontraditional work changed many of the women who did it, as did receiving the higher wages once reserved for men. . . . Coal mining, for example, was one of the most dangerous, demanding occupations in the United States; doing it well changed women's sense of themselves. "As I grow stronger," wrote one woman miner, "as I learn to read the roof [of the mine] like the palm of a hand, the confidence grows that I can do this work. . . . To survive, you learn to stand up for yourself And that is a lesson worth the effort to learn." . . . And for men, too, the entrance of women into these jobs led to adjustments in identity and social understanding. "Some of the men would take the tools out of my hands," a pipefitter recalled. "When a woman comes on a job that can work, get something done as fast and efficiently, as well as they can, it really affects them. Somehow if a woman can do it, it ain't that masculine, not that tough. . . .

As women in these struggles remade class and gender, they often found themselves tackling race as well: struggle led to deeper learning. Even when women's caucuses arose in predominantly white offices, for example, at least one, and sometimes a few, Black women were usually actively involved. Inquiries into sex discrimination uncovered racial discrimination as well, as in a landmark suit by Women Employed against the Harris Trust and Savings Bank in Chicago. Many women's groups thus quickly realized the need to establish ties with Black workers' caucuses or informal groups. . . . The resulting coalitions were rarely tension-free—particularly for Black women, who likely felt keenly the need for both groups and the limitations of each—but they were certainly educational and often effective at bringing greater rewards to the partners than they could have achieved alone. When full-time organizations developed, white women initially occupied all or most of the staff positions. This became a particular problem in the construction industry drive, because women of color made up a large proportion of the low-income constituency the organizations aimed to serve. Recognizing this, some of these groups consciously set out to reconstruct themselves by applying affirmative action internally.

At the same time, the nontraditional jobs effort enabled even predominantly white women's groups to develop alliances with Black and Chicano rights organizations fighting for fair employment. One case in point is the United Women Firefighters with whom this story began, who won support from the Black male firefighters of the Vulcan Society. Another example is the *New York Times* Women's Caucus, which coordinated its efforts with those of the Black workers' caucus throughout the struggle. . . . Alliances such as this could alter both parties, making the women's groups more antiracist and making the civil rights groups more feminist in their thinking and programs. . . .

I do not want to overstate the changes that occurred. If women tried to rewrite the script, so could men. Resistance was common, and sometimes fierce, as the example of the New York City firefighters illustrates. To take one obvious case: as if to certify their own now-uncertain masculinity and remind women of their place, some men turned to sexual harassment. Although hardly new, this tactic seemed to be used more aggressively and self-consciously where men found treasured gender privileges and practices in question—as in the case of the New York firefighters. . . .

. . . By and large, working women still face serious obstacles in trying to support themselves and their families. As much as occupational sex and race segregation have diminished, they have hardly disappeared, as any glance at a busy office or construction site will show. For women and men to be equally represented throughout all occupations in the economy today, 53 out of every 100 workers would have to change jobs. The absolute number of women in the skilled trades has grown, but they hold only 2 percent of the well-paying skilled jobs. In any case, these good jobs for people without higher education, as each day's newspaper seems to announce, are themselves an endangered species. In fact, although the wage gap between the sexes has narrowed, only about 40 percent of the change is due to improvement in women's earnings; 60 percent results from the decline in men's real wages. The persistent disadvantage in jobs and incomes contributes to another problem that has grown more apparent over the last two decades: the impoverishment of large numbers of women and their children, particularly women of color. Many of these poor women, moreover, are already employed. In 1988, more than two in five women in the work force held jobs that paid wages below the federal poverty level. So I am not arguing that some kind of linear progress has occurred and all is well.

Still, affirmative action was never intended as a stand-alone measure or panacea. From the outset, advocates were nearly unanimous in their insistence that it would work best in conjunction with full employment above all but also with such measures as pay equity, unionization, and improvements in education and training. Affirmative action's mission was not to end poverty, in any case, but to fight occupational segregation. And there it has enjoyed unprecedented, if modest, success. The best indicator is the index of occupational segregation by sex: it declined more in the decade from 1970 to 1980, the peak years of affirmative action enforcement, than in any other comparable period in U.S. history. As of 1994, women made up over 47 percent of bus drivers, 34 percent of mail carriers, and 16 percent of police—all jobs with better pay and benefits than most "women's work." This lags slightly behind nontraditional jobs requiring postsecondary training: women now account for nearly 40 percent of medical school students (20 percent of practicing physicians), nearly 50 percent of law school students (24 percent of practicing lawyers), and almost one-half of all professionals and managers. The ways that white women and women of color fit into these patterns complicate analyses based on sex alone. Yet whether in blue-collar, pink-collar, or professional jobs, white and Black women have gained benefits from breaking down sex barriers.

It would be absurd, of course, to give affirmative action exclusive credit for these changes. The policies described here came to life as the result of a broader history involving women's own determination to close the gap between the sexes in education and labor force participation, institutional fears of lawsuits for discrimination, new developments in technology and labor demand, and changes that feminism and civil rights brought about in U.S. culture. The mass entry of women into hitherto "men's work" in particular is deeply rooted in the breakdown of the family wage-based gender system. It is both result and reinforcement of a host of other changes: new expectations of lifelong labor force participation among a majority of women, the spread of birth control, the growing unreliability of marriage, the convergence in women's and men's patterns of education, the demise of associational patterns and sensibilities based on stark divisions between the sexes—even the growing participation of women in sports. But if it would be foolish to exaggerate the causative role of affirmative action, it would also be sophistry to deny or underrate that role. It has furthered as well as been fostered by these other developments. Women simply could not have effected the changes described here without its tools and the legal framework that sustained them. There are sound reasons why by 1975 virtually every national women's organization from the Girl Scouts to the Gray Panthers supported affirmative action, and why today that support persists from the African American Women's Clergy Association at one end of the alphabet to the YWCA at the other.

Yet there is a curious disjuncture between these organizations and the female constituency they claim to represent: repeated polls have found that white women in particular oppose affirmative action by margins nearly matching those among white men (which vary depending on how the questions are worded). No doubt several factors help to explain this paradox, not least of them the racial framing of the issue, which encourages white women to identify with white men against a supposed threat from nonwhites. The preference for personal politics over political economy at the grassroots has also led many women to interpret feminism in terms of lifestyle choices rather than active engagement in public life. Struggles for the ERA and reproductive rights ultimately eclipsed employment issues on the agenda of the women's movement in the 1970s. And most major women's organizations have come to emphasize service or electoral politics over grassroots organizing, and staff work over participation of active members. All these developments help to explain why today there is so little in the way of a well-informed, mobilized, grassroots female constituency for affirmative action—a vacuum that, in turn, has made the whole policy more vulnerable to attack.

Surely another reason, however, for the paradoxical gulf between national feminist organizations and grassroots sentiment on this issue is the historical amnesia that has obliterated the workplace-based struggles of the modern era from the collective memory of modern feminism—whether women's caucuses, clerical worker organizing, the fight for access to nontraditional jobs, or union-based struggles. If not entirely forgotten, these efforts on the part of working women are so taken for granted that they rarely figure prominently in narratives—much less interpretations—of the resurgence of women's activism. This disregard is especially ironic in that such struggles likely contributed more than we realize to our own era's heightened consciousness concerning the social construction and instability of the categories of gender, race, and class. Activists, that is, had begun the task of denaturalizing these categories and their associated hierarchies well before academics took up the challenge. If historians have now begun excavating the buried traditions of working-class women that can help us rethink the trajectories of modern feminism, there are still many, many more stories to be uncovered. . . .

The Female Orgasm in American Sexual Thought and Second Wave Feminism

JANE GERHARD

In 1968, Anne Koedt published "The Myth of the Vaginal Orgasm" in *Notes from the First Year,* a twenty-nine-page typed journal put out by New York Radical Women. By the time an expanded version appeared in *Notes from the Second Year,* Koedt's article had become a feminist classic. Koedt set out what would become

Jane Gerhard, "Revisiting 'The Myth of the Vaginal Orgasm': The Female Orgasm in American Sexual Thought and Second Wave Feminism," *Feminist Studies* 26, no. 2 (spring 1999): 449–473. Reprinted by permission of the publisher, Feminist Studies, Inc.

major concerns of the emergent movement—the meaning of sexual freedom, the political significance of sexual pleasure, and the psychological roots of male domination and female subordination. The vaginal orgasm, attained exclusively through intercourse, had long been a keynote in the clamor of expert ideas about female sexual health and normality. When Koedt attacked it as a myth, or more pointedly, as a fraudulent misinformation campaign that created a host of psychological problems for women, she appeared to challenge the very foundation of heterosexuality as it was understood in psychoanalytic, medical, and popular discourse. . . .

Using Koedt's article as a window into one moment of feminist sexual thought is important for a number of reasons. Koedt's piece clearly outlined a gender analysis of the historic discourse on female heterosexuality and articulated the stakes for feminists in it. Starting with Freud in 1905, the vagina had carried the double mission in expert discourse of naturalizing heterosexuality and essentializing the erotic underpinnings of reproduction. Psychoanalysts, physicians, and marriage experts who followed Freud used the diagnosis of frigidity, defined as the absence of an orgasm during intercourse, to establish the parameters of normal female heterosexuality. If psychoanalytic experts had made the vagina into a synechdoche for mature and healthy femininity, feminists in the late 1960s sought to make the clitoris the marker of the liberated and autonomous woman. To break out of male-defined notions of female pleasure, Koedt and others embraced the clitoris as a potentially unsituated site of sexual expression in women. Koedt was one of the first feminists to theorize clitoral sexuality as a form of sexual expression tied neither solely to heterosexuality nor homosexuality but to a kind of female sexuality that lay beyond or beneath social designations. The "discovery" of the clitoris as potentially unaligned to any specific sexual identity proved enormously useful to feminist sexual theories and constituted a major break in American sexual thought. . . .

In *Three Essays on the Theory of Sexuality* (1905), Freud set the terms for the psychoanalytic understanding of female sexuality, specifically the opposition between clitoral and vaginal sexuality as "immature" and "mature" forms of female development. In his third essay, "The Transformations of Puberty," Freud argued that the adolescent girl transferred her leading genital zone from the clitoris to the vagina. She, who had previously (if unconsciously) enjoyed the clitoris as the center of her fledgling libidinous pleasures, no longer did so. This shift constituted a profound change. Up to this point in her development, the girl had been, for all intents and purposes, "a little man." Like her brother, the girl was motivated by what Freud characterized as a "masculine" libido which was attached to her original love object, her mother. However, the girl's state of pre-Oedipal, libidinal attachment to her mother was short-lived. She quickly came to realize that her clitoris was inadequate in size and function to the penis. Freud postulated that at this point the girl gave up her mother in favor of her father and a powerful wave of repression carried her into her latency period. He suggested that when the girl emerged from latency, her erotic "transfer" would have been completed and she would find her vagina fully eroticized. The clitoris, in this context, would no longer be the woman's dominant sexual organ. . . .

The transfer theory introduced an unstated yet pervasive problem in Freud's conception of female sexuality. As a story of development, the transfer theory created a moment where the young girl stood outside of sexual categories. Her heterosexual identity would be consolidated only when the girl shifted her libido away from the mother and the clitoris and on to the father and the vagina. . . . Within the terms of psychoanalysis, the girl, for a brief moment, existed between sexual identities, she was neither purely masculine nor feminine, neither simply homosexual nor purely heterosexual, but somehow all of these at once. The outcome of such liminality, of temporarily existing between genders and sexualities, was an instability at the heart of the girl's heterosexual identity.

Freudians in the 1930s and 1940s tried to solve this problem by rooting an essential heterosexual identity in the female body. Toward this end, the vaginal orgasm and its shadow, vaginal frigidity, became two central components of Freudian femininity. Karl Abraham, Edmund Bergler, Marie Bonaparte, Helene Deutsch, Karen Horney, Eduard Hitschmann, and Clara Thompson, among others, selectively developed Freud's legacy for the psychoanalytic meaning of female sexuality for Americans in the interwar years. These experts first assumed and then detailed, among other things, the masculine character of the clitoris and its association with infancy, the shift from clitoral to vaginal sexuality as part of a biological imperative toward reproduction, and the association between women's psychological makeup and their entry into or rejection of heterosexuality. . . .

Psychoanalyst Helene Deutsch . . . was the first to use the vaginal orgasm as the metaphor for the healthy woman. As one of Freud's favorite students, Deutsch enjoyed his "blessings" on her work on femininity. . . . Deutsch's *The Psychology of Women* (1944), which built on her earlier work in the 1920s and 1930s, constituted her most comprehensive statement on the subjects of motherhood, female masochism and narcissism, and the vicissitudes of female sexuality. By the 1950s, *The Psychology of Women* had become a classic in the psychological literature on women: volume two on the psychoanalytic meaning of motherhood was reprinted eleven times by 1960.

In *The Psychology of Women,* Deutsch theorized a female sex drive rooted in the vagina. As did other Freudians, Deutsch infused female sexuality with the values of "healthy" subordination, passivity, dependency, and maternity. In her work, the vagina symbolically brought together women's reproductive and sexual identities, two aspects of women's psychology that psychoanalysis sought to harmonize under the rubric of innate heterosexuality. Like the master, Deutsch too cast the clitoris as the discarded lover in the sexual drama of healthy womanhood. Extending Freud's theories, Deutsch wrote that the young girl's body, quite simply, frustrated her active, clitoral sexuality. Without a penis the pre-Oedipal girl had no outlet for her aggressive sexuality. This drove her to unconsciously repress and convert her clitoral sexuality into passive and silent "readiness" for vaginal heterosexuality.

Unlike Freud, however, Deutsch used the vagina as a synecdoche for mature femininity. In her work, the healthy woman was herself as "passive" and "masochistic" as the vagina that signified her femininity. Deutsch laced her account of feminine passivity with a deep sense of women's innocence and child like naiveté in all sexual matters. Drawing on the romance of the Sleeping Beauty story, Deutsch explained that the innocent woman and the "silent" vagina passively waited to be "awoken" to heterosexual desire by the penis in a first experience of intercourse, ideally after a period of wooing and reassurances of love. "Just as in prehistoric times, women are more gratified when they grant sexual intimacy only after a long wooing . . . woman wants to be fought for and conquered and awaits her 'defeat' in joyful excitation. . . ." Deutsch explained that women's innocence in matters sexual was indeed so great that "the 'undiscovered' vagina is—in favorable instances—eroticized by an act of rape. . . . This process manifests itself in man's aggressive penetration on the one hand and in the 'overpowering' of the vagina and its transformation into an erogenous sexual zone on the other." Normal women, she went on, come to find what they first experienced as "an act of violence" as "an act of pleasure." Vaginal sexuality, at once mysterious and overpowering, transformed a girl into a woman through its capacity to bring sexual pleasure and reproduction together. The passive girl and the productive proto-mother became one in the face of full heterosexual pleasure. She wrote: "In the ecstacy of the orgasm, the woman experiences herself as a helpless child abandoned to her love partner—a deep experience in which her ego becomes the child that she conceives in her fantasy and with which she will continue to identify herself when her fantasies come true." . . .

One of the key indicators of an abnormal woman was the incapacity to renounce her clitoris as her dominant sexual organ. Freudians devoted much time and effort to discrediting the clitoris as a pathological site of female sexual feeling and none did so more doggedly than the team of [Eduard] Hitschmann and [Edmund] Bergler. Both had had psychoanalytic training in Europe, near Freud and his circle of analysts, and had emigrated to the United States in the late 1930s. Hitschmann and Deutsch had worked closely in Vienna for a number of years. Hitschmann and Bergler's 1936 monograph, *Frigidity in Women: Its Characteristics and Treatment,* translated and published in English in 1948, was the first to focus exclusively on the role of the clitoris in heterosexual women's neurosis. In this landmark text, they attempted to clarify the diagnostic criteria by which a woman could be called frigid and to set out a treatment plan for curing what they viewed as a burgeoning class of frigid women. Hitschmann and Bergler offered their readers a simple criterion: "It is of no matter whether the woman is aroused during coitus or remains cold, whether the excitement is weak or strong, whether it breaks off at the beginning or the end, slowly or suddenly, whether it is dissipated in preliminary acts, or has been lacking from the beginning. The sole criterion of frigidity is the absence of the vaginal orgasm."

Whereas Deutsch based her work on the power of the vagina, Hitschmann and Bergler based theirs on the potential of the clitoris to undermine healthy femininity. The pathology they detailed resonated with social catastrophe. Hitschmann and Bergler took Freud quite literally when they argued that the clitoris embodied women's refusal to accept their feminine roles. The clitoris represented to them the chaos of women behaving like men, or worse, of overpowering men. The social cost of frigidity, warned the authors, was nothing short of family destruction. Hitschmann and Bergler linked feminism and frigidity as related forms of sexual disorder. They concluded that frigid women, like feminists and lesbians, could not tolerate men being the leader in sexual matters and so instead they harbored neurotic fantasies about their own powers. The authors went so far as to declare that as psychoanalysis cured sexually dissatisfied women, "ridiculous manifestations of the woman's movement would [also] disappear." For Hitschmann and Bergler, the clitoris represented a point of convergence between pathological behaviors and abnormal identities. Implicitly, the vagina functioned as the productive counterpoint that made women feminine and heterosexual. . . .

Koedt's assault on the concept of the vaginal orgasm, then, came out of the ways in which, as a paradigm, it worked to police a specific set of gender traits—sexual dependency, passivity, maternal feelings—as normal, healthy, and essential. The meanings Freudians attached to female sexuality, particularly that of women's subordination to men, made it particularly important for feminists to challenge. Feminists like Koedt set out to reclaim the clitoris—and its association with autonomy, aggression, and feminism—from the jaws of Freudian pathologizing and use it for themselves to re-imagine a new kind of female sexuality.

According to Koedt, the psychoanalytic diagnosis of frigidity did not merely perpetuate an outdated view of women but had direct effects on the way many women viewed themselves. "The worst damage was done to the mental health of women," wrote Koedt, "who either suffered silently with self-blame, or flocked to psychiatrists looking desperately for the hidden and terrible repression that had kept from them their vaginal destiny." This situation left women feeling "sexually deprived" and inadequate. "Looking for a cure to a problem that has none can lead a woman on an endless path of self-hatred and insecurity. For she is told by her analyst that not even in her one role allowed in a male society—the role of a woman—is she successful." Nothing short of the mental health of women was at stake for Koedt and other feminists who rejected sexual expertise as poisoned by male chauvinism. Whether or not individual women faced an account of their "disordered" sexuality from a psychoanalyst or doctor, as a group, women encountered the messages of psychoanalysis in scholarly, literary, and popular writings, in parenting and marriage advice books, in Hollywood movies, and in mainstream magazines.

Koedt based her rejection of Freudian psychoanalysis on a new view of the sexually responsive female body generated by sexologists in the 1950s and 1960s. She drew on the sex studies of Alfred C. Kinsey (1953) and William Masters and Virginia Johnson (1966) for their "scientific" account of women's sexual physiology and behavior for her vision of women's sexual liberation. Koedt asserted that in contrast to Freud, sexologists started from the "facts" of women's bodies rather than from ideas about proper womanhood.

. . . Most importantly for Second Wave feminists, sexologists rejected the psychoanalytic pathologizing of the clitoris as a deviant form of sexuality and, in a historic reversal, claimed it as the centerpiece of female sexual response. . . . In a potentially radical statement which feminists like Koedt utilized in their view of female sexual liberation, Kinsey et al. suggested that vaginal intercourse was not necessarily the most pleasurable form of sexual practice for women. With illustrations and diagrams, they explained that the vagina was "insensitive" to touch and did not have the endowment of nerves to make it the center of female sexual response. The authors went so far as to suggest that the vagina was "of minimum importance in contributing to the erotic responses of the female. . . . [and] may even contribute more to the sexual arousal of the male than it does to the arousal of the female." This statement, buried on page 592 of the 800-plus *Sexual Behavior in the Human Female,* had the potential to alter substantially not just the heterosexual practice of sex but also the deeply entrenched associations between a woman's sexuality and her gender identity. . . .

. . . Much of the shock that *Sexual Behavior in the Human Female* generated came from the finding that women behaved sexually very much like men did: they masturbated, petted, had premarital sex and extramarital relations. Such behaviors flew in the face of years of expert accounts of women's disinterest in sexual matters. Masters and Johnson's research similarly challenged prevailing views of women's diminished sexuality. The researchers discovered that with proper stimulation of the clitoris, particularly during masturbation, women had the capacity for multiple orgasms. Significantly, women's capacity for multiple orgasms was something they did not share with men. In a passage remarkable for its departure from expert writings on female sexuality, the authors portrayed women as remarkably responsive. "The human female," they wrote in a now-famous quote, "frequently is not content with one orgasmic experience. . . . If there is no psychosocial distraction to repress sexual tension, many well-adjusted women enjoy a minimum of three or four orgasmic experiences before they reach apparent satiation." . . .

Sexologists, particularly Masters and Johnson, found themselves at the epicenter of shifting ideas about sexual liberation in the mid-1960s. . . . Most centrally, the consensus on keeping adult sexuality a marital affair had eroded. The postwar containment of sexuality in early marriages and through taboos against pre-marital and extramarital sex, which had been in place since the 1940s, no longer seemed unshakable as a generation of teenagers and young adults questioned the sexual categories and mores of their parents. Masters and Johnson's view of women as sexual athletes capable of multiple orgasms suddenly harmonized with the spirit of sexual freedom or, more accurately, sexual experimentation, sweeping the country.

Sexual liberationists reclaimed sex from the (rhetorical) confines of monogamous marriage and infused it with the symbolic values of authenticity, empowerment, and personal freedom. Radical psychoanalysts like Herbert Marcuse and Norman O. Brown infused sexuality with political significance when they pointed out the links between social and sexual repression. Student activists took up Marcuse's political analysis of pleasure and its role in overturning the mind numbing effects of conformity. They promoted sexual expressiveness, unencumbered by the "hang ups" of romance and monogamy, as a key value of the new society. Sexual liberationists also drew on the human potential movement led by Abraham Maslow and Carl Rogers in the 1950s and early 1960s. The "new psychology" saw humans as engaged in growth across a "life cycle." An important aspect of the new psychology was its tolerance of multiple routes to self-actualization. . . .

Anne Koedt's "Myth of the Vaginal Orgasm" appeared when the concern with sexual freedom as a weapon in the battle against repression had yet to be challenged as having gendered implications. Women learning to call themselves feminists found their immediate peer group of male student activists glibly linking social revolutions to sexual liberation without as much as a thought to its meaning for women. As historians of feminism have noted, many political women turned away from the New Left feeling diminished and belittled by their experience of sexism and sexual objectification. The combination of a revolutionary rhetoric that emphasized sexual freedom, on the one hand, and political women's experience of being ignored, patronized and sexually exploited, on the other, proved toxic for many women. Feminists claimed that women were entitled to both social and sexual independence. Women's desires, be it for emotional intimacy or for extended foreplay, for sex with men or with women, must dictate sexual practice. In this context, feminists recast the historic link between orgasm and femininity. Within early feminism, the female orgasm came to stand in for women's sexual self-determination. Sexual self-determination, in turn, held the promise of full equality with men. Feminists in the late 1960s joined sexual liberation to women's liberation, claiming that one without the other would keep women second-class citizens. . . .

In "The Myth of the Vaginal Orgasm," Koedt objected to the damage done to women and rejected psychoanalytic explanations of frigidity that refused to see women's sexual dysfunction as related to the larger societal dysfunction of sexism, homophobia, and enforced heterosexuality. Psychoanalysis, she complained, had pathologized women instead of addressing the problem of male indifference to women's desires. "Rather than tracing female frigidity to the false assumptions about female anatomy," wrote Koedt, "our 'experts' have declared frigidity a psychological problem . . . diagnosed generally as a failure to adjust to their role as women." According to Koedt, women must become full sexual agents, responsible for claiming their own pleasure. She wrote: "We must discard 'normal' concepts of sex and create new guidelines which take into account mutual sexual enjoyment. . . . We must begin to demand that if certain sexual positions now defined as 'standard' are not mutually conducive to orgasm, they no longer be defined as standard." . . . Male experts, according to radical feminists, denied the centrality of the clitoris to female sexuality because they felt threatened by the prospect of women as separate, desiring subjects. Koedt wrote: "It seems clear to me that men in fact fear the clitoris as a threat to their masculinity. . . . The establishment of clitoral orgasm as fact would threaten the heterosexual *institution*. For it would indicate that sexual pleasure was obtainable from either men or women, thus making heterosexuality not an absolute, but an option." Koedt thus articulated the links between patriarchy, male experts, and accounts of normal heterosexuality. She argued that the specter of an independent female sexuality, signified through the clitoris, threatened to alter the meaning of gender itself.

To liberate women from the Freudian view that women were naturally maternal, feminists emphasized women's capacity for orgasm and enjoyment of sex. . . .Yet as many women discovered, celebrating sexual pleasure as key to women's liberation did not necessarily eradicate what many women felt to be the sexism of the sexual revolution. Dana Densmore of Boston's Cell 16 complained that women were as oppressed by sexual liberation as they were by sexual repression. She wrote in 1971 that instead of being intimidated by psychiatrists for their lack of vaginal sexuality, women now found themselves oppressed by an "orgasm frenzy." "Our 'right' to enjoy our own bodies has not only been bestowed upon us," wrote Densmore, "it is almost a duty. . . . Everywhere we are sexual objects, and our own enjoyment just enhances our attractiveness. We are wanton. We wear miniskirts and see-through tops. We're sexy. We're free. We run around and hop into bed whenever we please . . . and people seem to believe that sexual freedom (even when it is only the freedom to actively offer oneself as a willing object) is freedom." Another writer explained that in the eyes of their male peers, women were "too sick to appreciate the benefits of free love" and needed enlightenment. "Suddenly men became concerned with my hang-ups and insistent that I accept their offers of instant liberation. Sexual exploitation was now disguised as participating in the new society." Roxanne Dunbar, also of Cell 16, complained that sexual liberation had come to mean "the 'freedom' to 'make it' with anyone, anytime." Women's liberation, she argued, could not simply be equated with sexual freedom because many women experienced sex not just as an arena of pleasure but as "brutalization, rape, submission, [and] someone having power over them."

Some feminists leery of the revolutionary potential of sexual pleasure reintroduced the idea that what women really wanted from sex was not orgasm but intimacy and love. Reworking a tradition of American sexual thought that emphasized romance over orgasm for women, elevated and celebrated by Deutsch in the 1940s, these feminists theorized psychological intimacy as a unique and unappreciated form of female sexuality. Rejecting traditional concepts of sexual pleasure, radical feminists sought to open up all feelings as sexual for women. Their vision of liminality cast the desire for intimacy as authentically female and the desire for something as tangible as orgasm an oppressive feature of male-dominated society. . . .

The feminist analysis of women's sexual self-determination, forged through their symbolic reworking of the clitoris, also revolutionized the meaning of lesbianism. This new version of lesbianism emerged out of the unmooring of female sexuality from heterosexual phallic sex. Once feminists had reintroduced the idea that psychological intimacy was the true origin of female sexual pleasure, the line demarcating heterosexual and lesbian women blurred. If sexual intercourse was an instrument of patriarchal control and orgasm a male myth. then emotional closeness became the basis for all sexuality. In this light, lesbianism became a form of resistance to male oppression, not an "illness." The Lavender Menace, which later became the Radicalesbians, offered in "The Woman-Identified Woman" an important challenge to the homophobia circulating in some feminists circles. This paper theorized lesbianism as an emotional and political choice rather than a (deviant) sexual object choice. A woman-identified woman, the paper explained, did not place hetero- or homosexuality at the center of her identity; rather she put her emotional relationships with other women first. "Only women can give to each other a new sense of self. That identity we have to develop with reference to ourselves, and not in relation to men." . . .

. . . [T]he emphasis on sexual freedom and the counterhegemonic possibilities of a liberated female sexuality was not uniformly adopted by all radical feminists. For radical women of color, the emphasis on sexuality was problematic. Francis M. Beal, for example, argued in 1969 that white women's groups must define overlapping structural forms of racial and sexual oppression and not conceptualize oppression only as the "vicarious pleasure" men derive from "'consuming [women's] bodies for exploitative reasons.'" Other radical Black women dismissed the revolutionary possibility of white feminism precisely because of its reliance on the fiction of the "universal" woman. Facing sexism and homophobia from their male colleagues in the civil rights and Black power movements, on the one hand, and racism from white feminists, on the other, by the mid-1970s Black radical women found themselves in an undeniable paradox where "all the men are black, all the women are white." Although Black feminists claimed sexual pleasure as a right and as important to female empowerment, they did so in and through the experiences of sexual exploitation and violently racist denial of their privacy and bodily integrity. This history shaped Black feminism as it emerged in the 1980s. . . .

Debates between feminists on the meaning of sexual freedom for women in the years between 1968 and 1973 foreshadowed tensions between radical and "cultural" feminists in the late 1970s and the battle lines between sex radicals and antipornography feminists in the early 1980s. The rise of cultural feminism, denoted by the antipornography movement in the mid-1970s, new psychological theories of women's essential differences, and lesbian feminism fundamentally changed the direction of feminist sexual theories. The historic critiques of sexual violence by cultural feminists left behind the earlier concern with orgasm. By the late 1970s, the vision of female sexuality as decidedly unlike male sexuality came to be ascendant: instead of pleasure, women pursued connection; instead of orgasm, women focused on intimacy; instead of phallic, sex became touching, looking, and kissing. This description of authentic female sexuality was not shared by all feminists in the late 1970s and 1980s. In reaction to what some dismissed as "politically correct sex," sex radicals, anticensorship feminists and those claiming the legacy of radical feminism's celebration of sexual expression mobilized in the early 1980s to revisit the radical possibility of sexual freedom for women. Tensions between competing groups of feminists broke out at the "The Scholar and the Feminist" conference on female sexuality held at Barnard College in 1982, which came to be known as "the Sex Wars."

However divisive and painful, the prosex/antisex labels bequeathed from the feminist sex wars should not be used as historical paradigms for reading radical feminism. To do so is to misremember that multiple analyses of sexuality existed simultaneously in radical feminism. The celebration of sexual freedom and the critique of sexual liberation, sex as pleasure and as danger, as liberation and exploitation, existed side by side in the years between 1968 and 1973. Cultural and radical feminists, antipornography and anticensorship feminists, lesbian separatists and sex radicals who battled in the late 1970s and the 1980s all derived a large part of their political vitality from this moment of sexual radicalism in early feminism where women dared to reinvent female sexuality. Our histories must remember that the radicalism of Second Wave feminism emerged, to no small degree, from the state of not knowing the boundaries of female sexual pleasure. After dismantling what they viewed as oppressive constructs reigning in female sexuality, feminists in the late 1960s took the radical position of questioning everything, trusting women's desires wherever they might lead, and sabotaging any theory that proposed to secure, at last, the true nature of female sexual pleasure.

◆ *F U R T H E R   R E A D I N G*

Bailey, Beth. *Sex in the Heartland* (1999).
Banner, Lois W. *Women in Modern America* (1984).
Carden, Maren Lockwood. *The New Feminist Movement* (1974).
Caron, Simone M. "Birth Control and the Black Community in the 1960s: Genocide or Power Politics?" *Journal of Social History* 31, no. 3 (spring 1998): 545–570.
Chafe, William. *Women and Equality* (1977).
Crawford, Vicki, Jacqueline Ann Rouse, and Barbara Woods, eds. *Women in the Civil Rights Movement: Trailblazers and Torchbearers, 1941–1965* (1990).
Daniel, Robert. *American Women in the Twentieth Century* (1987).
Davis, Flora. *Moving the Mountain: The Women's Movement in America Since 1960* (1991).
Davis, Martha. "Welfare Rights and Women's Rights in the 1960s," *Journal of Policy History* 8 (1996): 144–165.
Deckard, Barbara. *The Women's Movement* (1983).

D'Emilio, John. *Sexual Politics, Sexual Communities: The Making of a Homosexual Minority in the United States, 1940–1970* (1998).

Dewey, Scott Hamilton. "'Is This What We Came to Florida For?': Florida Women and the Fight Against Air Pollution in the 1960s," *Florida Historical Quarterly* 77 (1999): 503–531.

Dill, Bonnie Thornton. "The Dialectics of Black Womanhood," *Signs* 4 (1979): 543–555.

Douglas, Susan J. *Where the Girls Are: Growing Up Female with the Mass Media* (1994).

Echols, Alice. *Daring to Be Bad: Radical Feminism in America, 1967–1975* (1989).

———. *Shaky Ground: The Sixties and Its Aftershocks* (2002).

Evans, Sara. *Personal Politics: The Roots of Women's Liberation in the Civil Rights Movement and the New Left* (1979).

Evans, Sara, and Barbara J. Nelson. *Wage Justice: Comparable Worth and the Paradox of Technocratic Reform* (1989).

Garcia, Alma M. *Chicana Feminist Thought: The Basic Historical Writings* (1997).

Harrison, Cynthia. "A 'New Frontier' for Women: The Public Policy of the Kennedy Administration," *Journal of American History* 67, no. 3 (December 1981): 630–646.

———. *On Account of Sex: The Politics of Women's Issues, 1945–1968* (1988).

Hartmann, Susan M. *From Margin to Mainstream: American Women and Politics Since 1960* (1989).

———. *The Other Feminists: Activists in the Liberal Establishment* (1998).

Hoikkala, Paivi. "Feminists or Reformers? American Indian Women and Political Activism in Phoenix, 1965–1980," *American Indian Culture and Research Journal* 22 (1998): 163–186.

Hole, Judith, and Ellen Levine. *Rebirth of Feminism* (1971).

Honig, Emily. "Women at Farah Revisited: Political Mobilization and Its Aftermath Among Chicana Workers in El Paso, Texas, 1972–1992," *Feminist Studies* 22, no. 2 (summer 1996): 425–452.

Horn, Miriam. *Rebels in White Gloves: Coming of Age with Hillary's Class—Wellesley '69* (1999).

Horowitz, Daniel. *Betty Friedan and the Making of the Feminine Mystique: The American Left, the Cold War, and American Feminism* (1998).

Joseph, Gloria, and Jill Lewis. *Common Differences: Conflicts in Black and White Feminist Perspectives* (1981).

Linden-Ward, Blanche, and Carol Hurd Green. *Changing the Future: American Women in the 1960s* (1993).

McGlen, Nancy, and Karen O'Connor. *Women's Rights* (1983).

Murphy, Michelle. "Toxicity in the Details: The History of the Women's Office Worker Movement and Occupational Health in the Late-Capitalist Office," *Labor History* 41 (2000): 189–213.

Polatnik, M. Rivka. "Diversity in Women's Liberation Ideology: How a Black and White Group of the 1960s Viewed Motherhood." *Signs* 21 (1996): 679–706.

Rosen, Ruth. *The World Split Open: How the Modern Women's Movement Changed America* (2000).

Rothschild, Mary Aickin. "White Women Volunteers in the Freedom Summers: Their Life and Work in a Movement for Social Change," *Feminist Studies* 5, no. 3 (fall 1979): 466–495.

Rupp, Leila J., and Verta Taylor. *Survival in the Doldrums: The American Women's Rights Movement, 1945 to the 1960s* (1987).

Santillan, Richard. "Midwestern Mexican American Women and the Struggle for Gender Equality: A Historical Overview, 1920s–1960s," *Perspectives in Mexican American Studies* 5 (1995): 79–119.

Smith, Merril D., ed. *Sex Without Consent: Rape and Sexual Coercion in America* (2002).

Swerdlow, Amy. *Strike for Peace: Traditional Motherhood and Radical Politics in the 1960s* (1993).

Wandersee, Winifred D. *On the Move: American Women in the 1970s* (1988).

Weiss, Jessica. *To Have and to Hold: Marriage, the Baby Boom, and Social Change* (2000).

Yates, Gayle Graham. *What Women Want: The Ideas of the Movement* (1975).

CHAPTER
16

Women, Social Change,
and Reaction from the 1980s
to the New Millennium

During the 1970s, Americans who favored change in gender relations had reason to be optimistic: in 1972 Congress passed an equal rights amendment (ERA) and sent it to the states for ratification. The following year, the Supreme Court, in the landmark decision Roe v. Wade, *restricted states from prohibiting women's access to abortion during the first trimester of pregnancy. New federal policies were making it possible for women to advance toward equality with men in higher education, wage labor, and the professions. However, in the years that followed, a groundswell of opposition to changing gender roles developed and the feminist movement appeared to founder. Antifeminists with ties to fundamentalist Protestant churches, the Catholic Church, and the Republican Party mounted a political campaign that obstructed the ratification of the ERA. The women and men of the so-called New Right also pressured Presidents Ronald Reagan and George H. Bush to appoint conservative justices to the Supreme Court in hopes of overturning* Roe. *Emboldened social conservatives created a myriad of organizations devoted to advancing "family values" and embedding the moral precepts of evangelical Christianity in governmental policy. They condemned feminists for promoting immorality and selfish individualism, thereby undermining the cohesiveness of families and the well-being of the nation.*

Meanwhile, feminists continued to make some advances, for example, winning improvements in the research on, and treatment of, diseases that primarily affected women. Nevertheless, white middle-class feminists continued to struggle, often without great success, to comprehend and reach out to women in socially conservative faith communities or to women of color. For example, Arab American and Muslim women found themselves misunderstood by American feminists when they defended the right to wear the traditional hijab (head covering). And in the controversy surrounding Clarence Thomas's 1991 nomination to the Supreme Court, white feminists rallied to support Anita Hill's allegations of sexual harassment but failed to realize that Hill needed support not only as a woman, but also as a black woman. In the mid-1990s when conservative Republicans and so-called new Democrats worked on legislation to put an end to "welfare as we know it," many white feminists lent their support, even though women of color argued that the new legislation attacked the interests of poor and nonwhite women.

Why were thousands of women and men alienated by feminism during the last decades of the twentieth century, and how did the New Right speak to their anxieties about widespread patterns of change in women's lives? What impact did the New Right have on laws and policies that affected women's lives? Despite the growing opposition to feminism, to what extent did feminist activism continue to provoke positive change in America? Finally, how and why were white feminists in this era never fully able to acknowledge the needs and interests of women outside of the white middle class?

◆ *D O C U M E N T S*

Connaught C. Marshner explains the concerns and goals of social conservatives in 1988 (Document 1). Document 2 is an excerpt of Anita Hill's 1991 testimony before the Senate Judiciary Committee on the nomination of Clarence Thomas to the Supreme Court. In 1992 a divided Supreme Court reaffirmed the central holding of *Roe* v. *Wade* in *Planned Parenthood* v. *Casey* (Document 3), but gave states permission to enact rules and regulations that, short of imposing an "undue burden," encouraged women to seek options to abortion. In 2000 (Document 4), Nancy G. Brinker, a founding member of the Susan G. Komen Breast Cancer Foundation, testified before a subcommittee of the U.S. House of Representatives. In that same year, Asma Gull Hasan examined the lives of American Muslim women living simultaneously in two distinct cultures (Document 5). Document 6 presents the "personal story," published online in 2002, of Jamala McFadden, a welfare recipient of the early 1990s, and now a law student, who opposes the changes in welfare law that were implemented in 1996.

1. Connaught C. Marshner Explains What Social Conservatives Really Want, 1988

By now everyone knows that pro-family conservatives are a powerful political force. . . . What follows are the presumptions of the moral traditionalists.

The family is the fundamental institution of society; in the traditional society, it was your main source of comfort and strength. When you were a child, your father geared his life to providing shelter for your mother and you. As you grew, your family imparted the skills of survival, and gave you your religion and your politics. In your old age, someone with a blood connection would offer you a bed and a seat by the fire.

Today, these functions have atrophied. Your existence needn't cause your father to change his lifestyle, and in many circles it changes your mother's as little as she can possibly arrange. It is no reason for your father to stay with your mother; in the modern myth, she may even be more "fulfilled" without him around. If they do stay together, they play an increasingly small role in your upbringing: the public-education system, backed by the courts, positively puts obstacles in the path of parents wishing to exercise control over what their children read and study, while government-sponsored clinics are permitted to dispense contraceptives and perform abortions on teenagers without their parents' even being told. In your old age, Medicare will pay the costs of your medical treatment if you are put into an institution, but not if your relatives care for you at home. It's likely that your children and their spouses will all have careers anyhow, which means they can hire someone to look after you but can't spend time with you themselves.

In one area after another, functions once performed by the family are now provided by the government or government-style agencies and institutions. The goal of the pro-family movement is not to destroy these institutions but to restore to the family its proper functions, and to restore to the institutions an understanding of the proper proportion of their role.

The family fulfills many functions—social, psychological, and even economic—but these are *not* the reason for its existence. The family has one overriding task: raising children. It is each individual's entry point into society and the staging area of his personality.

Children are thus a gift and a responsibility, a long-term duty that arises from the nature of marriage. Marriage is not a contract, balancing conflicting interests, measuring competing obligations, forcing compliance with fear of consequences; it is a covenant, a permanent and exclusive union that sets no limits on what is to be given or forgiven by either party. The purposes of this covenant are the mutual support of the partners and the procreation, education, and rearing of children. Human nature being what it is, in practice many marriages are more reminiscent of contract than of covenant. But public policy should not seek the lowest common denominator and proclaim it as the model.

Modern society has, admittedly, lost sight of marriage in covenant terms. Fifty per cent of marriages in the U.S. today are second marriages for at least one of the partners. In 1984, over one million children were involved in the divorce of their parents; we can expect that over 11 million children—about one-fifth of the nation's total—will experience the misery of divorce over the next decade.

That trauma is rarely studied. In the famous California Children of Divorce Project, Dr. Judith Wallerstein of UC Berkeley followed children over a period of years after their parents divorced. Ten years after a divorce, 42 per cent of children were functioning poorly (exhibiting consistent depression, drug or alcohol abuse, sexual promiscuity, and/or poor performance in school); 15 per cent were functioning unevenly; and only 43 per cent were doing well most of the time. And the decline in upward mobility is just beginning to be noted: Dr. Wallerstein found in one study that, although 41 per cent of their divorced fathers were professionals, only 27 per cent of the children had professional aspirations.

A further result of the contract approach is no-fault divorce, which regards children as options that can be adjudicated like cars and stereos, with no long-term consequence to anyone. Some women may feel their "sense of self-worth" enhanced by bearing the costs of child-rearing alone, but their babies have no such illusions of self-reliance. Thanks to divorce and illegitimacy, children are the poorest class in America today: 20.5 per cent of all children were below the poverty line in 1986.

Nor are children the only victims. Stanford professor Lenore Weitzman, in her landmark study, *The Divorce Revolution,* found that in the year after a divorce, women experience a 73 per cent decline in their standard of living, while their former husbands experience a 42 per cent increase. The typical liberal response to this is to lament the feminization of poverty and wonder what the Federal Government is going to do to force fathers to pay child support. But even if every father met every child payment, 97 per cent of divorced women with children would still be in poverty. The real problem, again, is state laws and judges that adhere to no-fault divorce, expecting divorced mothers to function like young professional men. Despite what many would like to believe, traits of gender and the condition of motherhood make a tremendous difference in the way people can and will act. Any world view that pretends otherwise is either dishonestly or maliciously inviting human misery.

Another distortion in the public consciousness is population-bomb rhetoric: the idea that there are too many of us. Couples contemplating parenthood frequently decide against it out of deference to a vague sense of "society's" need. But decisions about fertility are properly the responsibility of husband and wife—those who will bear the responsibility of *raising* the children. Outside pressure—whether public or private—is inappropriate.

Actually, if the long-term good of the nation were the controlling factor, *large* families ought to be the goal. We have come to expect in retirement a standard of living that formerly was the reward of those who had raised a large family of successful and generous children. But maintaining Social Security and the rest of the welfare state requires constant population growth to keep the pyramid game going. The unfunded liability of our entitlement programs for the elderly alone is staggering. By the year 2010, two-thirds of the federal budget will be needed just to meet current entitlement promises.

The current tax cost of the welfare state is in fact making the future revenue base smaller, because it penalizes those who bear and raise children. Not only is there the loss of the second income and the expense of child-rearing, but mortgage rates for decent homes are geared to two incomes. At best, a young couple must choose prosperity or children—and many don't even have that choice.

A perverse dynamic is in place in our society: youthful lust is indulged, so long as fertility is controlled. Later, when fertility is desired, many find that it has been destroyed. One in four American couples is infertile, report the Centers for Disease Control, the most common cause being damage from venereal disease. And so begins the shrill demand to have a baby. Just as it was a "right" to be infertile when 18, it now is declared a "right" to be fertile at 28 or 35, as if nature could be turned on and off to suit one's preferences.

The lengths gone to and the amounts of money spent in pursuit of pregnancy can be astonishing. There is a growing demand for high-tech obstetrics—*in vitro* fertilization, embryo transfer, and even more alarming techniques—to say nothing of surrogate parenting. Let there be no confusion about this demand for babies, however: far too often, it is not a manifestation of pro-life sentiment, but of an ego in pursuit of an alter.

If couples yearning for children but unable to conceive were satisfied by adoption, theirs would be a noble impulse. But adoption remains unfashionable, and government policy does not encourage it. Federal funds are available to keep children in foster care, but not to place them in permanent homes, and some social workers establish standards for adoption so high that if nature held to such standards, few of us would have been born.

It should be an achievable goal that every baby born have an adult male responsible for it, that the norm be children nurtured by their own, married parents. But support for the traditional family flies in the face of the reigning orthodoxy by hinting that there is something inherently superior in children's being raised by their own parents in an intact family. Many professional women, single parents, and human-services personnel seem to take this praise of the ideal as an insult to the good they do. Many single parents *are* doing an excellent job of raising their children. But should we pretend that divorce and unwed motherhood are symptoms of social *strength?*

Liberalism since the Sixties has repudiated the validity of the ideal, anxious to placate feminism and the demand for instant pleasure without negative consequences. The facts of human nature do not change, however: to develop into stable, virtuous men and women, children need the constant, loving, particular attention of one or two consistent adults.

If we are to reassert the ideal, we must re-examine employment policies that lure mothers into the workforce, change tax policies that favor working mothers over full-time homemakers, and create tax oases for families of young children. Technology can come to our aid here, if it is not trammeled by politics as it has been in previous opportunities. Thirteen million new jobs could be created at home (presumably mostly for women) if government resists pressure from organized labor to outlaw home employment. Local laws restricting businesses operated out of the home—including computer work—must be corrected.

For those unmoved by social and moral arguments, there are hard dollars-and-cents considerations. If children are given the right formation they become a net plus to the public treasury; if not, they end up as a drain on it. According to University of North Carolina sociologist Peter Uhlenberg, there were in 1976 more than 260 programs administered by twenty different agencies of the Federal Government whose primary mission was to benefit children and adolescents, from recreation programs to drug and alcohol rehabilitation, job training, delinquency prevention, juvenile justice services, nutrition guidance, and so on. Real per-capita social-welfare expenditures in the country increased about five-fold between 1960 and 1980, with youth programs keeping pace. The government was doing more and more, and families were doing less and less. But did the well-being of the "beneficiaries" increase?

Among white adolescents aged 15 to 19, Uhlenberg found that, between 1960 and 1980, the death rate from suicide increased 140 per cent; from homicide, 232 per cent. The gonorrhea morbidity rate increased 199 per cent. Just between 1972 and 1979, the proportion of children aged 12 to 17 using alcohol increased 56 per cent; using drugs, 139 per cent. From 1970 to 1980, the arrest rate in that age group for violent crimes increased 60 per cent. This is the future we buy with our "investments."

It all comes down to values. Traditional values work because they are the guidelines most consistent with human nature for producing happiness and achievement.

Children who are not trained to traditional values are deprived of the best opportunity to understand their own nature and achieve that happiness. Children who *are* trained to these values are nonetheless free, upon maturity, to reject them: that is why, contrary to what the relativists insist, instilling them is not oppressive. But if these values are at least transmitted to all members of society, the possibility for a fundamental consensus on behavior exists.

Ronald Reagan got elected and reelected in large part because enough people agreed that the policies of the welfare state had failed, and enough wanted to hear more about traditional values. The public wanted government to shrink its role in their lives. That basic impulse has been developed for eight years now. In the meantime, we still have a welfare state that shows no signs of curing a single social ill, let alone withering away—it is, of course, intrinsically incapable of doing either. . . . This system perpetuates itself and the problems it pretends to solve; and yet we cannot follow the vision on which Ronald Reagan was elected until the way society organizes its approach to problems is changed—until people are again in charge of their own affairs, and those of their local community.

What can we do? An example comes from Texas. Jimmy Starkes runs the Dallas Life Foundation, a shelter for the homeless. It houses one thousand people, with over two hundred volunteers and fewer than fifty employees, many of both groups themselves former street people. Starkes estimates that out of every ten homeless people who come through his system, eight are employed and productive when he stops following them, whereas only one out of ten who go through a public shelter would have such a future. In 1987, Starkes raised $2 million in cash and in kind from the Dallas community to do this work—from people who are also paying taxes so government can do its ineffective work on the same mission.

Here is the answer: transfer, one by one, the functions of the welfare state from bureaucrats, whose vested interest is perpetuation of the problem, to service-oriented people whose only interest is solution of the problem in its current victims, and prevention of it in its future victims.

Sure, Jimmy Starkes gets the people he helps to commit their lives to Christ. Liberals would say that's unconstitutional; some conservatives would feel it's not fair. But Starkes would tell you that unless they do that first, he can't help them, because they're not willing to *let* him help them change their lives. Welfare agencies don't demand that change of heart, nor do they have Jimmy Starkes's low recidivism rate.

Liberal solutions don't work because institutions cannot change hearts or minds. *People* do that. That's why the family must hold onto as many functions as it can, and reclaim those that have been taken from it: because the consolidation of tasks in the family intensifies the interaction among members, and heightens awareness of and commitment to one another's welfare. That gives the long-range focus to our lives that connects us to society and enables us to extend our concern to our fellow citizens.

"Private-sector initiatives" is a fine watchword, but if it just means business voluntarily giving money to government-style programs, it is no solution to social problems. If it means empowering ancient institutions to do that which they do best, namely catalyze change in human hearts and actions, then it can invite a solution.

2. Anita Hill's Testimony Before the
Senate Judiciary Committee, 1991

Mr. Chairman, Senator Thurmond, members of the committee, my name is Anita F. Hill, and I am a professor of law at the University of Oklahoma.

I was born on a farm in Okmulgee County, OK, in 1956. I am the youngest of 13 children. I had my early education in Okmulgee County. My father, Albert Hill, is a farmer in that area. My mother's name is Erma Hill. She is also a farmer and a housewife.

My childhood was one of a lot of hard work and not much money, but it was one of solid family affection as represented by my parents. I was reared in a religious atmosphere in the Baptist faith, and I have been a member of the Antioch Baptist Church, in Tulsa, OK, since 1983. It is a very warm part of my life at the present time.

For my undergraduate work, I went to Oklahoma State University, and graduated from there in 1977. . . .

I graduated from the university with academic honors and proceeded to the Yale Law School, where I received my J.D. degree in 1980.

Upon graduation from law school, I became a practicing lawyer with the Washington, DC, firm of Wald, Harkrader & Ross. In 1981, I was introduced to now Judge Thomas by a mutual friend. Judge Thomas told me that he was anticipating a political appointment and asked if I would be interested in working with him. He was, in fact, appointed as Assistant Secretary of Education for Civil Rights. After he had taken that post, he asked if I would become his assistant, and I accepted that position. . . .

During this period at the Department of Education, my working relationship with Judge Thomas was positive. I had a good deal of responsibility and independence. I thought he respected my work and that he trusted my judgment.

After approximately 3 months of working there, he asked me to go out socially with him. What happened next and telling the world about it are the two most difficult things, experiences of my life. It is only after a great deal of agonizing consideration and a number of sleepless nights that I am able to talk of these unpleasant matters to anyone but my close friends.

I declined the invitation to go out socially with him, and explained to him that I thought it would jeopardize what at the time I considered to be a very good working relationship. I had a normal social life with other men outside of the office. I believed then, as now, that having a social relationship with a person who was supervising my work would be ill advised. I was very uncomfortable with the idea and told him so.

I thought that by saying "no" and explaining my reasons, my employer would abandon his social suggestions. However, to my regret, in the following few weeks he continued to ask me out on several occasions. He pressed me to justify my reasons

Testimony of Anita F. Hill, Professor of Law, University of Oklahoma, Norman, Okla., in *Hearing Before the Committee on the Judiciary, United States Senate, One Hundred Second Congress, First Session on the Nomination of Clarence Thomas to be Associate Justice of the Supreme Court of the United States, Oct. 11, 12, 13, and 14, 1991,* part 4 of 4, 36–40.

for saying "no" to him. These incidents took place in his office or mine. They were in the form of private conversations which would not have been overheard by anyone else.

My working relationship became even more strained when Judge Thomas began to use work situations to discuss sex. On these occasions, he would call me into his office for reports on education issues and projects or he might suggest that because of the time pressures of his schedule, we go to lunch to a government cafeteria. After a brief discussion of work, he would turn the conversation to a discussion of sexual matters. His conversations were very vivid.

He spoke about acts that he had seen in pornographic films involving such matters as women having sex with animals, and films showing group sex or rape scenes. He talked about pornographic materials depicting individuals with large penises, or large breasts involved in various sex acts.

On several occasions Thomas told me graphically of his own sexual prowess. Because I was extremely uncomfortable talking about sex with him at all, and particularly in such a graphic way, I told him that I did not want to talk about these subjects. I would also try to change the subject to education matters or to nonsexual personal matters, such as his background or his beliefs. My efforts to change the subject were rarely successful.

Throughout the period of these conversations, he also from time to time asked me for social engagements. My reactions to these conversations was to avoid them by limiting opportunities for us to engage in extended conversations. This was difficult because at the time, I was his only assistant at the Office of Education or Office for Civil Rights.

During the latter part of my time at the Department of Education, the social pressures and any conversation of his offensive behavior ended. I began both to believe and hope that our working relationship could be a proper, cordial, and professional one.

When Judge Thomas was made chair of the EEOC, I needed to face the question of whether to go with him. I was asked to do so and I did. The work, itself, was interesting, and at that time, it appeared that the sexual overtures, which had so troubled me, had ended.

I also faced the realistic fact that I had no alternative job. While I might have gone back to private practice, perhaps in my old firm, or at another, I was dedicated to civil rights work and my first choice was to be in that field. Moreover, at that time the Department of Education, itself, was a dubious venture. President Reagan was seeking to abolish the entire department.

For my first months at the EEOC, where I continued to be an assistant to Judge Thomas, there were no sexual conversations or overtures. However, during the fall and winter of 1982, these began again. The comments were random, and ranged from pressing me about why I didn't go out with him, to remarks about my personal appearance. I remember him saying that "some day I would have to tell him the real reason that I wouldn't go out with him."

He began to show displeasure in his tone and voice and his demeanor in his continued pressure for an explanation. He commented on what I was wearing in terms of whether it made me more or less sexually attractive. The incidents occurred in his inner office at the EEOC.

One of the oddest episodes I remember was an occasion in which Thomas was drinking a Coke in his office, he got up from the table, at which we were working, went over to his desk to get the Coke, looked at the can and asked, "Who has put pubic hair on my Coke?"

On other occasions he referred to the size of his own penis as being larger than normal and he also spoke on some occasions of the pleasures he had given to women with oral sex. At this point, late 1982, I began to feel severe stress on the job. I began to be concerned that Clarence Thomas might take out his anger with me by degrading me or not giving me important assignments. I also thought that he might find an excuse for dismissing me.

In January 1983, I began looking for another job. I was handicapped because I feared that if he found out he might make it difficult for me to find other employment, and I might be dismissed from the job I had.

Another factor that made my search more difficult was that this was during a period of a hiring freeze in the Government. In February 1983, I was hospitalized for 5 days on an emergency basis for acute stomach pain which I attributed to stress on the job. Once out of the hospital, I became more committed to find other employment and sought further to minimize my contact with Thomas.

This became easier when Allyson Duncan became office director because most of my work was then funneled through her and I had contact with Clarence Thomas mostly in staff meetings.

In the spring of 1983, an opportunity to teach at Oral Roberts University opened up. I participated in a seminar, taught an afternoon session in a seminar at Oral Roberts University. The dean of the university saw me teaching and inquired as to whether I would be interested in pursuing a career in teaching, beginning at Oral Roberts University. I agreed to take the job, in large part, because of my desire to escape the pressures I felt at the EEOC due to Judge Thomas.

When I informed him that I was leaving in July, I recall that his response was that now, I would no longer have an excuse for not going out with him. I told him that I still preferred not to do so. At some time after that meeting, he asked if he could take me to dinner at the end of the term. When I declined, he assured me that the dinner was a professional courtesy only and not a social invitation. I reluctantly agreed to accept that invitation but only if it was at the very end of a working day.

On, as I recall, the last day of my employment at the EEOC in the summer of 1983, I did have dinner with Clarence Thomas. We went directly from work to a restaurant near the office. We talked about the work that I had done both at Education and at the EEOC. He told me that he was pleased with all of it except for an article and speech that I had done for him while we were at the Office for Civil Rights. Finally he made a comment that I will vividly remember. He said, that if I ever told anyone of his behavior that it would ruin his career. This was not an apology, nor was it an explanation. That was his last remark about the possibility of our going out, or reference to his behavior.

In July 1983, I left the Washington, DC, area and have had minimal contacts with Judge Clarence Thomas since. I am, of course, aware from the press that some questions have been raised about conversations I had with Judge Clarence Thomas after I left the EEOC.

From 1983 until today I have seen Judge Thomas only twice. On one occasion I needed to get a reference from him and on another, he made a public appearance at Tulsa. On one occasion he called me at home and we had an inconsequential conversation. On one occasion he called me without reaching me and I returned the call without reaching him and nothing came of it. I have, at least on three occasions been asked to act as a conduit to him for others. . . .

It is only after a great deal of agonizing consideration that I am able to talk of these unpleasant matters to anyone, except my closest friends as I have said before. . . . Telling the world is the most difficult experience of my life, but it is very close to having to live through the experience that occasioned this meeting. I may have used poor judgment early on in my relationship with this issue. I was aware, however, that telling at any point in my career could adversely affect my future career. . . .

Perhaps I should have taken angry or even militant steps, both when I was in the agency or after I had left it, but I must confess to the world that the course that I took seemed the better, as well as the easier approach.

I declined any comment to newspapers, but later when Senate staff asked me about these matters, I felt that I had a duty to report. I have no personal vendetta against Clarence Thomas. I seek only to provide the committee with information which it may regard as relevant.

It would have been more comfortable to remain silent. . . . I took no initiative to inform anyone. But when I was asked by a representative of this committee to report my experience I felt that I had to tell the truth. I could not keep silent.

3. The Supreme Court Rules on Abortion Rights and State Regulation in *Planned Parenthood* v. *Casey,* 1992

Justice O'Connor, Justice Kennedy, and Justice Souter announced the judgment of the Court. . . .

Liberty finds no refuge in a jurisprudence of doubt. Yet 19 years after our holding that the Constitution protects a woman's right to terminate her pregnancy in its early stages, *Roe v. Wade,* that definition of liberty is still questioned. Joining the respondents as *amicus curiae,* the United States, as it has done in five other cases in the last decade, again asks us to overrule *Roe.*

At issue in these cases are five provisions of the Pennsylvania Abortion Control Act of 1982 as amended in 1988 and 1989. . . .

After considering the fundamental constitutional questions resolved by *Roe,* principles of institutional integrity, and the rule of *stare decisis,* we are led to conclude this: the essential holding of *Roe v. Wade* should be retained and once again reaffirmed.

It is . . . tempting . . . to suppose that the Due Process Clause protects only those practices, defined at the most specific level, that were protected against government interference by other rules of law when the Fourteenth Amendment was ratified. . . . But such a view would be inconsistent with our law. It is a promise of the Constitution that there is a realm of personal liberty which the government may not enter. . . . Our law affords constitutional protection to personal decisions relating to marriage, procreation, contraception, family relationships, child rearing, and

---

Planned Parenthood v. *Casey,* 1992, in Leslie Friedman Goldstein, *Contemporary Cases in Women's Rights* (Madison: University of Wisconsin Press, 1994), 99–151.

education. . . . Beliefs about these matters could not define the attributes of person-hood were they formed under compulsion of the State.

These considerations begin our analysis of the woman's interest in terminating her pregnancy but cannot end it, for this reason: though the abortion decision may originate within the zone of conscience and belief, it is more than a philosophic exercise. Abortion is a unique act. It is an act fraught with consequences for others: for the women who must live with the implications of her decision; for the persons who perform and assist in the procedure; for the spouse, family, and society which must confront the knowledge that these procedures exist, procedures some deem nothing short of an act of violence against innocent human life; and, depending on one's beliefs, for the life or potential life that is aborted. Though abortion is con-duct, it does not follow that the State is entitled to proscribe it in all instances. That is because the liberty of the woman is at stake in a sense unique to the human con-dition and so unique to the law. The mother who carries a child to full term is subject to anxieties, to physical constraints, to pain that only she must bear. That these sac-rifices have from the beginning of the human race been endured by woman with a pride that ennobles her in the eyes of others and gives to the infant a bond of love cannot alone be grounds for the State to insist she make the sacrifice. Her suffering is too intimate and personal for the State to insist, without more, upon its own vision of the woman's role, however dominant that vision has been in the course of our history and our culture. The destiny of the woman must be shaped to a large extent on her own conception of her spiritual imperatives and her place in society. . . .

The woman's right to terminate her pregnancy before viability is the most cen-tral principle of *Roe v. Wade*. It is a rule of law and a component of liberty we can-not renounce.

On the other side of the equation is the interest of the State in the protection of potential life. . . .

Though the woman has a right to choose to terminate or continue her pregnancy before viability, it does not at all follow that the State is prohibited from taking steps to ensure that this choice is thoughtful and informed. Even in the earliest stages of pregnancy, the State may enact rules and regulations designed to encourage her to know that there are philosophic and social arguments of great weight that can be brought to bear in favor of continuing the pregnancy to full term and that there are procedures and institutions to allow adoption of unwanted children as well as a cer-tain degree of state assistance if the mother chooses to raise the child herself. . . . It follows that States are free to enact laws to provide a reasonable framework for a woman to make a decision that has such profound and lasting meaning. This, too, we find consistent with *Roe's* central premises, and indeed the inevitable consequence of our holding that the State has an interest in protecting the life of the unborn.

We reject the trimester framework, which we do not consider to be part of the essential holding of *Roe*. . . . The trimester framework suffers from these basic flaws: in its formulation it misconceives the nature of the pregnant woman's interest; and in practice it undervalues the State's interest in potential life, as recognized in *Roe*. . . .

Numerous forms of state regulation might have the incidental effect of increas-ing the cost or decreasing the availability of medical care, whether for abortion or any other medical procedure. The fact that a law which serves a valid purpose, one not designed to strike at the right itself, has the incidental effect of making it more difficult or more expensive to procure an abortion cannot be enough to invalidate it. Only where state regulation imposes an undue burden on a woman's ability to make this decision does the power of the State reach into the heart of the liberty protected by the Due Process Clause. . . . .In our view, the undue burden standard is the appropriate means of reconciling the State's interest with the woman's constitutionally protected liberty. . . .

We permit a State to further its legitimate goal of protecting the life of the unborn by enacting legislation aimed at ensuring a decision that is mature and informed, even when in so doing the State expresses a preference for childbirth over abortion. . . . Requiring that the woman be informed of the availability of information relating to fetal development and the assistance available should she decide to carry the pregnancy to full term is a reasonable measure to insure an informed choice, one which might cause the woman to choose childbirth over abortion. This requirement cannot be considered a substantial obstacle to obtaining an abortion, and, it follows, there is no undue burden. . . .

The Pennsylvania statute also requires us to reconsider the holding in *Akron I* that the State may not require that a physician, as opposed to a qualified assistant, provide information relevant to a woman's informed consent. Since there is no evidence on this record that requiring a doctor to give the information as provided by the statute would amount in practical terms to a substantial obstacle to a woman seeking an abortion, we conclude that it is not an undue burden. . . .

Whether the mandatory 24-hour waiting period is . . . invalid because in practice it is a substantial obstacle to a woman's choice to terminate her pregnancy is a closer question. The findings of fact by the District Court indicate that because of the distances many women must travel to reach an abortion provider, the practical effect will often be a delay of much more than a day because the waiting period requires that a woman seeking an abortion make at least two visits to the doctor. The District Court also found that in many instances this will increase the exposure of women seeking abortions to "the harassment and hostility of antlabortion protestors demonstrating outside a clinic." . . .

These findings are troubling in some respects, but they do not demonstrate that the waiting period constitutes an undue burden. . . .

Section 3209 of Pennsylvania's abortion law provides, except in cases of medical emergency, that no physician shall perform an abortion on a married woman without receiving a signed statement from the woman that she has notified her spouse that she is about to undergo an abortion [or that she fit into one of the statute's exceptions]. . . .

In well-functioning marriages, spouses discuss important intimate decisions such as whether to bear a child. But there are millions of women in this country who are the victims of regular physical and psychological abuse at the hands of their husbands. Should these women become pregnant, they may have very good reasons for not wishing to inform their husbands of their decision to obtain an abortion. . . .

The spousal notification requirement is thus likely to prevent a significant number of women from obtaining an abortion. It does not merely make abortions a little more difficult or expensive to obtain; for many women, it will impose a substantial obstacle. . . . It is an undue burden, and therefore invalid. . . .

[As to parental consent w]e have been over most of this ground before. Our cases establish, and we reaffirm today, that a State may require a minor seeking an abortion to obtain the consent of a parent or guardian, provided that there is an adequate judicial bypass procedure. . . .

The judgment [of the Circuit Court] is affirmed. . . .

Justice Blackmun, concurring in part, concurring in the judgment in part, and dissenting in part. . . .

Three years ago, in *Webster v. Reproductive Health Serv.,* four Members of this Court appeared poised to "cas[t] into darkness the hopes and visions of every woman in this country" who had come to believe that the Constitution guaranteed her the right to reproductive choice. . . . All that remained between the promise of *Roe* and the darkness of the plurality was a single, flickering flame. Decisions since *Webster* gave little reason to hope that this flame would cast much light. . . . But now, just when so many expected the darkness to fall, the flame has grown bright.

I do not underestimate the significance of today's joint opinion. Yet I remain steadfast in my belief that the right to reproductive choice is entitled to the full protection afforded by this Court before *Webster.* And I fear for the darkness as four Justices anxiously await the single vote necessary to extinguish the light. . . .

Roe's requirement of strict scrutiny as implemented through a trimester framework should not be disturbed. No other approach has gained a majority, and no other is more protective of the woman's fundamental right. Lastly, no other approach properly accommodates the woman's constitutional right with the State's legitimate interests. . . .

Chief Justice Rehnquist, with whom Justice White, Justice Scalia, and Justice Thomas join, concurring in the judgment in part and dissenting in part.

The joint opinion, following its newly-minted variation on *stare decisis,* retains the outer shell of *Roe v. Wade,* but beats a wholesale retreat from the substance of that case. We believe that *Roe* was wrongly decided, and that it can and should be overruled consistently with our traditional approach to *stare decisis* in constitutional cases. We would adopt the approach of the plurality in *Webster v. Reproductive Health Services* and uphold the challenged provisions of the Pennsylvania statute in their entirety. . . .

In *Roe v. Wade,* the Court recognized a "guarantee of personal privacy" which "is broad enough to encompass a woman's decision whether or not to terminate her pregnancy." We are now of the view that, in terming this right fundamental, the Court in *Roe* read the earlier opinions upon which it based its decision much too broadly. Unlike marriage, procreation and contraception, abortion "involves the purposeful termination of potential life." *Harris v. McRae* (1980). . . . One cannot ignore the fact that a woman is not isolated in her pregnancy, and that the decision to abort necessarily involves the destruction of a fetus. . . .

We think, therefore, both in view of this history and of our decided cases dealing with substantive liberty under the Due Process Clause, that the Court was mistaken in *Roe* when it classified a woman's decision to terminate her pregnancy as a "fundamental right" that could be abridged only in a manner which withstood "strict scrutiny." . . . The Court in *Roe* reached too far when it . . . deemed the right to abortion fundamental.

4. Nancy G. Brinker Testifies in Favor of Increased Funding for Breast Cancer Research, 2000

Chairman Porter, Ranking Member Obey, and distinguished Members of the Subcommittee, thank you for the opportunity to testify before you today on the importance of federal health care funding. I began the Susan G. Komen Breast Cancer Foundation in 1982 after my older sister, Suzy, died of breast cancer at age 36. We didn't start with much—a couple of hundred dollars, an office in my bedroom, and a shoebox full of names. But we had something more important—a mission—to eradicate breast cancer as a life-threatening disease. To achieve that goal, we had to change both the clinical and cultural landscape of breast cancer, and we have.

Over the past 18 years, Komen has become one of the largest private funders of breast cancer research in America. We've raised and spent close to $214 million for research, education, screening and treatment programs often in partnership with the federal government.

At the time of Komen's inception, the federal government was only beginning to recognize the importance of funding breast cancer and other women's diseases. As the Foundation has grown over the past 18 years, so too has the federal commitment to women's health. Chairman Porter, Ranking Member Obey and Members of the Subcommittee, I thank you for your leadership and effectiveness in directing valuable federal resources towards the fight against breast cancer and other serious women's health issues. Chairman Porter, as you look back on your distinguished career in Congress, know that you have the sincere gratitude of those of us in the breast cancer movement and the thousands of breast cancer survivors you have helped because you cared enough to listen and to act.

I know that the Subcommittee is faced with competing demands and limited resources. When it comes to curing diseases and helping patients, there never seems to be enough to go around. So, it is important that every dollar is used wisely, effectively and efficiently. I am here today to show you how your investments in women's health care are yielding results far greater than the sum of their parts. By making significant federal funding commitments to breast cancer research and outreach, this subcommittee has built a strong foundation for private sector partnerships, like Komen's, that are producing real clinical results and a better quality of life for thousands of women living with breast cancer. My pledge to you is that we will continue to leverage your investments. Every dollar you dedicate will be a dollar well spent.

Today, I'd like to briefly tell you how Komen uses the dollars we raise to maximize our impact and yours. Most of you probably know Komen best for creating the "Race for the Cure," 5k races held all across America—in most of your districts—to raise funds for community breast cancer programs and international research grants. In fact, many of you have run or walked in Komen Races, and I want to thank you personally for your support. It means a lot to us.

This year, we expect more than a million participants in over 109 cities. But the people who will run and walk this year would tell you that what's important isn't how far they've run, but how far the money they've raised will go. So, I'd like to tell

Testimony of Nancy G. Brinker, Founding Chair, the Susan G. Komen Breast Cancer Foundation, Appropriations Subcommittee on Labor, Health, Human Services, Education, and Related Agencies, House of Representatives, March 14, 2000.

you how and where the Komen Foundation spends its funding—two major areas: cutting edge research and education, screening, and treatment programs.

Let me start with research. At Komen, we have awarded over $45 million in grants towards medical research, many working in conjunction with NIH, making it possible for world-class scientists in some of the nation's most prestigious research institutions to investigate exciting new fields of breast cancer research. At Komen, we have also worked to attract young scientists into breast cancer research, often offering the only source of funding for cutting-edge research for some of our newest and most creative scientists. Komen grants enable these young scientists to collect the critical data required by the National Cancer Institute (NCI) for the awarding of larger federal grants.

Federal support of cancer research is critical, and at Komen, we look to add value to your investment. We know that breast cancer can't be cured in the lab alone. Clinical trials are the only way to translate theoretical research progress into real cancer therapies; and, for many patients, they offer the best treatment available. Last year, the Susan G. Komen Breast Cancer Foundation launched a new grassroots initiative to increase enrollment in clinical trials—many of which are funded by NIH. Project CRAFT (Clinical Research—Affiliates Funding Trials) is a six-state demonstration project designed to raise awareness about clinical trials and help break down barriers that keep thousands of breast cancer patients from participating in clinical trials every year.

Thus, if NIH funds a clinical trial for breast cancer, Komen-funded community based organizations and medical institutions will help alert patients and physicians to this new opportunity, subsidize costs not covered by insurance, and even arrange transportation and child care needs for women so that they can participate. We hope to expand CRAFT to many more of our local affiliates because we believe that our committed volunteers and our supplemental financial support for NIH-sponsored and NIH-approved breast cancer clinical trials can help assure their success and increase participation in future trials.

Until a cure for breast cancer is found, Komen believes that we must do everything within our power to promote the life-saving message of screening and early detection. . . . One of the characteristics of Komen that sets us apart is our emphasis on a grassroots approach through our 113 affiliates. These affiliates identify local community needs and fund education and treatment programs to meet those needs, especially those of the most medically underserved in our communities.

The Centers for Disease Control and Prevention (CDC) has done an impressive job of advancing these goals, and it is my hope that the CDC will continue to be funded at an adequate level in fiscal year 2001. I urge the subcommittee to allocate $622 million for the important missions that CDC serves in cancer prevention awareness and early detection programs. In particular, the Komen Foundation joins with the entire cancer community in respectfully requesting at least $55 million for the National Program of Cancer Registries, $215 million for CDC's National Breast and Cervical Cancer Early Detection Program (NBCCEDP), and $352 million for CDC's other priority cancer control and prevention efforts.

In Washington, I understand that it can be difficult to see the difference federal funding is making in the lives of breast cancer patients and their families. On behalf of our 113 local affiliates working in the trenches to help each life touched by breast cancer, I assure you that this funding is making a difference. For example, CDC funding for the National Breast and Cervical Cancer Early Detection Program has not only provided funding for outreach and screening, but it has created a solid foundation for partnerships with Komen and others which have expanded the scope and depth of this program.

The Komen Foundation's Hispanic Outreach Program in Texas was initially funded through a CDC cooperative agreement grant. A three-year CDC grant in 1994 of just over $300,000 established a pilot program in two Fort Worth barrios to provide breast cancer outreach and education to medically underserved Spanish-speaking women. Since 1997, when funding for this pilot project ended, the Komen Foundation has kept the initiative alive by providing support for community-based organizations that continue this mission. Komen funding has contributed to the development of educational materials in Spanish, and dissemination of these kits has been extensive, spreading the message of early detection to a population that has often been difficult to reach. This initiative began with federal funding, but it keeps growing and keeps helping because we have been able to build on your foundation.

Komen funds many community-based organizations that partner with CDC to carry out and even expand the mission of the "Early Detection" program. For instance, some of our programs emphasize outreach to women who may not meet established program eligibility guidelines with respect to age but are at high risk for breast cancer. Other outreach programs target Asian, Hispanic, and African American women, in some cases developing written materials in their native language in a format that appeals to them. We have also financed promotional efforts at universities to increase awareness of the importance of early detection among students. The Komen Foundation has provided critical dollars to countless programs and support networks to address virtually every facet of breast cancer, and the CDC's Early Detection program has been the lynchpin of these programs.

Whether it's breakthrough research or grassroots education, screening and treatment programs, our progress at Komen or as a society is simply not possible without significant government support. For fiscal year 2001, I urge you to increase funding for the National Cancer Institute to $4.1 billion and expand funding for the National Institutes of Health (NIH) by fifteen percent over the fiscal year 2000 level. The NIH increase is necessary to keep on track with our five-year goal of doubling the NIH budget between fiscal year 1999 and fiscal year 2003.

Komen does not expect the government to develop a cure for breast cancer on its own—we have dedicated millions of our own hard-raised money towards breast cancer research, treatment, education, and screening. I assure you that we will continue in our mission. But I must also emphasize that we also can't do it alone. We need federal funding to continue in our battle against breast cancer and other women's diseases. I believe we are on the edge of real breakthroughs that could save thousands, millions of lives but we must have the funding to go the last mile. There are times when each of us must choose a course of action that requires a bolder stride to achieve a difficult goal. That time is now for cancer funding in America. If you will take that step with us, I assure you that you will not walk alone.

Thank you for your leadership and help in providing these valuable resources.

5. Asma Gull Hasan Comments on American Muslim Women Who Live "Between Two Worlds," 2000

American Muslim women are really between two worlds: the old world of traditions, preserved and passed down by immigrant parents or older members of the indigenous community, and the new world, as presented to us by the feminist movement, American emphasis on gender equality and by the Qur'an, in a sense, too.

The idea of a Muslim feminist also strikes Americans as odd. American Muslim women are in the unique and paradoxical position of living in a society where they are free to explore their religion but are stereotyped by the greater population of their country as oppressed women. The West cites its perceptions of arranged marriages, polygamy (actually polygyny, meaning a plurality of wives), veiling and other aspects of Islamic life that are perceived to degrade women as evidence of Islam's cultural inferiority.

At the same time as they encounter this criticism, American Muslim women are re-discovering the freedoms Islam gives them. Muslims believe that God revealed to Prophet Muhammad several provisions emphasizing a woman's independence, provisions which are recorded in the Qur'an. Of particular note is that in the Qur'an, Eve is created independently of Adam, providing no Qur'anic basis for women's existence as the result of the creation of men.

In the Qur'an, men and women are fully equal before God. Marriage is a contract to be negotiated, even to the woman's benefit, and, women have the right to divorce, one of many Qur'anic "innovations" that " . . . brought legal advantages for women quite unknown in corresponding areas of the Western Christian world," says Jane Smith. Other innovations include the right to property and the right to inherit money. According to Islamic law, a woman can keep her maiden name and her personal income. Islam also grants women the right to participate in political affairs (imagine, if we had all followed the Qur'an, there would have been no need for the suffragette movement), to stand equally with men in the eyes of the law, to receive child support in the event of a divorce, to seek employment and education, to take or turn down a marriage proposal and to live free from spousal abuse. Islam also gives women high status as mothers, to be respected and admired by their children. On two occasions the Prophet highlighted the mother's role, telling one follower to stay with his mother rather than join the military, " . . . for Paradise is at her feet." Muslim women also can draw on a history of strong women, particularly those women who lived in Muhammad's time. Some Muslims even support a woman's right to abortion because the procedure is believed to have been performed in the Prophet's time without his dissent.

However, along with Qur'anic tradition, one is also subject to other traditions that, over centuries of time, have come to be associated with being Muslim, though they may have nothing to do with Islam, like female circumcision (an African tribal custom) and an emphasis on marriage. Furthermore, women bear the brunt of traditional aspects of cultures associated with Islam—like wearing *hijab*. Algerian lawyer and specialist in Muslim women's rights for UNESCO, Wassyla Tamzali, told *The*

New York Times, " . . . [W]omen symbolize tradition and cultural identity. It is as if the whole burden of the Islamic tradition rests on their shoulders." Rifaat Hassan, an American Muslim scholar, writes, "Even when a Muslim woman is able to acquire an education and secure a job, she is seldom able to free herself from the burden of traditionalism that confronts her on all sides."

This coercive nature of traditional aspects of Islam manifests itself in America with an emphasis on marriage, in my opinion. Young Muslim women are bombarded with messages of not only the importance of marriage but marriage *at a young age.* Even with parents and families like mine, who show hardly any vestiges of traditionalism or conservatism . . . , the pressure for daughters to marry young is strong. That is a part of American-Muslim culture, for better or for worse. . . . There doesn't seem to be a really good reason to, other than marriage in our culture is a preferred alternative to dating, as sex outside of marriage is *haram* (unlawful). Marriage at a young age or marriage at all is not a religious obligation, but the centrality of family in Islamic culture makes marriage very important. In addition, marriage means acceptance into the Muslim social community. . . .

The importance of marriage in the American Muslim community is exemplified by the myriad ways the community has developed for finding a spouse: personal advertisements in Islamic publications, matrimonial booths at Islamic conferences, enlisting peers in a search or through "word of mouth" and mosque-arranged singles gatherings. American Islamic publications run how-to articles on finding a spouse. Marriage is so important that immigrant parents worry about a scarcity of young Muslim men for their daughters; some even wonder if the Islamic law allowing Muslim men to marry Christian or Jewish women should be rescinded in America.

However, today's Muslim woman is not necessarily doomed to failure because she marries young, according to traditional values. In many ways, it's good that the community is taking an active role in pairing off the young ones. As a result of parental flexibility and the perception of a scarcity of Muslims of similar ages, inter-ethnic marriages have become more popular, particularly intermarriage between racial backgrounds. That sounds like the American dream to me: young married people, sometimes of diverse backgrounds, with a stable financial footing and strong family setting.

A more subtle form of oppression against American Muslim women is carried out by American Muslim men who feel threatened by modern American culture. Rifaat Hassan writes, "Nothing perhaps illustrates men's deep insecurities . . . so well as the sternness and strictness with which they compel their women to cover themselves from head to foot and keep them confined to their houses." Kathleen Gough's essay, "The Origin of the Family," says that one of the characteristics of male power is physical confinement and prevention of movement of women; this characteristic is manifested by *purdah* (the separation of men and women at all gatherings especially during prayer, which has no solid Qur'anic basis but is practiced by most Muslims) and *hijab.* Muslim men, and eventually the females in their community, force *hijab* and severe forms of modesty on women that result in gender segregation. Such behavior is sometimes coerced through community attitudes onto Muslim women and chalked up to the noble purpose of protecting women. These attitudes are reminiscent of how the Christian male group, the Promisekeepers, allegedly protect their women. With both groups, a fine line exists between protection and encouragement versus oppression and suppression. . . .

Though the problems Muslim women face seem insurmountable, women can improve their situation by taking advantage of the opportunities a Muslim woman has in America. Living in the US is positively affecting the lives of American Muslim women in two ways: (1) American culture encourages female participation in religious activities and (2) Muslim women are readily able to learn Arabic, read the Qur'an and analyze the Qur'an for themselves.

One of the greatest phenomena occurring in the Muslim world today is Qur'anic exegesis by Muslim feminists. The Qur'an, a book regarded as the divine work for over 1400 years, is being interpreted from a non-male perspective on a large scale for *the first time ever.* A diverse group of the world's female Muslims are " . . . fundamentally rework[ing Islam] . . . from a feminist and egalitarian point of view." Their work is controversial because they are trying to prove that the Qur'an does not support oppression of women undermining or questioning the validity of the Qur'an itself, only certain interpretations. Some credit the Beijing United Nations Conference on women as bringing this intellectual, yet politically charged, dialogue to the surface, and now, the Ford Foundation, the National Endowment for Democracy and the Council on Foreign Relations are funding projects in this area.

I say it's about time. For 1400 years, men like my grandfather have told women like me what the Qur'an says. I'm not saying all those men are wrong. And frankly, the only interpretations I'm really interested in challenging are the ones regarding women's so-called inferiority. I'm just saying that now that women have an opportunity to be literate, to read the Qur'an in Arabic and tell us if they think God made men superior, let's have a listen!

The core complaint of these feminist Muslim theologians is that though the Qur'an is clear in its support of women's rights, men have been interpreting the Qur'an to their own advantage since its revelation. Amina Wadud-Muhsin, Philosophy and Religion Professor at Virginia Commonwealth University in Richmond, says, "[N]ow . . . many women are making the point that . . . men's interpretation of our religion . . . has limited women's progress, not our religion itself." For example, the gender segregation during prayer now suggests inferiority on women's part when, in actuality, the Prophet initiated the practice so that women would not have to prostrate in front of men. Realizing that a male perception of Islam has been used and accepted for centuries, Muslim women are taking back their right to Qur'anic education and interpretation.

6. Jamala McFadden Tells Her Story of Welfare Assistance in the 1990s, 2002

In 1991, at the age of fifteen, I had a child. My mother had five children and already received aid from the state of Illinois. My son was simply added to our family allotment. Even with the monthly cash, food stamps, and minimal child care subsidies, the amount was simply inadequate to support our family. I eventually supplemented

"Jamala McFadden's Story," Personal Stories, Welfare Made a Difference National Campaign, 2002. www.wmadcampaign.org/story01.html. Reprinted with the permission of Jamala McFadden.

the assistance by working and had enough money to buy, at most, diapers, milk, and other basic necessities for my child.

After two years, I completed high school and was fortunate enough to be able to go away to college. For four years (1994–98) I attended the University of Illinois at Urbana-Champaign. My son, two at the time, went along with me. Because my mother needed to provide for herself and my siblings, she was unable to provide financial support for my son and I. It was my responsibility to single-handedly supply all of our basic needs, including housing. As a full-time college student caring for a child alone, my needs were definitely not the needs of a traditional college student who had the financial support of her family. In Urbana, I was able to receive government assistance in my name for my child and myself. I was a full-time student caring for my child alone.

Welfare definitely made it easier for me to get through the critical transition period between high school and college and sustained me through undergraduate school. In my first year of college, there was no work prerequisite to receive aid. However, I worked anyway. During my second and third years, welfare recipients who were students were required to work a minimum of eight hours per week. That I did. However, by my last year, 1997–98, the state required that students work twenty hours per week. Fortunately for me, I was "grandfathered in" and wasn't forced to work the additional hours to receive assistance. I was told that "times are changing" and that "welfare as we know it was over." Indeed, college students were a very low priority for childcare subsidies. The perception was that "we didn't need it. . . . Getting a college degree was a personal decision—of no concern to the state." For the government at least, it was time to prioritize securing and maintaining a job over getting a good education.

Fortunately, I was successful. I finished college in four years. I finished before many of my peers who had little or no responsibilities and were completely supported by their families. Not only did I earn my college degree, I was active in several school organizations, co founding a single-parent support group on campus. I graduated with high distinction in political science, achieving a 3.7 G.P.A. I went on to law school at the University of Michigan—one of the top ten law schools in the country. If I had to work twenty hours per week, be a successful full-time student, and be a good mother to a small child, I doubt that I would have been as successful as I have been thus far.

Contrary to popular stereotype, welfare in no way held me back. I was fortunate and indeed blessed. Welfare made a difference in my life. Welfare made it easier for me to succeed and concentrate on what was important—my child and my education. For those who believe in the theory that welfare is cyclical and repeats throughout generations—for this family, the cycle is broken. Welfare helped me show my son, younger siblings, my community, and particularly other teenage mothers that anything is possible. For mothers, if it is necessary, welfare can be a stepping stone to great things in their lives.

E S S A Y S

Amy Sue Bix analyzes the shared values and tactics that enabled feminists and gay men to challenge medical authority and win increased funding and public support for the contemporary wars against breast cancer and acquired immunodeficiency syndrome.

Kathleen Moore argues that Muslim women in the United States have been unable to gain full religious liberty in the past several decades, despite existing laws that prohibit discrimination on the basis of religion. Gwendolyn Mink investigates why white feminists supported or did not support the Personal Responsibility Act of 1996, and she explores how the new welfare legislation denies critical freedoms to poor women and women of color.

Women, Gay Men, and Medical Authority in the Wars Against Breast Cancer and AIDS

AMY SUE BIX

Through the 1980s and early 1990s, the course of American health research was increasingly shaped by politically-aggressive activism for two particular diseases, breast cancer and AIDS (Acquired Immunodeficiency Syndrome). Even as national stakes rose, both in dollars spent and growing demands on the medical system, breast cancer and AIDS advocates made government policy-making for research ever more public and controversial. Through skillful cultivation of political strength, interest groups transformed individual health problems into collective demands, winning notable policy influence in federal agencies such as the National Institutes of Health (NIH) and Food and Drug Administration (FDA). Activists directly challenged fundamental principles of both government and medical systems, fighting to affect distribution of research funds and questioning well-established scientific methods and professional values. In the contest for decision-making power, those players achieved remarkable success in influencing and infiltrating (some critics said, undermining) both the politics and science of medical research. Between 1990 and 1995, federal appropriations for breast cancer study rose from $90 million to $465 million, while in the same period, NIH AIDS research rose from $743.53 million to $1.338 billion. . . .

[The] 1980s and early 1990s politicization of breast cancer was closely linked to general history of modern feminist concerns. Through the 1960s, as women organized around explicitly feminist motivations, they began scrutinizing gender dimensions of political, social and economic life, including health care. Under the maxim of "the personal as political," women's health was transformed from individual problems into a mutual concern and impetus for political action.

From its 1969 start, the Boston Women's Health Collective encouraged women to educate themselves about their physical well-being, to become informed health consumers who would refuse to tolerate condescending or inadequate treatment by the medical system. The group's 1974 reference *Our Bodies, Ourselves* described both medical details and women's own health experiences, from childbirth to contraception and more; within a decade, the text sold more than two million copies nationwide. In 1975, concerned parties established the National Women's Health Network to draw attention to female health issues and distribute information. Female-friendly

Amy Sue Bix, "Disease Chasing Money and Power: Breast Cancer and AIDS Activism Challenging Authority," *Journal of Policy History* 9, no. 1 (1997): 5–32. Copyright 1997 by The Pennsylvania State University. Reproduced by permission of the publisher.

health clinics became important providers of women's medical treatment and also worked to influence policy: rather than waiting for development of new contraceptives, feminist clinics helped promote cervical cap research.

Women's health mobilization also crystallized in response to two medical disasters: the Dalkon Shield, touted as a wonderful new 1970s IUD, turned out to cause miscarriage and pelvic inflammatory disease (some severe cases proving fatal), while the drug DES, once popularly administered to pregnant women in hope of avoiding miscarriage, was linked to cancer and reproductive problems extending even two generations down from users. Frustrated by seeming failure of doctors, lawyers, and politicians to provide information, health care, or compensation, concerned women formed grass-roots organizations such as DES Action to support affected women, raise public awareness, and maintain political, medical, and legal pressure.

By the late 1980s, feminist advocates argued that beyond disastrous products such as DES and the Shield, women's health had been systematically endangered by an entire medical establishment. Health was a gendered issue, critics contended; despite evidence of important medical differences between men and women on such matters as cholesterol levels, researchers often investigated health questions or tested new drugs on male subjects alone. The multi-year Physician's Health Study especially troubled women's advocates; the report relied on an all-male sample of 22,000 doctors and so offered no evidence whether aspirin's cardiovascular benefits held true for females. The project head . . . warned science would suffer if political pressure compelled researchers to alter studies, regardless of appropriateness, to fit a mandated gender balance; drug companies added their own cautions that potential harm to a fetus meant special risk in testing women of childbearing age.

Nevertheless, political forces . . . acquired momentum. In 1986, Public Health Service (PHS) officials spoke up for greater awareness of women's issues in medical studies, NIH then created policy encouraging all grant applicants to "consider the inclusion of women" and justify any research excluding female subjects. Four years later, however, a General Accounting Office (GAO) analysis confirmed women's suspicions that the new policy had been ineffective, that numerous research proposals still ignored gender considerations. The Congressional Caucus for Women's Issues subsequently introduced Women's Health Equity Act legislation which would, among other measures, create a special OB/GYN program at NIH and enforce rules for including female subjects in research. The Act drew growing attention, and soon House and Senate subcommittees adopted some of its provisions as part of NIH reauthorization. To try regaining credibility and demonstrate good faith on the question of women and research, NIH officials adopted strategy to separate and institutionalize responsibility for female health. In September, 1990, NIH established a new Office of Research on Women's Health, winning praise from Women's Caucus co-chair, Representative Patricia Schroeder, who had previously blamed male-dominated policy for leaving women's health "at risk."

The campaign for women's health united feminist advocates, sympathetic politicians such as Schroeder; individual doctors, scientists and medical researchers also supported the cause and organized groups such as the Society for the Advancement of Women's Health Research. By the 1990s, medical journals featured notable numbers of articles and editorials on the issue, as *JAMA* put it, whether there was "still too much extrapolation from data on middle-aged white men."

Interest groups made an ever-larger case, arguing that beyond women's under-representation in studies, gender bias extended to systematic inequity in federal health funds. . . . In 1991, one week after confirmation as first female head of NIH, Bernadine Healy announced the agency was creating a $600 million, fifteen-year Women's Health Initiative to redress history of gendered research imbalance. Healy called this NIH's "awakening to a simple fact . . . that women have unique medical problems." . . . Initiative research, planned to involve up to 160,000 women, would represent the biggest single clinical trial and research effort in NIH history.

While gratifying women's health activists, that fact met more dubious response from some scientific and medical quarters. The Initiative's giant scale and proposed structure drew criticism: with previous NIH work centering on relatively small-scale investigations proposed by researchers, why should the agency suddenly switch to an enormous undertaking directed top-down? . . . Other researchers expressed concern about initial scientific details, such as plans for overlapping clinical trials on 63,000 women to see how nutrient supplements, exercise, low-fat food regimens, and hormone treatment affected cancer, heart disease, and osteoporosis. Several dozen female epidemiologists worried such a complicated project would be undermined by both technical flaws (sorting out multiple factors) and practical difficulties (unlikelihood of convincing women to continue demanding lifestyle changes over ten or more years of study). . . . However valid the scientific criticism, the large Initiative satisfied NIH's political needs, addressing feminist demands for funding and research attention.

Within this context of activism for general women's health research, one particular disease, breast cancer, attracted increasing attention in the 1980s. New organizations were founded to focus public awareness and support concerned women; for example, the Susan G. Komen Breast Cancer Foundation, established in 1982, became known for organizing "Race for the Cure" runs in fifty-eight cities to raise money for research, education, and screening programs. Such groups gathered political strength, mobilizing to get government and public alike to recognize breast cancer as a unique concern and allocate special funds to fight the disease.

In this new political battle for breast cancer research, Susan Love, UCLA Associate Professor of Clinical Surgery and Director of the Revlon/UCLA Breast Center, established visibility and a dual identity as both doctor and political player. Historically, other practitioners, from occupational medicine pioneer Alice Hamilton to pediatrician Benjamin Spock, had combined professionalism with social and political expression. However, Love increasingly defined her medical and activist breast cancer work as inseparable, even as many health professionals still felt uncomfortable positioning themselves to challenge the political and medical order. Love linked her political awakening to her promotion of her 1990 reference book for women concerned about breast cancer; after she tossed off a line proposing a "march topless on the White House" to "make President Bush wake up and do something about breast cancer," she found female listeners ready to take her seriously. Calling this group "fed up . . . that this virtual epidemic was being ignored," Love became increasingly vocal about breast cancer being as much a political as medical battle.

Following broader campaigns for women's health research, breast cancer concerns maintained that government and medical authorities had ignored the disease even as it approached epidemic proportion; news commentator Cokie Roberts observed that women's 44,500 breast cancer deaths in 1991 exceeded the total of

American soldiers killed in Vietnam. Activists based their work on certain presumptions: without increased federal support, the country would make little progress on breast cancer, but given satisfactory resources, movement leaders promised, the disease could be conquered so modern women's daughters and granddaughters would not experience similar fear of breast cancer. To drive this agenda, Love helped establish the National Breast Cancer Coalition in 1991, linking separate advocacy groups to multiply their political effectiveness and muster parade rallies and other demonstrations of public support. Collecting thousands of signatures in petition drives to the President and Congress demanding more breast cancer research, the Coalition gained access to present its case to both Bill and Hillary Clinton.

Women's push for breast cancer money broke through partisan lines; Republicans such as Marilyn Quayle and Olympia Snowe joined Democrats Mary Rose Oakar and Schroeder. Senators such as Edward Kennedy and Tom Harkin (who lost several relatives to the disease) proved useful allies in Congress. Breast cancer groups also benefitted because their appeal coincided with a unique point in national politics; the 1991 nationally-televised hearings on sexual harassment charges in Clarence Thomas' confirmation as Supreme Court justice had left some Americans with an impression of Congress as insensitive to females' concerns. To mend political fences, some representatives turned to breast cancer funding to demonstrate willingness to listen to women's demands; Senator Arlen Specter, whose image had been especially damaged by harsh cross-examination of Anita Hill, especially highlighted his commitment to fighting breast cancer, Furthermore, in 1992, ongoing fallout over the hearings swept a number of women candidates into Congress; "the Anita Hill class" then established greater female representation on committees and subcommittees where they could speak up for women's health issues such as breast cancer,

As another advantage, no other advocates of specific women's diseases had achieved similarly high political profile by the 1990s, so breast cancer activists did not have to compete with other feminists for money and political consideration. Breast cancer could also be considered politically safe: while a campaign against women's lung cancer would have forced politicians to risk alienating Southern tobacco interests and defy the notoriously tough cigarette lobby, breast cancer did not seem to necessitate major confrontation. As Love acknowledged, advocates had demographics on their side; breast cancer had an image of affecting middle or upper-class Caucasian females, a crucial political constituency. For those reasons, supporting higher breast cancer funding became a way for politicians to exhibit awareness of women's issues. In 1991, government money for studying breast cancer rose $43 million, raising by half the previous level of $90 million; in 1992, funds soared to more than $400 million across various federal agencies. Within the National Cancer Institute (NCI) alone, breast cancer support jumped from $197 million to almost $263 million between 1993 and 1994; to place that in perspective, NCI devoted just over $90 million to lung cancer and under $50 million to prostate cancer in that same period. . . . Corporate sponsors such as Revlon enlisted in fighting breast cancer, providing research funds and other resources while highlighting their support as showing the female market they took women's issues seriously. Public commitment to breast cancer research became a "safe" yet powerful symbol of sensitivity.

Such a development contrasted sharply with previous American attitudes toward breast cancer; women affected in the early twentieth century had tended to keep the disease a close secret, afraid cancer reflected badly on them personally or simply considering it a private concern. . . . With ability and motivation to translate individual experience into group mobilization, transform concern into "demands," women's activists gave breast cancer new visibility and power to influence government funding decisions.

Just as feminist organizations provided both philosophical and practical impetus for activists to demand increasing funding and attention for women's health in general and breast cancer in particular, so AIDS activism reflected mobilization of America's gay community. While the 1960s and 1970s had represented an alternately heady and frustrating period of personal concern and political organization for gays, the 1980s brought what seemed the greatest challenge yet, a devastating and mysterious new disease. By 1981, West Coast doctors treating the gay population started noticing clusters of immune deficiency problems. Physicians and researchers at the Centers for Disease Control (CDC) found unusually frequent reports of rare pneumonia and cancer forms. CDC medical detectives initially had to sort through a variety of possible causes, from chemical poisoning to recreational drug use, and perceived the threat as sufficiently urgent to warrant special studies of what some referred to as "Gay-Related Immune Deficiency" (GRID). However, Reagan-era budget cuts threatened to force CDC staff layoffs, with devastating impact on agency plans and morale. NIH had no coordinated strategy for addressing the new disease, while clinic doctors were literally writing rules as they went along on how to treat the now-renamed "AIDS." Gay aides on Capital Hill tried pressing for increased federal research support. However, NIH representatives and Health and Human Services (HHS) Secretary Margaret Heckler officially assured skeptics that funding for AIDS work was "more than adequate." At various times, budget planners even proposed cuts of 10 percent or more. Meanwhile, between 1983 and 1985, United States AIDS cases jumped from three thousand to sixteen thousand, finally attracting significant national media coverage, especially after announcement of actor Rock Hudson's infection. Though Surgeon General C. Everett Koop began preparing to address the public on the nature and prevention of AIDS, concerned observers detected damning lack of leadership, if not outright sabotage, by the Reagan presidency and federal bureaucracy on research to fight the new fatal illness.

With increasing awareness of AIDS, 1980s gay community leaders mobilized resources for both medical and political efforts. Just as feminists had founded the Boston Women's Health Collective, National Women's Health Network, DES Action, and National Breast Cancer Coalition to call attention to women's health, so gay groups created new AIDS organizations. One West Coast group evolved into the San Francisco AIDS Foundation, while New York leaders established Gay Men's Health Crisis, along with the American Foundation for AIDS Research (Amfar).

The most brazen group, ACT-UP (AIDS Coalition to Unleash Power), had been organized in 1987, largely at New York writer/gay activist Larry Kramer's initiative. Members targeted public figures they believed had expressed insensitive attitudes or failed to show proper commitment to fighting AIDS, from Michael Dukakis and Ed Koch to George Bush and Jesse Helms. Hundreds of ACT-UP supporters took political confrontation to radical heights, designing strategies to draw media attention; most notably disrupting a December, 1989 mass at New York's St. Patrick's

Cathedral to condemn church positions on AIDS, condoms, and sex education. Protesters also broke into government hearings, prime-time network newscasts, and political speeches across the country to vent opinions on the AIDS crisis.

Behind such public protests, AIDS activists organized special committees to help care for patients, prepare and distribute preventive public health information, and support research on the disease. As advocates educated themselves about medical details, that sense of knowledge helped some approach health experts on an informed footing, winning professional respect for their seriousness. But the late 1980s proved discouraging; while laboratories turned up apparently hopeful clues to disease mechanisms, converting such findings into practical treatments continued to be difficult and slower than even some experts had predicted. Linking this medical impasse to lack of adequate research funding, frustrated activists blamed government apathy for extending the crisis; Kramer called federal efforts to fight AIDS "murderously slow."

Advocates complained that once developed, medical treatments took longer than necessary to reach desperate patients, due to dragging government regulatory processes. In addition to familiarizing themselves with medical facts, AIDS groups also started learning how NIH and FDA operated, to challenge those authorities more effectively. Incensed with seemingly unconscionable bureaucratic delay in approving new drugs, ACT-UP staged sit-ins at NIH and "die-ins" in front of FDA facilities to dramatize demands. . . .

The 1991 appointment of pediatrician and law professor David Kessler as new FDA commissioner led the agency to acknowledge and deal more explicitly with AIDS groups' pressure, just as Healy's NIH work both reflected and affected the changing political context of breast cancer concern. . . . Largely in response to such . . . pressure, FDA's average time before deciding to approve or deny new drug applications dropped 42 percent between 1987 and 1992, from thirty-three months to eighteen, the GAO reported. In December, 1995, the FDA proudly pointed to record speed in approving the new protease-inhibiting AIDS drug saquinavir, just over three months from the manufacturer's first submission. In fact, officials announced, all six anti-AIDS drugs approved in the preceding seven years had come through government review in six months or less. . . .

AIDS and breast cancer advocacy, of course, were not absolutely identical. For example, though women concerned with health issues were able to draw on increased female Congressional representation after 1992, gay groups could not count on having as many "natural" allies come forward in the political establishment. Overall, however, activist development for breast cancer and AIDS displayed significant parallels; in both cases, mobilized organizations transformed a group's specific medical problem into concerns defined as politically crucial. Both AIDS and breast cancer could leave victims feeling powerless, a sense reinforced by consciousness of women's and gays' status as "outsiders." Political activity offered a way to rechannel frustration, away from individual battles against an enemy inside (disease itself), into organized campaigns challenging stubborn outside forces ("the political establishment," "medical systems," or both). Even if policy changes and renewed research funding came too late to bring a particular patient/activist any personal medical help, organizations drew the individual into a broader fight, promising their commitment would broadly benefit entire groups of others, even curing or preventing future disease. Both breast cancer and AIDS activists operated from conviction that previous medical funding and research policy had been systematically biased against investigation of "their" disease. Some almost-moralistic undertones insisted government and medical authorities confess previous "injustices," then to be atoned for by generous new spending.

Similarities between AIDS and breast cancer activism should not be surprising. From the late 1980s on, leaders in the two camps studied each other's work, modelling new efforts in light of what had succeeded for the other cause. Breast cancer advocates adopted tactics initiated by AIDS activists and vice versa, cooperating where they saw common need for action. For example, members of Women's Health Action and Mobilization (WHAM!), sharing ACT-UP's aggressive political inclination, joined the 1989 St. Patrick's protest against certain Catholic moral precepts. Each movement developed special fund-raising and public awareness events (from breast cancer-benefit fashion shows, to AIDS-benefit theater, music, and art events). Both causes even acquired shorthand symbols of support: red ribbons for AIDS and pink for breast cancer, fashionable accessories among regular Americans and Hollywood celebrities wishing to display political and philosophical solidarity with activists. In both cases, AIDS and breast cancer activists achieved certain recognition by White House and Congressional politicians, doctors, FDA and NIH officials even as they harshly criticized government and medical authority. . . .

Breast cancer activists deserved credit for tangible progress in public awareness, both through the movement's own campaigns and the drive for increased media coverage. By the 1990s, the number of American women having mammograms rose significantly; up to 65 percent of females past age forty had breast exams. Earlier diagnoses, combined with better treatment options, were cited as factors in the 4.7 percent decline in breast cancer deaths between 1989 and 1992; fatality for women age thirty to fifty-nine dropped eight or nine percent. Clearly, through the mid-1990s, many important questions about breast cancer remained unanswered, especially relating to the exact nature of risk factors such as diet, environment, and genetics. Many doctors testified to need for further investigation; Susan Love stressed the goal of developing practical tests to screen breasts for cancer on a regular basis, analogous to the way Pap smears checked for cervical cancer.

As activists turned numbers into a political tool to gain clout, they established breast cancer funding as a key vote for politicians to show dedication to women's concern. However, Washington could support only so many key issues, and defining breast cancer as the primary principle risked in effect shunting aside other female health problems, arguably at least as serious. Similarly, American women themselves started thinking of breast cancer as their single greatest health danger, overwhelmingly out of proportion to actual risk. One study showed 46 percent of women convinced that breast cancer posed a major threat, though only 4 percent overall were likely to develop it; by contrast, while 36 percent could be expected to face heart disease, a mere 4 percent judged cardiac problems a serious risk. Of course, the very idea of cancer in general had acquired terrible emotional connotations, while some observers contended that breast cancer represented a uniquely terrifying form. Because of the significance attached to breasts in American culture, they argued, the cancer threatened the most vital physical and psychological sense of feminine identity.

Nevertheless, while breast cancer advocates established the issue at the center of women's health politics, drawing cover stories in *Newsweek* the *New York Times Magazine,* and *Ms.* (among other publications), heart disease remained the primary source of overall female death. . . . Moreover, medical reports emphasized that lung cancer, with increasing incidence and high mortality, actually accounted for more female deaths per year than breast cancer. . . . Such facts served as reminders that while activists had won new consideration for the important breast cancer issue, no comparable political clout had been mustered for other serious diseases in women such as lung cancer or heart disease. Activists such as Love dismissed fear that breast cancer might deplete other research, maintaining health should not be a zero-sum game and that funds could easily come out of "useless government spending." But while an ideal world might offer ample money to study all disease, 1990s political and financial reality, such as renewed attention to balanced budgeting, brought talk of tough review of scientific and medical spending. Nevertheless, through early 1996, breast cancer advocates in Congress had succeeded in largely protecting their gains in funding from the threat of harsh cuts. . . .

Fundamentally, AIDS and breast cancer activists were challenging and politicizing not only funding, but the structure and scientific values of research itself. . . . Some . . . activism explicitly challenged fundamental scientific method such as randomized research trials comparing new promising treatment against placebos or older drugs. AIDS groups objected that random tests might leave some patients stuck with ineffective medicine; a tombstone-shaped poster at one protest read, "I got the placebo." . . . In other cases, breast cancer . . . patients actually rejected scientific testing procedures. According to a 1995 report, NCI tests of bone marrow transplants as breast cancer treatment had been undercut because women feared they might be randomly placed in control sections receiving less aggressive therapy. When possible, patients simply chose to avoid enrolling in NCI trials, instead just finding providers willing to give them transplants directly. . . .

Beyond questions of research funding and testing procedures, some AIDS and breast cancer activists . . . directly challenged medical system motives. As *Nature* observed in 1991, women's health advocates often put "faith in the belief that disease can be prevented by appropriate behaviour, implying that the behavioural and social sciences are as important as the traditional biomedical sciences in creating a new research agenda . . . a view that would predicate a change in . . . NIH . . . mission." Some breast cancer advocates accused the medical establishment of systematically denying any evidence of nutrition and environmental pollution as causal factors. A 1993 *Ms.* article blamed cancellation of an NCI study on whether low-fat diets could lower cancer rates on clinicians "accustomed to having a virtual monopoly on the breast cancer research pie." . . . Another piece accused NCI and ACS of neglecting evidence linking breast cancer to organochlorine contamination. . . . In conspiratorial-sounding language, *Ms.* maintained that "a golden circle of power and money," including "mostly male" medical centers, doctors, drug companies, ACS and NCI, pursued mutually-beneficial political and financial interests while rejecting evidence which threatened their control. . . .

Questioning of medical authority on breast cancer and AIDS came in a period which also showed broader American skepticism of conventional medicine.

According to one 1990 report, over 33 percent of AIDS patients used unorthodox therapies such as acupuncture, imagery, megavitamin doses, and unapproved medicine. A more general 1993 study correspondingly shocked the medical profession, showing one-third of adults supplementing visits to regular physicians with chiropractic care, relaxation technique and other alternative treatments for physical pain (back and headaches) and other problems (anxiety, depression, and insomnia). Such therapy found a home within mainstream health institutions; by end of 1995, the relatively new NIH Office of Alternative Medicine had given out almost $8 million in research support, while Harvard, UCLA, and thirty other medical schools offered classes on unconventional treatments. . . . But for many scientists, the new NIH office and medical courses confirmed fear that non-scientific work was gaining a foothold in respectable institutions, violating the ultimate divide between objectivity and quackery.

For some feminists by the 1990s, the issue of what justified scientific authority had become a powerful philosophical issue. Critics such as Sandra Harding suggested that by definition, science could not be isolated from its historically male-dominated political and social context, so resulting sexist and racist bias undermined the system's supposed objectivity. Though such feminists maintained their analysis was meant to help improve scientific accuracy, some scientists interpreted it as academic-leftist "hostility," hopelessly misguided attacks out to destroy science.

While breast cancer and AIDS groups were not the first American organizations to fight for specific medical causes and research money, the 1980s–1990s activism was unique in two respects. First, as those organizations gained political power, they reached for unprecedented influence on government agencies, demanding a voice in distributing research funds, changing policy, and setting research agendas. While in earlier decades the March of Dimes had raised significant sums to fight polio, the group followed mainstream medical opinion on the best direction for using such research funds; by contrast, a 1996 breast cancer petition asked the President and Congress to "mandate that . . . breast cancer activists help determine how the money gets spent." Second, breast cancer and AIDS activists went beyond other medical causes in posing broad and direct challenges to scientific authority; again, polio groups had not disputed the objective value of research or fought to reverse specific rulings. Breast cancer and AIDS groups did not deny the ultimate value of medicine itself; in fact, they expressed repeated confidence that with significant increases in funding and national commitment, researchers would find better treatments, cures, and preventive measures for such terrible diseases. Yet to achieve such gains, activists contended, the medical community needed to reform its entire approach, even re-considering the value of randomized testing and supposedly "objective" results to accommodate sensibilities of patients and politics.

By the mid-1990s, breast cancer and AIDS activists had won significant power, reviewing and planning research along with scientists and officials. How had advocates achieved such change in so short a time? One doctor argued that "liberal" researchers and agencies had been "sympathetic to the plight" of seriously-ill patients and also "easily intimidated." While that explanation contained elements of truth, it did not fully reflect the power of AIDS and breast cancer activists in taking research to newly politicized heights. In part, these activists may have gained new influence in setting policy precisely because they were able to rally political clout behind such fundamental challenges to scientific method and federal authority. Smaller demands would not have attracted enough public attention to gain political credibility for winning major policy-making concessions, but activists' philosophical and political attacks on the medical system and government agencies resonated with many Americans' broader doubts about authority in the 1980s and 1990s. The activists' critiques alienated some scientists, who resisted what seemed unjustified interference by non-experts who failed to appreciate the value of objective method. But increasing numbers of researchers found some truth in activists' arguments about previous bias in the medical system, leading some doctors, agency officials and politicians alike to decide they could accommodate at least some demands of AIDS and breast cancer groups. By pressing their philosophical and political challenges to scientific and federal authority, AIDS and breast cancer groups won new policy-making authority themselves.

Muslim Women, the Hijab, and Religious Liberty in Late-Twentieth-Century America

KATHLEEN MOORE

Scholars have argued that developments since the 1960s in the judicial interpretations of the religion clauses of the First Amendment to the Constitution have produced a "more generous and accepting spirit" toward the religious practices of minority religions in the United States. It has further been said that certain statutes enacted by the federal government have gone beyond simply allowing free exercise (up to a point) to intervening in social and economic life to ensure that Americans are not deprived of certain rights because of the religious prejudices of their fellow citizens. Civil-rights and hate-crimes legislation have specifically targeted discrimination based on racial, ethnic, and national origins, and sexual, as well as religious, differences. The prescribed solution to discrimination of all types, according to these laws, is the creation of a uniform civil code of protection for all persons regardless of their ascribed characteristics (e.g., skin color) or religious beliefs. . . .

Yet recent appellate court decisions tell a different story. They belie the espoused commitment to neutrality and suggest that earlier research indicating a "more generous and accepting spirit" toward minority religions needs to be reconsidered in light of a conservative shift of late in the judiciary. In 1986 the U.S. Supreme Court told Orthodox Jews that they may not wear yarmulkes while on duty in uniform when this violates a military dress code. In a 1994 decision the Court denied public funding for a public school district, created exclusively for a community of Satmar Hasidic Jews, to run special needs educational programs for handicapped children of the Jewish sect. Native Americans who lost their jobs and subsequently were denied unemployment benefits because they used peyote in religious rituals sought relief through the courts, but were told that the state had acted rationally in firing

Kathleen Moore, "The Hijab and Religious Liberty: Anti-Discrimination Law and Muslim Women in the United States," in Yvonne Yazbeck Haddad and John L. Esposito, eds., *Muslims on the Americanization Path?* (Atlanta: Scholars Press, 1998), 129–158. Reprinted by permission of Kathleen Moore.

them. Sikhs and Muslims have suffered a similar fate, losing their livelihood and unemployment compensation when their religiously prescribed clothing conflicted with workplace regulations. . . .

Here I will examine the degree to which the concept of equality before the law has been honored and expanded in the law to include fair treatment for Muslims, granting legitimacy to religious practices as well as beliefs for a significant minority religion that is, more often than not, publicly represented as illiberal, anti-Enlightenment, misogynistic, and violent. The general point is to see whether and to what degree Muslims are allowed to act in accordance with particular religious convictions without its undermining their success in the economic and political institutions of the dominant society. This will entail a look at how Muslims have been treated in employment, an important area of law where the government has taken upon itself the task of eradicating discrimination. Specifically, I shall look at the status of Title VII anti-discrimination case law with regard to religious discrimination suits brought by Muslim women in the United States who have been fired or reprimanded at work for wearing Islamic attire. In some instances women have been prohibited from wearing the *hijab* or Muslim head scarf because of employers' dress regulations which forbid the wearing of clothing which attracts attention. Instituted in the 1960s, originally to prevent female employees from wearing miniskirts or other revealing attire, ironically this regulation has been enforced recently to hinder women who choose to conceal parts of their bodies for religious reasons. Under other circumstances women have been told not to wear the head scarf and other modest attire while at work because these articles of clothing clearly indicated their religious affiliation, which their employers did not wish to appear to endorse. For instance, in *EEOC v. Presbyterian Ministries, Inc.* (1992), a Presbyterian-operated retirement home forbade a receptionist from wearing the Muslim headscarf while at work because by doing so she was asserting non-Christian religious belief in a manner deemed inappropriate by her employer. In *EEOC v. Reads, Inc.* (1991), a public school district in Philadelphia refused to hire Cynthia Moore, a Muslim woman, as a third-grade counselor in two parochial schools (the school district provides parochial schools with auxiliary services such as counseling) because she would not agree to remove her headscarf during the work day. In these cases what seems to be crucial is the religious significance of wearing the headscarf and not the article of clothing itself; if a woman had chosen to wear a scarf as an expression of taste or fashion the problem of endorsement of a particular viewpoint would not have arisen. . . .

Title VII of the Civil Rights Act of 1964 was designed to protect employees in both the public and private sectors from discrimination in the workplace on the basis of race, sex, color, religion, or national origin. This piece of legislation radically changed our conceptions of discrimination as well as the larger civil rights movement that produced it. A heightened consciousness about racial equality and equal treatment of the sexes, as well as expectations about the utility and protection of the law, have influenced the debates about civil liberties, tolerance, and the law in a manner that suggests certain types of behavior and inhibits others. However, the critical issue of religious discrimination has received far less attention than race or sex discrimination in civil rights practice and scholarship. While a small but increasing number of complaints of religious discrimination have been filed with the Equal Employment Opportunity Commission (EEOC), and with state and county human relations or fair employment commissions, relatively few cases have been brought to the courts. Until recently, Muslims, who constitute a significant religious minority in the United States estimated to number over four million, have not been much heard from in equal employment opportunity debates and concerns over discriminatory treatment in the workplace.

The legal mobilization of Muslim claimants has accelerated of late, mainly in the form of women complaining of anti-hijab discrimination in a number of professions and occupations, including medicine, education, the hospitality industries (such as hotels and restaurants), retail sales, and secretarial work. The Council of American-Islamic Relations (CAIR) and the American Muslim Council (AMC), two advocacy groups, have documented several instances in which Muslim women were not allowed to wear the hijab at work, usually because it violated an employer's dress code, or were discriminated against because of their attire. Using press conferences, letter-writing campaigns, and the Internet to publicize offenses, these groups have brought pressure to bear upon employers in a bid to get them to accommodate the hijab. For instance, women who were not hired, or were fired, because they wore the hijab while on the job in hotels (e.g., at the reception desk or the hotel telephone switchboard) became the object of press conferences and letter-writing campaigns in 1996. At universities women have complained of ostracism and lost opportunities for advancement, which they attribute to anti-Muslim bias.

The following EEO religious discrimination case illustrates the changing conceptions of discrimination and the federal government's attempt to accommodate minority religious practices and what protections Title VII provides and what Title VII requires of employers.

In 1984 Alima Dolores Reardon, a Muslim who holds the religious conviction that Muslim women are required by their faith to wear a concealing headscarf and long, loose dress in public, was fired from her job as a substitute teacher in Philadelphia's public schools pursuant to Pennsylvania's "religious garb" statute. Originally enacted in 1895 at the peak of nativist anti-Catholic sentiments in the United States, the state law prohibits a public school teacher from wearing anything indicating adherence to any religious denomination.

This statute is not unique to Pennsylvania; it is one of four states with a religious-garb statute which proscribes the wearing of religious attire by public school teachers. While these statutes have been enforced very infrequently, their importance is more than symbolic. As a practical matter they have been used recently (seemingly in a disparate manner) by school boards to prohibit the practice of wearing religiously inspired or mandated clothing by a Sikh and, in the case considered in this section, by a Muslim school teacher. . . .

Reardon had been working in the Philadelphia school district for twelve years when she decided in 1982 to adopt the religious attire she believes her religion requires. She continued teaching after 1982 wearing a headscarf and long dress, and she received no complaints about this practice either "from the community or the school administration" for two years. At the end of 1984 Reardon was told, on three separate occasions by three different school principals, that she could not teach while wearing her religious attire. She was not allowed to teach as a substitute and was sent home on all three occasions because she arrived at the schools wearing her headscarf and concealing dress.

In November 1984 Reardon filed a Title VII complaint with the EEOC against the school district of Philadelphia charging discrimination on the basis of religion. The EEOC investigated the complaint and, finding Reardon's complaint to be valid, attempted reconciliation meetings with the school board. Reardon was reinstated as a substitute teacher in November 1985 and was permitted to teach full time in the Philadelphia school district while dressed in her religiously inspired clothing. However, she was not awarded back pay, nor did the school district concede that the religious garb statute was applied in a discriminatory fashion, nor did it promise not to continue to enforce the statute in like manner.

The EEOC transferred Reardon's complaint to the U.S. Department of Justice in order to sue the school board of Philadelphia in the federal district court in the Eastern District of Pennsylvania. The complaint in court included two theories of employer's liability: "(1) Failing or refusing to employ as public school teachers individuals who wear or who seek to wear garb or dress that is an aspect of their religious observance, and (2) failing or refusing reasonably to accommodate individuals who wear or who seek to wear garb or dress . . . that is an aspect of their religious observance or practice."

Initially Reardon's case was successful. The district court held that Title VII prohibited the enforcement of the Pennsylvania religious garb statute. Reardon received back pay for the period of time she was denied employment, and the school board was enjoined from continuing to enforce the religious garb statute. The district court noted that the school board's application of the religious garb statute to Reardon was selective and disparate treatment because "several others in the Philadelphia public school system wore religious garb and symbols without complaint or incident, [and] there was no evidence that any student perceived such attire as an endorsement of a particular religion." . . .

With respect to the reasonable accommodation provision of Title VII, the district court found that Reardon's employer must reasonably accommodate Reardon's religious practice unless the school board could show that such an accommodation would present an "undue hardship" to the schools. The school board had done nothing to accommodate Reardon and so had the burden of proving that it was unable to accommodate her religious practice without suffering undue hardship. The school board claimed that accommodation of Reardon's religious practices would hypothetically expose its administrators to the possibility of criminal penalties—convictions, fines, and expulsion from their profession—under Pennsylvania's religious garb statute. However, the district court rejected this argument, noting that no action had ever been taken to enforce the religious garb statute. The court concluded that "the specter of a penal sanction did not constitute undue hardship."

The district court also rejected the school board's argument that it would suffer undue hardship because an accommodation of Reardon's religious practice would force the school board to violate the establishment clause of the First Amendment to the U.S. Constitution. The establishment clause would be violated, the school board argued, by its acquiescence in Reardon's wearing of religious attire, which might lead schoolchildren to form the (mistaken) impression that the school board endorsed Reardon's religious viewpoint. The district court concluded that by allowing Reardon to wear religious attire the school board would not necessarily be communicating its endorsement of her convictions.

On appeal, however, the U.S. Court of Appeals accepted the school board's argument that accommodating Reardon's religious practices would constitute an undue hardship for the employer. The appeals court concluded that accommodation would work an undue hardship in two ways: (1) it would put the school board and the individual school principals in the position of violating a valid statute, thereby exposing administrators to the risk of criminal prosecution, fines, and the loss of their jobs pursuant to the religious garb statute; and (2) it would require the Commonwealth of Pennsylvania to sacrifice a compelling state interest in preserving the secular appearance of its public school system. While the courts have not accepted hypothetical undue hardship allegations in the past, this decision represents a departure from previous case law in the Third Circuit in this respect. The appellate court found that the prospect of criminal prosecution, no matter how remote, when combined with an interest in preserving the secular appearance of the schools, was sufficient to rule in favor of the employer. The appellate decision held that Title VII does not prevent the school board from denying Reardon the opportunity to teach while wearing the clothing she believes is mandated by her religious faith. In fact, the appellate court decision implies, but never explicitly holds, that Title VII's requirement of reasonable accommodation may place the public official in danger of violating the establishment clause by creating the impression that he or she endorses particular religious convictions.

Part of the Muslim community that was attentive to these court proceedings responded with dismay at the appellate court ruling. The *Muslim Media Watch* (published and distributed from Orange County, California), noted with considerable irony of the circuit court's decision to overturn the lower court ruling, "Free country, isn't it?" . . .

The Muslim headscarf case is only one example of changing conceptions of discrimination, equal treatment, and reasonable accommodation of religious practices in the workplace. The outcome in this case is that the headscarf—"a strong, loud, perhaps provocative expression of individual religious choice"—is not tolerated within the limits of nondiscrimination and religious liberty, but instead rejected as perhaps a threat of proselytism in public space and definitely as something which interferes with the secular nature of public education. This not only stigmatizes the headscarf, but also raises certain normative questions about the creation of a third position as an alternative to both liberalism and particularism, where reciprocal respect and recognition are exchanged and accommodation is allowed, and the adequacy of law to consider these claims and demands. The contextual analysis of the headscarf case indicates that the current status of Title VII law falls short of these tasks and presents observant Muslims in some instances with the necessity of choosing between breaking religious law and keeping a job.

Now the question is, what follows on the heels of litigation in terms of public action? In general, perhaps the most interesting effect has been the adaptation of legal norms and resources on the part of Muslims to change their environment, which has in turn contributed to an overall transformation of their self-identification. The result of a moderate record of success in litigation is that the plaintiffs become more attentive to the courts as an institution that legitimately defines and protects individual rights. However, the courts generally have not been very sympathetic to claims for reasonable accommodation of religious practices. EEOC plaintiffs claiming religious discrimination, over half of which seek accommodation on the part of their employers, lose an estimated 64 percent of their cases, which is a higher proportion of losses than in race and sex discrimination cases. . . .

What is lost in the American legal setting is the qualitative aspect of the stories Muslim women have to tell. The court records provide only a partial picture of the social realities encountered by Muslim women in the United States. The absence of narrative points to a loss for these women and for society at large, because they are treated as though they had no voice. Something is lost for pluralism even in those cases where the judicial outcome is favorable to Muslim women to the extent that the judicial proceedings have forced the issue of the headscarf into a problem that had to be managed and litigated, rather than leaving it as something that does not require separate attention and legal protection because it is simply part of social life. The "hegemonic" story—in other words, the court's interpretation of anti-discrimination law in a manner which allows school boards to prohibit the headscarf on the basis of a church/state separation claim, without hearing from the affected women what the headscarf means for identity—"reproduce[s] existing relations of power and in-equity, [and] fails to make visible and explicit the connections between particular lives and social organization." . . .

The intention in this essay and ongoing research is to bring the human factor into sharper focus by looking at the activity and divergent views of a significant re-ligious minority which has utilized legal structures in the United States to assert and protect its claims for equal protection. When we take into account the activity and views of Muslims as they interpret and act on law, we may apprehend the ways in which they, as a religious minority, signal and strengthen their relations with the larger society. As Harvard law professor Martha Minow explains, "Those claiming rights implicitly invest themselves in a larger community, even in the act of seek-ing to change it."

Rights claims, however, may challenge the exclusion from the workplace of some people who are "different," but fail to indicate how the workplace can be remade to accommodate difference. The unstated norms against which we define difference remain powerful. It is under these conditions that Muslims who file complaints of religious discrimination in employment have forged two paths: one toward equal treatment (seeking the right to be treated equally), and the other to-ward equal respect (seeking greater accommodation of their differences). Both of these paths imply slightly differing visions of pluralism. Historically, the path toward equal treatment has led to the right to receive uniform treatment—"to be treated the same way as the majority."

This outcome has failed to satisfy some members of subject groups, such as Muslims, who seek a broader conception of equality, one that includes a public recognition of collective identities and allows groups to maintain their distinctive ways of life. These would instead seek to follow the second path toward workplace policies that make accommodation of difference possible.

These features are increasingly important to comprehend as various societies worldwide face the growing pressures of the contemporary global migration. By focusing attention on the place of Islam in identity formation and negotiation with society at large and on the particular challenge this presents to the (re)constitution of the secular society, this inquiry provides a basis from which to theorize about the constitutive role of law in migration and acculturation.

Solving the problems of religious communal relations in multi-ethnic nation-states will become in the next century just as important in sustaining stable pluralistic societies as race relations have been in this century. The move toward greater accommodation of religious difference, articulated in the "reasonable accommodation" provision of Title VII, indicates an acknowledgment of American society as increasingly pluralistic. The intent here has been to lay the foundation for continuing examination of the role of law in mediating relations between a significant religious minority and the institutions of the state. While it would be incorrect to suppose that a heterogeneous population, such as the Muslims of the United States are, forms a single, unitary group, it ought not to be forgotten that Muslims constitute an important presence in a richly textured and complex society.

Feminists and the Politics of Welfare Reform in the 1990s

GWENDOLYN MINK

When the Personal Responsibility Act of 1996 transformed welfare, it also transformed citizenship. Flouting the ideal of universal citizenship, the act distinguishes poor single mothers from other citizens and subjects them to a separate system of law. Under this system of law, poor single mothers forfeit rights the rest of us enjoy as fundamental to our citizenship—family rights, reproductive rights, and vocational liberty—just because they need welfare. The law continues to injure poor single mothers' rights even after time limits end their access to benefits, for it directs them to forsake child raising for full-time wage earning. Both while they receive benefits and after they lose them, the Personal Responsibility Act (PRA) taxes poor women who have chosen motherhood and endangers their care and custody of children.

The PRA was the most aggressive assault on women's rights in this century. Yet it provoked only scanty protest from the millions of women who call themselves feminists. In fact, during three years of concerted debate leading up to enactment of the new welfare law, most feminists actually supported many of the restrictions contemplated by both the Clinton and the Republican versions of welfare reform. In their various roles as constituents, members of movement organizations, and even elected officials, they endorsed the core principles of welfare reform: child support rules that require welfare mothers to identify and associate with biological fathers even when they do not want to and work requirements that mandate work outside the home even at the expense of children.

The PRA's child support provisions exchange poor single mothers' income support from government with income support from individual men. Forwarding its statutory purpose of "encourag[ing] the formation and maintenance of two-parent families," the provisions compel each mother to associate not just with any man, but with *the* man the government tells her to: the biological father of her children. In addition to imposing potentially unwanted associations on mothers who need welfare, mandatory sperm-based paternal family headship impairs their sexual and family privacy. Under the PRA's child support provisions, mothers must help government identify biological fathers and locate their whereabouts so that government can collect child support from them. Where a mother is married, the establishment of paternity does not involve too much: paternity is a matter of public record, because the law assumes that a mother's husband at the time of her child's birth is the father, whether or not he is biologically related to the child. Where a mother has not been married, though, it means having to tell a welfare official or a judge about her sex life. It also means that government decides who belongs to welfare mothers' families and what those families should look like.

The PRA's work requirements further injure poor mothers' rights. For one thing, they deny poor mothers' parental choices about whether and how much outside employment is compatible with the needs of children. Further, like the child support provisions, the PRA's work requirements promote mothers' economic dependence on men, not independence through their own income. Sanctioning extramarital child raising, the act provides that where there are *two* parents, one may stay at home to care for children. Where there is only *one* parent, in contrast, the act says she *must* leave her home and children to work for wages. This means that if a poor single mother can't find reliable child care, or wants to raise her own children—if she needs or wants to work *inside* the home—she would be well-advised to get married.

What the new law means by "personal responsibility," then, is not personal responsibility at all. The Personal Responsibility Act makes *government* responsible for how poor mothers lead their lives. . . . Association, vocation, privacy, and parenting are basic constitutional rights—rights that are strictly guarded for everyone except mothers who need welfare.

The Personal Responsibility Act contradicts basic feminist axioms about the conditions for women's equality. Feminists long have argued that women's equality pivots on our ability to make independent choices. Constitutionally anchored liberties protect our choices, but we often cannot make them without having the means to do so. For thirty years, welfare was the currency for poor single mothers' choices, however constrained those choices may have been. Once the Supreme Court recognized welfare as an entitlement—a guarantee—to mothers and children based on economic need, poor mothers had the means to decide to not be dependent on particular men or to not risk their own or their children's safety. For these reasons, during the late 1960s and early 1970s, some feminists hailed welfare rights as part of their agenda for women's equality.

The connections between welfare rights and women's rights were never widely appreciated, however. Hence, when the Personal Responsibility Act directly invaded poor single mothers' rights, few feminists regarded that invasion as a problem for *women*. . . . Punitive welfare reform was not accomplished by one political party or by one side of the ideological spectrum. Republicans and Democrats, conservatives and liberals, patriarchalists *and feminists* were in consensus about basic elements of reform, including measures that interfere with the decisional liberties of poor women. Moreover, many feminists agreed with welfare reformers in both parties that welfare isn't "good for" women.

Not all feminists joined the welfare reform consensus, of course. Leaders of many national women's and feminist organizations—groups ranging from the American Association for University Women to the National Organization for Women—loudly and unwaveringly opposed the Personal Responsibility Act. They called press conferences, participated in vigils, appealed to their memberships, and lobbied Congress. Some leaders—like Patricia Ireland—even engaged in dramatic acts of civil disobedience. Other nationally visible feminists—including Gloria Steinem and Betty Friedan—joined the Women's Committee of One Hundred, a feminist mobilization against punitive welfare reform that was organized by feminist scholars and activists. As the cochair of the Women's Committee of One Hundred, I know firsthand that some feminists raised their voices in defense of poor single mothers' rights, including their entitlement to welfare. But I also know that feminist voices were relatively few.

. . . Sometimes by their silence and sometimes in their deeds, many feminists actually collaborated with punitive welfare reformers. The feminists I'm talking about form the movement's mainstream. Most are middle-class and white. Many have ties to formal organizations, contributing to NARAL or to Emily's List and participating in local NOW chapters. Others march for abortion rights, work for feminist candidates, or simply vote feminist. Some have high political positions—one is a cabinet secretary, several are members of Congress. Although feminism has many iterations, these feminists often speak for all of feminism. When mobilized, they can wield impressive political clout—creating gender gaps in elections and saving abortion rights, for example. Yet when it came to welfare, for the most part they sat on their hands. Ignoring appeals from sister feminists and welfare rights activists to defend "welfare as a women's issue" and to oppose "the war against poor women" as if it were "a war against *all* women," many even entered the war on the antiwelfare/antiwoman side.

Some examples: on Capitol Hill, all white women in the U.S. Senate—including four Democratic women who call themselves feminists—voted *for* the new welfare law when it first came to the Senate floor in the summer of 1995. In the House of Representatives in 1996, twenty-six of thirty-one Democratic women, all of whom call themselves feminists, voted *for* a Democratic welfare bill that would have stripped recipients of their entitlement to welfare. Meanwhile, across the country, a NOW–Legal Defense and Education Fund appeal for contributions to support an economic justice litigator aroused so much hate mail that NOW–LDEF stopped doing direct mail on the welfare issue.

Feminist members of Congress did not write the Personal Responsibility Act, of course. Nor did members of the National Organization for Women or contributors to Emily's List compose the driving force behind the most brutal provisions of the new welfare law. My claim is not that feminists were uniquely responsible for how welfare has been reformed. My point is that they were uniquely positioned to make a difference. They have made a difference in many arenas across the years, even during inauspicious Republican presidencies. They undid damaging Supreme Court decisions, for example, by helping to win the Civil Rights Restoration Act of 1988 after the Court gutted Title IX in *Grove City College v. Bell.* They even expanded women's rights while George Bush was president: in the Civil Rights Act of 1991, they won women's right to economic and punitive damages in sex discrimination cases. So they certainly could have made a difference under a friendly Democratic president who both needs and enjoys the support of women. Indeed, such feminists as were opposed to welfare reform did make a difference initially, in concert with antipoverty groups and children's advocates: President Clinton vetoed the first Republican version of the Personal Responsibility Act in November 1995. Had greater numbers of feminists cared that welfare reform harms poor mothers, we could have pressured the president to repeat his veto when a second bill crossed his desk in August 1996.

But welfare reform did not directly bear on the lives of most feminists and did not directly implicate their rights. The new welfare law did not threaten middle-class women's reproductive choices, or their sexual privacy, or their right to raise their own children, or their occupational freedom. So middle-class feminists did not raise their voices as they would have if, say, abortion rights had been at stake. This gave the green light to feminists in Congress to treat welfare reform as if it didn't affect women. . . .

Silence among feminists was not the only problem. At the same time feminists were generally silent about the effects of new welfare provisions on poor women's rights, some were quite outspoken about the need to reform welfare so as to improve the personal and family choices poor single mothers make. When feminists did talk about welfare as a women's issue, it often seemed that they were more concerned with reconciling welfare with feminism than with defending poor single mothers' right to receive it. Feminists I've talked to in communities and feminists I've listened to in Congress often reiterated the assumptions of welfare reformers: that welfare has promoted single mother's dependency on government rather than independence in the labor market; that it has discouraged poor women from practicing fertility control; and that it has compensated for the sexual and paternal irresponsibility of individual men. . . .

The welfare debate focused on the deficiencies of welfare mothers, rather than on the deficiencies of the welfare system. It trafficked in the tropes of "illegitimacy," and "pathology," and "dependency," and "irresponsibility," to deepen disdain toward mothers who need welfare. Feminists did not dispute the terms of the debate, although many tried to soften it. In Congress, feminists called for more generous funding for child care, for example. This would ease the effects of mothers' wage work on many poor families; but it did not contest the premise that poor single mothers should be forced to work outside the home. Hence, feminists did not fight for a policy that would enable poor mothers to make independent and honorable choices about what kind of work they will do and how many children they will have and whether they will marry. If anything, many feminists agreed with conservatives that welfare mothers do not make good choices.

Feminist reservations about welfare mothers' choices strengthened the bipartisan consensus that there's something wrong with mothers who need welfare and that cash assistance should require their reform. The two pillars of the new welfare law—work and paternal family headship—were born from this consensus. The harshness of the law's work requirements and the brutality of its sanctions against nonmarital child rearing by mothers may be Republican and patriarchal in execution. But the law's emphasis on women's labor market participation and on men's participation in families were Democratic and feminist in inspiration.

Feminists left their boldest imprint on the paternity establishment and child support provisions of the Personal Responsibility Act. For quite some time, feminists in Congress, like feminists across the country, have been emphatic about "making fathers pay" for children through increased federal involvement in the establishment and enforcement of child support orders. When Republicans presented a welfare bill without child support provisions, several feminist congresswomen embarrassed Republicans into adopting them.

The child support provisions impose stringent national conditions on nonmarital child rearing by poor women. The first condition is the mandatory establishment of paternity. Welfare law stipulates that a mother's eligibility for welfare depends on her willingness to reveal the identity of her child's father. Since the purpose of paternity establishment is to assign child support obligations to biological fathers, the second condition is that mothers who need welfare must cooperate in establishing, modifying, and enforcing the support orders for their children. The law requires states to reduce a family's welfare grant by at least 25 percent when a mother fails to comply with these rules and permits states to deny the family's grant altogether.

The "deadbeat dad" thesis—the argument that mothers are poor because fathers are derelict—is quite popular among middle-class feminists, as it is among the general public. Finding the costs of child bearing that fall disproportionately on women a wellspring of gender inequality, many feminists want men to provide for their biological children. Incautious pursuit of this objective aligned middle-class feminists behind a policy that endangers the rights of poor single mothers. . . .

. . . When middle-class women think of the circumstances that might lead them to welfare, they think of divorce—from middle-class men who might have considerable financial resources to share with their children. . . . The compulsory features of paternity establishment and child support enforcement may be unremarkable to a divorced mother with a support order: she escapes compulsion by choosing to pursue child support, and what matters to her is that the support order be enforced. But some mothers do not have support orders because they do not want them. A mother may not want to identify her child's father because she may fear abuse for herself or her child. She may not want to seek child support because she has chosen to parent alone—or with someone else. She may know her child's father is poor and may fear exposing him to harsh penalties when he cannot pay what a court tells him he owes. She may consider his emotional support for his child to be worth more than the $100 the state might collect and that she will never see.

"Making fathers pay" may promote the economic and justice interests of many custodial mothers. But *making mothers* make fathers pay means making mothers pay for subsistence with their own rights—and safety. The issue is not whether government should assist mothers in collecting payments from fathers. Of course it should. Neither is the issue whether child support enforcement provisions in welfare policy help mothers who have or desire child support awards. Of course they do. Nor is the issue whether it is a good thing for children to have active fathers—of course it can be. The issue is coercion, coercion directed toward the mother who doesn't conform to patriarchal conventions—whether by choice or from necessity. It is also coercion directed toward the mother whose deviation from patriarchal norms has been linked to her racial and cultural standing. . . .

. . . The mandatory maternal cooperation rule targets mothers who are not and have not been married, as well as mothers who do not have and do not want child support. Nonmarital mothers are the bull's-eye, and among nonmarital mothers receiving welfare, only 28.4 percent are white. This means that the new welfare law's invasions of associational and privacy rights will disproportionately harm mothers of color. Inspired by white feminist outrage against middle-class ex-husbands, the paternity establishment and child support provisions both reflect and entrench in equalities among women.

Feminists' general support for the claim that poor mothers need "work, not welfare" proceeded more from the internal logics of the late-twentieth-century women's movement than from specific policy goals. Feminists have long fought for women's right to work outside the home, and to do so on terms equal to men. Rather than demand honor and equity for all forms and venues of work, our bias has been toward work performed in the labor market. We've even been a little suspicious of the woman who doesn't work in the labor market—as if by working inside the home full-time she somehow undermines feminism. Often, we have demeaned her as "just a housewife."

The feminist work ethic made sense for the white and middle-class women who rekindled feminism in the 1960s. . . . Middle-class feminists understandably keyed on work outside the home as the alternative to domesticity—and therefore as the defining element of women's full and equal citizenship. . . .

Feminists of color have struggled alongside white feminists for equality in the workplace—for better pay, improved benefits, and due recognition of our merit. However, the idea that liberation hinges on work outside the home historically has divided feminists along class and race lines. Women of color and poor, white women have not usually found work outside the home to be a source of equality. To the contrary, especially for women of color, such work has been a site of oppression and a mark of inequality. Outside work has been required or expected of women of color by white society, though white society does not require or expect outside work of its own women. It also has been necessary for women of color because often their male kin cannot find jobs at living wages, if they can find jobs at all. And it has been exploitative because women of color earn disproportionately low wages. Since women of color have always worked outside their own homes—often raising other people's children—the right to care for their own children (to work inside their own homes) has been a touchstone goal of women of color struggles for equality.

For their part, white, middle-class feminists have been reluctant to make equality claims for women as family care givers. Still, they have never denied that women's family work has social value. During the early 1970s, for example, some feminists argued that the gross national product should include the value of women's work in the home. Many radical and socialist feminists challenged the sexual division of labor, illuminating connections between women's unpaid labor in the home and their gender-based inequality. Some on the feminist left drew the conclusion that "women's work" should be remunerated—that women should be paid "wages for housework." But across ideological divisions, most white, middle class feminists found the home to be the prime site of women's oppression and accordingly stressed the liberating potential of leaving it—for the labor market.

. . . Although feminism is fundamentally about winning women choices, our labor market bias has put much of feminism not on the side of vocational choice—the choice to work inside or outside the home—but on the side of wage earning for all women. In the Personal Responsibility Act, the feminist *right* to work outside the home has become poor single mothers' *obligation* to do so. . . .

To be sure, many feminists have fought ardently to attenuate the PRA's harshest provisions. For example, the NOW–Legal Defense and Education Fund has been working hard to get states to adopt the Family Violence Option, which exempts battered women from some of the most stringent welfare rules. Lucille Roybal-Allard in the U.S. House and Patty Murray in the U.S. Senate have fought hard to broaden the domestic violence exemption to include exemption from the PRA's strict time limit for welfare eligibility. Patsy Mink in the U.S. House has battled to secure vocational education funds for single mothers. At the local level, grassroots feminists and welfare rights activists have been struggling to enforce fair labor standards in welfare mothers' jobs.

If successful, all of these efforts could improve some women's fate in the new welfare system. But they do not disturb the principles behind the welfare law: they do not refute the idea that poor single mothers *should* seek work outside the home. . . . Nor has anyone paid serious attention to the racial effects of welfare principles. Although work requirements aim indiscriminately at all poor single mothers, it is mothers of color who bear their heaviest weight. African American and Latina mothers are disproportionately poor and, accordingly, are disproportionately enrolled on welfare. In 1994, adult recipients in AFDC families were almost two-thirds women of color: 37.4 percent white, 36.4 percent Black, 19.9 percent Latina, 2.9 percent Asian, and 1.3 percent Native American.

So when welfare rules indenture poor mothers as unpaid servants of local governments (in workfare programs), it is mothers of color who are disproportionately harmed. And when time limits require poor mothers to forsake their children for the labor market, it is mothers of color who are disproportionately deprived of their right to manage their family's lives, and it is children of color who are disproportionately deprived of their mothers' care.

What can we do now for poor mothers who need welfare? . . . [W]e need to defend the right to have children as a basic reproductive right; and we need to defend the right to raise one's own children as basic to family privacy as well as to associational and vocational freedom. But we also must argue further, that women's basic constitutional rights depend on a right to welfare—that a right to welfare is a condition of women's equality. . . .

We all know that care giving work—household management and parenting—takes skill, energy, time, and responsibility. We know this because people who can afford it *pay* other people to do it. Many wage earning mothers pay for child care; upper-class mothers who work outside the home pay for nannies; very wealthy mothers who don't even work outside the home pay household workers to assist them with their various tasks. Moreover, even when we are not paying surrogates to do our family care giving, we pay people to perform activities in the labor market that care givers also do in the home. We pay drivers to take us places; we pay nurses to make us feel better and help us get well; we pay psychologists to help us with our troubles; we pay teachers to explain our lessons; we pay cooks and waitresses to prepare and serve our food.

If economists can measure the value of this work when it is performed for other people's families, why can't we impute value to it when it is performed for one's own? In 1972, economists at the Chase Manhattan Bank did just that, translating family care giving work into its labor market components—nursemaid, dietitian, laundress, maintenance man, chauffeur, food buyer, cook, dishwasher, seamstress, practical nurse, gardener. The economists concluded that the value of family care givers' work was at least $13,391.56 a year (1972 dollars)—an amount well above the poverty line!

Once we establish that *all* care giving is work and that it has economic value—whatever the racial, marital, or class status of the care giver and whether or not it is performed in the labor market—we can build a case for economic arrangements that enable poor single mothers to do their jobs. In place of stingy benefits doled out begrudgingly to needy mothers, welfare would become an income owed to nonmarket, care giving workers—owed as a matter of right to anyone who bears sole responsibility for children (or for other dependent family members).

This would not require a radical restructuring of social policy, or an unprecedented departure from past practice. The survivors' insurance system—which has been around since 1939—does for widowed parents and their minor children exactly what I'm advocating for poor single mothers. Survivors' insurance is an entitlement and does not involve stigma and social control. Mothers who are eligible for survivors' insurance do not have to submit to governmental scrutiny to receive benefits and do not have to live by government's moral and cultural rules. Benefits are nationally uniform and are paid out automatically—much like social security benefits are paid out to the elderly. . . .

In my view, if widowed mothers are entitled to public benefits, poor single mothers should be, too. In fact, all family care givers are owed an income in theory, for all care giving is work. . . . A care giver's income would relieve the disproportionate burdens that fall on single mothers and in so doing would lessen inequalities among women based on class and marital status and between male and female parents based on default social roles. But although paid to single care givers only, this income support should be universally guaranteed, assuring a safety net to all care givers if ever they need or choose to parent—or to care for other family members—alone. The extension of the safety net to care givers as independent citizens would promote equality, as it would enable adults to exit untenable—often violent—relationships of economic dependency and to retain reproductive and vocational choices when they do. . . . It might even undermine the sexual division of labor, for some men will be enticed to do family care giving work once they understand it to have economic value. Offering an income to all solo care givers in a unitary system—to nonmarital mothers as well as to widowed ones—would erase invidious moral distinctions among mothers and eliminate their racial effects. Further, universal income support for single parents would restore mothers' constitutional rights—to not marry, to bear children, and to parent them, even if they are poor. It would promote occupational freedom, by rewarding work even when work cannot be exchanged for wages. So redefined, welfare would become a sign not of dependency but of independence, a means not to moral regulation but to social and political equality. . . .

Middle-class feminists were right to reject *ascribed* domesticity, and they have taught us well that fully independent and equal citizenship for women entails having the right *not* to care. So we must also win labor market reforms to make outside work feasible even for mothers who are parenting alone. Unless we make outside work affordable for solo care givers, a care givers' income would constrain choice by favoring care giving over wage earning.

The end of welfare, then, includes "making work pay," not only by remunerating care giving work but also by making participation in the labor market equitable and rewarding for women, especially mothers. Thus, for example, we need a minimum wage that provides a sustaining income—so that poor mothers can afford to work outside the home if they want to. We need comparable worth policies that correct the low economic value assigned to women's jobs. We need unemployment insurance reforms covering women's gendered reasons for losing or leaving jobs—such as pregnancy or sexual harassment. We need paid family leave so that the lowest paid workers can take time off to care for sick kids or new babies just as better paid workers do. We need guaranteed child care so that a parent's decision to work inside the home is truly a decision—not something forced on her because she can't find affordable and nurturing supervision for her children. We also need universal health care; full employment policy; a massive investment in education and vocational training; and aggressive enforcement of antidiscrimination laws.

This end to welfare will take us down many paths, in recognition of women's diverse experiences of gender and diverse prerequisites for equality.

◈ *F U R T H E R   R E A D I N G*

Ahmed, Leila. *A Border Passage: From Cairo to America—a Woman's Journey* (2000).

Bendroth, Margaret Lamberts. "Fundamentalism and the Family," *Journal of Women's History* 10, no. 4 (winter 1999): 35–54.

Berry, Mary Frances. *Why ERA Failed* (1986).

Boles, Janet. *The Politics of the Equal Rights Amendment* (1979).

Chun, Gloria Heyung. *Of Orphans and Warriors: Inventing Chinese American Culture and Identity* (2000).

Collins, Patricia. *Black Feminist Thought: Knowledge, Consciousness, and the Politics of Empowerment* (1990).

D'Amico, Francine, and Laurie Weinstein, eds. *Gender Camouflage: Women and the U.S. Military* (1999).

DeHart-Matthews, Jane, and Donald Mathews. *The Equal Rights Amendment and the Politics of Cultural Conflict* (1988).

Dill, Bonnie Thornton. "Race, Class, and Gender: Prospects for an All-Inclusive Sisterhood," *Feminist Studies* 9, no. 1 (spring 1983): 131–150.

Ehrenreich, Barbara. *Hearts of Men* (1983).

Eisenstein, Zillah. *The Radical Future of Liberal Feminism* (1981).

Faludi, Susan. *Backlash: The Undeclared War Against American Women* (1992).

Felsenthal, Carol. *Sweetheart of the Silent Majority: The Biography of Phyllis Schlafly* (1981).

Garcia, Alma M. *Chicana Feminist Thought: The Basic Historical Writings* (1997).

Giele, Janet. *Woman and the Future* (1978).

Hochschild, Arlie. *The Second Shift: Working Parents and the Revolution at Home* (1989).

Hoff, Joan. *Law, Gender, and Injustice: A Legal History of U.S. Women* (1991).

Hoff-Wilson, Joan, ed. *Rites of Passage: The Past and Future of the ERA* (1986).

hooks, bell. *Ain't I a Woman? Black Women and Feminism* (1981).

———. *Talking Back: Thinking Feminist, Thinking Black* (1989).

Hull, N. E. H., and Peter Charles Hoffer. *Roe v. Wade: The Abortion Rights Controversy in American History* (2001).

Kenny, Lorraine Delia. *Daughters of Suburbia: Growing Up White, Middle Class, and Female* (2000).

Klatch, Rebecca E. *Women of the New Right* (1987).

Klein, Ethel. *Gender Politics* (1984).

Lederer, Lauren. ed. *Take Back the Night: Women on Pornography* (1980).

Leidholdt, Dorchen, and Janice G. Raymond, eds. *The Sexual Liberals and the Attack on Feminism* (1990).

Lerner, Barron H. *The Breast Cancer Wars: Hope, Fear, and the Pursuit of a Cure in Twentieth-Century America* (2001).

Luker, Kristin. *Abortion and the Politics of Motherhood* (1984).

Maciel, David R., and Isidro D. Ortiz, eds. *Chicanas/Chicanos at the Crossroads: Social, Economic, and Political Change* (1996).

Mansbridge, Jane. *Why We Lost the ERA* (1986).

Mezey, Susan Gluck. *In Pursuit of Equality: Women, Policy, and the Federal Courts* (1992).

Mink, Gwendolyn. *Welfare's End* (1998).

———. *Hostile Environment: The Political Betrayal of Sexually Harassed Women* (2000).

Mohr, James. *Abortion in America* (1980).

Okin, Susan Moller. *Justice, Gender, and the Family* (1989).

Petchesky, Rosalind Pollack. *Abortion and Woman's Choice* (1990).

Rodriguez, Felix V. Matos, and Linda C. Delgado, eds. *Puerto Rican Women's History: New Perspectives* (1998).

Rosenberg, Harriet G. "From Trash to Treasure: Housewife Activists and the Environmental Justice Movement," in Jane Schneider and Rayna Rapp, eds., *Articulating Hidden Histories: Exploring the Influence of Eric R. Wolf* (Berkeley: University of California Press, 1995), 190–204.

Rosenberg, Rosalind. *Divided Lives: American Women in the 20th Century* (1992).

Ruiz, Vicki L. *From Out of the Shadows: Mexican Women in Twentieth-Century America* (1998).

Shakir, Evelyn. *Bint Arab: Arab and Arab American Women in the United States* (1997).

Sidel, Ruth. *Women and Children Last: The Plight of Poor Women in Affluent America* (1986).

Silverberg, Helene. "State Building, Health Policy, and the Persistence of the Abortion Debate," *Journal of Policy History* 9 (1997): 311–338.

Smith, Barbara. *Home Girls: A Black Feminist Anthology* (2000).

Smith, Barbara Ellen. "Crossing the Great Divides: Race, Class, and Gender in Southern Women's Organizing, 1979–1992," *Gender and Society* 9 (1995): 680–696.

Smith, Jane I. *Islam in America* (1999).

Snitow, Ann et al., eds. *Powers of Desire: The Politics of Sexuality* (1983).

Solinger, Rickie. *Beggars and Choosers: How the Politics of Choice Shapes Adoption, Abortion, and Welfare in the United States* (2001).

Tuan, Mia. *Forever Foreigners or Honorary Whites?: The Asian Ethnic Experience Today* (1998).

Vance, Carol, ed. *Pleasure and Danger: Exploring Female Sexuality* (1984).

Vogel, Lise. *Mothers on the Job* (1993).

Weitzman, Leonore J. *The Divorce Revolution: The Unexpected Social and Economic Consequences for Women and Children in America* (1985).